Curriculum in a New Key

The Collected Works of Ted T. Aoki

STUDIES IN CURRICULUM THEORY
William F. Pinar, Series Editor

Curriculum in a New Key

The Collected Works of Ted T. Aoki

Edited by

William F. Pinar
Louisiana State University

and

Rita L. Irwin
University of British Columbia

LAWRENCE ERLBAUM ASSOCIATES, PUBLISHERS

2005   Mahwah, New Jersey   London

Camera ready copy for this book was provided by the editors.

Lawrence Erlbaum Associates, Inc., Publishers
10 Industrial Avenue
Mahwah, New Jersey 07430

Cover art by Elysia Dywan: *Quadrant of Arms*. Used with permission.

Cover design by Kathryn Houghtaling Lacey

Library of Congress Cataloging-in-Publication Data

Aoki, Ted T.
  Curriculum in a new key : the collected works of Ted T. Aoki / edited
by William F. Pinar and Rita L. Irwin.
        p.   cm. — (Studies in curriculum theory)
Includes bibliographical references and index.
ISBN 0-8058-4741-3 (cloth : alk. paper)
ISBN 0-8058-4742-1 (pbk. : alk. paper)
1. Curriculum planning—Philosophy.   2. Education—Curricula—
  Philosophy.   3. Postmodernism and education.   4. Poststruc-
  turalism.   I. Pinar, William.   II. Irwin, Rita L., 1955– .   III. Title.
  IV. Series.
LB2806.15.A63   2004
375'.001—dc22
                                                              2003064150
                                                                    CIP

Books published by Lawrence Erlbaum Associates are printed on acid-free paper, and their bindings are chosen for strength and durability.

Printed in the United States of America
10   9   8   7   6   5   4   3   2   1

Ted T. Aoki

Contents

ACKNOWLEDGMENTS

We wish to acknowledge the contributions of curriculum scholars across Canada who have given generously of their time, energy, and commitment to the Canadian Association for Curriculum Studies. Along with Ted, we deeply appreciate the work of CACS members to the strength and vitality of curriculum studies in Canada.

In particular we wish to thank Nicholas Ng-A-Fook for his tireless work editing and formatting the volume. A Canadian, Nicholas took his BA in Classical Studies at the University of Ottawa, the MA in Education at York University, and is, currently, studying for the PhD at Louisiana State University. We also wish to thank three other Canadians, Labhir Bains, Sara Hambleton and Nicole McClelland, for their fortitude and attention to detail as the original documents were transferred into electronic format and copyright permissions were sought. Labhir, an undergraduate Arts student at UBC and single mother, Sara, a student teacher in elementary education at UBC, and Nicole, a new staff member in the Department of Curriculum Studies at UBC, have just the right mix of perseverance, dedication, and desire to achieve the near impossible in a project such as this. Without the help of these four remarkable individuals, this project would never have been realized. Thank you.

William F. Pinar
President, International Association for the Advancement of Curriculum Studies

Rita L. Irwin
President, Canadian Association for Curriculum Studies

March 2003

Grateful acknowledgment is made to the following for permission to reprint from previously published material:

Copyright © 2003. *A Lingering Note "Comments on the Collected Works of Ted T. Aoki"* by William F. Pinar. Reprinted with the permission of Educational Insights.

Copyright © 2003. *In a New Key: Ted T. Aoki* by Rita L. Irwin. Reprinted with the permission of Educational Insights.

Copyright © 1980. *Toward Curriculum Inquiry in a New Key* by Ted T. Aoki. Reprinted with the permission of Faculty of Education at the University of Alberta and Ted T. Aoki.

Copyright © 1983. *Curriculum Implementation as Instrumental Action and as Situational Praxis* by Ted T. Aoki. Reprinted with the permission of Faculty of Education at the University of Alberta and Ted T. Aoki.

Copyright © 1984. *Competence in Teaching as Instrumental and Practical Action: A Critical Analysis* by Ted T. Aoki. Reprinted with permission of University Press of America.

Copyright © 1986. *Interests, Knowledge and Evaluation: Alternative Approaches to Curriculum Evaluation* by Ted T. Aoki. Permission granted by the Journal of Curriculum Theorizing and the Corporation for Curriculum Research.

Copyright © 1987. *Toward Understanding "Computer Application"* by Ted T. Aoki. Permission granted by the Journal of Curriculum Theorizing and the Corporation for Curriculum Research.

Copyright © 1999. *Toward Understanding "Computer Application"* by Ted T. Aoki. Reprinted with permission by Peter Lang Publishing.

Copyright © 1986. *Teaching as In-dwelling Between Two Curriculum Worlds* by Ted T. Aoki. Reprinted with the permission of the British Columbia Teachers' Federation.

Copyright © 1991. *Teaching as In-dwelling Between Two Curriculum Worlds* by Ted T. Aoki. Reprinted with the permission of the Faculty of Education at the University of Alberta and Ted T. Aoki.

Copyright © 1991. *Layered Understandings of Orientations in Social Studies Program Evaluation* by Ted T. Aoki. Reprinted with the permission of Macmillan Publishing Company.

Copyright © 1991. *Layered Voices of Teaching: The Uncannily Correct and the Elusively True* by Ted T. Aoki. Reprinted with the permission of Faculty of Education at the University of Alberta and Ted T. Aoki.

Copyright © 1992. *Layered Voices of Teaching: The Uncannily Correct and the Elusively True* by Ted T. Aoki. Reprinted with the permission of Teachers College Press.

Copyright © 1993. *Legitimating Lived Curriculum: Towards a Curricular Landscape of Multiplicity* by Ted T. Aoki. Reprinted with the permission of the Journal of Curriculum and Supervision.

Copyright © 1991. *Signs of Vitality in Curriculum Scholarship* by Ted T.

Foreword

There is a problem with an American doing this work. Ted Aoki is a Canadian scholar, uniquely so. To be grasped in terms of Canadian intellectual life, his work must be situated within Canadian history and culture, specifically, within Canadian curriculum studies. I lack the expertise for such a project, and nor am I appropriately situated to undertake it. (I am not reiterating the view, held by some in cultural studies, that subject position is a prerequisite for expertise. But, of course, it matters.) I think Aoki's work is extraordinarily important for American as well as Canadian curriculum studies, as I trust the attention I gave to it in *Understanding Curriculum* testifies. In that textbook, I focused on Aoki's intellectual leadership in the effort to understand curriculum phenomenologically. Although acknowledging there the movement in his work from phenomenology toward poststructuralism, I confess I did not grasp the full extent of it.

Why? I attribute this lapse in judgment to the fact that, although I had access to a number of Ted's essays, I did not have access to them all. A number were in fact unpublished; and many were published in journals not readily accessible in the United States. Several of the most brilliant, in fact, I had not yet read when I composed the passages on Aoki's work for *Understanding Curriculum*. Now, thanks to Ted and to Rita L. Irwin, we have access to the entire body of work, entitled *Curriculum in a New Key*.

Aoki's leadership in the effort to understand curriculum phenomenologically is legendary. After having read everything now, I conclude that it is only part of the story. Aoki's scholarly work cannot adequately be described as "phenomenological," despite the strong and enduring influence that philosophical tradition exhibits in these collected essays. Aoki is enormously erudite; he is well read not only in phenomenology, but in poststructuralism, critical theory, and cultural criticism as well. Even these four complex intellectual traditions fail to depict the range and depth of his study and his intellectual achievement.

In my introduction to the collected essays of the man who taught us to "hear" curriculum in a "new key," I emphasize the range and depth of the work. I focus too on the deft pedagogical moves Aoki makes in these essays, most of which were speeches. I know of no other scholar who took as seriously as Aoki did the scholarly conference as an educational event. Often working from conference themes, Aoki takes these opportunities to teach, and with great savvy and subtlety. Of someone we might say that he or she is a fine scholar *and* a superb teacher. Of Aoki we must say that his brilliance as a pedagogue is inextricably interwoven with his brilliance as scholar and theoretician. It is the unique and powerful combination of the three that makes Aoki's work absolutely distinctive.

In taking seriously the scholarly conference and thereby construing our coming together as an educational event, Aoki acknowledges the centrality of the social in intellectual—and academic—life. In a time in which careerist self-interest and self-promotion animate and, for many, define professional practice, Aoki's generosity in acknowledging the presence of others is exceptional. It discloses not only his utter intellectual honesty, but his profound sense of the ethical as well. "There are new curriculum researchers," he tells his fellow conference goers in 1973, "with whose ventures I can strike a vibrant and resonant chord. Although not too long ago this chord sounded strange deep inside me, that strangeness is fading. I think it is partly because in being at a conference such as this, I feel a sense of emergent becoming." Already, in this early essay (the title essay of the collection), we hear the auditory characterization of education as "resonance." The last phrase—and its notion of "emergent becoming"—underscores the dynamic, developmental, and dialectical character of Aoki's intellectual formation.

I intend my introduction to the collected works to function in two ways. First, I hope it inaugurates a series of scholarly studies of Aoki's *oeuvre*. To situate Aoki's achievement within Canadian curriculum studies is a project I trust will be undertaken by several; to those of you reading, please know there is at least one (but, no doubt, not only one) book series editor committed to supporting such an effort. There should be comparative studies as well, such as of the intersections of (and differences) Aoki's and Huebner's work. As well, there need to be studies of Aoki's influence on generations of younger scholars, and not only in Canada. I would like to see extended studies of Aoki's intellectual life history. And certainly there is room for a biography of this uniquely Canadian intellectual and public pedagogue.

Especially in this time when the academic field of education is under savage attack by politicians (Aoki once described it as "open hunting season for education"), it is incumbent on us to maintain our professional dignity by reasserting our commitment to the intellectual life of our field. Such a reassertion of our intellectual commitment includes, perhaps most of all, the study and teaching of curriculum theory and history. Study in neither domain can proceed far without the careful consideration of the work of Ted T. Aoki.

Second, I trust my introduction will function as both teaching aid and study guide. This ambition may seem redundant, given how brilliantly Aoki himself teaches in these essays. Although that is the case, it is also true that Aoki's work is complex, nuanced, and profound, and students without backgrounds in phenomenology, poststructuralism, and critical theory may well benefit from my sketching of the thematic and pedagogical movements in Aoki's work. I hope that my long and "lingering note" will stimulate students to engage Aoki's essays more actively than they otherwise might.

As students of Aoki's work know, the title of the collection derives from an early essay that was widely read, including in the United States. But its visibility and familiarity were not the only reasons why Rita Irwin and I proposed it to Ted as the title of the entire collection. The concept of "key" is an auditory rather than visual one, and it is the primacy of the auditory in Aoki's work that constitutes one of his most important and unique contributions to the field. It is Aoki's critique of ocularcentrism in Western epistemology and his honouring of the auditory, and specifically the musical, that enable us to hear curriculum in a new key. Almost alone among curriculum theorists, Aoki appreciated that after the "linguistic turn" comes an auditory one.

Note that the organization of the essays is thematic, not chronological, and that the categories (parts A, B, C, D) and the sequencing of the essays were chosen by Aoki himself. Allow me to acknowledge my ambivalence regarding the length of my introduction: Although I wanted to honour Aoki's brilliance by taking seriously and slowly each essay, I worry I have "lingered" too long. Students and teachers of the text will be the judge of that. Allow me to note, too, that although Rita Irwin (whom I tried to persuade, without success, to list her name before mine, as this work would not have occurred without her) and I are editors, the royalties go to the Aoki family.

I am grateful to you, Ted, for allowing Rita Irwin and me to edit your life's work. Your collected essays make crystal clear that are you a master scholar, theoretician, pedagogue. Your life's work has influenced and will continue to influence those who encounter it. If there were a Nobel Prize in education, you would be a recipient.

William F. Pinar
Louisiana State University

Preface[1]

In the mid-1980s, I read an article that would influence my academic and personal life for all time. This article came to me with little fanfare. In fact, it was not given as a class handout or suggested to me by a professor. As I reviewed several monographs loaned to me, I happened on the article entitled: "Toward Curriculum Inquiry in a New Key" by Ted T. Aoki. Little did I know then that this article, its author, and the author's lifetime body of work would make such a profound difference to my life. I remember to this day my first reading of this article. It resonated with my very being. Suddenly, everything I had been learning came together in an elegant yet transformative way. It offered me insights into the worldview of others, myself, and the selves I was becoming. It provided a safe space for me to take on the role of interpreter and critic. But most importantly, it legitimated for me that art education was the powerful learning force I knew it to be. For this paper was originally written for a conference entitled "Phenomenological Description: Potential for Research in Art Education" hosted by the Fine Arts Graduate Studies Program at Concordia University (April 6–8, 1973). Some time later Ted would craft the paper into published form for the Curriculum Praxis Occasional Paper Series, No. 2 (University of Alberta). I am today, as I was then, quietly pleased to witness a curriculum scholar bridging curriculum concerns with art education, not only for those of us in art education, but for everyone interested in curriculum studies.

I did not know Ted then, but I came to learn of his teaching and leadership at the University of Alberta and the University of British Columbia (UBC). As a doctoral student at UBC I soon learned that Ted's work influenced generations of education scholars, some of whom taught me. In reading the article "Toward Curriculum Inquiry in a New Key" I realized that Walt Werner, an important curriculum scholar at UBC, had been another doctoral student of Ted's. In time, I came to appreciate that several scholars at the University of Victoria, where I completed my master's degree, also studied with Ted. These are only a few of the scholars Ted mentored who would in turn influence me, and many, many others. I am sure I am not exaggerating when I say that Ted's incredible ability to teach ideas through personal and theoretical inquiry has more than touched thousands of learners: his pedagogy has changed their thinking, their being, their lives. He embodies curriculum.

As I carried "Toward Curriculum Inquiry in a New Key" with me throughout my doctoral student and professorial life, I was reminded of the day when the excitement of Ted's ideas made me search out new directions for my

---

[1] An earlier version of this paper is published as: Irwin, Rita L. (2003). In a New Key: Ted T. Aoki *Educational Insights, 8*(2). [Available: http://ccfi.educ.ubc.ca/publication/insights/v08n02/celebrate/irwin.html]

work. The excitement was never boisterous, but then I am not boisterous. The excitement was teeming inside me, nurtured by an extraordinary human being, sharing his being, and his becoming, with others. Being in the presence of humble greatness inspires one to find one's own inner greatness. Ted's writing did that for me, and I am certain that Ted's mentorship of his graduate students and his many colleagues nurtured an excitement for curriculum that has never been replicated in Canada.

Although I first read Ted's work in the mid 1980s, it would be the mid 1990s before I met him. I have never been one to make myself known. I would rather do the work that needs to be done and, through the context of that work, meet and work with others. As I look back, I realize that Ted and I shared several institutional homes: Lethbridge School District 51 (he also taught in Rockyford, Taber, and Foremost, Alberta), where he was a teacher and vice-principal (he taught for 19 years across these school districts); the University of British Columbia, where he was the Director of the Centre for Curriculum and Instruction (3 years) and later, an adjunct professor (17 years); and the University of Alberta, where he obtained his bachelor of education degree (1949), his master of education degree (1963), was an assistant, associate, professor and chair of the Department of Secondary Education (18 years) and now holds professor emeritus status. One institutional home we did not share was the University of Oregon, where Ted completed his PhD (1969). Despite sharing some of the same institutional homes, our paths did not cross. Although I was a student, teacher, or professor in the same educational settings, I kept him on the pedestal I created for him. Then one day, following a talk we both attended, a colleague introduced us. Here was a gentle, soft-spoken man, who was shorter than me (and I am not tall). Yet his extraordinary reputation as a curriculum scholar imbued his aura: In front of me stood a great man.

In the intervening years Ted and I have been on a number of thesis committees together and have shared tales of leading a university department. He often writes me handwritten memos in which he shares his latest thinking or the latest book he has read or the connections he has made at a recent event. And several times a year, I slip away with Ted and June for a sushi lunch at their favourite restaurant. In these moments, his wisdom almost pours out of him. Although not the only reason, Ted's dedication for Canadian curriculum studies played a significant part in my personal recommitment to curriculum studies, a commitment that lead me to become active in the Canadian Association for Curriculum Studies (CACS). Through my conversations with Ted, I knew that the next surge of scholarship in Canadian curriculum studies would only happen if curriculum scholars took up the task of (re)conceptualizing the forgotten spaces lingering within the etymology of the words we hold dear, as well as the very premises from which we understand curriculum today. Inspired and energized, I took on the role of president of CACS, a position I hold today. I do not make any claims to changing curriculum scholarship in Canada, but in the compiling of this anthology I feel that Canadian scholars are recognizing a giant among us, a man whose career as a classroom teacher, vice-principal, scholar, teacher educator, and chair of a university department has touched the lives of countless Canadian educators and students. His influence has been felt not only in Canada, but internationally as well, and especially in the United States,

One of the most impressive attributes Ted has is his abiding dedication to curriculum studies and curriculum inquiry. Now in his 80s, Ted has continued to teach at the University of British Columbia, give talks at national and international conferences, mentor graduate students, and, perhaps most importantly, nurture inquiry in the many spaces experienced in a lived curriculum. Witnessing his passion, intellectual curiosity, and amazing pedagogical capacity even today, keeps his Canadian colleagues spellbound. In the 1970s when some considered curriculum studies to be moribund, Ted took up the challenge to reimagine what curriculum studies could become. He opened our minds to reconceptualizing curriculum, moving us away from curriculum-as-plan to the lived curriculum. He made room for curriculum to come alive in any learning opportunity. He had, and still has, the ability to move our minds and our hearts in amazing ways.

Although I was never fortunate enough to take a class from Ted, I know the power of his teaching. Over the years I have sent many students to his classes and lectures. In every case, students came back to me saying they had been in the presence of a profoundly amazing teacher. Ted's greatest gift was, and remains today, his ability to call out of each of us deeply felt teaching and learning concerns that are transformed through penetrating inquiry. He is a pedagogue of pedagogues, and because his pedagogy is so profound, it lingers with us as we go forward and teach. The genealogy of his powerful pedagogy is the legacy that Ted leaves in the minds and hearts of countless curriculum scholars, particularly in Canada. In celebration of his legacy, Ted has been recognized for his achievements, influence, and impact in a variety of ways. Ted holds honorary doctor of laws degrees from the University of Lethbridge (1988), the University of British Columbia (1991), the University of Alberta (1992), and the University of Western Ontario (1999). He is particularly proud of being given honorary Elder status by the Four Band Council, in Hobbema, Alberta (1975). Ted has been given a certificate of appreciation by the Korean Educational Development Institute (1984), the Distinguished Service Award from the Canadian Association for Curriculum Studies (1985), the Phi Delta Kappa of the Year Award by the University of Alberta Chapter of the Phi Delta Kappa (1985), the CEA Whitworth Award for Research in Education presented by the Canadian Education Association (1985), the Distinguished Service Award from the American Educational Research Association (1987), the Curriculum Theory Project Award presented by the Louisiana State University, Baton Rouge (2000), and a Mentoring Award from the International Institute for Qualitative Methodology (2001). In addition to these awards he holds honorary memberships in the International Honor Society in Education (1994) and the Social Studies Council of the Alberta Teachers' Association (2001), and was inducted into the Professors of Curriculum Circle (limited to 125 members) through the Association for Supervision and Curriculum Development (1988).

One other award Ted received, the *Journal of Curriculum Theorizing* Award, deserves special attention (1985). On this award may be found the following citation: "The *Journal of Curriculum Theorizing* honours Professor Ted T. Aoki for distinguished contributions to curriculum studies in the United States and Canada by establishing the Annual Aoki Award." This citation states what virtually all of the other awards seek to celebrate: the lifetime work of a distinguished and exceptional scholar whose practice has changed the landscape of curriculum studies. These accolades are particularly poignant when one considers that after Ted completed his first degree (bachelor of commerce, UBC) in 1941 he was subjected to the federal government's policy to evacuate Japanese Canadians from the west coast of British Columbia to southern Alberta immediately following the Japanese attacks on Pearl Harbor (1942).

Ted's ideas came into my life with little fanfare. Today, as a friend and colleague, I know that Ted never wants fanfare. It is his pedagogy that matters, his interactions with individuals, and his pursuit of new ideas. Even so, there is a community of scholars, now and in the future, who would benefit tremendously from reading Ted's body of work. Although it took some time to convince Ted of this, it is with his blessing that we bring to you his contributions to the field of curriculum inquiry. Although his scholarship is his own, Ted would be the first to acknowledge the love and support of his wife June, his sons Doug and Edward, and their wives and children.

This volume has given me the chance to work with two of the greatest curriculum giants in our field, William Pinar and Ted Aoki, and for that I am truly grateful. Through their generous spirits and intellectual rigour we have found profound professional respect and a lasting affectionate friendship.

In closing, the Canadian Association for Curriculum Studies stands as a national organization to which Ted's commitment to curriculum change was often directed. His national pride is very strong. Through him, and alongside him, Canadian curriculum studies became a field of study. In the past, Canadians often denied the power of their own ideas. Today, that has changed. We want to celebrate those who have made a difference and we want to conceptualize, perhaps reconceptualize, Canadian curriculum studies. What better way to do this than to celebrate the life's work of Canada's own Ted Aoki? Through this volume we pay tribute to Ted Aoki and his achievements. In the act of doing this, readers will witness the development of Ted's ideas over time. This could be the greatest contribution of all: to see firsthand how ideas developed, lingered, and found depth in the cracks within words most of us never knew existed. In his lingering notes, he nurtures continuous inquiry through the passions that ground our dedication and curiosity.

Ted, on behalf of countless teachers, administrators, and scholars in Canada, the United States, and a host of other countries, allow me to express our deepest gratitude, admiration, and affection.

Rita L. Irwin
University of British Columbia

"A Lingering Note":
An Introduction to the Collected Works
of Ted T. Aoki[2]

William F. Pinar

> On this bridge, we are in no hurry to cross over; in fact, such
> bridges lure us to linger.   Ted T. Aoki

Ted Aoki is a legendary figure in North American curriculum studies. You are about to understand why. A breathtakingly brilliant teacher and scholar, Aoki's interdisciplinary erudition enables us to understand curriculum not only as a verb (rather than a noun), but also as sound. As you will "hear," Aoki teaches theory as a master jazz musician plays his instrument.

In part A—Reconceptualizing Curriculum—we find the record of Aoki's significant and influential participation in the reconceptualization of North American curriculum studies, an approximately decade-long event (roughly the 1970s) during which the field was reconceptualized from a primarily bureaucratic support system to an interdisciplinary (often theoretical) study of educational experience (see Pinar, Reynolds, Slattery, & Taubman, 1995, chap. 4). In "Toward Curriculum Inquiry in a New Key" (chap. 1, first presented in 1973 and published in 1981), Aoki undertakes a "vitalized curriculum praxis."

To do so, Aoki turns to art education, citing Kenneth Beittel's call to uncover of the "root metaphors" in art education, "the experiential core of art," the "expressive situation." Aoki turns as well to Eliot Eisner, who had likewise called for an examination of the "conceptual underpinnings" and the "goals and assumptions of major orientation to curriculum." Aoki characterizes their work "a vibrant call" that questions "the constraining model of tradition" in the field. From the outset, the auditory echoes in Aoki's theorization.

"What seems to be needed in curriculum inquiry," Aoki writes, "is general recognition of the epistemological limit-situation in which curriculum research is encased. Accordingly, we need to seek out new orientations that allow us to free ourselves of the tunnel vision effect of mono-dimensionality." It is that work—the formulation of curriculum in a new key—to which Ted Aoki devotes himself for the next thirty years. At this opening moment of his remarkable and important career, Aoki characterizes his work as "search" that "beckons us to

[2] A shorter earlier version of this paper can be found at: Pinar, Bill (December 2003). "A Lingering Note" Comments on the Collected Works of Ted T. Aoki *Educational Insights, 8*(2).
[Available: http://ccfi.educ.ubc.ca/publication/insights/v08n02/celebrate/pinar.html]

probe and to clarify perspectives underlying research approaches." As you will see, such probing and clarification leads him to understand curriculum in a new key.

The occasion is the British Columbia Social Studies Assessment, wherein he poses the distinctly hermeneutical question: "What are possible ways of approaching the phenomenon of social studies in British Columbia?" After Habermas, Aoki poses three orientations, (1) the empirical analytic, (2) the situational interpretative, and (3) the critical theoretical. In his 1991 revisiting of this project (see chap. 7), Aoki reconfigures these categories and adds a fourth.

In this opening essay Aoki defines the "empirical analytic inquiry orientation" (the dominant one) as one in which "explanatory and technical knowledge" is sought. Like engineering, technical work has, as its basic cognitive interest, the control of objects in the world. In the second orientation, one of "situational interpretative inquiry," research is conducted as a "search for meaning," to be described phenomenologically. In the third, critical researchers question descriptive accounts in light of sociopolitical conditions, a process known as "critical reflection."

One of Ted Aoki's key contributions is his traversal of the theory–practice divide. He traverses it, as he might say, by dwelling within the space between the two. More than any contemporary figure, Aoki bridges (a word I use advisedly, in honour of Aoki's affection for it) the traditional and reconceptualized fields. As we later see, it is a verb on which he focuses in thinking about the Pacific Rim. But in chapter 2, at a Summer Institute for Teacher Education held in 1980, Aoki is discussing an old-fashioned curriculum concept in the sophisticated language of the new field. The term is "curriculum implementation" and Aoki is critiquing the concept as a form of "instrumental action" (too often its fate in the traditional field) and as "situational praxis," its phenomenological reconceptualization. He performs the "eidetic reduction" by "question[ing] the typically unquestioned," by asking, "How should implementation be understood?"

Aoki is clear that traditionally the dominant way of understanding curriculum implementation was instrumentally. In 1974 he suggested: "A basic problem in implementation of programs may be found in the producer–consumer paradigm underlying the view of implementation." He understood that instrumentalism was "a business metaphor," an expression of our cultural "intoxication" with the technical power of science and technology. So understood, curriculum implement amounted to a subset of business management techniques, "one in which curriculum producers offer something to curriculum consumers." Such instrumentalism amounts to a crisis of Western reason.

"This crisis," Aoki explained, amounts to "a fundamental contradiction" between our commitment to "technological progress" and our "commitment to the improvement of personal and situational life." This crisis of Western culture "shows as an internal crisis in curriculum." And key to understanding this issue is appreciating the inadequacy of the social theory undergirding "implementation," one in which the teacher is stripped "of the humanness of his being, reducing him to a being-as-thing, a technical being devoid of his own subjectivity." In the early work of Ted Aoki, we find not only a map of the field, but also an ingenuous linking of phenomenology and critical theory in his analysis of curriculum implementation:

> I wish to propose an alternative view of implementation, one, which is grounded in human experiences within the classroom situation. This is the experiential world of the teacher with his students who co-dwell within the insistent presence of "a curriculum X to-be-implemented." I propose an alternative view, which sees "implementation as situational praxis" of teachers.

Notice that in one paper Aoki has traversed the expanse between traditional and reconceptualized fields. His "walking stick" is a key bureaucratic term in the traditional field, one that did the dirty work of erasing academic, which is to say, intellectual freedom, in the name, presumably, of institutional efficiency. It is, in effect, the third of Ralph Tyler's "basic principles of curriculum and instruction," disingenuously phrased there as a question concerning the effective organization of educational experiences. What it means is that teachers are to do as they are told. Aoki has situated this conceptualization as an instance of instrumentality, a concept caught in the cultural contradiction between social and technological progress, a marker of the crisis of Western reason.

That is a long and complicated "walk," done rather swiftly and, apparently, effortlessly. But he is not finished. On the chance that not all his listeners have been able to accompany him, Aoki offers another major concept that might also function as a "walking stick" for those who might come along. This is the notion of "theory and practice." In the traditional, Tylerian field, "implementation" was the moment of "application" of theory to practice, in which practice came to resemble theory. It rarely did, of course, leaving the two split from each other in an unhappy marriage. Aoki integrates them:

> For many of us, to understand praxis requires an estrangement from the dichotomized view of "theory and practice" and embracing of that which sees them as twin moments of the same reality. Rather than seeing theory as leading into practice, we need now more than ever to see it as a reflective moment in praxis. In action-oriented language, praxis is action done reflectively, and reflection on what is being done.

Aoki's sophisticated critique of instrumentality and the crisis of western reason becomes a reflective moment in the classroom, an opportunity for teachers to understand what is happening to them and to the children they teach.

Rather than a fundamentally bureaucratic concept in which administrators rationalize their regulation of teachers' academic freedom, curriculum implementation has become, in the space of one essay, a form of praxis, an integration of the traditional binaries and one embedded in very different assumptions than those underlying instrumentalism. Aoki names three: (1) Humanization is the basic human vocation; (2) humans are capable of transforming their realities (in this instance, the self and the curriculum); and (3) education is never neutral. We can hear an echo of Paulo Freire here.

Indeed, Aoki employs Freirean language in his interpretation of "situational praxis" located "within the situation of a classroom." Here teachers and students become "co-actors as they dialectically shape the reality of classroom experience," creating together "a crucible of the classroom culture," animated guided by their "personal and group intentionalities." That last phrase would seem to portend a phenomenology of classroom life. "But," Aoki continues,

> what is equally important for teachers and students as they engage in interpretative acts is to be critically reflective not only of the transformed reality that is theirs to create, but also of their own selves. It is within this critical turn, a precious moment in praxis, that there exist possibilities for empowerment that can nourish transformation of the self and the curriculum reality. It is this critical turn that provides the power to affirm what is good in the reality experienced, to negate what is distorting therein, and to allow engagement in acts or reconstruction guided by an emancipatory interest.

In this passage we hear a sophisticated and original integration of Freirean pedagogical practice and Habermasian critical and autobiographical theory, presented, please recall, at a Summer Institute for Teacher Education in 1980. No one in North America is playing such a sophisticated theoretical hand as was Ted Aoki in the summer of 1980.

Characteristically, Aoki concludes his paper with a simple, even disarming, summary, one that understates his conceptual achievement by returning to the familiar—in this instance curriculum implementation—and restating its significance. "What I have attempted in this paper," Ted tells us, "is to portray implementation employing the distinction between 'instrumentalism' and 'praxis,' i.e., between instrumental action and situational praxis, between actions of beings-as-things and beings-as-human, signifying two frames of reference in which the reality of implementation activity can be constituted."

In so doing, Aoki has reconceptualized "implementation" from its obfuscation as a bureaucratic device by which teachers are rendered subservient to the intentions of others. Now "implementation" has become "competence in communicative action and reflection, and reality is constituted or reconstituted within a community of actors," an important advance in our thinking in itself. He adds in parting, "I see no place for the view of implementation as instrumental action. What we must have is a view or action which humanizes. Curriculum implementation as situational praxis is one such mode of action."

He is still not finished, "lingering" (to use one of his favourite gerunds, although it does not show up in this early paper) to introduce us to a major distinction he will develop in later essays, the distinction between curriculum-as-plan and curriculum-in-use. "Curriculum implementation," he notes, using two concepts that will figure prominently in the *oeuvre*, can be understood as "bridging the gap between curriculum-as-plan and curriculum-in-use."

In chapter 3, Aoki turns his attention to the term he introduced in the previous chapter, yet another term that figured prominently in the traditional field. Unlike "implementation," the concept of "competence" does not seem to have emerged within the internal history of the field. Rather, like other obnoxious political slogans (such as "standards"), the term was thrust on the field from the outside. Teacher education programs across the United States—at the time I was teaching in upstate New York and I remember the rush of meetings to supply Albany with the rhetoric it demanded—were being rewritten so as to "ensure" teacher "competency." It was as if we teacher educators had not before been concerned with the matter. What is obnoxious about the current "standards" movement is precisely the same implication: that until now teachers and teacher educators had had none.

The occasion for Ted's attention to "competency" was a conference on the subject, chaired by Penn State's Professor Edmund C. Short. Here Aoki was speaking to the largely American audience (I was in attendance), telling us, a decade before "place" and "situatedness" became key concepts, "I have become increasingly aware that I am North American." In later papers he will focus on his situatedness, on his identity, explicitly, but at Penn State this seems less like an assertion of selfhood than a pedagogical device to disarm a possibly sceptical audience. He does so by speaking not ideologically, but autobiographically: "Having lived in and where I find myself now within a world in which positivistic science and its derivative technological worldview is dominant, I find myself struggling against my own initial tendency to totalize *a* way of interpreting 'competence' into *the* way, the instrumental way." Here he is providing his listeners with an identificatory bridge, should they wish to traverse the distance between taken-for-granted (i.e. bureaucratic) acceptance of the commonsense term to a critical appraisal of it:

> [I] find myself caught within my own self-constituted limit-situation, and in attempting to understand "competence" differently, I am experiencing a struggle to attempt to break through my self-imposed walls. Fundamental to this struggle are the contradictory meanings of competence that dwell within me. What follows is a portrayal of this contradiction.

This is powerfully performative pedagogy. By disclosing his own struggle, his own dwelling in the gap between common sense and critique, Ted invites his listeners to distance themselves from their uncritical acceptance of the term, to create a gap where, before, there might not have been one, where they might "learn."

While evidently not caught in the same rhetoric game as were we at the University of Rochester in the late 1970s, the University of Alberta education faculty were nonetheless engaged in a revision of their teacher education program, documented in a report entitled "A Report on the Revision of the B. Ed. Program." In the 1978 report, Aoki identifies two contradictory interpretations of competence. The first, evident in Segment 1 of the program, is evident in a compulsory core course in "basic skills and strategies of teaching," imagined to be: (1) classroom management and discipline, (2) curriculum planning, (3) instructional strategies or methods, and, paralleling Tyler's fourth "basic principle," and (4) assessing and evaluating student behaviour. This course illustrates an interpretation, Aoki notes, of competence as instrumental action.

There was in the report (not present, I assure you, in the New York State Plan of the same period), a Segment 2, entitled "The Senior Elective," an opportunity for undergraduate students to bring together the various program elements in a course "committed to integration and synthesis." Ted quotes from the report; we learn that in this senior elective should provide an experience enabling the student (1) to "combine personal action and reflection on action," (2) to analyze the "assumptions and values regarding the role of the teacher, especially as "leader," (3) to "link the universal with the particular, the concrete, day-to-day world of personal action with the world of ideas, values, symbols, or, more generally, with systems of meaning." Aoki notes that "teaching as reflected in Segment 2 no longer espouses the instrumental and technical view of competences was reflected in Segment 1," that this represents a view of competence as *praxis*.

So far, Aoki has confined his discussion to a report, the kind of institutional documentation most administrators can appreciate. But in his discussion of the report, Aoki has built a bridge to a very different, non-administrative conception of competence. Now he goes to work, phenomenologically. "To help explore this view of competence," he begins, gently, "let us uncover the root etymology of *competence*." The Latin root reveals, he suggests, with Heideggerean irony (that the West is in decline, that to renew ourselves we must return an ancient past we have foolishly fled), a "fresh view." He notes that the Latin root is *competere*, *com* meaning "together," and *petere* meaning "to seek." In a root sense, Aoki points out, to be competent means to be able "to seek together or to be able to venture forth together." Such a conception—"competence as communal venturing"—represents a radical departure from what the American bureaucrats had in mind, but Aoki, the master pedagogue, concludes subtly that it "holds promise for a fresh view of what it means to be a competent teacher."

In shock, I suspect, at finding themselves in the presence of a decidedly nonAmerican view, Aoki's mostly American listeners are now transported to Poland, as Ted, again most modestly, says he "seeks support from a phenomenological scholar whose works I have recently come to know." He is referring to Polish scholar Karol Wojtyla, who proposed (Aoki tells his audience) that humanity's authentic vocation is self-disclosure and self-governance, the fashioning of personal and social lives worth living. "By emphasizing both the communal condition of man and the irreducible transcendence of the human person with respect to the current of social life," Aoki continues, "Wojtyla counteracts the deviant, reductionist tendencies so prevalent in contemporary philosophy and culture. Furthermore, he sees man as a historical being, man as a marker of his own history, who together with others are seen as co-makers of history."

It is to such an understanding of "acting and reflecting," Aoki suggests, "we must turn to make sense afresh of competence in teaching." So understood, the concept of competence is anchored in the situated "interaction" of teachers and students, "mediated by everyday language, oriented toward practical interest in establishing open intersubjectivity and nonviolent recognition on which communicative action depends."

Once again, Ted has moved swiftly, deftly, and a far distance, formulating a sophisticated integration of phenomenology and critical theory grounded in respect for the everyday life of teachers and students. The situated interactivity of teachers and students, he emphasizes, is:

> rooted in a network of meanings actors within that situation
> give. Hence, understanding the day-to-day life of teachers and
> students in the classroom requires at least understanding the
> terms of meaning structures actors in the classroom gives.
> However, to be able to venture forth together in the meaningful
> way Wojtyla speaks of requires not only an understanding of
> his meaning structure but also action rooted in critical
> reflection on these meaning structures.

Aoki returns the ontological ground of action to teachers and students and their relatedness, insisting that their meaning structures, and their reflection upon them, constitute "competence." In this "critical venturing together," as he puts it, "both teachers and students become participants in open dialogue." Through "open dialogue," then, teachers and students "examine the intentions and assumptions underlying their acts." In such "critical reflection," the everydayness of routinized conduct is placed in "brackets," in an effort, Aoki notes, "to go beyond the immediate level of interpretation." "In this sense," he concludes, "critical reflection is thoughtful action, i.e., action full of thought."

Once again Ted concludes in a modest tone, no small trick given the scope of his accomplishment. "What I have attempted to do," he begins, "is to portray *competence* employing the categorical distinction between 'technique' and 'praxis,' i.e., instrumental action and practical action, between beings-as-things and beings-as-no-things, signifying two frames of reference in which reality is constituted." Within the world of "technique" or "instrumental action," he notes, "reality is objectified, that is, it is constituted as the being of things according to nomological laws." To invoke the concept of competence within this worldview, construes actions as the behaviours of "beings-as-things oriented toward interests in control, efficiency, and certainty."

In contrast, in the worldview of "praxis" or "practical action," social reality is constructed by the "intersubjective actions of beings-as-humans, oriented toward cognitive interests in understanding." Within this worldview, *competence* is reconceptualized as "communicative action and reflection, reality is constituted as a community of actors and speakers." Invoking Habermas's notion of "emancipatory" interest, Aoki affirms competence as critical-reflective labour toward "de-naturalizing" of the commonsensical, that reiteration of the social surface in which alternative realties are dismissed as "impractical." In the commonsensical worldview, the historical predicament is "pulverize[d] into a multitude of mini-problems [that] can be articulated in purely instrumental terms."

This is, I submit, a major paper, from both conceptual and pedagogical points of view. In it, Aoki invites his listeners to identify with him as he situates himself as "North American," an invitation that denaturalizes their own commonsensical understanding of "competence." He initiates this move in two steps: First he discusses a teacher education revision document, a kind of bureaucratic artefact familiar to all in the audience, and one that starts off familiarly enough: teacher competence as classroom management and evaluation. But then it moves to an integrative seminar—not common then or now in American teacher education—in which critical reflection is required.

At this early point in the paper, the audience remains "safe" in a bureaucratic document and in a proposal for a course safely lodged in Canada. Now Aoki takes his next step, to that familiar artefact, the dictionary, where he notes, commonsensically enough, the Latin root of the word at hand. But in the dictionary, competence means to "be able to seek together or to be able to venture forth together." Now we've left State University USA, and, in the held breath that, I suspect, ensued, he showed them just how "situated" as Americans they are. It's to Poland we have to go to reunderstand "competence." There, he points out, Karol Wojtyla critiques instrumentality itself, insisting that humanity's authentic vocation is self-disclosure and self-governance, and from that phenomenological understanding of the humanity, Aoki has moved to refashion not just the cóncept, but the very life-world in which "competence" has meaning and creates effects in the lives of teachers and students. At Penn State, in 1980, Ted Aoki has, through his sounding of a complex note comprised of critical theory, phenomenology, and classroom experience, reimagined the world of the school.

In chapter 4, Aoki revisits his experience evaluating the British Columbia Social Studies curriculum. He does so in order to provide "an exemplar of how multiple perspectives can guide curriculum evaluation." He and his colleagues began their evaluation tasks by administering paper-and-pencil questionnaires that sought teachers', parents' and students' views of social studies, and, in particular, students' knowledge of social studies content. Then they made on-site visits, guided, he points out, "by concerns for meanings people who dwell within classroom and school situations give to Social Studies." Finally, the evaluation team conducted a critical analysis of the Ministry of Education's official curriculum documents, in order to lay bare the "official" perspectives embedded in them. "Now, some years after the completion of the evaluation," he notes, "we are in a position to provide a reconstructed version, possessing to some degree a clarity and tidiness, which only a reconstruction can give."

In this reconstructed version, Aoki revisits the three orientations he has outlined in chapter 1, a schema for understanding evaluation that anticipates by several years Patti Lather's (1991) somewhat similar construal of educational research into (a) "a realist tale," not unlike Aoki's "ends-mean's orientation" in this commonsensical representation of "reality"; (b) "a critical tale," not unlike Aoki's "critical orientation"; (c) "a deconstructionist tale," which, although avowedly poststructuralist in conceptualization (an influence not yet visible in the field when Aoki and colleagues conducted the BC assessment in 1978), echoes his "situational interpretative" and "critical" orientation, and, finally (d) "a reflexive tale," again suggestive of Aoki's situational-interpretative and critical perspectives. It is a tribute to Aoki's scholarship and intellectual prescience that he is able to anticipate such widely read work as Lather's, and years in advance of it.

Next Aoki elaborates the "ends-means (technical) evaluation orientation" in some detail, emphasizing its interest in efficiency, effectiveness, predictability, and certainty, which he sees in the service of *control*, a theme on which my colleague Bill Doll (1993, 1998, 2002) would focus nearly a decade later. Within this orientation, the form knowledge takes is that of "empirical data." The harder they come, Ted notes, presumably the more objective they fall. "Knowledge is objective," he summarizes succinctly, "carrying with it the false dignity of value-free neutrality, reducing out as humanly possible contamination by the subjectivity of the knower."

In the "situational interpretative evaluation orientation" the primary interest are those meanings ascribed to the situation by those engaged in the curriculum. In order "to gain insights into human experiences as they are experienced by insiders, as they are lived within the situation," Aoki and his BC Social Studies Assessment team "experimented with two situation evaluation approaches: (1) an ethnographic approach in which we sought out views of the curriculum-as-plan and curriculum-in-use as interpreted by parents, students, teachers and administrators, and (2) an approach using conversational analysis of the meaning structures of the existential life of teachers and students."

Aoki summarizes the situational interpretative orientation in terms of cognitive interest, form of knowledge and mode of evaluation concerned with (a) "the meaning structure of intersubjective communication between and among people who dwell within a situation"; (b) "situational knowing, within which understanding is in terms of the structure of meaning," working "to strike a resonant chord by clarifying motives and common meanings"; and (c) "the quality of meanings people living in a situation give to their lived situations."

In the "critical evaluation model orientation," the evaluator asks six questions:

1. What are the perspectives underlying a particular curriculum?
2. What is the implied view of the student or the teacher held by the curriculum planner?
3. At the root level, whose interests does the particular curriculum serve?
4. What are the root metaphors that guide the curriculum developer, the curriculum implementer, or curriculum evaluator?
5. What is the basic bias of the publisher/author/developer of prescribed or recommended resource materials?
6. What is the curriculum's supporting worldview?

Although this orientation is rooted in critical social theory, its anticipation of poststructuralism in education—and, in particular, deconstruction—is audible when Aoki writes that the critically–oriented evaluator, him/herself, becomes a subject of evaluation research. "The evaluator," he writes, "in becoming involved with his subjects, enters into their world and attempts to engage them mutually in reflective activity." From their report of the BC Social Studies Assessment, Aoki and his colleagues assert: "The curriculum developers' perspective toward the social world should not, in other words, be hidden from the users of the curriculum."

Not only has Aoki anticipated by years important work in research methodology (the situatedness of the investigator in his/her investigation), he has extended and concretized Habermas's characterization of "cognitive" interests that renders another key concept in the traditional field—evaluation—reconceptualized. No longer can those conducting curriculum evaluation imagine their work as the simple accumulation of data, or even the faithful rendering of others' experience, or only an ideological analysis of curriculum content. As Aoki has reformulated it, curriculum evaluation includes all these cognitive interests, not only separately but in combination, which, to anticipate his later work, creates spaces among the three, in which the subjectivity of evaluators themselves is linked to the social reality embedded both in the curriculum and in its assessment.

"In our efforts to give an accurate portrayal," Aoki reflects, "we have employed not only traditionally accepted techniques, but also more personalized ones aimed at seriously attempting to 'hear' what the people of the province are saying about the subject." The subjective and the social become linked his attending to the public sphere. He concludes by quoting the report (the words are David G. Smith's):

We know that the true magic of the educating act is so much more than a simple, albeit justifiable, concern for improved resources, more sensitively stated objectives, better pre-service and in-service training for teachers, or improved bureaucratic efficiency. Rather it is has to do with the whole meaning of a society's search for true maturity and responsible freedom through its young people.

In chapter 5, "Toward Understanding of 'Computer Application,'" Aoki confronts the "blindness of high fashion in the world of curriculum," wherein endorsements of the educational potential of the computer are "bandied about with almost popular abandon." These are strong words for this gentle pedagogue, who asserts that most computer enthusiasts are "without a deep understanding of what they are saying." Strong words, but accurate ones, and composed 7 years before we discuss the history of technology in schools in *Understanding Curriculum* (see Pinar et al., 1995, pp. 704–719). Aoki provides his readers with his own history.

"Within the Faculty of Education wherein I dwell," he writes, for the moment regaining phenomenological calm, "I have experienced in the last quarter century three waves of technological thrusts." The imagery is perfect and, I suspect, not without humor. "We first witnessed the grand entrance"—a saviour has come!—"of educational media instruments such as the overhead projector, the film projector, the slide projector, the listening labs." Like now, the hype then meant hiring faculty specialists in the area and "the creation of media resource centers," which, he notes drolly, "now exist as mausoleums of curriculum packages and instructional hardware."

"The second wave," Aoki recalls, "was the TV thrust," once again employing that term overused in popular educational journalism (that sometimes passes for scholarship). "Educational TV," he reminds, was supposed "to deliver the message." What "message" was delivered? "Today," he reminds, "we see, in our faculty classrooms, platforms mounted in corners, empty holding places for TV monitors that no longer sit there, monitors that for some reason could not replace professors. They stand as museum pieces in the wake of unfulfilled hopes of dispensing education via TV. Today, the third wave is upon us."

The third wave—the image suggests drowning as well as surfing—Aoki characterizes, quite rightly, as a "frenzy," a word that underlines the profoundly irrational and antieducational quality of enthusiasm (especially among politicians) for computers in the classroom. Having made that point, Aoki focuses on the term "computer application," a familiar phrase Ted chooses to question, to press for "understanding" by asking: "How shall I understand computer technology? How shall I understand application?"

Inspired by Heidegger's meditation on technology, Aoki suggests that "we must seek the truth by understanding computer technology not merely as means but also as a way of revealing." "How, then," he asks us, "is this essence [of computer technology] revealed?" Aoki answers:

It is revealed as an enframing, the ordering of both man and
nature that aims at mastery. This enframing reduces man and
beings to a sort of "standing reserve," a stock pile of resources
to be at hand and on call for utilitarian ends. . . . But by so
becoming, man tends to be forgetful of his own essence, no
longer able to encounter himself authentically. Hence, what
endangers man where revealing as ordering holds sway is his
inability to present other possibilities of revealing. In this, it is
not computer technology that is dangerous; it is the essence of
computer technology that is dangerous.

The third wave, then, overwhelms—"drowns"—us. We are no longer able
to encounter ourselves as authentic beings; we encounter ourselves as elements
of "standing reserve," interchangeable units ready for application in a complex
technological world of instrumental action.

Aoki notes that "application" means the reproduction of "something general
in a concrete situation," as in old-fashioned understandings of "theory into
practice." Application as reproduction divorces the phenomenon from
"understanding, and, in fact, follows it." "It is," he underscores, "an instrumental
view." Drawing on Gadamer's (1975) *Truth and Method*, Aoki asks us to
understand computer application "as a hermeneutic problem," wherein
"application thus is an integral part of understanding." As a hermeneutic
problem, application occurs in "the tension between the language of computer
technology on the one hand and, on the other, the language of the situation,"
what later Aoki will characterize as "the third space."

Aoki appreciates that he must move slowly here. "What is being said here,"
he notes, "is that computer technology, to be understood properly, must be
understood at every moment, in every particular situation in a new and different
way." In this sense, he adds, "understanding is always application." So enframed
in Gadamerian language, "the meaning of computer application and its
application in a concrete situation are not two separate actions, but one process,
one phenomenon, a fusion of horizons." Before "fusion," however, is
"mindfulness," a phenomenological meditativeness that enables us to remember
"that being in the situation is a human being in his becoming. This mindfulness
allows the listening to what it is that a situation is asking."

Aoki knows that this theorization is subtle, and, possibly, elusive for his
readers, as he offers, modestly, gently, "Hopefully, the meaning of application is
clearer." He reiterates that the meaning of application is not the reproduction of
the general in a specific concrete situation. The meaning of application, he
writes, "is the actual understanding of the general itself that a given situation
constitutes for us. In this sense, understanding shows itself as a kind of effect
and knows itself as such." Understanding application as a hermeneutic
movement avoids the reductionism of instrumentality "by vivifying the
relationship between computer technology and the pedagogical situation."
Rather than forcing the situation to become a replica of another, Aoki animates

the computer by casting it as part of the "livedness" of educational experience, an occasion of "understanding." It is to that term he turns as, ever rooted in the process of teaching, "I begin to talk about concluding."

He points out that he has, thus far, neglected "a key term in the title I have chosen for this paper." Before we turn to that term and his discussion of it, I want to focus on this characteristic Aokian move. Just as he vivifies the machine by rendering the situation in which it is embedded as a hermeneutic, which is to say, an educational one, just as he vivifies what for many of us are routine assemblies by taking seriously conference titles and themes, here he dwells on the title of the talk he himself is giving.

By doing so, he demonstrates his pedagogical savvy. First, by engaging in a critical reflection (or, in his phenomenological moments, an eidetic reduction) of the title, he distances himself from it, enabling him to understand his own embeddedness in the discursive formations and crosscurrents that comprise the field. Second, by bringing the reader's and listener's attention back to the title, he performs a recursive reiteration of the main themes of his "lesson," enabling his "students" to both retrieve what has occurred so far and integrate it in a final, concluding and synthetical moment. These tactics are those of the high theorist and supreme pedagogue.

These moves are discernible in the final paragraphs what must be, for the instrumentally structured reader/listener, an elusive paper. "One of my agendas leading to the coming into being of this paper," he tells us, "was to flirt with the question, 'What does it mean to understand both epistemologically and ontologically?'" To answer, he moves from Gadamer and Heidegger, recalling that a "coming to appearance of any phenomenon is also a concealing," and that "in the very appearing of the phenomenon is concealed the essence of what is." One way, he continues, "to understand the essence of 'what is' without violating the appearance of the phenomenon or the phenomena itself is to allow the essence to reveal itself in the lived situation." It appears we have returned to the situation as hermeneutical.

This time Aoki enters the situation, and dwelling within it he notices "that my question 'What is it?' is 'caught in the *it*,'" which is say, that when "being" is "caught by the question 'what is *it*?'" we have "surrender[ed]" to the *it*. For Huebner (1999), this problem is one of being caught in the "whatness" to the exclusion of the "moreness," what for him is "the lure of the transcendent." While there is no theological language in Aoki's formulation, the powerful point is present. "To be caught in the question 'What *is* it?' is," he teaches us, shifting our attention from the "what" to the "is," "to dwell in an ontological world of the *is* and *not yet*." "This appearance," he writes, teasingly I think, as in the *lure* of the transcendent, "beckons me to move beyond mere flirtation."

As he so often does, Aoki is moving from the abstract to the concrete, here turning his attention to the teaching of a doctoral student in the department named Carol Olson. Ever humble, he wishes "to reveal what she has taught me." It is an example that makes clear that, despite his strong critique of computers, the man is no Luddite. Olson, he reports, has, for 12 years, been "a child of haemodialysis technology," sustained by a dialysis machine at the University of Alberta Hospital. Olson wrote: "We (her three sisters have also been so treated) acknowledge our indebtedness to technology; we refuse to be enslaved by technology." In this doubled relation of dependency and independence, of gratitude and defiance, Olson understands the "application" of technology. Aoki says it simply: "What Carol teaches us is the significance of that which is beyond the technological in the technological." Even in the hospital, even when one's "interiority" is being routed through a machine, one discerns the lure of the transcendent.

The distinction between the "whatness" and the "isness" of educational experience is elaborated in chapter 6, a paper dated a year earlier. Here Aoki invites us to understand "teaching as in-dwelling between two curriculum worlds." The first of these is the curriculum-as-plan, the origin of which, he notes, is outside the classroom, in the Ministry of Education or a school district office. It is "given." Originating elsewhere, it travels to the classroom, in this instance, Miss O's classroom. "This curriculum-as-plan is the curriculum," Aoki reminds, "which Miss O is asked to teach the Grade 5 pupils who are entrusted to her care."

The curriculum-as-plan represents the "what" of educational experience and Miss O's classroom personifies the "is." Returning to the concept of "implementation," Aoki notes that "if the planners regard teachers as essentially installers of the curriculum, implementing assumes an instrumental flavour . . . that is, there is forgetfulness that teaching is fundamentally a mode of being." The understatement makes the point compellingly.

"The other curriculum world," Aoki continues, "is the situated world-as-lived that Miss O and her pupils experience." He provides a glimpse of this world from the inside, so that its "appearance" may reveal the "isness" of the lived world:

> For Miss O it is a world of face-to-face living with Andrew,
> with his mop of red hair, who struggles hard to learn to read;
> with Sara, whom Miss O can count on to tackle her language
> assignment with aplomb; with popular Margaret, who bubbles
> and who is quickly to offer help to others and to welcome
> others' help; with Tom, a frequent daydreamer, who loves to
> allow his thoughts to roam beyond the windows of the
> classroom; and some 20 others in class, each living out a story
> of what it is to live school life as Grade 5.

Miss O is clear, Aoki tells us, that she is an employee of an institution, thereby "accountable" for what and how she teaches. But Miss O is no ordinary school employee, Aoki continues, as "she also knows that the Ministry's curriculum-as-plan assumes a fiction of sameness throughout the whole province, and that this fiction is possible only by wresting out the unique," that is, the specificity of the classroom as lived. In the sameness of the curriculum-as-plan, the teacher becomes "one of the thousands of certified teachers in the province." "Worse," Aoki adds, "children like Andrew, Sara, Margaret and Tom [become known] merely as Grade 5 pupils, children without unique names, without freckles, without missing teeth, without their private hopes and dreams."

Miss O knows that these children *are* individuals; she knows that they "are counting on her as their teacher." For Aoki, that means that that these children "trust her to do what she must do as their teacher to lead them out into new possibilities, that is, to educate them." As for Miss O, dwelling within the situation of responsibility, "she knows that whenever and wherever she can, between her markings and the lesson planning, she must listen and be attuned to the care that calls from the very living with her own Grade 5 pupils." Although deeply respectful, there is no sentimentalism here; Aoki invokes Miss O to make an educational point:

> Miss O in-dwells between two horizons — the horizon of the curriculum-as-plan as she understands it and the horizon of the curriculum-as-lived experience with her pupils. Both of these call upon Miss O and make their claims on her. She is asked to give a hearing to both simultaneously. This is the tensionality within which Miss O inevitably dwells as teacher. And she knows that inevitably the quality of life lived within the tensionality depends much on the quality of the pedagogic being that she is. Here the "third" space, the space in-between, has entered Aoki's theorization, and this theorization will become ever more prominent in the final phase of Aoki's *oeuvre*.

The educational point is not to overcome the tension of the zone between curriculum-as-plan and curriculum-as-lived-experience; the educational point, Aoki teaches us, is to dwell "aright within it." He suggests that an overconcern for mere survival in the maelstrom of the classroom is not enough, a point Christopher Lasch (1984) makes in a different context. Survival for what? The educational question is one of meaning. It has an ethical meaning, as the teacher recognizes her or his moral obligation to recognize the individuals in the teacher's midst, to acknowledge their dependency, their trust, their hopefulness. But in such ethical recognition the teacher does not disappear into the concrete world of the everyday; he or she remains attentive to the curriculum-as-plan, but not obsessively so. The teacher works from within; he or she resides "in-between." Aoki admonishes: "We must recognize the flight from the meaningful and turn back again to an understanding of our own being as teachers."

Now Aoki moves to make a harsh criticism of—or is it a sharp warning to?—curriculum planners, but he does so indirectly. "We are beginning to hear that in Canada," he reports,

> some architects—developers of lived space who have claimed
> disciplined understanding of human space, guided by their zeal
> for high technology—have constructed buildings (places-to-
> experience-life) that are now called sick buildings. We hear
> that the architects of these buildings were not attuned to the
> fundamental meaning of space-as-lived-experience. What does
> this say to curriculum architects?

He doesn't answer the question directly, but points out that for those curriculum planners who appreciate "the nuances of the in-dwelling of teachers in the Zone of Between, the challenge seems clear." If the quality of curriculum-as-lived-experience is, in fact, the quality of education, curriculum planners must take as their central concern making a contribution "to the aliveness of school life as lived by teachers and students." The authority of curriculum developers derives not from technical expertise, Aoki continues, but from

> a deeply conscious sensitivity to what it means to have a
> developer's touch, a developer's tact, a developer's
> attunement that acknowledges in some deep sense the
> uniqueness of every teaching situation. Such a sensitivity calls
> for humility without which they will not be able to minister to
> the calling of teachers who are themselves dedicated to
> searching out a deep sense of what it means to educate and to
> be educated.

As he pointed out in the essay on computer application, the uniqueness of the situation *is* its educational import, and by living through that situation critically, self-reflexively, attuned to revelation of reality, one comes to understand the deeper meanings of "curriculum development."

One of the most evocative and, for me, beautiful images in the Aoki *oeuvre* appears chapter 8, entitled "Layered Voices of Teaching: The Uncannily Correct and the Elusively True." As is the case with so many of the papers collected here, the original version was presented to teachers, this one at a conference sponsored by the British Columbia Teachers' Federation. Aoki begins, as he so often begins, gently, making manageable a point of fact that is, in fact, highly unpleasant. "In our busy world of education," he notes, providing an initial opportunity for identification, a moment that we continues into the next phrase: "we are surrounded by layers of voices."

The first association his teacher/listeners might make of the image might well be that of the classroom. Aoki seems to work from this possibility in the next, elliptical phrase, when he describes these voices as "some loud, some shrill." But these are not our students, for however loud they may become, they rarely become shrill. "Shrill" seems to be a quality of adults, disingenuous adults, who "claim to know what teaching is." Now we know to whom he refers but before we can fasten on that fact, he returns us to ourselves: "Awed, perhaps, by the cacophony of voices, certain voices become silent and, hesitating to reveal themselves, conceal themselves."

Here he has said a brave thing, as few teachers want to admit that they have indeed become silenced, that, by and large, they have remained silent despite their public defamation. But there, he has said it to them. But he does not allow them to linger there, perhaps because it might invite humiliation or melancholy. Quickly he calls to them: "Let us beckon all these voices to speak, particularly the silent ones, so that we may awaken to the truer sense that stirs within each of us." Poetically, politically, this is a pedagogue with savvy, courage, and compassion.

"Before we visit the place where the silent voices dwell," he counsels his listeners, "let us uncover the outer layers of voice—all voices claiming to know what teaching is." Having moved from the public to the private, from the social to the subjective, deftly, in three sentences, he moves to reassure his listeners that he will walk with them across the bridge from defamation to affirmation. "I will try," he says softly, reassuringly, "to uncover layer by layer, from the outside in, from the top to the ground, from the abstract to the concrete place where teaching truly dwells."

Aoki does not become angry—not in public, not directly—with those whose shrill voices claim knowledge and authority but have neither. Instead, he blames his own colleagues, who have, he suggests, "shied away from the live but complex world of the classroom." These people have focused on the "outcomes" of teaching rather than on "understanding of teaching." Disclosing his knowledge of Marxist critique, he notes: "Likening the school to a factory or a knowledge industry, they assumed that what counts are effects and results in terms of investments made."

From the obsession with "outcomes," Aoki takes us to the second layer, one focused on teaching itself, but as technique. He points out that the notion of "effective teaching" derives from the behaviouristic conceptions of motivation and retention, in which teaching is reduced to "doing." Acknowledging that "the notion of effectiveness has a seductive appeal of essential simplicity," he chides those who espouse this view by pointing out that "such a focus may be neglectful of the fact that the effectiveness of teaching may have more to do with the being of teacher—who a teacher is."

Now he grasps our hand and takes us into the inner layer, a layer he characterizes as a journey "on the way to understanding teaching as mode of being." In order to begin this journey, we must understand that the first two layers—"scientific and technical understandings of teaching"—derive from manipulation and control. "What we need to do," he advises, is "to break away from the attitude of grasping, and seek to be more properly oriented to what teaching is, so that we can attune ourselves to the call of what teaching is." He emphasizes the verb, enabling us to see that these voices have grasped us around our throats, squeezing our voices silent. This is a not a matter of simply changing one's mind; it requires, make no mistake about it, "breaking out of the seductive hold of an orientation to which we are beholden."

Having now said another brave and dramatic thing, Aoki withdraws slightly, giving us space to breathe without the constriction we suffer amid layers one and two. He withdraws, not in retreat, but to give us room to breathe. He does so by speaking to us indirectly, through stories. In doing so, he enables us to retreat slightly, to listen for our own voices, silenced by others. He wishes to "offer" these stories, he tells us, as they suggest "what it means to be properly oriented to the essence of teaching that may itself reveal itself to us." He retreats again, however, giving us yet more space: "All I can do is point, hoping that the pointing will help us to begin to hear the voice of teaching that lurks concealed but, nevertheless, calls upon us."

As he will do many times, Aoki takes an everyday word—we have seen him do it already with "implementation" and "competence"—and works it, sometimes by investigating its etymological meaning, on other occasions by situating it in a hegemonic Western episteme (instrumentality and the crisis of Western reason), and here by emphasizing one word that usually is silent: "is." He points out that the question "What is teaching?" emphasizes the "whatness" of teaching. But "What *is* teaching?" emphasizes the "is." "With this new question," he tells us (teaching us the centrality of posing questions in pedagogy), "I feel much more oriented, I hope more properly oriented, to be in the presence of the beingness of teaching." Having provided us with a simple guide by which we may listen, he proceeds to tell three stories, stories providing us with "a glimmer of what teaching essentially is."

For the sake of space, I will focus on only one, the second narrative, in which describes a reunion with an elementary-school teacher named Mr. McNab. It is a story told by Ted's wife June, who recalls that, 44 years ago, Mr. McNab encouraged his Japanese Canadian students to share their culture with Anglo and other students. Reunited with him 44 years later, Aoki tells the retired teacher that in the interim "I often recalled the image of his watchfulness clothed in care that lived in vividly within me." Who among his listeners could not have been moved by this story, a story in which we as teachers can identify both with McNab and with Aoki, identify both as teacher and as student. Aoki enables us to accompany him on his journey by providing us multiple sites of identification. He tells us:

> I feel blessed being allowed 44 years ago to be in the presence of a teacher whose quiet but thoughtful gesture had touched me deeply. Today I feel doubly blessed being allowed to relive the fullness of this moment in the regained presence of Mr. McNab, rooted as I am in memories of my teacher of 44 years ago.

But the story is not about Ted; at least he is not employing it so. He asks us to join him in wondering, "What insights, what deeper seeing into teaching does this story allow?" He provides two answers for our consideration, two themes, as he puts it phenomenologically, "I wish now to dwell within . . . that speak to essential features of teaching that this story reveals: teaching as watchfulness and teaching as thoughtfulness."

For Aoki, "watchfulness" seems akin to vigilance, and it is gendered feminine. "Such," he writes, "is the watchfulness of mother with child; such is the watchfulness of teacher with student." Formulating what might be described as a phenomenological ethics, Aoki continues: "Authentic teaching is watchfulness, a mindful watching overflowing from the good in the situation that the good teacher sees. In this sense, teachers are more than they do; they are the teaching."

When teaching is thoughtfulness, Aoki suggests, teaching is "an embodied doing and being, thought and soul in oneness of the lived moment." The "lived moment" Aoki articulates involves the same Mr. McNab who had encouraged the Japanese Canadian children in his class to be proud of their culture. Aoki escorts us to the lived moment when Mr. McNab was forced to witness the midyear departure of those Japanese Canadian students relocated to Alberta during World War II. Although the victim in this moment, Aoki does not speak from that position, but, rather, from the position he imagines as the teacher's. He suspects that even though Mr. McNab

> had become attuned to the annual departure of his students at the end of school year, somehow the departure of these students in mid-year must have been for him a different experience. And, as a teacher . . . he was caught in this living difference, experiencing the solitude, left alone to make sense of the breakup that happened in his classroom beyond his willing.

What an excruciating moment Aoki has communicated to us, and in a psychologically manageable way. His move is not unlike the identificatory invitation in the film *Schindler's List*, wherein Christian viewers are psychologically enabled to face what Christians did to Jews in Nazi Germany by identifying with a Christian character who, like Mr. NcNab, was caught in a situation "beyond his willing."

Some of us might wonder if Steven Spielberg's motives were more commercial than pedagogical, although his own Jewish identity necessarily complicates any such speculation. In Aoki's case, he has nothing to gain but a lesson well taught. What he teaches to those who were present (and those of us who are present each time we read this moving piece) is the timeliness, at this historical moment (note that the "lived moment" he explicates, both in the McNab story and in this opening to the talk to teachers in which this story appears, is a historical *and* phenomenological moment), of understanding what teaching truly is, how it speaks from within autobiographical memory and lived experience, and provides the fundamental layering of our professional calling and experience. Aoki says it so much better than can I:

> I have suggested that what seems urgent for us at this time is
> understanding what teaching truly is, to undertake to reattune
> ourselves such that we can begin to see and hear our doings as
> teachers harboured within the pedagogical presence of our
> beings, that is, of who we *are* as teachers.

Having sounded the call, Aoki might have worried that his own voice lingered in
the outer layers of his listeners' lived worlds, as he, again, retreats from this
direct encounter, and invites his listeners to "work from within." He provides a
pedagogical, meditative exercise in which the silenced voices within can now
speak:

> I ask you now to think of a really good teacher you experienced
> in your own time. Allow him or her to be present now before
> you. I feel sure that the truth of this good teacher of yours is in
> the measure of the immeasurable. And now, say to him or her:
> he is the teaching; she is the teaching. After having said these
> words, in the silence allow the unsaid to shine through the said.
> Savour now the elusively true, the mystery of what teaching
> essentially is.

Three years later (in publication dates, at least), Aoki will once again
invoke the image of "layered," this time not as layered voices but (in chap. 7)
"Layered Understandings of Orientations in Social Studies Program
Evaluation." Here he returns to and expands the schema of orientation or
cognitive interest that he employed in the British Columbia Social Studies
Assessment project. He begins by noticing the prominence of the word
assessment in many evaluation schemes, pointing out that it "speaks of the
epistemological tradition to which many evaluators hold allegiance." Leaning on
Habermas, as he puts it, Ted recasts the empirical analytic orientation as an
ends–means model, retains the critical-reflective orientation as *praxis*, while
unfolding the situational-interpretative orientation into *emic* and *critical-
hermeneutic* evaluation orientations. "Moreover," he continues, "rather than
merely suggest a plurality of alternative orientations, the orientations have been
gathered, admittedly loosely, into layers that suggest some distinction between
the world of concretely lived experience and the formulations of evaluation that
are abstractions of and somewhat distant from lived experience."

Following the spatial metaphor that informed his "voices of teaching"
essay, Aoki works from the outside in, the closest in or "ground" being the inner
layer of lived experience. From outside in, they are listed: (a) ends-means
evaluation orientation, (b) praxical evaluation orientation, (c) emic evaluation
orientation, and (d) critical hermeneutic evaluation orientation. The interest of
the "ends–means" orientation is "control as reflected in values of efficiency,
effectiveness, certainty, and predictability." It is rooted in positivism. The

interest of the "praxical" is "emancipatory action that improves human condition," and it is rooted in neo-Marxism.

Ted realizes that for many *emic* will be a new word, so he defines it. An anthropological term referring to insiders' subjective understanding of a situation anthropologists are studying, "emic" refers to the "quality of everyday cultural life." The fourth evaluation orientation, the "critical-hermeneutic," involves, he tells us, the "disclosure of existential meanings in lived experience." It involves the "quality of human Beingness." Positioning this layer closest in, Aoki seems to be returning to phenomenology as primary in this conceptual tool chest.

In the critical-hermeneutic orientation, the evaluator does not stand aloof; he or she is no mere observer, as typical in the ends–means evaluation scheme and in the situated participation of emic evaluation. Rather, the critical-hermeneutic evaluator "must enter deeply into intersubjective conversation with the people in the evaluation situation." Such conversation "moves beyond the chit-chat that so often remains at the informational level as simply exchanges of messages, not requiring true human presence." In such conversation, "language is not merely a tool of communication in which thoughts are put into words, nor is it merely a bearer of representational knowledge." Recalling Heidegger's conception of language as a House of Being, Aoki characterizes language as "a way humans live humanly in this world."

Within the 1970s British Columbia Studies Assessment, Aoki recalls, "a modest attempt" was made to employ the critical-hermeneutic orientation, guided by an understanding of existential realms of being as first, a "passive realm of being" wherein "one lives out the expectancies of others. Values and meanings are perceived as given in the situations in which one exists." Second, Aoki posits an "immediate realm of being," wherein one "tends to be concerned only about pleasurable experience to fight off boredom. In this realm it is the present that is of paramount importance, and little responsibility is taken for choices made."

In the third realm, what Aoki calls a "responsible realm of being," key qualities include "decisiveness and self-determination." Here a person makes choices and assumes full responsibility for them in terms of other people's welfare. Such a person knows that others are affected by his or her decisions. The fourth and final layer is an "immanent realm of being," wherein "a person experiences the self truly. Experiences in life are vivid. Choices are increasingly based on trusting personal understandings and on a sense of the spiritual dimensions of living. Authentic being with others is the person's prime concern."

In his concluding note, Ted suggests that the four evaluation orientations reflect what he terms the polysemic nature of both social studies and evaluation. He acknowledges the influences of Habermas and (for the first time) of Foucault, Derrida, Lyotard, Deleuze, and Guattari, whose works, he suggests:

challenge the centrality of the metaphysical grounds of western tradition. We live in a turbulent and exciting time. Implications for social studies and evaluation abound . . .. At stake is what our children and adolescents experience in the name of social studies education. Hence, there is, at this time, a deep challenge confronting social studies evaluators.

In chapter 9, "Legitimating Lived Curriculum: Towards a Curricular Landscape of Multiplicity" (first published in 1993), Aoki is speaking to the 1992 annual convention of the Association for Supervision and Curriculum Development (ASCD), a group of school administrators, classroom teachers, and other school personnel. He starts by using an anecdote to teach a complicated and, I think, radical idea. He anticipates that the idea might be disturbing for this audience, so he claims the disturbance for himself, a pedagogical move that provides opportunities for listeners to identify and disidentify at the same. The ambivalence this school-based audience might have felt as Aoki challenges unquestioned assumptions regarding the organization of the curriculum is situated in himself. Watch this consummate pedagogue at work.

"Science must be taught as a humanity," Aoki quotes Stuart Smith as saying, noting to his listeners that Smith is both a scientist and chair of the Association of Universities and Colleges of Canada. "Of course," Aoki acknowledges, "many of us would be interested in the full report. But, for me, a sometimes curriculum person, the anecdote evokes reflection. Two thoughts come forth, each in its own way disturbing our curriculum landscape." By "landscape" Aoki means nothing less than the academic disciplines themselves. "We are familiar with this curriculum topography," even though "the reference here is to the university setting." "We can sense," claiming the shared identification he has invited his readers to assume at the outset:

> that what is at stake is fundamentally the lure of Western epistemology, our beliefs about knowing and knowledge, which has given our universities and schools a striated curricular landscape. . . . We have deeply set images reflecting the way this curricular landscape is inscribed in us.

Maintaining a relaxed, even folksy tone—he refers to "us" as curriculum "people"—Aoki gently insists that Dr. Smith's call is indeed a challenge. "Should we 'integrate' the two disciplines?" he asks. Affirming the possible distress that those who have accepted the separate school subjects as sacrosanct, Aoki offers, "I am hard pressed to ask good questions." While he thinks of what to ask, he moves from being relaxed to being humorous, defusing any discomfort by telling us "I have a tongue-in-cheek response. How would it be if we brought together a scientist, a novelist, and a bottle of scotch at a café on Bourbon Street?"

Having spent more than few hours on Bourbon Street myself, I was amused by Aoki's juxtaposition of what C. P. Snow characterized as "two cultures" in the decadent culture of the New Orleans's Vieux Carré. Lest we think Aoki himself has "gone native," he adds, quickly and seriously: "Less playfully, what Dr. Smith's remark evokes in me is what some call a crisis of modernity in the Western world, a questioning of the way of life we have constituted as modernism."

Juxtaposing the conception of curriculum-as-plan with the lived curriculum (again he refers to Miss O), he moves to a third element, and it's not the scotch. He invokes what he characterizes as a "curricular landscape of multiplicity (C&C landscape)." This is no add-on, but already extant in the lived curriculum: "A critical feature of Miss O's curricular landscape, which is already populated by a multiplicity of curricula, is the very word multiplicity itself." Then he poses the question: "How shall we understand this cumbersome sounding word, *multiplicity?*"

Noting that in the curriculum-as-plan conception, "curriculum-related activities such as 'instruction,' 'teaching,' 'pedagogy,' and 'implementation' [have] become derivatives in the shadow of the curriculum-as-plan," Aoki asks how we can "displace" its "primacy." He suggests a distinctly Deleuzian idea, "a curricular landscape of multiplicity (which grows in the middle)." How to understand this concept? "We might begin," he answers, "by heeding the words 'multiplicity is not a noun,' a claim by Gilles Deleuze, for whom, like Heraclitus, life is constantly in flux."

The use of the passive voice in the following passage is strategic, I suggest, enabling his listeners to undergo the questioning at a distance, through another, namely, Aoki himself. "Increasingly," he writes, "we are called upon [note the passive voice framing this process as a matter of 'calling' and 'profession' to reconsider the privileging of 'identity as presence' and to displace it with the notion of 'identity as effect.'" This is subtle, sophisticated stuff, the heart of the Derridean critique of the Western metaphysics of presence. Ted suspects his audience must be squirming, so he stops and asks a question that acknowledges their own possible confusion: "What is being said here?" He doesn't allow the question to linger long (assessing, probably correctly, that his audience does not know the answer), but in the very next sentence explains, again employing the passive voice to enable the audience's identification with him and participation in this educational experience:

> We are being asked to consider identity not so much as some*thing* already present, but, rather, as production, in the throes of being constituted as we live in the place of difference. For example, according to this understanding our identities as teachers or curriculum supervisors are not so much in our presences; rather, our identities, who we are as teachers and as curriculum supervisors, are ongoing effects of our becomings in difference.

In this passage Aoki seems to have moved past the phenomenology of the early papers; the conception of "selfhood" as "authentic being" who is "grounded" in "lived experience" has become movements of self-constitution within spaces of difference. Who we are, this view suggests, is not some anterior or essential "soul." Rather, who we are is produced by the effects of our movements among layers of difference. As he has done before, Aoki employs a list to make this complex idea accessible. The first "line of movement"—"in difference between discourses"—Aoki characterizes as "C&C landscape, a landscape embodying the curriculum-as-plan and curricula-as-lived, indeed, an open landscape of multiplicity."

In the second line of movement—"in the difference between metanarratives and narratives"—Aoki returns to Deleuze to remind us that "multiplicity grows from the middle." Drawing on Lyotard, Aoki suggests that these are not either/or. Rather, "it is time not to reject but to decenter the modernist-laden curricular landscape and to replace it with the C & C landscape that accommodates lived meanings, thereby legitimating thoughtful everyday narratives."

We have traveled a far distance in a short period of time, and perhaps Aoki is sensitive to the possible "exhaustion" (intellectual and psychological) among his listeners, and so returns to the beginning. "In this context," he explains:

> we might reinterpret Dr. Smith's statement, "Science must be taught as a humanity." I now hear Dr. Smith (1) recognizing the unwarranted privileging of the techno-scientific curriculum mind-set understood almost totally in terms of objective meanings, and (2) calling for a de-privileging such that a clearing can be opened up to allow humanly embodied narrative to dwell contrapuntally with metanarratives.

Then he returns, briefly, to phenomenological language, suggesting that Smith's call that "science must be taught as a humanity" seems to "beckon questioning from the ground up. Such a questioning, it seems to me, puts not only the structure of the university but also the structure of curriculum at all levels into turbulence, opening possibilities of a fresh line of movement for curriculum."

Now that he has questioned not only the curriculum organization but the metaphysical grounds for our (modernist) identities as educators, now that he has questioned the organization of the curriculum (and thereby creating the conditions for a fundamental reconceptualization of institutional education), Aoki returns to familiar ground, a move no doubt welcomed by his listeners. His sense of humor returns, as he confesses that "I do not know if Miss O has read anything of Jean-François Lyotard, but somehow in her wisdom she knows the significance for herself as a teacher of allowing space for stories, anecdotes, and narratives that embody the lived dimension of curriculum life."

In paying this respect to Miss O—and to thoughtful teachers everywhere—Aoki distinguishes himself from those university-based researchers who are ready to use teachers to make their own "empirical" or ideological points. True, Aoki is making a point, but it is one grounded in his own humility and respect and appreciation for teachers, from Mr. NcNab to Miss O. And it is no cheap compliment; he is suggesting that, without knowing it, thoughtful educators understand what is at stake dwelling within spaces between curriculum-as-plan and curriculum-as-lived. "In her wisdom," he tells us, the educator seems to know how to proceed "in the middle," amid various "lines of movement."

Aoki acknowledges that 3 years have passed since he first wrote about Miss O, who is now a vice-principal. From this position, she "leads" a beginning teacher named Laura into "that place of difference between metanarratives and narratives, beckoning her to struggle and flourish on her own in a line of movement that has its own zigzags." In her coming of age in the profession (or, Ted terms it, "a practicing teacher grows in wisdom"), Laura will travel what Aoki characterizes as "polyphonic lines of movement," lines such as (1) "experiencing differences in kind in the tension between the master story and the daily stories, (2) experiencing pedagogic reaching as a mode of becoming, (3) pedagogic reaching as a letting go and a letting be, (4) pedagogical listening as a responding to others and (5) hearkening to the call of calling."

Drawing on scholarship that questions the primacy of the visual in the epistemology of modernism, Ted notes that the young teacher "is drawn into what seems to be an architectonics of lines of movement that we feel sure Deleuze also would hear rather than see as a multiplicity growing in the middle." Both bodies of work—Deleuze's and the critique of the visual—become increasingly key in Aoki's work, as we will see.

In the third line of movement—entitled "In the Difference between Faceless Others and Faces of Others"—Aoki points to the spaces between C & I landscapes, wherein "students become faceless others," and those lived curricula, wherein "teachers and students are face to face." To question the "synthesized totality" of intersubjectivity fused into "we," Aoki invokes Miss O again, suggesting that she "worries that there might be something remiss in the synthesized totality." That something remiss is supplied, in part, by Levinas, through whose work "Miss O sees a decentering of the self ego, allowing acknowledgment of the teacher's responsibility to others, the students." Not only Miss O—evidently a concrete person—feels keenly her responsibility to others.

Through his invocation of Miss O, through his portrayal of her as embodying the wisdom curriculum theory articulates and to which it aspires, Aoki performs his own responsibility to his colleagues in the schools. At first blush, his choice of a woman to personify the educator is traditional and mirrors the educator's gender in the public mind. But in more subtle gender terms, this seems to me a transgressive choice, insofar as the university professor (gendered male in the public mind) is "becoming-woman" (a Deuleuzian concept) in his choice of Miss O. In contrast to the more typical theory–practice relationship in which (male) university professors often ask (female) public school teachers to accept positions of "gracious submission," in Aoki the relationship is not "vertical," but "horizontal." Moreover, although Miss O exists and is, in literary terms, a foil for Aoki, she is, at the same, also Aoki. He has never forgotten his years in school classrooms. He has never disconnected his theorizing from that remembrance. I suggest that the theorizing of Ted Aoki is a complex pedagogical performance of that rich remembrance, rearticulated through what he has studied as a university-based scholar and theorist.

To conclude: Does Ted ever want to render a "conclusion"? Or is his regular use of "A Lingering Note" a pedagogical rather than psychological device, asking his listeners and readers not to rush to the end, to think that they have "acquired" knowledge, asking us to dwell in the moment of questioning and reflecting, between the C & I landscape (his paper perhaps?) and the C & C landscape (their experience of listening or reading it), and to see what "grows in the middle." What he says, however, is rather didactic, guy-to-guy talk, but in "her" honour:

> Curriculum developers and curriculum supervisors should heed
> thoughtful practicing teachers who already seem to know that
> the privileging of the traditional C&I landscape may no longer
> hold, but must give way to a more open landscape that offers
> possibilities by, in part, giving legitimacy to the wisdom held
> in live stories of people who dwell within the landscape. . . .
> [W]e are already in the age where *episteme* will not be able to
> stand alone. It needs to stand together with *sophia*, for it seems
> that the name of the game is no longer knowledge alone but,
> rather, the belonging together of knowledge and wisdom.

Lest he has pushed his listeners away with talk of sophia and relationality and wisdom, Aoki brings them back Bourbon Street, "where our scientist, a person of knowledge, and our novelist, a person of wisdom, are supposed to be in conversation about 'science must be taught as a humanity.'"

So that his humor should not be coded as disavowal, Aoki invokes not scotch or music—probably the two most common associations with New Orleans's Vieux Carré (and the former one of which Aoki employed at the outset of this essay)—but philosophy. The association is with France. "Since it is in the French Quarter," he suggests, "our friends from France, Jean-François Lyotard and Gilles Deleuze, may have already joined our scientist and novelist in conversation." Note that he has hardly backed off the complexity of what he told his ASCD listeners but in fact has "multiplied" it. Instead of using the Quarter as an opportunity to flee serious thought and conversation, Aoki recasts the Quarter as Paris's Left Bank and suggests:

> Possibly, we might be allowed to listen to their improvised
> lines of movement growing from the middle of their
> conversation. And possibly, just possibly, there might be a new

language with a grammar in which a noun is not always a noun, in which conjoining words like *between* and *and* are no mere joining words, a new language that might allows a transformative resonance of the words *paradigms, practices,* and *possibilities*. If that be so, we should all move to the French Quarter, so that we can not only listen, but also join them right in the middle of their conversation.

Although hardly the only brilliant piece, this one is among the most brilliant in the collection, a virtuoso performance of pedagogy. His ever-shifting position—even "vacating" it in the persona (and actuality) of Miss O—disables his listeners from pinning him down so they can reject his "lesson." As he shifts—high theory to humor, from Canada to France, from science to the humanities, from the binary of curriculum as-plan/curriculum-as-lived experience to what "grows in the middle"—Aoki speaks a sophisticated jazz, highly disciplined, carefully focused, ever-shifting creatively, communicatively, theoretically. By starting with the idea of science as one of the humanities, Aoki scrambles the curriculum code, but makes it palpable for his American listeners by making it Canadian. By invoking Miss O he invites his mostly male audience to feel safe, assured that God's scheme of men thinking and women working is safe and sound. But it is Eve who does the thinking, and "Adam" is her secretary, communicating to us knowledge God herself wants us to know.

Finally, I confess I am flabbergasted at the audacity of using Deleuze's notion of "growing in the middle" with a group we might surmise are, by and large, rather determined to prevent something from "growing in the middle." Subtle does not mean timid, and in introducing this notion that eats, like a termite, at the primacy of binaries in the Western episteme, Aoki has questioned the entire modernist, indeed, Western project. He has used humour to do so, and his references to the decadence of the New Orleans's Old Quarter—a site of both displacement and disidentification (few Americans consider New Orleans as exactly "American") and placement and identification (his listeners are in New Orleans: what Aoki is saying is, however, not in Canada or in France but here)—shift the very ground on which his listeners locate their professional activity.

A genius of improvisation, Aoki tells this audience of school administrators, district supervisors, and classroom teachers (the theorists long ago fled ASCD: for a brief history of ASCD see Pinar et al., 1995, pp. 142–143, 172–173, 208ff) that they must abandon their hierarchical positions of authority and honour their colleagues in the classroom by joining them in a journey toward wisdom. I spoke at an ASCD conference twice and on one of those occasions fully one-third of my audience (of several hundred; it is a large organization and a well-attended conference) had loudly departed by mid-speech. I wasn't there for Ted's speech, but I bet his radical proposal sounded sweet to them, and not one person moved. I can see the twinkle in his eye.

The second section (part B) of these collected essays—Ted entitles it "Language, Culture and Curriculum"—begins a decade before the last chapter. We're still at ASCD, however, and I was at this one, Ted. (This was the other time I spoke at ASCD, a "face off" with Ralph Tyler.) The sounds of "reconceptualization"—although loud and dissonant in AERA—were just plain inaudible at ASCD, except at the leadership levels (which arranged the "debate" between Tyler and me). In other words, Ted is facing an audience without a clue as to what they're about to hear. Ted seems to know that, as he begins gently a speech entitled "Toward Understanding Curriculum Talk Through Reciprocity of Perspectives."

Aoki starts by employing the disarmingly simple metaphor of "bridging two worlds" ("bridge" is a term to which he returns several times over the years and on which I comment later) to characterize what is involved when two people meet. But as soon as he has offered it, he questions it: "[I] fear the bridging metaphor is more opaque than transparent and fails to lead us too far in our understanding." A familiar experience—meeting another person—becomes defamiliarized.

We learn that the speaker is not thinking of everyday interpersonal encounters at all, but "cross-cultural awareness," which he warns if limited to observation and "contact alone" is "but a tourist's surface sense of awareness of culture." He thinks Maruyama's notion of "trans-epistemological process" might help us understand what is involved in "bridging two ways of knowing." Perhaps his listeners imagined meeting a colleague in the hallway, but Aoki has whisked us away to another country, and where the familiar image of the tourist won't do, he adds. Before his listeners vaporize in the warp speed of his movement, he returns them to the hallway. "My interest in this paper," he says, "is to understand more fully what it means when two people from different lands meet in a face-to-face situation to make sense together of school and curriculum."

Now Aoki sets to work theorizing. A face-to-face encounter is, he says (after John O'Neill), "a conversation of mankind" in which language and reason are connected. Ted asks: "How shall we understand such conversation as a meeting of mankind?" To answer, he provides three narratives, the first of which is "A Conversation with Graduate Students in Curriculum Studies." In it he reveals he is an administrator (a fact that must pique the interest of many in the ASCD audience), but as soon as he offers that familiar image he complicates it, reporting that "I find myself occasionally in what I call a trans-national situation when I encounter students from beyond North America."

It turns out "beyond North America" includes Kenya, Zambia, Ghana, Thailand, Korea, East India, Malaysia, Afghanistan, Iraq, Lebanon, and Egypt. Once again offering himself as a site of identification (and, simultaneously, disidentification, given his ethnicity and citizenship), he tells his fellow administrators and classroom teachers:

> Their visits help me to arrest the almost mindless instrumental
> mode of life that I routinely live as administrator. They help to
> remind me of the centeredness of conversation in any educative
> process. Somehow a student's visit transforms, as by magic,
> the physical environment labelled office into a human
> situation.

Once again Aoki has managed to question the taken-for-granted reality of many
administrators through the use of self-disclosure. By contextualizing his critique
of instrumental rationality and administrative control in the context of his own
daily life as a department chair, Aoki offers his listeners the opportunity to
question their own submergence in institutional "reality." The office becomes a
"human situation."

His description of meeting graduate students is phenomenological, and
poetically so. This quality is prominent throughout the entire Aoki *oeuvre*,
whether he is working from critical theory, poststructuralism, or
phenomenology. The dignity and beauty of the man, his delicacy, nuance and
profound respect for whomever he encounters, are movingly present in his
poetic prose:

> In a situation within which we as strangers meet, each with his
> own culturally conditioned horizon, how can we being to make
> sense common to us? And in our reaching out for each other
> through gesture, silence and talk, how can we become aware of
> our reachings, knowing fully that our reachings never fully
> reach?

Anticipating the postcolonial theory that will become fashionable 10 years later
(although this is the year Edward Said's *Orientalism* appears), he confides to his
audience that he worries that these students might study uncritically, that they
will see their "mission" as taking home Western curriculum knowledge as a
"commodity." "Underlying this view," he notes, "is a naive assumption of the
universality of knowledge—a notion that is tenuous and dangerous." In
conversation with students, "the initial turn takes us usually to talk of program
and such. But to remind ourselves of who we are in conversation, I ask that we
turn the conversation to ourselves. 'How will you know that what we consider
'good' here is 'good' in your homeland?'"

The second situation Aoki narrates to his ASCD audience in St. Louis in
1981 concerns a conversation with Francis Lampi of Zambia, a young
curriculum scholar now at the University of Zambia, with whom he has been
"engaged in a conversation through correspondence." Through their
correspondence Aoki finds him, "though not physically present, vividly present
before me. I can see him at times serious, and, at times, smiling. I can hear his
deep voice become softer when he becomes serious, become effervescent when
he laughs." Lampi had taken a curriculum theory seminar with Aoki during

which time he studied phenomenology and critical theory. Returning to Zambia, he found that his colleagues at the University of Zambia and the Ministry of Education were "entrenched" in positivism, including behaviourist psychology and Bloom's taxonomy. Lampi bemoaned the imperialism of the scientistic educational agenda.

From school colleagues meeting in the hallway to tourists exploring cultures "beyond North America," from Canada and to Africa, Aoki's American listeners have learned (a) that they do not know what "reciprocity of perspectives" actually means and (b) that what they have been taught to think education is, is actually a problem for others around the world.

Lest his listeners think that it is only Africans who are sensitive about the imperialism of scientism (with its fantasies of universality), Aoki provides a second example of the imperialism of North American constructions of "manpower," "planning," and "development." This time we are in South Korea, working from a paper by Bom Mo Chung. Chung deplores, Aoki reports, the reduction of admirable human traits and qualities to "knowledge and skills" demanded in "job settings," a consequence of treating human beings as means, ends. "For me," Aoki tells his audience, "these remarks by Dr. Chung are momentous. They speak fundamentally to Francis Lampi's concerns at the University of Zambia. They speak to us deeply." From Canada to Zambia to South Korea, the globalization of instrumental rationality in education threatens the very existence of education itself.

Ted concludes this speech to American schoolpeople by calling them to conversation. "If East–West conversation in curriculum is to be authentically East-West dialogue, if North–South conversation is to be authentically North–South dialogue," he suggests, then "such conversation must be guided by an interest in understanding more fully what is not said by going beyond what is said." Without such "going beyond," those engaged in conversation will not be able to take into account "unspoken" and "taken-for-granted" assumptions, including "ideology," what Aoki characterizes as that "the cultural crucible and context that make possible what is said by each in the conversational situation."

Once again, Aoki has made an "end run" around the possible recalcitrance of his American listeners by asserting that all educators—worldwide—must not succumb to their own, and to others' assumptions, but, rather, to engage what is "not said." Returning to phenomenological language, he reminds that "authentic conversation is open conversation," one in which the participants in the conversation engage in a "reciprocity of perspectives." Invoking one of his favourite metaphors, he ends: "I understand conversation as a bridging of two worlds by a bridge, which is not a bridge." Conversation is a passage from here to there and elsewhere, but it is not "here" or "there" or "elsewhere." It is the traversal of the shifting spaces separating us.

In chapter 11, entitled "Signs of Vitality in Curriculum Scholarship," Aoki takes the opportunity of being awarded the Canadian Association for Curriculum Studies (CACS) Award for Distinguished Contribution to Canadian Curriculum

Theory and Practice, an award presented at the 1985 CACS/CSSE Conference in Montreal. Aoki takes this opportunity to speak to the state of the field.

His first point is that curriculum is the "locus of scholarship in education." Given the marginalization of the field in too many United States schools of education (in the U.S. instruction and learning continue to dominate the broad field of education), this is an important assertion to make. Given the erasure of the academic freedom of teachers, including their professional control of the curriculum and the means by which its study is assessed, it is an important political point to make.

Ted summarizes the intellectual achievements of the field, the "questionings" that "have been taking place in curriculum studies." He identifies four: (1) questioning of "the technological orientation that prevails in curriculum rooted in instrumental reasoning"; (2) questing (rather than questioning) for the "original ground of curriculum as a human study"; (3) the questioning of the primacy of "epistemological over ontological considerations" in "curriculum understanding"; and (4) the questioning of "the adequacy of the assumptions underlying the domain of curriculum studies." This first theme suggests a field that is itself in revolution but, as well, a field that calls its sister specializations in the broad field of education to reconceptualize their (to use Schwab's language) substantive content and methodological structures.

The second theme concerns the "increasing recognition of curriculum scholarship in many faculties of education." He notes that for too long curriculum and instruction departments have been understood as "methods" specialists, "technicians, really, relegated to teaching 'how to' courses." Referring to the Faculty of Education at the University of Alberta, Aoki notes that the departments of educational psychology, educational foundations, and educational administration have been labelled the "basic" departments, relegating curriculum and instruction departments (at Alberta, of course, elementary and secondary education are housed in separate departments) to a "derivative" status, presumably "secondary" to the "basic."

Like Dwayne Huebner (and a younger generation of scholars; see Kumashiro, in press), Aoki takes note of the "privileged place" of educational psychology, "somehow separated from educational foundations, where a motley crew of sociologists of education, historians of education, et al. try to dwell together." His humour here is simultaneously deprecating and aggressive, it seems to me. Like Huebner, he understands that the preeminence of educational psychology can be attributed, in part, to the centrality of the concept of "learning" in education. He declines to mention psychologists' aggressive self-promotion of the term—and their field. In such a view, "teaching" becomes, merely, "the flip side" of "learning." Aoki has carefully studied Huebner's work, as he acknowledges: "I am reminded of the ardent pleas of curricularist Dwayne Huebner whom, I feel, not many have given a deserved hearing. What is to be noted here is that it has taken a curriculum scholar to dare to question the hegemony of the notion of 'learning' in education."

The third theme Aoki identifies concerns "the celebration of the mundane in curriculum studies," by which he means the "dialectic between the first and second–order curriculum worlds," curriculum-as-plan and curriculum-as-lived, "twin moments of the same phenomenon, curriculum." Due to the phenomenological movement which he—as scholar, teacher and administrator— he helped make important, he is able to say, if with characteristic modesty, "[I] feel that, as a group of curriculum scholars, we have begun to attend more seriously to the domain of everyday life in the curriculum world, in a sense, in celebration of the mundane world where peoples' lives are lived." This celebration does not disavow, however, the "first curriculum world," that of planning. Rather, it is "the tensionality in the dialectic" between the two that intrigues Aoki.

The fourth theme concerns "researching the meaning of the commonplaces of curriculum practice," an obvious reference to Schwab's work (as he acknowledges in the essay). Apparently devaluating "theory," Aoki asserts: "Curriculum essentially belongs to the world of the practical. Hence, curriculum studies, if they are authentic, must return to the concrete world of the practice." But the devaluation is apparent only, as quickly becomes clear. He names "two current developments" that "deserve our notice," the first of which is "a serious effort to re-understand practice," surely a theoretical endeavour if there ever was one. In this work, "practice is no longer understood merely as *applied theory*, i.e., a theory applied to situation." In fact, Aoki notes, "I now find 'application' a bothersome word," a point he made in his essay on computers (chap. 5). Rather than application of theory, "practice" becomes an element in *praxis*, a moment of action in which theory becomes enacted, now we would say (after Judith Butler), performatively.

In another effort to re-understand practice, the "focus is on the commonplaces of curriculum practice and action," by which Aoki means "curriculum development, curriculum improvement, curriculum implementing, curriculum evaluation, curriculum piloting, and curriculum policy–making." "In the past," he notes, "these commonplaces typically fell prey to a mean–ends interpretation, understandably given the almost oppressive technological ethos that prevails and enframes us." Now these commonplaces are to be reconstituted, he reports, "firm in their insistence of recognizing the presence of people who subjectively act."

"I applaud these scholars on two counts," Aoki tells us in rare moment of intra-field partisanship. First, he applauds those who have acknowledged "the mundane commonplaces of curriculum practice as a worthy dwelling place for scholars," a place, as he has taught us, in tensionality between curriculum-as-plan and curriculum-as-lived. Second, he makes a rare criticism by applauding those scholars who have not forgotten that

> the world of curriculum practice that was the raison d'être of
> the coming into being of curriculum scholarship in the first
> place, and thus, not yielding to the lure of the siren-voices of

the human science disciplines as some of our colleagues have
done—a movement I refer to as the "flight" from the
curriculum field.

This is a concern I have shared (see Pinar, 1979, p. 99). Never one to end on
a discordant note, Aoki praises the field overall, specifically "the vitality of the
curriculum field to which we have committed our lives as educators." In that
phrase and in the sentence to follow, Aoki speaks, it seems to me, of the
fundamental theme of his own career, a life's work in which he has always
brought an authentic and powerfully pedagogical presence to an academic field
dedicated to the world of practice. Utilizing his notion of "tensionality" to think
about the field as a whole, he concludes that, as a field, curriculum studies is
"vital," "a field of dynamic tensionality wherein curriculum scholars are
experiencing new beginnings that promise new possibilities. The debates and
discussions are lively. These are indeed exciting times for curriculum people."
Indeed they were and are exciting times, in no small measure, thanks to Ted
Aoki. In the final moment he returns to the occasion of his speech, and hands the
torch, as it were, to those assembled, reminding them—in the reference to
scholarship—that this field devoted to practice is an academic field: "I thank you
once more for the honour you have bestowed upon me. May I wish you and the
Association many, many rewarding years of curriculum scholarship."

In chapter 12, entitled "The Dialectic of Mother Language and Second
Language: A Curriculum Exploration," we remain in the mid-1980s (the paper is
dated 1984), and Aoki is bringing to bear on second language school programs
the insight of phenomenological curriculum theorists regarding "language as the
ground that makes possible the revelation of life experiences of human beings."
It is, as well, he suggests, an opportune moment to explore language as a way of
understanding curriculum orientations, using second language school programs
as the paradigm.

He reiterates (in terms of this collection—see chap. 5—but in terms of the
chronology of his *oeuvre*, he names for the first time) three "waves" of
educational technology. (He cites an example of the first wave the slide-tape
program *Voix et Image*" his children suffered in junior high school; the second
wave was TV; the third is computer). Here he links them to second-language
programs. "Within the predominant presence of machinery," Aoki suggests, the
"dominant understanding of language in second language curricula" relegates
language to a linguistic code. With such a view, planners of second-language
curricula incorporate instrumental conceptions, such as "language-as-a-tool,
linguistic teaching strategies, word-referent relationships, and language
expressing thought."

So enframed, the second-language curriculum becomes about "linguistic
competence wherein learning is understood as achievement of the vocabulary
and grammatical rules of the code." Language becomes reduced to a means to an
end. Second-language curriculum and instruction become technocratic, "the
world order of technical human being given to gaining technical competence in

the use of the second-language." As an example, Aoki points to English "immersion programs" designed to enable students (especially immigrants) to learn a second language quickly and efficiently. Such programs tend to be "utilitarian and technical," and result, presumably, in improved job opportunities. "The overriding aim," he charges, "is the removal of the accent of the mother tongue." He comments:

> Oriented instrumentally, these programs see the second language apart from its culture. Hence, language and culture are alienated, remaining in a nondialectical relationship, closed to the dynamic tension between the languages. The teaching/learning milieu becomes entrapped in a technical scheme of means–ends, detached and de-ontologized.

Given such instrumentality, he adds, "what seems urgent is the recovery of the fullness of language." To that end he turns his attention in the final section of the paper.

He starts by reminding us that "each of us is born into [the] language of our mother tongue," a tongue or language in which we are at home. By "home" he is referring to a community, as the mother tongue is "a language of sharing, a language of familiarity, a vernacular of daily conversation, a language with a profound respect of the other as self." The Heideggerean antecedents echo here, but there are others, as I hear a member of an ethnic and political minority speaking here. But this is no summons to the *Volk*. This becomes clear when he acknowledges that our mother tongue leaves us "homeless" when we travel elsewhere. "Such an understanding of the mother language," he writes, referring to his linking of language to community, "allows us to see how language, nourishing us, makes of the life-world or home—set within the comfort of the taken-for-granteds, while it simultaneously disorients us into becoming virtual strangers within another's life world." It is to this experience of disorientation, of being a stranger in a strange land, that he turns his attention next.

"The crucial question" concerns our understanding of the notion of "second language." Rather than regarding, in the case of immigrants, the second language as replacing the mother tongue, Aoki emphasizes that "any second language will always remain second, and it should be accorded what is appropriate to secondness." Although in meaningful relation to the first language, he notes, the second language "cannot replace the mother language that allowed it to come into being as a second language."

Now Aoki is ready to redefine bilingualism as"dialectic of complementarity. Such a definition, he suggests, "begins to bring into fuller view the contextuality of the lived situation that the instrumental and scientific understanding utterly neglects." He refines this definition by asserting that "bilingualism is a hermeneutic dialectic." He explains:

> To venture forth into the world of the second language thus is
> an endeavour which entails the "is," the "is not," and the "not
> yet." It is a circular journey in which there is always a turning
> homeward, a return. But unlike the vicious circle, the circle
> here is a hermeneutic one, re-entering home always at a
> different point, thus coming to know the beginning point for
> the first time.

Within the hermeneutic circle, the student of a second language has "at
every moment" the possibility of moving back to one's own mother tongue,
one's own self. One is simultaneously in the world of the mother language, and
in the world of the second language. "By questioning the mother language and
the second language," Aoki advises, "by contrasting one with another, the
resultant dialectic allows possibilities of a deeper awareness of who one is, and
of a fuller understanding of the conditions shaping one's being." Gone now is
the technical view of second language learning as linguistic competence to be
exchanged for employment opportunities in the adopted country. Present is an
educational view in which study provides opportunity to understand self and
society through the juxtaposition of first and second languages. Aoki asks us to
teach and study in the middle: "Because I live in tension at the margin,
questioning becomes central to my way of life. This questioning is the dialectic
between the familiar and the unfamiliar."

In this paper we see a nuanced extension of curriculum theory to second-
language learning. But Aoki evidently senses the possibility that the discursive
movement of this extension might be experienced by second-language
specialists as rendering their field "secondary" to curriculum studies. I speculate
so because in the final sentences of this impressive paper Aoki turns the table, as
it were, suggesting that bilingualism itself offers the opportunity to
reconceptualize curriculum studies from a technical instrumentalism to an
authentic educational experience of being-in-the-world. Understanding second-
language programs in terms of a "dialectic between the mother language and the
second language," he writes, promises

> an understanding of education as a leading out and a going
> beyond the merely instrumental or immersion stage to the truly
> authentic. I see here a glimmer of a way of understanding
> education as a dialectic between the language of epistemology
> and the language of ontology. I thus feel the coming into being
> of this understanding of education is eminently a bilingual
> matter.

Through being bilingual—by occupying the lived and educational spaces
between mother and second tongues—one defamiliarizes the familiar while
making a new home out of a strange new land. There is an echo here of the early
Maxine Greene (1973), but the "plague" to which Aoki is responding is not only

the taken-for-grantedness of the bourgeois life, it is the self-erasure that often accompanies cultural assimilation.

In chapter 13 we move some years ahead. The occasion for "Five Curriculum Memos and a Note for the Next Half-Century" was the first of the Curriculum Lecture Series inaugurated on September 27, 1991, by the Department of Secondary Education in celebration of the 50th year since the establishment of the Faculty of Education at the University of Alberta, the first such faculty in Canada. In 1991, Aoki has been, in an official sense, "retired" for 6 years, but, as we know from this collection, he is hardly retired. Indeed, Aoki has never "retired" from active engagement with the intellectual life of his field. His repositioning (which might be a more accurate characterization of his post-Alberta period in Vancouver) enabled him to reflect on his field, from the distance of his new, perhaps more private life, and from his continued study, uninterrupted by administrative and regular teaching duties.

"To mark this anniversary," he begins, speaking to many of his former colleagues and, I should think, with a full heart, given his long sojourn both in Alberta and at the university in Edmonton, "I join you on this vibrant threshold standing between the past and the future." Acknowledging that his title is a half-echo of a book that his son Edward (with whom I once spent a remarkable two hours listening to Beethoven while watching the beautiful Edmonton sunset) urged him to read, Italo Calvino's *Six Memos for the Next Millennium*, in Memo 1 (entitled ED SEC or "Where Did ED CI Go?"), Ted begins autobiographically, recalling that "it was in the summer of 1945, not quite 50 years go, that the Faculty of Education became part of my life. I was then a student."

Aoki recalls a number of significant moments in his professional life history. "But what I remember most," he tells us (grounding autobiography in history),

> about my experiences of the summer of 1945 in the midst of the summer session courses was the night of raucous celebration on Jasper Avenue. The bombs that landed on Hiroshima and Nagasaki had done their jobs. I remember, amid the noise of celebration, the Hiroshima I had seen 11 years earlier while meeting friends of the family that lived there.

What a brilliantly pedagogical juxtaposition of images, one for which we are unprepared, as we had, I suspect, been lulled into thinking we were going to hear life history, not History, not trauma. The juxtaposition of "raucous celebration" on Jasper Avenue and the memory of a pre-bombed Hiroshima shock us into a third space between Canada and Japan, between then and now.

But we stay in Edmonton for only a moment, as Aoki transports us through time and space to Hiroshima itself. The year is 1986 and the former schoolteacher is serving as program chair for the Hiroshima Conference of the World Council for Curriculum and Instruction (WCCI; see Overly 2003). Employing a typically and powerfully Aokian idea—lingering—he returns to the same spot, where the juxtaposition of then and now could not be made more vivid:

> While there, I visited along, within walking distinct of the Hiroshima railway station, a Japanese garden I had visited as a youngster in 1934. I lingered, facing one memorialized tree, no longer a tree—stark, twisted, black remnant of a tree, without foliage, with only a few twisted limbs. A memorial to what? Man's capacity for inhumanity?

We are left on our own to ponder this question and this image, as Aoki transports us back to Alberta. We are back in Edmonton, but the year is 1964, the year Aoki joined the University of Alberta Faculty of Education after 19 years of teaching experience in southern Alberta, most of these devoted to the teaching of the social studies. "I was thinking," he confides, "that my 19 years of practical teaching experience would be sufficient to allow me to be a teacher of teachers." Given the vocationalism of teacher education, one is likely to agree, but Aoki will have none of it, as once again he shifts abruptly, if gently. He tells us: "I remember almost to the day when I was emptied of confidence."

In a passage laced with humour, Aoki uses autobiographical reminiscence to challenge the vocationalism of much teacher education. Although on this occasion he was speaking to the "converted," perhaps he was mindful that his readers might not be. He tells us that what he thought were methods courses had this prefix before their numbers: ED CI 266 and ED CI 466. "For the first time," he tells us, "I was transfixed upon the prefix ED CI—Curriculum and Instruction." I can hear his audience chuckle as he reports: "I twisted it; I turned it upside down I tried many things to answer the question: 'How do I understand CI?'" (These are, incidentally, not bad as descriptors of Aoki's impact on curriculum studies.) In the midst of his "quandary," he recalls, Schwab came to campus, and Aoki recalls listening to his lecture, which in its employment of phrases such as the *structure of knowledge*, *the structure of the disciplines*, and *epistemology*, seemed to Aoki to be composed in a foreign language. (How many of our students make the same comment today, and not just about Schwab!)

Those who may have misinterpreted Aoki's allegiance to the life-world of teachers and students in classrooms as a phenomenological version of vocationalism are corrected now, as Aoki makes clear that, although invaluable, his 19 years of teaching experience did not prepare him intellectually for participation in the academic field of curriculum studies. "So I began my career as a teacher educator," he tells us, "with some practical understanding of social studies and social studies teaching, but with little understanding of curriculum and instruction in a curriculum instruction department called Secondary Education."

Rather than playing his practice card, Aoki begins to study, asking several senior professors for guidance. In the United States, (especially junior) faculty tend to mention mentors as currency in a careerist system, but the retired Professor Aoki does so here out of respect. He recalls the mentorship of Lawrence Downey, the department chair, acknowledging that he "open[ed] doors for me, leading me particularly to scholars in curriculum associated with the University of Chicago such as J. J. Schwab and Elliot Eisner." A noted scholar in linguistics and language education, Marion Jenkinson advised him to read Mauritz Johnson's *Curriculum and Instructional System.* He remembers being impressed by Downey's understanding of the structure of knowledge and by Johnson's general systems theory which took seriously the conjunction and of "C and I." (Aoki would work that conjunction himself in the decades to follow.) In a footnote, he acknowledges that his initial work antedated his critique of general systems theory as a "generalized abstraction" that emptied "C and I" of the concrete and lived experience of teachers and students.

"Today," Aoki acknowledges, "I am thankful that, with all its limitations, there was the label EDCI attached to all courses in our Department; more thankful that I became aware of my own ignorance of a field that was to hold my deep interest for years to come." What a wise man this is! Teaching experience (even 19 years of it) does not necessarily make one knowledgeable about teacher education and curriculum studies. This speech is an act of mentoring itself, affirming to the junior faculty and students in his audience that "ignorance" is a position chosen to position one as ready to study, ready to accept guidance and mentoring, ready to teach.

In the second memo, Aoki reports (again, somewhat humorously, I suspect) to "Curriculum in the News," wherein he returns (given the sequence he has chosen for this book) to the idea that "Science Must be Taught as a Humanity." In actual chronology, this is the occasion in which he introduces this idea for the first time, an example, he suggests, of "curriculum turbulence at the university." For the sake of space, I refer you to the earlier description (chap. 9). Suffice to say here that the reference here functions to broaden the significance of what can seem to some as highly specialized (that is, socially removed) debates and ideas, showing that they operate and influence university curricula but are, in fact, "newsworthy" (as Aoki reports hearing about the report over the Canadian Broadcasting System [CBC]).

In the third memo, he turns his attention to the role of narrative in curriculum research and scholarship, a memo in which, he tells us in the title, he will "lean on Lyotard." (Lest his former colleagues and the new students think that this man has in fact retired, he will demonstrate just how contemporary his thinking is. It is not only contemporary, it is *avant-garde.*) From that "position," Aoki associates modernity with the commodification of educational experience associated with "objectified research, legitimated by metanarratives." "If Lyotard makes sense," he tells us, "it is time not to reject, I insist, but to consider decentering, the modernist view of education and to open the way to include alternative meanings, including lived meanings, legitimated by everyday narratives—the stories in and by which we live daily." By such "decentering" is opened a "clearing" in which we allow "humanly embodied meanings to dwell contrapuntally with objective meanings."

As he so often does, Aoki introduces a folksy element that functions, I speculate, to make him seem less intimidating. He reports a TV program (recall he has reported earlier a CBC radio program on teaching science as a humanity) in which he hears a Ms. Fiona Nelson, a Toronto School Board member, raise questions about the contemporary obsession with assessment. Afterward, Aoki writes a short letter to Ms. Nelson, from which he quotes: "Allow me to applaud you for asking for space for localized situational evaluation, questioning the possibility of the dominance of the totalitarian standardized testing program that may misfire in the name of education." This is both folksy and serious, an example of civic engagement few of us in the academy can claim. The assessment obsession means, in Aoki's words, "pedagogical suffocation." He is here explicitly a "public intellectual," although I contend that in connecting the subjective to the social, in grounding autobiography in history and culture, Aoki performs throughout these speeches and essays the pedagogy of the public intellectual. In *What Is Curriculum Theory?* I name Aoki and Maxine Greene as the primary public intellectuals in education in North America today.

In the fifth memo, Aoki turns his attention a British Columbia Ministry of Education document entitled *Year 2000*, subtitled *A Curriculum and Assessment Framework for the Future*. In a rare moment of frustration (no doubt they were not rare, but in the writing they almost inaudible), Aoki recalls his career:

> As I mentioned earlier, since 1964 I have been toiling with interested colleagues within this faculty and beyond to make sense of the multiple ways in which words *curriculum* and *instruction* can be understood. We've twisted and turned the word *curriculum* this way and that way . . . [W]e've tried curriculum praxis, curriculum as ideology, we've tried curriculum-as-plan and curriculum-as-lived . . . Likewise we've looked at *instruction*, and have tried replacing it with *teaching*; we've tried restoring the word *pedagogy*. And what has it added up to? Assessment!

After expressing this frustration, Aoki gathers himself, as he returns to work, pointing out that the conjunction "and" presumably joins elements of equal weight (or importance) to promote a balance. "Curriculum and assessment," he notes, are "two separate words, like two separate branches, but somehow connected." "And" functions here as both "separator and co-joiner."

"But when we become more thoughtful," he continues, "we may begin to see *and* in motion, moving from left to right in a linear fashion . . . If we continue our gaze upon *and*, we may begin to see the flow moving in the opposite direction, from assessment to curriculum." This right to left movement (it works politically, does it not?) was visible, he reports, only a few months prior to this occasion, at a BC Teachers' Federation-sponsored "student assessment" conference. There, he continues, an assessment professor made an explicit statement on this right-to-left flow: "Assessment should direct curriculum."

In a footnote, Aoki adds culture to history (postmodernity being, in part, a historical moment, *after* modernity: see Doll, 1993) but pointing out that "in curriculum thinking, we in North America are becoming aware of the dominance in our discourse of Eur-Ameri-centricity and the need for openness to others. In this connection, it is of interest to see how postmodernist scholars are exploring premodernist East Asian thought." This cultural analysis will be elaborated in other papers, but for this occasion, "at this moment, I await a response from Fiona Nelson of the Toronto School Board. And as I wait, I pause to remember some of the ands in the five previous memos." They are:

> Memo 1: Curriculum *and* Instruction EDCI *and* ED SEC.
> Memo 2: Science *and* Humanity Curriculum-as-Plan *and* Curriculum-as-Lived.
> Memo 3: Metanarratives *and* Narratives Modernity *and* Postmodernity.
> Memo 4: National Testing *and* Situational Evaluation.
> Memo 5: Curriculum *and* Assessment.

No longer leaning on Lyotard, or anyone else, Aoki floats free from the binaries, dwelling in the *and*, cautioning himself (he tells us) not to get caught in the dualisms. "I jump up and down in the *and* and let more *ands* tumble out. I rewrite."

> Memo 1: *and* Curriculum and Instruction *and* Memo 2: *and* Science and Humanity *and* C-as-P and C-as-L *and* Memo 3: *and* metanarratives *and* Narratives *and* Modernity *and* Postmodernity Memo 4: *and* National Testing *and* Situation Evaluation Memo 5: a*nd* Curriculum *and* Assessment *and* . . . AND . . . AND . . . AND . . .

I can see him now; the frustration is gone and that twinkle is back in his eye as he bids his colleagues and their students farewell for now: "I revel in the writing space that seems to dissolve beginnings and endings, that proliferates and disseminates *ands* here, there, and in unexpected places. I am now thinking, maybe I would like to play in and among the *ands* for a while, at least for a part of the next 50 years." It has been nearly 15 years since that Edmonton speech, Ted, and playing in and among the "ands" you have been, as this collection testifies.

As are so many of these papers, chapter 14, entitled "In the Midst of Slippery Theme-Worlds: Living as a Designer of Japanese Canadian Curriculum," is a speech, on this occasion to the Designing Japanese Canadian

Curriculum Conference, held on May 21–23, 1992, in suburban Toronto. In a now familiar mix of profundity and modesty, Aoki opens his address:

> To be called to a national meeting of curriculum experts dedicated to the production of Japanese Canadian curricula and to be drawn into the midst of the life of curriculum praxis and curriculum theorizing is for me to experience a resonance that seems to touch the core of my being as a sometimes Japanese Canadian educator and student of curriculum.

He recalls (characterizing it as an "echo") his first day as a teacher some 40 years before, in the spring 1945. World War II is not yet over, and he remembers facing "30 some Occidental faces, Grades 1–8." He wonders what it is like for these students to be facing a Japanese Canadian teacher: "I did not ask my students this phenomenological question," he tells his us, but "perhaps I should have. But what now provokes me to thought is how the silent question some 40 years ago is a reminder of an era, at least in British Columbia, when Japanese Canadians were not allowed to be teachers of Occidental students." Recall that, like Japanese Americans, Japanese Canadians were "relocated" during the war, Aoki to Alberta.

"Now, today, 40 some years later," he asks, "within what questions are we inhabiting as Japanese Canadian educators?" "What a leap . . . from 1945 to 1992," he emphasizes. "I delight in this leap, prompting me to wonder about the texture of the lived landscape of designers of Japanese Canadian curriculum. This is the focus of my address today." Such wondering "draws me to language. Why language, we might ask?" He reports that during his career "curriculum scholars have opened themselves to the realm of language, linguistics, discourse and narratives to understand their own field." Playing on the notion of "linguistic turn," Aoki continues: "Within this curricular turn, language is understood not so much as a disembodied tool of communication caught up in an instrumental view of language, but more so language understood in an embodied way—a way that allows us to say, 'we are the language we speak" or "language is the house of Being.'"

To illustrate, he quotes Basho, a haiku artist, who wrote:

> When I look carefully
> I see nazuna blooming
> By the hedge.

The choice of haiku is no arbitrary one: "And as I am so drawn, I remember well 60 years ago, bowing with my father before Basho's simple grave beside a mountain path somewhere near Mito, north of Tokyo."

A moment of intimacy between father and son becomes a public lesson in subject–object dualism in Western epistemology, as he dwells on the distinction between the "I who looks" and the "I who sees." In the translated haiku, he asks:

"is it I, the subject, that looks at an object of the looking? Is it I, the subject, that seems an object of the seeing?" He remarks on the "anthropo-centeredness" of this dualism, "inscribed with the makings of an ego-centered universe that is ever in danger of slipping into narcissism," recalling Christopher Lasch's (1978) widely read study of the American culture of narcissism. "[I] am left with a tinge of shudder," he confides.

He returns to Basho's words, suggesting that the subject–object dualism evident in the translation is "subordinate perhaps to a larger movement," that is, "the blooming of the nazuna by the hedge." Aoki offers that it is "the being in nature in bloom that holds and sustains the gaze. It seems, too, that it is not so much of the voice of the subject who looks and sees, but rather the voice of nature that is speaking." He continues with the metaphor of the garden even as he returns to the conference room: "You can see how I have already slipped into the texture of the landscape of multiculturalism . . . let me note how I've become more aware of how slippery is the very name 'Japanese Canadian,' a theme-word of our conference." ("Landscape" is a metaphor of which Maxine Greene, too, was fond [see Greene, 1978]; Aoki uses it extensively throughout this collection, as a glance at the index will indicate.)

As he does so regularly, Aoki focuses on a theme-word of the conference: "Japanese Canadian." To do so, he recalls an occasion several years before when he served as an external examiner at the University of Toronto's Ontario Institute for Studies in Education (OSIE) for an interesting phenomenological study in multicultural education. It was at this event, he reports, that, recalling his own title, he "experienced slipperiness." The study had been conducted by a young Israeli scholar and was entitled: "Ethnic and National Identity among Jewish Students in Ontario." What struck Aoki was the term employed by the researcher to refer to the Canadian-born students he had studied: "Canadian Jews." "In our multicultural context," he asks, "does it make a difference whether 'Canadian' is a noun or an adjective? . . . And remembering where I now am, I am urged to ask, 'How should we as curriculum designers approach our tasks when we know that our theme-words slide about, refusing to stand still?'"

From Toronto Ted moves to New Orleans, where he recalls a recent conference in New Orleans of the Association for Supervision and Curriculum Development (ASCD), the same meeting to which he had spoken in 1981 and would do so this same year (1992). Aoki tells us he "was struck by our American neighbours' surge of curricular interest in multiculturalism," noting our struggle "to slide away from a melting pot metaphor of multiculturalism to one of mosaic, a metaphor of some long legitimacy in Canada." The subtle patronizing tone—hardly unique to this Canadian citizen—is not my interest (it is, after all, hardly inappropriate), but how he uses the reference as a device to suggest solidarity among his listeners, most of whom were, no doubt, Canadian. Talk of Japanese Canadians and Canadian Jews might splinter the already splintered (between French and English, for starters) Canadian identity, and

Aoki, the great pedagogue, wants his audience to feel, for a moment at least, together.

He wants that, I speculate, because he is about to pull the proverbial rug out from underneath them, as he dismisses the view probably many in the audience hold, what he terms "the museum approach" to multiculturalism curriculum. In this approach "curiosities are displayed museum-fashion to be looked at by subjects from an objective distance, promoting what smacks of a breed of voyeurism based on the subject–object dualistic epistemology mentioned earlier." He is critical as well of the emphasis upon "identity" in multiculturalism, pointing out that "to be oriented toward the identity view of 'multiculturalism' is to be attracted to the noun view or the thing view of ethnic identities. Such a way of positing identities is, we are told, a cultural habit of modernism grounded in the metaphysics of presence."

Now the "rug" is not only not underneath one's feet, it's no longer in the room, as Aoki draws on the work of Gilles Deleuze to suggest multiculturalism as a "multiplicity is not a noun." After Deleuze, Aoki asks his audience "to displace ourselves from our fondness of noun-oriented, thing-oriented entities . . . and to place ourselves in the midst, between and among cultural entities. He says, living in such a place of *between* is a living in the midst of differences, where . . . multiplicity grows as lines of movement."

Now Aoki himself leaves the room, returning to the hedge in Basho's haiku, from where he suggests that "we might be creatively productive in the difference, growing uniquely Japanese Canadian lines of movement, among which might be a new language, a minority's English, which is neither Japanese nor the English of the dominant majority." Recalling his speech at Edmonton, he slips and slides amid conjunctions: "Now, I am beginning to understand the landscape of multiculturalism in the language of AND . . . AND . . . AND . . ., each AND allowing lines of movement to grow in the middle."

From Basho Aoki moves to Bach, whose music "resound[s] in a parallel polyphony that refuses closure—lines that refuse synthesis into a symphonic unity." He asks: "Canadian polyphony? Canadian polyculturalism? Canadian multiculturalism? For me, Bach's fugue with its fugal polyphony serves as an icon of Canadian multiculturalism, a textured landscape always in flux, a landscape of multiple possibilities in a shifting web of nomadic lines of movement."

From "nomadic lines of movement," Aoki explicates the various formulations of the curricular landscape, explaining to these nonspecialists in curriculum studies the role of "implementation" (associated with the language of management employed by school administrators) in curriculum-as-plan and curriculum-as-lived. "Allow me to sketch two lines of movement," he tells his listeners, "that I have found growing in the middle between the curriculum-as-plan and the lived curriculum, which may speak to curriculum designers." The first "line of movement is itself the intensity that lies in the difference between two kinds of discourse: the discourse of the curriculum-as-plan and the discourse of the lived curriculum."

This first line leads to a second line of movement, and that is what Aoki is asking of the curriculum designers assembled that day. "Curriculum designers in a landscape of multiplicity," he explains, offering a rather different model of "implementation" than that associated with school managers, "are asked to heed their relationship with others, primarily the teachers and the students out there." In the management model, he points out, "teachers and students . . . are only implied in words like 'implementation,' 'instruction,' and 'assessment.'" In this bureaucratic scheme, students and teachers become secondary to the curriculum-as-plan being designed, "faceless others" who are "reducible to some kind of sameness." Nowhere is this more obvious, he points out, that "when assessment time comes, when all students are subjected to the district-wide, province-wide, or even nation-wide tests."

From Deleuze, Aoki moves to Levinas, who speaks of "responsibility before freedom," "responsibility before rights." "We can sense here," Aoki points out, "a different tone of 'self/other' relationship in a language breaking with the subject–object dualism. This is the kind of ethical consideration that seems to be possible in the curricular landscape of multiplicity." Having dispensed with the subject–object binary in Western thought, having dismissed the assessment craze as anti-multicultural, having redefined multiculturalism itself as a verb and as an ethics of responsibility, Aoki is not quite ready to depart. Once again, he offers—and I find myself always delighted when he uses the phrase, as I never want him to go—"a lingering note."

After briefly (and modestly) summarizing what he has done, he asks if the "designers of Japanese Canadian curricula here assembled" can participate in the creation of a curriculum language that is "neither the language of the dominant culture nor the Japanese language of our heritage, but one that grows in the middle." Although this language will be English, it may be a non-Western version of English "wherein the noun is not always a noun, where joining words like 'BETWEEN' and 'AND' are not merely conjoining words." "Could it be," he concludes, "that this kind of creative participation is what it means to be designers of Japanese Canadian curricula?"

Chapter 15—entitled "The Child-Centered Curriculum: Where Is the Social in Pedocentricism?"—is also a speech, this time given in 1993 to the Richmond (British Columbia) Elementary Social Studies Association. I am struck once again by Aoki's modesty and his pedagogical savvy, this time focused on the conception of this occasion. I use that gendered noun deliberately, as Aoki opens this talk by recalling the telephone call (the moment of conception) during which he was invited to speak to these suburban Vancouver teachers. This section is entitled "Birthing of the Title," in which he appears to align himself as a woman, either as a mother giving birth or a midwife (conceivably a man but most commonly a woman) enabling the birth. He also positions himself as a student, unable, at first, to give a proper reply to the teacher's question. "Putting the phone down, I sank into my chair 'to think about it awhile.' What began to crowd into my thoughts were voices of media that declared that January 1993 shall be open hunting season for education." He assumes here what in Western culture is the man's position, as he engages in a moment of public jousting over a public issue: education.

"Hunting season" is an apt description, especially in the United States. I hope the "hunt" is gentler for the "game" in Canada than it is in the United States. Probably Aoki has more emotional distance from it than I, as I can share only the first moment of his response: "[I] found myself both annoyed and delighted—delighted that education and miseducation are of public interest; annoyed by the way hypermedia tend to slither about a bit on the surface." He does not stay long with this unhappy state of affairs—I argue that it is, in part, simple scapegoating (Pinar, 2004)—but focuses instead on the prominence of the phrase "child-centered" in public discussions. He asks a theorist's question: "What kind of discourse makes it possible for us to speak of child-centeredness? Of pedocentricism?"

In this talk to teachers, Aoki asks this question three times, each time teaching a sophisticated lesson in curriculum politics and theory. The "first moment" of questioning Aoki entitles "Pedocentricism and Competing Curriculum Centers," citing a *Vancouver Sun* article in which a "critic" is reported as alleging that "child-centeredness" sacrifices academic achievement. The critic's argument is a tired but long-lived one, namely that the centre of the curriculum should not be the child but the school subjects. Many American teachers are vulnerable to such academic vocationalism, unless they know curriculum history and theory, as Aoki does. He recalls the 1960s national curriculum reform movement in the United States, a school subject-centered curriculum organized around "the structure of the disciplines" (see Pinar et al., 1995, chap. 3).

The three traditionally "competing curriculum centers" Aoki names are the teacher-centered curriculum, the subject-centered curriculum, and the child-centered curriculum. Aoki regards the three as constituting "an irreducible triad that are at play in every pedagogical situation." In naming any one of the three as central, he adds, "we risk becoming indifferent to the others." Moreover, "life in the classroom is not so much *in* the child, *in* the teacher, *in* the subject; life is lived in the spaces between and among." As a consequence, we need to abandon the language of competing curriculum centers. Indeed, "we ought to *decenter* them *without erasing them*, and to learn to speak a non-centered language."

To illustrate, he attends to the everyday language of teaching. "When we say 'a child is interested' or 'a teacher is interested," he tells his teacher-listeners, we might attend to the etymology of the phrases. "Interest," he explains, derives from "*inter/esse*" (*esse*—to be), being in the "*inter*." That means "to be interested" is to dwell "in the intertextual spaces of inter-faces," those lived spaces where "and" is no mere grammatical conjunction, but "a place of difference, where something different can happen or be created, where whatever is created comes through as a voice that grows in the middle. This middle voice is the sound of the "interlude" (inter/ludus—to play), the voice of play in the midst of things—a playful singing in the midst of life." From the commonsensical thinking of competing curriculum centres Aoki has moved to "a playful singing in the midst of life." Even after a day of teaching, his listeners must have felt elated.

There is a strong phenomenological echo in this poststructuralist notion of "decentered curricular landscape," evident in the reference Aoki makes to the decision he and his coeditor faced in naming these narratives of teaching published by the British Columbia Teachers Federation. Deciding between *Voices of Teachers*, and *Voices of Teaching*, Aoki chose the latter, "preferring to decentre the teacher and to move into the space which is alive with teaching, hopefully in the neighbourhood of the call of the calling that is teaching."

In the "second moment" of questioning pedocentrism, Aoki attends to "child-centeredness and the language of individualism," asking "what is it to understand a 'child' as an 'individual?'" He notes the taken-for-granted character of the notion of "individual" in Western cultures. "We feel rather comfortable with these words," he notes, "maybe, too comfortable." He asks his listeners to take a moment to consider "the language of non-individualism in another culture," noting that, for instance, in Samoan language there are no terms corresponding to Western conceptions of "self" or "personality" or "character." In contrast to Socratic injunction to "know thyself," Samoans advise: "Take care of relationships."

Aoki's concern, he tells the assembled teachers, has nothing to with establishing the superiority of either view. Rather, his interest is in "how meanings of words are culturally constituted, and how the very words and language we are born into may be shaping us." Here, it seems to me, Aoki is performing a sophisticated version of the social studies teacher, infused with phenomenology (i.e., the notion of language as house of being). Not only his interdisciplinarity is sophisticated, so is his pedagogy.

To continue and complicate his discussion of "individualism" and the cultural embeddedness of language, Aoki refers to Charles Taylor's *The Malaise of Modernity*, "a book that my friend Craig Worthing, vice principal at Cook Elementary School, Richmond, offered me last summer." Legitimating the book as one of value to school professionals reduces the distance between him as university-located scholar and his school-based listeners with limited time to read. Aoki quotes Taylor's characterization of the Western uncritical acceptance of "individualism" as a "worry," as "narrowing our lives" and "less concerned with others in society." "Here," Aoki cautions, "Taylor is not attacking all forms of individualism; he is questioning that meaning of 'individualism' that has flattened and narrowed our lives . . . [and as] less concerned with the social."

At this point Aoki returns to the public debate over education—child-centeredness versus subject-centeredness—and suggests that "the critical point for us is not to turn away from it, but to move more deeply into this language, so that we become more aware of our caughtness in a language." (This is a fine theoretical point, although in Aoki's *oeuvre* admittedly the distinction between theoretical points and practical ones fades.) Instead, we teachers might "try to move towards the edges of that language" where, "re-positioned at the margin where the hold of the language of narrow individualism weakens," we might "open ourselves to a re-positioned landscape where may voices of 'self and other' call upon us for attentive listening."

The "third moment" of this questioning of "pedocentrism" Aoki entitles "Self and Other in a Polyphonic Landscape." He performs four "voices," the first one of which is the "individualistic self and individualistic other." Such atomized conceptions of "self and other" are "saturated" with what Taylor described as "the dark side of individualism that in centring on the self . . . [becomes] less concerned with others in society." After Christopher Lasch (1978), perhaps, Aoki terms this "the centered self, the narcissistic self."

The second voice speaks a romantic view of "self and other" in which, after Gadamer, separate subjectivities are fused into "a unity, a harmonious oneness, a wholeness." "There is something nice and fuzzily warm about it," Aoki admits. But there is a danger in such fusion. In political terms, "self and other" can become "selves and others," who, in turn, become "we who are inside," and "others who are outside." There is a second danger as well: The conjunction "and" disappears. "[In] the wake of its disappearance," Aoki points out, "there lurks danger that we may become indifferent to the differences between self and other that ought not to be erased."

In the third voice, Aoki focuses on the ethics of "self and other," drawing on the work of Emmanuel Levinas, which, Aoki notes, affords primacy to "the self's responsibility to others." "Responsibility" comes "before rights," including responsibility to those whom one has never met. In Levinas, Aoki sees additional "cracks" in individualistic conceptions "self and other." "Individual identity begins to dissolve," he observes, "and the 'and' in 'self and others' becomes loaded with ethicality."

In the fourth voice, entitled "Self and Other in a Divided Subject," Aoki turns to Julia Kristeva's questioning of the "undivided individual," replacing that untenable idea with what she calls a *divided subject*, no longer an "individual." By this notion of "divided subject," Aoki explains:

> Kristeva asserts that one's *subjectivity* is constituted by *both* self and other . . . In each one of us there is always a part that is stranger to the self—other than self . . . For Kristeva, our world is filled with strangers, whether we call them foreigner, aliens or simply "others." She tells us that we shall never be able to live at peace with the strangers around us if we are unable to tolerate the otherness in ourselves.... Each of us a divided subject, constituted by both self and other.

Having performed pedagogically his notion of a decentered curriculum landscape filled with the "voices of teaching," Aoki concludes, once again, with "a lingering note." He reminds his teacher-listeners "how Janet pressed me into delivering a title for this talk." Invited by a teacher, and in the midst of public discussion—allegations—concerning the curriculum (whether it should be "child-centered" or "subject-centered"), Aoki brings sophisticated theory to bear on the question: "What is the condition that makes it possible to say 'child-centered curriculum?'"

This speech is a remarkable performance. Not only does it advance our understanding of the discursive formations of taken-for-granted concepts in curriculum studies, it performs pedagogically the theory Aoki invokes. What a telling fact about the character of Ted Aoki, that one of his major papers is given to a local meeting of elementary social studies teachers. What respect he pays his colleagues in the schools by presenting them his best work!

Chapter 16, entitled "Humiliating the Cartesian Ego," was also a speech, also given in 1993. Here Aoki recalls teaching reading with his Grade 1 students. The textbook was entitled *We Think and Do*, a version, it occurs to him now, of "I think; therefore, I am." He chides himself for not appreciating the Cartesian character of that textbook: "What a teacher of reading! Humiliating!" Such either/or worldview "seduces many of us into the language of either 'boosters of technology' or 'knockers of technology.'" Aoki affirms that, for him, technology "is both a blessing and a burden." He ask us to abandon either/or binaries in favour "of the landscape of 'both this and that, and more, . . . which does not exclude the either/or but regards it as one among many ways of being in the world."

"What does all this say to a curriculum person like me?" he asks, referencing the genesis of curriculum studies in Denver in the 1920s in an administrative interest to manage proliferating curricula. He answers, again using the metaphor of which Maxine Greene was also fond:

> Acknowledging both the lived curricula of students and the designed curriculum places us in a different landscape, one populated by a multiplicity of curricula. For want of a name, I call it the C and C landscape (the c-as-plan and c-as-lived landscape). This is but a version of "both this and that, and more."

Positioned in the "and," he continues, "how shall we begin to think anew?" (How lovely and remarkable that he asks this question, at this point in his career, some 8 years after his official retirement.) To answer, he recalls Deleuze, whose notion of multiplicity emphasizes not the constituent elements of things, "but the space between, a place of difference, a place of bind, a place of tension . . . *and* as a place of difference." Given such a conception, what language can curriculum designers use to position them "in the middle that is neither the discourse of the curriculum-as-plan nor the discourse of the lived curriculum?" "It will have to be a language of humility," he answers.

Now, as he so often does, he returns to his title, and he does so with humour. "Many of you may be asking, and rightly so, why I have not dealt with the word *humiliation*," he offers. He admits he has "not been explicit, but this is, in part, because I have been sliding about in my talk with the word humiliation in my back pocket, looking for a site that might allow the word itself to erupt somewhere with new meaning."

This moment of playfulness ends, and the great theorist and pedagogue turns to his very serious point, his interest in "reunderstanding" the word humiliation. In doing so, he avoids anthropocentricism, declining to be trapped in discourses wherein humans are assumed to be central, declining to be caught in subject–object dualisms wherein humiliation means the debasement of another. Wanting to escape such traps, "I have been looking for a site where the usual meaning of humiliation connected with human-centeredness dissolves somewhat, so there is room for emergence of new lines of meaning."

New lines have emerged, and playfully so, as Aoki is not finished having fun: "But I have just noticed that over the journey so far, I have had a hole in my back pocket. Pieces of humiliation have been slipping out, growing new sprouts of meaning at different sites, so it seems." "Pieces of humiliation slipped out when I was telling you of my humbling experiences teaching Grade 1," he suggests:

> still more pieces slipped out, landing on the fertile soil of *and*.
> And lingering in this space of lived tensionality, I am able to
> hear the rhythmic measure of the earth, our place of dwelling,
> where its earthly humus provides nurturance to new meanings
> of humiliation that are springing forth.

Having been privileged to visit Ted and June at their home in Vancouver, I recall that he is quite the gardener. Here his theory garden is sprouting in abundance.

Positioned among at the many "ands" where the human-centered conceptions of humiliation move in tension, where the human subject is no mere self-involved ego, no narcissistic subjective "I" who thinks he exists *because* he thinks, "humiliating" shifts its meaning. Now, he suggests, the word requires one to consider the questions of ethics, questions:

> concerned with lived space where people dwell communally,
> where dwelling is a dwelling with others on earth under the
> sky, where we find *humus* that nurtures *humans*, where humans
> caught up in binds sometimes chuckle, where we can hear
> laughter at the thought of humans thinking they can master the
> world.

"What kind of place is this?" Aoki asks. It is a place where "there is room for words like *humouring human, humus, humility* to live together." In such a place, to humiliate the Cartesian ego is to be reminded that we are communal and ecological, "that the rhythmic measures of living on Earth come forth polyphonically in *humour* and *human* and *humus* and *humility*." It is a place called "and," "a place of tension between this and that. And here, I hope, *humiliation* is no longer a word that merely sounds negative; in its repositioned sense, *humiliation* can indeed be a sign of our humanness." Indeed.

It is 2 years later in chapter 17, but once again we are listening to the great man speak, this time at a conference on "Imagining the Pacific Community: Representation and Education," held at on the campus of the University of British Columbia. His speech is entitled "In the Midst of Doubled Imaginaries: The Pacific Community as Diversity and as Difference." Aoki is now 75 years old.

He begins by reminding his listeners of the political character of history, of global migrations and military conquests, and of the arbitrariness of triumph. The idea circulating among some is that "The Regime of the Pacific Will Come." It legitimates, he notes, "the binary of the Occident and the Orient." Despite the name of the province in which he is speaking, "new language codes are at work, for within public schools' curricular scene exist legitimated spaces for East Asian languages such as Japanese, Mandarin, Cantonese and Korean." In a certain sense, he suggests, "we are in a position to transform the saying from the future tense, 'The Regime of the Pacific Will Come,' into the present tense, 'The Regime of the Pacific Has Come.'"

This idea, he continues, "is enframed within the imaginary of a linear historical movement of centers of civilization: from the Mediterranean to the Atlantic, and then to the Pacific." But the "regime in the Pacific" is no mere linear extension of the Mediterranean—Atlantic—Pacific thesis, he explains. The notion of "Pacific Community" cannot be understood in Western terms solely. Although my gloss of this chapter shows little evidence of Aoki's pedagogy, when you read the chapter you will see that Aoki is here a poet, playing with words, performing his "thesis" and his teaching poetically.

In Western terms, the notion of "Pacific Community" is a metaphor of "diversity." "But if we heed post-colonial scholars such as Stuart Hall and Homi Bhabha," Aoki advises, "we need to question this very imaginary that construes the Pacific Community as diversity." Such an imaginary—the metaphor of community-as-diversity—presumes "a silent norm that both contains and constrains differences on the underside of diversity," despite its "seeming liberal openness and tolerance of others."

After Bhabha, Aoki worries that such tolerance "is inevitably coupled by a constraint," "one that tends to be indifferent to community *as* difference." "The universalist pluralism espoused by liberalism," Aoki suggests, "paradoxically permits diversity but masks differences." Given this dynamic, "what is necessary," he continues, is "a disruption, a displacement" away from notions of "plurality" and "diversity" to "the imaginary of community as difference." This is, he offers:

> an enunciatory space of language in movement, a space of signifying activity, a space of interlanguage translation. It is an enunciatory space of cultural and language differences—in my case, the space which is neither Japan nor Canada, neither

Japanese nor English, but that interspace where the otherness
of others cannot be buried, as is done within the imaginary of
community as diversity.

In these "enunciatory interspaces of difference" the Pacific Community
acknowledges and honours "difference," historical difference, political
difference, cultural difference, difference articulated "in multiple ways,
positively and negatively, progressively and regressively, often conflictually,
sometimes even incommensurably." Moreover, "such spaces are liminal spaces,
inhabited often by the colonized, the minorities, the migrants in a diasporic
community."

"What is this all about?" he asks, articulating for his audience the question
some may be posing silently. To work in "the enunciatory space of the
imaginary of difference requires a positioning at a margin," he answers. In
particular, "we are challenged to be explicit about the imaginaries that allow
articulations of the *other*." Aoki worries that in the language of "individualism,"
the "other" is "beyond the self, distanced and objectifiable as in a display." In
"interspaces" of "difference," in contrast, "the other is already present, albeit
ambiguously, within the person."

Such theorization permits Aoki to "transform the sting of the strap I got for
speaking Japanese at school recess decades ago into a generative rhythm such
that the sting is no more. Instead, in my own becoming, I feel I am beginning to
speak a vitally new language." Aoki does not stay here long, returning in his
final comments—these are termed "a meditation"—to the occasion for his
remarks, the conference.

The title of the conference "challenged me," he reports, "coaxing me to
resituate myself and to reflect upon my own narrative imaginary within which
I've been inventing stories of personal experiences of my schooling days, and,
as well, upon my own life experiences as a Canadian with the label of an Asian
minority." Acknowledging the scholarly sources of his theorization—the work
of Charles Taylor, Homi Bhabha, Trinh Min-ha, Rey Chow, Masao Miyoshi—
he tells his listeners: "I now seek further help. Hence, I look forward to coming
sessions of this conference over the new few days and plan to join you as you
engage in articulating your imaginaries of the Pacific Community." In his
humility, Aoki once again honours the conference as an educational event.

Chapter 18 is a speech Aoki gave a year later on the Eastern side of the
Pacific Ocean. Entitled "Imaginaries of East and West: Slippery Curricular
Signifiers in Education," the occasion was an International Adult and
Continuing Education Conference, sponsored by Chung-Ang University in
South Korea. He begins by recalling his parents, who predicted, "that the era of
the Pacific will come." Influenced by his parents and their view of the future,
Aoki recalls studying commerce—he focused on international trade—at the
University of British Columbia. For his parents and for himself, "international
trade" meant working the Pacific east and west. But for his professors,

"international trade meant plying the Atlantic." "Then the War came," he continues:

> and my dream was shattered, beckoning a physical displacement that landed me in the prairies of Alberta in the field of education. In the latter years, I was "professing" education as a member and, later, chair of a curriculum department at the University of Alberta. While so situated, suppressed traces of the dreams about the Pacific surged forth. Let me offer two short narratives.

The first, entitled "A Binary Image of East and West," involves Aoki's service on a Ministerial Curriculum Committee engaged in revising a humanities program. In an effort to expand the sphere of students' attention, the committee focused on "internationalization" and "globalization." When the time came for entitling the new course, the Committee hair proposed: "Western and non-Western Civilizations." Aoki offered: "Eastern and non-Eastern Civilizations." Awkwardness followed, punctuated by expressions of concern for the disappearance of the word "West." The committee compromised and settled for "Western and Eastern Civilizations."

Even in the new title, Aoki suggests, there remained a residue of Eurocentrism. Recalling Edward Said's influential study *Orientalism*, Aoki points out that in the West there is a tendency to regard the "Orient" as the other side of the West. In addition to the binary, Aoki is concerned with the final word, which, he points out, is often presumed "is a universal." "Civilization" is a term associated, he acknowledges, "with the Western imaginary of liberal democracy."

In the second narrative, Aoki recalls Korean students coming to the University of Alberta to study curriculum. Aoki expresses a concern: "But the very thought of them [Korean students] coming to us from Korea to study Western scholarship and return the same, was, it seemed, reducing education to a commodity view of education." He asked, "insistently" (a frequently used word in the Aoki *oeuvre*, a word underscoring the urgency of these concerns), that in the Korean students' doctoral dissertations there must be attention to "the experiences of Korean scholars living life at a Western university. For us it was an opportunity to question ourselves seriously: What is it to invite Eastern scholars in our midst?"

Now Aoki returns to the "key signifier" in the title of the conference: "East and West." He suggests that the term "East and West" connotes "separate preexisting entitles," which can then "be bridged or brought together" by the use of the conjunction "and." This "imaginary" has, he suggests, predominated in Western modernity, and is evident in the works of many historians, anthropologists, and others who study "culture." He focuses on the "image" of "crossing" between East and West, an image suggesting the "cross-cultural, emphasizing movement in getting across from one culture to another."

Now he turns to what is for me one of the most beautiful and "lingering" images in Aoki's work: the bridge. Before, he has employed the word to discuss the possibilities of conversation; here, his use is both literal and metaphoric. He acknowledges that in his parents' time his appearance at a conference on the Eastern shore of the Pacific Ocean would not have occurred very easily: "Today, we revel in the remarkable speed . . . and give thanks to all these bridges." Surely, transportational infrastructure enables "cross-cultural" conversation.

There are other bridges, such as those found in Japanese and other Asian gardens, "aesthetically designed, with decorative railings, pleasing to the eyes." There are bridges that are only functional, referring to "the many bridges that cross the Han River in Seoul." It is a metaphoric bridge he walks now: "But on this bridge, we are in no hurry to cross over; in fact, such bridges lure us to linger." This metaphoric bridge is, in my view, "a site or clearing in which earth, sky, mortals and divine, long to be together, belong together."

After "a short interlude on sign theory" in which he introduces the work of Sassure and Lacan (Aoki is always teaching!), he returns to the title. He tells his listeners "I can see myself trying to move away from the identity-centered 'East and West' and into the space between East and West," and thereby "trying to undo the instrumental sense of 'bridge.'" This noninstrumental sense of "bridge" is implied by the conjunction and. Focusing on the space between "East and West," understanding "and" as "both 'and' and 'not-and,'" Aoki proposes a lived space of "both conjunction and disjunction."

"So enframed," he thinks of the bridges of the Pacific Rim "as being both bridges and non-bridges." He thinks of the Korean graduate students who studied with him and his colleagues at the University of Alberta, "rethink[ing] their spaces as third spaces between Western and Eastern scholarship." Quoting Stuart Hall, Aoki suggests that in these "third spaces" the notion of "identity" is "no mere depiction of the vertical, but more so 'identification,' a becoming in the space of difference." This is "tensioned space of both 'and/not-and,' a space "of conjoining and disrupting, indeed, a generative space of possibilities, a space wherein in tensioned ambiguity newness emerges." Indeed.

Next we move across the Pacific. It is May 27, 2000. The occasion is the President's Symposium at the annual meeting of the Canadian Association for Curriculum Studies (CACS). With his former colleague Ken Jacknicke (who succeeded Aoki as department chair at the University of Alberta), Aoki discusses "Language, Culture, and Curriculum." Employing a now familiar tactic, Aoki begins: "We look at the title of our presentation." To do so, Aoki turns from high to popular culture, and quotes the Canadian poet and songwriter Leonard Cohen. In "The Anthem," Cohen writes:

"There's a crack, a crack in everything: That's how the light Comes in."

"Heeding Cohen," Aoki reports, "we re-read our title." Now it reads:

Langu/age . . . Cul/ture . . . Curri/culum . . .

He and Jacknicke wonder "what it may be like to be enlightened, living in the spaces between, marked by cracks in the words."

Next Aoki introduces the concept of metonymy, a dictionary definition of which is "a figure of speech consisting of the use of the name of one thing for that of another of which it is an attribute or with which it is associated." In "Metonymic Moment #1: Midst Curriculum-as-Plan/Curriculum-as-Lived," Aoki asks, intriguingly, "pedagogy is the fold between the two?" In "Metonymic Moment #2: Midst Presence/Absence," Aoki refers to the "modernist imaginary" in which "presence is absence." In "Metonymic Moment #3: Opening Up to the Third Space Midst Representational/Nonrepresentational Discourses," he suggests "the metonymic space of verticality and horizontality." Such space exists between representational discourse and nonrepresentational discourse; it is, after Homi Bhabha, a "third space of ambivalent construction."

In "Metonymic Moment #4: Midst Western Knowledge/Aboriginal Knowledge," Aoki and Jacknicke recall the inseparable relation between culture and history, focusing on the divergence of Aboriginal and Western worldviews. Nowhere is this more obvious than in the "emphasis of Western ideology on physical presence or objectivity reality," what some have call "outer space." In contrast to Western materialism is the more "metaphysical" character of Aboriginal knowledge. Such knowledge "places a premium on the spirit, self, and being, or 'inner space.'" A second difference concerns the Western emphasis on the isolated individual: "Aboriginal cultures support inclusiveness and connectedness through the life-force in all living things."

In "Metonymic Moment #5: Translation/Transformation," we are returned to Aoki's ongoing critique of Western individualism. He points out that for the Japanese, "a person is a twofold of self and other." In contrast, the English word *individual* implies an entity unto itself, a self "indivisible," a "totalized self." This critique seems in sync with Madeleine Grumet's (1990) characterization of the individual's voice as a "chorus." "We need not dissolve identity," Grumet (1990, p. 281) pointed out, "in order to acknowledge that identity is a choral and not a solo performance." Translation—intersubjective, cultural, and linguistic— is, Aoki points out, a "transformation," "an ambivalent construction," "a signification that is ever in-complete and ongoing."

Aoki concludes with "a lingering moment," recalling that he and Jacknicke had begun "boldly" with a title promising to lay out "Language, Culture and Curriculum." But during their "journey in/through" five metonymic moments, "our boldness trembled and quaked a bit, transforming both ourselves and our understandings of these words." These metonymic moments were "moments of transformation, wherein form and formlessness insistently interplayed." Now lingering at the moment of farewell, this noun-oriented signification— "Language, Culture, and Curriculum"—has been transformed by the "living moments of life." We leave you with a new title: "The Interplay of Languages and Cultures Midst Curricular Spaces: Five Metonymic Moments."

This chapter is a strong example of Aoki's powerfully performative pedagogy in which he enacts the theory he is explaining. The noun-dominated title, which is associated with the totalizable identities of Western individualism, is transformed through the experience of teaching. This experience of teaching transforms both the teacher and knowledge (the title) itself as it translates the complex mix of idea and experience into the "chorus" that is this presentation. The complexity of this mix of idea and experience is made vivid in the next chapter.

Aoki entitles the third part (part C) "Sounds of Pedagogy in Curriculum Spaces," and he opens it with a 1979 address to the Canadian Ethnic Studies Association. Entitled "A Japanese Canadian Teacher Experiencing Ethnicity," this paper is powerfully autobiographical. Aoki begins by recalling "when, as a youth, I first walked the sidewalks of crowded Tokyo, I experienced a strange feeling that stemmed from being thrust into a sea of black heads, a feeling of belonging and not belonging." Questioning this feeling, he turns to his own experience in Canada. Perhaps, he suggests, he felt as if he did and did not belong "because for me to be one with the dominant mainstream group has never been my way of life, ever since I was born."

Still, the experience of being in Japan differed from the experience of being in Canada; in Japan he experienced himself as "an ahistorical being." The "space-time coordinates" of Japanese experience "didn't ring" with his. "And yet," he qualifies himself, "when I traveled north from Tokyo, I felt, at times, a vibrant resonance with certain things and people of Japan." He recalls visiting Matsushima, "where the blue sea and the dotted islands sing a song of unspeakable but bounteous beauty and joy." But most vivid for him was his visit to Hirosaki Castle at the northern end of Honshu, "whence my mother came." There he came upon a sculpture, a photograph of which he had viewed in his family album as a child on Vancouver Island. This sculpture is of Aoki's grandfather.

> I was told, later, that when I saw the "dozo" (statue), I shouted "ojisan" (grandfather) and ran to him across the plaza to be with him. In some mysterious way, I felt, through that piece of ground, a presencing in oneness of both him and me, of both his past and my past, of both Cumberland and Hirosaki. That I richly and deeply remember.

"And yet," Aoki contrasts this experience of homecoming with a narrative of alienation, as "back in Tokyo, I recall watching, puzzled, parades of elementary school children, boys and girls, toting on their shoulders wooden guns, led by lady teachers also toting wooden guns, marching along the streets of Tokyo to the rhythm of 'oichi-ni, oichi-ni' (one-two, one-two)." In this period of Japanese militarism, many Japanese were avidly reading a book entitled *Should Japan and America War*? "As a preteen Japanese Canadian youngster," he tells us, "I couldn't make sense of school and marching; they didn't seem to go together. Nor could I make sense of a naval fleet in the beautiful Inland Sea."

As a British Columbia-born Japanese Canadian in Japan, Aoki felt "both Japanese and non-Japanese, both insider and outsider." It was a feeling not limited to that visit to Japan, as Aoki recalls the moment—during World War II—of "evacuation," when Japanese Canadians were relocated away from the Pacific Coast. Aoki narrates an incident that renders explicit Anglo-Canadian attitudes at this time:

> Early in the fall of the 1941, our Commanding Officer, Colonel Shrum, summoned me. In the basement of the present University [UBC] Administration Building I appeared before him. He fired me a terse question with his typical bard: "Aoki, what would you do should there be a war between Japan and Canada?" I responded in what I thought was a voice assured: "I am a Canadian, Sir." That was a damn good honest answer, I thought. But I guess my old physics professor didn't think so. For about two weeks later I got a piece of paper—an honourable discharge from his Majesty's service—this before Pearl Harbor!

Nearly 25 years ago, at the dawn of identity politics in North America during which time many victimized groups would (understandably) retreat into separatism and rage, Aoki stands his ground, and characterizes his situation as an "opportunity." With a sagacity I find staggering, Aoki tells his listeners:

> This kind of opportunity for probing does not come easily to a person flowing within the mainstream. It comes more readily to one who lives at the margin — to one who lives in a tension situation. It is, I believe, a condition that makes possible deeper understanding of human acts that can transform both self and world, not in an instrumental way, but in a human way.

It is to this project of "deeper understanding of human acts that can transform both self and world" that Aoki has dedicated his life.

It would be to Alberta that Aoki would be relocated and live for most of his professional life, teaching in the public schools of southern Alberta and at the University of Alberta in Edmonton. But British Columbia was always Aoki's home, it seems, as he and June kept their house on Beechwood Street in Vancouver while renting a spacious apartment in Edmonton. And it will be to Vancouver Island, where Aoki grew up, that he will be returned when he lingers with us no more.

After relocation to Alberta, Aoki became a teacher. "What does it mean to become a teacher?" Aoki asks. He notes the "ritual" through which one is permitted "entry into a culturally—shaped and culturally—legitimated world," a ritual involving "years of training, certification, automatic membership in a teachers' association, apprenticeship, scrutiny and evaluation by legitimated seniors, and so on." But recalling the ritual of becoming a teacher ignores the experience of it, "the unique flavour of the experiences of becoming a teacher in my time and in my own historical situation. My experiences are centered within my own experiential horizon and under-girded by my own biography of past experiences and my own aspirations and hopes." A decade before autobiography would become fashionable, Aoki demonstrates a strong understanding of its structure and function.

It was the autumn of 1971, at a "chance" meeting with Maurice Wolfe, Chief of the Ermineskin Band, the largest of the four bands of the Hobbema Indian Reserves south of Edmonton, when Aoki was returned to the moment when history and politics became personified in the figure of the schoolteacher he would become. He reports that he and Chief Wolfe spoke "freely of many things, mainly about matters other than mounting a curriculum project." Then the conversation turned to World War II, and the experiences of the Japanese Canadian evacuees, including the expropriation of Japanese Canadian properties on the Coast. Chief Wolfe drew a "parallel between the Japanese Canadian experience and his own forbearers' experience."

After the "invocation" in Canada of the Emergency War Measures Act in 1941, Aoki was relocated to Alberta, where he was employed as a sugar-beet worker. During the war, the province faced a critical shortage of teachers; in response, the Alberta Government passed a School Emergency Measure. During the winter of 1944 Aoki was cutting timber at Burmis in the Crows Nest Pass area; he saw a newspaper advertisement for teaching jobs.

> I dropped my bucking saw and double bit axe and off I went to Calgary. Here, I faced an unanticipated problem—a becoming a teacher problem for a Japanese Canadian, that of "where to live?" Calgary's bylaws forbade residence of any Japanese Canadian within the confines of Calgary City proper. Aoki was able to live with a Japanese couple just outside the city limits, from where he commuted to Calgary.

While studying, he applied to the Calgary City Council for temporary permission to reside within Calgary. A report of the City Council deliberations was published in the city newspapers—the *Calgary Albertan* and the *Calgary Herald* –on February 7, 1947, and, Aoki reports, he became a *cause célèbre* at the Normal School. By a six-to-five vote, the council referred his case to the city commissioners, suggesting that "if in conference with Royal Canadian Mounted Police and city police, there is no objection to the individual's character, he is permitted to attend Calgary Normal School for a period of two and one half months." By April of that year, Aoki had attained temporary certification as a teacher. But soon enough, "I learned quickly that when the government spoke of a shortage of teachers, they had in mind 'typical' teachers. There was no shortage of Japanese Canadian teachers. In fact, there was one too many."

Despite his bachelor's degree from the University of British Columbia, despite his certification as a teacher, despite the fact that the teacher shortage in Alberta was so acute that Grade 11 secondary school students were being recruited into teacher training, Aoki was offered jobs not in the public schools, but in broadcasting (by the BBC in London to translate propaganda into Japanese) and in nonpublic school settings. The first of these latter two was offered by the Canadian Intelligence Service, where he would teach Japanese; the second was made by a Hutterite school (see also chap. 13). This one he accepted. There he served as caretaker, teacher, principal, launching a most remarkable pedagogic career, "a move . . . I have never regretted taking."

At the Hutterite school, Aoki remained isolated, enjoying little contact with fellow teachers or the mainstream of the Hutterite community's social world. This was, for him, "not an unaccustomed kind of experience—for living apart from the mainstream had been the lot of most Japanese Canadians." The next school year finds him in Foremost, during which time—the fall of 1947—Aoki is attending a teachers' convention in Lethbridge. With colleagues at the Marquis Hotel in downtown Lethbridge, Ted is refused service due to his ethnicity. During the winter of 1946, Aoki considers attending the 1947 Summer Sessions Studies at the University of Alberta. Given the restrictions on students of Japanese ancestry living in Edmonton, he is told by the registrar that he must apply to the City of Edmonton to live there while a student. Aoki comments:

> To all my children, Douglas, Michele, and Edward, Harry Ainlay means a large composite high school in Edmonton (dedicated to this one-time mayor) and it has for them mixed memories there of life as Sansei students. For me, however, the name Harry Ainlay means "he who granted me the privilege of temporary residence" in Edmonton to attend Summer School in 1947.

Aoki knows he was not, is not, alone. "These experiences I narrate," he reports, "and the experiences of my fellow Japanese Canadians attest to the psychic walls and constraints that kept us caged in or caged out, depending on one's perspective—unwanted strangers in our homeland." Whatever wounds remain with Ted Aoki are not audible. Here he says simply, with restraint: "These experiences we experienced; silently but bone deep we experienced them."

After Foremost, Aoki moved to Lethbridge, where he taught 13 years. When he left Lethbridge in 1945, he was a "budding" assistant principal of the Lethbridge Collegiate Institute whose duties included locker keys, student attendance, and student assemblies. Unsurprisingly, he had "not really enjoy[ed] being assistant principal." Moreover, he had been "a total stranger in Lethbridge's world of teachers and teaching." After teaching in Taber, he returned to Lethbridge as a junior high school social studies and physical education teacher at Hamilton Junior High School. He was "the first teacher or oriental origin to be hired in Lethbridge," hired "as a test case."

From the junior high school Aoki moved to the University of British Columbia, where for 3 years—1975-1978—he served as a professor of curriculum studies. While there, "I often wondered my way to Nitobe's Garden." He asks us: "Walk with me now." He recalls the man for whom the garden is named, Dr. Nitobe, and his book *Bushido: The Soul of Japan*. There he reflects upon two flowers: the sakura and the rose, two flowers that, for him, symbolized two ways of seeing, two ways of knowing, two ways of living. He tells us that—and here I learn why he has managed not to be scarred by his experience—he has worked to keep "the rose [the symbol of Europe and the West] and the sakura [the symbol of Japan] in view simultaneously." He continues:

> Instead of the power of mono-vision, the power of double vision may be what I should seek. The significance to me of making sense of ethnicity as a Japanese Canadian in this way may well lie in the ever-present dynamic between the sakura way and the rose way. . . . Such an approach may reveal more fully within my lived human condition, self-imposed or socially-imposed distortions that call for action—action that in the very acting will empower me to become a maker of my own history, a historical being engaged in his own personal and human becoming. Maybe being a Japanese Canadian is just that— maybe experiencing ethnicity as Japanese Canadian is just that.

With those "flowers" in hand, he turns (in "a lingering note") to a flower—a cherry blossom—he lost. He tells his audience that "I have a daughter; rather, I had a daughter. Three years ago, Michele Novuko, like a cherry blossom that had its brief moment, parted with life, untimely, at the call of nature." Of her 19 years of life, Michele spent 3 years in Vancouver, one of them on the campus of the University of British Columbia. When in 1978 the Aoki family returned to Alberta, where Ted would chair the Department of Secondary Education, "she came with us, but urged us to retain our house in Vancouver as a symbol of 'home.' We did." In one of the most deeply personal and moving passages in all of Aoki's work, he imagines their reunion:

> We have taken her home and have buried her on the coast. Beside her is a plot. It is mine. I intended to come home to B.C., and when I come home, I want to view the sakura and the rose, so beautiful and bountiful are they in British Columbia. But in seeing them, I will be seeing myself—for I know that what I see and how I see is because of who I am. I am what I see. I am how I see. And when I see them, I will likely reflect

> upon what it means for me to experience ethnicity in British
> Columbia as a human being endeavouring to become more
> human.

Here he names his lifelong project in poetical terms, a project born in particular historical circumstances: evacuation and the loss of home, mistreatment by his fellow citizens as not fully human. Despite the discrimination, despite the ignorance around him, despite the double loss of home (Japan and Canada, British Columbia and the family residence) and his daughter, Aoki never forgets he is "at home" inside himself.

"For me, being and becoming [note the order] a teacher and teacher educator has been an experience made *richer* by the fact of my ethnicity," he tells his audience (emphasis added). "In my being and becoming," he continues, "the tensions that were there created a dynamic world within which I acted, which has, after all is said and done, turned out to be my life as I have experienced it." And he acknowledges as he reflects upon this experience, that he has given meaning to it, "doing my damnedest in my own personal becoming." There have been several moments in reading this work where I have been deeply moved, but here—even when I return to its revision—I tear, moved by his courage, his humility, his deep sense of loyalty to daughter, to humanity.

In chapter 21, we find Aoki speaking, once again by invitation and to an ethnic studies meeting, this time to the national conference of the National Association of Japanese Canadians, held in Vancouver in 1987. Entitled "Revisiting the Notions of Leadership and Identity," this paper begins abruptly. Aoki asks his audience: "What authorizes me, silver-haired and vintage Nisei that I am, to stand before you?" No doubt engaging his audience's attention, he asks a second—his main—question: "What is it to lead?" He takes his question to school.

There, he notes, the principal was once understood as "the principal teacher, a leading teacher." Although "a specially recognized teacher," the principal remained, "first and foremost, a teacher." How the adjective "principal"—as in "principal teacher"—"became detached and turned into a noun is a bit of a mystery," Aoki muses. This detachment, however, "was a prelude to the linking of 'principal' to 'administration,' a term *au courant* in the world of business." Am I alone is discerning an aggressive humor here, also embedded in his use of "mystery" to describe how we ended up with a business manager rather than a teacher as "principal"? Then simply, if emphatically, Aoki announces the tragedy of our time: "Education became a business, an educational enterprise to be managed."

Aoki illustrates his point with an allusion to legislation renaming the principal as "administrative manager" and removing the category from eligibility for membership in the teachers' association, the British Columbia Teachers Federation. He finds it "hilarious" that in the legislation those principals—he reminds us that the term meant "principal teacher" at one time— who fail as administrators are demoted to "teacher." Aoki comments: "It can only happen in Fantasyland!" I have not read a more precise designation for the reactionary political terrain in which schools have become businesses.

"In my world of education," Aoki tells us, "the notion of 'educational leader' is a redundancy, repeating the same thing twice, for to educate itself means in the original sense, to lead out (ex-ducere)." He likens the meaning of leadership to "a mother's true leading of a child, a leading that follows the voice of the hand-in-hand of mother and child as they cross a busy street." With this moving and gendered characterization of leadership, Aoki returns to the question: "What authorizes a person to be leader?"

What we seek in a leader is not so much "official" authority, authority conferred by appointment or position or credentials. What we seek in a leader is "lived" (my term, not Aoki's) authority, authority "that flows from insightfulness and wisdom that knows the good and the worthy in a situation that must be followed." Moreover, in recognizing authentic leaders whom we might follow, we are demonstrating our own leadership.

"Leadership [is] linked to authentic followership," Aoki asserts. To link "leadership" to "identity," Aoki turns to "three concrete episodes," the first concerning the question: Canadian Japanese or Japanese Canadians? Here he recounts the story of the Israeli doctoral student who made "Canadian" a modifier for "Jews." To "re-understand the question 'Who are Japanese Canadians?'" he focuses, in episode two, on the emphasis in the question. Is it on the "whatness" of the question, i.e. on "what" are Japanese Canadians or Native Indians, or on the verb, as in "Who are Native Indians?" This second emphasis, he suggests, "urges me to be attuned to a different world, a world of being and becoming, a world of human beings. In this world nouns tend to conceal themselves."

In the third episode, entitled "Beyond Identity," Aoki articulates the possibility of identity "in-between" two nouns. Such a subject position suggests "dwelling in tensionality in the realm of between, in the tensionality of difference." Here "it is the difference that really matters," and our work as educators is "not so much the elimination of differences, but, more so, the attunement of the quality of the tensionality of differences that makes a difference." This is the work of leadership.

Chapter 22, entitled "Inspiriting the Curriculum," was a speech given at an Alberta Teachers Association (ATA) seminar on March 4, 1989. He begins autobiographically, recalling his work at the Hutterite school where he used a primer, We Work and Play, to teach reading, noting that, at that time, he had not realized he was, in addition to reading, teaching an ethic that separated work from play. He recalls that he and other teachers, as had soldiers in warfare, employed "strategies" and "tactics," "guided by targeted ends (many of them behavioural), the achievement of which meant victory and the failure to achieve, defeat." Although Aoki is making this association reflecting in the aftermath of World War II, it is quite apt to the depict conflation of Cold War politics and national curriculum reform in the late 1950s and early 1960s United States (see Pinar, 2004, chap. (3).

In teaching reading as a mere skill, Aoki recalls, "I was being caught up unconsciously in a technological ethos which, by overemphasizing 'doing,' tended toward a machine view of children as well as a machine view of the teacher." In such an ethos, he notes, teachers and children become "things" rather than human beings. He asks: "Is this not 'education' reduced to a half-life of what it could be?"

Working within this "technological" ethos, it is not only play that is separated from work; theory is separated from practice. "What I was teaching," Aoki concludes, "was a way of life that sees thinking as theorizing and doing as practicing. Hence, *We Think and Do* can be seen as merely a mundane version of what could be entitled *We Theorize and Practice*." In teacher education, this binary means that university coursework is sometimes viewed as "theory," which is then to be "applied" in school settings. In the structure of the university, the binary is reflected in the distinction between "basic faculties (such as the Faculty of Science and the Faculty of Arts) and practitioners in the applied faculties; which we have typically labelled professional schools (such as medicine, law, commerce, nursing and education)." And in the schools, the binary produces a sharp distinction between academic and vocational programs. He asks, "insistently": "Must we caught up totally in the linearized form of 'from theory into practice?'"

"The time is ripe," Aoki offers, "to question the traditional way of understanding *We Think and Do*, and move forward to embrace a more edifying and inspired sense of theorizing." He adds: "Education that alienates must be considered 'mis-education' and education must be transformed by moving toward a reclaiming of the fullness of body and soul." Such work will require an "inspirited curriculum," he suggests, a curriculum that "can influence the ways people can be attuned to the world." In such a curriculum, "teaching is understood not only as a mode of doing but also a mode of being-with-others . . . Teaching is a tactful leading out—leading out into a world of possibilities, while at the same time being mindful of the students' finiteness as mortal beings."

Chapter 23, entitled "*Sonare* and *Videre*: A Story, Three Echoes and a Lingering Note," is the keynote address to the 1991 annual conference of the British Columbia Music Educators' Association. (An earlier version appeared in Willis and Schubert—Aoki, 1990). In the 1989 address to Alberta teachers (chap. 22), Aoki praised the BC elementary music curriculum for speaking of "soul." His appreciation for thinking musically becomes evident as he recalls the 1981 winter session at the University of Alberta when he learned that Bobby Shew, a jazz trumpeter, was visiting the music department. Explaining to an evidently puzzled music department chair why the chair of secondary education wanted Shew to spend a couple of hours there, Aoki offered: "There are two questions we would like Bobby Shew to speak to, sing to or play to. The first question is, 'When does an instrument cease to be an instrument?' and the second question is, 'What is it to improvise? What is improvisation?'"

Aoki conveys to Shew "how in the field of curriculum we have come under the sway of discourse that is replete with performative words such as goals and objectives, processes and products, achievement and assessment—works reflective of instrumentalism in modernity—and that some of us were exploring ways of breaking out of such instrumentalism." (Aoki humbly omits that he is chief among those so exploring.) "Perhaps," he tells Shew, "if we can come to know how an instrument can cease to be an instrument, maybe that might provide us clues for a way out." Why improvisation?

> I told him that in education, and in curriculum particularly, under the hold of technological rationality, we have become so production oriented that the ends-means paradigm, *a* way to do, has become *the* way to do, indifferent to differences in the lived world of teachers and students. Could improvisation be a way to create spaces to allow differences to show through?

Aoki's narrative of Shew's visit is vivid and I will leave it to you to read it. Suffice to say here that after performing on his trumpet, Shew told assembled education faculty and students that in improvisation no two performances are alike. When improvising, Shew said "he and his fellow musicians resound not only to each other, but also to whatever calls upon them in that situational moment, and that, for him, no two situational moments, like life lived, are exactly alike." Sounding like Deleuze, Shew explained: "Exact repetition, thank God, is an impossibility. It's a remarkable feature that ought not to be suppressed!" In language his listeners could no doubt appreciate, Aoki comments: "It was an inspirited curriculum seminar that we truly lived and enjoyed, a seminar whose resonant echoes, even now, 10 years later, sound and resound."

The first of three "echoes" Aoki names moves "Through Disembodied Instrumentalism to Embodied Meaning." Here he calls upon us to "seek curriculum words that can sound and resound in an inspirited way." Here are echoes not only of the jazz trumpeter Shew, but of Heidegger and Huebner. Aoki's use of "echo" underscores the auditory, as does the notion of "lingering note," and, recalling the title to this collection, "key."

Here we learn a reference for this notion of "inspirited," as Aoki recalls the fiction of Milan Kundera, who portrayed "dispirited lives lived daily by Czechoslovakians in a regime that, in its exercise of instrumental totalitarianism, became indifferent to the beingness of humans. The result, nihilistic existence—disembodied existence, hollow existence." Aoki recalls the instrumentality of curriculum language—"implementation" specifically—and suggests that

> [w]e should recall Bobby Shew whose notion of improvisation reverberates within us and animates us. Instead of "curriculum implementation," how about "curriculum improvisation?" Such a change provokes in us a vitalizing possibility that causes our whole body to beat a new and different rhythm . . . If what I have been saying is worthy of Bobby Shew's teaching to us,

then more than ever we need the help of music educators such
as you to help us in the creation of new curriculum language—
a language that resounds bodily.

The second "echo" Aoki entitles "Polyphonic Curriculum: Responding to
the Call for Curriculum Integration in 'Year 2000.'" Here his humor is audible;
he quips that a "curriculum talk in BC that doesn't mention the government
document 'Year 2000' risks being labelled 'irrelevant.'" He tells us that he has
been noticing, "from a comfortable distance," "a flurry of activities" associated
with the document, among them the formulation of an evidently central concept:
"curriculum integration." He attended a tri-university conference on the topic;
Aoki notes, wryly, "I didn't see Bobby Shew there."

As a visitor to the conference, he remained silent, he tells us. We know
better, and a line later he admits he did ask one question: "Is integration always
good?" "I was asking," he points out, "the question of the integrity of the very
notion of 'integration' in curriculum talk." In poetic language, he asks us: "Shall
we integrate the strands into a sonic unity? Shall we allow the strands to sing
polyphonically and pray that, on occasion, they glow white-hot from within?"

Aoki makes the auditory theme explicit in an "interlude" entitled
"Conversation Pieces." He quotes Levin's 1989 *The Listening Self* to make the
point that conversation is primarily (although not exclusively; think of nonverbal
communication) an auditory phenomenon. He also quotes Derrida, Kierkegaard,
Heidegger, all emphasizing the significance of the ear and listening in lived
experience. In "Echo 3: *Sonare* and *Videre*," Aoki continues the auditory
emphasis:

I pause [a musical term] to reflect. Lingering in the reflection, I
confess that, over the years of schooling and teaching, I have
become beholden to the metaphor of the I/eye—the I that sees
. . . For myself, I too had become enamoured of the metaphor
of *videre* (to see, thinking and speaking of what eyes can see).

Referring to Wittgenstein, he concludes: "I am convinced now that in becoming
enchanted with the eye, there lurks the danger of too hurriedly foreclosing the
horizon where we live as teachers and students." But, unlike some who have
studied the auditory and the visual in the epistemology of modernity (see, for
instance, Levin, 1993), Aoki is not privileging one mode over the other. He tells
us: "The time is ripe for us to call upon *sonare* to dwell juxtaposed with *videre*."
He closes—in "A Lingering Note"—quoting a poem about a first-grade
experience in music. It sounds, as he hopes it does, "like the ring of a temple
bell, echoes and re-echoes as it fades into silence."

Chapter 24, entitled "Taiko Drums and Sushi, Perogies and Sauerkraut:
Mirroring a Half-Life in Multicultural Curriculum" was a talk given to the
Alberta Teachers Association's (ATA) Multicultural Education Council's 1990
annual conference. Aoki is thinking of Czechoslovakia, referring again to

Kundera and Vaclav Havel. He discusses Havel's (1989) essay "Words on Words," focused on one word—socialism—whose meaning for Czechoslovakians was shifting. Havel recalled that for decades socialism "rang" as "a call for revolutionary and emancipatory change; of how the word later became a totalitarian, ideological, political slogan." (The quoted words are Aoki's.) Recently in Czechoslovakia "socialism" had become laughable. Aoki quotes Havel: "What a weird fate can befall certain words."

"Havel's words on words," Aoki comments, "provoke us to thought." He wonders: Are "the bread-and-butter words for Multiculturalism and Citizenship Canada, words like 'multiculturalism" and "ethnicity,' [undergoing] a bit of turbulence? I think they are. Havel's remarks on 'words' echo and re-echo." Like "socialism" in Czechoslovakia, "multiculturalism" is shifting in meaning in Canada, no longer as respected as the term once was.

The dominant perspective on multiculturalism Aoki characterizes as "the museum approach." "Like a museum display," he explains, "the interesting cultural curios were arrayed as objects of study." It was this perspective that led him to entitle his talk: "Taiko Drums and Sushi, Perogies and Sauerkraut." These words reflect multiculturalism taught in terms of "heritage-day celebrations" and "ethnic festivals." Multiculturalism textbooks devote to a chapter each for Japanese Canadians, Ukrainian Canadians, German Canadians and so on. Drawing on his critique of Western epistemology (in particular, the subject–object split, the visual–auditory distinction in epistemology), Aoki worries that "the museum approach assumes the structure of the viewer-viewed, of subject-object separation. As such, it is reductive—reducing others to objects." Not only are these cultures objectified; so are those who study them.

Aoki wants to move "beyond mere manyness to cross-culturalism." As he so often does, he draws his listeners' attention to the conference theme, noting that "a key theme word of this conference is 'cross-culturalism.' I am drawn to it for the way it promises to open us to others." He is interested in how a conception of "multiculturalism as cross-culturalism" enables teachers and students to focus on "the crossings" between cultures. Now Aoki imagines "multiculturalism as dwelling in the midst of interculturalism." In poetical language he tells us:

> Now I slide away from the crossing, and sink into the lived
> space of between—in the midst of many cultures, into the *inter*
> of interculturalism. In-dwelling here is a dwelling in the midst
> of differences, often trying and difficult. It is a place alive with
> tension. In dwelling here, the quest is not so much to rid
> ourselves of tension . . . but more so to seek appropriately
> attuned tension, such that the sound of the tensioned string
> resounds well.

Here we hear the tension of being in Tokyo but not being (only) Japanese, of being in Canada but "evacuated" because he is Japanese Canadian, of studying in Calgary but having to apply for permission to live there.

In this chapter, Aoki returns to the question of cultural identity, recounting the OSIE incident in which he wonders about the positioning of modifiers and nouns: Canadian Jews? Jewish Canadians? Canadian Japanese? Japanese Canadians? He asks his listeners: "Does the episode draw you into what we have been calling the tensionality in the midst of differences in the 'inter?'" Then he turns to a different set of nouns: "Canadian," "Nation," "Land." These are, he suggests, "more turbulent words: in the midst of polysemic differences."

To illustrate, Aoki recalls that two summers ago in a graduate seminar in curriculum studies he taught at the University of Victoria—while retired from the University of Alberta Aoki continued to teach courses across Canada—there was a Native Indian scholar-educator enrolled, a superintendent of Band Schools, who viewed Western individualism as a narcissistic "I." When other students asked him about his identity, "he was thoughtfully silent." As that silence echoes in Aoki:

> I return to the silence where now I find more questions. "What
> do we mean by "nation" when we say "the Canadian nation?"
> I remind myself that the notion of nation-state is a Western
> cultural artefact . . . And here in Canada, I ponder the word
> "nation" in . . . "the first *nations*," "the Canadian *nation*." . . .
> Beneath me, I feel the earth tremble as the words "Canadian,"
> "nation," "land" breed uncertainty and ambiguity.

These two episodes "portray what might be meant by 'inter' in inter-culturalism, a living in the midst of differences." He follows them with a moving story of "Experiencing Differences in the Midst of Two Language Worlds: A Child's Story of a Pedagogical Experience," concluding his speech with "A Lingering Note."

Chapter 25—"The Sound of Pedagogy in the Silence of the Morning Calm"—was presented in 1990 at the International Conference on Korean Studies sponsored by the Academy for Korean Studies. In this poetic paper Aoki presents three themes, the first of which he entitles "Lingering in the Story's Pedagogical Theme." The story in question—Anjin's story—Aoki has told in seminars "in curriculum and pedagogy at the University of Victoria, the University of Alberta, and at Louisiana State University." I leave the story to you to read; let us focus here on the narrative Aoki composes to describe the educational event:

> Picture me, if you will, in a seminar of master's and doctoral
> students, calling upon them to read the story. They read in
> silence. Then ensures a hushed silence, a different silence. But
> talk-oriented as we professors are in our pedagogical situations,

> I break the silence and beckon them to a discussion. Silence
> continues to prevail. I sense their hesitation to break the
> sanctity of the silence, preferring instead to allow the story to
> linger where it seem truly to belong—in the silent mystery that
> is teaching.

What a nuanced narrative this is, a precise portrait of educational experience as lived. It is such a welcome contrast to the ugliness of "instruction" and "learning."

In Anjin's story, Aoki focuses on the authority of the teacher, a theme he has visited before (when he has focused on educational "leadership" in chap. 21). In this story, Aoki suggests:

> pedagogical authority flows from somewhere else altogether —
> from the wisdom of having lived well, from the being that
> deeply understands what it is to live truly, a poet who not only
> wrote and sang poetry but who also lived piously and dwelt
> poetically on this earth, on this land of the morning clam.
> Authority so understood is not concerned with delegating or
> sharing power, as if it were a commodity, but, rather, it leads us
> to understand authority in terms of the wisdom that comes from
> having lived well as a very human being.

I suggest this is a strong description of Aoki himself.

Aoki was not thinking of himself, but his discussion of "pedagogical leave-taking" in the story seems to me reverberates throughout his own career. The year is 1990 and Aoki will continue to teach for another decade. Although he remains very much engaged in the intellectual life of the field for another 10 years, the time before him must seem shorter than the time past. At times, he tells us, the pedagogue

> must take leave . . . he must withdraw, such that in the very
> event of withdrawal, there may inhere a pedagogic creativity, a
> coming into being that is vibrant with pedagogic possibilities.
> Hence, pedagogic withdrawal may, within a seeming negating
> of self, confer in the silence of the pedagogue's absence an
> opening wherein the student can truly learn what it is to stand,
> what it is to be in one's becoming.

We do not want you to withdraw, Ted.

The second theme Aoki "unfolds" provides an "excursus" into his concern for "*belonging* together" and "belong *together*," and for his interest in attempting to think the unthought. Concerning the former, Aoki notes that "the habitual way many of us understand 'belonging together' is 'belonging *together*,' enframed in the primacy of togetherness." In this way "belonging" is "secondary," implying fitting in a preexistent order. The notion of "relation" becomes secondary. "How," he asks, "are we to be released from the hold of this metaphysical totality that reduced belonging together to the eminence of belonging *together*?" He answers: "By thinking differently."

Aoki calls upon Heidegger here, suggesting that we transform "belonging together as enframing" into "*belonging* together" as an event of appropriation, by which he means "vibrating within itself." Belonging's homage to together is loosened, making possible the recovery of belonging in its fuller . . . [B]elonging takes precedence over together, thereby revealing the "being" of "belonging." Having now taught us this key piece of Heidegger's thought, Aoki moves to employ it. In doing so, Aoki is performing his unique "improvisation" of the poetical and the didactic. After laying out ideas and themes for the listener/reader, after "making an argument," he "poetizes" them to leave a lasting impression.

This pedagogical movement is evident in Theme 3, entitled "Decrying the Dawn in the Evening Land of the Occidental." Here he suggests that the foregoing "excursus into the realm of '(pedagogical) belonging together' offered us an opening," wherein we might feel "the turbulence" shaking "the ground of two thousand years of Western tradition beginning with Plato and Aristotle." He quotes a Heideggerean scholar named David Krell who situates Heidegger at "the outermost point in the history of the Occident or Evening-land . . . the land of dawn." By this phrase—"the land of dawn"—is meant that moment or terrain "that allows the yet unthought in Western thought." In particular, Aoki wonders about "the interplay between Tao and Heidegger's Being" as one "pretextual realm that welcomes the belonging together of the language of the East and the language of the West."

To finish this "excursus" into the "unthought," Aoki returns to Anjin's story, suggesting that it incorporates this "interplay" between East and West in its portrait of "that pedagogical relationship that reverentially knows its attunement to Being." Its "gentle lesson" is that we seek that "piety of thinking" that allows an authentic sense of pedagogy to be revealed, "freed of the calculated measure of [Western] logic." In that sense, we become "face to face with the primal mystery of Being," aware that the "language which has served us well to describe the phenomena of the world begins to falter; at best, it merely points and then passes into silence." In poetic prose unmatched in the scholarly literature, Aoki stands before us:

> I am left with a petal of thought that the appropriate topos for such piety of thinking is the silence of the morning clam. Anjin Yoo, a pedagogue that she is, has led me by her hand to the brink of this silence. And at this moment in the shimmering presence of her absence, I stand—midst the silence—alone but not alone.

You are not alone. Your students are here.

Chapter 26, entitled "Narrative and Narration in Curricular Spaces," is an invited address delivered in 1996 at the University of British Columbia. Here Aoki returns to central Europe, intellectually speaking, as he has been reading, he tells us, Slavoj Zizek's *Tarrying with the Negative*. Characteristically, he juxtaposes this abstraction with something concrete; while reading Zizek he receives a postcard from Ljubljana, sent by two of his former colleagues at the University of Alberta. Zizek opens his book with an "uncanny image," what Zizek calls "the most sublime image," depicting the political upheaval in Eastern Europe—in Romania specifically—during violent overthrow of the Ceausescu regime. Quoting Zizek, Aoki presents the image: "The image of the rebels waving the national flag with the red star, the communist symbol, cut out, so that instead of the symbol standing for the organizing principle of national life, there was *nothing but a hole in its center* (emphasis added)."

Now Aoki returns from the abstract to the concrete, recalling that he has, over "the last couple of years," been calling "home" the University of British Columbia's Asia Pacific Education Graduate Program, straddling the Centre for the Study of Curriculum and Instruction (CSCI) and the Centre for the Study of Curriculum and Instruction and the Department of Language Education (LANE). Just as Aoki takes seriously conference titles and themes, he reflects here on the APE program brochure. He notes that there arc three "master signifiers," "language," "culture," and "curriculum," and that he and his colleagues have been rethinking not only the meanings of each, but their interdisciplinary interrelationships. To specify this point he quotes Roland Barthes (1986, p. 26):

> Interdisciplinary work, so much discussed these days, is not about confronting already constituted disciplines (none of which, in fact, is willing to let itself go). To do something interdisciplinary, it is not enough to choose a subject or a theme and gather around it two or three sciences. Interdisciplinary consists in creating a new object that belongs to no one.

Aoki reports: "We in the program have been asking: where is this interdisciplinary space, where is the creation of newness possible?"

He sees this "newness" in the Ph.D. dissertation research of Erika Hasebe-Ludt, in published work by Jean François Lyotard, Deborah Britzman, Homi Bhabha, and of David Jardine, whose essay—"Reflection on Education Hermeneutics, and Ambiguity: Hermeneutics as a Restoring to Life to Its Original Difficulty"—William Reynolds and I included in our 1992 collection *Understanding Curriculum as Phenomenological and Deconstructed Text*.

Aoki reports that his class "discussed whether the [Jardine] article belonged to Part I [phenomenology] or Part II [poststructuralism], or where it might be better located in the "and" between Part I and Part II. Neither strictly phenomenological nor postmodern, most students felt it was 'growing' in the ambivalent space of "and/not and," between Part I and Part II." It seemed so to me too, which is why I located it as the last essay in the phenomenological section, the nearest to the "deconstructed" section.

Working with Jardine's reflection on "original difficulty," Aoki recalls the death of his daughter Michele Novuko (see chapter 20), and recalls students in that 1993 class who suffered loss and difficulty, among them George Fedoruk, who lost a son in a car accident and Margo Rosenberg, whose mother died in Chicago. He quotes from an article by P. D. Hershock (sent to him by David Smith): 'In this sense, suffering is . . . neither objective nor subjective, but profoundly and immediately personal and shared . . . As such, and this is crucial . . . personhood becomes a centerless space of dramatic interplay."

"If that be so," Aoki suggests, "while my suffering is always uniquely embedded in a story in which I am the seeming narrator, it is never mine alone but always ours." If that be so, he continues, "the locus of suffering is not the objective so-called 'natural' world of individual people and things, but, rather, the fathomless intimacy of narration." In this view, subjectivity itself becomes "narration, a centre-less space of dramatic interplay." He reports: "I now find myself in the space of what for me is a metonymic site of 'narrative and narration,' a site midst doubled signifiers. How was this space so constituted?" For Aoki, this site is constituted pedagogically.

How many of us acknowledge the formative role teaching plays in our intellectual lives, except to speak in generalities? Rarely do we speak in specific cases, or so it seems to me. In answering the question above—"how was this space so constituted?"—Aoki does speak specifically, paying tribute to that 1993 class and the students participating in it:

> It was born, if at all born, in that curriculum class of 1993 when it found itself located in that space of ambiguity and original difficulty David Jardine spoke of. It was within this space that George Fedoruk and Margo Rosenberg began to tell their experiences of loss and grief, later nourished by the tale of suffering Kisagotami [a young woman who lost her mind due to the death of her child, a story told in the Hershock article quoted earlier,] experienced and came to understand.

Now, "dwelling in the midst of 'narrative and narration,'" with images of a person as a centerless space, and person as the fathomless intimacy of narration," Aoki returns to Zizek of Ljubljana, "beckoned," Aoki tells us, "by his sublime image of the centerless flag—the flag with the master signifier cut out." Zizek calls upon us, Aoki notes, to "occupy all the time . . . the place of this hole; i.e., to maintain a distance toward every reigning master-signifier" (Zizek, p. 4). Aoki asks: "How might we . . . read and interpret Zizek's poignant remarks?" If we understand ourselves as spaces of "centerless narration" who "rush to fill the voice of narration with narrative, what then?" Now Aoki moves to a space in-between phenomenology and poststructuralism: "It is here I hear

Zizek urging us that we, as humans, are duty bound, ethically bound, to undergo the difficulty—to try to occupy all the time the centre-less space of narration." Is this the sense in which Aoki dwells in the lived and intellectual space of "lingering," in Zizek's term, of "tarrying?" Aoki uses both his gerund and Zizek's gerund in his conclusion:

> Short as this paper is, I experienced, in the writing of narratives, of life/not life, many pauses, spaces where I was drawn to linger a while. Where were these moments? Most of them were occasion when I tarried with negatives embedded in the doubling of "things and no-things," of "and and not-and," of "enjoining and disjoining," of the ambiguity of "this and that" instead of "this or that," of the difficult space of "life and not-life," of "center and the centerless," of "the invisible and the invisible," but, most lingeringly, in the metonymic space between "narrative and narration."

These are the spaces and moments that define education for the Aoki of the mid-1990s.

Chapter 27 is also a speech and was also given in 1996. Returning to a term he has used before (*inspirited*), Aoki entitles the performance "Spinning Inspirited Images in the Midst of Planned and Live(d) Curricula." Addressing the Fine Arts Council on the campus of the University of Alberta, the speech was preceded by a drum performance by David Thiaw, originally from Senegal, Africa. Ted Aoki was introduced to the stage by Thiaw's drumbeats, which Aoki acknowledges:

> Within me, the sound of David Thiaw's drumbeats sounds and resound . . . So inspired and so inspirited by the Senegalese drumbeat, I am beckoned by another rhythm, this from far-off Asia. Join me in a play with images and sounds of just one word, an ideograph that comes to us as a Chinese character. In Japanese, it reads "shi," literally translated as "poetry" or "that which evokes earthly rhythm."

From "indwelling ideographically"—focused on the writing of ideas—Aoki invites us to consider writing artistically, or calligraphic writing.

"June, my wife, has long been fond of Chinese and Japanese calligraphy," he reports. Mrs. Aoki prefers, he tells us, the phrase "brush sculpting" to calligraphy, emphasizing the material movement and the art over the idea. For over a decade, June has been studying "brush sculpting" with Chinese and Japanese masters. Every morning, Ted reports, she "writes." "What has long puzzled me," he admits, is how she stays at her desk writing and rewriting, repeating the same word or words 10, 20, and even more times. In this seemingly tensioned repetition, she appears not so much concerned with what is being written but, rather, seem enraptured in a world of sculpturing in space with her brush and ink as partners. Writing as sculpturing in space? Calligraphy? Considering writing as both "idea" and "artistic practice," Ted dwells "in the midst of doubled imaginaries."

He considers the "double meanings" of "live(d) experience." The first of these is "*lived* experience," he notes, "referring to past experiences that are assumed to be historically recollectable. The second is '*live* experience,' referring to ongoing experiences of the moment." "Now as I pause to reflect," he tells us, "I myself lingering in the fold of doubled imaginaries—the *ideo*graphic . . . and the calli*graphic.* I find myself in a vibrant tension of in-between, the seemingly same word refusing to fuse—a pleasant confusion! Similar, yet different at the same time!"

Now he turns to the concept of curriculum, asking "Why is it that we seem to be caught up in a singular meaning of the word curriculum?" Revealing the influence of Deleuze in this thinking at this time, he likens "the single curriculum to a single tree dominating the landscape," and he calls such a landscape "arboreal." Within this landscape, the single dominating tree "casts its benign shadow over the landscape such that 'teaching' becomes 'implementation' and 'instruction' becomes in-structuring students in the image of the given," what Aoki has described in other essays as the "curriculum-as-plan."

This obsession with sameness, he suggests, returning to the drums that opened his talk, "fails to heed the feel of the earth that touches the dancing feet differently for each student." Still "resounding" with the drumbeat, Aoki advises: "This landscape needs a bit of earth quaking such that other meanings of 'curriculum' can surface." And his words "quake," as he asks us to shift "our attention from the image of the arboreal landscape of planned curriculum to the image of live(d) curriculum. By live(d) curriculum, I mean the situated image of the live(d) curricular experiences of teachers and students." He points out that the word "experience" itself is a hybrid in the sense that it has embedded within it both the notion of "past experiences" (*lived* experiences) and that of "ongoing experiences" (*live* or *living* experiences). "But," he adds, "what matters significantly lies beyond mere 'past' and 'ongoing.'"

To suggest what that is, Aoki turns to Jonathan Culler (1982, p. 83) who argued that "experience is divided and deferred—always behind us as something to be recovered, yet still before us as something to be produced." Always the teacher, Aoki asks: "What is he saying?" "First," he answers, those "past experiences, assumed to lie in the depth of the past, await recovery through careful archaeology." And second, the "meanings of experiences ongoing horizontally are being produced in the spaces between signifiers," in the present instance, between ideographic and calligraphic, between "live(d) curriculum" and "curriculum-as-plan."

"Such a curricular landscape," he continues, "is replete with a multiplicity of curricula." After Deleuze, he call this landscape "rhizomean," a term to signify not only "multiplicity," but as well "that textured web of connecting lines that, like rhizomean plants, shoot from here to there, and everywhere working through, nourished by the humus." So understood, we are positioned "in the midst of and between planned and live(d) curricula." To shift our attention from the nouns to the con/disjunction, Aoki "slips into the language of 'and/not and,' and into the language of 'conjunction' and 'disjunction,' a difficult ambivalent space but a space nonetheless." In this space it is no longer possible "to cross smoothly and quickly from 'planned curriculum' to 'live(d) curriculum' through 'implementation or instruction.'"

Taking very seriously Huebner's injunction to create new curricular language, Aoki enters "a space textually accented with a mark: /, a graphically tectonic space, a space marked by differences neither strictly vertical nor strictly horizontal, a space that may allow generative possibilities." It is a space "of generative interplay between planned curriculum and live(d) curriculum," space "where newness can come into being." Connecting this new formulation with phenomenological language he has used in earlier essays he notes: "It is an inspirited site of being and becoming."

To help us "better understand the generative though ambiguous, ambivalent space between this and that, between planned curriculum and live(d) curriculum," Aoki provides a list:

- I now see inspirited hybrid brush writing that occurs in that space of ambivalence between ideographic writing *and* calligraphic writing;
- I see inspirited dancing that happens in that space between dancing about an event *and* dancing as performative;
- I see inspirited singing as that creative singing in the space between singing a song *and* live(d) singing;
- I see inspirited acting as enaction in that space between acting by script *and* live(d) acting; and
- I see inspirited painting as that generative creation in that space between panting an object *and* painting as living experience.

Such spaces, he underlines, are "edgy spaces, located at margins and boundaries, space of doubling, where 'this or that' becomes 'this and that,' ambiguously, ambivalent—difficult places but nonetheless spaces of generative possibilities."

Aoki concludes his remarkable speech with "a plea to art educators." In an effort to escape the hegemony of curriculum-as-plan, he notes, scholars in the university have focused on "pedagogy." "No doubt much good and promising work has gone on and is ongoing," he allows. "But so oriented and so directed," he continues, importantly, "many have neglected the word *curriculum*, and by their neglect, they may have complicit in solidifying the hold of curriculum-as-plan." Rightly associating "curriculum" with the "yearning for new meanings," he notes that such yearning "feels choked, out of breath, caught in a landscape wherein 'curriculum' as master-signifier is restricted to planned curriculum with all its supposed, splendid instrumentalism." (This is the second occasion on which he has used the imagery of "suffocation" to describe the situation of the public school teacher.) Drawing together the various images and ideas of the speech, Aoki makes his plea:

> I call on fine arts educators in particular, with their strong sense of poetics, to offer inspiration and leadership in the promising work of creating a new landscape wherein "live(d) curricula" can become a legitimated signifier. We seek your guiding hand in re-shaping and re-constituting the landscape such that in generative third spaces earth's rhythms can be heard, at times in thunderous rolls and at other times in fingertip whispers, not only in fine arts classes but also throughout the school wherever teachers and students gather in the name of inspirited education.

Chapter 28, entitled "Locating Lived Pedagogy in Teacher 'Research': Five Metonymic Moments," was presented at a Teacher Research Conference held in Baton Rouge, Louisiana, in April 2000, concurrent with the Louisiana State University (LSU) Conference on the Internationalization of Curriculum Studies, on the final evening of which I presented Ted the LSU Curriculum Theory Project Award for a Lifetime of Achievement in Internationalization of Curriculum Studies (see Appendix). June Aoki had also made the trip; I sat next to her while we listened to Ted's speech.

In this speech Aoki summarizes several of his theoretical initiatives that we have read in the speeches of the 1990s. As would his son Doug, Ted turns to psychoanalysis, and the work of Jacques Lacan in particular, to underline the significance of "situatedness" in understanding curriculum. Aoki notes that for Lacan, the question is not "who am I?" but "where am I?" "To help understand the where," Aoki asks, "allow me to journey through five metonymic moments."

In the first—"living pedagogy midst curriculum-as-plan/curriculum-as-live(d)"—Aoki returns to Leonard Cohen's poem, enabling him to "crack" the concept of curric/ulum. In the "crack" are "sites of living pedagogy," the "pedagogical 'where' between the curriculum-as-plan and the live(d) curriculum." In the second, he recalls June Aoki's calligraphy in order to question Western traditions of representation and the privileging of presence. In the third, he enters the site between "representational discourse/nonrepresentational discourse." This "third space" is the site of "living pedagogy," a site of "original difficulty" or, after Bill Doll, "chaos." "As for me," he says, "it is the site of metonymy, of metaphoric writing, metonymic writing."

In the fourth moment—"self/other"—Aoki return his critique of Western individualism, and in the fifth—"A Double Reading of a Zen Parable"—Aoki recalls an invitation of several years ago to teach a course at McGill University titled "Curriculum Foundations." Ted accepted the invitation, "providing I could change the title to 'Curriculum Foundations without Foundations,'" a shift in "master signifiers" to denote "indwelling" in the "third space." Certainly that is one legacy of the work of Ted Aoki: He has shifted the "master signifiers" in curriculum studies, including the central concept itself, so that we now hear "curriculum" in a "new key."

In Part D—Miscellaneous Essays—opens with a letter Ted writes to Mrs. Elsie McMurphie, then president of the British Columbia Teachers Federation (BCTF) regarding Bill 19, which legislated the creation of an administrators' association separate from the BCTF (see chap. 21). He points out that "education [is] a venture different from business." To construe the school principal as business manager, "by itself, misunderstands education. As such, it is dangerous." In "Bridges that Rim the Pacific," presented at a 1988 international conference n social studies, Aoki makes explicit what is an key theme of his work: "It is my wish to serve as a bridge over the Pacific Ocean." In an interviewed conducted by *Teacher Magazine* in 1994 on the occasion of his induction into the Education Honor Society, Aoki's modesty is unmistakable. He does not "linger" there long, however, and turns to the persisting issues of "theory" and "practice," pointing out, with disarming simplicity, the nature of their relationship: "Thinking and doing are entwined." He speaks of "the limits of phenomenology," the dualism of the Western epistemological tradition, the significance of situatedness. Then he turns to the ecological:

> I think we need to break away from that narrow version of humanness by reconstituting the meaning of *human* in terms of, perhaps, our relation to the earth. If we were to link the word *human* with related words like *humility*, we begin to see a new relationship between self and others. It may help us to remember that *human* has kinship with *humus* and *humor*. We need to move to an earthly place where we can have fun and laugh, too.

In that sentence he speaks for the first time of the significance of humor. I have called attention to Aoki's wry and subtle sense of humor. Here he makes a general point regarding the significance of laughter, but I cannot but read the passage as also self-referenced. "Why do we laugh?" Aoki asks. In the answer we hear several themes in the collected works: truthfulness, tension, and difference.

> Laughter emerges from the notion of difference, difference from what we expect somebody to say, and what he or she does say. Because of the difference, we laugh; laughter is truthful. And like laughter, life is paradoxical, caught in the midst of tensioned differences. Without the tension we'd be dead.

Living in-between and amidst difference—the generative educational potential of dwelling in that "third space" of tension—has been a constant and powerful theme in Aoki's work.

Aoki's commitment to and grounding in classroom teaching sound loud and clear throughout his career. On this occasion, speaking to *Teacher Magazine*, it is crystal clear that this commitment is not in the least vocational but, rather, profoundly theoretical. He explains to the teachers reading the magazine, simply but with intellectual integrity, a central feature of post-modernism. He tells the interviewer: "But keep in mind that in post-modernism, it's less you and me talking, but more your text and my text in inter-textuality—a dialogue of texts. And in the dialogue two things can happen—new texts are created *and* you and I are transformed."

Echoing Huebner and anticipating Elizabeth Ellsworth's 1997 critique of "communication," he adds: "We need to break away from the privilege we've given language as a tool of communication and re-understand language." As if to illustrate and, in the process, distilling much of the what the contemporary field of curriculum studies is now saying, Aoki concludes: "Teachers can also think of the experience as ongoing, right now, in the present. It's a living experience ongoing now. And in the now, teachers are somewhere in life, somewhere in the midst of differences, in that space constituting and reconstituting themselves and the program."

In a 1999 interview with the *Kappa Delta Pi Record* entitled "Rethinking Curriculum and Pedagogy," Aoki attributes one of his key conceptualizations to teachers, telling the interviewer: "Sensitive teachers have told me that teaching in a live situation is midst the planned and unplanned, between the plannable and the unplannable." He quickly elaborates in sophisticated theoretical language:

> For me, these are telling marks, signally the tensioned textured spaces teachers are already indwelling in their pedagogical practices. Where? In that metonymic space of doubling, between curriculum-as-plan and curriculum-as-lived, then, is a call to recognize that textured site of lived tension—so often ambiguous, uncertain, and difficult—and a call for struggle in tension but, nevertheless, a generative site of possibilities and hope.

Like Huebner, Aoki appreciates teaching as a calling (he notes that "vocation" derives from the Latin *vocare*/to call), and he characterizes the "voices of teaching" in as having "sought ways of attunement that will allow them to hear, even faintly, the call of the calling." Speaking of those who contributed to the collection, Aoki is also, it seems to me, speaking about himself when he writes: "the authors of *Voices of Teaching* offer us narrative of some moments in their experiences of teaching, thereby opening themselves to the lived meanings of teaching." Aoki's theorizing is always profoundly pedagogical, deeply grounded in concrete and specific educational events, occasions for experiencing the lived meanings of teaching.

Disengaging himself from teaching as a bureaucratized profession, Aoki opened himself to his own lived experience of teaching, at first in the Hutterite school east of Calgary, then in the public schools of southern Alberta, 19 years in all as teacher and assistant principal. After accepting a professorship at the University of Alberta, Aoki understood immediately that his "job" was not narrowly vocational, but profoundly theoretical, and that there was no unbridgeable divide between theory and practice.

In characterizing these "voices of teaching," Aoki describes the work of finding themes in others' work as "theming," disclosing his fondness for gerunds rather than nouns, emphasizing the *live* in lived experience. "Theming," he writes, "is understood as a lingering intimately in embedded thoughtfulness in the story—as thoughtful listening in the nearness of the calling. Such theming is, as some would say, reflective thoughtfulness." The labour of "theming," Aoki concludes, involves

> what we might call a hermeneutic returning to the lived ground of human experience within the story — a place wherein inhabits a tensionality of both distance and nearing. It understands such a place as a resonant place where emerging from the silence may be heard the movement of melody and rhythm — polyphonic voices of teaching. Where might such a place be? Paradoxically, the place is where we already are — a place so near yet so far that we have forgotten its whereabouts. Reflecting theming may allow us to come to know how sufficiently as humans we inhabit where we already are as teachers.

This paragraph expresses several of the major themes of Aoki's remarkable career, among them the primacy of "lived experience," a distant but near "place" of "resonance," sounding in unmistakable if silent rhythms the "polyphonic voices of teaching." Where is this "lived experience," this "place" where we can hear the call of teaching? It is where we are "already."

These are deeply evocative themes, recalling phenomenology's critique of contemporary life in the West as estranged from its ground, lost in the chimera of the mundane everyday world. Nowhere is that inauthentic social world more "suffocating" (to use another gerund of Aoki's) than in those classrooms regulated by proliferating bureaucratic protocols, institutionalizations of Western (mis)conceptions of "individualism" and "competence." It is Aoki's voice—no unitary sound, indeed, polyphonic—that sounds the call of our vocation, that calls us back to its lived ground where we are already, if muffled by the distractions and obsessions of the maelstrom that structures inauthenticity. There, where we are already, we can dwell in a conjunctive space, not one splintered by binaries, a lived space marked by generative tensions that we can incorporate, embody, and personify in our dialogical encounters with students and colleagues.

This "third space" space within which we can dwell both incorporates and leads us to the world outside. It is the space between political and bureaucratic stipulation—it is, as Aoki notes, "open season" on education—and the classroom reenactment of those contractual obligations, the space between what Aoki so usefully characterizes as "curriculum-as-plan" and "curriculum-as-lived." It is the space where we work (and play) to understand the educational meaning of our being together, in classrooms, at conferences, in seminars, engaged in improvisation, that disciplined and creative reconstitution of the past in anticipation of a future waiting to be heard in the present. "It is," Aoki explains, "a space of doubling, where we slip into the language of 'both this and that, but neither this nor that' . . . The space moves and is alive."

It is to this profoundly spatial, temporal and vibrant character of curriculum to which Aoki's work testifies. Significantly, it is not temporality severed from history. Aoki's narratives of his own schooling (the story of Mr. NcNab), the family's "evacuation" during World War II and his encounters with ignorance and prejudice, his mention of specific events (such as the Challenger disaster and the Columbine murders) all keep "time" grounded in "history," but never collapse the two. There is always in Aoki's work an attunement to time that exceeds historicity, an attunement that renders Aoki not only a philosopher, but a historian, an autobiographer, always the sophisticated theoretician, in each instance answering the call of pedagogy, speaking in the voice(s) of teaching.

Ted is always teaching. Nearly all of these essays are speeches; they are, in a profound sense of the word, "lessons." And even though the lessons he teaches are complex, never does he seem distracted by that complexity. Indeed, he is always attentive to the concreteness and singularity of the situation at hand. Invariably he acknowledges (respectfully) the occasion on which he is speaking, often referring to the conference title or theme, and organizing his "lesson" around those "signifiers." He proceeds with the sophistication and savvy of the veteran classroom teacher he is, sometimes disarming his listeners with a folksy story, sometimes taking on their own incomprehension as his own, embodying in himself their struggles to understand the lesson he is presenting, to bridge the distance between where they are and where he invites them to visit. Ted's pedagogical movements from the concrete to the abstract and back again, and into the spaces among and between them, dazzle me, enable me to linger longer, listening to this master "musician" play.

In that "music" we hear echoes of pieces he has played before, but there is never simple repetition. As in jazz (as the visiting trumpeter made explicit), the narratives Aoki reiterates sound differently each time he speaks them, each time in new context, serving a different purpose, while reconceptualizing an enduring theme. There is in Aoki's *oeuvre* a robust recursive movement, as Aoki returns to lessons past in making points present, anticipating ideas yet to come. It is this temporal enactment of his pedagogy—organizing these speeches into "moments" and "echoes"—that enables listeners to understand the lessons he has to teach.

I had suggested to Aoki that he organize the essays chronologically so students could see how his thought evolved over time. Too linear, I could hear him say in the silent twinkling of his eye. After rereading the foreword to *Voices of Teaching* I know why; he was "theming," reflecting the gatherings that stimulated his thought, the clustering of concepts, the reconfiguring of melodies, creating new sounds of dissonance and difference out of juxtapositions a simple chronology would have silenced. I am grateful Aoki declined my suggestions and stayed his course, a course, like the one he taught in Montreal, without foundations, in this instance, temporal foundations.

"Foundations" would be too reductionistic, too binary. He is, after all, a "bridge," understood both a noun and a verb. This theme shows up in the chapters on conversation, on the Pacific Rim; he is "a person," as Aoki's puts it, who is "both self and other." "It is my wish," he offered in 1988, "to serve as a bridge over the Pacific Ocean." Aoki lives on the Pacific Rim, Japanese *and* Canadian (as he makes clear, a slippery set of signifiers), well aware of the Western individualism (the limitations he has insistently pointed out), well aware of the Eastern side of the Rim. He quotes Roshin, a Taoist teacher, to make his point: "Humanity's greatest delusion is that I am here and you are there." There is no American-style narcissism here, in which the "other" disappears into my "self." Aoki invokes Levinas to ensure that his Western listeners and readers do not mistake the profoundly ethical, relational, indeed, ecological character of "self *and* other."

It is this enduring sense of the ethical that enables Aoki to occupy a space between history and time, between continents, between the public school classroom and the university seminar room, between a field in collapse in the 1960s, its reconceptualization in the 1970s, and its rejuvenation today. Aoki's career started in the Tylerian past, but he never seems to have been seduced by the apparently commonsensical purposes to which Tyler's work was put, namely, the conversion of the school into a factory. Over and over again Aoki points out that education is not a business, that a school principal is not an administrative manager (but, rather, a principal teacher). He knew that we needed not to see a new curriculum model, but to hear curriculum in a new key. The new key Aoki has composed is breathtakingly beautiful in its sonorous poeticity, powerfully and provocatively multiplying in its concepts.

In the postscript/rescript, composed in late 2002 and early 2003, Aoki recalls his public school teaching life, his early years at the University of Alberta, and the primacy of students—including Max Van Manen—in his intellectual life. He recalls the special issue of *Journal of Curriculum Theorizing* (JCT) devoted to him, an issue featuring the proceedings of a special session held at the *JCT*/Bergamo Conference in Dayton, Ohio, in honour of his retirement from the University of Alberta in 1985. His participation in the calligraphic design of the cover of that issue, and a second one in 1995, provokes reflection on issues of East/West, representation/nonrepresentation, "a cursive figuration often invoking the 'is not.'" His reflection performs *currere* in its profoundest sense.

Aoki's influence on students and theirs on him are evident in the doctoral dissertation research he describes in the postscript/rescript. As important as students are to his intellectual life, Aoki's influence is not limited to them, but extends to his colleagues worldwide. He closes by mentioning the formation of the International Association for the Advancement of Curriculum Studies, but he declines (his modesty, again) to mention the significant role he played in its coming to form; he represented North America on the Provisional Executive Committee that drafted a constitution that resulted in the establishment of the association. From the public school classrooms of southern Alberta to the seminar rooms of universities in Canada and the United States, Ted Aoki's participation in the "complicated conversation" that is the academic field of curriculum studies has been pivotal and worldwide.

Because the concept communicates the significance of the auditory in Aoki's theory and teaching (and because it is a central concept in contemporary curriculum studies in the United States), I close this "lingering" introduction by focusing on the notion of "conversation." In the collection it shows up first in chapter 4, where Aoki revisits his experience during the 1970s evaluating the British Columbia Social Studies curriculum. In what he characterizes as the "Situational Interpretative Evaluation Orientation," the primary interests are those meanings ascribed to the situation by those engaged in teaching and studying the curriculum. In order to represent those meanings, Aoki and his BC Social Studies Assessment team employed "conversational analysis."

Disclosing the primacy of phenomenology in his thinking even at this early stage, Aoki notes that the conversation he has in mind is not "chit-chat," nor is it the simple exchange of messages or only the communication of information. None of these, he suggests, requires "true human presence." Nor is language only a tool by means of which thoughts are recoded into words. Curriculum as conversation, in this formulation, is no conveyor belt of "representational knowledge." It is a matter of attunement, an auditory rather than visual conception.

In chapter 10, Aoki brings this phenomenological critique of "conversation" to bear on issues of intercultural education, specifically as these surfaced in the internationally-attended graduate program in curriculum studies at the University of Alberta. Revealing his characteristic pedagogical movement from the abstract to the concrete, from the theoretical to the anecdotal, here from the local to the global, Aoki conceives of graduate study as "a conversation of mankind" in a "transnational situation."

Speaking with students who have come to Alberta from beyond North America, Aoki is reminded of the instrumentality of his assignment as an administrator and of the centrality of conversation in the process of education. In this intercultural educational experience, Aoki worries about the erasure of originary identities. "To remind ourselves of who we are in conversation," he suggests to these students, "I ask that we turn the conversation to ourselves." He poses to them what might be the central curriculum question in an era of globalization: "How will you know that what we consider 'good' here is 'good' in your homeland?'"

In this same essay, Aoki employs "conversation" to think about what might comprise an "authentic dialogue" among scholars worldwide. "If East-West conversation in curriculum is to be authentically East–West dialogue, if North–South conversation is to be authentically North–South dialogue," he suggests, then "such conversation must be guided by an interest in understanding more fully what is not said by going beyond what is said." Here he is using a phenomenology of language—and specifically its depth imagery—to remind us that the social surface of speech is precisely that. Authentic conversation requires "going beyond" the surface to take into account "unspoken" and "taken-for-granted" assumptions, including "ideology," what Aoki characterizes as "the cultural crucible and context that make possible what is said by each in the conversational situation." With the inclusion of the concept of "ideology," Aoki is disclosing a complication of his initial phenomenological formulation, here by critical theory, specifically the work of Habermas.

Aoki reminds us that "authentic conversation is open conversation," never "empty," always one in which the participants engage in a "reciprocity of perspectives." Invoking one of his favourite metaphors, he tells us: "I understand conversation as a bridging of two worlds by a bridge, which is not a bridge." Conversation is a passage from here to there and elsewhere, but it is not "here" or "there" or "elsewhere," but in the conjunctive spaces in-between.

Aoki employs "bridge" in both literal and metaphoric senses; the idea seems to foreshadow the bridging movements in his own work. That movement is evident in chapter 9, a 1992 speech to the Association for Supervision and Curriculum Development (ASCD). It is, in my judgment, a most remarkable speech, in which Aoki moves deftly between high abstraction and amusing anecdote. Among the abstractions he introduces to this audience of school personnel is interdisciplinarity, specifically, the teaching of science as one of the humanities.

Lest he run off his audience of administrators by such talk, Aoki creates a scenario on Bourbon Street. (Given that this conference was being held in New Orleans, he is enabling his audience to "run off" while remaining seated.) In this scenario, a scientist and a novelist are engaged in conversation, yes, about science taught as one of the humanities. Here he seems to be using "conversation" commonsensically, but this seems to me strategic, and it doesn't last long. Quickly this concrete sense of conversation becomes abstract "under the influence," not of drink (as one might suspect, being on Bourbon Street), but of the philosophy of Gilles Deleuze.

For in this encounter between scientist and novelist, Aoki imagines, as he puts it, "improvised lines of movement growing from the middle of their conversation." Such improvisation in conversation requires, he tells us, "a new language," still a phenomenological theme, but now emitting a decidedly post-structuralist sound. The language Aoki hears in this interdisciplinary conversation on Bourbon Street has, he tells us, "a grammar in which a noun is not always a noun, in which conjoining words like *between* and *and* are no mere joining words, a new language that might allow a transformative resonance of the words *paradigms*, *practices*, and *possibilities*" (a reference to the subtitle of William Schubert's widely read 1986 study). If that be so," he concludes, returning us from the abstract to the concrete with humor, "we should all move to the French Quarter, so that we can not only listen, but also join them right in the middle of their conversation."

Conversation understood as authentic attunement to "true human presence" was, let us remember, a radical idea in the 1970s; for many trapped in the school-as-a-business it remains so today. By characterizing the exchange of "information" as "chit-chat," Aoki was, in the 1973 essay, calling to us to rethink not only what we mean by "evaluation," but, as we reflect on his later questionings of technology (in chap. 5), to rethink the so called Age of Information in which we presumably live. In 1992, not blocks from Bourbon Street, he is employing poststructuralism to disperse disciplinary identities and to create interdisciplinary spaces between the humanities and the sciences, spaces that include both sets of disciplines.

Twenty years after his initial and important formulation of the concept of "conversation" as evocative of and attuned to "true human presence," Aoki (presumably retired, mind you) is speaking of conversation in less sombre tones. By the early 1990s Aoki is speaking of conversation as a version of jazz, a notion that first shows up in the 1991 Bobby Shew anecdote (see chap. 23) and a discussion of improvisation, although the language he employs in the New Orleans speech to ASCD is Deleuzian. Rather than returning to something lost or at least in jeopardy ("true human presence"), Aoki now focuses on something futural, something to be created, a "new language," and through improvisation.

There is no question for Aoki of working from *either* phenomenology *or* from poststructuralism. The interest in language and, more specifically, the analysis of the conjunctions of apparently mutually exclusive binaries through deconstruction is present in Heidegger (if in the service of retrieving "true human presence"), as John Caputo (1987) and others have made clear (see Pinar et al., 1995, chap. 8). Aoki never abandons phenomenology, but he follows it to its edge where conversation as hermeneutics becomes conversation as "improvisation."

"Improvisation" is a powerful notion that not only allows us to emphasize the creativity of teaching, but enables us to "hear" the relation between theory and practice. As Aoki notes in the title essay (if in visual terms): "Rather than seeing theory as leading into practice, we need now more than ever to see it as a reflective moment in praxis." In the sounds of our conversation we honour the past by self-reflectively reformulating it in the present, animated by our own and others' "true human presence." That is the jazz of praxis.

If we focus on the auditory character of Aoki's metaphors, we see continuity as well as change in the essays. From the beginning, Aoki is critical of scientistic observation (and its privileging of the visual), emphasizing instead the sound of conversation (and its privileging of the auditory). He makes this critique explicit in a 1991 speech to the British Columbia Music Educators Association, where he points out that conversation is primarily an auditory experience. In this important paper, Aoki quotes Derrida, Kierkegaard, and Heidegger to emphasize the significance of the ear and of listening in educational experience. He writes:

> I pause [a musical term as well] to reflect. Lingering in the reflection, I confess that, over the years of schooling and teaching, I have become beholden to the metaphor of the I/eye—the I that sees . . . For myself, I too had become enamoured of the metaphor of *videre* (to see, thinking and speaking of what eyes can see).

This formulation represents a major theoretical advance in our understanding of curriculum as conversation. In creating a "new language" in which *sonare* becomes as least as important as *videre*, Aoki has changed everything. Gone are decades of behaviourism and its residues in observational analysis. Questioned is the very subject–object binary in Western epistemology, imprinted as that is throughout the school curriculum and mainstream educational research. Questioned is the relegation of classroom teaching to "implementation," a bureaucratic bridge between objectives and assessment.

Present are the sounds of complicated conversation in which teachers are bridges between curriculum-as-plan and curriculum-as-lived, between the state and the multitude, between history and culture. "Conversation," Aoki explains, "is a bridging of two worlds by a bridge, which is not a bridge." "Bridge" here is both noun and verb; it is both literal and metaphoric. It is both spatial and temporal. As *Webster's* points out, "bridge" is defined as "time, place, or means of connection or transition." Aoki himself performs, indeed personifies, such temporal and spatial connections and transitions: between the traditional and reconceptualized fields, between phenomenology and poststructuralism, between theory and pedagogy, between the West Coast and the prairies, between Canada and the United States, between East and West.

To bridge East and West, Aoki moves away from a focus on the separate identities of the binary and into the spaces between them. As he puts it, he is "trying to undo the instrumental sense of 'bridge.'" Such a nuanced sense of "bridge" is implied by the conjunction "and" in the binary. By focusing on the conjunctive space *between* "East and West," and by understanding "and" as "both 'and' and 'not-and,'" Aoki proposes a bridging space of "both conjunction and disjunction." This is, Aoki explains, a space of tension, both "and/not-and," a space "of conjoining and disrupting, indeed, a generative space of possibilities, a space wherein in tensioned ambiguity newness emerges."

That last phrase describes, I think, the space Aoki has created in his work, wherein we can now listen as if with new ears to conversation across terrains of difference, a complicated conversation in which both separation and belonging together exist in generative tension. The latter phrase is explicated in a 1990 paper, beautifully entitled "The Sound of Pedagogy in the Silence of the Morning Calm" (chap. 25), in which Aoki privileges the gerund "belonging" over the noun "together." "Belonging" takes precedence over "together," he explains, thereby revealing the "being" of "belonging." In his subtle and sophisticated conceptualization, "being" vibrates like a violin string, and in its sound, honours the complexity and integrity of individual identity and social relationality.

"Bridge" is a musical term as well, defined by Webster's as "an arch serving to raise the strings of a musical instrument." Aoki raised us, the individual strings of the field, attuning us to our calling as educators. Aoki has ennobled us by his labour, enabled us to "be" in our belonging together, engaged in creative and disciplined "improvisation" as we traverse the terrain of our lived differences as educators.

"There are other bridges," he notes, such as those found in Japanese gardens, including one to which he refers in chapter 20: the bridge in the Japanese—Nitobe's—garden on the University of British Columbia campus. In Aoki's bridging movements from the abstract to the concrete, from the metaphoric to the literal, from history to culture, he has advanced, as he has complicated, our understanding of our pedagogical and scholarly calling. Ted Aoki's work is a bridge, and, like the bridge he describes in chapter 18, "we are in no hurry to cross over; in fact, such bridges lure us to linger." This metaphoric bridge is "a site or clearing in which earth, sky, mortals and divine, long to be together, belong together." Aoki's work has created such a clearing in curriculum studies. Please, enter it now.

REFERENCES

Aoki, D. (2002). The price of teaching: Love, evasion, and the subordination of knowledge. *Journal of Curriculum Theorizing*, 18 (1), 21–39.

Aoki, T. T. (1990). Sonare and videre: Questioning the primacy of the eye in curriculum talk. In G. Willis & W. H. Schubert (Eds.), *Reflections from the heart of educational inquiry: Understanding curriculum and teaching through the arts* (182-189). Albany, NY: State University of New York Press.

Barthes, R. (1986). *The rustle of language.* New York: Hill and Wang.

Caputo, J. (1987). *Radical hermeneutics: Repetition, deconstruction and the hermeneutic project.* Bloomington: Indiana University Press.

Doll, W. E. Jr., (1993). *A post-modern perspective on curriculum.* New York: Teachers College Press.

Doll, W. E. Jr., (1998). Curriculum and concepts of control. [Assisted by Al Alcazar.] In W. F. Pinar (Ed.). *Curriculum: Toward new identities* (pp. 295–323). New York: Garland.

Doll, W. E. Jr., (2002). Ghosts and the curriculum. In W. E. Doll, Jr., & N. Gough (Eds.), *Curriculum visions* (pp. 23–70). New York: Peter Lang.

Ellsworth, E. (1997). *Teaching positions: Difference, pedagogy, and the power of address*. New York: Teachers College Press.

Greene, M. (1973). *Teacher as stranger*. Belmont, CA: Wadsworth.

Greene, M. (1978). *Landscapes of learning*. New York: Teachers College Press.

Grumet, Madeleine R. (1990). Voice: The search for a feminist rhetoric for educational studies. *Cambridge Journal of Education*, 20 (3), 277–282.

Jardine, D. (1992). Reflections on education, hermeneutics, and ambiguity: Hermeneutics as a restoring of life to its original difficulty. In W. F. Pinar & W. M. Reynolds (Eds.), *Understanding curriculum as phenomenological and deconstructed text* (pp. 116–127). New York: Teachers College Press.

Kumashiro, K. (in press). *Anti-oppressive teaching*: New York: RoutledgeFalmer.

Lasch, C. (1978). *The culture of narcissism: American life in an age of diminishing expectations*. New York: Norton.

Lasch, C. (1984). *The minimal self: Psychic survival in troubled times*. New York: Norton.

Lather, P. (1991). Deconstructing/deconstructive inquiry: The politics of knowing and being known. *Educational Theory*, 41 (2), 153–173.

Overly, N. V. (2003). A history of the World Council for Curriculum and Instruction (WCCI). In W. F. Pinar (Ed.), *International handbook of curriculum research*. Mahwah, NJ: Lawrence Erlbaum Associates.

Pinar, W. F. (1979). What is the reconceptualization? *Journal of Curriculum Theorizing*, 1 (1), 93–104.

Pinar, W. F. (2004). *What is curriculum theory?* Mahwah, NJ: Lawrence Erlbaum Associates.

Pinar, W F., & Reynolds, W. M. (Eds.), (1992). *Understanding curriculum as phenomenological and deconstructed text*. New York: Teachers College Press.

Pinar, W. F., Reynolds, W. M., Slattery, P., & Taubman, P. (1995). *Understanding curriculum*. New York: Peter Lang.

Schubert, W. H. (1986). *Curriculum: Perspective, paradigm, and possibility*. New York: Macmillan.

Zizek, S. (1993). *Tarrying with the negative*. Durham, NC: Duke University Press.

Part I

Reconceptualizing Curriculum

Chapter 1

Toward Curriculum Inquiry in a New Key[1] (1978/1980)

> "There are some good indications that educational research
> may have reached a crisis stage with its major Fisherian
> experimental design tradition and perhaps that the paradigm
> has never worked."[2]

Whether we agree or not with A. J. Magoon that educational research is in a crisis stage, there are no doubt noteworthy indications of search efforts for alternative research possibilities in education. The convening of this conference, Phenomenological Description: Potential for Research in Art Education, is in itself such an indication.

The theme of the conference reminds me of Aldous Huxley, who some years ago admonished us to:

> intensify our ability to look at the world *directly*, not through
> the half-opaque medium of concepts which distort every given
> fact into the all too familiar likeness of some generic label or
> explanatory abstraction.[3] [Emphasis mine]

---

[1] Reprinted from: Aoki, Ted T. (1980). Toward curriculum inquiry in a new key. *Curriculum Praxis Occasional Paper No. 2*. Edmonton, Alberta: Department of Secondary Education, Faculty of Education, University of Alberta. The paper was originally presented at the Conference on Phenomenological Description: Potential for Research in Art Education sponsored by the Division of Graduate Studies in the Fine Arts, Concordia University, April 6–8, 1978.

[2] Magoon, A J. (1977). Constructivist approaches in educational research. *AERA Review of Educational Research*, 47 (4), 653. Magoon's examination of research approaches is of interest for its breadth and detail. Unfortunately, his discussion of phenomenological approaches is framed in the control orientation of empirical-analytic research, which belies the dominant perspective toward which he himself is biased.

[3] Aldous Huxley, *The Doors of Perception*. Huxley's admonition is fundamentally phenomenological and is reflective of his concern for reductivism through abstraction.

In these words Huxley reflects a research attitude with a familiar ring to phenomenologists: "to the things themselves," which as a mode of inquiry, H. Spiegelberg has described thus:

> The *direct* investigation and *description of phenomena as consciously experienced*, without theories about their causal explanation and as free as possible from unexamined preconceptions and presuppositions.[4] [Emphasis mine]

Some educational researchers have begun to show serious interest in "the directly experienced," marking for education a real advance. In this paper I wish to explore, from a curriculum generalist's perspective, some thoughts on possible new directions in curriculum inquiry. This personal exploration has been motivated, in part, by my general disenchantment with the lack in recent years of fundamentally significant advances in curriculum inquiry and, in part, by my fervent hope that the talks and discussions at this conference act as a spur toward vitalized curriculum research praxis.

SOME BELLWETHER SIGNS IN CURRICULUM INQUIRY

Since Ralph Tyler's formulation in 1950 of the curriculum rationale,[5] curriculum writings over the last quarter century have been abundant, making it increasingly difficult to make sense of the path or paths being trodden. The bulk of this literature, however, has been devoted to the elaboration of Tyler's language of ends–means relationships through the use of increasingly sophisticated but reified languages of systems theory, games theory, decision theory, and the like.

However, since the 1960s there have been bellwether signs in curriculum, a few of which we should take serious note of. We who are in the domain of curriculum studies remember the early 1960s when much was made of Jerome

---

[4] Spiegelberg, H. (1975) *Doing Phenomenology: Essays on and in Phenomenology*, p. 3. The Hague: Martinus Nijhoff. 1975, p. 3. Spiegelberg's book discusses the practice of phenomenology.

[5] Tyler, Ralph. (1949) *Basic Principles of Curriculum and Instruction.* Chicago: University of Chicago Press. The Tyler rationale for curriculum development is comprised of four steps based on a commonsensical ends–means schema. They are as follows: (a) determine purposes, (b) identify learning experiences, (c) organize these learning experiences, (d) evaluate achievement in terms of purposes stated. It is the predominant paradigm in curriculum literature.

Bruner's *The Process of Education,*[6] wherein the understanding of the "structure of the disciplines" was considered to be the open sesame to Curriculum Studies. Not many of us remember, however, how Bruner in 1971, 10 years after the publication of *The Process of Education,* announced what amounted to a refocus away from his earlier stance:

> If I had my choice now in terms of a curriculum project for the 1970s, it would be to find a means whereby we could bring society back to its sense of values and priorities in life. *I believe I would be quite satisfied to declare, if not a moratorium, then something of a de-emphasis on matters that have to do with the structure of history, the structure of physics, the nature of mathematical consistency, and deal with it rather in the context of the problems that face us . . .. We might put vocation and intention back into the process of education, much more firmly than we had it there before.*[7]
> [Emphasis given by Jerome Bruner]

Likewise, J. J. Schwab, heavily involved in the 1960s with science–oriented curricula (e.g., Biological Sciences Curriculum Studies), advocated, as did Bruner, curriculum thought controlled by the codification of disciplined knowledge.   However, by the onset of the 1970s, we find him grimly commenting to curriculum people:

> . . . [T]he field of curriculum is moribund, unable by its present methods and principles to continue its work and desperately in search of new and more effective principles and methods. . . . The field has reached this unhappy state by inveterate and unexamined reliance on theory in an area where theory is partly inappropriate in the first place and where the

---

[6] Bruner, Jerome. (1963). *The Process of Education.* New York: Vintage Books. A report of a curriculum conference at which noted disciplinarians assembled and, as expected, it recommends rigor in a knowledge centered curriculum, knowledge defined within the empirical analytic orientation.

[7] Bruner, Jerome. (1971). The process of education revisited. *Phi Delta Kappan,* September, p. 21. A talk given at the A.S.C.D. Conference in St. Louis, MO, March 1971.

theories extant, even where appropriate, are in-adequate to the
tasks which the curriculum field sets them.[8]

At the turn of the present decade then, we find both Bruner and Schwab
giving recognition to the inadequacies of existing curriculum inquiry modes but
unable at that time to suggest fundamentally new directions.

Among the few educators who, early in this decade, called for the need for
probing into the deep structure underlying curriculum research thought are two
educators, Kenneth Beittel and Elliot Eisner, both grounded in art education. I
have found them seriously questioning underlying presuppositions of the
dominant tradition in curriculum conceptions and research calling for close
examination of curriculum orientations at the root level.

In *Alternatives for Art Education Research*,[9] Beittel urged the uncovering of
"the root metaphors in art education," "the experiential core of art," "the
expressive situation," and in *Conflicting Conceptions of Curriculum*,[10] Eisner
asked for surfacing "conceptual underpinnings" and "the goals and assumptions
. . . of major orientations to curriculum." Theirs has been a vibrant call for
calling into question the constraining mould of tradition.

In like vein, curriculum generalists labeled "Reconceptualists" have begun
recently to press for recognition of the deep level value and intent base of
underlying curriculum perspectives. For instance, James Macdonald, one of the
senior members of the Reconceptualist School has commented:

> In the field of curriculum we have been fussing about with the
> problem of values and perspectives for some time . . . It is
> clear that curriculum thinkers have been unaware of the

---

[8] Schwab, J. J. (1972). The practical: A language for curriculum." In D. E.
Purpel & M. Belanger (Eds.), *Curriculum and the Cultural Revolution* (p. 79).
Berkeley CA: McCutchan. Schwab has a series of papers on "The Practical" of
interest to curriculists.

[9] Beittel, K. R. (1973). *Alternatives for Art Education Research* (p. vii).
Dubuque, IA: Wm. C. Brown. What Beittel has to say about art education
research is applicable to general education research.

[10] Eisner, E. W & Vallance, E. (Eds.). (1974). *Conflicting Conceptions of
Curriculum* (p. 2). Berkeley, CA: McCutchan. Eisner has been a foremost critic
of the behavioural objectives movement and the accountability type approach to
curriculum evaluation.

different levels and kinds of value perspectives that are involved in curriculum thinking.[11]

Likewise, Michael Apple, concerned with the assumptions that educators bring to their curriculum work, pointed to the fundamental difficulty of curriculum thought modes that rest on the models and language systems that are applied to designing educational environments and to a large portion of educational research. He has called on curriculum researchers to become aware of the latent dilemmas involved in the modes of discourse they employ, discourse that tends to obscure fundamental human interests. He has argued that:

1. Educators, especially members of the curriculum field, have taken an outmoded positivistic stance that disarms critical self-reflection and have given it the name and prestige of *the* scientific method.

2. Because of our lack of reflectiveness, we have perceived our dominant style of scientific rationalizing as being interest free, when this may not be the case, thereby contributing to an already strongly manipulative ethos of schooling.

3. Educators may find it necessary to seek new forms of rationality that are less restrictive than those on which they have drawn so heavily in the past if they are, in fact, to design more humane educational environments.[12]

It is quite apparent that the foregoing authors, particularly Beittel, Macdonald, and Apple, have identified the crisis in curriculum research as related to the mono-dimensional effect of the dominance of the traditional

---

[11] Macdonald, James (1975). Curriculum and human interests. In William Pinar (Ed.), *Curriculum Theorizing: the Reconceptualists*, (p. 283). Berkeley, CA: McCutchan. Macdonald is one of leading curriculum thinkers who have countered the Tyler rationale.

[12] Apple, Michael. (1975). Scientific interests and the nature of educational institutions (p. 121). In W. Pinar (Ed.), *Curriculum Theorizing: The Reconceptualists*. Berkeley, CA: McCutchan. Among curriculum theorists Apple is a leading critical social theorist.

orientation to research, what Paulo Freire[13] has termed a "limit-situation" within which many curriculum researchers seem encapsulated.

What seems to be needed in curriculum inquiry, therefore, is general recognition of the epistemological limit-situation in which current curriculum research is encased, that is, a critical awareness that conventional research has not only a limiting effect but also to some degree a distorting effect on new possibilities in curriculum research. Accordingly, we need to seek out new orientations that allow us to free ourselves of the tunnel vision effect of mono-dimensionality.

Such a search beckons us to probe and to clarify perspectives underlying research approaches. Fortunately, we in North America, witnessing a reverse-Columbus phenomenon, have discovered European scholars and their disciples whose scholarship Radnitzky[14] has collectively identified as the "Continental Schools of Metascience." These Continental scholars have been concerned with "ways of looking at science," and their insights into these ways have provided us with a rich avenue that could open up possibilities for curriculum research. Notable among these scholars is Jurgen Habermas, an anthropological philosopher, whose tri-paradigmatic framework is discussed in this chapter.

CENTERING CURRICULUM THOUGHT

The term *curriculum* is many things to many people. In attempts to give focus curriculum people have tried to center their thoughts on the teacher (as in the "teacher-centered curriculum"), on the child (as in the "child-centered curriculum"), on the structure of the disciplines (as in the "discipline-centered curriculum"), on society (as in the "society-centered curriculum"), and so on. I find these centering attempts too confining, and I believe that in spite of some years of activity based on these centers, these research activities have failed to make significant advances in curriculum thought. I criticize these "centers" for

---

[13]In Paulo Freire's curriculum thought see *Pedagogy of the Oppressed*. (New York: Herder and Herder, 1972), or *Education for Critical Consciousness* (New York: Seabury Press, 1973).
[14]Radnitzky, G. (1968). *Contemporary Schools of Metascience*, 2 Vols. Gotesberg: Akademiforiaget. In this book Radnitzky identifies two categories of schools of metascience: (a) Anglo-Saxon schools of metascience wherein the empirical analytic approach to epistemology is paramount, and (b) Continental schools of metascience wherein the interpretive and dialectic traditions are paramount. Dr. Helmut Wagner, a Schutzian scholar, reflects a tradition rooted in the Continental Schools.

not providing sufficient scope and contextuality that allow entertainment of views of human and social acts we call "education." Hence, I find it important to center curriculum thought on a broader frame, that of "man/world relationships," for it permits probing of the deeper meaning of what it is for persons (teachers and students) to be human, to become more human, and to act humanly in educational situations.

Given this center, which I consider to be irreducible, I am able to view people situated in their world and acting upon themselves and their world. Translated into a school situation (see Fig. 1.1) I can view two persons, one typified as teacher (Pt) and the other as student (Ps) with their intentional acts directed towards each other and a displayed object (D), be it canvas, a painting, or guiding image or idea. I can see the teacher and the student, as Dr. Wagner stated in his conference paper as "humans with their volitions, aspirations, goals, feelings and intentions."[15] Such a center will allow me to view a teacher or the student as "an individual in his dual appearances as a thinking and willing being within the immediate spheres of his experience and as a social actor involved in interchanges with others in face-to-face relations."[16]

If curriculum is given such a center, we can begin to unfold manifold ways of viewing *"man/world relationships"* (including man-man relationships), making possible the discovering of perspectives that undergird curriculum thought.

Displayed object to which act is directed

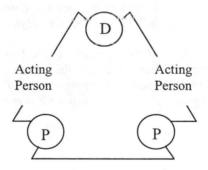

Acting   Acting
Person   Person

FIG. 1.1 Intentional acts of a teacher and a student.

[15] Dr. Helmut Wagner in his conference paper. "A Phenomenological Approach to Art" describes Alfred Schutz's endeavours in breaking through the individualistic confines of phenomenological psychology.

[16] Wagner, Helmut (1973). The scope of phenomenological sociology. In L. G. Psathas (Ed.), *Phenomenological Sociology: Issues and Applications.* New York: John Wiley and Sons.

In this chapter, concern is, of course, for alternative curriculum research perspectives or orientations.   Hence, it is appropriate to ask: Is there a formulation of orientations that can advance our search?

MULTIPLE ORIENTATIONS IN CURRICULUM EVALUATION RESEARCH: AN EXEMPLAR

> No program can be evaluated in its entirety.   But we can increase our vision of whatever we are viewing through the employment of as many perspectives as we can find appropriate and utilize for our purposes.[17]

A province-wide curriculum evaluation research we just conducted can serve as an exemplar of how multiple perspectives can guide curriculum inquiry, in this case an evaluation of a provincial school curriculum.   In launching the British Columbia Social Studies Assessment,[18] we initially posed the question: What are possible ways of approaching the phenomenon of social studies in British Columbia?

We took our cue from what Beittel called appropriately the "Rashomon effect," a notion borrowed from Kurosawa's acclaimed film in which the same event is disclosed interpretively from different perspectives.   Simultaneously, we were mindful of the need to counterbalance the dominant orientation in evaluation a point M. Q. Patton ably pointed out recently:

> The very dominance of the scientific method in evaluation research appears to have cut off the great majority of practitioners from serious consideration of any alternative research paradigms.   The label "research" has come to mean

---

[17] Aoki, T. T. (Ed). (1978). *Curriculum Evaluation in a New Key* (p. 2). Vancouver: Center for the Study of Curriculum and Instruction, U.B.C. A monograph of papers presented at the College and University Faculty Association Symposium, Annual Conference of the National Council of the Social Studies, Cincinnati, November 1977.

[18] Aoki, T. T. et al. (1977). *British Columbia Social Studies Assessment.* Victoria: Ministry of Education, 1977 Books I, II, and III and Summary Report.

the equivalent of employing the Scientific Method . . . of
working within the dominant paradigm.[19]

We began our evaluation work aware of the need for multiple perspectives,
and of the potential of Jurgen Habermas's tri-paradigmatic framework[20] in
providing alternative orientations appropriate for our evaluation research
interests.

Guided by these orientations we projected evaluation plans, conducted
evaluative activities and compiled six reports. Figure 1.2 shows how the reports
match the framework containing the three paradigmatic orientations.[21]

FIG. 1.2 Orientational framework of the reports included in the B.C.
          Social Assessment 1978.

[19]Patton M. Q. (1972). *Alternative Evaluation Research Paradigms* (p. 6).
Grand Forks: University of North Dakota press. This is a book in a series
developed by the North Dakota Study Group on Evaluation.

[20]Habermas, Jurgen (1972). *Knowledge and Human Interest* (p. 1972). Boston:
Beacon Press. The paradigmatic framework is found in the well-known
appendix in this book.

[21]Aoki, T. (1978). Toward new conceptions for evaluation in social studies. In
Ted T. Aoki (Ed.), *Curriculum Evaluation in a New Key*, p. 4. (see footnote 17).

A. Teacher Views of Social Studies
B. Teacher Views of Prescribed Social Studies
C. Views of Goals of Social Studies
D. Student Achievement and Views in Social Studies
E. Interpretive Studies of Selected Situations
F. "An Interpretation of Intents of the Elementary and Secondary Curriculum Guides" (in Summary Report, 1978)

The orientational framework we used provided three root orientations: the empirical analytic orientation, the situational interpretive orientation, and the critical reflective orientation.

It is to these orientations that we must now turn.

THREE CURRICULUM INQUIRY ORIENTATIONS

> Man has been set in this world that surrounds him, with its rich and varied activities. It may be conceived by the human intelligence and formed by human action and endeavour. Schleiermacher calls this world, as opened to our reasoning, understanding and to our activity, *the universum*. . . . It signifies that great totality of being and becoming, of nature and of history in which we ourselves are partly links and partly masters that forge the chain. Our relation to this *universum* . . . is manifold.[22]

Man's relation to the world is manifold and man relates to this world through varied activities. The quality of the relationships and the kind of activity depend on the orientation man assumes in establishing his relationship with this world.

In curriculum inquiry, there is an array of orientations that a researcher might adopt (see Fig. 1.3). Here are three possibilities. First, there is the empirical analytic inquiry orientation in which explanatory and technical knowledge is sought. This research mode is familiar to us as "science." Second, there is the situational interpretive inquiry orientation in which research is conceived of as a search for meaning, which people give in a situation. Such an account is called phenomenological description. Third, there is the critical

---

[22] Otto, Rudolf. (1972). Religion as numinal experience. In W. H. Capps (Ed.), *Ways of Understanding Religion* (p. 22). New York: Macmillan. In this article Otto is describing the thoughts of Schleiermacher, an able scholar in religious studies.

inquiry orientation, which is gaining some visibility in research literature. Researchers within this orientation are concerned with critical understanding of fundamental interests, values, assumptions, and implications for human and social action. These orientations are discussed briefly in the following sections and a chart summarizing these discussions is included (Table 1.1).

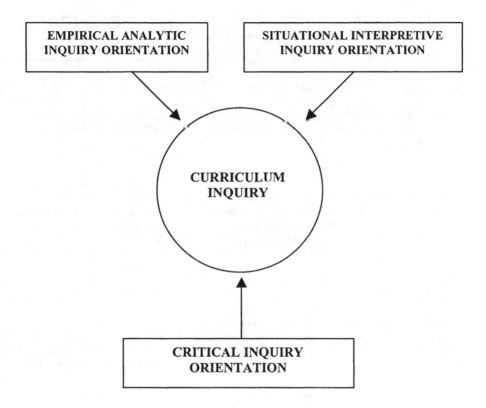

FIG 1.3 Possible orientations to curriculum inquiry.

TABLE 1.1

Three Orientations to Curriculum Inquiry

"Man experiences three root activities: Work, Communication and Reflection. These activities yield three forms of knowledge: Nomological, Situational Interpretive, and Critical."

EMPIRICAL ANALYTIC (Technical) ORIENTATION	SITUATIONAL INTERPRETIVE ORIENTATION	CRITICAL ORIENTATION
Root activity:	*Root activity*:	*Root activity*:
Intellectual and technical work (relating man to natural world).	Communication: (relating man to social world).	Reflection (relating man to self and social world).
Interest:	*Interest*:	*Interest*:
In intellectual and technical control of world. Interest also in efficiency, certainty, and predictability.	In experientially meaningful, authentic intersubjective understanding (in terms of meanings to actors)	In improving human condition by rendering transparent tacit assumptions and hidden assumptions and by initiating a process of transformation designed to liberate man.
Knowledge form:	*Knowledge form*:	*Knowledge form*:
Nomological knowledge (facts, generalizations, cause and effect laws, theories).	Situational knowledge. Knowing of structure of interpretive meanings.	Normative knowledge. Knowledge of thought and action to improve humanness and human/social condition.
Understanding:	*Understanding*:	*Understanding*:
Is in terms of facts, etc.	Is in terms of meanings people give to situations.	Is in terms of reflection.
Knowing:	*Knowing*:	*Knowing*:
Empirical knowing.	Giving meaning.	Critical knowing that combines reflection and action.
Explaining:	*Explaining*:	*Explaining*:
Giving causal, functional or hypothetico-deductive reasons.	Striking a resonant chord by clarifying motives, common meanings and authentic experiences.	Tracing to underlying unreflected aspects to call to action.

Table 1.1 (*continued*)

Man/world relationship "man and world"	Man/world relationship "man-in-his-social world"	Man/world relationship "man-in-his-world, with his world"

Reality is out there.

Life in this world can be explained with certainty, predictability.

Theoretical studies

Behavioural Theory
Systems Theory
Cybernetics
Structural Functionalism

Some Scholars

Descartes (I think; therefore I am)
Locke
Skinner
Vienna Scholars

Evaluation (ends–means)

Achievement oriented
Goal based evaluation
Criterion referenced
evaluation
Cost–benefit evaluation

Reality is intersubjectively constituted.

Life is a mystery.

Theoretical studies

Phenomenology Sociology of knowledge Ethno methodology Linguistic Analysis Hermeneutics

Some Scholars

Schutz, Berger, and Luckman Garfinkel, Goffman, Husserl (to the things themselves) Spiegelberg, Cicourel Palmer, Hirsch

Evaluation (situational interpretive)

Phenomenological
Interpretive   Evaluation

Reality is in praxis (thought and action).

Life can be improved.

Theoretical studies

Critical theory
Critical social theory
Psychoanalysis

Some scholars

Gouldner, Adorno, Wellmer, Marcuse, Habermas Frankfurt Scholars, Utrecht Scholars, Paulo Freire.

Evaluation (critical)

Discovering Underlying Assumptions, interests, values, motives, perspectives, root metaphors, and implications for action to improve human condition. Uncovering ideologies

EMPIRICAL ANALYTIC INQUIRY ORIENTATION

Of the three orientations, the empirical analytic is without doubt the dominant one in education research communities throughout North America. The "scientific" enterprise, as most educators know it, is embedded in this orientation and carries with it the weight of tradition and prestige. Research in education is typically defined in terms of this orientation, and in typical graduate research seminars in education, we find faculty and graduate students devotedly engaged in mastering the rules and techniques of complex and sophisticated designs and analyses appropriate for this orientation. By rigor in research is often meant understanding tile complex research designs and sophisticated mathematics based statistical analyses appropriate for this orientation.

According to Habermas, the root human activity of those engaged in empirical analytic research or its utilitarian derivatives (applied sciences) is intellectual or technical *work*. Seen as a productive process, intellectual or technical work has as its basic intent a cognitive interest in *control* of objects in the world. By acting upon the objectified world man through work transforms it, in the process generating empirical analytic and technical understandings that enhance efficiency, certainty and predictability. Thus, the form of knowledge sought is nomological and law-like knowledge that gives man explanatory power, understood within this orientation as equivalent to giving cause-and-effect, functional, or hypothetico-deductive statements.

Within this orientation is technical interest in the utilization of predictive knowledge, as in behaviour modification, technology, engineering, and the like. In support of this interest in technical control has developed a number of control-oriented theories such as cybernetic engineering, management theory, general systems and structural-functionalism.

A researcher within this orientation assumes a detached stance toward his world, which, through his intellect and will, attempts to subdue it. Intellectual control of this world is approached indirectly, mediated by conceptual constructs, and knowledge about the world is gained through guided observation and carefully designed and controlled manipulation. The scientific experiment is the exemplary paradigm. Hence, the researcher approaches his world objectively, distancing his own subjectivity from the objectified world. Validation of knowledge gained in this orientation proceeds through the ground of corroborative empirical evidences found within this objective world.

Life is viewed differently from one orientation to another. Within this orientation there exists a view that human and social life can be explained away with degrees of certainty, probability and predictability.

When a researcher becomes engaged in empirical analytic research, he defines his research world through a statement of his researchable problem accompanied by a description of and the research method associated with it. The problem and the method determine the limits of what he sees in the research situation. Circumscribed by the problem and methodology used, he collects relevant data. These data are then transformed into second-order descriptions guided typically by predetermined theoretical constructs. What this means is that these second-order descriptions (generalizations and idealizations) are once removed from the first order descriptions of those who dwell in and who experience life within the situation defined as the research situation. When scientist Adolphe Patmann said, "Life is always more than what science can say at any given time," he was referring to how in order to arrive at these generalizations and idealizations, the uniqueness and messiness of any lived situations tend to be reduced out.

Knowing of the reductionism that goes on in second order research ventures, the curriculum researcher needs to be concerned about what second order knowledge fails to reveal.

SITUATIONAL INTERPRETIVE INQUIRY ORIENTATION

At this very moment I find myself situated in my world of "conferencing" people. In this world of mine, my "I" is at the center. I am experiencing life as I am living it now guided by my commonsense-typified knowledge about educators' conferences. I define my life now by giving meaning to my paper presentation, to you who are listening or not listening to me, and to ongoing events here as I notice them. I am continuously involved in meaning-giving activities as I construct my personal world of meanings. The structure of these meanings is my present reality.

At this moment I see you sitting across from me, in my visual and auditory presence, experiencing your life of "conferencing." You are situated with yourself as center and that central point is your "I." You are experiencing life as you are now living it in your commonsense conferencing way, defining it by giving your own meaning to things, people, and events about you. You, too, are continuously involved in meaning–giving activities as you construct your own personal world of meanings. The structure of these meanings is your present reality.

Hence, in a social situation wherein things, people, and events move together, there are many ways in which they are given meaning by the people in the situation. In other words, people are continuously interpreting the events that they experience, and these interpretations differ from person to person. A researcher oriented toward situational interpretive research must keep two significant features in mind: (1) people give personal meanings to each situation experienced, and (2) people interpret the same event in different ways.

Although the most human activity of concern within the empirical analytic orientation is man's productive intellectual and technical capacity to work, the activity of concern for those in the situational interpretive framework is *communication* between man and man. Because research-guiding interests of the situational interpretive researcher are insights into human experiences as they are lived, he needs to direct his efforts toward clarifying, authenticating and bringing to full human awareness the meaning structures of the constructive forces of the social cultural process. The form of knowledge sought is not nomological law-like statements but deep structures of meaning, the way in which man meaningfully experiences and cognitively appropriates the social world. Hence, when he comes to know situationally, he knows his world in a different form and in a different way compared with those of the empirical analytic researcher.

The view of man/world in lived situations is one of man-in-his-world of fellow men. Although in the empirical analytic stance, as we have seen, man and world are given second-order constructions through the medium of conceptual constructs, in the situational world man and social world are seen as united. This is not to deny the objectivity of the social world but rather to say that the subjective "I-in-my-world" is in a dialectic relationship with another's "I-in-my-world." This means, for instance, that in my lived world, I (as subjective) am active, and act upon my social world; hence, I am able to "name" my world. But I realize, however, that my fellow man subjectively acts upon his world, names his world, and influences me. In this sense my "I" and his "I" are dialectically related. Communication is indeed intercommunication between people in face-to-face situations.

In seeking out, therefore, the structure of meanings, which are not accessible to empirical analytic science, researchers in the situational interpretive orientation must attempt to provide explanations of an interpretive kind. That is, although "explaining" within the empirical analytic orientation means giving causal, functional, or hypothetic-deductive statements, in the situational orientation "explaining" requires striking a responsive chord among people in dialogue situations by clarifying motives, authentic experiences, and common meaning. The researcher, hence, cannot stand aloof as an observer as is done in empirical analytic research, but must enter into intersubjective dialogue with the people in the research situation.

Within the situational interpretive orientation there are different approaches, each allowing a description of the meaning structure in a situation. There is a growing interest among educators in theoretical studies that fall within the phenomenological attitude. The phenomenology of social understanding requiring investigation of meaning-giving activities in the everyday world is the main research interest of some social and cultural ethnographers, particularly ethnomethodologists who follow the tradition established by Garfinkel and Goffman. Interpretation of text and text analogues embodied in social-cultural phenomena is the guiding interest of those who engage in hermeneutics.

Such interpretations are called phenomenological descriptions, providing accounts of first-order experiences people experience, without which, it seems to me, second-order descriptions are deprived of content. The situationally interpretive oriented research is vitally complementary to empirical analytic research and deserves close attention by curriculum researchers, particularly for those whose interests lie in the study of curriculum-in-use, curriculum development *in situ*, or curriculum evaluation *in situ*.

CRITICALLY REFLECTIVE INQUIRY ORIENTATION

The third form of research is within the orientation represented by critical theory. Although in the empirical analytic research mode the root activity is productive work, and in the situational interpretive, the activity of *communication*, that of critical theory is *reflection*. In reflection, the actor through the critical analytic process uncovers and makes explicit the tacit and hidden assumptions and intentions held.

We have noted that researchers within the empirical analytic orientation are interested in second-order descriptions of social phenomena, that is, nomological law-like statements resulting from mediated and systemized theoretical interpretations of experience. On the other hand, researchers within the situational interpretive orientation are interested in generating first-order descriptions of social phenomena, that is, descriptions of immediate interpretations of experience. These first-order accounts are, we noted, commonsense-typifications of meanings which an actor gives to situations in terms of his immediate acts in his daily ongoing life. Critical researchers are interested in questioning these descriptive accounts, whether they be second-order or first-order, and in probing for the underlying biases in order to reveal tacitly held intentions and assumptions. This process is what some refer to as critical reflection.

In critical inquiry the researcher himself becomes part of the object of inquiry. The researcher in becoming involved with his subjects enters into their world and engages them in mutually reflective activity. He questions his subjects and himself. Reflection by himself and participants allows new questions to emerge, which, in turn, lead to more reflection. In the ongoing process, which is dialectical and transformative, both researcher and subjects become participants in an open dialogue.

However, it is important for the researcher to remember that critical perspective is a two-bladed knife, cutting both ways. Werner states:

> We must be reflective of the very perspective we use for
> critical sense-making. Any clarifying of perspective of others
> or within programs is itself perspective guided. In arguing for
> point-of-viewism one cannot presume himself free of a
> viewpoint. One way to deal with this dilemma is to make

explicit and reflect upon the theoretical, and methodological
beliefs within which our own thinking is situated.[23]

Reflection in the sense used here is not the kind of activity that people as
actors engage in their daily life. For in their day-to-day existence, actors deal
with their concerns in routine ways without probing beyond the immediate
exigencies. Missing is a conscious effort to examine the intentions and
assumptions underlying their acts. However, in critical reflection the everyday
type of attitude is placed in "brackets," as it were, and examined in an attempt to
transcend the immediate level of interpretation. Critical reflection leads to an
understanding of what is beyond; it is oriented towards making the unconscious
conscious. Such reflective activity allows liberation from the unconsciously
held assumptions and intentions that lie hidden. These may be repressive and
dehumanizing aspects of everyday life that man needs to face in his personal and
social life. For example, at the personal level the content of reflection may be
the "rationalizations" an actor uses to hide underlying motives for his action.
Or, at the societal level, the content of reflection may be the "ideology" used to
speak for social policies and practices, rendering obscure society's coercive
interests that lie beneath. In this case critical reflection demonstrates interest in
uncovering the hidden "true" interests embedded in some given personal or
social condition.

Reflection, however, is not only oriented toward making conscious the
unconscious by discovering descriptions of underlying assumptions and
intentions, but is also oriented toward the implications for action guided by the
newly gained consciousness and critical knowing. It is interested in bringing
about a reorientation through transformation of the assumptions and intentions
upon which thought and action rest. These may be preconceived norms, values,
images of man and the world, assumptions about knowledge, root metaphors
and perspectives. Critical reflection, then, with its research-guiding interest to
liberate man from hidden assumptions and techniques, promotes a theory of man
and society that is grounded in the moral attitude of liberation.

Curriculum research within this orientation would ask that focus be given
not only on the knowledge structure of life experiences, but also on the
normative structure as well. Thus, in such bifocal context, phenomenological
description of educational phenomena may be regarded as incomplete, but
significant in making possible critical reflective activity. For instance, van
Manen describes the work of the School of Utrecht led by Langeveld,[24] whose

---

[23] Werner, Walter (1976). Evaluation: Sense-making of school programs. In
Ted T. Aoki, (Ed.), *Curriculum Evaluation in a New Key,* p. 20. (see note 17).
[24] The account of Langeveld's conception of phenomenological pedagogy is
described in Max van Manen, "A Phenomenological Experiment in Educational

interest lies in phenomenological pedagogy. Langeveld is said to argue that phenomenological disciplines are constructed within the dialogical context of an ongoing situationally interpretive activity but guided by some meaningful purpose of what it means to educate within the critically reflective orientation. In describing Langeveld's pedagogical research position,   van Manen states: "Educational research must always be structured pedagogically; that is, it should be grounded reflectively in the emancipatory norms toward which all education is oriented."[25]

As I understand the field of critically reflective social theory—and I speak as a novice in this realm—I see it as a broad domain, essentially one of the manifold attitudes that man can assume in relating to his world. Hence, it can have related but diverse frameworks such as those reflecting disciplines such as the sociology of knowledge, literary criticism, critical social theory, praxiology, psychoanalysis, and phenomenological pedagogy. These disciplines deserve close examination by educational researchers for what they can offer in providing a research perspective oriented toward human and social transformation and change.

A PERSONAL REFLECTION

I have given an array of research orientations. By relating to this array, I wish to conclude with a personal note by making observations and reflections upon the biography of my research interests and my personal transformation over the last several years as mirrored in a set of doctoral students' reports of their research constructs, which in academia go by the name of "dissertations."[26] They are listed as follows:

Doctoral dissertations:

> *Study* 1. "A Comparison of Bales' and Flanders' Systems of Interaction. Analysis as Research Tools in Small Group Instruction," (University of Alberta, Robert Anderson). Completed 1972.

> *Study* 2. "A Tri-Dimensional Interaction Analysis of the Valuing Process in Social Studies,"   (University of Alberta, Raymond Hanson). Completed 1975.

Theory: The Utrecht School."   Paper presented at the Annual American Education Research Conference, Toronto, Ontario, March 27–30,1978, p. 5.
[25]Ibid.
[26]Studies 1 to 7 are unpublished doctoral studies, Department of Secondary Education, University of Alberta. Study 8 is an interdepartmental study, Center for the Study of Curriculum and Instruction, University of British Columbia.

Study 3. "Toward a Cybernetic Phenomenology of Instruction,"
(University of Alberta, Max van Manen). Completed 1973.

Study 4. "Knowledge Organization and Instructional Systemics: A Problem
in the Epistemology of Curriculum," (University of Alberta,
Andrew Hughes). Completed 1975.

Study 5. "Toward a Conceptualization of Ideal Styles of Curriculum Design
Making in Small Groups" (University of Alberta, Douglass
Ledgerwood). Completed 1975.

Study 6. "Emic Evaluative Inquiry: An Approach for Evaluating School
Programs" (University of Alberta, Donald C. Wilson). Completed
1976.

Study 7. "A Study of Perspectives in Social Studies." (University of
Alberta, Walter Werner). Completed 1977.

Study 8. "Toward an Existential Phenomenological Approach to
Curriculum Evaluation." (University of British Columbia, Peter
Rothe). Completed 1979.

I view Studies 1 and 2 as attempts by Bob Anderson and Ray Hanson to
investigate life-in-the-classroom by examining school programs-in-use. In their
studies they approached teachers and students as their objects of study from an
etic stance.[27] In so doing they examined classroom life as experienced by
teachers and students using second-order constructs codified as interaction
analysis systems of Bales, Flanders, or Flanders modified. The first-order lived
experiences of the actors in the classroom went unexamined.

In Study 3, two perspectives were adopted, one "etic" and the other "emic."
Max van Manen's interest in contextuality led him to entertain General Systems
Theory as a way of exploring interrelated subsystems within the instructional
system. To complement the etic posture, he included another perspective to
view the phenomenon of instruction. As a part of the study, van Manen
examined phenomenologically the pedagogical relationship between Don Juan
and Castaneda as he interpreted the text of *The Teachings of Don Juan: A Yaqui*

---

[27]The terms "Etic" and "Emic" frames were coined by anthropologist Pike who
abstracted them from "phonetic" and "phonemic" as used in language; "Etic"
refers to the stance of an outsider who observes the ongoing events; "Emic"
refers to the stance of the insider who lives within the ongoing flow of lived
experiences.

Way of Knowledge.[28] Wherever appropriate the dissertation was written in the "first person singular," a brow-raiser in some research quarters.

Study 4 was influenced conceptually by Basil Bernstein's interpretations of codified knowledge within the framework of sociology of knowledge. Andrew Hughes examined the types of codified knowledge embodied in Social Studies curricula and made an empirical analytic study of curricula-in-use in the classroom. In Study 5 Douglass Ledgerwood set out a culturally based frame of "life-styles" and examined ethnographically acts of group members involved in curriculum development. In Study 6, Donald C. Wilson reinterpreted the etic/emic framework of Pike and the elucidatory/evaluative framework of Gene Glass, and ethnographically studied two cases of curriculum implementation. Wilson set aside the "installation" view of implementation and, instead, adopted the view of situationally interpreted meanings teachers give to programs received.

In Study 7 Walter Werner explored literature widely in an endeavour to grasp the meaning of "perspective." He initially brought to his task two orientations, the empirical analytic from his earlier graduate work and the hermeneutic from his theological interests. He extended his orientation base by exploring sociology of knowledge, philosophical anthropology, and critical theory. His total effort was focused on an analysis of perspectives that man-in-his-world employs. In Study 8 Peter Rothe, who was concerned with the ontological condition of teachers and students in the situation of a curriculum-in-use, studied existentialism (particularly as expressed by Heidegger), existential phenomenology of Merleau-Ponty, phenomenology of Alfred Schutz, etc., enabling him to explore the lived experiences of actors in the classroom. Through the use of sociocultural ethnography and ethnomethodology, he analyzed the day-to-day lived experiences of teachers, students and administrators.

These are young curriculum scholars who have good familiarity with the literature of the curriculum field, who because of the tendency for abstracted reification in curriculum thought have grounded themselves for substantive content in at least one school subject area, and who have strengths in the domain I refer to as "the conduct of inquiry." In this connection, we are in accord with the general public in sounding the slogan "to the basics," but in our bailiwick, by this we mean a thrust into the underlying epistemic, axiological, telic, and ontological bases that reveal for us in increasing fullness orientations such as the ones we examined in this paper.

In the brief accounts of the doctoral studies is reflected, too, a biography of the transformation of our own research orientation. Increasingly, we have come to give a phenomenological emphasis. But at times we felt "suspended as in

---

[28]Castaneda Carlos (1968). *The Teachings of Don Juan: A Yaqui Way of Knowledge.* Berkeley: University of California Press.

brackets," wondering whether or not we were constructing a mystified dream world, in the process estranging ourselves from the mainstream flow of educational researchers. At other times we found ourselves frustrated, finding difficulty trying to make sense to colleagues how we see our research world. In the process, we have become more sensitive to the urgency of coming to know how to communicate cross-paradigmatically at the level of deep structure. We feel there are significant educational implications for such a concern.

At this point in time we are asking the question: "Descriptive knowledge, phenomenological or otherwise, what for?" We take a cue from the first line of Tao. "The way that can be described is not the way." We find this relevant to education because we believe education to be a moral enterprise concerned about what it means to educate and to be educated. In this connection, some of us feel that the inherent logic of "application" often found in education talk—the notion of "applying thought to practice"—should be made problematic, at least when reference is made to the world of people. We feel that for too long "thought" and "practice" have been set apart, an act that has tended to invite reified "thought" on the one hand, and a-theoretical utilitarian "practice" on the other. For too long, we have not been aware that second-order thoughts were being "applied" to the first-order social world of practice. A phenomenological study of the phenomenon of "application" is called for. Such an explanation might provide us insight into possibilities of contextualizing "thought" and "practice" within a new framework wherein the relatedness of the situational interpretive and the critically reflective orientations may lead us further along the way. This is our current interest and thrust in curriculum inquiry.

Today, I no longer feel discomforted as I did once when Bruner called for a moratorium, when Schwab pronounced the fact of the moribund state of curriculum inquiry, or when Magoon cried "crisis" in educational research. There are now curriculum researchers with whose ventures I can strike a vibrant and resonant chord. Although not too long ago this chord sounded strange deep inside me, that strangeness is fading. I think it is partly because in being at a conference such as this, I feel a sense of emergent becoming. By being here, I am becoming. I am experiencing a sense of committed involvement in cocreating research paths upon which we might meaningfully tread, as before us unfolds a clearer vision of a different research reality.

Chapter 2

Curriculum Implementation as Instrumental Action and as Situational Praxis[1] (1983)

MAKING CURRICULUM
IMPLEMENTATION PROBLEMATIC

Allow me to offer a brief portrayal of a scenario that typifies curriculum implementation as I know it. Within a Curriculum Branch of the Ministry of Education, someone in an administrative role as curriculum director summons a group of teachers and perhaps a university professor of education hand-picked for their reputed excellence in teaching (not necessarily for excellence in curriculum development), sets them the task of developing a curriculum in a subject area. Usually, there is included a token evaluation (pilot testing is the legitimated jargon) done usually by hand-picked teachers. Minor revisions are made, Band Aid fashion. (Full-scale revisions are usually impossible because the time-line administratively pre-set prevents such an overhaul.) Then, the massive undertaking of implementing the program in all the schools of the province is begun. In school districts implementation inservice days are declared. The experts-in-the-know hop from school district to school district providing "communiqués" to assembled teachers who, under a high level of anxiety and frustration, attempt to understand it all in a one or two day session. In the meantime, the Assessment Branch's psychometricians develop achievement tests to measure teacher effectiveness indirectly by measuring student learnings directly. The teachers on whom the success of the

[1]The original version of this paper was presented at the Symposium on Strategies for School Improvement Inservice in a New Context, the Summer Institute for Teacher Education (SIE), Simon Fraser University, 1980. This version was presented at the symposium entitled Understanding Situational Meanings of Curriculum Inservice Acts: Implementing, Consulting, Inservicing, AERA Conference, Montreal, Canada, April 11, 1983. This version is reprinted from Ted T. Aoki, Terrance R. Carson, & Basil J. Favaro, with an introduction and response by Louise M. Berman (1983), *Understanding Situational Meanings of Curriculum In-service Acts: Implementing, Consulting, Inservicing. Curriculum Praxis Monograph Series, Monograph 9* (pp. 3–17). Edmonton, Alberta. Department of Secondary Education, Faculty of Education, University of Alberta.

implementation depends try their damnedest to make sense of the new curriculum, wondering if they should commit themselves to the new curriculum, or if they should make visible token commitments, or if they should make the program relevant to their own students, or if they should compromise between what they have been doing and what they are expected to do.

The foregoing scenario, repeated throughout Canada under the label "curriculum implementation," has become a ritual for attempting to bridge the gap between curriculum-as-plan and curriculum-in-use.

Curriculum implementation problems, like most curriculum problems, are typically seen as practical problems of the curriculum field. For such practical problems, solutions are sought pragmatically. More likely than not, taken for granted and not questioned is the understanding of what "curriculum implementation" itself is.

In this paper, I question the typically unquestioned—"implementation" itself is made problematic, leading us to ask, "How should implementation be understood?"

To explore this question, we situate ourselves in the ambience of a classroom so that we can begin to make sense of the experiences of the teacher in the presence of both students and a curriculum-to-be-implemented. How we come to understand the teacher's experience within his [or her] situation depends wholly on the perspective employed to guide our interpretation of the experience of the teacher engaged in implementation. Two perspectives will be explored. The first perspective yields an understanding of "implementation as instrumental action," and the other, an understanding of "implementation as situation praxis."

UNDERSTANDING IMPLEMENTATION AS INSTRUMENTAL ACTION

How is curriculum implementation conceived of in the dominant way of understanding it? What is the mainstream perspective that allows this kind of understanding? Within this perspective, how is the teacher engaged in implementation viewed?

At a curriculum decision-making conference in Alberta 8 years ago, I was asked to pinpoint major issues in the curriculum decision-making process. I identified, as one among several issues, "curriculum implementation," urging that although increasing attention was being given to day-to-day problems of implementation, there has been little attempt to make "implementation" itself problematic. At that time, I stated the issue as follows: "A basic problem in implementation of programs may be found in the producer-consumer paradigm underlying the view of implementation" (Aoki, 1974, p. 37).[2]

---

[2] I recall being blamed for academic jargonese for using the term paradigm, but not for using the language of producer/consumer.

I pointed to this paradigm as being embedded in a business metaphor, one in which curriculum producers offer something to curriculum consumers, and added that this paradigm:

> views implementation in terms or a unidirectional flow. It is analogous to the producer-consumer paradigm we have in business and in industry. In this paradigm experts produce for non-experts who consume. It is the paradigm of the relationship between the haves and the have-nots. In program development under this paradigm, curriculum experts produce programs for the consumers—the teachers and students.
>
> Implementing a program under this paradigm presents a basic problem of how to communicate effectively with people who have not been involved in setting goals, nor in designing resources, nor teaching/learning strategies, nor evaluation plans. (House, 1979)[3]

Within this framework, the problem of implementation is often seen in terms of the effectiveness of communiqués.

Recently, in an article entitled "Technology versus Craft: A Ten Year Perspective on Innovation" (1979), Ernest House referred to this metaphor borrowed from business and industry as "technological," committed to a systematic rational approach to change. He claimed that the technological perspective underlying the notion of implementation flourishes in education as in competency-testing movement, management by objectives, and the like, were spawned as dimensions of the back-to-the-basics curriculum thrust. These can be traced, according to House, to the efficiency movement of industrial engineering.

Within this perspective, a competent teacher-implementer is one who has skills and techniques oriented toward efficient control. Such a know-how-to-do view of implementation is embedded in scientific and technological thought/action framework that reduces human competence to instrumental reason and instrumental action. Here, the teacher is seen as a rule-oriented, rule-governed being cast within a manipulative ethos, an ethos in which even his [or her] future is conceived in terms of rules.

It is to this kind of instrumentalism dominant in our culture that men such as Edmund Husserl, Jurgen Habermas, Trent Schroyer, Michael Apple and others have been referring as the crisis of Western reason. According to them, the crisis is manifested in a fundamental contradiction between a perspective

---

[3] In this article, House describes three implementation modalities which he identifies as "technological," "political," and "cultural."

committed to technological progress and that committed to the improvement of personal and situational life.

Of the two, the paramount mainstream reality is the technological, devoted to the belief that problems and conflicts can be managed through purposive rational action based on precise quantification and systematic decision–making. What is damaging in this interpretation of reality is the fact that emphasis on it effectively submerges the ideology of sociocultural values, leaving in its wake the "neutral" standards of purposive rational action and instrumental reason.

This crisis, manifested as a reflection of the contemporary image of advanced industrial society, shows as an internal crisis in curriculum. Central to understanding this issue is the question of the adequacy of the social theory, undergirding "implementation." By social theory I mean the philosophical presuppositions and root metaphors that inform the notion of "curriculum implementation."

To date in the field of curriculum the dominant social theory has been guided by idioms of behaviorism, structural functionalism, systems theory and the like, which support the instrumental notion of reason. By adopting technocratic strategies and allied decision–making social theories, we are asked to admit the rational necessity of extending centralized management theories to more and more areas of the life of teachers, students, and administrators in the classroom and the school, including implementation. This assumption has been reinforced by positivistic thought, by an "intoxication" with the technical power of science and technology, and by the development of business management techniques. To question this position requires a radical reexamination of the foundations of social theory and an exploration of alternative modes of inquiry and sociocultural organization.

The technological paradigm entrenched among mainstream thought in North America is reflected in the dominance of the R and D model, more fully elaborated by Egon Guba as the R.D.D.A model (research, development, diffusion, and adoption). I made reference to the R.D.D.A. model in an article about an implementation oriented symposium of Project Canada West, the Canada Studies Foundation's western arm, dedicated to the notion of teacher-centered curriculum development and implementation. I commented:

> The idea for this implementation symposium/workshop arose
> . . . as a reaction to the typical difficulties confronted by
> implementers who see the act of implementation as a phase of
> a natural linear schema of practical events whereby "one
> builds a program and then puts it into practice." In this
> common sense schema, "implementation" is seen simply as a
> process of "putting a program into practice." At a more
> elaborate level we find people speaking of the R.D.D.A.
> model. In this conception, implementation carries the fancier

labels of diffusion and adoption. The PCW (Project Canada West) recognized the conceptual problem of implementation and made attempts to overcome the traditional difficulties encountered by program developers who . . . tend to assume the stance of a "salesman" hawking his wares as a means of promoting curriculum change. (Aoki, 1977)

Ernest House, considering the R.D.D.A. approach within his examination of implementation in the United States, has made a telling comment:

In practice the R.D.D.A. approach has not worked very well. The federal laboratories and centers have created thousands of new educational products, but these have not been widely used by teachers in the schools. The approach requires the belief that one can create generalizable and easily diffused products that can be used in a great number of settings, a doctrine of transferability. (House, 1979)

In this connection, what ought to be of critical interest to us is Egon Guba's rejection of his own R.D.D.A. model after 10 years, for its inadequacies in the field of education. He has raised serious issue with the unified-systems view, which, according to him, "presupposes to effect a linked set of productive agents, each of which assumes discrete responsibility for a segment of R.D.D.A. effort to achieve a commonly agreed upon goal" (Guba & Clark, 1975). He argued that this view has set into motion a cycle of failure in educational knowledge production and utilization productivity (implementation, in other words).

Regarding the rational-logical underpinnings of the unified system view as not being upheld by empirical and experimental examination, he states bluntly: "The unassailable rational base is not the way the world is" (Guba & Clark, 1975, p. 6). He called for setting aside of the "unified-system view" and for a radical reformulation of the conceptual structure.

I agree with Guba and House that implementation as instrumental action is not the way the world is. I agree with them for I feel that the instrumental view of implementation minimizes or neglects the interpretive activities the teacher is engaged in when he [or she] encounters Curriculum X. What is objectionable is the fact that viewing the teacher instrumentally effectively strips him/her of the humanness of his/her being, reducing him/her to a being-as-thing, a technical being devoid of his/her own subjectivity. Reduction to activities within the instrumentalist process renders irrelevant the subjectivity of the teacher. I find such reductive rendering oppressive.

CURRICULUM IMPLEMENTATION
AS SITUATIONAL PRAXIS

If, returning to Guba, "implementation as instrumental action" is not the way implementation is, then we are faced with the question of how to understand it. If we were to take seriously Kierkegaard's remark of "that which is known must be known in a mode appropriate to the thing known," then we must ask: What will be an appropriate mode for understanding "implementation"?

I wish to propose an alternative view of implementation, one that is grounded in human experiences within the classroom situation. This is the experiential world of the teacher with his students (Fig. 2.1), who co-dwell within the insistent presence of "a curriculum X to-be-implemented."[4]

I propose an alternative view, which sees "implementation as situational praxis" of teachers.

To say "praxis" today is to restore that which prevailed among the ancient Greeks.[5] Recalling Aristotle reveals for us a tradition that has become concealed, disappearing from the recesses of our memory. In his days, Aristotle saw different forms within which a reflective subject can relate with the objective world as ways of knowing. I wish to refer to two of these ways:

1. *Theoria*—a way of knowing in which the subject comes to know through a contemplative, nonengaged process, as a spectator as it were, guided by the *telos* of theoretical knowledge itself.

2. *Praxis*—a way of knowing in which the subject within a pedagogic situation (like a classroom) reflectively engages the objective world guided by the telos of ordering human action. Here, theory and practice are seen to be in dialectical unity.

For Aristotle, praxis was a holistic activity of the total person—head, heart, and lifestyle, all as one—given to an ethical life within a political context. It is this sense of practice as praxis that I feel we need to restore (Table 2.1).

---

[4] For the development or Figure 1, which reflects the notion "curriculum center," see T. Aoki (1978), initially presented at the Conference on Phenomenological Descriptions: Potential for Research in Art Education, sponsored by the Division of Graduate Studies in the Fine Arts, Concordia University, 1978. See Proceedings, Aoki, (1979).

[5] For philosophical roots of praxis, see Groome (1980, chap. 8).

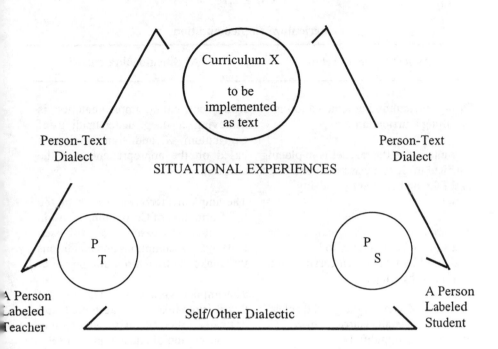

FIG. 2.1 Situational Experiences

TABLE 2.1

Curriculum Implementation

As Instrumental Action	As Situational Praxis
Doing curriculum implementation is installing Curriculum X.	Doing curriculum implementation is achieving a deep understanding of Curriculum X and transforming it based on the appropriateness to the situation.
The interest of the teacher is in placing Curriculum X in a classroom of school faithfully and efficiently (fidelity view).	
	The implementer's interest is in the transformation of Curriculum X within the situation based on disclosed underlying assumptions and conditions that make the transformation possible.
The implied view of curriculum is that of a situation commodity to be dispensed by teachers and assumptions consumed by students.	
The implied view of the good teacher is one who installs Curriculum X efficiently and faithfully.	The implied view of Curriculum X is that it is the text to be interpreted, and critically reflected on in an ongoing transformation of curriculum and self.
To explain "implementation" within this framework is to give a cause–effect relationship.	The implied view of teacher is that of an actor who acts with and on Curriculum X as he [or she] reflects on his own assumptions underlying action.
The implementer's subjectivity is irrelevant, as implementing Curriculum X is seen as an objective process.	
	The implied form of the theory/practice relationship is that theory and practice are in dialectic relationship. To implement within this framework is to reflect critically on the relationship between curriculum-as-plan and the situation of the curriculum- in-use.
The implied relationship between theory and practice underlying this view of implementation is one in which to implement is to put into practice curriculum-as-plan (i.e., to apply to a practical situation an ideal construct).	
The typical approach to implementation studies is through	The interpreter's central activity is reflection on his [or her] subjectively based action with and upon Curriculum X.

examination of the degree of fidelity of the installed curriculum compared with the master curriculum. The master curriculum is typically nonproblematic.

To evaluate implementation within this framework is to examine the quality of the activity of discovering underlying assumptions, interests, values, motives, perspectives, root metaphors, and implications for action to improve the human condition.

In passing, it is well to remember that Aristotle himself contributed to the dichotomizing of theory and practice for he essentially gave preference to *theoria* over *praxis*. This, however, must be understood in the context of his time, for he was reacting against the Sophists of his day who had reduced knowing to instrumentalism. In giving primacy to *theoria*, Aristotle paved the way for the mode of intellectualism that is so dominant in our culture, such that only a few see difficulty with "One should know theory first and then apply it to practice." In this way he helped to lay the ground for the prevailing mind-set of Western thought, that to guide action in the world, one should begin with intellectual knowing and then apply it, if it has any application, from outside experience to practice. We now need to negate the sense of theoria that reduces practice to a secondary role, and reaffirm practice as praxis as an anchor for developing the notion of implementation as situational praxis.

To understand "praxis" in the contemporary sense, it is well to be reminded of Paulo Freire, who remarked, "Praxis is reflection (thought) and action (practice) upon the world in order to transform it" (Freire, 1972). I am mindful that Freire is critical of dualism by separating theory and practice, all owing the coming into view of "practice as applied theory" or the coming into view of a-theoretical practice. We should remember Freire's enjoinder that "All educational practice implies a theoretical stance on the educator's part. This stance in turn implies-sometimes more, sometimes less explicitly—an interpretation of man and the world. It could not be otherwise" (Freire, 1972, pp. 205–206). It is this Greco sense of the theory/practice nexus under the label "praxis" that Freire helped with others to restore, a happening in education that holds promise in our effort to gain a renewed sense of "implementation."

To gain a firmer hold on praxis, I seek support of a phenomenological scholar whose work I have recently come to know. He is Karol Wojtyla, a Polish theologian and scholar (Pope John Paul II) who speaks, of course, in a spiritual context of what education deeply means. His denouncement of instrumental action has meaningful relevance for our search. Wojtyla became extremely skeptical of the reductive tendencies of instrumental reason embedded in materialistic and positivistic thought, inherited from the 19th century, which spread pervasively and insidiously penetratingly into the life world of the Polish people. He had recognized that since Descartes, knowledge of man and his world has been identified with a narrow view of cognition, and in the ensuing centuries was exclusively extended in the familiar rhetoric of behaviorism, utilitarianism and determinism. His efforts to transcend instrumental reason appear in his books *The Acting Person* (Wojtyla, 1979), and *Toward a Philosophy of Praxis* (1981), both dealing with the personal and communal venturing of man as he experiences life through action and reflection on his experiences. Unraveling the network of, man's constitutive tendencies and strivings, Wojtyla attempted to reveal man's status in the world, the meaning of emancipation and of human fulfillment. He probed, by means of ontological hermeneutics, the constitutive dynamism integrated by the acting person. Believing that man is no mere creature of circumstances, conditioned and encapsulated by his personal and social milieu, he proposed man's worthy life venture as self-disclosure and self-governance as he fashions a personal and social life worth living. By emphasizing both the situationally human condition of man and the irreducible transcendence of the human person with respect to the current of social life, he counteracted reductionist tendencies so prevalent in contemporary Western culture. Furthermore, he saw man as a historical being, man as a maker of his own history, who, together with others, is seen as co-makers of history.

For many of us, to understand praxis requires an estrangement from the dichotomized view of "theory and practice" and embracing of that which sees them as twin moments of the same reality. Rather than seeing theory as leading into practice, we need now more than ever to see it as a reflective moment in praxis. In action-oriented language, praxis is action done reflectively, and reflection on what is being done. Within this view, knowing arises not from inward speculation but from intentional engagement with, and experience of, lived reality. It is thus a practical way of knowing guided by its own telos. Hence, praxis has as its main interest further praxis.

If we were to interpret curriculum implementation as praxis, we must acknowledge assumptions that differ markedly from those underlying instrumentalism:

Assumption 1: Humanization is the basic human vocation. Within this view the teacher called on to implement Curriculum X must be seen not in terms of a being-as-thing but as a human being interested in his [or her] own and others' becoming. The instrumental view of implementation, by technicizing the teacher, denudes him [or her] of subjectivity.

Assumption 2: People are capable of transforming their realities (in our case, the self and Curriculum X). Within this view, we see the teacher as a person-who-acts, and thus as a creator of his [or her] own reality. As such, he [or she] interprets from within his [or her] horizon Curriculum X, and engages situationally in its transformation.

Assumption 3: Education is never neutral. Within this assumption, curriculum implementation is a political act. Within a social relational context, the activity of implementation is a matter of power and control.

I would now like to interpret situational praxis more concretely within the situation of a classroom (see Fig. 2.1). Within the perspective of praxis, the presence of Curriculum X in the classroom situation can be seen as a penetration into the lifeworld of the teacher and students. This penetration can be seen as an event that can occasion interpretive activities, efforts at sense-making of Curriculum X. Teachers and students can be seen as co-actors acting with and on Curriculum X, as they dialectically shape the reality of classroom experiences embedded in a crucible of the classroom culture of which they are a part and in which they have inserted themselves. This reality is the situation meaning that the teacher and the students cocreate, guided as they are by their personal and group intentionalities.

But what is equally important for teachers and students as they engage in interpretive acts is to be critically reflective not only of the transformed reality that is theirs to create, but also of their own selves. It is within this critical turn, a precious moment in praxis, that there exist possibilities for empowerment that can nourish transformation of the self and the curriculum reality. It is this critical turn that provides the power to affirm what is good in the reality experienced, to negate what is distorting therein, and to allow engagement in acts or reconstruction guided by an emancipatory interest. In this sense the end of praxis is more praxis.

Thus, in praxis, our teacher needs to place his [or her] everyday type of attitude in "brackets," as it were, and examine it in an attempt to go beyond the immediate level of interpretation of Curriculum X. Critical reflection and action as action full of thought, and thought full of action, leads to an understanding of what is beyond, allowing disclosure of tacitly held assumptions and intentions of the authors of Curriculum X, which likely are hidden from view. Or such reflectivity can allow disclosure of the teacher's own unconsciously held assumptions and intentions that underlie his [or her] interpretation of Curriculum X. Either or both of these may be repressive constraints, which our teacher needs to face. For example, the content of reflection may be the "rationalization" the teacher uses to hide underlying motives for his own action, or it may be the "ideology" used by those who developed Curriculum X, rendering obscure the developer's interests that lie beneath. In this sense, critical reflection demonstrates interest in discovering the hidden "true interests" embedded in some given humanly lived situation.

Reflection, however, is not only oriented toward making conscious the unconscious by disclosing underlying assumptions and intentions, but it is also oriented toward the implications for action guided by the newly gained critical knowing. It is interested in bringing about a reorientation through clarification of the assumptions and intentions upon which thought and action rest. These may be preconceived norms, values, images of man and world, assumptions about knowledge, root metaphors, and perspectives.   Implementation of Curriculum X as situational praxis has an interest in liberation of the teacher from hidden assumptions and intentions, promoting a social theory grounded in the moral attitude of liberation and fulfillment.

CONCLUSION

What I have attempted in this paper is to portray implementation employing the distinction between "instrumentalism" and "praxis," that is, between instrumental action and situational praxis, between actions of beings-as-things and beings-as-human, signifying two frames of reference in which the reality of implementation activity can be constituted.

In the framework of instrumental action, implementation is objectified; that is, it is constituted as action according to an ends–means framework. Competence in implementation within this framework assumes actions of beings-as-things oriented toward interest in control, efficiency and certainty. In contrast, the framework of situational praxis is oriented toward interest in mutual understanding, and also towards practical interest in securing authentically the always precarious intersubjectivity.   In this framework, competence in implementation is seen as competence in communicative action and reflection, and reality (of Curriculum X) is constituted or reconstituted within a community of actors.

Within the framework of praxis and emancipating actions, these actors are oriented toward "de-naturalizing" that which common sense declares to be human nature they explore and condemn the commonsensical dismissal of alternate realities, and they attempt to restore the legitimacy of those existential issues that common sense, following human historical predicament, tends to pulverize into a multitude of mini-problems as can be articulated in purely instrumental terms.

Ultimately, competence in curriculum implementation as situational praxis as I have outlined it is a metaphor I have chosen to oppose in humanity. Hence, if a school is seen as a community of very human beings, I see no place for the view of implementation as instrumental action. What we must have is a view or action that humanizes. Curriculum implementation as situational praxis is one such mode of action.

REFERENCES

Aoki, T. (1974). Pin-pointing issues in curriculum decision-making. In
    Curriculum decision making in Alberta: A Janus look. Alberta: Alberta
    Department of Education.
Aoki, T. (1977). Theoretic dimension or curriculum: Reflections from a micro-

perspective. *Canadian Journal of Education*, 2(1).

Aoki, T. (1979). Toward curriculum inquiry in a new key. *Occasional Paper No. 2*. Edmonton, Alberta: Secondary Education, Faculty of Education, University of Alberta.

Editorial: Statement of agreement by professionals in the field of educational dissemination. (1977, November). *Educational Researcher*, pp. 6–10.

Groome, T, H.   (1980). *Christian religious education. Sharing our story and vision.* San Francisco: Harper & Row.

Freire, P. (1972). *The pedagogy of the oppressed.* New York: Herder & Herder.

Guba, E., & Clark, C. (1975, April). The configurational perspective: A new view of educational knowledge production and utilization. *Educational Researcher.*

House, E. (1979). Technology versus craft: A ten year perspective on innovation, *Journal of Curriculum Studies,* 1 (11).

Schroyer, T. (1973). *The critique of domination: The origins and development of critical theory.* Boston: Beacon Press.

Wojtyla, K. (1979). *The acting person.* Boston: D. Reidel.

Wojtyla, K. (1981). *Toward a philosophy of praxis.* New York: Crossroad.

Chapter 3

Competence in Teaching as Instrumental and Practical Action: A Critical Analysis[1] (1984)

Competent, adj. 1. Having sufficient ability or authority. 2. Possessing the requisite natural or legal qualifications; qualified. 3. Sufficient; adequate. [MF competent competens, -entis, ppr. of *competere*. Be fit, be proper. *Com-* together *petere* go, seek.] (Britannica World Language Dictionary)

In discussing "competence," from the perspective of critical social theory, I have felt tension, doubly: first, because I experienced this tension as an alien to a strange country might experience it. Trained as a teacher and teacher educator mainly in the tradition of, broadly speaking, positivistic science, I have been finding the world of critical social theory somewhat foreign to me, and my initial coming to an understanding had been as that of a North American visiting Continental Europe for the first time. I become increasingly aware that I am North American. Schooled as I have been in psychosocial theories applied to education in the tradition of North American scholarship, I have been dwelling in a world somewhat distanced from the domain of critical social theory. Hence, as many monopolarized strangers are wont to be, I know I am suspect in my occasional and maybe frequent tendency to reduce what to me is new by interpreting it within the framework of what has been familiar to me. Knowing this, you will appreciate my uneasiness.

Second, I also experienced tension because of my initial inclination to give meaning to the term "competence" within a framework wherein I have been making-sense of activities such as "*competency*-based curriculum development," "*competency*-based testing," "*competency*-based teacher education," "management by *competency*-based objectives," and the like. My first inclination has been to make sense of "competence" by reducing it to the instrumental sense of techniques and skills. Thus, having lived in and where I

---

[1] Reprinted from: Aoki, Ted T. (1984). Competence in Teaching as Instrumental and Practical Action: A critical analysis. In Edmund Short (Ed.). *Competence: Inquiries into its Meaning and Acquisition in Educational Settings.* (pp. 71-79). Lanham: University Press of America, Inc.

find myself within a world in which positivistic science and its derivative technological worldview are dominant, I find myself struggling against my own initial acculturated tendency to totalize *a* way of interpreting "competence" into *the* way, the instrumental way.

Thus, I find myself caught within my own self-constituted limit-situation, and in attempting to understand "competence" differently, I am experiencing a struggle to attempt to break through my self-imposed walls. Fundamental to this struggle are the contradictory meanings of competence that dwell within me. What follows is a portrayal of this contradiction.

COMPETENCE AS INSTRUMENTAL ACTION

In discussing teaching competence within a concrete program, allow me to ground my discussion in two segments of the undergraduate teacher education program in our own Faculty of Education at the University of Alberta, Canada, from which I hail. For the past few years, our faculty has been engaged in the revision of the teacher education program guided by the content of a faculty-approved report entitled *A Report on the Revision of the B. Ed. Program.*[2] In it are two contradictory interpretations of competence in teaching. My interest is to illuminate the contradictions.

Segment 1

Segment 1 describes briefly a compulsory core course in curriculum and instruction. It prescribes a repertoire of "basic skills and strategies of teaching," thought to be key to the classroom-teaching situation. These basic teaching skills and strategies read as follows:

1. *Classroom management and discipline.* This would include such topics as organizing and managing routine tasks and physical arrangements, individualizing and grouping for instruction, behaviour management and/or modification, and pupil reinforcement.

2. *Curriculum planning.* Included in this area would be the development of skills in relation to goal setting, writing lesson objectives, lesson and unit planning, motivation of students, and selection of appropriate materials and aids.

---

[2] *A Report on the Revision of the B. Ed. Degree.* Committee on Basic Skills and Knowledge of the Faculty of Education, University of Alberta, Edmonton, 1978.

3. *Instructional strategies or methods.* Students should be provided examples of and opportunities to practice different skills related to the presentation and discussion of information. Included would be such items as questioning, explaining, and demonstrating, along with methods of achieving lesson closure and giving directions.

4. *Assessing and evaluating student behaviour.* This would include observation and listening skills, other diagnostic techniques and record keeping.[3]

The notion of "competence" exhibited in the foregoing as management skills, planning skills, instructional skills, and assessing skills is legion and is of the same order as many typified expressions we find in current educational literature—"competency-based teacher education," "competency-based curriculum development," "competency-based testing," "management by competency-based objectives," and their many derivatives. As such, "competence" reflects what might be seen as the current mainstream metaphor of teaching, schooling, and curriculum thought.

This metaphor sees "competence" as means to given ends, skills and techniques oriented toward interest in efficient control. Such a knowing-how-to-do view of competence is embedded in scientific and technological thought and action within the framework of which curricular competencies such as "teaching competence" "curriculum development competence," or "curriculum evaluation competence" are seen strictly within a technical ends–means framework, reducing competence to instrumental reason and instrumental action. As such, the teacher, the curriculum developer, or the curriculum evaluators are seen as rule-oriented, rule-governed beings cast within a manipulative ethos, an ethos in which even the future is conceived in terms of rules.

It is to this kind of phenomenon dominant in North America that men such as Edmund Husserl, Jurgen Habermas, Trent Schroyer, Michael Apple, and others have been referring as a crisis of Western reason (Henry Johnson, in questioning, "What's good for General Motors is good for the school," was also pointing to this crisis.)

Trent Schroyer in *The Critique of Domination* speaks of this crisis as reflected in two symbolic events of the 1960s, man's landing on the moon and the founding of the Woodstock nation. According to Schroyer, the first, the moon-landing feat, represents the zenith of technical progress; the latter, popular or not, the affirmation of a communal sentiment. These, according to Schroyer,

---

[3] Ibid, Appendix III, pp. 1 and 2.

mark a fundamental contradiction between an orientation committed to technological progress and that committed to the improvement of personal and communal life.[4]

Of the two, the paramount mainstream reality seems to be the technological, devoted to the belief that problems and conflicts can be managed through purposive rational action based on precise quantification and systemic decision making. What is here reductive and damaging is the fact that emphasis on technical strategy as a means for efficient decision making effectively submerges the ideology of sociocultural values, and leaves the "neutral" standards of purposive rational action, what could be called "competence as instrumental reason."

This same crisis manifested as a reflection of the contemporary image of advanced industrial society shows as an internal crisis in the curriculum world indicated by, although still few, an increasing number of curriculum scholars.[5] Central to this crisis, writ large or small, is the issue of the adequacy of the social theory or social theories undergirding it. By social theory I mean the philosophical presuppositions and root metaphors, which inform curriculum and pedagogy.

To date in the field of education the dominant social theory has been guided by an instrumental notion of reason which, I believe, impoverishes us by submerging or even denying the meaning of cultural reality. By adopting technocratic strategies and allied decision-making social theories, we are asked to admit the rational necessity of extending centralized management theories to more and more areas of the life of teachers, students, and administrators in the classroom and the school. This assumption has been so reinforced by positivistic thought and action, by our intoxication with the technical power of science and technology, and by the unreflective adoption of business management techniques that it has become a mainstream doctrine of educational thought. To question this position requires a radical reexamination of the foundations of social theory and an exploration of alternative modes of inquiry and sociocultural organization.

Those of us in the realm of curriculum who are wedded to an instrumental concept of competence[6]—that is, competence viewed as naive scientism of our technocratic guidance system—should become vitally sensitive to the limit-situation that blocks our capacity to recognize the sociocultural significance of the living acts of teachers and students. It is a new metaphor of teachers and

---

[4] Schroyer, T. (1973). *The Critique of Dominance.* New York: George Braziller, 1973.

[5] For the work of critical scholars, see William Pinar (Ed.). *Curriculum Theorizing: The Reconceptualists.* Berkeley, CA: McCutchan, 1975.

[6] See extract from *Britannica World Language Dictionary* at the beginning of this paper.

students we need—one that will avoid reduction of teachers and students from beings-as-humans to being-as-things.

COMPETENCE AS PRACTICAL ACTION (PRAXIS)

I now wish to turn to another segment in our faculty report previously mentioned for undergraduate teacher education program revision in an attempt to secure a more vital sense of competence.

Segment 2

Segment 2 in the report is entitled "The Senior Elective." It reflects a desire to provide undergraduate students in their final year of their 4-year program opportunities to bring together the diverse program elements in which they have been immersed in a course "committed to integration and synthesis." Here is an extract from that document:

1. A suitable SENIOR ELECTIVE experience is one in which a student combines personal action and . . . reflection on action;

2. A suitable SENIOR ELECTIVE experience should expand the student's awareness of the teacher's role by . . . analysis of assumptions and values; by reconceiving the role of the teacher as a skilled leader and by being aware of the dynamics of organizations and of human relationships therein;

3. A suitable SENIOR ELECTIVE should seek to link the universal with the particular, the concrete, day-to-day world of personal action with the world of ideas, values, symbols, or more generally, with systems of meaning.[7]

What is the notion of teaching competence to which this textpoints? What is the underlying perspective of this text on "competence?"

Even from this sketchy text from Segment 2, we can begin to trace the contours of the underlying view of competence in teaching and the teacher situated in the everyday commonplace of the classroom and the school. To view the "teacher" as "actor/reflector on action" or "teaching" as "action and reflection with others in a social context" is sharply in contrast with the view of

---

[7] Karol Wojtyla. (1979). *The Acting Person.* Boston: D. Reidel Publishing Co. *(Analecta Husserliana, The Yearbook of Phenomenological Research*, Vol. X)

"teacher" as "behaviour modifier" or "teaching" as "instrumental skills" so paramount in Segment 1. Teaching as reflected in Segment 2 no longer espouses the instrumental and technical view of competence as was reflected in Segment 1. No longer is teaching viewed merely in terms of technical skills of classroom management, questioning, "behaviour modification," and the like.

To help explore this view of competence, let us uncover the root etymology of "competence." The disclosure of the Latin root reveals a fresh view. The Latin root is "com-petere," "com" meaning "together," and "petere" meaning "to seek." In a root sense, then, to be competent means to be able to seek together or to be able to venture forth together. This root meaning of "competence" as "communal venturing" holds promise for a fresh view of what it means to be a competent teacher. (This, I feel, is embedded in the question Henry Johnson posed: "What does it mean to be human?")

I now seek support from a phenomenological scholar whose works I have recently come to know. He is a Polish scholar, by name Karol Wojtyla, who speaks in a context broader than that of education. Yet his denouncement of competence as instrumental action has meaningful relevance for us. I understand that Wojtyla became skeptical of the reductive tendencies of instrumental reason embedded in materialistic and positivistic thought inherited from the 19th century and spreading into all domains of thought in Poland. He had recognized that since Descartes, knowledge of man and his world has been identified with cognition, the ensuing post-Cartesian attitude extending it as reflections in behaviourism, utilitarianism, and determinism. His efforts to transcend objectivism appear in his book *The Acting Person* dealing with the *communal venturing of man* as experienced through acting and reflecting throughout one's life. Unraveling the network of man's constitutive tendencies and strivings, Wojtyla, in his book, attempted to reveal man's status in the world, the meaning of emancipation, and of human fulfillment. He probed by means of ontological hermeneutics the constitutive dynamism integrated by the acting person. Believing that man is no mere creature of circumstances conditioned and encapsulated by his social milieu, he proposed man's worthy life venture as self-disclosure and self-governance as he fashions a personal and social life worth living. By emphasizing both the communal condition of man and the irreducible transcendence of the human person with respect to the current of social life, he counteracts the deviant, reductionist tendencies so prevalent in contemporary philosophy and culture. Furthermore, he sees man as a *historical being*, man as a maker of his own history, who together with others are seen as co-makers of history.

It is to this framework of acting and reflecting that we must turn to make sense afresh of competence in teaching. Within such a framework, competence in teaching is anchored in a situation of interactions among teachers and students mediated by everyday language, oriented toward practical interest in establishing open intersubjectivity and nonviolent recognition on which communicative action depends. But these inter-actions are rooted in a network of meanings actors within that situation give. Hence, understanding the day-to-day life of teachers and students in the classroom requires at least understanding in terms of the meaning structures actors in the classroom give. However, to be able to venture forth together in the meaningful way Wojtyla speaks of requires not only an understanding of this meaning structure but also action rooted in critical reflection on these meaning structures.

I would like to interpret what I can now refer to as critical venturing together more concretely, within this critical framework. The teacher in becoming involved with his [or her] students, enters into their world as he [or her] allows them to enter his and engages himself with students mutually in action-reflection oriented activities. He [or she] questions students as well as himself as he [or she] urges students to question the teacher and themselves. Mutual reflection allows new questions to emerge, which, in turn, leads to more reflection. In the ongoing process, which is dialectical, and transformative of social reality, both teacher and students become participants in open dialogue.

However, it is important for the teacher to remember that a critical perspective is a two-bladed knife, cutting both ways. Werner stated:

> We must be reflective of the very perspective we use for critical sense making. Any clarifying of perspective of others . . . is itself perspective guided. In arguing for point-of-viewism one cannot presume himself free of a viewpoint. One way to deal with this dilemma is to make explicit and reflect upon the theoretical and methodological beliefs within which our own thinking and acting are situated.[8]

Reflection in the sense used here is not the kind of activity that teachers and students as actors engage in their typical daily life. For in their day-to-day existence, acting persons deal with their concerns in routine ways often without probing beyond the immediate exigencies. Often, actions are without thought. Missing is a conscious effort to examine the intentions and assumptions underlying their acts. However, in critical reflection the everyday type of attitude is placed in "brackets," as it were, and examined in an attempt to go beyond the immediate level of interpretation. In this sense, critical reflection is thoughtful action, that is, action full of thought. Critical reflection thus leads to an understanding of what is beyond; it is oriented toward making the unconscious conscious. Such reflective activity allows liberation from the

---

[8] Werner W. (1978). Evaluation: Sense-making of school programs. In T. Aoki (Ed.). *Curriculum Evaluation in a New Key*. (a monograph, p. 20). Vancouver: University of British Columbia, Center for the Study of Curriculum and Instruction.

unconsciously held assumptions and intentions that lie hidden. These may be repressive and dehumanizing aspects of everyday life that man needs to face in his [or her] personal and social life. For example, at the personal level the content of reflection may be the "rationalizations" an actor uses to hide underlying motives for his [or her] action. Or at the societal level, the content of reflection may be the "ideology" used to speak for social policies and practices, rendering obscure society's coercive interests that lie beneath. In this sense, critical reflection demonstrates interest in discovering the hidden "true" interests embedded in some given personal or social condition.

Reflection, however, is not only oriented toward making conscious the unconscious by discovering underlying assumptions and intentions, but it is also oriented toward the implications for action guided by the newly gained consciousness and critical knowing. It is interested in bringing about a reorientation through transformation of the assumptions and intentions on which thought and action rest. There may be preconceived norms, values, images of man and the world, assumptions about knowledge, root metaphors, and perspectives. Competence as critical venturing together, then, with its interests in liberating man from hidden assumptions and techniques, promotes a theory of man and society that is grounded in the moral attitude of liberation.[9]

CONCLUSION

What I have attempted to do is to portray competence employing the categorical distinction between "technique" and "praxis," that is, instrumental action and practical action, between beings-as-things and beings-as-no-things, signifying two frames of reference in which reality is constituted. (See table 3.1, which contrasts these two "perspectives on competence.")

In the framework of "technique" (instrumental action), reality is objectified—that is, it is constituted as the being of things according to nomological laws. Competence within this framework assumes actions of beings-as-things oriented toward interests in control, efficiency, and certainty. In contrast, in the framework of "praxis" (practical action), reality is constituted by the intersubjective actions of beings-as-humans, oriented toward cognitive interests in mutual understanding, and also the practical interest in securing authentically the always precarious intersubjectivity. In this framework of

---

[9] Aoki T. (1978), Toward curriculum inquiry in a new key." In J. Victoria & E. Sacca (Eds.), *Phenomenological Description: Potential for Research in Art Education, University of Concordia, Montreal, Series Presentations on Art Education Research,* pp. 47–75. Also published as *Occasional Paper No.2,* Department of Secondary Education, Faculty of Education, University of Alberta, Edmonton, Canada.

competence as communicative action and reflection, reality is constituted as a community of actors and speakers.

Within the framework of "praxis" and emancipatory actions, these actors and speakers are oriented toward "de-naturalizing" that which common sense declares to be human nature; they explore and condemn the commonsensical dismissal of alternative realities, and they attempt to restore the legitimacy of those existential issues that common sense, following human historical predicament, pulverizes into a multitude of mini-problems as can be articulated in purely instrumental terms.

Ultimately, critical competence or competence as praxis as I have outlined it is for people for whom the way competence is known is not reason enough for the way competence is known by mainstream America. In essence, critical competence is the way we choose to act to oppose inhumanity in songs and acts of joy, be they in the everyday idiom of music, art, play, poetry, pottery, or everyday language.

TABLE 3.1

Perspectives on Competence

Perspective A	Perspective B
Competence as Instrumental Action (Theory and Practice in Linear Relationship)	Competence as Practical Action (Praxis) (Theory and Practice in Dialectical Relationship)
Interest in	**Interest in**
Interest in *controlling* teaching situation through theory(ies).	Interest in "venturing forth" together with psychosocial students.
Instrumental interest in applying reason to teaching practice (thought to action) effectively, efficiently.	Interest in self-improvement by reflecting on and freeing itself from self or socially imposed constraints.
Interest in applying theoretical understandings in curriculum and instruction into classroom practice.	Interest in the teacher interpreting the classroom world, acting with and on that world, and reflecting and acting on both self and world.

TABLE 3.1 (*continued*)

ASSUMPTIONS ABOUT TEACHER AND CLASSROOM WORLD	ASSUMPTIONS ABOUT TEACHER AND CLASSROOM WORLD
The classroom is a world, which can be changed with certainty by the application of theory.	The teacher as acting person in dialectical relationship with the classroom world.
Thought and action (theory and practice) are separate realms linearly connected.	Assumes reality is not given directly in appearance, hence requires critical reflection to enable the teacher to discover deep structure not given in *appearance*.
"Practice" is actualization of theory.	
The theoretical world is paramount reality (therefore, theoretical knowledge is more important than applied knowledge).	Theory and practice are in integrated unity (praxis). (Praxis is thoughtful action; action full of thought.)
Instrumental knowledge is "applied" knowledge.	The teacher has unlimited possibilities for growth.
	The teacher is engaged in the writing of his [or her] own history.
Teacher is instrument of theoretical knowledge.	Praxical knowledge is "critically reflected" knowledge.

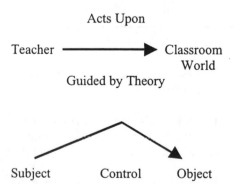

Acts Upon

Teacher ⟶ Classroom World

Guided by Theory

Subject   Control   Object

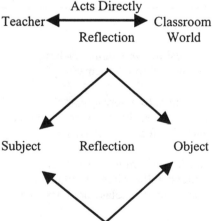

Acts Directly

Teacher ⟷ Classroom World
Reflection

Subject   Reflection   Object

APPROACH

Teacher applies theoretical rules to
Practical
situations; therefore, instrumental in
approach.

Planning lessons, managing class, and
teaching guided by "theoretical rules."

EVALUATION QUESTION

TYPE: How efficiently was "theory"
implemented in "practice"?

APPROACH

Acting and reflecting upon the world
the teacher helps students to construct
and transform reality.

Becoming aware of own teaching acts
as possible object-in-view.

Reflection as going beyond the
framework of everyday instrumental
action.

Seeks moment for conscious
connecting of teacher's awareness and
the teacher's intentional world.

Becoming aware of the writing of
history in which he [or her] is
engaged—the history that is the
activity through which the teacher
creates himself [or herself]. (Teacher
is maker of own history.)

Becoming aware that personal praxis
involves social praxis.

Becoming aware of the personal,
social, cultural, and political context in
which praxical activity is conducted.

EVALUATION QUESTION

TYPE: What is the quality of the
underlying perspective of my action?
What makes it possible for me as a
human being to act the way I do in my
pedagogical activities? Is it adequate?

Chapter 4

Interests, Knowledge and Evaluation: Alternative Approaches to Curriculum Evaluation[1] (1986)

In any serious discussion of school improvement, improvement of curriculum is implied. Curriculum improvement, in turn, implies curriculum evaluation.

In spite of the many years of curriculum evaluation activities at local, provincial, and national levels, it is only in recent years that the notion of "curriculum evaluation" itself has been made problematic and subjected to rigorous scrutinizing. It is this meta-level concern in curriculum evaluation that is the focus of this paper, guided by an interest in understanding more fully what is meant when we say "curriculum evaluation."

In recent years, some of us have come to question the tendency of educators to reduce the idiom of educational evaluation to the paradigm of scientist research. In our search flowing from our questioning, we have come to know some Continental European scholars who did not succumb to the persuasions of logical positivism expounded by members of the Vienna Circle as did North American scholars. Among these is Jurgen Habermas, a German scholar affiliated with the Frankfurt School.[2] He, together with others such as Horkheimer, Marcuse, and Adorno, announced what they saw as a serious crisis in the Western intellectual world so dominated by instrumental reason based on scientism and technology. Habermas appealed to philosophical anthropology to reveal knowledge constitutive of human interests embedded in basically different paradigms. In our endeavour to transcend the dominant tradition in curriculum evaluation, we appropriated Habermas's paradigms, and relabeled them for our purposes.

These we have termed:

1. Ends–Means (technical) evaluation orientation.
2. Situational interpretive evaluation orientation.

---

[1] Reprinted from Aoki, T. (1986). Interests, knowledge and evaluation: Alternative approaches to curriculum evaluation. *Journal of Curriculum Theorizing*, 6, (4), pp. 27–44.

[2] I have been influenced greatly by the writings of Jurgen Habermas, principally *Knowledge and Human Interests* (Boston: Beacon Press, 1972). The reader will note the relationship between the title of the book and the title of this paper.

3. Critical theoretic evaluation orientation.

I wish to discuss these orientations by grounding my discussion in a concrete evaluation experience: the assessment of the British Columbia Social Studies program.

Public school educators in British Columbia are very aware of the many evaluation activities spawned by the office of the Assessment Branch of the Ministry of Education over the past several years, in response, in part, we sense, to the public clamour for accountability in education.

Our experiences in evaluating the British Columbia Social Studies[3] provide an exemplar of how multiple perspectives can guide curriculum evaluation. From the outset, as we ventured into various centers in British Columbia, seeking out and trying to make sense of concerns about social studies expressed by teachers, students, parents, school trustees, administrators, and professors of social studies education, we seriously posed ourselves a question: "What are the evaluation frameworks and approaches we should employ in evaluating the phenomenon called social studies in British Columbia?"

We took a cue from what Kenneth Beittel[4] called, appropriately, the "Rashomon effect," a notion borrowed from Kurosawa's acclaimed film in which he disclosed the same event from several perspectives. Simultaneously, we were mindful of the risk of reductionism of evaluation possibilities to the dominant ends–means orientation in evaluation research, a point M. Q. Patton made in the following way:

---

[3] *The British Columbia Social Studies Assessment: A Report to the Ministry of Education, 1977*, is comprised of six reports in four volumes. The reports are as follows:

- *Views of Goals of Social Studies*
- *Teachers' Views of Social Studies*
- *Teachers' Views of Prescribed Social Studies Curriculum Resources*
- *Student Achievement and Views in Social Studies*
- *Interpretive Studies of Selected School Situation*
- *British Columbia Social Studies Assessment: Summary Report*

The Contract Team consisted of Ted T. Aoki, Chairman, Caroline Langford, David M. Williams, and Donald C. Wilson, and the reports were submitted to the Ministry of Education, Government of British Columbia, Victoria, B.C.
[4] Beittel, K. R. (1973). *Alternatives for Art Education Research* (p. vii). Dubuque, IA: Wm. C. Brown. What Beittel has to say about art education research is applicable to evaluation studies.

> The very dominance of the scientific method in evaluation research appears to have cut off the great majority of practitioners from serious consideration of any research paradigm. The label "research" has come to mean the equivalent of employing the Scientific Method ... of working within the dominant paradigm.[5]

We approached our evaluation activities mindful of the importance to us of ourselves being open to fresh possibilities. We began our evaluation tasks guided by paper-and-pencil-oriented questionnaires that sought teachers', parents' and students' views of aspects of Social Studies, and also students' views and knowledge of Social Studies content. We extended ourselves to include on-site studies, guided by concerns for meanings people who dwell within classroom and school situations give to Social Studies. Further, we added a critical evaluation dimension, seeking out underlying "official" perspectives embedded in the Ministry's official curriculum documents.

These activities led to the formulation of five reports and a special paper as follows:

Report A: *Teacher Views of Social Studies*
Report B: *Teacher Views of Prescribed Social Studies Curriculum Resources*
Report C: *Views of Goals of Social Studies*
Report D: *Student Achievement and Views in Social Studies*
Report E: *Interpretive Studies of Selected School Situations*

Special Paper: "An Interpretation of Intents of the Elementary and Secondary Curriculum Guides" in *The Summary Report: B.C. Social Studies Assessment.*

Now, some years after the completion of the evaluation, we are in a position to provide a reconstructed version, possessing to some degree a clarity and tidiness, which only a reconstruction can give. In fact, it is through such a reconstruction that we were able to provide a portrayal of our evaluation approaches interpreted within a framework of evaluation paradigms.[6]

We must now turn to an effort to illuminate to some extent these three evaluation orientations.

---

[5] Patton, M.Q. (1975). *Alternative Evaluation Research Paradigms* (p. 6). Grand Forks: University of North Dakota Press. This is a monograph in a series developed by the North Dakota Study Group on Evaluation.

[6] See Aoki, Ted T. (1978). Toward curriculum inquiry in a new key. In *Phenomenological Description: Potential for Research in Art Education*, Montreal: Concordia University, p. 54.

ENDS–MEANS (TECHNICAL)
EVALUATION ORIENTATION

Evaluators acting within an ends–means orientation reflect their interests by entertaining a set of evaluation concerns.

Ends–Means Concerns:

1. How efficient are the means in achieving the curricular goals and objectives?

2. How effective are the means in predicting the desired outcomes?

3. What is the degree of congruency between and among intended outcomes, the content in the instructional materials and the teaching approaches specified?

4. How good is Curriculum A compared with Curriculum B in achieving given ends?

5. Of given curricula, which one is the most cost-effective and time-efficient?

6. What valid generalizations can be made for all schools in a district?

7. How well are inputs organized to achieve organizational goals?

8. What are the principal means used to achieve goals? How do we know that these means are actually enacted, with what frequency, and with what intensity?

These ends–means concerns reflect an orientation to evaluation, which can be characterized as technical or instrumental. As such, these concerns reflect the dominant evaluation approach in use, going hand-in-hand with the technically oriented mainstream curriculum development/evaluation rationale, known popularly as the Tyler Rationale. We know it by Tyler's sequentially arranged four-step formulation[7]:

---

[7] From Tyler, Ralph W. (1949). *Basic Principles of Curriculum and Instruction.* Chicago: University of Chicago Press.

Step 1. What educational purposes should the school seek to attain?

Step 2. How can learning experiences be selected which are likely to be useful in attaining these objectives?

Step 3. How can learning experiences be organized for effective instruction?

Step 4. How can the effectiveness of learning experiences be evaluated?

The ends–means evaluation orientation has for the pragmatically oriented a commonsensical ring carrying with it the validity of popular support. Further, its congruency with the mainstream social theory idioms of basically instrumental reason, such as behaviourism, systems thinking, and structural functionalism borrowed heavily by educators, lends end–means evaluation a credibility that assumes the status of consensual validity of legitimated educator "scholars." Such legitimated authenticity has led many evaluators to regard this evaluation orientation as *the* orientation.

But what does this orientation imply in terms of cognitive interests and assumptions held tacitly? I suggest that underneath the avowed interest in efficiency, effectiveness, predictability, and certainty, as reflected in the list of concerns we examined, is a more deeply rooted interest—that of *control*. It is saturated with a manipulative ethos that leads evaluators of this orientation to value evaluation questions such as: How well have the ends been achieved? Which is a better program, Curriculum A or Curriculum B?

Within this framework, the form of knowledge that is prized is empirical data; the "harder" they are, the better, and the more objective they are, the better. Data are seen as brute facts. In scientific terms the form of knowledge assumes nomological status, demanding empirical validation and seeking levels of generalizability. Knowledge is objective, carrying with it the false dignity of value-free neutrality, reducing out as humanly as possible contamination by the subjectivity of the knower.

Evaluators who subscribe to the ends–means view are technologically oriented, primarily interested in seeing how well the system is able to control components within the system as it struggles to achieve its goals. In their tasks, these evaluators seek efficient tools and instruments such as tests and questionnaires, and seek rigor by bringing to bear the expertise of psychometricians and statisticians. They tend to resort to measurable quantitative data subjected to sophisticated statistical analyses.

In our B.C. Social Studies Evaluation, we administered achievement tests to Grade 4, 8, and 12 classes randomly selected throughout the province, and we sent questionnaires to randomly selected teachers in order to seek the teachers' assessment of instructional resources. These are illustrations of the instruments we used in the technically oriented dimension of our evaluation.

In summary, we might say that the ends–means evaluation mode just considered is framed within the orienting perspective of the following cognitive interest, form of knowing, and mode of evaluation: *Interest* in the ethos of *control* as reflected in the values of efficiency, effectiveness, certainty, and predictability. *Form of knowing* emphasized is that of empirical nomological knowing. Understanding is in terms of facts and generalizations. *Mode of evaluation* is ends–means evaluation, which is achievement oriented, goal based, criterion referenced, and cost benefit oriented.

SITUATIONAL INTERPRETIVE EVALUATION ORIENTATION

In contrast, to the technical interests and concerns reflected in the ends–means approach to evaluation, those evaluators oriented toward the situational interpretive mode of evaluation register interest in the following kinds of concerns:

Situational Interpretive Concerns:
1. How do various groups such as teachers, the ministry, parents, students, and administrators view Curriculum X?
2. In what ways do various groups approve or disapprove the program?
3. How do the various groups see Curriculum X in terms of relevance, meaningfulness, and appropriateness?
4. What are the various groups' perceived strengths and weaknesses of the program?
5. What questions do administrators and significant others have about Curriculum X?

The situational concerns expressed in these evaluation concerns reflect an orientation to evaluation that we can characterize as situational interpretive. As such these concerns reflect an approach to evaluation in which evaluators show interest in the meanings those living in the situation give to a given curriculum.

Although the technical evaluator assumes a posture as an outsider external to the situation (i.e., as a disinterested observer or as a stranger), the situational interpretive evaluator attempts to gain insights into human experiences as they are experienced by insiders, as they live within the situation.

For example, at this very moment as I write I find myself situated within my world of teacher educators. In this world of mine, my "I" is at the center. I am experiencing life as I am now living it, guided by my commonsense-typified knowledge about educators' writings and about people who read such writings. I define my life now by giving meaning to my paper on evaluation, as I sit at my desk awaiting words to come into view, and to ongoing events about me as I experience them. I am continuously involved in meaning-giving activities as I am subjectively engaged in constructing my personal world of meanings. The structure of these meanings is my present reality.

I can also picture you seated with the text of this writing before you as you are experiencing the reading of my paper. You are situated with yourself at center, that central point of your being that allows you to say "I." You are experiencing life as you are now living it in your typical "reading" way, giving your own meaning to the text of what you are reading. You, too, are continuously involved in meaning-giving activities as you construct your own personal world of meanings. The structure of these meanings is your present reality.

In a social situation, which a classroom or school significantly is, there are multifold ways in which things, people, and events are given meaning by those who are living in the situation. In other words, people are continuously interpreting events that they experience, and these interpretations differ from person to person. Hence, an evaluator oriented toward situational interpretation must keep two significant features in mind: (1) People give personal meanings to each situation experienced, and (2) people interpret the same event in different ways.

Although, as we have seen, the human activity of central concern within the ends–means orientation is man's technical productive capacity to achieve ends, the activity of most concern for evaluators in the situational interpretive framework is communication between man and man. Because evaluation-guiding interests of the situational interpretive evaluation are insights into human experiences as socially lived, the evaluator needs to direct efforts toward clarifying, authenticating, and bringing into full human awareness the meaning structures of the constructive activities of the social actors in the situation. Thus, the form of knowledge sought by the evaluator within this situation is not nomological statements, but rather structures of meaning as man meaningfully experiences and cognitively appropriates the natural and social world. Hence, when the situational interpretive evaluator comes to know situationally, he [or she] knows the world in a different form and in a different way compared with the knowledge gained by the ends–means evaluator.

In seeking out, therefore, the structure of meanings, which are not accessible to ends–means evaluators, those in the situational interpretive orientation must attempt to provide explanations of a different kind. That is, although "explaining" within the ends–means orientation means giving causal, functional, or hypothetico-deductive statements, within the situational orientation, "explaining" requires the striking of a responsive chord among people in dialogue situations by clarifying motives, authentic experiences, and common meanings. The evaluator, hence, cannot stand aloof as an observer as is done in the ends–means evaluation, but must enter into intersubjective dialogue with the people in the evaluation situation.

Within the situational interpretive orientation, there are different approaches, each allowing a description of the meaning structure in a situation. There is growing interest among evaluators in studies that fall within the phenomenological attitude.   The phenomenology of socially constructed understanding, requiring investigation of meaning-giving activities in the everyday world, is the main interest of sociologists of knowledge such as P. Berger, T. Luckman, and A. Schutz, ethnomethodologists such as H. Garfinkel, I. Goffman, and Cicourel, and hermeneutists such as F. Schleiermacher, H. Palmer, and Hans-Georg Gadamer.

Such interpretations of situations are called phenomenological descriptions, providing first-order experiences people directly experience. Evaluators of this persuasion are interested in the quality of life-as-lived in the classroom or school, life experienced by those who dwell within the situation.

Within the B.C. Social Studies Assessment, we experimented with two situational evaluation approaches: (1) an ethnographic approach in which we sought out views of the curriculum-as-plan and curriculum-in-use as interpreted by parents, students, teachers and administrators, and (2) an approach using conversational analysis of the meaning structures of the existential life of teachers and students. The inclusion of these reports represented our attempt to portray more fully the social studies phenomenon as it existed in British Columbia.

We can summarize the situational interpretive framework in terms of its cognitive interest, form of knowledge, and mode of evaluation as follows:

> *Interest* in the meaning structure of intersubjective communication between and among people who dwell within a situation.

> *Form of knowing* is situational knowing, within which understanding is in terms of the structure of meaning. Within this orientation, to explain is to strike a resonant chord by clarifying motives and common meanings.

> *Mode of evaluation* is situational evaluation, which seeks the quality of meanings people living in a situation give to their lived situations.

CRITICAL EVALUATION MODE ORIENTATION

Evaluators thinking and acting within the critical mode reflect their interests by committing themselves to a set of evaluation concerns that differ markedly from either the technically or the situationally oriented evaluators. The following concerns illustrate the interest of critical evaluators:

Critical evaluation concerns:

1. What are the perspectives underlying Curriculum X? (What are underlying root interests, root assumptions, and root approaches?)
2. What is the implied view of the student or the teacher held by the curriculum planner?
3. At the root level, whose interests does Curriculum X serve?
4. What are the root metaphors that guide the curriculum developer, the curriculum implementer, or the curriculum evaluator?
5. What is the basic bias of the publisher/author/developer of prescribed or recommended resource materials?
6. What is the curriculum's supporting worldview?

The evaluation concerns just illustrated reflect an orientation to evaluation that we can characterize as critical or critical theoretic, rooted in critical social theory, an emerging discipline area. These concerns reflect an approach to evaluation in which the evaluators are interested in bringing into full view underlying perspectives of programs that are typically taken-for-granted and therefore, hidden from view. Implied within a "perspective" are root metaphors, deep-seated human interests, assumptions about man, worldview, and knowledge, as well as stances that man takes in approaching himself or his world. Critical evaluators are interested in making these visible. But they do not stop here.

As we have noted, although evaluation is seen in ends–means evaluation within the framework of instrumental or technical action, and in situational evaluation within the framework of communicative action, in critical theoretic evaluation it is seen within the dialectical framework of practical action and critical reflection, what Paulo Freire refers to as *praxis*. In critical reflection, the actor, through the critical analytic process, discovers and makes explicit the tacit and hidden assumptions and intentions held. Such reflective activity is guided by interest in revealing the root condition that makes knowing possible, or in revealing the underlying human and social conditions that distort human existence, distortions that tend to alienate man. Thus, critical evaluators attempt to determine when theoretical statements grasp invariant regularities of human and social action or when they express ideologically frozen relations of dependence that can, in principle, be transformed. Richard Schaull captures aptly this critical orientation in the following way:

> There is no such thing as a *neutral* educational process. Education either functions as an instrument which is used to facilitate the integration of the younger generation into the

logic of the present system and bring about conformity to it, *or* it becomes "the practice of freedom," the means by which men and women deal critically and creatively with reality and discover how to participate in the transformation of their world.[8]

Thus, a critically oriented evaluator becomes a part of the object of the evaluation research. The evaluator, in becoming involved with his [or her] subjects, enters into their world and attempts to engage them mutually in reflective activity. The evaluator questions subjects and self, and encourages subjects to question him [or her] and themselves. Reflection by the evaluator and by participants allows new questions to emerge from the situation, which, in turn, leads to further reflective activity. Reflection, however, is not only oriented toward making conscious the unconscious by discovering underlying interests, assumptions and intentions, but it is also oriented toward action guided by the newly gained conscious, critical knowledge. Hence, in the ongoing process, which is dialectical and transformative, both evaluator and subjects become participants in an open dialogue.

Reflection in the foregoing sense is not the kind of activity school people, as actors, engage in their ongoing lives. In their everyday existence, actors deal with their concerns in routine ways, guided by the commonplace recipes that sustain them in good stead. What is missing is a conscious effort to examine critically the assumptions and intentions underlying their practical thoughts and acts. They may be reflective but not critically reflective. Critical reflection leads to an understanding of what is beyond the actor's ordinary view, by making the familiar unfamiliar, by making the invisible visible. Such reflective activity not only allows liberation from the unconsciously held assumptions and intentions that lie buried and hidden. For example, at the personal level the content of reflection may be the "rationalization" an actor uses to hide underlying motives for his actions. Or at the societal level, the content may be the "ideology" used to support social practices and policies, rendering obscure society's manipulative ethos and interests that lie beneath. Critical interest thus sees interest in uncovering the "true" interests embedded in some given personal or social condition.

But more than that, it is interested in bringing about reorientation through transformative action of the assumptions and intentions upon which reflection and action rest. Critical orientation, then, with its evaluation-guiding interest to liberate people from hidden assumptions and intentions, promotes a theory of man and society that is grounded in the moral attitude of emancipation.

---

[8] Schaull, Richard. (1968). Foreword to Paulo Freire, *Pedagogy of the Oppressed*. New York: Herder and Herder.

Curriculum evaluation within this orientation would ask that focus be given to the dynamic of the dialectic between the knowledge structure of life experiences and the normative structure as well. Within this critical framework, phenomenological description of educational phenomena will be regarded as incomplete, but significant in making possible critical reflection and action. Within such a framework of interest the pioneer work of Langeveld, associated with the School of Utrecht, makes sense. He has argued that phenomenological disciplines are conducted within the dialogical context of an ongoing situational interpretive activity but guided by some normative purpose of what it means to educate and to be educated within the critically reflective orientation. As van Manen states, referring to Langeveld's pedagogical position: "Educational activities must always be structured pedagogically; that is, it should be grounded reflectively in the emancipatory norms toward which all education is oriented."[9]

Within the British Columbia Social Studies Assessment, critical evaluation was included under the innocuous title "An Interpretation of Intents of the Elementary and Secondary Curriculum Guides," and exists as an afterthought, an addendum to the summary report. In it we examined the official text of the social studies curriculum-as-plan and gave it a critical look.

To get a sense of the flavour of this evaluation, read the concluding statement of the critical analysis:

> The B.C. Social Studies program approaches the study of man-in-his-world from three different perspectives: scientific, situational and critically reflective knowing. Through each of these, students are exposed to various interpretations of how the social world has been constructed. The program, however, does not provide a balance among these perspectives: rather, it emphasizes scientific knowledge. Through such an emphasis teachers and students are made dependent on one particular way of viewing the social world. Such dependence limits the possibilities which the participants have available for exploring their social environment. The extent to which the perspectives influence classroom presentations (passive vs. active, non-committal vs. committal) stresses the importance

---

[9] An account of Langeveld's conception of phenomenological pedagogy is described by Max van Manen (1978, March). A phenomenological experiment in educational theory: The Utrecht school, (p. 5). Paper presented at the Annual Conference of the American Education Research Association, Toronto, on.

of providing a balance of knowledge perspectives in the program.[10]

What we have done is to bring the official B.C. Social Studies Program into fuller view by revealing the tacitly held assumptions and intentions. Following the comment we added, as a recommendation to the ministry, the following:

> To aid teachers in moving towards consideration of perspectives, it is recommended that a full description of the perspectives incorporated into the B.C. Social Studies program be carefully described in the Curriculum Guides. Students and teachers are entitled to a full explanation of the curriculum developers' knowing stance. The curriculum developers' perspective toward the social world should not, in other words, be hidden from users of the curriculum.[11]

We might summarize the third evaluation mode discussed here as follows:

Critical evaluation: As Summary:

Interest in emancipation from hidden assumptions or underlying human conditions.

Form of knowing is critical knowing in the sense of understanding hidden assumptions, perspectives, motives, rationalizations, and ideologies. To explain within critical knowing is to trace down and bring into fuller view underlying unreflected aspects.

Mode of evaluation is critical theoretic evaluation, which involves (1) discovering through critical reflection underlying human conditions, assumptions, and intentions, and (2) acting on self and world to improve the human conditions or to transform the underlying assumptions and intentions.

In this paper I have attempted to trace out a post hoc reconstruction of three orientations that undergirded the evaluation we conducted. By embracing these perspectives we acknowledged multiple human interests, each associated with a

---

[10] Aoki, T. and Harrison, E. (1977). The intents of the B.C. Social Studies Curriculum Guides: An interpretation. In Aoki, T. et al., *The British Columbia Social Studies Assessment: A Summary Report, 1977*, p. 62.
[11] Ibid.

form of knowledge. We stated that within the ends–means evaluation approach, the implied interest is intellectual and technical control, and the implied form of knowledge is generalizable objective knowledge. Within the situational interpretive approach, the implied interest is authentic communicative consensus, and the form of knowledge, situational knowledge in terms of meaning. Within the critical orientation, the implied interest is emancipatory, based on action that brings into fuller view the taken-for-granted assumptions and intentions. The knowledge flowing from this activity is critical knowledge.

It has been said that an educator's understanding of his [or her] task as educator is most clearly demonstrated by his [or her] method of evaluation. If that be so, the evaluation approaches we used disclose our understanding of possible ways of understanding what it means to be an educator and what it means to be educated. In our efforts we employed evaluation orientations that reflect to some extent our commitment to our understanding of evaluation as human intentional activities grounded in multiple human interests. So committed, we directed our efforts to go beyond technical instrumentalism, to which we educators in North America have been so prone.

We feel that we have gained a fuller and richer understanding of curriculum evaluation and a sense of how this understanding might help in efforts toward school improvement. And yet, in reaching out for a fuller understanding, we have a gnawing sense flowing from having experienced a reaching out that never fully reaches.

We acknowledge that our effort in conducting this evaluation was a human effort and, as such, subject to the weaknesses and blindness to limit situations that all humans, being human, suffer.

And so, when we felt the task was done, we asked ourselves these questions: Has the job been done? Has the picture of Social Studies in British Columbia been adequately drawn? We replied:

> Certainly in our efforts to give an accurate portrayal, we have employed not only traditionally accepted techniques, but also more personalized ones aimed at seriously attempting to "hear" what the people of the province are saying about the subject.
>
> There may be dissatisfactions. Some may feel that this is "just another assessment" and thereby dismiss it. Others may argue quite rightly that the findings do not represent the true picture as they see it. But all this is as it should be.
>
> Whenever we see a picture of ourselves taken by someone else, we are anxious that justice be done to the "real me". If there is disappointment, it is because we know that there is so much more to the "real me" than has been momentarily captured by the photographer's click. So too with this

assessment: there are deeper and wider dimensions to the total subject than can be justly dealt with from such a hasty glance. Any ensuing dissatisfaction should not be simply taken as a measure of the assessment's failing but as testimony to that crucial vitality of the subject that eludes captivity on paper. We know that the true magic of the educating act is so much more than a simple, albeit justifiable, concern for improved resources, more sensitively stated objectives, better pre-service and in-service training for teachers, or improved bureaucratic efficiency. Rather it has to do with the whole meaning of a society's search for true maturity and responsible freedom through its young people.[12]

---

[12]Aoki, T., et al., (1977). *The British Columbia Social Studies Assessment: A Summary Report.* This was written for the project by David Smith, currently professor of education at University of Lethbridge, Canada.

Chapter 5

Toward Understanding
"Computer Application"[1] (1987/1999)

I have labelled my paper, "Toward Understanding 'Computer Application." The title appears simple, perhaps even simple-minded. Ten years ago, even 5 years ago, would not have thought such a title worthy of a talk, for then, I would have assumed that everyone understands what computer application is. Today, I am provoked to ask the question "How shall we understand 'computer application?'" I am provoked by what I see as partial blindness of high fashion in the world of curriculum wherein I see bandied about, with almost popular abandon, expressions linked to the computer without a deep understanding of what they are saying.

Within the faculty of education wherein I dwell, I have experienced in the last quarter century three waves of technological thrusts. We first witnessed the grand entrance of educational media instruments such as the overhead projector, the film projector, the slide projector, and the listening labs. The hold of this instrumental interest led to the bringing in of ed. media professors and to the creation of media resource centers, which now exist as mausoleums of curriculum packages and instructional hardware. The most atrocious instrumentalization of a school program within my knowledge during this wave was the "*Voix et Image*" French as a second language program (the slide tape program) my children underwent in junior high school. The second wave within our faculty was the TV thrust. Educational TV was looked on to deliver the message. Today, we see, in our faculty classrooms, platforms mounted in corners, empty holding places for TV monitors that no longer sit there, monitors that for some reason could not replace professors. They stand as museum pieces in the wake of unfulfilled hopes of dispensing education via TV. Today, the third wave is insistently upon us. The times are such that *Time* magazine is led to announce without qualm the computer as the man of the year. In our own faculty of education, a Computer Needs Committee proposes the creation of a teaching department in Computer Education. The Provincial Minister of Education doles out millions of dollars as matching grants to schools buying

[1]First printed in Aoki, Ted T. (1987). Toward Understanding "Computer Application." *Journal of Curriculum Theorizing, 7* (2). Reprinted here from Aoki, Ted T. (1999). Toward understanding "computer applications." In William F. Pinar (Ed.), *Contemporary Curriculum Discourses: Twenty Years of JCT* (pp. 168–176). New York: Peter Lang.

Apples, Commodores, IBMs, and the like. In schools, "computer literacy" curricula have the teachers in a semipanic. And, in the United States, the Commission on Educational Excellence announces "computer science" as a component of the New Basics.

Reflecting this ferment, the curriculum world picks up on in-language of alphabets—CL (computer literacy), CAI (computer-assisted instruction), CE (computer education), FUC (friendly use of computers), all implying *application* in schools of the *microcomputer*. Computer application is the focal curriculum third-wave activity.

In all this frenzy, the term *computer application* itself is assumed to be readily understood and stands naively unproblematic. I choose to question.

But what am I questioning when I ask what computer application essentially is? I wish to press for an understanding by entertaining two questions:

> How shall I understand computer technology?
> How shall I understand application?

Hopefully, these questionings will lead me to a deeper understanding of what we mean when we speak of computer application.

UNDERSTANDING THE COMPUTER AS TECHNOLOGY

Acknowledging the microcomputer as a high-tech product, I pose the question: "How shall we understand computer technology?" In dealing with the question, I lean heavily on Heidegger's well-known essay, "The Question Concerning Technology" (Heidegger, 1977).

We are aware of the commonplace answers to the question. The first says that the microcomputer is a high-tech tool. As a tool, it extends man's capabilities in rule governed behaviour. It is a sophisticated man-made means empowering man to achieve specified ends. Hence, as Heidegger would say, this means–ends embedded interpretation is an instrumental definition of computer technology.

That computer technology is a human activity is another commonplace interpretation, one that is related to the foregoing instrumentalist definition. According to Heidegger:

> To posit ends and procure and utilize the means to them is a human activity. The manufacture and utilization of equipment, tools and machines, the manufactured and used things themselves, and the needs and ends that they serve, all belong to what technology is. (Heidegger, 1977, pp. 4–5)

Computer technology as human activity is what Heidegger refers to as an anthropological definition of technology.

Today, so pervasive are the instrumental and anthropological understandings, according to which computer technology is both a means and human activity, that they can be referred to as the current conception of computer technology. This conception, rooted in man's interest in means, reflects his will to master, to control, and to manipulate.

Pointedly, Heidegger says that this current conception is uncannily correct but not yet true. What does Heidegger mean by this? According to him:

> the correct fixes upon something pertinent in whatever is under consideration. However . . . this fixing by no means needs to uncover the thing in question in its essence. Only at the point where such an uncovering happens does the true come to pass. For that reason the merely correct is not yet the true. (Heidegger, 1977, p. 6)

Accordingly, the instrumental or anthropological conception of computer technology fails to disclose its essence, although the way to the true is by way of the correct. And because the essence of computer technology is not computer technology as means, we must seek the true by understanding computer technology not merely as means but also as a way of revealing. As a mode of revealing, computer technology will come to presence where revealing and unconcealment can happen, that is, where truth can happen.

If, as Heidegger suggests, the essence of computer technology is not computer technology, we must let go of the seductive hold of the whatness of "computer technology" when we are inclined to ask, "What is computer technology?"

How, then, is this essence revealed? It is revealed as an enframing, the ordering of both man and nature that aims at mastery. This enframing reduces man and beings to a sort of "standing reserve," a stockpile of resources to be at hand and on call for utilitarian ends. Thus, the essence of computer technology reveals the real as "standing reserve," and man, in the midst of it, becomes nothing but the orderer of this "standing reserve." But by so becoming, man tends to be forgetful of his own essence, no longer able to encounter himself authentically. Hence, what endangers man where revealing as ordering holds sway is his inability to present other possibilities of revealing. In this, it is not computer technology that is dangerous; it is the essence of computer technology that is dangerous.

Hopefully, our exploration, albeit brief, allows us some sense of what it means to understand the computer as technology in its correctness and in its essence. We turn, now, to explore what computer application essentially means.

UNDERSTANDING COMPUTER APPLICATION

Understanding Computer Application as a Technical Reproduction

In the prevailing way of thought in Western culture, the very idea of making "application" problematic befuddles many. They ask, is not application simply application? What is there really to query about except how well application is accomplished?

Those who see application as nonproblematic are apt to be caught up within a theory/practice nexus wherein *practice* is thought to be *applied* theory, a secondary notion deriving its meaning from the primacy of *theory*. Within this scheme of things, the term *application* is seen as a linear activity, joining the primary with the secondary. Within this framework, computer application in a mathematics curriculum, for example, is understood as a linear and technical act of joining the computer with the mathematics education curriculum. Applying is to bring into the fold (*plicare*) or crucible of a concrete situation.

But when a phenomenon like computer technology is enfolded in a situation like a mathematics education curriculum, how should we understand application? The traditional view has been that we understand application as the problem of applying computer technology to a particular situation. Application here means adapting the generalized meaning of computer technology to the concrete situation to which it is speaking. Hence, applying is reproducing something general in a concrete situation. This reproductive view of application embraces the view that application is separated from understanding, and, in fact, follows it. It is an instrumental view.

Understanding Computer Application as a Hermeneutic Problem

For another view of application, I wish to turn to the work of Hans-Georg Gadamer, who in *Truth and Method* explored the hermeneutic problem of application. In it he recollects the early tradition of hermeneutics which, according to him, "the historical self-consciousness of . . . the scientific method completely forgot" (Gadamer, 1960/1975, p. 274). Gadamer confronts squarely the hermeneutic problem of application in the context of understanding, interpretation and application, which, to him, are all moments of the hermeneutic act.

He states that "understanding always involves something like the application of the text to be understood to the present situation of the interpreter" (Gadamer, 1960/1975, p. 274) and that application is an "integral or part of the hermeneutical act as are understanding and interpretation" (Gadamer, 1960/1975, p. 275).

Within this view the task of application in our context is not so much to reproduce computer technology, but to express what is said in a way that considers the situation of the dialogue between the language of computer technology and the language of the mathematics education situation. Application thus is an integral part of understanding arising from the tension between the language of computer technology on the one hand, and on the other, the language of the situation. Computer technology is not there to be understood historically, but to be made concretely valid through being interpreted. What is being said here is that computer technology, to be understood properly, must be understood at every moment, in every particular situation in a new and different way. Understood in this way, understanding is always application, and the meaning of computer technology and its application in a concrete curriculum situation are not two separate actions, but one process, one phenomenon, a fusion of horizons.

The question concerning application surfaces the hermeneutic problem of the relationship between the general and the particular. At the heart of this problem is the notion that the general must be understood in a different way in each new situation. Understanding is, then, a particular case of the application of something general to a particular situation.

We can now see that a serious shortcoming of application as reproduction is the way in which the engagement in reproductive activities can obscure the demands to understanding the situation itself makes. What the situation demands must not be ignored, for the general risks meaninglessness by remaining detached from the situation.

Ignoring the situational prevents the person in the situation from recognizing that application as technical reproduction is forgetful of the being in the situation. Mindfulness of the situation allows the person in the situation to recognize that application is a hermeneutic act, remembering that being in the situation is a human being in his becoming. This mindfulness allows the listening to what it is that a situation is asking. In a human situation, which is often a situation of action, it asks of us to see what is right. But in order to be able to see what is right in a situation, one must have one's own rightness; that is, one must have a right orientation within oneself. Not to be able to see what is right is not error or deception; it is blindness.

Within this view, application is not a subsequent nor a merely occasional part of understanding but codetermines it as a whole from the beginning. Here, application is not the mere relating of some pregiven generalized notion of the particular situation. In our case, then, to understand computer technology, one must not seek to disregard oneself and one's particular hermeneutic situation. One must relate computer technology to this situation, if one wants to understand it at all. And if, as it has been earlier given, the general must always be understood in a different way, understanding computer technology will necessarily have to be restated in each new subject area situation.

Interpretation is necessary where the meaning of "computer technology" in a situation cannot be immediately understood. It is necessary wherever we are not prepared to trust what a phenomenon immediately presents to us. Thus, there is a tension between the appearance that presents immediately to us and that which needs to be revealed in the situation.

Hopefully, the meaning of application is clearer. It is not the applying to a concrete situation of a given general that we first understand by itself, but it is the actual understanding of the general itself that a given situation constitutes for us. In this sense, understanding shows itself as a kind of an effect and knows itself as such (Gadamer, 1960/1975, p. 305).

For those of us confronted with the application of computer technology in curricular situations as the task at hand, understanding of application as a technical reproduction problem shows itself as instrumentally reductive, and inadequate. Understanding of application as a hermeneutic problem seems to overcome the shortcomings of the technical by vivifying the relationship between computer technology and the pedagogical situation.

CONCLUSION

Understanding "Understanding" as Essential to Understanding Computer Application

As I begin to talk about concluding, I need to point to my neglect in addressing, thus far, a key term in the title I have chosen for this paper. I have mentioned so far the "computer" and "application." I now feel inclined to say a word about "understanding," the third term of the title, for one of my agendas leading to the coming into being of this paper, such as it is, was to flirt with the question, "What does it mean to understand both epistemologically and ontologically?"

Within the frame of this questioning, I have been guided by a minding of how a coming to appearance of any phenomenon is also a concealing, of how in the very appearing of the phenomenon is concealed the essence of what is, and of how a way to understanding the essence of "what is" without violating the appearance of the phenomenon or the phenomenon itself is to allow the essence to reveal itself in the lived situation.

I feel that as a novice I have begun to come to understand that in my question "What is it?" to be caught in the "it" (i.e., being caught by the question "What is *it*?") is to surrender to the "it." But I am beginning to understand, too, that only an authentic surrender to "it" frees me from my own caughtness, allowing me to see before me even for a moment the "isness" of the it (i.e., being caught by a different question of "What *is* it?" is to dwell in an epistemological world; to be caught in the question "What *is* it?" is to dwell in an ontological world of the is and not yet). This appearance beckons me to move beyond mere flirtation.

My exploration of computer technology and application was situated to some extent in the question concerning understanding. I feel that my reaching for a fuller understanding of computer technology and application was simultaneously a reaching for a fuller understanding of understanding. In this reach for an understanding, it is well for me to remember Gadamer who, quoting Heidegger, said, "We live in an era, according to Heidegger, when science expands into a total of technocracy and thus brings on the cosmic night of the forgetfulness of being" (Gadamer, 1982, p. xvi).

A Lesson Learned From Carol Olson

To be allowed to sense concretely what computer technology essentially is, I wish to turn to Carol Olson, a doctoral student in our department, to reveal what she has taught me.

Carol has been for 12 years a child of hemodialysis technology. She and her three siblings had been sustained by a dialysis machine at the University of Alberta Hospital, a teaching-research medical institute.

She recently wrote of her experiences with technology: "We acknowledge our indebtedness to technology; we refuse to be enslaved by technology."

Deep understanding seems to come to those who come to know and feel the limits of their horizon, for it is at the point of limit that a phenomenon reveals itself through the dialectic of the being that is and the being yet to be.

I somehow feel that the children of technology, like Carol, are the first to see beyond technology for they know technology with their lifeblood. It is people like Carol who are able to say authentically, "We acknowledge our indebtedness to technology."

So she understands deeply, with her lifeblood she understands, that most people understand technology as "applied science," that is, as "means to ends," strictly an instrumental interpretation. She acknowledges that this interpretation is correct but not yet true. These understandings she has, for she understands that the truth of technology is in the essence of technology, as Heidegger insisted, in the revealing of things and people as only resources, as standing reserves that can be objectified, manipulated, and exploited. Demanding this of subjectivity, man within the world of technology becomes being-as-thing, no longer human.

So through her own experiences in the teaching-research ward of the hospital, Carol knows, for she writes: "Within technology, we become 'standing reserve'—units of labor" (as in concentration camps); "teaching material and interesting care" (as in the teaching-research hospital).

Carol struggles against such narrow determination of life. She knows the strong presence of the overwhelming power of consensus among medical personnel and the presencing of the machine itself. To become *empty* in such a situation is, according to her, to block our spiritual pain. One who is spiritually empty knows only physical pain, that pain that leads one to ask, "More Demerol, please."

So when she refuses to be enslaved by technology, it is her spiritual presence that speaks, calling for the right even in pain to live life humanly beyond the technological (Aoki, 1983).

What Carol teaches us is the significance of that which is beyond the technological in the technological.

REFERENCES

Aoki, T. (1983, June). Beyond the technological lifestyle: Re-shaping lived experiences in schools. An invited paper at Futurescan '83 Conference, Saskatoon. Saskatchewan. Sponsored by the government of Saskatchewan, the University of Saskatchewan, and the Saskatoon School Board.

Gadamer, H. (1975). *Truth and method*. New York: (Original work published 1960) Seabury Press.

Gadamer, H. (1982). *Reason in the Age of Science*, Cambridge MA: MIT Press.

Heidegger, M. (1977). The question concerning technology. In *The question concerning technology and other essays* (pp. 3–35). New York: Harper Textbooks.

Chapter 6

Teaching as Indwelling Between Two Curriculum Worlds[1] (1986/1991)

Even before day 1 of the term, our teacher, Miss O, walks into her assigned Grade 5 classroom. Because Miss O is already a teacher, by her mere presence in the classroom as teacher, she initiates a transformation of a sociocultural and physical environment into something different. Even before a pupil walks in, she silently asks: "Can I establish myself here as a teacher?" and the classroom's desks, walls, chalkboards, floor, books, and resources jointly reply, albeit wordlessly, by what they are. They respond to Miss O's intention and presence. And when the pupils arrive, things and pupils arrange themselves, as it were, around Miss O's intention. They become "suitable," "teachable," "harmful," "difficult," "hopeful," "damaging." The environment ceases to be environment, and in its place comes into being a pedagogic situation, a lived situation pregnantly alive in the presence of people.

Within this situation, Miss O soon finds that her pedagogic situation is a living in tensionality—a tensionality that emerges, in part, from indwelling in a zone between two curriculum worlds: the worlds of curriculum-as-plan and curriculum-as-lived-experiences.

CURRICULUM-AS-PLAN

The first of these, the curriculum-as-plan, usually has its origin outside the classroom, such as the Ministry of Education or the school district office. But whatever the source, it is penetratingly and insistently present in Miss O's classroom. This curriculum-as-plan is the curriculum that Miss O is asked to teach the Grade 5 pupils who are entrusted to her care.

---

[1] This invited article first appeared in *The B.C. Teacher*, 65 (3), April/May issue, 1986, a publication of the British Columbia Teachers' Association. The article was inspired through conversations with Miss "O," a Grade 5 teacher at Westwind School in Richmond, BC. Miss "O," now Mrs. S. Chamberlain, was principal of Maple Lane Elementary School, Richmond, B.C. at the time. This article is reprinted from: Aoki, Ted T. (1991). "Teaching as indwelling between two curriculum worlds." In Ted, T. Aoki (Ed.), *Inspiriting Curriculum and Pedagogy: Talks to Teachers* (pp. 7–10). Edmonton, Alberta: Department of Secondary Education, University of Alberta.

In curriculum-as-plan are the works of curriculum planners, usually selected teachers from the field, under the direction of some ministry official often designated as the curriculum director of a subject or a group of subjects. As works of people, inevitably, they are imbued with the planners' orientations to the world, which inevitably include their own interests and assumptions about ways of knowing and about how teachers and students are to be understood. These interests, assumptions, and approaches, usually implicit in the text of the curriculum-as-plan, frame a set of curriculum statements: statements of *intent* and *interest* (given in the language of "goals," "aims," and "objectives"), statements of what teachers and students should do (usually given in the language of *activities*), statements of official and recommended *resources* for teachers and students, and usually, implicitly, statements of *evaluation* (given, if at all, in the language of ends and means).

If the planners regard teachers as essentially installers of the curriculum, implementing assumes an instrumental flavour. It becomes a process, making of teacher–installers, in the fashion of plumbers who install their wares. Within this scheme of things, teachers are asked to be doers, and often they are asked to participate in implementation workshops on "how to do this and that." Teachers are "trained," and in becoming trained, they become effective in trained ways of "doing." At times, at such workshops, ignored are the teachers' own skills that emerge from reflection on their experiences of teaching, and, more seriously, there is forgetfulness that what matters deeply in the situated world of the classroom is how the teachers' "doings" flow from who they are, their beings. That is, there is a forgetfulness that teaching is fundamentally a mode of being.

CURRICULUM-AS-LIVED-EXPERIENCE

The other curriculum world is the situated world of curriculum-as-lived that Miss O and her pupils experience. For Miss O it is a world of face-to-face living with Andrew, with his mop of red hair, who struggles hard to learn to read; with Sara, whom Miss O can count on to tackle her language assignment with aplomb; with popular Margaret, who bubbles and who is quick to offer help to others and to welcome others' help; with Tom, a frequent daydreamer, who loves to allow his thoughts to roam beyond the windows of the classroom; and some 20 others in class, each living out a story of what it is to live school life as Grade 5s. Miss O's pedagogic situation is a world of students with proper names—like Andrew, Sara, Margaret, and Tom—who are, for Miss O, very human, unique beings. Miss O knows their uniqueness from having lived daily with them. And she knows that their uniqueness disappears into the shadow when they are spoken of in the prosaically abstract language of the external curriculum planners who are, in a sense, condemned to plan for faceless people, students shorn of their uniqueness, or for all teachers, who become generalized entities often defined in terms of performance roles.

On one side of Miss O's desk are marked class assignments ready to be returned with some appropriate remarks of approval or disapproval—some directed to the whole class, others directed to selected pupils. And on her desk, too, sits a half written memo eventually to be delivered to the office to make sure that a film ordered 3 months ago will be available for the first class in the afternoon.

Living within this swirl of busyness where her personal life and her life as teacher shade into each other, Miss O struggles with mundane curriculum questions: What shall I teach tomorrow? How shall I teach? These are quotidian questions of a teacher who knows, from having experienced life with her pupils, that there are immediate concerns she must address to keep the class alive and moving.

DWELLING IN THE ZONE OF BETWEEN

In asking these questions our teacher, Miss O, knows that an abstraction that has distanced but "accountable" relevance for her exists, a formalized curriculum, which has instituted legitimacy. She knows that, as an institutionalized teacher, she is accountable for what and how she teaches, but she also knows that the ministry's curriculum-as-plan assumes a fiction of sameness throughout the whole province, and that this fiction is possible only by wresting out the unique. This kind of curriculum knowing she understands, for she knows that generalized knowing is likely disembodied knowing that disavows the living presence of people, a knowing that appeals primarily to the intellectual. So she knows that this generalized knowing views a teacher like her as one of the thousands of certificated teachers in the province, and children like Andrew, Sara, Margaret and Tom merely as Grade 5 pupils, children without unique names, without freckles, without missing teeth, without their private hopes and dreams.

But she knows deeply from her caring for Tom, Andrew, Margaret, Sara and others that they are counting on her as their teacher, that they trust her to do what she must do as their teacher to lead them out into new possibilities, that is, to educate them. She knows that whenever and wherever she can, between her markings and the lesson plannings, she must listen and be attuned to the care that calls from the very living with her own Grade 5 pupils.

So in this way Miss O indwells between two horizons—the horizon of the curriculum-as-plan as she understands it and the horizon of the curriculum-as-lived experience with her pupils. Both of these call on Miss O and make their claims on her. She is asked to give a hearing to both simultaneously. This is the tensionality within which Miss O inevitably dwells as teacher. And she knows that inevitably the quality of life lived within the tensionality depends much on the quality of the pedagogic being that she *is*.

Miss O knows that it is possible to regard all tensions as being negative and that so regarded, tensions are "to be got rid of." But such a regard, Miss O feels, rests on a misunderstanding that comes from forgetting that to be alive is to live in tension; that, in fact, it is the tensionality that allows good thoughts and actions to arise when properly tensioned chords are struck, and that tensionless strings are not only unable to give voice to songs, but also unable to allow a song to be sung. Miss O understands that this tensionality in her pedagogical situation is a mode of being a teacher, a mode that could be oppressive and depressive, marked by despair and hopelessness, and at other times, challenging and stimulating, evoking hopefulness for venturing forth.

At times Miss O experiences discouragement by the little concern the public seem to display for teachers' well-being—zero salary increases, colleagues' layoffs, and problems of too few teachers resolved simply by increasing class size with little regard for the quality of the curriculum-as-lived experiences. Yet even in such greyness, her blood quickens when she encounters Andrew's look, Sara's rare call for help, Margaret's smile, Tom's exuberant forgetfulness, when light that comes from contacts with children glows anew.

And Miss O knows that some people understand teaching for the second year a Grade 5 class, as she is doing, is teaching the same class as last year, in the same room as last year, in the same school as last year, with the same number of pupils as last year. But Miss O knows that although technically people may talk that way, in teaching this year s Grade 5 class, the seemingly same lessons are not the same, nor are the Grade 5 pupils though they sit in the same desks, nor is Miss O herself for she knows she has changed from having reflected upon her teaching experiences last year with her Grade 5s. She no longer is the same teacher. Miss O knows that "implementing" the curriculum-as-plan in this year's lived situation calls for a fresh interpretive work constituted in the presence of very alive, new students.

Our Miss O knows that some of her colleagues who faithfully try to reproduce the curriculum-as-plan are not mindful of the lived situation, and that in so doing, they are unaware that they are making themselves into mere technical doers. In so making, they embrace merely a technical sense of excellence matched by a sense of compliance to the curriculum-as-plan, which exists outside of themselves. They tend to forget that gaining such fidelity may be at the expense of the attunement to the aliveness of the situation.

She knows, too, that some of her colleagues who are tuned into the pragmatics of what works in everyday school busyness—the curriculum grounded in the pragmatics of life as experienced in everyday life—may become skilful in managing the classes and resources from period to period—and survive well—keeping the students preoccupied and busy. But our teacher, Miss O, wonders whether a concern for total fidelity to an external curriculum-as-plan and a lack of simultaneous concern for the aliveness of the situation do not extinguish the understanding of teaching as "a leading out to new possibilities," to the "not yet." She wonders, too, if an overconcern for mere survival in the lived world of experience may not cause a teacher to forget to ask the question, Survive? What for?—the fundamental question of the meaning of what it is to live life, including school life. Miss O realizes the challenges and difficulties that living within the Zone of Between entails, but she learns, too, that, living as a teacher in tensionality is indeed living teaching as a mode of being that with all its ever-present risks, beckons the teacher to struggle to be true to what teaching essentially is. Miss O, our teacher, knows that indwelling in the zone between curriculum-as-plan and curriculum-as-lived experience is not so much a matter of overcoming the tensionality but more a matter of dwelling aright within it.

COMMENTS

In our effort to understand the world of curriculum, we joined our teacher Miss O in her indwelling between two curriculum worlds: the world of curriculum-as-plan and the world of curriculum-as-lived experiences. We have seen a glimmer of what it is like for a teacher to be situated in the Zone of Between. The calling into presence of two curriculum forms, even though often singularly understood—like the reading curriculum, the social studies curriculum, the music curriculum, and so on—allows us to understand more fully teachers' curriculum life. Some features of this life are sketched next.

1. We can see in Miss O's story, how truncated our understanding becomes when we see only a single curriculum-as-plan awaiting implementation. In this truncation, teachers are often technicized and transformed into mere technical implementers, and good teaching is reduced to mere technical effectiveness. The portrayal of Miss O's indwelling in the Zone of Between calls on us to surmount such reductionism to seek out a more fully human understanding of who a teacher is and what teaching truly is.

2. The portrayal of Miss O's indwelling shows us, too, how the appeal of commonplace logic can, at times, give credibility to simplistic and mechanical understandings of pedagogic life, which sees a linear movement *from* curriculum-as-plan *to* curriculum-as-lived experience. The story of her indwelling in the Zone of Between, by revealing the naiveté of the linear understanding with its linear logic, calls on us to take heed of understanding indwelling as a dialectic between complementaries with a logic of its own. For many of us, grounded in linear logic, such an understanding may seem to

be a totally new way of understanding. Hence, many of us may need to open ourselves to this fundamental way in which we all experience life.

3. We also can see in Miss O's story how indwelling dialectically is a living in tensionality, a mode of being that knows not only that living school life means living simultaneously with limitations and with openness, but also that this openness harbours within it risks and possibilities as we quest for a change from the is to the not yet. This tensionality calls on us as pedagogues to make time for meaningful striving and struggling, time for letting things be, time for question, time for singing, time for crying, time for anger, time for praying and hoping. Within this tensionality, guided by a sense of the pedagogic good, we are called on as teachers to be alert to the possibilities of our pedagogic touch, pedagogic tact, pedagogic attunement—those subtle features about being teachers that we know, but are not yet in our lexicon, for we have tended to be seduced by the seemingly lofty and prosaic talk in the language of conceptual abstractions. We must recognize the flight from the meaningful and turn back again to an understanding of our own being as teachers. It is here, I feel, that teachers can contribute to fresh curriculum understandings.

4. In Miss O's indwelling in the Zone of Between we see the teacher's dwelling place as a sanctified clearing where the teacher and students gather—somewhat like the place before the hearth at home—an extraordinarily unique and precious place, a hopeful place, a trustful place, a careful place—essentially a human place dedicated to ventures devoted to a leading out, an authentic "e(out)/ducere(lead)," from the "is" to new possibilities yet unknown.

5. We are beginning to hear that in Canada, some architects—developers of lived space who have claimed disciplined understanding of human space, guided by their zeal for high technology—have constructed buildings (places-to-experience-life) that now are called sick buildings. We hear that the architects of these buildings were not attuned to the fundamental meaning of space-as-lived-experience. What does this say to curriculum architects?

For curriculum planners who understand the nuances of the indwelling of teachers in the Zone of Between, the challenge seems clear. If, as many of us believe, the quality of curriculum-as-lived experiences is the heart and core as to why we exist as teachers, principals, superintendents, curriculum developers, curriculum consultants, and teacher educators, curriculum planning should have as its central interest a way of contributing to the aliveness of school life as lived by teachers and students. Hence, what authorizes curriculum developers to be curriculum developers is not only their expertness in doing tasks of curriculum development, but more so a deeply conscious sensitivity to what it means to have a developer's touch, a developer's tact, a developer's attunement that acknowledges in some deep sense the uniqueness of every teaching situation. Such a sensitivity calls for humility without which they will not be able to minister to the calling of teachers who are themselves dedicated to searching out a deep sense of what it means to educate and to be educated. To raise curriculum planning from being mired in a technical view is a major challenge to curriculum developers of this day.

Chapter 7

Layered Understandings of Orientations in Social Studies Program Evaluation[1] (1991)

Since the mid-1960s, about the time of the publication of Scriven's *Perspectives of Curriculum Evaluation* (1976), the field of evaluation in education has begun to come into its own. In program evaluation in particular, significant advances have been made, led by scholars such as Eisner (1979), Stake (Stake & Easley, 1978), MacDonald and Walker (1974), House (1973), Apple (1974), Hamilton (Hamilton, Jenkins, King, MacDonald, & Parlett (1977), and Patton (1975). Within this growing field, it has become increasingly challenging for curriculum evaluators not only to become acquainted with the burgeoning literature, but also to be insightful in trying to understand the world-views from which approaches to evaluation have been propounded. Social studies evaluators have an added challenge for they find themselves in the midst of multiplicities: multiple understandings of evaluation approaches and multiple interpretations of social studies. The intent in this chapter is not to provide a compendium of evaluation models or of social studies evaluation reports, or a history of evaluation approaches in social studies education, but to begin to address the social studies evaluators' challenge by attempting to disclose orientations toward evaluation.

More than a decade ago in a probing article, "Research on Teaching Social Studies," Shaver and Larkins (1973), concerned with the confining nature of traditional approaches to research in social studies including evaluation research, called for an opening up of the basic research frame. In the field of evaluation practice in social studies, in spite of the numerous evaluation activities in social studies at the local, state/provincial, and national levels, the call of Shaver and Larkins seems to have gone largely unheeded. It is only within the last decade that those in the field of social studies curriculum evaluation have begun to put to serious questioning the notion of "evaluation" itself.

Social studies evaluators, like other researchers, have been prone to approach their evaluation tasks with their favorite evaluation models, approaches, and techniques. In education, the prevailing research ethos is technological. Evaluation is a part of this ethos, and evaluators have approached

---

[1] Reprinted from Aoki, Ted T. (1991). Layered understandings of orientations in social studies program evaluation. In James P. Shaver (Ed.), *Handbook of Research on Social Studies Teaching and Learning: A project of the National Council for the Social Studies* (pp. 98–105). New York: Macmillan.

their tasks from that perspective. In fact, the prominent use of "assessment" in its strict instrumental sense within the language of evaluation speaks of the epistemological tradition to which many evaluators hold allegiance.

In itself there is little reason to be concerned about the dominance of any single mode of evaluation. What is of concern is that the dominance may lead evaluators to forget that the form of evaluation should be appropriate to the phenomenon to be evaluated and that the evaluation approach should be responsive to the interests to be served by the evaluation. In accord with what Kaplan (1964) has termed "the law of the instrument" (p. 28), in educational research the availability of a research tool often determines the nature of the research done and how research is understood; so, too, in evaluation, the evaluation methods and instruments available may determine the nature of the evaluation done and how evaluation is understood. We need to be alert to the law of the instrument in social studies evaluation.

In recent years, some have questioned the tendency of educators to reduce educational evaluation to the paradigm of scientific research. Much of this questioning has come from Continental European scholars who did not succumb, as did many North American scholars, to the persuasions of logical positivism expounded by members of the Vienna Circle. Among these is Jurgen Habermas (1972), a German scholar affiliated with the Frankfurt School. He, together with others such as Horkheimer and Adorno (1972) and Marcuse (1968), decried what they saw as a serious crisis in Western intellectualism because of the domination of instrumental reasoning based on scientism and technology. Habermas appealed to philosophical anthropology, a cultural study of philosophic orientations, to reveal knowledge—constitutive human interests embedded in basically different orientations. His list's threefold orientations (the empirical-analytic, the critical-reflective, and the situational-interpretive) have inspired many human scientists in their endeavours to reexamine not only the issue of research frameworks noted by Shaver and Larkins (1973), but also the issue of evaluation frameworks.

In this chapter, which leans heavily on Habermas, the empirical-analytic orientation has been recast as an *ends–means* model, the critical reflective orientation has been retained under the name of *praxis,* and the situational interpretive-orientation has been unfolded into *emic* and *critical-hermeneutic* evaluation orientations. Moreover, rather than merely suggest a plurality of alternative orientations, the orientations have been gathered, admittedly loosely, into layers that suggest some distinction between the world of concretely lived experience and the formulations of evaluation that are abstractions of and somewhat distant from lived experience.

As might be expected, the world of lived experience is considered as the ground for the four evaluation orientations, layered as follows:

1. Ends–means evaluation orientation.

2.   Praxical evaluation orientation.
3.   Emic evaluation orientation.
4.   Critical-hermeneutic evaluation orientation.

Each of these evaluation orientations is discussed briefly. To provide some contact with the practical world of evaluation, illustrations are provided from the province-wide British Columbia Social Studies Assessment of which the author was team director (Aoki, Langford, Williams, & Wilson, 1977a, 1977b).

Our experiences in evaluating British Columbia social studies, guided by Habermas's interpretation of multiple interests, provide an exemplar of how evaluation can be viewed from multiple perspectives. From the outset as we ventured into various centers of British Columbia seeking out and trying to make sense of social studies interests expressed by teachers, students, parents, school trustees, administrators, and professors of social studies education, we seriously asked ourselves: "What evaluation frameworks and approaches should we employ in evaluating the phenomenon called *social studies* in British Columbia?"

We took a cue from what Beittel (1973, p. 6) called appropriately the "Rashomon effect," a notion from an acclaimed film by Kurosawa in which he disclosed the same event from several perspectives. Simultaneously, we were mindful of the possibility of inadvertently reducing our evaluation to the dominant ends–means orientation. As early as in the mid-1970s, Patton (1975) had pointed out this concern in the following way:

> The very dominance of the scientific method in evaluation research appears to have cut off the great majority of practitioners from serious consideration of any alternative research paradigm. The label "research" has come to mean the equivalent of employing the Scientific Method—of working within the dominant paradigm. (p. 6)

In the following sections, the four evaluation orientations, which are summarized in Table 7.1, are illuminated.

ENDS–MEANS EVALUATION ORIENTATION

The interests of evaluators acting within the ends–means orientation are reflected in the evaluation questions they entertain. The following questions illustrate these interests:

1.   How effective and efficient are the means used in achieving the curricular goals and objectives?

2. What is the degree of congruency between and among intended outcomes, the content of the instructional materials, and the teaching approaches specified?

3. How good is Curriculum A compared with Curriculum B in achieving given ends?

4. Of given curricula, which one is the most cost-effective and time-efficient?

5. What valid generalizations can be made for all schools in a district?

These ends–means interests reflect an orientation to evaluation that can be characterized as technical or instrumental. As such, they reflect the dominant evaluation approach in use, going hand in hand with the technically oriented mainstream curriculum development/evaluation rationale, known popularly as the Tyler Rationale. We know it by Tyler's (1949) sequentially arranged four-step formulation. The steps are as follows:

1. What educational purposes should the school seek to attain?

2. How can learning experiences be selected that are likely to be useful in attaining these objectives?

3. How can learning experiences be organized for effective instruction?

4. How can the effectiveness of learning experiences be *evaluated*?

The ends–means evaluation orientation has for the pragmatically oriented a commonsensical ring that carries with it the validity of popular support. Further, its congruency with the mainstream social theory idioms of basically instrumental reason, such as behaviourism, systems analysis, and structural functionalism—from which educators have borrowed heavily—lends ends–means evaluation a credibility that assumes the status of consensual validity. Such legitimated authenticity has led many evaluators to regard this evaluation orientation reductively as *the* orientation.

But what does this orientation imply in terms of interests and assumptions usually held tacitly? Underneath the avowed interest in efficiency, effectiveness, predictability, and certainty, as reflected in the preceding list of interests, is a more deeply rooted interest—that of *control*. The orientation is immersed in a manipulative ethos that leads evaluators of this orientation to value such evaluation questions as, "How well have the ends been achieved? Which is a better program, Curriculum A or Curriculum B?"

TABLE 7.1

A Summary of Layered Understandings of Evaluation Orientations

Evaluation Orientation	Evaluation Interests	World of Knowing	Mode or Evaluation
Ends–means	Control as reflected in values of efficiency, effectiveness, certainty, and predictability. Fidelity between ends and means.	Finite world of facts, information, concepts, generalizations, laws, and theories. Objectives are often stated in terms of knowledge, skills, and attitudes. Possibility of progress is key belief.	Measurement of discrepancy between ends and means. Goal-based, criterion-referenced, cost-benefit assessment of achievement.
Praxical	Emancipatory action that improves human condition. Quality of reflection and action.	Critical knowing in the sense of understanding hidden assumptions, perspectives, motives, rationalizations, and ideologies. Critical knowing coupled with action.	Uncovering of ideology underlying knowledge and action.
Emic	Quality of everyday cultural life. Tacit rules people live by in daily life.	Thick, descriptive knowledge of lived cultural layer. Social life understood as socially constructed rules of everyday living	Ethnographic case studies approach. Ethnomethodological approach.

TABLE 7.1 (*continued*)

Critical-hermeneutic	Disclosure of existential meanings in lived experience. Quality of human beingness	A world of insights (rather than generalizations) into unique human situations. Correctly lived world as earth dwellers. Infinite world of being.	Phenomenological-Hermeneutic approach. Critical quest for what it means to be human.

Within this framework, the form of knowledge that is prized is empirical data; the harder and the more objective the data, the better. Data are seen as brute facts. In scientific terms, the form of knowledge confers nomological status, with empirical validation demanded and levels of generalizability sought. Knowledge is assumed to be objective, carrying with it the dignity of value-free neutrality

Evaluators who subscribe to the ends–means view are technologically oriented, primarily interested in seeing how well the system is able to control its own components in struggling to achieve system goals. These evaluators seek efficient tools and instruments such as tests and questionnaires, and seek rigor by bringing to bear the expertise of psychometricians and statisticians. They tend to resort to measurable quantitative data subjected to sophisticated statistical analyses.

In our British Columbia Social Studies Assessment, we administered achievement tests to randomly selected classes in Grades 4, 8, and 12 throughout the province and we sent questionnaires to randomly selected teachers in order to seek the teachers' assessment of instructional resources. In our evaluation project, the largest portion of the evaluation grant budget was allocated to this phase, indicating how we, ourselves, were held in the sway of this orientation.

In summary, the ends–means evaluation mode is framed within the framework of the following interests, world of knowing, and mode of evaluation.

> *Interests in:* The ethos of control as reflected in the values of efficiency, effectiveness, certainty, and predictability. Fidelity to given ends is a major concern.

> *World of knowing:* Assumed is a finite world of nomological knowing. Understanding is in terms of facts, generalizations,

concepts, laws, and theories.   Objectives are often given in terms of knowledge, skills, and attitudes

Mode of evaluation: Ends–means evaluation that is achievement-oriented, goal-based, criterion-referenced, and cost-benefit-oriented.

PRAXICAL EVALUATION ORIENTATION

Evaluators thinking and acting within the praxical mode express their interests by committing themselves to a set of evaluation concerns that differ markedly from those of technically oriented evaluators. The following questions illustrate the concerns of praxical evaluators:

1. What is the orientation underlying Curriculum X in terms of root interests, root assumptions, and root approaches?
2. What is the implicit view of the student or the teacher held by the curriculum planner?
3. At the most basic level, whose interests does Curriculum X serve?
4. What are the fundamental metaphors that guide the curriculum developer, curriculum implementer, or curriculum evaluator?
5. What is the basic bias of the publisher, author, or developed or prescribed or recommended resource materials?
6. What is the world view underlying the curriculum?

These evaluation interests reflect an orientation to evaluation that is rooted in neoMarxian critical social theory.   In this approach to evaluation, the evaluator attempts to bring into fuller view the underlying elements of programs that are typically taken for granted and, therefore, hidden from view. Implied within any curriculum or evaluation orientation are root metaphors, deep-seated human interests, assumptions about humans, worldviews, and knowledge, as well as stances that people take in approaching self or world.   Praxical evaluators are interested in making these visible. But they do not stop there.

In ends–means evaluation the task is seen within the framework of instrumental or technical action; in praxical evaluation, it is seen within the dialectical framework of practical action and critical reflection, what Paulo Freire (1968) referred to as *praxis*. In critical reflection, the actor through the reflective process discovers and makes explicit tacit and hidden assumptions and intentions.   Such reflective activity is guided by an interest in revealing the ideological condition that makes knowing possible, or in revealing the underlying human and social conditions that distort human existence, distortions that tend to produce alienation.   Thus, praxical evaluators attempt to determine the regularities of human and social action that express ideologically frozen relations of dependence that can be transformed. Schaull (1968) captured aptly this praxical orientation in the following way:

> There is no such thing as *neutral* educational process. Education either functions as an instrument, which is used to facilitate the integration of the younger generation into the logic of the present system and bring about conformity to it, *or* it becomes "the practice of freedom," the means by which men and women deal critically and creatively with reality and discover how to participate in the transformation of their world. (p. 15)

Thus, a praxically oriented evaluator's self may become apart of the object of the evaluation research. The evaluator, in becoming involved with his or her subjects, enters into their world and attempts to engage them mutually in reflective activity. The evaluator questions the subjects and self, and encourages subjects to question him or her and themselves. Reflection by self and the participants allows new questions to emerge from the situation that, in turn, lead to further reflective activity. Reflection, however, is oriented not only toward making conscious the unconscious by discovering underlying interests, assumptions, and intentions, but also toward action guided by the newly gained conscious and critical knowledge. Hence, in the ongoing dialectical and transformative process, both evaluator and subjects become participants in an open dialogue.

Reflection in the foregoing sense is not the kind of activity in which school people typically engage in their ongoing daily lives. In their everyday existence, people deal with their concerns in routine ways guided by the commonplace recipes that sustain them. What is missing is a conscious effort to examine critically the assumptions and intentions underlying their practical thoughts and acts. Evaluators may be reflective but not necessarily critically reflective. Critical reflection leads to an understanding of what is beyond the actor's ordinary view by making the familiar unfamiliar, by making the invisible visible. Such reflective activity allows liberation from the unconsciously held assumptions and intentions that lie buried and hidden. For example, at the personal level the content of reflection may be the rationalization an actor uses to hide underlying motives for his or her actions. At the societal level, the content reflected on may be the ideology used to support social practices and policies that render obscure society's manipulative ethos and the underlying interests.

But more than that, such critical reflection is intended to bring about the reorientation, through transformative action, of the assumptions and intentions on which reflection and action rest. The praxical orientation to evaluation, then, with its guiding interest of liberating people from hidden interests and approaches, promotes a theory of individuals and society that is grounded in the moral attitude of emancipation.

Within the British Columbia Social Studies Assessment, praxical evaluation was included under the innocuous title "An Interpretation of Intents of the Elementary and Secondary Curriculum Guides." In that part of the project we examined the official text of the social studies curriculum-as-plan. The concluding statement of the praxical analysis gives a sense of the flavour of this evaluation:

> The British Columbia Social Studies program approaches the study of man-in-his world from three different perspectives: scientific, situational and critically reflective knowing. Through each of these, students are exposed to various interpretations of how the social world has been constructed. The program, however, does not provide a balance between these perspectives: rather, it emphasizes scientific knowledge. Through such an emphasis teachers and students are made dependent on one particular way of viewing the social world. Such dependence limits the possibilities which the participants have available for exploring their social environment. The extent to which the perspectives influence classroom presentations (passive vs. active, non-committal vs. committal) stresses the importance of providing a balance of knowledge perspectives in the program. (Aoki & Harrison, 1977, p. 62)

We tried to bring the official B.C. Social Studies Program into fuller view by revealing the tacitly held assumptions and intentions. Following the comment just given, we added as a recommendation to the Ministry of Education the following:

> To aid teachers in moving towards consideration of perspectives, it is recommended that a full description of the perspectives incorporated into the British Columbia Social Studies program be carefully described in the Curriculum Guides. Students and teachers are entitled to a full explanation of the curriculum developers' knowing stance. The curriculum developers' perspective toward the social world should not, in other words, be hidden from users of the curriculum. (Aoki & Harrison, 1977, p. 62)

The praxical evaluation orientation can be summarized as follows:

Interests in: Emancipation from hidden assumptions of underlying human conditions that distort human life. Quality of reflection/action.

World of knowing: Critical knowing in the sense of understanding hidden assumptions, perspectives, motives, rationalizations, and ideologies.   To explain within critical knowing is to trace down and bring into fuller view the underlying ideology.   As praxis, this critical knowing is coupled with action.

Mode of evaluation: Praxical evaluation involves (a) discovering through critical reflection the underlying human conditions, assumptions, and intentions and (b) acting on self and world to improve the human condition or to transform the underlying assumptions and intentions.

EMIC EVALUATION ORIENTATION

In contrast to the technical interests of evaluators in the ends–means approach to evaluations and the emancipatory interests of those in the praxical approach, the central interest of emic evaluators is in seeking understanding of the situated cultural activities, values, and beliefs of participants in social studies. (*Emic* is an anthropological term referring to the insiders' subjective understanding.) Hence, these evaluators are guided by interests embedded in such questions as the following:

1.   How can we understand the quality of this social studies class as a microculture of the classroom?

2.   How do various groups such as teachers, students, parents, and administrators view Curriculum X?   How worthy are these views?

3.   In what ways do various groups approve or disapprove the school's social studies program?

4.   How do the various groups view Curriculum X in terms of relevance? How worthy are these views?

5.   How do the various groups understand the strengths and weaknesses of the social studies program?

6. What are the group-constructed rules for the social studies activities in this class?

The interests expressed in these questions reflect an approach to evaluation in which evaluators show interest in the ethnocultural patterns of life in the social studies situation. Hence, many of these evaluators have a kinship with cultural anthropologists or sociologists whose interest is in the social construction of reality. Characteristically, rather than be strictly objective observers, these evaluators attempt to place themselves in situ in order to be near the culture or society they wish to understand, while at the same time attempting to maintain a distance that will enable them to observe the construct of interest. Case studies are frequent within this orientation.

Related to the work of ethnographers is the work of ethnomethodologists, who attempt to understand group life as a game consisting of tacitly acknowledged socially constructed rules. They also place themselves in situ. Tactically, they often introduce a break in the pattern of living and observe how members of a group respond to the break, attending to the way they reconstitute their way of life. In this reconstitution, the ethno-methodologically oriented evaluator seeks out the socially constructed rules of the game that is life.

In the British Columbia Social Studies Assessment, we attempted to be sensitive to the etic/emic (outsider/insider) perspectives distinguished by cultural anthropologists. (The etic/emic perspective in this study was a contribution of Donald C. Wilson, who, in his doctoral study [1976], explored epistemological issues underlying etic and emic approaches to research and evaluation.) In our emic effort, we strove to capture aspects of the subjective world of teachers, students, parents, and administrators as they lived in their social studies situations in school. In rendering emic views of their lives, we came to recognize a way of knowing that countered the standardized way in which people recognize correctness and incorrectness based on the strict outsiders' objective format that dominates the view of knowing stressed in ends–means evaluation.

A flavour of our effort in emic evaluation is offered in the following excerpt from a summary of the "Interpretive Studies of Selected School Situations" subreport of the B.C. Social Studies Assessment (Aoki et al., 1977b). It is:

> an account of five in-depth studies in school situations . . . .
> Each study is based on a series of school visits and interviews with educators and students. This personal contact provides evaluative information consisting of the thoughts and experiences individuals have of learning and teaching Social Studies in particular situations. Information concerned with the everyday activities of students and teachers enriches and

therefore complements the generalizations arising from information obtained from the paper-and-pencil instruments. Hence, each study outlines the setting of the situation and describes the nature of the Social Studies programs, and interprets the meaning or significance which educators and students ascribe to them. Conclusions are made in terms of the schools visited in each particular situation and not with reference to all schools in British Columbia. . . .

In most cases, paper/pencil instruments collect data according to certain reporting categories identified as important prior to collection procedures. Understanding, therefore, becomes expressed in terms of relational knowledge that can become generalizable to other situations. . . . Based on the premise that educators and students interpret social studies according to their experiences within their social context, the [interpretive] studies not only describe particular situations according to what was observed by evaluators and stated by teachers and students, but also interpret those descriptions with reference to frameworks that acknowledge the process of instruction and the "insiders'" perspective. (p. 26)

A framework, "used to interpret how teachers view a program" is described next:

1. *Intents:* These are expressions of desired goals or possibilities for a program. They may be manifestations of written instructional objectives or implicit desires of individuals.

2. *Resources:* These are resource materials that display a particular means with which students and teachers interact in an instructional setting. A resource might be a picture, a page in a textbook, a map, or a film that displays, some object of the environment.

3. *Activities:* This component of a program refers to student and teacher activities defined in the context of intents and resources. Class activities may either be predefined by teachers or result from interactions of students and teachers. Activities that are often a part of a social studies program as lectures, class discussions, field studies, or simulations.

These components of a program do not exist in isolation but are closely interrelated. For example, the intent a teacher has for teaching social studies will also be manifested in his or her view of resources and desired class activities. Again, the concern for certain kinds of resources and class activities will reflect certain interests one has for teaching social studies. It is this "total picture" of how teachers interpret a program in a particular context that becomes the focus of the interpretation (Aoki et al., 1977b, p. 27).

In approaching emic evaluation with a preset framework, we were mindful of the risk of imposition of external categories and attempted to be open to the insiders' interpretations of our categories and sensitive as well to their own categories.

The emic evaluation orientation can be summarized as follows:

Interest in: The quality of everyday cultural and social life or of the tacit rules people live by in their daily lives.

World of knowing: Thick descriptive knowledge of a cultural layer; understanding of socially constructed rules governing everyday living.

Mode of evaluation: In situ evaluation that embodies ethnographic and/or ethno-methodological approaches.

CRITICAL-HERMENEUTIC EVALUATION ORIENTATION

Within the critical-hermeneutic orientation, the evaluators' interest is directed not so much to the level of attainment of knowledge, skills, or attitudes; nor to the merit of ideological interests, assumptions, and approaches; nor to in situ portrayals that constitute the cultural lives of people. Rather, the interest is in seeking out the quality of ontological meanings in the lived experiences of students, teachers, administrators, and parents. The interests in the nature and quality of the beingness of human beings are reflected in questions such as the following:

1. What is it like being a teacher or student of social studies in this school?
2. What is it like to experience social studies classes in this school?

3. What is the quality of the lived experiences of teachers and students in social studies?

4.   What *is* social studies? (Not, *what* is social studies?)

5.   In what ways do teachers and taught belong together pedagogically?

Within this orientation, social studies is understood not so much in terms of studies *about*, cast within the realm of positivistic objectivity, somewhat distanced from the lives of teachers and students, but in terms of life as humanly lived in social studies classes. Labels such as *social living* or *social education* that have appeared in the social studies lexicon in the past can be seen as early efforts to break out of the reductive objectivity from which social studies is understood as studies *about*. Hence, evaluators within this orientation try to transcend evaluation modes that are oriented to objectivity.

Because the guiding interests of critical-hermeneutic evaluation are insights into human experiences as humanly lived, the evaluators direct their efforts toward clarifying, authenticating, and bringing into human awareness the meaning structures of lived experiences of people in the situation. Thus, the form of knowledge sought by the evaluator within this orientation is not nomological statements, but rather the structures of existential meaning as people meaningfully experience and appropriate the natural and social world. Hence, a critical-hermeneutic evaluator comes to "know" the evaluated reality in a different form and in a different way than the knowledge gained by, for instance, an ends–means evaluator.

In seeking out understandings that are not accessible from an ends–means evaluation orientation, those in the critical-hermeneutic orientation attempt to provide explanations of a different kind. Although *explaining* within the ends–means orientation means giving causal, functional, or hypothetico-deductive statements, within the critical-hermeneutic orientation *explaining* requires the striking of resonance among people in dialogue situations by clarifying motives, authentic experiences, and common meanings. The evaluator, hence, cannot stand aloof as an observer, as is done in the ends–means evaluation and the in situ participation of emic evaluation, but must enter deeply into intersubjective conversation with the people in the evaluation situation.

Conversation that is hermeneutic moves beyond the chitchat that so often remains at the informational level as simply exchanges of messages, not requiring true human presence. Exchanges of computerized messages based on bits and bytes characterize our Age of Technology and the Age of Information. Acknowledgment of the informational structure of our age and attempts to humanize the age can be seen in the efforts toward "user-friendly" techniques. Hermeneutic conversation is a dialectic of questions and answers that in their interpretive turnings are attempts to move to deeper ontological realms of meanings. Successful hermeneutic conversations lead conversationalists, human beings that they are, toward questions concerning who they are. In such conversations existential themes often emerge, and the questionings and the answering are guided by these emerging themes. Critical hermeneutics is an activity that deepens existential themes, as the source of our human beingness is sought in the realms of the finite and infinite.

The enterprise for critical hermeneutic evaluators is often linguistic. That is, for them language is not merely a tool of communication in which thoughts are put into words, nor is it merely a bearer of representational knowledge. Language is a way that humans live humanly in this world. We are reminded of Heidegger (1971), who called language a House of Being. The challenge to evaluators of this persuasion is to disclose life as lived in and through language, thereby disclosing in some way what it means to be human. These evaluators, therefore, are called on to work beyond the prosaic language of representation and to dwell in a language world of metaphors. Hence, they entertain questions such as, "What is it *like to be* a teacher or student in social studies classes?"

Within the British Columbia Social Studies Assessment, a modest attempt was made to embody the critical-hermeneutic evaluation orientation. We were guided by an understanding of existential realms of being as follows:

> *Passive realm of being:* From this stance a person does not view self as the one who lives out the expectancies of others. Values and meanings are perceived as given in the situations in which one exists.

> *Immediate realm of being:* Within this attunement to the world, a person tends to be concerned only about pleasurable experiences to fight off boredom. It is the present that is of paramount importance, and little responsibility is taken for choices made.

> *Responsible realm of being:* Here, decisiveness and self-determination are key qualities. Such a person makes choices and assumes full responsibility for them in terms of other people's welfare. Such a person knows that others are affected by his or her decisions.

> *Immanent realm of being:* Living in this realm, a person experiences the self truly. Experiences in life are vivid. Choices are increasingly based on trusting personal understandings and on a sense of the spiritual dimensions of living. Authentic being with others is the person's prime concern. (Adapted from Aoki et al. [1977b, pp. 27–28]. This segment of the report was contributed by Peter Rothe [1979],

who made existential phenomenology the core of his doctoral
study. An evaluation study incorporating critical hermeneutics
was reported by Stephen W. Y. Bath [1988]. He was
concerned with the immanence of ethical being-with-others in
evaluation situations.)

The following brief extract from the B. C. Social Studies Assessment
Report (Aoki et al., 1977a) provides a flavour of what we meant by realms of
being:

> An interpretation of grade 4 responses indicates a wide range
> of meanings Social Studies has to pupils. Their varied
> responses suggest a "shift" in meanings when discussing
> Social Studies subject matter . . . and classroom activities
> indicating differing concerns about different aspects of a
> social studies class, usually presupposed or overlooked by
> educators. For example, when pupils were asked questions
> concerning what social studies topics they would like to spend
> more time studying their answers suggested an immediate area
> of being. Their replies focus on momentary enjoyment
> personal and appealing aesthetics. . . .
>
> Uncommitted reasons of ephemeral interest and boredom
> indicating classroom meanings within the Immediate area
> were also evident when pupils responded to the questions: "Of
> all the topics you have studied, what topics would you *not* like
> to spend more time studying?" "Why did you select this
> topic?" . . .
>
> Reasons constituting meanings within the Responsible
> rather than Immediate area of being were prevalent when the
> grade 4 pupils interviewed were asked what classroom
> activities they prefer to participate in when doing Social
> Studies. Their responses indicate committed and responsible
> efforts to acquire maximum learning. It seems that the grade 4
> pupils interviewed gave responsible meanings to
> circumstances involving relevant areas. . . of classroom
> activities but uncommitted ephemeral responses indicating
> immediate meanings when answering . . . questions pertaining
> to curricular subject matter. (pp. 76-78)

Even the brief extract just given suggests that pupils interpret social studies
according to their experiences within their social contexts. Individuals give
meanings to social studies based on their daily life situations, comprised of
activities with people, leanings, social tasks, physical objects, and

circumstances. For evaluators interested in the quality of life lived in social studies, inclusion of the critical-hermeneutic mode is a desirable possibility.

The critical hermeneutic evaluation framework can be summarized in terms of its interests, world of knowing, and mode of evaluation as follows:

Interest in: Disclosure of existential meanings in lived experiences.

World of knowing: A world of insights (rather than generalizations) in each unique, personal situation as it is lived concretely. It is an open world, infinite in its layers of beingness.

Mode of evaluation: A critical quest for what it means to be human. Often called existential inquiry or phenomenological hermeneutics.

A CONCLUDING NOTE

A modest attempt has been made in this chapter to trace out four evaluation orientations, reflecting the polysemic nature of both social studies and evaluation. The discussion of the orientations is not meant to exhaust all possibilities. What it does point to is the possibility of openness of discourses in social studies program evaluation.

At the outset, the contribution of Continental European scholarship in the human sciences, notably that of Jurgen Habermas, was acknowledged. Social studies educators and evaluators should open themselves to discussions in the human sciences that have provided us with disciplines such as critical social theory, phenomenology, sociology of knowledge, and hermeneutics. More recently, led by scholars such as Foucault (1972), Derrida (1978), Lyotard (1984), and Deleuze and Guattari (1987), there have been new stirrings with scholarship in postmodernism, poststructuralism, and deconstructionism that challenge the centrality of the metaphysical grounds of western tradition. We live in a turbulent and exciting time. Implications for social studies and evaluation abound.

It has been said that educators' understanding of their task as educators is most clearly demonstrated by their favoured mode of evaluation. Conversely, evaluators' understanding of what evaluation is discloses their understanding of what it means to be an educator and what it means to be educated. At stake is what our children and adolescents experience in the name of social studies education. Hence, there is, at this time, a deep challenge confronting social studies evaluators.

At the end-point of the British Columbia Social Studies Assessment, we asked ourselves this question: "Has the job of evaluation been done?" In response, we made the following admission, which is a fitting conclusion to this chapter:

> Whenever we see a picture of ourselves taken by someone else we are anxious that justice be done to the "real me." If there is disappointment, it is because we know that there is so much more to the real me than has been momentarily captured by the photographers click. So too with this assessment: there are deeper and wider dimensions to the total subject than can be justly dealt with from such a hasty glance. Any ensuing dissatisfaction should not be simply taken as a measure of the assessments failing but as testimony to that crucial vitality of the subject that eludes captivity on paper. We know that the true magic of the educating act is so much more than a simple, albeit justifiable, concern for improved resources, more sensitively stated objectives, better pre-service and in-service training for teachers, or improved bureaucratic efficiency. Rather, it has to do with the whole meaning of a society's search for true maturity and responsible freedom through its young people. (Aoki et al., 1977b, p. 49)

REFERENCES

Aoki, T. T., & Harrison, E. (1977). The intents of the BC Social Studies Curriculum Guides: An interpretation. In T. T. Aoki, C. Langford, D. M. Williams, & D. C. Wilson (Eds.), *The British Columbia Social Studies assessment summary report: A report to the Ministry of Education* (pp. 55–63). Victoria, BC: Ministry of Education.

Aoki, T. T., Langford, D., Williams, D. M., & Wilson, D. C. (Eds.). (1977a). *The British Columbia social studies assessment: A report to the Ministry of Education* (Vol. 1). Victoria, BC: Ministry of Education.

Aoki, T. T., Langford, D., Williams, D. M., & Wilson, D. C. (Eds.). (1977b). *The British Columbia social studies assessment summary report: A report to the Ministry of Education.* Victoria, BC: Ministry of Education.

Apple, M. W. (1974). The process and ideology of valuing in educational settings. In M. W. Apple, M. J. Subkoviak, & H. S. Lufler, Jr. (Eds.), *Educational evaluation: Analysis and responsibility* (pp. 3–34). Berkeley, CA: McCutchan. Bath, S. W. Y. (1988). *Justice in evaluation: Participatory case study evaluation.* Unpublished doctoral dissertation, University of Alberta, Edmonton. Beittel, K. R. (1973). *Alternatives for art education research.* Dubuque, IA: Wm. C. Brown.

Deleuze, G., & Guattari, F. (1987). *A thousand plateaus: Capitalism and schizophrenia*. Minneapolis: University of Minnesota Press.

Derrida, J. (1978). *Writing and difference*. Chicago: University of Chicago Press.

Eisner, E. W. (1979). *The educational imagination on the design and evaluation of school programs*. New York: Macmillan.

Foucault, M. (1972). *The archaeology of knowledge*. London: Tavistock.

Freire, P. (1968). *Pedagogy of the oppressed*. New York: Herder & Herder.

Habermas, J. (1972). *Knowledge and human interest*. Boston: Beacon.

Hamilton, D., Jenkins, D., King, C., MacDonald, B., & Parlett, M. (Eds.). (1977). *Beyond the numbers game: A reader in educational evaluation*. Berkeley, CA: Scotchman.

Heidegger, M. (1971). *On the way to language*. San Francisco: Harper & Row.

Horkheimer, M., & Adorno, T. (1972). *Dialectic of enlightenment*. New York: Continuum.

House, E. R. (Ed). (1973). *School evaluation the politics and process*. Berkeley, CA: McCutchan.

Kaplan, A. (1964). *The conduct of inquiry*. San Francisco: Chandler.

Lyotard, J. F. (1984). *The post-modern condition: A report of knowledge*. Minneapolis: University of Minnesota Press.

MacDonald, B., & Walker, R. (Eds.). (1974). *SAFARI papers one: Innovation, evaluation, research and the problem of control*. Norwich, England: University. of East Anglia (CARE).

Marcuse, H. (1968). *Essays in critical theory*. Boston: Beacon.

Patton, M. Q. (1975). *Alternative evaluation research paradigm*. (Monograph of the North Dakota Study Group on Evaluation). Grand Forks: University of North Dakota Press.

Rothe, P. (1979). *An exploration of existential phenomenology as an approach to curriculum evaluation*. Unpublished doctoral dissertation, University of British Columbia, Vancouver.

Schaull, R. (1968). Foreword. In P. Freire, *Pedagogy of the oppressed* (pp. 9–15). New York: Herder and Herder.

Scriven, M. (1976). *Perspectives of curriculum evaluation*. Chicago: Rand McNally.

Shaver, J. P. & Larkins, A. G. (1973). Research on teaching social studies. In R. M. W. Travers (Ed.). *Second handbook of research on teaching* (pp. 1243–1262). Chicago: Rand McNally.

Stake, R., & Easley, J. (1978). *Case studies in science education: Vol. 2. Design overview, and general findings*. Urbana-Champaign: University of Illinois, Center for Instructional Research and Curriculum Evaluation.

Tyler, R. W. (1949). *Basic principles of curriculum and instruction*. Chicago: University of Chicago Press.

Wilson, D. C. (1976). *Emic evaluation inquiry: An approach for evaluating school programs*. Unpublished doctoral dissertation, University of Alberta, Edmonton.

Chapter 8

Layered Voices of Teaching:
The Uncannily Correct
and the Elusively True[1] (1992)

I have been asking myself twice, three times, and more, "What authorizes me to speak to educators of teaching?"

Could it be that with over 40 years of teaching I have become preoccupied with so many answers to the question "What is teaching?" that I have forgotten to question my own understandings of the question itself?

Could it be that in the years of questioning that accompanied my experiences of teaching, I have come to an understanding not so much of what teaching is, but rather what teaching is not? Could it be that this sort of understanding—a negative understanding—is a stage on the way to an understanding of what teaching is? Is this the sort of understanding that allows us to begin to see the uncannily correct but not yet true?

Or could it be that in my questioning, I have become more sensitive to the seductive hold of the scientific, technological ethos that enframes education, and thereby our understandings of teaching? And could it be that because of this sensitivity, I have come to seek a way to be more properly attuned, not only to see but also to hear more deeply and fully the silent call of our vocation, teaching?

---

[1] Reprinted from Aoki, Ted T. (1992). Layered voices in teaching: The uncannily correct and the elusively true. In W. F. Pinar & W. Reynolds (Eds.), *Understanding Curriculum as Phenomenological and Deconstructed Text* (pp. 17–27). New York: Teachers College Press. An earlier version of this article was originally published in *Education New Brunswick*, June 1988, published by the New Brunswick Department of Education. The original paper was presented at the Program for Quality Teaching Conference, sponsored in Vancouver, BC, by the B.C. Teachers' Federation. The article was also reprinted in: Aoki, Ted T. (1991). Layered voices of teaching: The uncannily correct and the elusively true. In Ted T. Aoki (Ed.), *Inspiriting Curriculum and Pedagogy: Talks to Teachers* (pp. 1–6). Edmonton, Alberta: Department of Secondary Education, University of Alberta.

LAYERS OF UNDERSTANDING

In our busy world of education, we are surrounded by layers of voices, some loud and some shrill, that claim to know what teaching is. Awed, perhaps, by the cacophony of voices, certain voices became silent and, hesitating to reveal themselves, conceal themselves. Let us beckon these voices to speak to us, particularly the silent ones, so that we may awaken to the truer sense of teaching that likely stirs within each of us.

Before we visit the place where the silent voices dwell, let us try to uncover layer by layer—three layers—from the surface to the place where teaching truly dwells.

THE OUTERMOST LAYER:
UNDERSTANDING TEACHING AS A BLACK BOX

Some of us can remember the days when researchers shied away from the live and complex world of the classroom. These researchers were primarily interested in the outcomes of teaching rather than in the understanding of teaching itself. Likening the school to a factory or a knowledge industry, they assumed that what counts are effects and results in terms of the investments made. Hence, they typically cast their studies into a before-and-after design, concealing the domain of teaching in a black box, nonessential for research purposes, and thereby willfully ignoring the lived world of teachers and students.

Even today the black box image persists, characterized by the yearly visits to schools by assessors—usually measurement experts who style themselves in the language of psychometrics—who seem to revel in their technicized vocation. They heed the call of the instrumental rules of tests and measurements but ignore the call of teachers and students who dwell within the crucible of their own concretely lived situations. Without these voices we lack the understanding of meaning.

I feel that this kind of willful ignoring reflects the hold of an attunement in life, including school life, governed by goals and objectives, and consequently by measures of successful achievement.

In this black-box view of teaching, what I resent is the way in which, by ignoring the lives of teachers and students, they are cast into nothingness. That which I consider to be most vital is devitalized into nonexistent darkness. For me, the black box reflects a frightening ignorance of so-called educational assessors and researchers, who, as assessors and researchers, are forgetful that they are not merely researchers, but educational researchers. They forget the adjective. And by being forgetful, they deny the humanness that lies at the core of what education is.

We are less naive today. But still we see about us efforts that place teaching in a gray box, if not a black box, wherein teachers are mere facilitators to teaching built into programmed learning packages. These are teacher-proof packages wherein the preference is for noncontamination by teachers' presence. This is akin to a technological understanding of teaching whose logical outcome is the robotization of teaching: schools in the image of Japanese automobile factories—heaven forbid!

THE MIDDLE LAYER: UNDERSTANDING TEACHING THEORETICALLY AND SCIENTIFICALLY

In recent years we have had a surge of interest in expounding what teaching is. Books such as *Life in Classrooms* by Philip Jackson (1972) gave legitimacy to scholars to move daringly into the black box to make sense of the happenings there. Many psychologists, sociologists, anthropologists, and the like have approached the question of what teaching is from their own favored perspectives. Often the psychologists are oriented toward understanding teaching behavior, the sociologists toward understanding the roles of teachers, and the anthropologists toward an understanding of teaching as human activity. In disciplined ways they have attempted to offer complex portrayals, even models, of what teaching is. In so doing they have imposed on the lived situations of teachers and students abstract, preset categories of their disciplines. Thus a psychological understanding of teaching is popularly framed within the psychological concepts of motivation, reinforcement, retention, and transfer. These are, incidentally, the titles of a monograph series on teaching by Madeleine Hunter (1982). An understanding of teaching framed within the sociopsychological concepts has given birth to a whole array of interaction analysis systems, founded by Ned Flanders (1960); a sociological understanding of teaching based on role analysis often sees teaching in terms of the roles of classroom management, lesson planning, classroom discipline, surrogate parenting, mediating knowledge, and so on, popular themes that occupy a large terrain of the teacher education curriculum and instruction syllabi. An anthropological understanding of teaching frequently sees teaching as cultural activity, ethnographically understandable.

As such, all of these are knowledge formulations of behavior, roles, and activities that provide some understanding of human doings: observable, measurable, and within the grasp of reasoned control. They present, indeed, a seductively scholarly and intellectual quality and legitimacy that make the understanding of teaching uncannily correct. But we must remember that these portrayals, although correct, although illuminative, are all distanced seeing in the images of abstract conceptual schemes that are idealizations, somewhat removed, missing the preconceptual, pretheoretical fleshy, familiar, very concrete world of teachers and students.

THE INNERMOST LAYER: UNDERSTANDING
TEACHING TECHNIQUES, STRATEGIES, SKILLS

This understanding of teaching is of special interest to us because it is taken-for-granted hereabouts, popularized in the language of "teaching competence" and "effective teaching."

The notion of "effective teaching" flows from the behaviouristic theories of motivation, retention, and the like, transformed into the language of teaching as doing. Within it is the admission that the psychological concept of learning behavior is central and that teaching is the flip side of learning. A proponent of this view, Madeleine Hunter, revealingly states that decisions based on learning theory are decisions of how to teach.

That is quite a sweeping statement to make. The notion of effectiveness that she presents has a sense of practical urgency about it that teachers readily recognize. It is no doubt a word that reminds us that teaching is a deeply practical vocation, that our predicament as teachers is a very pragmatic one.

In the first flush of thought, the notion of effectiveness has a seductive appeal of essential simplicity that suggests the possibility of a focus that can be grasped. It suggests, too, that effectiveness is mainly a matter of skill and technique, and that if I can but identify the components of effective teaching and if, with some concentrated effort, I can but identify the skills, maybe in a three- or four-day workshop, my teaching can become readily effective.

Reorienting the Search for the Essence of Teaching

All of these scientific and technical understandings of teaching emerge from our interest in intellectual and manipulative grasp and control. But in so understanding, we must be attuned to the fact that although those understandings that can be grasped are uncannily correct, the essence of teaching still eludes our grasp. What we need to do is to break away from the attitude of grasping and seek to be more properly oriented to what teaching is, so we can attune ourselves to the call of what teaching is. And so we set aside these layers that press upon us and move to indwell in the earthy place where we experience daily life with our colleagues and students, and begin our search for the "isness" of teaching, for the being of teaching. This search calls for a break away from the orientation that may blind us. But what is it to experience a break?

When we are writing and the pencil breaks, suddenly the content of our writing disappears and goes into hiding, and the pencil that we really did not see before comes out of hiding to reveal itself to us. What we see here is how the experience of breaking can help us in breaking out of the seductive hold of an orientation to which we are beholden. I wish to offer short narratives—stories— that point to, more than they tell, what it means to be oriented in a way that allows the essence of teaching to reveal itself to us. I say this because prosaic words are often inappropriate when describing certain phenomena. I find it so when I try, as I am doing here, to talk *about* the essence of teaching. All I can do is point, hoping that the pointing will help us to begin to allow ourselves to hear the voice of the essence of teaching that lurks concealed, but nevertheless calls upon us.

But before I tell the stories, allow me to try to reunderstand the question that is holding our attention. I now return to our original question: What is teaching? To this point I have been guided by the question *"What is teaching?"* (with the whatness of teaching emphasized). This is the typical way in which most of us understand the question. The question so understood beckoned me to focus on the "whatness" of teaching and yielded to us an understanding of teaching as a black box; as psychological, sociological, anthropological conceptions; and as modes of doing. I wish to ask the same question differently, unavoidably making it a different question. I ask; What *is* teaching?, emphasizing "Is."

This new question asks that I reorient myself that I break from my usual orientation to the question and seek that which not only offers me a different orientation but also draws me to a deeper level, a level that allows the essence of teaching to speak to me. With this new question, I feel much more oriented, I hope more properly oriented, to be in the presence of the beingness of teaching.

So placed, I may be allowed to hear better the voice of what teaching essentially is. The question understood in this way urges me to be attuned to a teacher's presence with children. This presence, if authentic, is being. I find that teaching so understood is attuned to the place where care dwells, a place of ingathering and belonging, where the indwelling of teachers and students is made possible by the presence of care that each has for the other.

A notion of pedagogy might be helpful here. Pedagogy means, in the original Greek sense, leading children. Teaching is truly pedagogic if the leading grows out of this care that inevitably is filled with the good of care. Teaching, then, is a tactful leading that knows and follows the pedagogic good in a caring situation.

The narratives that follow are meant to point to rather than to describe what teaching more truly is. But this pointing is more an allowing of a concretely lived place to speak to us—a disclosure that allows us a glimmer of the essence of teaching.

NARRATIVE ONE: A LOOK THAT HEARS

To help further our effort to reorient ourselves properly, let me tell a story mother told me years ago. I title it "A Look That Hears."

In Feudal Japan there lived a monk, famed for his temple garden of morning glories, and a lord at a nearby castle. The lord, upon hearing of the bountifulness and beauty of the garden, sent forth to the temple a message that on the day following the full moon, he would arrive in early morn to view the garden.

On that appointed day, the monk, upon early rising, went directly to the garden and plucked all the morning glories but one. When the lord arrived, the monk guided him to the garden, fresh laden with morning dew, beckoning him to savor to the fullest what his eyes could behold.

The mass of foliage denuded of the multitude of flowers he had imaged beckoned the lord to break the silence to ask of the monk, "Where are the morning glories for which you have gained renown?"

The monk, gesturing to the lord to savor the lone flower, said softly, so as not to tread upon the silence unduly, "My lord, if you but allow the morning glory to speak, the flower will disclose to you the essence of the being of the morning glory that it is."

The lord paused, allowing his eyes to rest upon the flower, and listened with care to the speaking of the morning glory. Then he turned to the monk, bowed a little more deeply than a lord typically is wont to bow, and said quietly, "I know better now what it is to hear when I look." With that he left, upon his lips a faint smile.

In a true sense, our monk was a pedagogue, a person who leads. He asked his lord to push aside the seductive hold of those understandings that claim correctness and to approach with bowed humility, with an attitude of surrender, the sound of the voice that calls. What yielded to him was a deep seeing into, an insight, that if he is properly oriented and if he listens carefully—that is, a listening filled with care, the care that brought the lord and flower together— understanding will be granted to him.

The monk as pedagogue taught the lord, a leader of men, what it is to lead—that in a world of beings, to lead is to hearken and to follow the voice of the *logos;* that he who cannot follow the voice of *logos* is not an authentic leader; and that what authorizes him to be a leader is not so much the title or position, but rather his attunement to the care that silently dwells.

NARRATIVE TWO: CHRISTA MCAULIFFE— SHE IS THE TEACHING

January 28, 1986: the breakdown of the *Challenger*. All of us experienced shock, sorrow, and deep pain. The whole world mourned. We lost Christa McAuliffe, a teacher and colleague. In death, life?

I feel personally touched by Christa McAuliffe, whose absence speaks to me with a strong presence of what her teaching essentially was and is.

This social studies teacher, who ventured forth on what is typically understood as a scientific mission, cared about how science and technology, held in objective regard, should be more fully understood in the context the beingness of humans. Hers was a teacher's hope to break away from the bonds of the technological perspective and to offer to our children a reoriented vision.

But this reoriented seeing was not so much geared to a seeing of the earth from the perspective of space, although that was a part of her mission, but one more oriented to a deeper sense of seeing. In this regard, we recall her thoughtful words uttered with care, "I want to humanize the technology of the space age." That is what she said.

She planned to do this not so much by observing from high above what she would see below, but by writing in a journal her experiences of what it might mean for her as a human being to be involved in a technological venture. Indeed, she wanted to understand how human beings are embedded in human beingness. Her interest, and this is my interpretation, was to listen to what her writing might say, to listen therein to the voice that called upon her as teacher and as ordinary citizen. She had hoped to seek a deeper understanding of what it means to be beholden to science and technology.

A cruel accident has taken the life of a fellow teacher, but I am sure she is even now very much present in all of us, touching the inner soul and being of each of us. I am convinced that this kind of touching comes from the deep care people have for the teachers in whose trust they place their young. What speaks here in the truest sense is the truest sense of being pedagogues, the being of those who in leading the young abide by the *logos* of care that tells us what is pedagogically good in our relationship with children.

Christa McAuliffe helped me to see a glimmer of the essence of teaching, of what it means to be attuned to the call of care that is present in every authentic pedagogic situation.

NARRATIVE THREE:
JUNE'S STORY AND TWO PEDAGOGICAL THEMES

The third narrative begins with the story of a bewildered child, as June Aoki recalls a break in the dailiness of her school life as a junior high school student. Drawn into the story, I linger on two themes: pedagogical watchfulness and pedagogical thoughtfulness. Here, then, is June's story: "A Re-Meeting with Mr. McNab, My Grade 7 Teacher."

It was a cloudy day in early April, 1942. I was 13 then, going on14, in Grade 7 at Fanny Bay School, a two-room school about 40 miles from Nanaimo in British Columbia.

It was a bewildering day for many of us. Our Japanese Language School had already been ordered closed by the Ministry of Education. My father had already been sent to a road camp near Blue River in the far-off wilds of the Rockies. We had been hearing rumors that we were to be moved, first to Vancouver, then somewhere to the interior of British Columbia and possibly beyond. We had been trying not to believe Charlie Tweedie, who told my brother, Tim, that all the Japanese would be herded en masse to Hastings Park, and who had said, teasingly perhaps, "That way only one bomb will do it!"

On this day in April, I went to school solely for the purpose of leaving school. As soon as school began, we cleaned out our desks, returned texts that belonged to the school, gathered our books and belongings while our Occidental schoolmates silently watched our movements. With our arms full, we left our classroom, taking footsteps that seemed to know that these might be the last, at least in this classroom. Cautiously, we moved step by step down two flights of stairs and wended our way along the worn path of the school playground, homeward bound.

The leaving this day was different from our usual taking leave at the end of the school's day. Somehow I felt I was leaving a place to which, like home, I belonged. Why was it that my usually happy feet had no skip to them? I guess we were experiencing emptiness in leaving behind what had become so much a part of our everyday existence. As I walked, I felt the school's tug and this walking home was like hands that slip away in parting, knowing not what to say in a silent farewell.

I was about to leave the schoolyard. Something called upon me to turn around for a last look. On the balcony of the school stood my teacher Mr. McNab, alone, watching us as if to keep guard over us in our departure.

I almost felt I did wrong in stealing a look, so without a wave of good-bye, I resumed my walk homeward. I wondered, "What is Mr. McNab thinking right now?"

I cannot really recall my other teachers in all the years of my schooling, which began in Fanny Bay. But Mr. McNab, I remember. He was the one I recall. He was the teacher who urged us in school to display our Japanese kimonos and to perform some "odori" to Japanese music. He was the one who on the annual district sports day insisted on taking all the students, the athletic and the not so athletic, breaking with the tradition of sports days for elite athletes. For us, the event was something special. It mattered little whether we won or lost. All of us were grateful that Mr. McNab took us—swift ones and slow ones, dumpy ones and lean ones, tall ones and short ones.

Recently, we returned to the Coast, in a way a touching again the earth and water we once knew. Coming home, I wondered if by chance I could make contact with Mr. McNab, of whom I had heard not a thing over more than four decades.

Through the British Columbia Teachers Federation offices we learned that William McNab, a retired teacher, lived in North Vancouver. I felt a stirring in my heart. I phoned him. Most graciously he listened to my story. For him it must have been puzzling after 44 years to sort me out from a mountain of memories of hundreds and thousands of students who called him "teacher." But he was my Mr. McNab, my teacher.

He kindly visited us. I experienced a deep inward joy of thanks when my hand grasped the hand of the man [who] silently watched over us as we left his school that April day 44 years ago. I felt he did not know that over all those years the memory of his watching stayed vividly with me. For me, the singular moment reflected his being as teacher.

I told Mr. McNab how over 44 years, I often recalled the image of his watchfulness clothed in care. Mustering courage, I asked him if he remembered the moment. There was a moment of silence. Then he simply said, "That was a sad day." That was all he would say. The rest he left unsaid. But I felt that in the silence he said much.

I felt blessed being allowed after 44 years to be in the presence of a teacher whose quiet but thoughtful gesture had touched me deeply. Today I feel doubly blessed being allowed to relive the fullness of the moment in the regained presence of Mr. McNab.

What deeper seeing into, what deeper hearing of teaching does this story allow? I wish to dwell on two themes that speak to what teaching is: pedagogical watchfulness and pedagogical thoughtfulness.

Theme 1: Pedagogical Watchfulness

What is the voice of teaching that this story speaks? Surely it is more than a nostalgic remembrance of a past. Surely it is more, much more than a recording of a minor historical event in the lives of a teacher and a few students.

Why is this particular story of a single moment worth a remarking? Could it be that that which is remarkable is the indwelling presence of the shimmering being of teaching that is open to those whose listening is attuned aright?

How shall we understand the voice of Mr. McNab's teaching? Could it be that it is not so much what he did—"watch"—but more so the person he was as he watched?

We might see a glimmer of the person he was as teacher if we listen with care to his "watching." His watching was not so much watching as observing, a looking *at* that which is apart from his self, although in part it was, as he watched the students wind homeward. It was a watching that was watchfulness—a watchfulness filled with a teacher's hope that wherever his students may be, wherever they may wander on this earth away from his presence, they are well and no harm will visit them.

Teachers understand the meaning of the presence of absence growing out of their own experiences of watchfulness. Teachers know that pupils come to them clothed in a bond of parental trust, and parents know that they, in entrusting their children to teachers, can count on the watchful eyes of teachers. So, too, teachers know that at the end of the year, they and their students will part, the students to the next grade or to another school. Yet it is their very leaving that allows them the possibility to return—a turning again to the experiences of the present. And the teachers know that watching the students depart at the end of the year is a watchfulness that is filled with the hope that wherever they may be the students will do well and be well, and no harm will befall them.

Authentic teaching is watchfulness, a mindful watching overflowing from the good in the situation that the good teacher sees. In this sense, good teachers are more than they do; they are the teaching. When Mr. McNab watched, he was the teaching. No less, no more.

Theme 2: Pedagogical Thoughtfulness

Let us recall the question put to Mr. McNab: "What were you thinking when you watched us leave?"

June's story speaks also to thinking that was a part of Mr. McNab's watchfulness. But it speaks not of the form of thinking that holds sway in most quarters wherein educators and non-educators dwell—the form of thinking that has kindred modality to what we call rational thinking, logical thinking, or critical thinking, although in part it is. Thinking typically understood in our Western tradition has a seductively intellectual ring to it. As some psychologists tell us, the bulk of the behavior we call thinking is cerebral, all in the head above the neck, as it were, holding in lower regard anything below the neck as being secondary attachments. As analytical philosophers tell us, there is a logic in reason that makes thinking a reasoned forward movement, so that with every click of the synapse, we can hammer out a linear path to a logical conclusion.

"Thinking" so understood is so familiar to us that when we say "thinking," we can think no other thought about thinking but that. In fact, we tacitly subscribe to this understanding of thinking such that we forget that we have been seduced into having a love affair with such an understanding. And in the blindness that usually accompanies such affairs, we fail to see other possibilities of understanding "thinking."

What seems to be concealed and hence unseen and unheard is an understanding of thinking that might be understood as thoughtfulness— thoughtfulness as an embodied doing and being—thought and soul embodied in the oneness of the lived moment.

When Mr. McNab watched his students leave, his watching was a watching with thoughtfulness—a thoughtfulness that spoke silently from deep within, a thoughtfulness that reached out without gesture or motion, a thoughtfulness filled with both hope and sadness: hope for the well-being of the departing student, and sadness that he must now live in the empty presence of his students' absence.

Although he had become attuned to the annual departure of his students at the end of the school year, the departure of these students at midyear must have been for him a different experience. As a teacher, it is likely that for some time, he was caught in this living difference, experienced the solitude, and was left alone to make sense of this unwilled break-up that happened in his classroom.

So why was it, when remembering a moment of 44 years ago, our teacher Mr. McNab merely said, "That was a sad day?"

A LINGERING NOTE

In the foregoing I have attempted to unfold layers of understandings about teaching. I began with an understanding wherein teaching is hidden, willfully ignored, in the dark recesses of the black box.

In the unfolding we explored teaching understood as behavior, as role, as human activity, wherein disciplined abstractions of teaching hold sway, somewhat forgetful of the lived world of teachers and students that was the source of their interest in the first place. We explored, too, understandings of teaching that flow out as applied versions of these abstractions. We noted also the seductive appeal of these understandings—of suggestions of simplicity and pragmatic usefulness—all uncannily correct.

I have suggested that what seems urgent for us at this time in understanding what teaching more truly is, to undertake to reorient ourselves so that we overcome mere correctness so that we can see and hear our doings as teachers harbored within pedagogical being, so we can see and hear who we *are* as teachers.

I ask you now to think of a really good teacher that you have experienced in your time. Allow him or her to be present before you. I believe that the truth of this good teacher of yours is in the measure of the immeasurable. And, now, say to him or her: He *is* the teaching; she *is* the teaching. And, after you have said these words, allow the unsaid to shine through the said. Savor now the elusively true, the mystery of what teaching essentially is.

REFERENCES

Flanders, N. A. (1960) *Interaction analysis in the classroom: A manual for observation*. Minneapolis: University of Minnesota Press.
Hunter, M. (1982). *Mastery teaching*. El Segundo, CA: TIP.
Jackson, P. (1972). *Life in classrooms*. New York: Holt Rinehart and Winston.

Chapter 9

Legitimating Lived Curriculum: Toward a Curricular Landscape of Multiplicity[1] (1993)

"The lived curriculum" . . . "the other curriculum" . . . These words inscribed in the title of this article speak to the way I have already been claimed by curricular landscapes of practicing teachers and their students. So claimed, I ask that I be allowed to dwell near, if not in the midst of, these landscapes, so that I may, by listening more thoughtfully to sayings of teachers and students, become more alert to the archi-texture of curricular landscapes within which activities like curriculum supervision, curriculum development, curriculum implementation, and curriculum evaluation are said to take place.

"SCIENCE MUST BE TAUGHT AS A HUMANITY": A CURRICULUM ANECDOTE

A short anecdote from my journal speaks to a curricular landscape at the university level, although in its import, it speaks as well to the curriculum at the school level. Highlighting a saying in the anecdote, I title it, "Science must be taught as a humanity":

> During a late breakfast early last year, I was tuned to radio news coverage on the CBC (the Canadian Broadcasting Corporation). My ears twitched a bit as I listened, more carefully than I am wont to do for radio news, to a report of Canada wide curriculum study.
> We were told that the study was a response to the finding that of the high school graduates entering the Faculty of Science undergraduate programs across Canada, by the end of the third year, nearly one-third of the students were dropping out. Such a happening triggered a questioning of why students successful in high school science were dropping out of the university science programs. A national study was launched

[1] Reprinted from Aoki, Ted T. (1993). Legitimating lived curriculum: Towards a curricular landscape of multiplicity. *Journal of Curriculum and Supervision*, 8 (3), 255–268.

to seek out why. We were told that the researchers sought out
dropouts to listen to their stories of their experiences.

They heard, among other comments, the following:

- "We found science a touch boring; we just did assigned
  experiment after assigned experiment. We felt science
  has to be more than that."
- "We felt in the name of science we were overemphasizing
  skills and techniques."
- "We felt science experiences were bit irrelevant to what
  we see as human crises in these times."

In other words, the researchers found that according to these ex-students, what
they experienced as university science was a bit out of touch with their own
lives. Reflecting upon the report, Dr. Stuart Smith, a scientist himself and chair
of the sponsoring Association of Universities and Colleges of Canada, said:
"Science must be taught as a humanity."

Of course, many of us would be interested in the full report. But for me, a
sometime curriculum person, the anecdote evokes reflection. Two thoughts
come forth, each in its own way disturbing somewhat our curriculum landscape.

DISTURBING THE CATEGORIES
THAT POPULATE THE C & I LANDSCAPE

The first line of thought turns to Dr. Smith's remark, "Science must be taught as
a humanity." These words claim me, cause me to pause and to question the way
we have traditionally textured the curriculum landscape into epistemic
categories, writ large, often labeled Faculties—the Faculty of Science, Faculty
of Arts and Humanities, Faculty of Engineering, Faculty of Education, and so
on. We are familiar with this curriculum topography. And although the
reference here is to the university setting, we can sense that what is at stake is
fundamentally the lure of Western epistemology, our beliefs about knowing and
knowledge, which has given our universities and schools a striated curricular
landscape. Particularly at the secondary school level, we are familiar with the
privileged curriculum categories that mirror the landscape of the university:
courses or subjects we call science, mathematics, history, geography, literature,
and so on.

Dr. Smith's remark, "Science must be taught as a humanity," disturbs the
traditional landscape that separates science and the humanities into distinct
categories. Even in our own minds, many of us feel we can readily spot science

students or humanities students on campus by the way they comport themselves! We have deeply set images reflecting the way this curricular landscape is inscribed in us.

For me, Dr. Smith's call to teach science as a humanity is more a question than a statement. It calls into question the underlying condition that allows science and the humanities to exist in separate domains. For curriculum people like us, Dr. Smith's call is indeed a challenge. Should we "integrate" the two disciplines? Should we search for a different condition that will allow science and the humanities to come together as one? Should we search for a different space that allows science and the humanities to be separate, yet together? I am hard pressed to ask good questions.

Even before the questioning is settled, I have a tongue-in-cheek response. How would it be if we brought together a scientist, a novelist, and a bottle of scotch at a café on Bourbon Street? Wouldn't it be fun to listen to what they might talk about? Hopefully, after a round or two (or three), they get around to talking about "science must be taught as a humanity." And if this should come to pass, I would love to hear how they sing or dance the "belonging togetherness" of science and humanities.

Less playfully, what Dr. Smith's remark evokes in me is what some call a crisis of modernity in the Western world, a questioning of the way of life we have constituted as modernism. Today, we have curriculum scholars who seem attuned to the same soundwave as Dr. Smith. Some of them are engaged in the modernist/postmodernist debates. How they interpret Dr. Smith's remark, "Science must be taught as a humanity," may well influence how we might reunderstand our curricular landscape. We, as curricular people, would be wise to be attentive to these debates.

Disturbing the Landscape that Privileges the Curriculum-as-Plan

Another line of thought that flows from the anecdote concerns the architectonics of the curriculum landscape. In the anecdote we heard that the researchers approached students to listen to their stories of their lived experiences as science students. In other words, the researchers sought out what may be called the lived curriculum of the students. This lived curriculum, of course, is not the curriculum as laid out in a plan, but a plan more or less lived out. It deserves the label "curriculum" as much as the plan deserves the label "curriculum-as-plan." But what I have said, I am afraid, is too glib.

For more intimate understanding of the curriculum landscape, let us visit Miss O, who, as a grade 5 teacher, lives amidst a landscape that knows both the curriculum-as-plan and the curriculum-as-lived. Let me quote a few paragraphs from an earlier effort of mine to portray Miss O's curricular landscape in an article I titled "Teaching as Indwelling Between Two Curriculum Worlds:"

Even before Day 1 of the term, our teacher, Miss O, walks into her assigned Grade 5 classroom. Because Miss O is already a teacher, her presence in the classroom initiates a transformation of a socio-cultural and physical environment into something different. Even before a pupil walks in, she silently asks: "Can I establish myself here as a teacher?" and the classroom's desks, walls, chalkboards, floor, books and resources jointly reply, albeit wordlessly, by what they are. They respond to Miss O's intention and presence. And when the pupils arrive, things and pupils arrange themselves, as it were, around Miss O's intention. They become "teachable," "promising," "difficult," "hopeful," "challenging." The environment ceases to be environment, and in its place comes into being a pedagogic situation, a lived site presently alive. Within this site, Miss O soon finds that her pedagogic situation is a living in tensionality—a tensionality that emerges, in part, from indwelling in the difference between two curricula: the curriculum-as-plan and the lived curriculum.

Curriculum-as-Plan

The first of these, the curriculum-as-plan, usually has its origin outside the classroom, such as the State Department of Education or the school district office. But whatever the source, it is penetratingly and insistently present in Miss O's classroom. This curriculum-as-plan is the curriculum, which Miss O is asked to teach the Grade 5 pupils who are entrusted to her care.

The curriculum-as-plan is the work of curriculum planners, often selected teachers from the field, under the direction of some official often designated as the curriculum director or curriculum supervisor. As a work of people, inevitable, it is imbued with the planners' orientations to the world, which inevitable include their own interests and assumptions about ways of knowing and about how teachers and students are to be understood. These interests, assumptions, and approaches, usually implicit in the text of the curriculum-as-plan, frame a set of curriculum statements: statements of *intent and interest* (given the language of "goals," "aims," and "objectives"), statements of what teachers and students should do (usually given the language of *activities*), statements of official and recommended *resources* for teachers and students, and usually implicitly, statements of *evaluation* (given, if at all, in the language of ends and means).

The Lived Curriculum

The other curriculum is really a multiplicity of lived curricula that Miss O and her pupils experience. For Miss O it is a world of face-to-face living with Andrew, with his mop of red hair, who struggles hard to learn to read; with Sara, whom Miss O can count on to tackle her language assignment with aplomb, with popular Margaret, who bubbles and who is quick to offer help to others and to welcome others' help; with Tom, a frequent daydreamers who loves to allow his thoughts to roam beyond the windows of the classroom; and some 20 others in class, each living out a story of what it is to live school life as Grade 5's. Miss O's pedagogic situation is a site inhabited by students with proper names—like Andrew, Sara, Margaret and Tom—who are, for Miss O, very human, unique beings. Miss O knows their uniqueness from having lived daily with them. And she knows that their uniqueness disappears into the shadow when they are spoken of in the prosaically abstract language of the external curriculum planners who are, in a sense, condemned to plan for faceless people, students shorn of their uniqueness or for all teachers, who become generalized entities often defined in terms of generalized performance roles.[2]

In this portrayal of her curriculum situation, we can see how in her class, Miss O as a practicing teacher is alert to the lived curriculum, the other curriculum that

---

[2] Aoki, Ted T. (1986). Teaching as indwelling between two curriculum worlds. In *The B.C. Teacher*, April/May (Vancouver: British Columbia Teachers' Association); republished in Aoki, Ted T (1991). *Inspiriting Curriculum and Pedagogy: Talks to Teachers* (Edmonton: University of Alberta, 1991), p. 7. Miss O, the practicing teacher referred to in this excerpt, was a Grade 5 teacher at Westwind School and later vice-principal at Lord Byng Elementary School in Richmond, BC, Miss O, now Mrs. S. Chamberlain, is now principal of Maple Lane Elementary School, Richmond, B.C. I consulted her throughout the preparation of this report.

she in her practical wisdom knows. And so knowing, she knows that there are many lived curricula, as many as there are self and students, and possibly more.

Acknowledging the lived curricula as Miss O has done offers us a retextured landscape, populated by a multiplicity of curricula, disturbing the traditional landscape, with its single privileged curriculum-as-plan awaiting implementation. It is to this promising disturbance of the curricular landscape I now turn.

FROM THE C & I LANDSCAPE TO A CURRICULAR LANDSCAPE OF MULTIPLICITY (C & C LANDSCAPE)

A critical feature of Miss O's curricular landscape, which is already populated by a multiplicity of curricula, is the very word *multiplicity* itself. How shall we understand this cumbersome-sounding word, *multiplicity?*

The C & I Landscape

Before we explore the word *multiplicity*, let us remember where we now are. For many of us, *curriculum*, in spite of its inherent indefiniteness, has become definitive, so much so that we speak with ease of *the* curriculum, *the* curriculum-as-plan. And when we so speak, we seem to be heedless of the way we have been drawn into a curricular landscape where in privileged aplomb stands, a tree does, a single curriculum. In this arboreal landscape, curriculum-related activities such as "instruction," "teaching," "pedagogy," and "implementation" become derivatives in the shadow of the curriculum-as-plan. Consider these familiar curricular phrases: "teaching the curriculum," "implementing the curriculum," "assessing in terms of fidelity to the curriculum." Do we not hear the chiseled motif of the striated linear instrumentalism deeply inscribed into our landscape?

Over the years, this instrumental landscape has become the working framework in many quarters. So prominent is instrumentalism woven into the fabric of curriculum work that we will not be remiss to call this landscape the *C & I Landscape*. The C & I landscape frames many curriculum and instruction course in teacher education. The same C & I landscape has become the curriculum developers' framework, framing curriculum development and implementation. The same C & I framework has become the curriculum supervisors' framework, framing supervision, the overseeing of activities related to curriculum and instruction, curriculum, and implementation.

A Curricular Landscape of Multiplicity (Which Grows in the Middle)

How can we displace the C & I landscape's primacy? We might begin by heeding the words "multiplicity is not a noun," a claim by Gilles Deleuze, for whom, like Heraclitus, life is constantly in flux.[3] With such a saying in mind, let us open ourselves to understandings of "multiplicity." To be noun-oriented, thing-oriented, or positivistically oriented is to be culturally conditioned to see multiplicity as multiple identities. So conditioned, in Miss O's landscape, we may be first attracted to the identities of the curriculum-as-plan and the lived curricula, much as we are drawn to ethnic identities when we speak of multiculturalism. Such a way of positing identities in the landscape is, we are told, a habit of modernism grounded in the metaphysics of presence. That is, we are drawn into a view that any identity is preexistent presence—a presence we can represent by careful scrutiny and copy.

Increasingly, we are called upon to reconsider the privileging of "identity as presence" and to displace it with the notion of "identity as effect." What is being said here? We are being asked to consider identity not so much as some*thing* already present, but rather as production, in the throes of being constituted as we live in place of difference. For example, according to this understanding our identities as teachers or curriculum supervisors are not so much in our presences; rather, our identities, who we are as teachers and as curriculum supervisors, are ongoing effects of our becomings in difference.

But where in multiplicity is such a place? In *Dialogues*, Deleuze states: "In a multiplicity what counts are not . . . the elements, but what there is between, the between, a site of relations which are not separable from each other. Every multiplicity grows in the middle."[4]
This saying reminds us of Miss O, our Grade 5 teacher, who found her place in the middle—in the midst of a multiplicity of curricula, between and among curriculum-as-plan and the lived curricula. Miss O's indwelling as teacher is indeed a living in difference, in the midst of curricula, where, according to Deleuze, multiplicity grows as lines of movement.

Line of Movement #1: In Difference Between Discourses

In noting the between as a place of difference, we might listen more fully to what Deleuze has to say elsewhere.

---

[3] Deleuze, Gilles and Parnet, Claire. (1987). *Dialogues*, p. vii. New York: Columbia University Press.
[4] Ibid, p. viii

- "We tend to think in terms of more or less, that is, to see difference in degree where there are differences in kind."[5]

- "Each time that we think in terms of more or less, we have already disregarded differences in kind between the two orders, or between beings, between existents."[6]

- "Conceiving everything in terms of more or less, seeing nothing but differences in degree . . . where, more profoundly, there are differences in kind is perhaps the most general error of thought, the error common to science and metaphysics."[7]

Deleuze's remarks alert us to how differently "difference" might be understood, and further, how, if one understands difference only as difference in degree, one may become indifferent to difference in kind.

With this understanding of difference, let us return to Miss O's curricular landscape to listen to her language carefully. For Miss O, her indwelling in difference is *not* a monochromed difference in degree. Let us recall that Miss O knows "the uniqueness of her pedagogical situation from having lived daily with Andrew, Sara, Margaret and Tom and others," and so living "she knows that their uniqueness disappears into the shadow when they are spoken of in prosaic abstract language of the external curriculum planners who are in a sense, condemned to plan for faceless people, students shorn of their uniqueness or teachers who become generalized entities often defined in terms of performance roles."[8]

For Miss O, to live in the middle between the language of the curriculum-as-plan and the language of lived curricula is to live amidst discourses that are different in kind.

On one hand is the prosaic discourse of the external curriculum planners, whose techni-scientific language of planning is the striated language of ends–

---

[5] Deleuze, Gilles (1988). *Bergsonism*, p. 21. New York: Zone Books. p. 21.
[6] Ibid, p. 20.
[7] Ibid.
[8] Aoki, Ted T., (1986). "Teaching as indwelling between two curriculum worlds. In *The B.C. Teacher*, April/May (Vancouver: British Columbia Teachers' Association); republished in Aoki, Ted. T. (1991) *Inspiriting Curriculum and Pedagogy: Talks to Teachers*, p. 7. Edmonton: University of Alberta.

means. Further, this prosaic language is abstract, written for faceless people in a homogeneous realm.

On the other hand is the language of the lived curriculum, the more poetic, phenomenological and hermeneutic discourse in which life is embodied in the very stories and languages people speak and live. These two discourses are different in kind; they resist integration.

At this point we might remember our friends, the scientist and the humanist, whom we left in conversation at a table on Bourbon Street. We wonder if they have moved to discuss how two discourses, the discourse on science and the discourse on humanity, may "belong together," if indeed they belong together at all. But let us return to Miss O.

Surely Miss O's open curriculum landscape is different in kind from the traditional C & I landscape that enframes many curricular activities. Rather, Miss O's curricular landscape is a multiplicity of betweens. This landscape, so different from the striated C & I landscape, is textured by a multiplicity of lines moving from between to between, is ever open, knowing no beginning and no end, resisting enframing. In contrast to the C & I landscape, I might call this the C & C landscape, a landscape embodying the curriculum-as-plan and curricula-as-lived, indeed, an open landscape of multiplicity.

Within such a retextured curricular landscape, how should a curriculum developer re-attune as a curriculum developer? How should a curriculum supervisor re-attune as a curriculum supervisor? How should a teacher re-attune as a teacher?

Line of Movement #2: In the Difference Between Metanarratives and Narratives

I return to Deleuze to remind myself that "multiplicity grows from the middle." So reminded, I ask you to join another moving line in the midst of the discourse of curriculum-as-plan and the discourse of the lived curriculum. In this line of movement, I lean on Jean François Lyotard, who chooses as his focus not the "will of power" that Nietzsche espoused, nor the "instrumental reason" that Habermas and the neo-Marxists favoured, but rather the principle of legitimacy of narratives, a principle that in my language, boils down to "who says what stories count and don't count."

In his book *The Postmodern Condition*, Lyotard speaks to the way of life we in the West have historically characterized as modernism, with its 2,500 years of tradition from the time of Socrates and Plato, accelerated in more recent times by the Age of Enlightenment and the Age of Reason.[9]

---

[9] Lyotard, Jean François. (1984). *The Postmodern Condition: A Report on Knowledge*. Minneapolis: University of Minnesota Press.

According to Lyotard, modernity is marked by the advance of a techno-scientific mind-set, which the past has relied on metanarratives to legitimate itself. By the technoscientific mind-set he is referring to the way we tend to constitute our world in terms of Cartesian subject–object dualism, the way we constitute realms of objective meanings or of subjective meanings. Our C & I landscape reflects this modernism. By metanarratives he means the grand stories through which we have come to accept certain notions about "truth," "progress," "goals," "rationality," "unity and totality," "subjectivity," "objectivity," "end-means," and so son—master narratives that cradle modernism.

Lyotard boldly states:

> Simplifying to the extreme, I define postmodernism as incredulity toward metanarratives.   This incredulity is undoubtedly a product of progress in the sciences . . .. To the obsolescence of the metanarrative apparatus of legitimation corresponds most notably the crisis of metaphysical philosophy and of the university institution that in the past relied on it.[10]

By "the obsolescence of the metanarrative apparatus of legitimation," he means the diminishing legitimacy of the master stories about "progress" (progress is always good for us); about "goals" (we as humans are driven by goals); about "rationality" (by sound reasoning we can arrive at all truths); about "truth" (somewhere there is a thing called "the truth," which, by our striving, we can discover); about "unity" (unity is not only possible but desirable; hence we should strive to connect things and people into a totality); about "end-means" (our world is striated technically; everything boils down to ends–means.) These are examples of grand narratives whose privileged primacy Lyotard questions. Legitimation by these and other metanarratives, says Lyotard, has led to delegitimation of understandings we come to through narratives and stores we daily tell and hear.

For us, the modernist/postmodernist dialogue allows deeper awareness of how the modernist vision of the world has dominated our curriculum landscape shaped in the manner of the curriculum-as-plan and instructional strategies—a landscape legitimated by metanarratives. If Lyotard makes sense, as he does to me, it is time not to reject but to decenter the modernist-laden curricular

---

[10] Lyotard, Jean François (1984). *The Postmodern Condition: A Report on Knowledge*. Minneapolis: University of Minnesota Press.

landscape and to replace it with the C & C landscape that accommodates lived meanings, thereby legitimating thoughtful everyday narratives.

In this context, we might reinterpret Dr. Smith's statement, "Science must be taught as a humanity." I now hear Dr. Smith (1) recognizing the unwarranted privileging of the techno-scientific curriculum mind-set understood almost totally in terms of objective meanings, and (2) calling for a de-privileging such that a clearing can be opened up to allow humanly embodied narratives to dwell contrapuntally with metanarratives. For the university founded within a metaphysical philosophical framework that is fragmented into categories called faculties, like the Faculty of Science and the Faculty of Arts and Humanities, Smith's call that "science must be taught as a humanity" seems to beckon questioning from the ground up. Such a questioning, it seems to me, puts not only the structure of the university but also the structure of curriculum at all levels into turbulence, opening possibilities of a fresh line of movement for curriculum.

In this context, we again recall Miss O, who sees herself in "face to face living with Andrew, . . . with Sara, . . . with Margaret, . . . with Tom, . . . and with some 20 others in class, each living out a story of what it is to live school life as Grade 5's." I do not know whether Miss O has read anything of Jean François Lyotard, but somehow in her wisdom she knows the significance for herself as a teacher of allowing space for stories, anecdotes, and narratives that embody the lived dimension of curriculum life. As far as she is concerned, these narratively structured lived curricula have legitimacy in her class, even thought the curriculum-as-plan is silent about lived curricula. Miss O flourishes in vibrant lines of movement in the midst of her C & C landscape of multiplicity, and she offers us practical wisdom.

Three years after my earlier portrayal, Miss O, by this time a vice-principal, leads Laura, a beginning teacher, into that place of difference between metanarratives and narratives, beckoning her to struggle and flourish on her own in a line of movement that has its own zigzags. Listen to Laura, who, by the way, holds a science degree and is now a third-year teacher in an elementary school, speak of her own experiences as a beginning teacher of social studies:

Polyphonic Lines of Movement: A Practicing Teacher Grows in Wisdom

> The June before I began my first year of teaching, I was introduced to the narrative as a way of moving into that space between curriculum-as-plan and the lived curriculum of a child. I had finished my teacher education program in April, and in June I was substituting in the school where I would be teaching in September.

The teachers there reached out to me. They shared with me their way of transforming curriculum in to the form of a master story. During three weeks, I was immersed in stories; stories surrounded me, stories that hopefully reach into the world of the child.

In the last days of school, Vice-Principal Miss O sat with me and helped me create a plan for the year to come. The plan was a long story that would take ten months to tell. I remember my amazement and delight as I saw those areas of study listed in the curriculum guides woven into a master story on a large sheet before us. . . . I held this plan in anticipation of the year to come.

Thus I began my first year of teaching with a master story that was my curriculum-as-planned and daily stories to create by students and myself as we went along. Creating these stories was for me difficult. Each story attempted to reach into the worlds of a roomful of children, each child different from any other. I struggled with the role of the storyteller; it did not come easily for me. But I remember at least a couple of times when my struggling as storyteller was rewarded with coming into being of a kind of tension I had never experienced before.

I think back to one of these times. There were 28 of us in the room and together we were involved in a story about the early voyageurs in Canada and the extreme conditions they lived within. We were questioning what life might have been like for the voyageurs. Every child was tense, leaning toward, silent, looking right at me, the storyteller. Something had clicked and there we all were gathered together by a tension holding us in a way that we did not want to let go. I felt I was reaching them.

The story was more than 30 minutes long and the children's thoughts and questions that followed led me to believe they had considered deeply the question we were exploring. I was delighted.[11]

---

[11] Richter, Laura. (1990). Pedagogical reaching as a mode of being. unpublished manuscript, University of Victoria, BC. Laura Richter is a teacher at Lord Byng Elementary School in Richmond, B.C. She is a master's student in Curriculum Studies at the University of Victoria, BC. The story presented here was originally written for a graduate course.

Miss O gently led Laura to that tensioned place in the curricular landscape between the curriculum guide and the lived curricula. And in that between grew this story, which is for Laura already a line of movement we might call a thesis-in-the-making. Laura as a graduate student in curriculum studies has placed herself in the openings the story offers. And at this moment, her interest is in understanding the lived meaning of the click we heard in the tension as she and her children indwelt between curriculum-as-plan and the lived curriculum. And in that space in the middle of her curricular landscape, she is now beginning to hear more deeply echoes of the sound of the click as it opens up into a polyphony of lines of movement, lines such as:

- Experiencing differences in kind in the tension between the master story and the daily stories.

- Experiencing pedagogic reaching as a mode of becoming.

- Pedagogic reaching as a letting go and a letting be.

- Pedagogic listening as a responding to others.

- Hearkening to the call of calling.

At this moment, Laura is drawn into what seems to be an architectonics of lines of movement that we feel sure Deleuze also would hear rather than see as a multiplicity growing in the middle.

Line of Movement #3: In the Difference Between Faceless Others and the Faces of Others

For another line of movement in our C & C landscape, let us move into the difference between what I call "the faceless others" and "faces of others." We return to Miss O in her curricular landscape and recall these words about faces of others:

> External curriculum planners are condemned to plan for faceless people, students shorn of their uniqueness, . . . teachers who become generalized entities. . . . The other curriculum is . . . the lived curriculum, a world of face-to-face living with Andrew, . . .

with Sara, . . . with popular Margaret, . . . with Tom . . . and some
20 others . . ..[12]

What is this saying? In the C & I landscapes, students become faceless
others; in the lived curricula, teachers and students are face to face.

We can see that for a teacher like Miss O, the face of the other is already
inscribed in the "other" of "the other curriculum," the lived curriculum. Implicit
in such an understanding of face is the question of our understanding of
"self/other," the question of how we should understand the pedagogical
relationship of the teaching self and the other, the student. Such a question
places Miss O in curricular site of multiple meanings of "self/other."

In our everyday understanding of "self/other," the self is often understood
as an individualized being bestowed with the self's rights and freedoms. But
Miss O wonders whether or not, in such an understanding, the self may already
be reduced, pared down to an identifiable ego who, in the very act of becoming
an ego, distances others into faceless, objectified others. In this everyday
understanding of self/other, there seems to be subject/object dualism that is
inscribed in the familiar positivistic Cartesian saying: "I think; therefore, I am."

Miss O also knows another everyday understanding of "self/other," one that
intertwines the self as subject and the other as subject—an inter-subjectivity,
which, in the hermeneutic language of Hans Georg Gadamer, is understood as a
fusion of horizons, an intersubjectivity fused into a "we."[13] And although such
romanticized understanding may be tantalizingly holistic, Miss O worries that
there might be something remiss in the synthesized totality.

For Miss O, both of these understandings of "self/other"—the "self/other"
in distanced solitude and the "self/other" in integrated wholeness—express
differences between self and other in terms of more or less, in terms of degree,
neglectful possibly of the irreducible surplus in the difference. Hence, Miss O
seeks to displace and replace these understandings of "self/other" with one that
considers difference in kind as a possibility.

In this, Miss O recalls the challenging remarks of Heidegger, whose works
have long haunted her. She recalls him saying of teaching, teacher, and taught:

---

[12] Aoki, Ted T. (1986). Teaching as indwelling between two curriculum
worlds," *The B.C. Teacher*, April/May (Vancouver: The British Columbia
Teachers' Association); republished in Aoki, Ted. T. (1991). *Inspiriting
Curriculum and Pedagogy: Talks to Teachers*, p. 7. Edmonton: University of
Alberta.
[13] Gadamer, Hans Georg. (1975). *Truth and Method.* New York: The Seabury
Press.

> Teaching is even more difficult than learning. . . . Teaching is
> more difficult than learning because what teaching calls for is
> this; to let learn. . . . If the relation between the teacher and the
> learner is genuine . . . there is never a place in it for the authority
> of the know-it-all or the authoritative sway of the official. . . . It
> . . . is an exalted matter . . . to become a teacher . . . which is
> something else entirely than becoming a famous professor. . . .
> We must keep our eyes fixed firmly on the true relation between
> teacher and taught.[14]

Heeding Heidegger's call "to keep our eyes fixed firmly on the true relationship
between teacher and taught," the between in "self/other," Miss O sets aside the
language of rights, that is, the language of the privileged ego, and beckons a
language of pedagogy that might help her reunderstand "self/other" and embrace
the otherness of others. Feeling a bond of ethicality in her own relationship with
her students, she wonders if it is not in responding to other responsibility that a
teacher finds promise in ethical pedagogy. Is this what Heidegger was pointing
to when he said, "We must keep our eyes fixed firmly on the true relationship
between teacher and taught?" Remembering that etymologically, *pedagogy*
comes from the Greek words *agogue*, to lead, and *pedae*, children, she wonders
about the ethical moment in the difference between teacher and taught, between
self and other. She remembers Emmanuel Levinas, who ethicality in
"self/other" hinges on the self's responsibility to the otherness of others.[15]

In Levinas, Miss O sees a decentering of the self's ego, allowing the
acknowledgement of the teacher's responsibility to others, the students. Hence,
she sees pedagogic leading not so much as asking the followers to follow
because the leader always knows the way. Rather, she sees it as a responsible
responding to students. Such a leading entails at times a letting go that allows a
letting be in students' own becoming. Miss O asks, "In such a leading, is not a
teacher called upon as leader to hearken to the call of the calling that is
teaching?" And in such leading, is there not entailed a humility of obeisance as
a teacher responds to the call of the calling? Is this pedagogic leading a
pedagogic wisdom that comes to thoughtful teachers who, in the midst of the
practice of teaching, listen with care to the voice of the silent other? Is this what
Heraclitus, the Greek philosopher of flux, meant when he told his students in
Athens, "Do not listen to me; listen to the logos?" It is indeed wisdom Miss O
seeks.

---

[14] Heidegger, Martin. (1968). *What is Called Thinking?*, pp. 15-16. New York:
Harper and Row.

[15] Levinas, Emmanuel (1981). *Otherwise Than Being or Beyond Essence*. The
Hague: Martinus Nijhoff.

The Chinese knew well what it is for humans to live in wisdom, for in their language, wisdom is inscribed in a family of words: *human, humility, humus,* and *humor,* all etymologically related as they are, too, in our language. The Chinese characters of a wise leader read *sei-jin* (𤤇)—a person who, indwelling with others (人), stands between heaven and earth (土), listening (耳) to the silence, and who, upon hearing the word, allows it to speak (口) to others so others may follow.

Miss O knows this is but one understanding of pedagogy, one understanding of "self/other" in a curricular landscape that allows multiplicity to grow in the middle.

A LINGERING NOTE

Claimed by a curricular landscape that includes the lived curricula of teachers and students, we dwelled for a while in the midst of a multiplicity of curricula, a landscape radically different in kinds from the traditional, instrumental C & I landscape that has long contained us. We have listened to practicing educators who found themselves in sites of openness between and among the multitude of curricula that grace the landscape. And in those sites we saw insights and heard resonant sounds of "multiplicity growing from the middle."

It is urgent now that those curriculum developers and curriculum supervisors encompassed in the traditional C & I curriculum framework take heed, for in light of the growing skepticism regarding the privileging of modernism, the very curriculum landscape that sustained them may be slipping into obsolescence.

Curriculum developers and curriculum supervisors should heed thoughtful practicing teachers who already seem to know that the privileging of the traditional C & I landscape may no longer hold, but must give way to a more open landscape that offers possibilities by, in part, giving legitimacy to the wisdom held in live stories of people who dwell within the landscape. But most importantly, curriculum developers and curriculum supervisors need to learn to listen to the wisdom of practicing educators, for we are already in the age where *episteme* will not be able to stand alone. It needs to stand together with *sophia,* for it seems that the name of the game is no longer knowledge alone but, rather, the belonging together of knowledge and wisdom.

If that be the case, we should go back to Bourbon Street, where our scientist, a person of knowledge, and our novelist, a person of wisdom, are supposed to be in conversation about "science must be taught as a humanity."

But who knows, because it is in the French Quarter, our friends from France, Jean Francois Lyotard and Gilles Deleuze, may have already joined our scientist and novelist in conversation. Possibly, we might be allowed to listen to their improvised lines of movement growing from the middle of their conversation. And possibly, just possibly, there might be a new language in the making—growing in the middle—a language with a grammar in which a noun is a not always a noun, in which conjoining words like *between* and *and* are no mere joining words, a new language that might allow a transformative resonance of the words *paradigms, practices*, and *possibilities*. If that be so, we should all move to the French Quarter, so that we can not only listen, but also join them right   in   the   middle   of   their   conversation.[16]

---

[16] This article is a distinguished lecture presented by invitation at the 1992 ASCD Annual Conference in New Orleans. The conference theme was "Transforming Learning: Paradigms, Practices, Possibilities."

Part II

Language, Culture, and Curriculum

Chapter 10

Toward Understanding Curriculum: Talk Through Reciprocity of Perspectives[1] (1981)

When two strangers meet, indeed two worlds meet. How is it when two worlds meet? I have heard that a bridge is necessary only when there are two worlds to begin with and when there is a committed interest in bridging the two worlds.

The metaphor of "bridging two worlds" begins to provide us with an image to help us understand what it means when two people meet. But like the everyday metaphor of "understanding each other through contact," I fear that the bridging metaphor is more opaque than transparent and fails to lead us too far in our understanding. I recall Robert G. Hanvey in a paper, "An Attainable Global Perspective," which he presented at a recent WCCI Conference, emphasizing: "Contact alone will not do it. Even sustained contact will not do it. There must be a readiness to respect and accept and a capacity to participate. . . ."[2] Cross-cultural awareness through contact alone results in but a tourist's surface sense of awareness of a culture. There lacks an understanding that penetrates beyond the tourist bureau's gloss.

Often it is said that to understand a person from another land or culture, one must be empathetic. Understanding in our situation must be beyond empathy for as anthropologist Magorah Maruyama says, "Empathy is a projection of feelings between two persons within one epistemology. For understanding in a trans-national or trans-cultural situation, what we need is trans-spection, which is a trans-epistemological process."[3] I interpret Maruyama's "trans-epistemological process" to mean a way of bridging two ways of knowing.

---

[1] Taken from Aoki, Ted T. (1981, March). *Toward understanding curriculum talk through reciprocity of perspectives.* A paper presented at a symposium entitled Toward Understanding Trans-National Curriculum Talk: An Exploration in Cross-Paradigmatic Communication. Presented at the Annual Conference of the Association for Supervision and Curriculum Development, St. Louis, MO.

[2] Hanvey, Robert G. An attainable global perspective. In D. W. Bulam & R. P. Seymour (Eds.), *World Study Action*, linked with World Council for Curriculum and Instruction. Alexandria, VA: Association for Supervision and Curriculum Development.

[3] Maruyama, Magorah. (1970). Towards a cultural technology. Given at the Cultural Technology Symposium, 1970, American Anthropological Association National Meeting, published by Training Center for Community Programs, University of Minnesota. Readers will enjoy Maruyama's paper entitled

My interest in this paper is to understand more fully what it means when two people from different lands meet in a face-to-face situation to make sense together of school and curriculum.

John O'Neill, a phenomenologist and critical social theorist at York University in Toronto, talks of such talk as being essentially "a conversation of mankind" connecting language and reason.[4] How shall we understand such conversation as a meeting of mankind? Approaching such a situation with the image of problem solving or with the image of scientific inquiry is apt to pulverize the lived wholeness of the conversation. I surrender my notion of the "meeting of mankind" to the image of "conversation" that Michael Oakeshott so marvelously furnishes us in "The Voice of Poetry in the Conversation of Mankind." Listen to what he says:

> As civilized human beings, we are the inheritors of a conversation, begun in the primeval forests and extended and made more articulate in the course of centuries. It is a conversation, which goes on both in public and within each of ourselves. It is the ability to participate in this conversation, and not the ability to reason cogently, to make discoveries about the world, or to contrive a better world, which distinguishes the human being from the animal and the civilized man from the barbarian. Indeed, it seems not improbable that it was the engagement in this conversation (where talk is without a conclusion) that gave us our present appearance, man being descended from a race of apes who sat in talk so long and so late that they wore out their tails. Education, properly speaking, is an initiation into the skill and partnership of this conversation in which we learn to recognize the voices, to distinguish the proper occasions of utterance, and in which we acquire the intellectual and moral habits appropriate to conversation. And it is this conversation which, in the end, gives place and character to every human activity and utterance.[5]

Using "conversation" as my paradigm case, I wish to explore three concrete situations.

Paradignatology and its Application to Cross-Disciplinary, Cross-Professional and Cross-Cultural Communication.

[4] John O'Neill, in *Making Sense Together: An Introduction to Wild Sociology* (New York: Harper & Row, 1974), discusses how we make sense together within a framework of conversation.

[5] Michael Oakeshott in "The Voice of Poetry in the Conversation of Mankind" in his *Rationalism in Politics and Other Essays* (London: Methuen & Company, 1962, p. 199).

SITUATION 1. A CONVERSATION WITH
GRADUATE STUDENTS IN CURRICULUM STUDIES

In my work as chairman of a curriculum and instruction department, I find myself occasionally in what I grandiloquently might call a transnational situation when I encounter students from beyond North America—from nations such as Kenya, Zambia, Ghana in Africa; Thailand, Korea, East India, Malaysia in Asia; Afghanistan, Iraq, Lebanon, Egypt in the Middle East. These are graduate students, dedicated educators, who come with profound interest in curriculum studies in an M.Ed. or Ph.D. program, committed to return home following study with us.

Their visits help me to arrest the almost mindless instrumental mode of life that I routinely live as administrator. They help to remind me of the centeredness of conversation in any educative process. Somehow a student's visit transforms, as by magic, the physical environment labeled *office* into a human situation.

What does it mean to understand how an environment becomes a situation? Let us note Strasser's portrayal:

> In 1804 Saint Bruno went to establish himself as a hermit in a savage region of the French Alps. By the very fact that Saint Bruno seeks a place where he and his companions can devote themselves undisturbed in their meditations, the environment (physical geography) ceases to be an environment. The saint asks the mountains and valleys a question: "Where can I establish myself as a hermit?" The mountains and the valleys reply, albeit wordlessly. They reply by what they are. Thus there begins a dialectic, in which things are involved negatively and positively. They are opposed to, or in favour of a certain human intention. They are "useful," "safe," "harmful," "unsuitable," "dangerous." Precisely because things arrange themselves, as it were, around an intention, a "situation" is born."[6]

In a situation within which we as strangers meet, each with his own culturally conditioned horizon, how can we begin to make sense common to us? And in our reaching out for each other through gesture, silence, and talk, how can we become aware of our reachings, knowing fully that our reachings never fully reach?

Fortunately for me each of these graduate students comes to talk in English, although typically his sayings carry an "English" English accent, already

---

[6] Strasser, Stephen. (1963). *Phenomenology and the Human Sciences*, Trans. Henry J. Karen. Pittsburgh: Duquesne University Press.

indicating something of his historical tradition. Beneath the English language he uses an accent of the tribe I would like to hear, the language of the cultural-historical crucible into which as a child he was thrust, within which he likely learned to speak a language, a language in which and through which he lived and experienced life, the language in which and through which he learned to make sense of his lived reality.

I sometimes worry that these educators coming to study with us see their mission as taking home, virtually as "commodities," notions of education and curriculum educators in the Western world espouse. Underlying this view is a naive assumption of the universality of knowledge—a notion that is tenuous and dangerous.

In our conversational situation, the initial turn takes us usually to talk of program and such. But to remind ourselves of who we are in conversation, I ask that we turn the conversation to ourselves. For instance, I ask: "Why are you here in a North American University to study education and curriculum? Are you intending to return to your homeland? Upon your return, what do you intend to do with what you learn here? Would you be concerned about North American intellectual 'imperialism'? Would you be concerned about becoming an instrument of that imperialism? How will you know that what we consider 'good' here is 'good' in your homeland?"

My interest, you see, is in promoting conversation that is a dialogue between two worlds, that ought not to be reduced to a monologue, spoken only in the language of one world, the language of the university professor.

SITUATION 2. A CONVERSATION
WITH FRANCIS LAMPI OF ZAMBIA

I wish now to ask you to enter into another conversation situation. In recent months, Francis Lampi, a young curriculum scholar now at the University of Zambia, and I have been engaged in a conversation through correspondence. In my writings to him, and in my reading of his writings, I find him, Although not physically present, vividly present before me. I can see him, at times serious, and at times smiling. I can hear his deep voice become softer when he becomes serious, become effervescent when he laughs.

Francis wrote to me just recently:

> "I was appointed a junior lecturer in our university (Zambia) .
> . .. My colleagues not only from the University of Zambia but
> from the Ministry of Education as well have all a "real"
> empirical view of knowledge. They are behavioural
> psychologists, believing that the only "effective" teaching can
> be done the Bloom's Taxonomy way, with objectives and
> means to attain them. I feel alone with my concerns . . .."

I replied:

> Your portrayal of your Zambian colleagues' orientation does
> not surprise me a bit. They must have received a powerful bit
> of "behavioural mod" education in the Anglo world. I can
> understand what it is like to feel loneliness.[7]

In trying to make sense of this talk, it may be helpful for you to know that
Francis in his master's program joined me in a curriculum theory class. In our
seminars we cast ourselves within a framework of multiple socio-cultural
realities, paying serious attention to what anthropological philosophies had to
say about the shape of each notion of reality. In this exploration we were
influenced by Continental European thought, which we found less enamoured of
scientism and technology, and much more deeply concerned about what makes
possible our very human thoughts and actions, our human doings and our human
beings.

For instance, we were impressed with Husserl's questioning of the
Cartesian objectivist world and his urgings to bracket out abstracted reifications
so we can move toward understanding "the things themselves," the concreteness
of the concrete world of reality. He led us to suspect that much of our own
everyday curriculum talk, by objectifying and abstracting teachers and students
and their activities, tended to miss the mark.

We have been impressed also by a new breed of sociologists—sociologists
of knowledge and sociological phenomenologists, like Basil Bernstein, Peter
Berger, Thomas Luckman, Alfred Schutz and his disciples, where notions of
beings as actors engaged in the construction of reality made for us much more
sense than the social theorists who tended to reduce out the situational life and
experiences of people.

We were also impressed by critical social theorists like Jurgen Habermas,
Horkheimer, Marcuse, Adorno of the Frankfurt School, who, noting a crisis in
the human sciences, called for emancipation from instrumental and technical
rationality into which so many of us in the Western world have been driven by
our sociocultural tradition to a dialectic rationality of praxis that sees unity in the
dialectic between theory and practice. Within this praxis framework, we began
to appreciate the Third World curriculum efforts of people such as Paulo Freire,
who to us spoke anew with vigour about the educative act.

These interests grew out of our serious effort to heed Husserl's call of "to
the things themselves." In the search for the origin, we have begun to consider
the ontological basis of human thought and action. Such interests have led us to
explore the works of scholars such as Heidegger, Ricouer, and Gadamer, who
seek to understand the essence of our being in language. As David Smith in his
paper indicated, we are what we say.

For Francis Lampi, his colleagues, and me, the effort of turning to the
concrete meant, too, our own personal unfolding, revealing to us new vistas that

---

[7] From personal correspondence.

allowed us, we felt, more adequately to respond to our quest to understand more fully "what it means to educate" and "what it means to be educated."

So when Francis Lampi, my friend from Zambia, upon his return, bemoaned that his colleagues at the University of Zambia and the Ministry of Education are entrenched in a empirical view of knowledge characterized by behavioural psychologism as reflected in Bloom's Taxonomy, he was questioning the imperialism of the scientistic mode of thought characteristic, I daresay, of much of educational thought in North America. It is the thought mode underlying notions such as competency based assessment, competency-based teacher education, management by objectives, and behavioural-objectives-based curriculum development and the like. In effect, he was questioning the orientation to education as thought and practice wherein the fundamental ethos is that of manipulation and control. Within this perspective, assumed is the split between body and mind, body and soul, the separation between the knower and the objective reality out there. Also assumed is that the only acceptable form of understanding is knowledge of facts and theory, and the desirable approach to the world that leads to understanding that of detached but carefully calculated observation.

If I understand what Francis is saying, the kind of teacher education program Zambian students are undergoing should be no different from many of the mainstream pre-service teacher education classes in North America.

If this be so, what seems critically necessary is a serious reflection upon the question, "What is it that makes possible the University of Zambia teacher education curriculum to be like that of mainstream North America?" "An After-Thought"[8] by Bom Mo Chung allowed his thoughts to dwell on the well-worn concepts of development education, "haunted" as he says by imported terms such as "manpower," "planning," "development," "development education" which had guided educational thought in Korea. So infatuated with this language are policy planners in Korea that "higher educational plan" is not called as such but as "higher manpower training plan."

This infatuation is reflected, says Dr. Chung, in the view of education as "instrumentalistic thinking [which] . . . tends to alienate students and teachers from absorbed, committed and joyful learning, estranging them." What is instrumentalism to Dr. Chung? He views it in the following way:

> Instrumentalism is to see the present moment of life as means
> to the next, including the present job, status, residence, human
> relatives and even you yourself. What you do and have now is

---

[8] Bom Mo Chung in "Development Education: An After Thought." In an endeavour to retain as much as possible of the speaking of Dr. Chung, I have liberally used phrases and passages from his paper. To prevent the paper from being punctuated by *ibid*, I have not referenced them. If this nonconventionality disturbs the-reader, I extend apologies. Dr. Chung's paper will appear as an Occasional Paper in the Curriculum Praxis Series, Department of Secondary Education, Faculty of Education, University of Alberta, Edmonton, Alberta.

of no intrinsic value of its own but only of instrumental value to the future. . . . Life seen strictly from such a view has no value, no meaning of its own.

Out of instrumentalism so defined, what we call culture would not be born nor thrive. . . . Those who do not see intrinsic value in whatever he is doing . . . are effectively severed from cultural life, creation and enjoyment. . . . They are alienated persons . . . haunted by ontological doubts about one's own being.

Within this instrumentalist framework, Dr. Chung says,

Whenever the concept of manpower is used, invariably it is a constricted notion that prevails reflected in education as constricted schools, constricted curricula, constricted learning activities, and constricted human beings.

He deplores the reduction of desirable human traits and qualities to "knowledge and skills supposedly required in the job settings," creating the philosophical problem of treating man as means, not an end.

For me, these remarks by Dr. Chung are momentous. They speak fundamentally to Francis Lampi's concerns at the University of Zambia. They speak to us deeply.

Dr. Chung continues in his inner dialogue to confront directly two understandings of "educational planning," one based on the traditional Western social science paradigm of systems thinking, and the other based on Indian religious philosophy. The dialectic is revealing.

Dr. Chung himself trained as an educational planner based on Western thought, characterizes educational planning in the Western idiom in the following way:

After lengthy consideration of needs, forecasts, constraints, resources, forces and what not . . . [educational planners should] come out with some plan for figures of student enrollments, financial investments, policies and so on.

This approach to planning, which he describes as "playing the role of a god-like prophet looking crystal clear into the future," distresses him.

Hence, he seeks an alternative: an understanding of planning that more befits his Asiatic heritage. He employs the notion of "karma" which has to do, he says, with "the secular doctrine of reincarnation" understood as "historical causation." Within this understanding he speaks of social changes: "What makes change successful . . . is not change itself but the historical undercurrent, the necessary Karma, that has been slow in the making." It is an approach that allows Dr. Chung to ask: "What really makes changes possible?"

In answer to the question, he says:

> "History will not respond favourably to those calculating and utilitarian minds who do something today with an eye to the quick and easy return in the future. History responds favourably to something simply because it is the thing that "ought" to be done now and is "desirable" to be done now to the best of your personal, moral and social judgment, and to the best of your calculation."

To Dr. Chung, this karma-based understanding of planning is "in part a philosophy of anti-planning."

Pointing to a concrete instance of karma-based influence, he speaks of the establishment of elementary education in the 1950's (which permitted a populace ready for the transformative decades of the 1960's and 1970's). This action was based, he says, on the "traditional valuation among Korean parents and the need for the educated man in democracy," not because of "calculated manpower needs for economic development." I feel that the Korean parents spoke as embodied people—with blood coursing through them.

With glee Dr. Chung says that it was fortunate that Koreans were not saddled in the 1950's with an Economic Planning Board for Economic Development, for if they were so saddled, planners "would have swayed the glittering sounds of 'five year plans,' 'manpower,' 'investment priorities,' and would have thrashed the 'consumptive' elementary investment and probably put the relative emphasis on the more 'investive' secondary and higher education that would give Koreans manpower in a matter of a few years instead of waiting 15 or more years."

He also looks at two understandings of "development." He finds in South Korea that typically development is understood in practice as: "economic development foremost, overriding other aspects of development—political, social, cultural, intellectual." In fact, he says, these other aspects are taken to be the means to economic development. Dissatisfied with this understanding of development, Dr. Chung proffers another: "Development is creating those social conditions wherein the people in society can achieve the fullest possible self-realization."

Very significantly, Dr. Chung points out that in this realization of the self, what is important is the giving of a second thought, that is, thought that is reflective, thought that has a critical turn. It is only then, he believes, that we come to understand our own crisis in values.

It is this kind of critical turn that allows one "to wonder why only Gross National Product is predominantly assumed to be the indicator of national growth and development." He presses on by adding:

> What about GNS, gross national satisfaction; GNH, gross national happiness, and GNW, gross national welfare that some people have proposed out of desperation? What about gross national learning, gross national reading, gross national

> love, gross national dance and drama performance, gross
> national park stroll, gross national research, exploration,
> expedition . . .?[7]

He continues: "I know these sound a little facetious, but after all, are these not
what people do and value primarily for which economic means are needed?"

He asks social scientists, including educators, to address this problem
squarely—without squinting.   He asks them to be concerned about
instrumentalism run rampant among developmentalists, those who see the
present moment of life as means to the next, including the present job, status,
residence, human relations, and even the person himself. He asks of social
scientists and educators:

> When life from birth to death is seen strictly from an
> instrumentalist's point of view, does it not total up to having
> no value, no meaning of its own? Would not life be a chain of
> void heading toward death, which is itself a supreme void?
> Several from cultural life, creation and enjoyment, are not
> instrumentalists alienated persons . . . haunted by ontological
> doubts about their own being with no room for ontological
> sympathy and commitment?"

This is my understanding of Dr. Chung. Interestingly salient is Dr. Chung's
inner conversation, guided by his interest in coming to a fuller understanding of
"developmental educational" in his own situation:

1. His disclosure of the culturally bound ideologies within
    which each understanding of developmental education is
    embedded.

2. His understanding of the relationship between the two
    modes of understanding developmental education as a
    dialectic movement—without which he would have been
    left with but two monologues. This dialectic tension is at
    the heart of all dialogical conversation.

If East–West conversation in curriculum is to be authentically East–West
dialogue, if North–South conversation is to be authentically North–South
dialogue, I contend that such conversation must be guided by an interest in
understanding more fully what is not said by going beyond what is said.
Without this going beyond, the participants in conversation will not be able to
penetrate each others' unspoken taken-for-granted, that is, each other's ideology,
which is the cultural crucible and context that make possible what is said by
each in the conversational situation.

Essentially, then, authentic conversation is open conversation although not empty conversation. Authentic conversation is one in which the participants in the conversation engage in a reciprocity of perspectives.

Within Dr. Chung, this reciprocity can be seen as a dialectical one empowering him to understand the reciprocity between two deep understandings. It is a dialectic in the sense, too, that in his private conversation the meaningfulness of one understanding comes into view illuminated by the whole context; and the meaningful of the whole comes into view illuminated by a part. It is in this sense that I understand conversation as a bridging of two worlds by a bridge, which is not a bridge.

Chapter 11

Signs of Vitality in Curriculum Scholarship[1] (1985/1991)

You honor me greatly by the award you presented me. I feel grateful that you regard my thoughts and efforts in the field of curriculum worthy of the domain for which CACS stands. My deepest gratitude to you all.

President Richard Butt offered me an opportunity to give a few remarks on what I see as significant features in the curriculum landscape today. If I were to give this talk a title, I would call it, "Signs of Vitality in Curriculum Scholarship." May I offer four themes.

THEME 1—CURRICULUM AS THE LOCUS OF SCHOLARSHIP IN EDUCATION

The happening that has exploded upon the educational scene within the last two decades has resulted from a crisis in what some call "the human sciences." It is characterized by a critical questioning of the ground within which "the human sciences," including education, are situated. Among educators in North America, curriculum scholars have been the first to heed this crisis, giving serious recognition to their work.

What questionings have been taking place in curriculum studies? Let me identify a few:

1. The questioning of the dominance of the technological orientation that prevails in curriculum rooted in instrumental reasoning.

2. The quest for the originary ground of curriculum as a human study.

3. The questioning of the priority to curriculum understanding of epistemological considerations over ontological considerations.

---

[1] This address was first given on the occasion of Professor Aoki's receipt of the Canadian Association of Curriculum Studies Award for Distinguished Contribution to Canadian Curriculum Theory and Practice May 28, 1985, at the CACS/CSSE Conference in Montreal. This version is reprinted from: Aoki, Ted T. (Ed.). (1991). *Inspiriting Curriculum and Pedagogy: Talks to Teachers* (pp. 23–28). Curriculum Praxis, Department of Secondary Education, Faculty of Education, University of Alberta, Edmonton.

4.   The questioning of the adequacy of the assumptions
     underlying the domain of curriculum studies.

In my view this sort of questioning marks the cutting edge of promising
scholarship. I have no doubt that curriculum scholars must be reckoned with
and that they cannot be ignored.

THEME 2—INCREASING RECOGNITION
OF CURRICULUM SCHOLARSHIP
IN MANY FACULTIES OF EDUCATION

For a long time, C & I people in Faculties of Education have been labeled
"methods" people—technicians, really, relegated to teaching "how to" courses.
In our own faculty, the departments of educational psychology, educational
Foundations, and educational administration have been labeled the "basic"
departments, relegating teaching departments like C & I departments to a
derivative position, secondary to the "basic." The C & I departments tended to
be suspended, unrooted, reduced to instrumental reasoning.

Historically, educational psychology has enjoyed a privileged place of its
own, somehow separated from educational foundations, where a motley crew of
sociologists of education and historians of education try to dwell together.

One wonders if the preeminence of educational psychology cannot be
attributed to the way in which the concept of "learning" has become a central
concept in education, a concept so central that many feel that life in education
just cannot go on without the word "learning." In fact, teaching is often seen as
the flip side of "learning." I have a feeling that many believed and still believe
that to understand teaching is to understand learning. When we realize that
learning theory courses are usually mandatory in undergraduate teacher
education programs, one wonders how strongly psychologism prevails. I am
reminded of the ardent pleas of curricularist Dwayne Huebner, to whom, I feel,
not many have given a deserved hearing. What is to be noted here is that it has
taken a curriculum scholar to dare to question the hegemony of the notion of
"learning" in education.

Educational foundations have also gained preeminence over the years. Yet,
increasingly, there is a questioning of the ground of educational foundations.
What I am really asking is: How foundational are educational foundations?
Two points might be raised.

First point. We are increasingly aware of the vigorous interests of
foundations people in curriculum. Educators of the sociological,
anthropological, historical, philosophical persuasions are contributing much to
curriculum studies. They bring disciplined perspectives to understanding of
curriculum, but when they do, we must remember that they are essentially doing
sociology, anthropology, history, philosophy—abstractive studies that try to
understand in disciplined ways something *about* the curriculum world, the

livedness of the everyday life of teachers and students. (Note the preposition "about," which suggests distancing).

Second point. A question flowing from the foregoing is the question of the meaning of "foundation" in foundational studies. Calvin O. Schrag, whom I respect, points to the myth of so-called foundations, indicating the lack of groundedness in the experiences of the people about which they sociologize, anthropologize, historicize, or philosophize. He is saying that the *foundational* are not *foundational enough* and that the originary ground needs to be sought.

Many curriculum people are showing concerted interest in the points I am making and have begun to participate earnestly in the questioning. The vitality of curriculum scholarship has invigorated the field to such an extent that I heard that at the recent AERA in Chicago there is concern for the increasing empowerment of Division B, the curriculum studies division!

I note too that in both Canada and in the United States faculties of education seem to be seeking "curriculum scholars with a new vitality" (not any curriculum scholar).

Even in the subject areas (like language education, social studies education, or home economics education), advertisements call for good familiarity with the field of general curriculum as well as the subject area C & I. We need to assist administrators in their understanding of curriculum scholarship.

I am convinced that where "learning" had the ownership of the center of talks among educators, curriculum is now moving in, and receiving some prominence if not center stage prominence.

THEME 3—THE CELEBRATION OF THE MUNDANE IN CURRICULUM STUDIES (A DIALECTIC BETWEEN THE FIRST AND SECOND ORDER CURRICULUM WORLDS)

We are all familiar with *curriculum-as-plan*. We understand it as it comes in all sizes and shapes—as programs of study, curriculum guides, lesson plans, and unit plans. Curriculum-as-plan is an abstraction yearning to come alive in the presence of teachers and students. What it lacks is situatedness.

A situated curriculum is a curriculum-as-lived. It is curriculum in the presence of people and their meanings. It is an experienced curriculum. I like to call it the first-order curriculum world.

Recently, as many of you know, science educators in Canada conducted a national study of school science-as-lived. It was a fascinating study in two ways: (1) It provided portrayals of school science as distinct from the conceptualized renditions of science typically reflected in curriculum-as-plan, and (2) it provided opportunities to curriculum researchers to employ new human science approaches that I referred to in Theme 1.

Just a month ago, I had the pleasure of hosting the Seventh Annual CACS Symposium. We titled the symposium "Understanding Curriculum-as-Lived," attempting to focus on the first-order world of curriculum. Canadian researchers from coast to coast displayed fine first-order curriculum scholarship in the subject areas of drama education, multicultural education, art education, science education, and social studies education. Demonstrated were the human science research approaches including the autobiographic method, hermeneutics, phenomenology, critical theory, sociology of knowledge, and ethnomethodology. They showed not only epistemological concern but ontological concerns as well.

I feel that, as a group of curriculum scholars, we have begun to attend more seriously to the domain of everyday life in the curriculum world, in a sense, in celebration of the mundane world where people's everyday lives are lived.

I feel that we are now in a position to move towards a juxtaposition of curriculum-as-plan and curriculum-as-lived, which can be explored as twin moments of the same phenomenon, curriculum. I feel that each moment calls for its own form of understanding, but together they seem to unfold as a dialectic unity. It is to this possibility that I say it may be worthwhile to explore *the tensionality* in the dialectic between the First and Second Curriculum Worlds.

THEME 4—RESEARCHING THE MEANING
OF THE COMMONPLACES
OF CURRICULUM PRACTICE

Curriculum essentially belongs to the world of the practical. Hence, curriculum studies, if they are authentic, must return to the concrete world of the practical. Such is my belief.

As curriculum scholars dedicated to the practical, we are mindful of Schwab's caution some years ago that the curriculum world of practice is moribund lacking adequate theories, and that curriculum theories extant are unable to speak of authentically to curriculum practice. We are aware of Schwab's urgings to understand the practical within a deliberative framework. Many have heeded Schwab, and interesting work seems to be ongoing.

In my view, two current developments also deserve our notice. First, of all, there is a serious effort to reunderstand practice. These efforts recognize the inadequacies of "practice" understood merely as *applied theory, that is*, a theory applied to a situation. Within such a view "practice" is understood merely as a derivative of theory—theory holding its monarchical position. I now find "application" a bothersome word. The world in that word puzzles me.

One of the promising reunderstandings of "practice" views practice as *praxis*. Wherein even the notion of theory requires a reunderstanding. I see at this time two major interpretations of praxis—one in tune with the critical social theory of the new Marxist persuasion, and the other, hermeneutic praxis, which seems to flow out of the existential posture of Heidegger and Gadamer. I note that at this cutting edge, forceful work is ongoing. The debates and discussions show promise.

Second, there is another effort to reunderstand practice. In *this* effort, focus is on the *commonplace of curriculum practice and action*. I refer to practices such as curriculum development, curriculum improvement, curriculum implementing, curriculum evaluation, curriculum piloting, and curriculum policymaking. In the past, these commonplaces typically fell prey to a means–ends interpretation, understandably given the almost oppressive technological ethos that prevails and enframes us.

For me, what has been encouraging is the increasing number of scholars who have refused to surrender to the taken-for-granted understandings of these curriculum practices, and have made these very terms problematic. I like the daring in this critical stance.

There is ongoing a *deinstituting* of the traditional understanding of "development," "implementing," "evaluation," and so on, and a *reconstituting* of these commonplaces of curriculum practice, firm in their insistence of recognizing the presence of people who subjectively act.

I applaud these scholars on two counts: for their acknowledgement of the *mundane commonplaces* of curriculum practice as a worthy dwelling place for scholars, and for not being forgetful of the world of curriculum practice that was the raison d'être of the coming into being of curriculum scholarship in the first place, and thus, not yielding to the lure of the siren voices of the human science disciplines as some of our colleagues have done — a movement I refer to as the "flight" from the curriculum field. Our young scholars believe that essentially, curriculum scholarship is not armchair stuff; there is need to return to the messy but alive world of the mundane. I dwelled upon four themes:

1. Curriculum as a locus of scholarship in education.

2. The increasing recognition of curriculum scholarship in many faculties of Education.

3. The celebration of the mundane in curriculum studies: a dialectic between the first-order and second-order curriculum worlds.

4. Researching the meaning of the commonplaces of curriculum practice.

I have traced but a few themes, but I hope sufficiently to portray my sense of the vitality of the curriculum field to which we have committed our lives as educators. Indeed, as a vital field, it is a field of dynamic tensionality wherein curriculum scholars are experiencing new beginnings that promise new possibilities. The debates and discussions are lively. These are indeed exciting times for curriculum people.

I thank you once more for the honor you have bestowed upon me. May I wish you and the association many, many rewarding years of curriculum scholarship.

Chapter 12

The Dialectic of Mother Language and Second Language: A Curriculum Exploration[1] (1987/1991)

In recent years leading curriculum theorists have been calling upon educators to move away from the dominant technicist understanding of the world, and to reorient themselves to a world grounded in the dwelling place of humans. Efforts to understand these human dwelling places have led to a beginning of awareness that the lived experiences of people are made opaque by a conceptual sheath that allows only a prosaic understanding of life-as-lived. There is now an urgent need to penetrate this sheath in an effort to disclose the "*lebenswelt*." Guided by a phenomenological interest, curriculum theorists have begun to consider language as the ground that makes possible the revelation of the life experiences of humans. It is an opportune moment, therefore, to explore language as a way of understanding curriculum orientations, using second-language school programs as the paradigm.

This paper is a venture, first, in asking about the condition that allows a technicist, curriculum-oriented second-language program to dominate the current curriculum scene, and secondly, in exploring an alternative curriculum orientation that understands the wellspring of life, when the relationship is understood dialectically between the second language and the mother language.

CURRICULUM ORIENTATION BASED ON THE TECHNICAL UNDERSTANDING OF LANGUAGE

Within the faculty of education where I dwell, I have experienced three waves of technological change over the past quarter century. We first witnessed the grand entrance of educational media instruments such as the overhead projector, the film projector, the slide projector, and the second-language listening laboratory. The attraction of these instrumental additions led to the hiring of Educational

[1] This invited paper was presented at the 1984 Ottawa Conference on Language, Culture and Literary Identity in Canada and published in Aoki, Ted T. (1987). *The Dialectic of Mother Language and Second Language. Canadian Literature,* Supplement No. 1/May (UBC Publication). It was subsequently printed in Aoki, Ted T. (Ed.). (1991). *Inspiriting Curriculum and Pedagogy: Talks to Teachers* (pp. 23–28). Curriculum Praxis, Department of Secondary Education, Faculty of Education, University of Alberta, Edmonton.

Media professors and to the creation of media resource centers. The most atrocious instrumentalization of a school program within my knowledge during this wave was the *Voix et Image* French-as-a-second-language program, a slide–tape program, which my children experienced in junior high school. The second wave within our faculty was the TV thrust. Education TV was looked upon as the means for delivering the message. Today we see, in our classrooms platforms mounted in corners, empty holding places for TV monitors that no longer exist—monitors that for some reason could not replace the teachers. They stand as museum pieces representing the unfulfilled hopes dispensing education via television. Today, the third wave is insistently upon us. A little over a year ago, *Time* announced without qualm that the computer was the "Man of the Year." In our own faculty a computer needs committee proposes the creation of a teaching department in computer education. The Provincial Minister of Education doles out millions of dollars as matching grants to schools buying Apples, Commodores, IBM, and the like. In the schools, "literacy" curricula—including computerized second language programs—have the teachers in a panic. And in the United States, the Commission on Excellence announces "computer literacy, . . . a new language," as a basic component of the "New Basics."

The language listening labs, the slide–tape second-language program, computerized literacy programs—these reflect the ambience of the situation within which I live, an ambience so dominant that I am urged to say that "the technological ethos permeates everyday existence and orders the agenda of daily life in schools."[2]

Within the predominant presence of machinery, an increasingly dominant understanding of language in second-language curricula sees it as a linguistic code. Within this understanding, the languages of our world exist as multiple codes, each of which can be analyzed into atomic units, and subsequently synthesized into larger units. Languages can be encoded and decoded. Curriculum developers who approach language in this way insist that linguistic codes be learned as codes. Inevitably within this orientation, second-language curriculum discussion becomes dominated by instrumental language such as language-as-a-tool, linguistic teaching strategies, word–referent relationships, and language expressing thought.[3]

Within this understanding, the second-language curriculum fosters linguistic competence wherein learning is understood as achievement of the vocabulary and grammatical rules of the code. Language thus becomes a means to an end, a tool to permit the expression of preexisting thought. Second-language curriculum and instruction thus join technocracy, the world order of

---

[2] Aoki T. T. (1983). *Beyond the Technological Lifestyle: Reshaping Lived Experiences in Schools.* Futurescan Conference, Saskatoon.

[3] Martel, Angeline. (1983). *On Becoming Bilingual: Reflections in Education, Curriculum Praxis Monograph Series Paper No.4.* (1983). (Edmonton University of Alberta, Faculty of Education, Department of Secondary Education.

technical human being given to gaining technical competence in the use of the second language. This curriculum orientation allows the view that language competence in any language essentially involves the learning of purely technical skills. So we find in an Alberta Education curriculum document:

> Many of the skills used in learning another language are the same as those used in learning one's first language. Through the learning of French, the learner can become conscious of those skills and how they apply to any language learning. In this process, the learner develops the ability to listen for meaningful sounds, to understand different elements of a sentence, and to analyze a message so as to group its meaning. Analyzing messages, reconstructing sentences, and situations enhance the development of problem solving skills.[4]

One cannot help but note in this document the way in which technicist language is used to understand language as code, and the way in which instrumentalized language is disembodied of the social and cultural crucible that alone engenders life within language.

CURRICULUM ORIENTATION
IN IMMERSION PROGRAMS

By *immersion programs* I refer to short but intensive programs given to the learning of a second-language quickly and efficiently. Utilitarian and technical in approach, the interest of such a programs is typically in the improvement of job opportunities. Language is understood instrumentally as a tool to facilitate practical communication in job situations. The learner penetrates into the horizon of the second language as a stranger, not so much with openness to the culture that cradles the second-language, but rather with interest in subordinating that strangeness into the scheme of his or her own mother language. The immersion program is an obvious answer to contemporary expectations of efficiency and hence is prone to the technically oriented, technological methodologies of instruction, such as language laboratories, and audiolingual and audiovisual approaches. The overriding aim is the removal of the accent of the mother tongue, the most obvious sign of strangeness.

Oriented instrumentally, these programs see the second language apart from its culture. Hence, language and culture are alienated, remaining in a nondialectical relationship, closed to the dynamic tension between the languages. The teaching/learning milieu becomes entrapped in a technical scheme of ends–means, detached and deontologized. Literacy in a second

---

[4] Alberta Education, *French as a Second Language: Program of Studies* (Edmonton: Alberta Education, 1983), p. 23.

language is understood in much the same way as computer literacy is typically understood, as a gaining of competence in "how to do."

In such an immersion program, the acquisition of second-language competence is seen merely as gaining an additional tool, subordinate to the first language. Hence, it is encapsulated in a monolinguistic and monocultural framework, driven by a tendency toward singular totality and a singular interpretation. Metaphorically, immersion can be likened to taking a bath from which one emerges superficially changed, but essentially no different from the moment of immersion. In a fundamental sense, immersion program have become submersion and even submission.

Such observations are not intended to suggest that immersion programs are inevitably doomed to an instrumental orientation of learning merely another code. What these programs do recognize is that a second language is different. But in understanding this difference in code, they have not appreciated a more promising difference among languages: differences in culture. Such an appreciation goes beyond instrumentalism, promising a dialectic at the cultural level, where the others as strangers can call upon us to understand them within the strangers' own interpretive scheme. It is to this possibility that we must now turn.

BILINGUALISM AS A DIALECTIC
OF COMPLEMENTARITY BETWEEN TWO WORLDS

To understand a second language—or for that matter, any language—as an objectified tool of communication, as a language code, or as a linguistic structure may be technically correct. But, in my view, such an approach commits an unwarranted reductionism by transforming human beings into things. What seems urgent is the recovery of the fullness of language.

I begin with the insight of Humboldt that a view of language is essentially a view of the world. Emphasizing that language is human from its very inception he recognized that a human world without language is not possible, and the fact that man has a world at all depends upon language. Acknowledging the linguisticality of the human world, Hans-Georg Gadamer stressed:

> language has no independent life apart from the world that
> comes to language within it. Not only is the world "world"
> only insofar as it comes into language but language, too, has
> its real being only in the fact that the world is represented
> within it.[5]

Understanding the linguistic nature of the human world, the way in which the human world presents itself in language, the way the world appears in language

---

[5] Hans-Georg Gadamer, *Truth and Method*, translation ed., Garrett Barden and John Cumming (New York: Continuum, 1975),   401.

and is constituted by it, paves the way for understanding the mother language more deeply and more completely.

Each of us is born into a concrete language of our mother tongue. This mother language with which we are at home is the language belonging to a community—a language of sharing, a language of familiarity, a vernacular language of daily conversation, a language with a profound respect of the other as self.

> Language has its true being only in conversation, in the exercise of understanding: between people. . . . Communication . . . does not need any tools, in the real sense of the word. It is a living process in which a community of life is lived out. . . . All forms of human community of life are forms of linguistic community: even more they constitute language. For language, in its nature, is the language conversation, but it acquires its reality only in the process of communicating. This is why it is not a mere means of communication.[6]

Such an understanding of the mother language allows us to see how language, nourishing us, makes of the life-world our home-set within the comfort of the taken-for-granteds, while it simultaneously disorients us into becoming virtual strangers within another's life world.

Hence, when a reporter in reference to the recent Manitoba language issue commented, "Westerners have a virtually unilingual view of Canada," we can understand such a remark in terms of a world of solitude characterized by an imprisonment within the finitude of a world of monolanguage. More serious is the fact that this world of solitude assumes a world without margins, a world without possibility for encounters of unfamiliarity, a world that submerges the "is not" and thus the "not yet." It is a world that is unable to speak authentically of first and second languages.

The crucial question remains: How shall we understand a second language? Any second language will always remain second, and it should be accorded what is appropriate to secondness. Although it is always related to the first language, it cannot replace the mother language that allowed it to come into being as a second language. Coming to know a second language is indeed a coming to know a way to enter a new world. As such it goes far beyond learning a new language as merely a preexistent tool for designating a world already somehow familiar to us, but rather it represents "acquiring a familiarity with the world itself and how it confronts us."[7]

---

[6] Gadamer, p. 404.
[7] Gadamer, p. 405

At the same time, we should bear in mind that learners of a second language do not alter their relationship to the world, but rather enrich and extend it through the world of the foreign language. It is in this sense that George Herbert Mead, half a century ago, was prompted to say, "A person learns a new language and, as we say, gets a new soul . . . he becomes in that sense a different individual. You cannot convey a language as a pure abstraction; you inevitably, in some degree, convey also the life that lies behind it."[8]

In this context, it is helpful to listen to the voices of parents who seem to have an intuitive grasp of the relationship between the mother language and the second language. A Czechoslovakian Canadian parent, for example, voices anguish about the erosion of the self as his son's mother tongue fades:

> My son was born in Canada. When he started school he could speak Czech and English. Now he is in grade five. Now he can listen, speak, read and write in English but can only listen to some Czech. This is not fair. There is so much friend pressure to speak English that he won't even try to speak Czech. He won't bring his friends home and his mother and I are having problems. His self concept is as a half boy. This is not right. Can we not teach English and still have our children proud of their ancestry and mother tongue?[9]

A Japanese Canadian parent speaks from a sense of the ontological realm when he says:

> Together we can teach Japanese and English to complement each other. Like Yin and Yang, together, they will be in harmony. Teach English so that it adds to our being and makes us more whole. Take care not to teach English so that takes away from our being and makes us less than what we can be.[10]

A Mexican Canadian parent speaks of the mutuality of the mother language and the second language in the following way:

> In a few words I believe both the school and the parents are responsible for the complete development of the child—and this includes his languages, culture and all skills and goals.[11]

---

[8] George Herbert Mead, *Mind, Self and Society* (Chicago: Univ. of Chicago Press, 1934), p. 156.

[9] Bruce Bain, *English as a Second Language Needs Assessment: Alberta Hopes* (Edmonton, 1981), p. 26.

[10] Bain, p. 32.

[11] Bain, p. 30.

Those educators who have given of themselves to the instrumental and scientific understanding of language need to listen with care to the way these people understand language. Do not the educators, by intellectualizing, tend to put themselves within a prosaic mentality, where as the lay people speak more from the ground of poetics? Although the educators speak from a technologized or scientifically oriented discipline, do not the parents speak from the ground of their own being? These parents seem to be speaking to "languaging" as communal venturing from an ontological understanding of what it means to speak two languages, enfolded as their lives are existentially as beings engaged in their own becomings as Canadians.

The understanding of bilingualism as a dialectic of complementarity, or as Yin and Yang, begins to bring into fuller view the contextuality of the lived situation that the instrumental and scientific understanding utterly neglects. We are solicitously reminded of the impressionist artist Seurat, whose understanding of the twofoldness of colours has metaphorical relevance in our context.

> Seurat was far more concerned with incomplete mixture, the
> effect that adjacent colors have on each other. . . . Colors
> mutually influence one another when placed side by side, each
> imposing its own complementarity on its neighbour. . . . If the
> two are juxtaposed, each will "reflect" upon the other, with the
> result that both seem strengthened and intensified.[12]

Such an understanding of dialectic as complementarity reminds us in a most profound way of Heidegger, who portrayed his own reactions of translating from one language into another. He speaks of this experience in the following way:

> While I was translating, I often felt as though I were
> wandering back and forth between two language realities, such
> that at moments a radiance shone on which let me sense that
> the wellspring of reality from which these two fundamentally
> different languages arise was the same.[13]

In Heidegger's sense of dialectic, what is central is the revealing of the "wellspring of reality," the source of being from which language comes. It is here that Heidegger shows us in his celebrated way that the essence of language is linguistic but indeed existence.

Revealing as these instances of the dialectic of complementarity might be, what still seems concealed within this formulation is the nature of the relations

---

[12] Robert Wallace. (1969). *The World of Van Gogh, 1853-1890*, p. 73. New York: Time-Life.

[13] Heidegger, Martin (1982). *On the Way to Language*, p. 24. San Francisco: Harper & Row.

between the secondness and firstness of the languages, without which the historicality of the lived situation cannot come authentically alive.

BILINGUALISM AS A HERMENEUTIC DIALECTIC

To speak of a dialectic of complementarity, or its popularized form "unity in differences" (often used to describe Canadian multiculturalism), is to give it a form neglectful of the hermeneutic experience of beings rooted in their mother language—the vernacular world of the language of love, the language of anger, the language of humour, the language of being at one with the language that nurtured and nurtures. From the standpoint of the speaker of the vernacular of his or her own tongue, how are we to understand the experience of the world of the second language?

I take a cue from Gadamer, who claimed that this other world that is experienced is not simply an object of knowledge. It is impossible, he argues, to understand what the language of the other world has to say if it does not speak into a familiar world that provides a point of contact with the text. Accordingly, the other world of the second language is always understood, if at all, from the familiar world of the mother language. Gadamer incisively states:

> However much one may adopt a foreign attitude of mind, one still does not forget one's own view of the world and of language. Rather the other world we encounter is not only strange, but also different in its relations. It has not only its own truth in itself, but also its own truth for us.[14]

Within this understanding of encounter, to be sure, the dialectic we seek is "twofold always," as William Blake would have it, but it is a part–whole dialectic that is situated historically in the realm of the mother language.

To venture forth into the world of the second-language thus is an endeavour that entails the "is," the "is not," and the "not yet." It is a circular journey in which there is always a turning homeward, a re-turn. But unlike the proverbial vicious circle, the circle here is a hermeneutic one, re-entering home always at a different point, thus coming to know the beginning point for the first time. Thus, this hermeneutic circle becomes a fundamental principle of one's man's understanding of one's own nature and situation.

Within this circle, one who studies a second language has at every moment of the study the possibility of a free movement back to one's own self. He [or she] is at once both here in the world of the mother language, and there in the world of the second language. Within this dialectic, the possibility opened up is one of a deeper insight. By questioning the mother language and the second language, by contrasting one with another, the resultant dialectic allows possibilities of a deeper awareness of who one is, and of a fuller understanding

---

[14] Gadamer, p. 400.

of the conditions shaping one's being. It is in this sense that Gadamer speaks of the possibilities of returning home as a changed being:

> If, by entering into foreign linguistic worlds, we overcome the prejudices and limitations of our previous experience of the world, this does not mean that we leave and negate our own world. As travelers we return home with new experiences.[15]

Bilingualism, in this sense, is indeed a mode of being-and-becoming-in-the-world.

For me personally, learning a second language has been an entering into the strange world of unfamiliarity. Gradually, the new language sheds its unfamiliarity as I see more deeply into another perspective of the world and see with new eyes an already familiar world. Two perspectives dance before me and press forward upon me, and when I find difficulty with one perspective, the other lends a willing hand.

Being bilingual in the sense we are now talking about is to meet the unfamiliar second language at the margin of the horizon of the mother language. It is to belong to two worlds at once and yet not belong to either completely. It offers an opportunity to fall back on the only person I must depend on, myself. Being bilingual asks of me that I live while probing life and life experiences. Because I live in tension at the margin, questioning becomes central to my way of life. This questioning is the dialectic between the familiar and the unfamiliar.

Hence, for me, being bilingual is not becoming like the native in a second language, even if I am competent and comfortable in it. Inevitably, I am viscerally linked with my mother language in my "dwelling aright," as Heidegger put it. As Martel summarizes:

> My second language is a vehicular language, my mother tongue is vernacular even though I could claim my mother tongue is not a *patois* and that my second language is often a dialect. This makes of me a bilingual person but not a bicultural being.[1]

As I see it, bilingualism is a mode of being, fully engaged in a twofold dialectic. On the one hand, there is the dialectic between the mother language and the second language, and on the other hand, there is a dialectic between self and the context of the first dialectic.

---

[15] Gadamer p. 407
[1] Martel, p. 50

TOWARD AN AUTHENTIC EDUCATION

Having explored, albeit sketchily, orientations that attempt to make sense of the relationship between the mother language and the second language, I wish now to come back to my own world of curriculum to explore the sense of how curriculum people entertain second-language programs. I find it revealing to listen to the language of school curriculum developers as they constitute and institute second-language programs. Allow me to draw upon a segment of a formal document called the Alberta Program of Studies, issued by the Minister of Education [Extracts from text of "French as a Second Language, Program of Studies," Alberta Education, French A.1 (Junior High)]:

> *Second Language As A Way of Understanding Another Culture:* "In learning French, one gains a new awareness and a greater understanding of culture through the realization that there are similarities and differences between French and English speaking peoples."

> *Second Language As A Way To Openmindedness and Flexibility:* "Awareness that the pattern of living of each group are based on one's environment and experiences will . . . lead to greater openmindedness, flexibility and readiness to understand and accept others as they are."

> *Second Language As Means For Communication:* "Languages are tools which enable the user to elicit and receive information, to express his or her opinions and feelings; in effect to communicate."

> *Second Language As A Way To Jobs:* "With widespread mobility, knowledge of more than one language is becoming increasingly valuable: tourists, technicians, business people, civil servants, diplomats, athletes—people from all walks of life—are going abroad more frequently to visit or to work . . . knowledge [of a foreign language] . . . may well be the deciding factor in obtaining employment in a world where the job market is becoming more competitive."

What is of interest to us is how efforts such as these to constitute and institute second-language program reflect understandings of what we mean by education.

In the first place, in second-language programs where language is understood instrumentally, education itself is likely also to be understood instrumentally. Teaching a second language is viewed as the transmission of a set of codes, and learning is viewed as the achievement and employment of these codes. Education is thus seen as involving a transference and consumption of a commodity called language. Heightened are acts of cognition on the part of both teachers and students, but this heightening is accompanied by a de-ontologizing. Missing is a willing admission of the whole beings of teachers and students. Teaching tends to be reduced to instruction and is understood as a mode of doing. An understanding of teaching as a mode of being is virtually eliminated.

In the second place, the second-language *immersion* program is one given to both extending the language potential as code and to submerging the second-language to a position of an addendum to the first language. So understood, it tends to neglect the potentiality of tension between the mother and second languages. Education becomes acquisition, as in "language acquisition." Understanding the relationship between the mother language and the second language as a situated dialectic would force educators to focus on the tension rather than the acquisition. Moreover, such a tension points to the dialectic between the self and the world, allowing the understanding of *education as "ex-ducere"* (a leading out and an unfolding) speaking ontologically, that is, speaking from within the ground of being of a person who in his being can be seen as coming into his own personal being.

Finally, constituting and instituting a second-language program rooted in the notion of the dialectic between the mother language and the second language seems, as I understand it, to promise *an understanding of education as a leading out and a going beyond* the merely instrumental or immersion stage to the truly authentic. I see here a glimmer of a way of understanding education as a dialectic between *the language of epistemology* and *the language of ontology*. I thus feel that the coming into being of this understanding of education is eminently a bilingual matter.

Chapter 13

Five Curriculum Memos
and a Note for the Next Half-Century[1] (1991)

I am honoured to be called upon to participate in the Department of Secondary Education's celebration marking the 50th anniversary of the coming into being of our Faculty of Education, the constitution in Canada of the first teacher education faculty in a university setting. To mark this anniversary, I join you on this vibrant threshold standing between the past and the future.

On my part, allow me to gather random thoughts in what I call "Five Curriculum Memos and a Note for the Next Half-Century." The title is a half-echo of a book that my son Edward, because of my recent interest in "reflective narratives and curriculum," urged me to read: Italo Calvino's (1988) *Six Memos for the Next Millennium*.[2]

MEMO 1: ED SEC OR "WHERE DID ED CI GO?"

It was in the summer of 1945, not quite 50 years ago, that the Faculty of Education became a part of my life. I was then a student.

1945. Early in that year, I had left the logging camp at Burmis in the Crowsnest Pass, laid down the double-bit axe and eight-foot felling saw, and hiked to the Calgary Normal School, becoming a part of the last gasp of the disappearing normal school system. I understand that it was planned to phase the school out a few years earlier, but it was given a last gasping life by the provincial War Measures Act that tried to address the shortage of teachers created by the war. It was a 2-month program meant to put warm bodies as temporary teachers with temporary certificates in Alberta's rural classrooms—a program augmented by three summer sessions at its northern mother institution in Edmonton, the Faculty of Education—the only one then in Alberta.

I remember well the summer of 1945. For me it was following a 4-month stint as a teacher of Grades 1–8 in a one-room Hutterite school at Hines Creek in the Wheatland School District about 60 miles east of Calgary. That summer I

---

[1] From: Aoki, Ted T. (1991). *Five Curriculum Memos and a Note for the Next Half-Century. Occasional Paper No. 46, Curriculum Praxis.* Department of Secondary Education, Faculty of Education, University of Alberta. This paper was originally presented as the first of the Curriculum Lecture Series inaugurated on September 27, 1991, by the Department of Secondary Education in celebration of the 50th year since the establishment of the Faculty of Education at the University of Alberta in Edmonton, Canada, the first such faculty in Canada.

[2] Calvino, I. (1988). *Six Memos for the Next Millennium.* Cambridge, MA: Harvard University Press.

landed in Corbett Hall on campus to continue the teacher certification program I had begun in January and February at the Calgary Normal School.

Among my instructors was Superintendent James McKay of Sangudo in northwest Alberta. He must have been desperate, for he offered me a principalship of a three-room school. Another instructor was Superintendent Tim Byrne of Foremost in southern Alberta, later the highly respected Deputy Minister of Education, and more recently president of Athabasca University. I worked for top marks in his class, got them, and then applied for a job in his school system. I got a junior high school job as social studies teacher in Foremost.

But what I remember most about my experiences of the summer of 1945 in the midst of the summer-session courses was the night of raucous celebration on Jasper Avenue. The bombs that landed on Hiroshima and Nagasaki had done their jobs. I remembered, amid the noise of celebration, the Hiroshima I had seen 11 years earlier while meeting friends of the family that lived there.

Leap now to 1986. I was again in Hiroshima, this time as program chair for the Hiroshima Conference of the World Council for Curriculum and Instruction (WCCI). While there, I visited alone, within walking distance of the Hiroshima railway station, a Japanese garden I had visited as a youngster in 1934. I lingered, facing one memorialized tree, no longer a tree—a stark, twisted, black remnant of a tree, without foliage, with only a few twisted limbs. A memorial to what? Man's capacity for inhumanity?

I leap back to 1964 when the University of Alberta came to mean more for me. I joined the staff as the most junior staff member in the Faculty and the Department, claiming 19 years of teaching experience in southern Alberta, most of those years as a social studies teacher.

I remember priming myself and primping myself getting ready to teach teachers to be. Think, if you will, of my blind naiveté-oozing confidence, thinking that my 19 years of practical teaching experience would be sufficient to allow me to be a teacher of teachers.

I remember almost to the day when I was emptied of the confidence. I was given my teaching assignment in social studies methods: two undergrad classes and one AD (After Degree) class. What I thought were methods courses were labeled ED CI 266 Social Studies and ED CI 466 Social Studies—and, for the first time, I was transfixed upon the prefix ED CI—curriculum and instruction. I twisted it; I turned it upside-down; I tried many things to answer the question: "How do I understand CI?" I remember well that while I was in the midst of my quandary, J. J. Schwab, a renowned educator from the University of Chicago, came to campus. I recall taking in his lecture, which was for me in a foreign language. He used words like *concepts, conceptualization, the structure of knowledge, the structure of disciplines,* and *epistemology*—a new lexicon for a CI professor.

So began my career as a teacher educator with some practical understanding of social studies and social studies teaching, but with little understanding of curriculum and instruction in a curriculum and instruction department called Secondary Education.

But begin I did. I solicited my senior professors for help. I read Dr. Lawrence Downey's (1965) book *The Secondary Phase of Education*[3]; I pored over an article Marion Jenkinson of Elementary Education gave me titled "Curriculum and Instructional Systems,"[4] written by Mauritz Johnson, Jr. I remember being impressed by Downey's understanding of the structure of knowledge and by Johnson's general systems thinking. Johnson not only depicted "curriculum" as a system, "instruction" as a system, but he also took the little conjunction *and* of "C *and* I" and generated a system out of a coordinating conjunction. Marvelous, I thought.

Today I am thankful that, with all its limitations, there was the label *ED CI* attached to all the courses in our department; more thankful that I became aware of my own ignorance of a field that was to hold my deep interest for years to come.

Last spring I was invited to teach on campus again. Ken Jacknicke, current chair of the department, handed me my assignment. It read "ED SEC 600." I had to ask him, "Where did ED CI go?"

And I reflected. If back in 1964 Lawrence Downey had given me my teaching "assignment" as ED SEC 266/ED SEC 466 instead of ED CI 266/ED CI 466, look at all the anguish and study I could have avoided trying to get to know what C & I really meant.

MEMO 2: CURRICULUM IN THE NEWS: "SCIENCE MUST BE TAUGHT AS A HUMANITY." CURRICULUM TURBULENCE AT THE UNIVERSITY LEVEL?

Earlier this year, I heard over CBC radio a report of a Canada-wide curriculum study at the university undergraduate level. We were told that it was launched by an alarm over the finding that of the high school graduates entering the faculty of science undergraduate programs in Canada, by the end of the third year one-third of the students were dropping out. This apparently triggered a

---

[3] Lawrence Downey was Chair of the Department of Secondary Education, University of Alberta (1961-1966). He has been a long-time mentor, opening doors for me, leading me particularly to scholars in curriculum associated with the University of Chicago such as J. J. Schwab and Elliot Eisner.

[4] It was Marion Jenkinson, a noted scholar in linguistics and language education, who led me to several curriculum writers. Among them was Mauritz Johnson, Jr., whose article titled "Curriculum and Instructional Systems" led me to general systems thinking and curriculum. At that time I admired the holism Johnson brought to curriculum and instruction as he interpreted it through general systems theory. I was, however, less aware then of how the generalized abstraction emptied "C and I" of the concretely lived life of teachers and students.

questioning of why students "successful" in high school science were opting out of the university science programs. So a national study was directed to find out why this was happening, and the researchers involved sought out dropouts to hear their stories of why they dropped out. Those dropouts, we were told, began to say things like:

> We found science a bit boring; we just did experiment after experiment, all preset. We felt our curriculum experiences were not too relevant to our lives. We felt we were just being taught skills and techniques focusing mainly on "how to do's."

In other words, the researchers found that according to these ex-students, university science was somehow out of touch with their own lives. Of course, we don't know how out of touch with life these students themselves were. On reflecting upon the research report, Dr. Smith, the chair of the National Science Research Council, said flatly, "Science must be taught as a humanity."

Of course, it would be of interest to many of us to seek out the fuller texture of the report. But for us, the point of the anecdote is that in this study, to make sense of the university-level science curriculum, the researchers sought out students' portrayals of the science curriculum as experienced (i.e., the lived curriculum).

What is being acknowledged here is the presence of at least two curricula, the curriculum-as-plan and the curriculum-as-lived. We all know of the curriculum-as-plan often manifested in the syllabus, the course outline, or the course text, typically reflecting objective understandings. On the other hand, the curriculum-as-lived is one that students experienced situationally. It is a part of this situated curriculum that the researchers heard when students told their stories of being bored, of experiencing detachment from their life interests and activities.

We in the curriculum world are led to ask the place of stories and narratives in understanding curriculum or doing curriculum research.

MEMO 3: LEGITIMATING NARRATIVES IN CURRICULUM? LEANING ON LYOTARD

I lean on Jean François Lyotard of France whose book *The Postmodern Condition* (1984) is influencing thoughtful curriculum thinkers.[5] In it he casts his eyes over the way of life characterized as modernism with its 2,500 years of tradition from the time of the Greeks, accelerated in modern times by the Age of Enlightenment and the Age of Reason.

Lyotard chooses as his focus not the "will to power" that Nietzsche espoused, not "instrumental reason" that Habermas and the neo-Marxists made as their central questioning, but rather the principle of legitimacy of narratives.

---

[5] Some readers might be interested in a shorter version entitled "The Postmodern Condition" in Baynes, Bohman, and McCarthy (1987).

I feel sure that if Lyotard were to hear "Science must be taught as a humanity," he might entertain questions such as "What legitimated university science curriculum in the past, and how was it legitimated?" and "What needs new legitimation, and how might we go about such legitimation?"

According to Lyotard, modernity is marked by the advance of a scientific and technological mind-set, which in the past has relied on metanarratives to legitimate itself. By the scientific mind-set, he is referring to the way we tend to constitute our world in terms of subject–object dualism, the way it constitutes realms of objective meanings or of subjective meanings. By metanarratives he means the grand stories through which we have come to believe things about "truth," "progress," "rationality," "unity and totality," "subjectivity," " objectivity," "theory–practice" and so on—grand narratives that cradle modernism. He states that legitimation of metanarratives has led to delegitimation of understandings we come to through narratives and stories we daily tell and hear.

Lyotard (1984) boldly states:

> Simplifying to the extreme, I define postmodernism as incredulity toward metanarratives. This incredulity is undoubtedly a product of progress in the sciences. . . . To the obsolescence of the metanarrative apparatus of legitimation corresponds most notably the crisis of metaphysical philosophy and of the university institution that in the past relied on it. (p. 74)

By the obsolescence of the metanarratives of legitimation, he means the diminishing legitimacy of the grand stories about "progress" (progress is always good for us); about "rationality" (by sound reasoning we can arrive at all truths); about "truth" (somewhere there is a thing called "the truth," which by our striving we can discover); about "unity" (unity is not only possible but desirable; hence we should strive to connect things and people into a totality); about "theory" (we should strive for theory, for predictability and applicability throughout the universe are made possible by theory). These are illustrations of grand narratives whose privileged primacy Lyotard questions.

In the West these grand stories support metaphysical philosophy within whose framework the university institution, as we know it, came into being. With the questioning of the credulity of metaphysical philosophy legitimated by metanarratives, the university institution itself is in crisis, so claims Lyotard.

For us, the modernist/postmodernist dialogue allows us to become more deeply aware of the primacy of the modernist vision of the world that has come to dominate education, including curriculum with objectified meanings and objectified research legitimated by metanarratives. If Lyotard (1984) makes sense, it is time not to reject, I insist, but to consider decentering the modernist view of education and to open the way to include alternative meanings, including lived meanings, legitimated by everyday narratives—the stories and narratives in and by which we live daily.

In this context, we might reinterpret what Smith said when he said, "Science must be taught as a humanity." I now hear Smith (a) as recognizing the unwarranted centrality of the scientistic and technological curriculum mind-set understood almost totally in terms of objective meanings, and (b) as calling for a decentering such that a clearing can be opened up to allow humanly embodied meanings to dwell contrapuntally with objective meanings. For the university institution founded within a metaphysical philosophical framework that is fragmented into categories called *faculties* like the Faculty of Science and the Faculty of Arts and Humanities, Smith's call that "science must be taught as a humanity" seems to beckon questioning from the ground up on how the university institution is constituted. Such a questioning, it seems to me, puts not only the structure of the university but also the structure of curriculum at all levels into turbulence, setting another line of movement for curriculum quest in the next half-century.

MEMO 4: CURRICULUM ASSESSMENT ON NATIONAL TV: CRACKS IN NATIONWIDE TESTING?

Just a few days ago, I saw/heard on national TV a brief discussion of the national testing program being promoted, so I understand, by the Canadian Council of Ministers of Education. On the TV program emanating from Toronto were Ms. Fiona Nelson, a Toronto School Board member, and an assessment expert from OISE.

After listening to their stances on national testing, I sent a short letter to Ms. Nelson. It reads:

> Ms. Fiona Nelson
> Toronto Board of Education
> Toronto, Ontario
>
> Dear Ms. Nelson:
>
> I chanced to see/hear you on national TV when you and an evaluation professor from OISE were being interviewed about the national testing movement. Allow me to applaud you for asking for space for localized situational evaluation, questioning the possibility of the dominance of the totalitarian standardized testing program that may misfire in the name of education. In this view, you seem to concur with the Minister of Education of your province who announced a few months ago hesitancy to go along with the national standardized testing program.

I interpreted your stance as one concerned with the possibility that a nation-wide standardized consensus may become indifferent to the situational differences from province to province, from school to school, from classroom to classroom. In an era that seems to have given of itself to instrumental efficiency much too much, it is indeed encouraging to hear of educational leadership that is deeply concerned for the quality of situated living of teachers and students.

I have requested the BC Teachers' Federation to send you a copy of *Voices of Teaching, Vol. II.* In Part B are teacher narratives that speak thoughtfully to teachers' experiences of externally imposed assessment

I wish you and the Toronto Board of Education well.

Cordially yours,

Ted T. Aoki

I look at *Voices of Teaching, Vol. II* (Aoki & Shamsher, 1991)[6] where Part B is titled "Assessment That Is Indifferent to the Lived Situation of Teachers and Students." Within this part is a short but sensitive narrative by Wendy Mathieu, now a practicum associate in the Department. Wendy wrote this 4 years ago when she was engaged in her M.Ed. program in the Department. She titled it "Approaching D-Day: Experiencing Pedagogical Suffocation."[7]

Listen to her narrative:

It's day one of the new semester. Over the past thirty minutes or so, my Grade 12 English students have discussed and questioned with interest the course outline and materials we will be using this term. I've tried to give them a sense of the experiences that we as a class will encounter through all the strands of the language arts: reading, writing, viewing, speaking, listening, acting and thinking. They appear to be interested as we talk about the titles of some of the short stories in our text and about the possible novels and plays we

---

[6] Aoki and Shamsher (1990, 1991) are collections of narratives written by teachers. In these, their efforts were to allow voices of teaching to be heard through the voices of teachers. Underlying is the understanding that teaching as vocation (from Latin *vocare*) is a calling and it is the voice of this calling that speaks to what teaching truly is. For an effort on the place of "listening," see Aoki (1991).

[7] Wendy Mathieu, "Approaching D-Day: Experiencing Pedagogical Suffocation" in Aoki and Shamsher (1991). This sensitive article also appeared in *The Teacher*, 3(5), a magazine publication of the BC Teachers' Federation in 1991.

might read. There are only a few minutes until bell time and I think I've made it . . . but no, the inevitable question that has been lurking under the surface, the one that no one (including me) has addressed, is finally vocalized: "Aren't you gonna tell us anything about the Diploma Exam we'll be writing at the end of June?" Although I've been expecting it, the question still brings to mind my many criticisms of the exam as well as the frustrations that I experience in teaching an English course that ends in a mandatory exam.

My immediate thoughts run to the component of the exam that involves readings and multiple choice questions based on those readings. It irritates me to think that we should ask students to respond to something they have read by answering multiple choice questions that limit their response. This seems so counter to our classroom ambience, which stimulates open-ended discussions allowing each student to explore the many interpretations that can be given to anyone piece of literature. Personal response to literature has been our focus. Where is there room for the voice of the student in this type of exam?

Another feature involving the actual writing of this part of the exam quickly surfaces. In my classroom I am constantly encouraging my students to take advantage of the literary tools at their disposal, a dictionary and a thesaurus, to help them in their understanding of the literature they are reading. This component of "the exam" strictly forbids them from utilizing such tools. When my students ask me why they can't use them, I find it troublesome to have to rationalize the reasons for something I don't really believe in. It's difficult to be genuine in my explanation to them because I am tom between what I have been expecting of them all year and what is allowed by the rules of the exam.

The rules for writing the multiple choice section of the test lead me to think about a prohibition that concerns the written component. As an English teacher in the eighties, and now in the nineties, I've become excited about the advantages and benefits that come from writing with a word processor. In fact, I've been encouraged to implement it in my classroom. It is another tool that has helped some of my students become better writers. The day for the written exam comes and again, its use is prohibited. At this point I worry about my students for whom handwriting is such an arduous task.

The format for writing the written component of "the exam" annoys me even more. All of my teacher education and the research in composition emphasize that the process of writing, not just the product, is what is important. "The exam" though asks for the three finished writing products—in two and a half hours! Again, I agonize because of my belief that writing is a recursive process that requires time for revising and editing. What does this say for the many hours we've spent working with peer editing and stressing the need for more than one draft?

Over the five months we're together, I encourage my students to be creative and original in their writing—to break away from the old ways—and to find their own voice in writing. I wonder if the people who mark my students' papers are able to recognize the attempts made by the writers to develop their own voice and style. What if the markers still believe in the old five-paragraph essay? What if they don't believe that a sentence fragment can be an element of style?

"The exam" leaves no opportunity for my students to demonstrate the gains they have made in the acting speaking and listening strands of the program, areas in which some of their greatest achievements have been made through the year. As a teacher I am given fifty percent of the student's final mark to assess these areas, but that is not enough. Although I am expected to teach one hundred percent of the course, I am left to determine only half of each student's final grade and the exam only tests three of the language arts strands. My students (and I) sometimes begin to question whether or not much of what we do all year is inane in light of the exam at the end. I believe I could be appeased if the diploma exam only counted for the thirty percent of my students' final grade. Ah yes! Perhaps this mental tirade of criticisms and complaints about "the exam" touches only the surface of the struggle I am having with it.

Experiencing Pedagogical Suffocation

The problem centers more closely around the futility I feel as a teacher in trying to teach an integrated and individualized curriculum which, in the end, is evaluated by a cold and impersonal exam. Maybe, what is really bothering me is that I am upset by the notion that some outside exam could even attempt to "measure" the lived experiences that have occurred within my English classroom over the course of the term. Perhaps that's not the root of the frustration either. Maybe, I am really afraid that my teaching and many students' learning are being suffocated by the omnipresence of the impending exam. Emotionally, I am angry that "the exam" has become the most important thing to students (and to some teachers too!). How has this exam gained the prestigious position of being the finale for my students' high school English experience?

My physical reaction of teeth clenching belies the calmness with which my response comes. Underneath my nearly composed exterior is the ongoing personal struggle I am experiencing with this all pervading force—"The Diploma Exam." Having expected this question from my students, though, I am prepared with copies of the materials the "department" has sent us to administer to our students. Things that explain all the what, where, and when. I pass them out (knowing that they will have lost them by the end of the semester when we might glance at them). I explain to the students that we need not concern ourselves with this now, but come June, I will teach them how to succeed at "the exam." This satisfies them, and so until "D-Day" (my students' term for Diploma Exam day), we get on with living and experiencing what it really is to live and learn the joys that can evolve in a high school English classroom. I have come to terms that life in my classroom will continue before (and after) "the exam."

MEMO 5: "CURRICULUM AND INSTRUCTION" GOES; UP POPS "CURRICULUM AND ASSESSMENT"

The anecdote involving Fiona Nelson and Wendy Mathieu's narrative remind me of the BC curriculum document that goes by the futuristic label *Year 2000* (BC Ministry of Education, n.d.),[8] marking the next millennium—a touch of Italo Calvino's interest! If we slide under the captivating title *Year 2000*, we find as subtitle: "A Curriculum and Assessment Framework for the Future."

A "Curriculum and Assessment Framework?" Is this the C & I framework in a new guise? As I mentioned earlier, since 1964 I have been toiling with interested colleagues within this Faculty and beyond to make sense of the multiple ways in which the words *curriculum* and *instruction* can be understood. We've twisted and turned the word *curriculum* around this way and that way. We've tried curriculum as *currere*[9]; we've tried different ways of understanding curriculum development, curriculum implementation, curriculum evaluation, curriculum assessment, curriculum policymaking; we've tried curriculum praxis, curriculum as ideology[10]; we've tried curriculum-as-plan and curriculum-as-lived.

---

[8] *Year 2000: A Curriculum and Assessment Framework for the Future* is a curriculum document published by the BC Ministry of Education (n.d.) following discussion throughout the province with parents, educators, and the public. It serves as a "blueprint for provincial curriculum and assessment work leading into the next century."

[9] In the most notable pioneering work in curriculum in North America have been the efforts of Bill Pinar, currently of Louisiana State University. His *Curriculum Theorizing: The Reconceptualists* (1975) marked a turn away from instrumentalism that was the hallmark of curriculum to literary and linguistic discourse, nurturing thereby the life of language in curriculum. His work is being carried on most notably by scholars such as Madeleine Grumet, Joanne Pagano, and Janet Miller, all of who have been visiting scholars in curriculum studies at the University of Alberta by invitation of the Department of Secondary Education. Without doubt the linguistic turn in curriculum discourse they have been advancing will blossom further in the 1990s.

[10] Undoubtedly the work of Michael Apple of the University of Wisconsin beginning with his publication *Ideology and Curriculum* (1979) became a dominant line of curriculum thought and action in the 1980s. Flowing from the neo-Marxist critical social theory framework aligned with the Frankfurt School in Germany, Apple pioneered the establishment of a discourse of praxis with its distinctive flavour of "reflection." Apple and his fellow workers, like Nancy King and Glenn Hula, have been visiting scholars in the Department of Secondary Education, University of Alberta.

CHAPTER 13

Likewise we've looked at *instruction,* and have tried replacing it with *teaching*; we've tried restoring the word *pedagogy,*[11] knowing of the Continental European's penchant for it (in North America, Max van Manen of our Department has been the driving force in legitimating the word *pedagogy*).

And without doubt, many members of this department and faculty have opened up clearings for new modes of understanding "curriculum and pedagogy," "curriculum and teaching," thereby moving beyond the instrumentalism that underlies "curriculum and instruction."

Now we have before us a seemingly new framework labeled *curriculum and assessment,* a framework that seems to flow from prelegitimated existence of branches within some ministries like the Curriculum Branch and the Assessment Branch.

As we have boldly faced words like *curriculum* and *pedagogy* in the past, perhaps it is time that we began to explore more fully the question of the legitimacy of frameworks such as "the C & I framework" whose traces still remain after erasure under the label *curriculum and assessment framework.*

When we see an expression such as *curriculum and assessment,* we often succumb to the lure of the substantive terms *curriculum* and *assessment.* Some say that this fondness for substantive terms is a reflection of what some anthropological linguists say about western cultures' bent toward nouns with interest in the "whatness" of things compared with other cultures' bent toward relations and relational words like prepositions and conjunctions. Here I am reminded of Marcus and Fischer (1986), who in *Anthropology as Cultural Critique* wrote: "The Samoan language has no terms corresponding to 'personality,' 'self,' 'character;' instead of our Socratic 'Know thyself,' Samoans say, 'Take care of the relationship.'"[12]

---

[11] The word *pedagogy* as a key lexicon in North American curriculum discourse today resulted in the main through the efforts of Max van Manen of our department. I recall an early conversation with Max, who himself is a product of the Continental European tradition, about how the word *pedagogy* seems to have been set aside in North American educational discourse in favour of the more instrumentalist word *instruction.* As founding editor of *Phenomenology + Pedagogy,* he has not only introduced the word pedagogy textured in the language of phenomenology, but has promoted a notion of theorizing that breaks with the traditional understanding of theory in "theory and practice." His books *Researching Lived Experience* (1990) and *The Tact of Teaching* (1991) are no doubt major contributions to curriculum discourse.

[12] In curriculum thinking, we in North America are becoming aware of the dominance in our discourse of Euro-Ameri-centricity and the need for openness to others. In this connection, it is of interest to see how postmodernist scholars are exploring premodernist East Asian thought. See, for example, Miyoshi and Harootunian (1988).

In keeping with such saying, I interrupt the gaze upon the nouns in "curriculum and assessment," and turn my attention to the *and*, reminiscent of Mauritz Johnson who included a concern for *and* when he explained the expression *curriculum and instruction.* Such a gaze places the *and* into a bit of turbulence. Let's play a bit with multiple meanings of *and*.

And, we were taught, is a conjunction, a word that relates. It is, moreover, a coordinate conjunction, said to cojoin things of equal weight to promote a stilled balance. *Curriculum* and *assessment*, two separate words like two separate branches, but somehow connected. "And" as separator and co-joiner.

But when we become more thoughtful, we may begin to see *and* in motion, moving from left to right in a linear fashion. Our thinking might go, "We develop curriculum first and at the end we assess." We are well aware of this form of thinking. It is of the same breed of thinking as the following: curriculum development, curriculum implementation, and curriculum evaluation, sequentially arranged. It has a neat linear logic of its own.

If we continue our gaze upon *and*, we may begin to see the flow moving in the opposite direction "from assessment to curriculum." A few months ago, at a BC Teachers Federation-sponsored "student assessment" conference, an assessment professor made an explicit statement on this flow. He almost shouted: "Assessment should direct curriculum." Again, *and* in linear movement, better said: "from this to that."

If we continue not so much to ponder upon the *and* but rather to slip underneath it or slide elsewhere, we are apt to come to sense that the label of the framework *curriculum* and *assessment* suggests, too readily perhaps, the presence of two identities that could be bridged by *and*. But accepting the two identities and situating ourselves in that geographic space between *curriculum* and *assessment*, we are led to ask, "Which understanding of *curriculum* is allowed? What sort of narrative legitimates it? What understandings of the word *curriculum* are erased?" So with the word assessment we can ask, "Which understanding of assessment is allowed? What metanarrative legitimates it? What understandings of the word *assessment* are erased?" With these questions, we become mindful not only of the multiplicity of meanings of each word in "curriculum and assessment," but also of how this multiplicity can proliferate the interplay among these meanings.

I feel convinced that we are at the threshold that calls for serious questioning of the curriculum frameworks that under different guises seem entrenched in our educational discourse.

A NOTE FOR THE NEXT HALF-CENTURY ...
AND ... AND ... AND ...

At this moment, I await a response from Fiona Nelson of the Toronto School Board. And as I wait, I pause to remember some of the *and* in the five previous memos:

Memo 1: Curriculum *and* Instruction
         ED CI *and* ED SEC

Memo 2: Science *and* Humanity
         Curriculum-as-Plan *and*
         Curriculum-as-Lived

Memo 3: Metanarratives *and* Narratives Modernity
         and Postmodernity

Memo 4: National Testing *and* Situational
         Evaluation

Memo 5: Curriculum *and* Assessment

As I move to dwell in the *and*, I sense I need to caution myself, for I seem to be caught in all the risks of dualism. I jump up and down in the *and* let more *ands* tumble out. I rewrite:

Memo 1: *and* Curriculum and Instruction *and*

Memo 2: *and* Science *and* Humanity *and*
         and C-as-P *and* C-as-L *and*

Memo 3: *and* Metanarratives *and* Narratives *and*
         Modernity *and* Postmodernity *and*

Memo 4: *and* National Testing *and* Situational
         Education *and*

Memo 5: *and* Curriculum *and* Assessment *and* . . .
         . . . AND . . . AND . . . AND . . .

I revel in the writing space that seems to dissolve beginnings and endings, that proliferates and disseminates *and* here, there, and in unexpected places. I am now thinking, maybe I would like to play in and among the *and* for a while, at least for a part of the next 50 years.

REFERENCES

Aoki, T. T., & Shamsher, M. (Eds.). (1990). *Voices of teaching, volume I.* BC Teachers Federation.
Aoki, T. T., & Shamsher, M. (Eds.). (1991). *Voices of teaching, volume II.* BC Teachers' Federation.
Apple, M. W. (1979). *Ideology and curriculum.* London: Routledge & Kegan

Paul.

Baynes, K., Bohman, J., & McCarthy, T. (1987). *After philosophy: End of transformation.* Cambridge, MA: MIT Press.

BC Ministry of Education. (n.d.). Year 2000: *A curriculum and assessment framework for the future.* Victoria, BC: Author.

Calvino, I. (1988). *Six memos for the next millennium.* Cambridge, MA: Harvard University Press.

Downey, L. (1965). *The secondary phase of education.* New York: Blaisdell.

Lyotard, J. F. (1984). *The postmodern condition.* Minneapolis: University of Minnesota Press.

Miyoshi, M., & Harootunian, H.D. (Eds.). (1988). *Postmodernism and Japan.* Durham, NC: Duke University Press.

Marcus, G., & Fischer, M. (1986). *Anthropology as cultural critique.* Chicago, IL: University of Chicago Press.

Pinar, W. (1975). *Curriculum theorizing: The reconceptualists.* Berkeley, CA: McCutchan.

Van Manen, M. (1990). *Researching lived experience.* New York: State University of New York Press.

Van Manen, M. (1991). *The tact of teaching.* New York: State University of New York Press.

Chapter 14

In the Midst of Slippery
Theme-Words: Living as Designers
of Japanese Canadian Curriculum[1] (1992)

OPENING UP TO THE SITE OF DESIGNERS

To be called to a national gathering of curriculum experts dedicated to the production of Japanese Canadian curricula and to be drawn into the midst of the life of curriculum praxis and curriculum theorizing is for me to experience a resonance that seems to touch the core of my being as a sometime Japanese Canadian educator and student of curriculum.[2]

An echo that still resounds within me is a personal memory of the first day as a licensed teacher forty 40 years ago. It was in spring 1945. The war in the Pacific was still waging. I can still remember, as I stood facing 30 some Occidental faces, Grades 1-8, a question that lurked silently within me: "I wonder what it is like for them, my students, to be facing a Japanese Canadian teacher?" I did not ask my students this phenomenological question. Perhaps, I should have. But what now provokes me to thought is how the silent question some forty years ago is a reminder of an era, at least in British Columbia, when Japanese Canadians were not allowed to be teachers of Occidental students.

Now, today, 40-some years later, within what questions are we inhabiting as Japanese Canadian educators? At this conference we are immersed openly in curricular questions as we participate in the construction of Japanese Canadian curricula. What a leap in the texture of the questions from 1945 to 1992, telling us something of the situated lives of Japanese Canadian teachers! I delight in this leap, prompting me to wonder about the texture of the lived landscape of designers of Japanese Canadian curriculum. This is the focus of my address today.

---

[1] An invited paper originally presented as: Aoki, Ted T. (1992). *In the midst of slippery theme-words: Living as designers of Japanese Canadian curriculum.* An invited paper presented at Designing Japanese Canadian Curriculum Conference held on May 21, 22, and 23, 1992, at the Novotel Hotel, North York, Ontario.

[2] Ted Aoki, persuaded that in spite of theorizing in curriculum and in pedagogy over the past half century, there persists instrumentalism in the geopolitics of curriculum discourse, called for the questioning of the frozen, striated curricular landscape in "Legitimating the Lived Curriculum: The Other Curriculum that Teachers in Their Practical Wisdom Know," an invited paper presented at the 47th Annual ASCD Conference in New Orleans (April 1992).

TOWARD UNDERSTANDING LANDSCAPES:
A LINGUISTIC TURN

How shall we understand the texture of the landscape of designers of Japanese Canadian curriculum? Such a question calls upon us as curriculum people to bring to the fore at least two related landscapes:

1. The landscape of *multiculturalism* within which we dwell as Japanese Canadians and/or as designers of Japanese Canadian curricula.
2. The landscape of *curriculum* within which we as curriculum designers have situated ourselves.

The call to unfold the texture of the landscapes draws me to language. Why language, we might ask?

In recent years, increasingly, curriculum scholars have opened themselves to the realm of language, linguistics, discourse and narratives to understand their own field. Within this curricular turn, language is understood not so much as a disembodied tool of communication caught up in an instrumental view of language, but more so language is understood in an embodied way—a way that allows us to say, "We are the language we speak" or "Language is the house of Being."

Language so understood allows us a way to understand the texture of the two landscapes of our interest, and at the same time, to reveal to us by the very language we speak, who we indeed are as human beings.

But this talk is too glib, too abstractive. Allow me to try to incarnate what I have been saying.

For this, I lean on Basho, a favourite poet of mine, a haiku artist who in one of his many haikus sang:

良く見れば なづな花咲く 垣根かな

When I look carefully
I see the nazuna blooming
By the hedge.

First, may I ask, what did you experience when these texts appeared before you? Does your ongoing experience right now have anything to do with your own linguistic makeup, how you are the language you speak, the language you read, the language you write?

Allow me to offer my reading. I was first drawn to my favourite haiku as Basho wrote it:

良く見れば なづ女花咲く垣根かな

(Yoku mireba nazuna hana saku kakine kana.)

And as I am so drawn, I remember well 60 years ago, bowing with my father before Basho's simple grave beside a mountain path somewhere near Mito, north of Tokyo. I revel in the inscribed pulsation of the 5/7/5 rhythm, marveling at how Basho made the seeming constraint of the preset rhythm a counterpoint to poetic flight. I also revel in the flow of the strokes of the "fudé" (brush), a veritable calligraphic dancing—done by a Nisei who is even now studying calligraphy with a Chinese master and a Japanese master.

Then I read: "When I look carefully, I see the nazuna blooming by the hedge," and in this reading, I feel I am drawn into another world—a discourse world in the English language.

In this reading, what looms large for me are the "I who looks" and the "I who sees." And I wonder if this way of living in language is not a reflection of the subject–object dualism that has long dominated the Western way of knowing. In the translated haiku, is it I, the subject, that looks at an object of the looking? Is it I, the subject, that sees an object of the seeing? It seems it is a way of understanding self-in-world that privileges a person-centered universe, an anthropo-centeredness that marks this language. It seems it is inscribed with the makings of an ego-centered universe that is ever in danger of slipping into narcissism. And I am beckoned to remember Christopher Lasch, who in his book, *The Culture of Narcissism: American Life in the Age of Diminishing Expectations* (1979) spoke of the minimalization of the self. I am left with a tinge of shudder.

I allow myself to return to Basho's words. I note in "yoku mireba" a dispersal of the subject "I." What we are left with is "gazing," a gentle movement subordinate perhaps to a larger movement, "the blooming of the nazuna by the hedge." I feel that it is the being of nature in bloom that holds and sustains the gaze. It seems, too, that it is not so much the voice of the subject who looks and sees, but rather the voice of nature that is speaking.

I am led to wonder if indeed these are different ways of understanding, different linguistic worlds, and different discourses with different grammars. I find myself flowing in the midst of these discourses, and I feel that I am in that little open space between the words "Japanese" and "Canadian" in "Japanese Canadian."

It is here that we might lean on thoughtful people like Joy Kogawa who writes

not　おばさん　nor "auntie," but "obasan"; not　いつか

nor "sometime," but "itsuka." Could it be that this subtle linguistic turn is already flowing as a minority language of Japanese Canadians growing in the middle some place?

THEME-WORDS IN THE LANDSCAPE OF MULTICULTURALISM

You can see how I have already slipped into the texture of the landscape of multiculturalism. But because since I have already begun to quest the meaning of what it is to be a Japanese Canadian, let me note how I've become more aware of how slippery is the very name "Japanese Canadian," a theme-word of our Conference.

The Theme-Word: "Japanese Canadian"

For most of us, the term "Japanese Canadian" has a stable finiteness in the realm of multicultural Canada, and we can define the term with relative ease in sayings such as "Canadians of Japanese ethnic origin" or "Canadians with Japanese heritage."

I experienced slipperiness when a few years ago, OISE (the Ontario Institute of Studies in Education) asked me to serve as an external examiner for an interesting phenomenological study in multicultural education. The text of our focus was a doctoral study by a young Hebrew scholar from Israel, titled "Ethnic and National Identity Among Jewish Students in Ontario." What struck me from the outset of my reading was the way in which the Canadian-born students were referred to by the researcher. Through some 300 pages, these students were called "Canadian Jews."

So as external examiner, usually given the privilege of opening a conversation with the candidate, I began:

> Mr. Shamai, I have been calling myself a Japanese Canadian, and people like me have become accustomed to being called Japanese Canadians, not Canadian Japanese. In your dissertation, you referred to the students all born in Canada as "Canadian Jews." In our multicultural context, does it make a difference whether "Canadian" is a noun or an adjective? Or is it merely a semantic matter, as some would say?

I leave the episode itself suspended, for the point is not so much to define who we are, but more so to acknowledge what some linguists tell us—the inherent ambiguity of any word, even proper names like "Japanese Canadians" that slide about in their slipperiness.

and that in this context "words (signifiers) slip over the signified endlessly."

What does this mean to us? It means that every word has possibilities of multiple meanings and that a choice of which meaning is to count is a legitimating process, a political process, conscious or unconscious. Such a thought provokes us to thought about other theme-words that we thrive on in the landscape of multiculturalism—theme-words like "ethnicity," "ethnic identity," "heritage," "the Canadian nation," "minorities and minority rights," and, of course, "multiculturalism." And remembering where I now am, I am urged to ask, "How should we as curriculum designers approach our tasks when we know that our theme-words slide about, refusing to stand still?"

The Theme-Word: "Multiculturalism"

I wish to touch on another of these theme-words, "multiculturalism." As we well know, the word "multiculturalism" has gained a moment of legitimacy. It gained some measure of political legitimacy when it became a part of the lexicon of the federal bureaucracy—as, at first, the Multicultural Branch became an arm of the Department of the Secretary of State. And later, it gained more legitimacy when a full-fledged Department of Multiculturalism and Citizenship came into being, producing and distributing a newsletter titled *Together*, a word implying a dream of multicultural unity in Canada.

At a recent conference in New Orleans of the Association for Supervision and Curriculum Development, I was struck by our American neighbours' surge of curricular interest in "multiculturalism." I chuckled to myself, noting their effort to slide away from a melting-pot metaphor of multiculturalism to one of mosaic, a metaphor of some long legitimacy in Canada.

But understandings of "multiculturalism" discomforting to many are surfacing. Shall we ignore them or allow dialogue to flow made possible by their surfacing? Let me cite two concrete situations:

First, about a year ago there appeared in the *Vancouver Sun* an article on a new TV series titled *Diversity,* supported in part by Multiculturalism and Citizenship Canada. The caption read, "TV Program offers *Diversity* minus the dirty culture words." The article began:

> For the staff of *Diversity,* the dirty words are the M-word and the E-word. They don't want words like "multicultural" or "ethnic" used to describe their new information series. Such words conjure up scenes of festive clothing, special holidays, Easter egg painting contests, clog dancing festivals and other happy imagery of Canada's vertical mosaic. So we won't use these words here. (*Vancouver Sun*, October 6, 1990, p. B-10)

These words of the article caused me to pause and to wonder. Are the bread-and-butter words for Multiculturalism and Citizenship Canada, theme-words like "multiculturalism" and "ethnicity," in a bit of turbulence?

In the *Together* magazine covering the same TV *Diversity* program, I found the word "multiculturalism" fully restored. Its article read:

> *Diversity* will bring the positive aspects of multiculturalism to the screen. . . . Instead of dwelling on ethnic food and exotic costumes, this program will present multicultural news items, in-depth reviews of current affairs and studio interviews. (*Together,* Multiculturalism and Citizenship Canada, Fall, 1990, p. 19)

Midst the sliding of the word "multiculturalism" in both articles there is a tone critical of curricula composed of ethnic foods and exotic costumes, the kind of program we in the field of curriculum refer to as the museum approach in multicultural curriculum (Werner et al., 1977). Why "museum"? Because of the approach in which curiosities are displayed museum-fashion to be looked at by subjects from an objective distance, promoting what smacks of a breed of voyeurism based on the subject-object dualistic epistemology that was mentioned earlier. There is an aethicality that is obscured by the supposed neutrality in objectivity.

Second, another discomforting item. Over these past months, we have been witness to national constitutional discussions that have included talk of erasing "multiculturalism" from the lexicon of the Federal Government structure. In fact, in a recent nomination meeting for a political party in Vancouver, a candidate called out in his victory speech: "Multiculturalism should be wiped out in Canada. Why should we cater to heritages of the ethnics that they left behind to come to Canada? They should be all Canadians."

I interpreted this candidate in part as questioning "multiculturalism" that understands multiplicity strictly as cultural identities, a multiplicity that slips into the language of heritages, a multiplicity that slips into a display of national flags!

As for me, I am supportive of the understanding of Canada as a multiplicity of cultures, particularly as a counterpoint whenever the dominant majority cultures become indifferent to Canada's minorities. I suppose I reflect a minority voice that asks that minorities not be erased. But I am supportive of multiculturalism for another reason. Let me try to unfold it in a roundabout way as I question the way we have tended to understand the multicultural landscape as a multiplicity of cultural identities, large and small, visible and invisible.

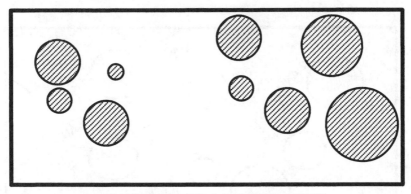

MULTIPLICITY AS IDENTITIES

To be oriented toward the identity view of "multiculturalism" is to be attracted to the noun view or the thing view of ethnic identities. Such a way of positing cultural identities in a landscape is, we are told, a cultural habit of modernism grounded in the metaphysics of presence (Bernstein, 1992, p. 225). That is, we are drawn into a view that an identity is a preexistent presence—a presence we can re-present by careful scrutiny and copy. Multiculturalism as multiple identities is the privileged way of understanding multiculturalism.

But what if we were to heed a saying, "multiplicity is not a noun," a claim made by Gilles Deleuze, for whom, like the Greek Heraclitus, life is ever in a movement of flux? With such a saying, can we remove ourselves to a different place where multiplicity is not a noun?

Where is such a place of multiplicity? In *Dialogues,* Deleuze (1987) states: "In a multiplicity what counts are not the elements, but what there is between, the between, a site of relations which are not separable from each other. Every multiplicity *grows in the middle*" (p. viii).

Deleuze is urging us to displace ourselves from our fondness of noun-oriented, thing-oriented entities, that give us a thing-oriented view of multiculturalism, to decenter ourselves from such an established metaphysical view, and to place ourselves in the midst, between and among the cultural entities. He says, living in such a place of between is a living in the midst of differences, where, according to Deleuze, multiplicity grows as lines of movement.

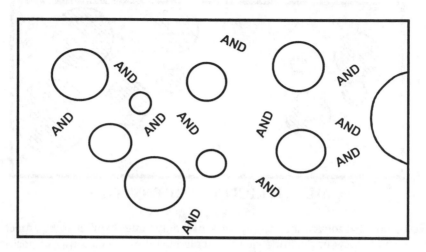

MULTICULTURALISM AS MULTIPLICITY

In noting the between as a place of difference, we might listen more fully to what Deleuze (1988) has to say elsewhere about difference:

- "We tend to think in terms of more or less, that is to see difference in degree where there are differences in kind" (p. 21).
- " . . . each time that we think in terms of more or less, we have already disregarded difference in kind between the two orders, or between beings, between existents " (p. 20).
- "Concerning everything in terms of more or less, seeing nothing but difference in degree . . . where, more profoundly, there are differences in kind is perhaps the most general error of thought, the error common to science and metaphysics" (p. 20).

Deleuze, in calling upon us to think differently, alerts us to how differently "difference" might be understood, and further, how to be seduced to understanding "difference" as difference in degree may be to become indifferent to difference in kind.

Allow me now to return to Basho's haiku where we noted that the two versions are different. We can note that this difference is not so much a difference in degree but a difference in kind, two different discourses that ought not to be integrated into a homogeneous oneness. Rather, we might be creatively productive in the difference, growing uniquely Japanese Canadian lines of movement, among which might be a new language, a minority's English, which is neither Japanese nor the English of the dominant majority. And, as we said earlier, this minority English may have a grammar wherein a noun is not always a noun, where joining words like "between" and "and" are not merely joining words.

Now, I am beginning to understand the landscape of multiculturalism in the language of AND . . . AND . . . AND . . ., each AND allowing lines of movement to grow in the middle. Within such an understanding, Canadian multiculturalism is a polyphony of lines of movement that grow in the abundance of middles, the "betweens" and "AND" that populate our landscape.

I liken the foregoing to certain of Bach's fugues in which musical lines of movement, we are told, resound in aparallel polyphony that refuses closure— lines that refuse synthesis into a symphonic unity. Canadian polyphony? Canadian polyculturalism? Canadian multiculturalism? For me, Bach's fugue with its fugal polyphony serves as an icon of Canadian multiculturalism, a textured landscape always in flux, a landscape of multiple possibilities in a shifting web of nomadic lines of movement.

IN THE CURRICULAR LANDSCAPE

We have lingered long on the first of the two landscapes I earlier mentioned, the landscape of multiculturalism. Allow me, even briefly, to turn to the other landscape, the curricular landscape, within which curriculum designers are situated.

C & I Landscape
(Curriculum & Instruction/Implementation Landscape)

I think it is well to remember how in North America the word "curriculum" entered into the language of education as a management category set up by school administrators. We are told that the first curriculum personnel was named "curriculum director" in the Denver school system. So originating, from the outset, "curriculum" was cast in a management framework of "ends–means," a striated instrumentalism that is inscribed in the curriculum landscape even today. Curriculum designing has been textured often within the language of input and output within a production system. The consequent reduction of very human designers to instruments was not at all surprising as it mirrored the technical and technological ethos that prevails in the Western world, wherein even the notion of "education" has become instrumentalized.

With these words I have already intoned a curriculum landscape inscribed by striated linearity, a landscape dominated by a single master curriculum that stands in splendour as a tree stands in its own landscape. All else like branches become derivative. In such an arboreal landscape, curriculum theme-words like "implementation," "instruction," or "assessment" flow derivatively from the curriculum. I call such a landscape a C & I landscape (a curriculum and instruction/implementation landscape). As you well know, this is the established landscape for many curriculum designers.

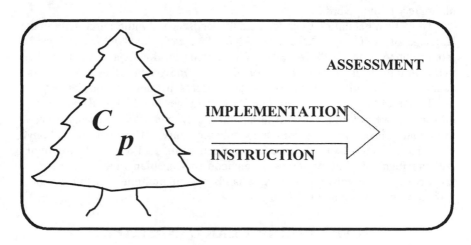

C AND I LANDSCAPE

But let us pause and weigh with care how limited this landscape might be. Allow me to take a short detour.

C & C Landscape:
The Landscape of the C-as-Plan and C-as-Lived

We all know that if you were to ask students questions like, "What is your Social Studies 9 curriculum like this year?" we get responses such as the following:

- "We're into multiculturalism, and because so many of the kids in our class are from Pacific Rim countries, we hear lots about what it's like to be ethnic. We learn a lot from each other. Some of the ethnic students have a tough time mixing."
- "I like Socials 9 except when we have to stuff into our heads a lot of facts about China, Japan, Thailand and so on to get ready for the big test at the end."
- "We find Socials 9 mostly exciting. We discuss things like the meaning of what it is to experience prejudice. At one time I thought all prejudices were bad, until I learned that every understanding has some kind of prejudgment, some kind of prejudice. The challenge is to learn to see which prejudgments are acceptable, which ones are not."

These sayings of students narratively told reflect lived experiences, what to them are their *lived curricula*. So understood we can see that if there are 25 students in the class, there are apt to be 25 lived curricula. Quite a multiplicity!

Each of these lived curricula deserves the label "curriculum" as much as the "curriculum-as-plan" deserves the label "curriculum."

Acknowledging both the lived curricula of students and the designed curriculum places us in a different landscape, one populated by a multiplicity of curricula. For want of a name, I call it the C & C Landscape (the C-as-Plan and C-as-Lived Landscape).

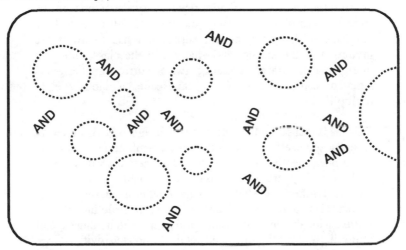

C AND C LANDSCAPE

The very word "multiplicity" reminds us of our earlier discussion of "multiplicity" in the multicultural landscape. Again, were remind ourselves of what Deleuze said when he said that multiplicity is not a noun; that what counts in multiplicity are what there are in the betweens; that multiplicity as lines of movement grow in the middle.

To offer my sense of lines of movement, allow me to sketch two lines of movement that I have found growing in the middle between the curriculum-as-plan and the lived curriculum, which may speak to curriculum designers.

1. One line of movement is itself the intensity that lies in the difference between two kinds of discourse: the discourse of the curriculum-as-plan and the discourse of the lived curriculum. We all know of the rather disembodied, prosaic language of the typical curriculum-as-plan that speaks of goals and objectives, teacher and student activities, and teaching resources. The discourse of the lived curricula, on the other hand, speaks a somewhat different language—a more concretely situated, embodied and incarnated, often narratively told.

Given these discourses, what new kind of discourse can designers grow in the middle which is neither the discourse of the curriculum-as-plan nor the discourse of the lived curriculum? For one thing, this language cannot be indifferent to the possibilities of the lived curricula even before the curriculum is experienced.   It will need to be open to possibilities of lived curricula, which vary depending on the situated lives of teachers and students. It will have to be a language of humility, as the curriculum has to await the invitation of the teacher and students in the classroom. An interesting discursive challenge awaits curriculum designers situated within the C & C landscape, a landscape of multiplicity.

2.   This leads to a second line of movement; indeed, what the C & C landscape itself may be asking of curriculum designers. As it has been mentioned, curriculum designers are often placed such that they are in a sense "condemned" to design for faceless teachers and students. On the other hand, the teachers in their classroom situation are in a more intimate face-to-face setting with students. Curriculum designers in a landscape of multiplicity are asked to heed their relationship with *others*, primarily the teachers and the students somewhere out there.

In the rather disembodied language world of the C & I landscape, the *others*—teachers and students—are only implied in words like "implementation," "instruction" and "assessment." These *others* become secondary to the curriculum-as-plan being designed.   Further, these *others* become faceless *others* and thus are reducible to some kind of sameness. This becomes very discernible when assessment time comes, when all students are subjected to the district-wide, provincewide, or even nationwide tests.

It was when I was in the midst of a concern for reductive facelessness emerging from too strong an allegiance to the C & I landscape that I watched and heard a CBC TV program, a short discussion regarding National Testing in Canada. The discussion struck home to me. On the TV program were Fiona Nelson, a Toronto School Board member, and an assessment expert from a local institute. After listening to their stances on national testing, I sent a short letter to Ms. Nelson. It reads (Aoki, 1992):

Dear Ms. Nelson:

I chanced to see/hear you on national TV when you and an evaluation professor . . . were being interviewed about the national testing movement. Allow me to applaud you for asking for space for localized situational evaluation questioning the possibility of the dominance of the totalitarian standardized testing program that may misfire in the name of education. In this view, you seem to concur with the Minister of Education of your province, who announced a few months ago hesitancy to go along with the national standardized testing program.

I interpreted your stance as one concerned with the possibility that in legitimating a nation-wide standardized consensus, we may become indifferent to the situational differences from province to province, from school to school, from classroom to classroom.

In an era that seems to have given of itself to instrumental efficiency much too much, it is indeed encouraging to hear of educational leadership that is deeply concerned for the quality of situated living of teachers and students.

I have requested the BC Teachers Federation to send you a copy of *Voices of Teaching, Vol. II.* In Part B are teacher narratives that speak thoughtfully of teachers' experiences of externally imposed assessment.

I wish you and the Toronto Board of Education well.

Cordially yours,

Ted. T. Aoki

Among these voices of teachers' experiences of external examinations is a narrative written by Wendy Matthieu, a Secondary School English teacher in Alberta. From the title, you will sense Wendy's concern. The title: "Approaching D-Day: Experiencing Pedagogical Suffocation" (Matthieu, 1991, p. 24).

For me, the voices of people like Fiona Nelson and Wendy Matthieu are calls for a recognition of the curricular landscape that we are now calling the C & C landscape, the one that legitimates and brings into fuller view both the curriculum-as-plan and the lived curricula, including, thereby, the lived space where teachers and students dwell in face-to-face situations.

It seems to me that underlying this discussion is the question of how we should understand the "designer–other" relationship, that is, the question of "self/other."

How is the "self/other" understood in the C & I landscape? This landscape is a manifestation of the subject–object framework that emerges from the Cartesian subject–object dualism, grounded in the saying, "I think; therefore, I am." (I touched on this earlier when we engaged Basho's haiku.) In this framework, the other is an object, at a distance from the subject, what I have begun to call the "faceless," even when the other is human. The C & I landscape reflects this dualism, monochromed in the colour of the subject's choice, where the lone curriculum tree sets the monotone of the total landscape.

To so understand "self/other" is to be preconditioned by what some call the language of modernity, which, although it has empowered us in many ways by enhancing our control over things and people, has encouraged indifference to other ways of understanding "self/other."

Among the other ways of understanding "self/other" I would like to mention Emmanuel Levinas (1981), who speaks of the otherness of others. Claiming the aethicality of the subject–object framework that characterizes modernism, he calls for an opening up to an understanding of "self/other" in which central is the subject's responsibility to the other, even before the subject meets the other. As we can see, this is a deeply ethical concern, ethics that are not a list of external rules of good behaviour to be applied in a situation, but rather ethics that are immanent in the human situation. Within such a thought, Levinas speaks of "responsibility before freedom," "responsibility before rights." We can sense here a different tone of "self/other" relationship in a language breaking with the subject–object dualism. This is the kind of ethical consideration that seems to be possible in the curricular landscape of multiplicity. There is, then, in the C & C landscape, an opportunity for the coming into being of a designer's language that responds responsibly to faceless others. This is an opportunity not as possible for those in the dominant language but an opportunity open to those who have the possibility for production of a minority language.[3]

A LINGERING NOTE

I have dealt with any two possible lines of movement within a curricular landscape of multiplicity: first, a line of movement between the disembodied discourse of the curriculum-as-plan and the embodied discourse of lived curricula. Second, I tried to trace a line of movement between "self/others" in which the others are faceless, and "self/others" in which the otherness of others

---

[3] The emergent sense of minority language as a line of movement in a landscape of multiplicity is offered by Gilles Deleuze and Claire Parnett in *Dialogues* (New York: Columbia University Press, 1987). They claim: "We must pass through . . . dualism because they are in language . . . in order to trace a vocal or written line which will make language flow between these dualisms, and which will define a minority use of language . . . .. [It] is always possible to undo dualisms from the inside, by tracing the line of flight which passes between two terms or the two sets, the narrow stream which belongs neither to the one nor to the other, but drawn both into a nonparallel evolution, into a heterochromous becoming" (pp. 34–35). Could designers participate in creating a minority language, which moves beyond instrumentalism?

makes a claim of responsibility on the self. The possibilities of the lines of movement are limitless—such is the open landscape of multiplicity.

This leads me to ask, can designers of Japanese Canadian curricula here assembled by their happy minority status participate in the creation of a minority curriculum language that, I believe, only minorities can speak and understand? Such a language would be, I suspect, neither the language of the dominant culture nor the Japanese language of our heritage, but one that grows in the middle. For sure, this minority language will be English, but it may be in that style of English wherein the noun is not always a noun, where joining words like "between" and "and" are not merely conjoining words, where words like "obasan" and "itsuka" may come to flourish.

Could it be that this kind of creative participation is what it means to be designers of Japanese Canadian curriculum? Could it be that this kind of thought in action be what designers of Japanese Canadian curriculum can contribute by placing new lines of movement in the curricular landscape? Is this a minority's opportunity not available to the dominant majority to participate in the creation even in a small way of what it means to be a Canadian educator? Could it be that here we are touching upon a larger mission of what it means to be designers of Japanese Canadian curricula?

I salute you for your commitment to an educational endeavour that is wrought with deep meanings. May I wish you a venture that is vitalizing and edifying for both you and the multitude of others, teachers and students, who await your creative curricular designs. "Gumbatté."

REFERENCES

Aoki, T. T. (1992). Five curriculum memos and a note for the next half-century. In M. van Manen (Ed.), *Phenomenology + pedagogy*. Edmonton: Faculty of Education Publication Services, University of Alberta. Also published as Occasional Paper/Curriculum Praxis #46 by the Department of Secondary Education, University of Alberta.

Bernstein, J. M. (1992). *The Fate of Art: Aesthetic Alienation from Kant to Derrida and Adams*. University Park: Pennsylvania State University Press.

Deleuze, G. (1987). *Bergsonism*. New York: Zone Books.

Lasch, C. (1979) *The culture of narcissism: American life in "the age of diminishing expectations."* New York: W. W. Norton.

Levinas, E. (1981). *Otherwise than being or beyond essence*. The Hague: Martinus Nijhoff.

Matthieu, W. (1991). Approaching D-Day: Experiencing pedagogical suffocation. In T. Aoki & M. Shamsher (Eds.), *Voices of teaching vol. II*. Vancouver: BC Teachers Federation Press.

Werner, W., et al. (1977). *Whose culture? Whose heritage?* Vancouver: Center for the Study of Curriculum and Instruction, Faculty of Education, University of British Columbia.

Chapter 15

The Child-Centered Curriculum: Where Is the Social in Pedocentricism?[1] (1993)

(This invited talk was presented in February 1993, at the Lecture series sponsored by the Richmond Elementary Social Studies Association. Ted Aoki engages the logos, "The Child-Centered Curriculum," attributed to Year 2000, to ask, "What is at work that allows us to speak of 'child-centered curriculum?'" So . . . in-sited, Aoki appeals to the Richmond Elementary Social Studies teachers to loosen our seeming "hang-ups" for "centering" and for "self-centered individualism." In so doing, he takes his cue from what Charles Taylor calls The Malaise of Modernity.*)*

BIRTHING OF THE TITLE

Early last month, Janet Cullis phoned me, inviting me to speak to a small group of Elementary Social Studies teachers. On the phone, Janet couldn't read my lips when I was silently saying: "Social Studies. Social Studies teachers. What impressive thing can I say about Social Studies to Social Studies teachers?" And like a student without an answer besieged by a probing teacher, I told Janet, "Let me think about it a while." (You experienced teachers know that's another way of saying "I'm empty of thoughts right now.")

Putting the phone down, I sank into my chair "to think about it a while." What began to crowd into my thoughts were voices of media that declared that January 1993 shall be open hunting season for education, particularly *Year 2000.*

Prominent among these media voices was the New Year issue of *Maclean's* magazine[2] with its education bashing words on the cover: "What's wrong at school?" together with its sub-text, "Why many parents give failing grades to their children's teachers."

I am annoyed with the negativism of publicity mongering. But annoyed though I am, or because I am annoyed, I am drawn in, and thumbing through the

---

[1] Aoki, Ted T. (1993). The child-centered curriculum: Where is the social in pedocentrism? In Ted T. Aoki & Mohammed Shamsher (Eds.), *The Call of Teaching* (pp. 67–76). Vancouver: British Columbia Teachers Federation.
[2] Maclean's *Magazine*, January 11, 1993.

many pages of *Maclean's*, I paused on page 38 to read: "Year 2000 or Bust: Controversy Dogs a B.C. Program." In it I read:

- "Under the program . . . classes will be organized according to the theories of 'child-centered' learning." (There it is—child-centered psychologism.)
- "Psychologist James Steiger of UBC . . . opposes the abandonment of grading. Steiger said that the noncompetitive atmosphere will make it easier for students to graduate, but it will not prepare them for the future." (Almost to say if teachers make it easier for students to graduate, teachers are not doing their job.)
- "The curriculum of Year 2000 is a child-centered curriculum." (There it is—pedocentricism)

And in another medium, *The Vancouver Sun* of January 8th, appears a caption: Critic Calls *Year 2000 Program* "Dangerous."[3] And in the article, I read:

- "The *Year 2000* . . . is designed to avoid academic excellence and that's dangerous."
- "Price [the North Vancouver critic] is dissatisfied with the *Year 2000* which talks about a 'learner focused curriculum.'" (Child-centeredness again.)

And on the morning CBC Radio talk show, the radio host, taking a cue from *Maclean's magazine*, welcomes talk on his open talk show *enclosed*, in a predefined question, "What's wrong with our schools?" I say "enclosed" for such a question is more closed than open, closed to a simplistic binary either/or—either good or bad; either black or white; either positive or negative; either achievement centered or child-centered.

Situated midst the texture of these media texts, I found myself both annoyed and delighted—delighted that education and miseducation are of public interest; annoyed by the way hypermedia tend to slither about a bit on the surface, suggesting a questionable premise that openness to people on talk shows assures surfacing of the truth.

Nonetheless, what provoked me was the way in which the words "child-centered" highlighted the verbal landscape. And reminding myself of the *social*-mindedness of social studies teachers, I phoned Janet to offer her the title of this talk, "Child-Centered Curriculum: Where Is the Social in Pedocentricism?" But sinking deeper in my chair, I asked myself, "What am I really interested in?" Then, this question came forth: "What kind of discourse makes it possible for us to speak of child-centeredness? of pedocentricism?"

---

[3] *The Vancouver Sun*, January 8, 1993, p. B4.

I will ask this question three times, each hopefully provoking a discursively live moment.

FIRST MOMENT: PEDOCENTRICISM AND COMPETING CURRICULUM CENTERS

In the already cited *Vancouver Sun* article, "Critic Calls *Year 2000 Program* Dangerous," Price, the named critic, said, "The Year 2000 . . . is designed to avoid academic excellence." In so saying, he is saying that "child-centeredness" sacrifices academic achievement. For him, there is a more desirable curriculum center—that of the academic subjects, the school subjects, the disciplines as they are often called. Price is opting for a subject-centered curriculum, which has undergone different labels, such as the discipline-centered curriculum (we remember the New Math, Chem Study, B.S.C.S., MACOs, etc.); the core curriculum (advocating a central core of basic subjects like the three R's); or the interdisciplinary curriculum (sometimes termed the combined program). We recall the time when we fell in love with words such as "concepts," "conceptual structure," "the structure of disciplines." And by falling in love with the language of the disciplines, we were swept up into the ivory tower's realm of universalizing abstractive reason, forgetting, at times, that our feet were no longer touching the earth where students and teachers live. And before that, not too long ago it seems, there used to be talk of the teacher-centered curriculum— the teacher from whom all rays emanated.

So in the world of curriculum over the years we have slid about, and today we now slide about, from center to center—the teacher as center, the subject/discipline as center, the child as center. Such talk of competing curriculum centers flows from a landscape populated by identifiable entities that stand as discrete units: the school subject, the teacher, and the child. Over the years and even now, people have debated which of these should be the center, assuming there has to be a center, and further assuming that each of teacher, subject, and child is a completely separate entity, each having a solid identity of its own.

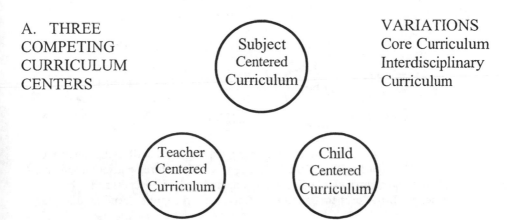

A. THREE COMPETING CURRICULUM CENTERS

Subject Centered Curriculum

Teacher Centered Curriculum

Child Centered Curriculum

VARIATIONS
Core Curriculum
Interdisciplinary Curriculum

I differ from the foregoing on at least two counts.

1. In my view, these three (teacher, subject, and child) form an irreducible triad that is at play in every pedagogic situation. So when we name any one of these as *the* center, we risk becoming indifferent to the others.

2. Further, life in the classroom is not so much *in* the child, *in* the teacher, *in* the subject; life is lived in the spaces between and among. What we ought to do, then, is to slip out of the language of curriculum centers. We ought to *decenter* them *without erasing them*, and to learn to speak a noncentered language. For instance, we might begin to be more alert to where we are when we say "a child is interested" or "a teacher is interested." "Interest" comes from "*inter/esse*" (*esse*—to be), being in the "inter." So "to be interested" is to be in the intertextual spaces of inter-faces, the places where "betweens" and "ands" reside, the spaces where "and" is no mere conjoining word but, more so, a place of difference, where something different can happen or be created, where whatever is created comes through as a voice that grows in the middle. This middle voice is the sound of the "interlude" (*inter/ludus*—to play), the voice of play in the midst of things—a playful singing in the midst of life.

B. DISSOLVING THE IDENTITIES: A DECENTERED CURRICULAR LANDSCAPE

You can see or, better, you can hear the striving for a shift in the tonality of language. The questioning of the language of child-centered curriculum led us, first, to a prosaic curricular landscape populated by child, teacher, and subject— a landscape that allows the language of curriculum centers. And as our gaze shifted from the triad to the open field, we began to reposition ourselves in a different landscape, in a *decentered* landscape that allows us to escape the language that gives primacy to substantive identities called teacher, subject and child. As we begin to live in the landscape populated by "ands," the solid identities of:

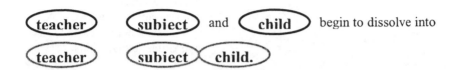

teacher   subject and   child   begin to dissolve into

teacher   subject child.

The solid line that bound the child in pedocentricism becomes less firm, solid, and stable. The center no longer holds, yielding place to a new decentered curricular landscape. (See Diagram B.)

One short example: Recently, the British Columbian Teachers Federation published narratives of teaching told by teachers. As editors, we had two possible titles: *Voices of Teachers,* and *Voices of* Teaching.[4] We chose the latter, preferring to decenter the teacher and to move into the space that is alive with teaching, hopefully in the neighborhood of the call of the calling that is teaching.

SECOND MOMENT: CHILD-CENTEREDNESS AND THE LANGUAGE OF INDIVIDUALISM

Let us move away from the curricular landscape of "centers" and decentered centers to consider another condition that allows us to say "child-centered curriculum." In this consideration, let us ask, "What is it to understand a 'child' as an "individual?" Or, for that matter, any person as an individual.

To begin to savor the significance of our question, let us play with some of the key words in the lexicon of social studies:

Some Social Studies Words:

- Rights   (individual)
- Democracy   (individual)
- Liberalism   (individual)
- Private ownership   (individual)
- Competitive economy   (individual)
- Sovereignty   (individual)

---

[4] Aoki, T. T., & Shamsher, M. (1991). *Voices of Teaching Vol. 2.* Vancouver, BC: BC Teachers Federation Press.

First, let me invite you to play in the interlude between each of these social studies terms and the word "individual" to see what might come forth (as I have done below).

- Rights   (individual) I think of individual
                                          rights, omens' rights,
                                          Native Indian rights,
                                          minority rights, gay
                                          rights, prisoners rights,
                                          legal rights, equal rights. . .

- Democracy   (individual) I think of government
                                          of, for, by the people—"people"
                                          meaning a collection of individuals,
                                          each with individual rights. . .

- Liberalism   (individual) I think of freedoms, autonomy . . .

- Private ownership   (individual) I think of individual ownership,
                                          privatization . . .

- Sovereignty   (individual) I think of individual sovereignty,
                                          national sovereignty, ethnic
                                          sovereignty , sovereign rights. . .

In all these words are inscribed traces of "individualism," which we much value in our culture—a notion that allows us to understand a "child" or any "person" as a "self," an "individual." We feel rather comfortable with these words—maybe too comfortable.

Let me break the comfortable mood and tonality of what we are experiencing by asking you to be heedful of the language of nonindividualism in another culture: "The Samoan language has no terms corresponding to 'personality,' 'self' (individual), or character. . . . Instead of our Socratic 'know thy*self*,' Samoans say, 'take care of relationships'" (take care of *AND*s) (Marcus & Fischer).[5]

Here, my concern is not whether we are right or the Samoans are right. Rather, my interest is in how meanings of words are culturally constituted, and how the very words and language we are born into may be shaping us.

With that said, let me draw your attention to a book that my friend Craig Worthing, vice principal at Cook Elementary School, Richmond, offered me last

---

[5] Marcus, G. F. & Fischer, M. (1986). *Anthropology as Cultural Critique: An Experimental Movement in the Human Sciences.* Chicago: University of Chicago Press.

summer. Titled *The Malaise of Modernity*,[6] written by Charles Taylor, it is a series of lectures aired on the CBC-Idea Series a little more than a year ago. By modernity he means the cultural lifestyle dominant in the West—a lifestyle that can be traced to the logos of modern Western culture: "*I* think; therefore, *I* am." In this book, Taylor speaks of three malaises of modern culture, one of which is "self-centered individualism," and discusses what he sees as the tyranny of "individualism" so deeply inscribed in the logos of Modernity: "I think; therefore *I* am," the Cartesian ego, the atomized individual that is considered to exist as an entity in itself.

Let's listen carefully to what Taylor says about the malaise of individualism:

> A source of worry is individualism . . . what many consider
> the finest achievement of modern civilization. We live in a
> world where people have a right to choose for themselves their
> own pattern of life, to decide in conscience what convictions
> to espouse, to determine the shape of their lives in a whole
> host of ways. . . . And these rights are generally defended by
> our legal systems. . . .
>
> The worry has been . . . that the individual lost something
> important along with the larger social horizons of action. . . .
> People no longer have a sense of a higher purpose, of
> something worth dying for . . .
>
> . . . People lost the broader vision because they focused
> on their individual lives. . . . Democratic equality . . . draws
> an individual towards himself. . . . In other words, the dark
> side of individualism is a centering on the self, which both
> flattens and narrows our lives, makes them poorer in meaning,
> and less concerned with others in society. (pp. 3–4)

Let's be cautious. Here Taylor is not attacking all forms of individualism; he is questioning that meaning of "individualism" that has flattened and narrowed our lives. He is questioning "individualism" that is overly centered on the self. He is questioning "individualism" that by centering on the self, the "I," the "me," becomes "less concerned with others in society," less concerned with the social.

So when I see "child-centered curriculum" voiced in *Year 2000* and hear Taylor's concern about "individualism," even if many consider it "the finest achievement of modern civilization," I become a touch uneasy when I recall our ministry's 1987 statement "designed to set a 'context for curriculum

---

[6] Taylor, Charles. (1991). *The Malaise of Modernity*. Concord, ON: House of ANANSI Press, Ltd.

development' in British Columbia." Recall the ministry's version of the educated person that appeared in your *BCTF Teacher*[7]:

> The educated person is one who is a thinking individual, capable of making independent decisions based on analysis and reason. The individual is curious, capable of, and interested in learning, capable of acquiring and imparting information, and able to draw from a broad knowledge base. The individual appreciates and is able to contribute to creative expression. The individual is self-motivated, has a sense of self-worth, pursues excellence, strives to be physically healthy and is able to achieve satisfaction through achievement. The individual has sound interpersonal skills, morals and values, and respects others who may be different, understands the rights and responsibilities of an individual within the family, community, nation and the world and is aware of Canada's cultural heritage. The individual is flexible, and has skills necessary to function in and contribute to the world of work. (Ministry of Education, *BCTF Teacher Magazine*, 1987, Vol. 67, No. 1, p. 22)

And among more recent ministry documents concerning the Primary Program Goals and Foundation Statements, we find a translation of the foregoing expressed in a multifold development of an educated child as an individual, cast in the language of "aesthetic and artistic development," "emotional and social development," "intellectual development," and "physical development."

Even with this cursory excursion, we can begin to see how *Year 2000*, in its well-intentioned aspirations, might be caught up in the individualist language of modernity. The crucial point for us is not to turn away from it, but to move more deeply into this language, so that we become more aware of our caughtness in a language, and try to move towards the edges of that language as Charles Taylor has done. So, repositioned at the margin where the hold of the language of narrow individualism weakens, let us open ourselves to a repositioned landscape where many voices of "self and other" call upon us for attentive listening.

THIRD MOMENT: "SELF AND OTHER" IN A POLYPHONIC LANDSCAPE

VOICE #1. Individualistic Self and Individualistic Other

This "self and other" is saturated with the kind of individualism we have been talking about. Let's recall the "self and other" that Taylor described: "The dark

---

[7] *BCTF Teacher Magazine*, 67(1) (1987).

side of individualism that in centering on the *self* . . . [becomes] less concerned with *others* in society."

We see here the centered self, the narcissistic self, the me-centered egocentricism of the self that relegates others as being secondary to my "I." In such a "self *and* other," the "and," pretending conjunctive equality, conceals the primacy of the self, relegating the other as object as viewed from the self's subjective center.

Inscribed in this understanding of "self and other" is the structure of "subject and object" wherein "I," the subject, is the first person and the "other" is the objective third person, reduced to a passivity where existential presence depends on the will of the subject. Recall Taylor portraying the way in which within this framework the individual has the right to choose, the right to decide, the right to determine—manifestations of "I think; therefore, I am." Taylor's worry is that this centered self that wills may diminish concern for others. There may well be a deep reason why we don't hear of a *Charter of Responsibilities* although we have a *Charter of Rights*, and why we don't hear of the *Bill of Responsibilities*, although we hear of the *Bill of Rights*.

VOICE #2. "Self and Other" in Romantic Intersubjectivity

Another understanding of "self and other," the one I call romantic, comes forth in the language of "intersubjectivity." Within this language, the subjectivity of the self and the subjectivity of the other (the "I" of the "self" and the "I" of the "other") intersubjectively become a "we." As Gadamer, a noted hermeneut, said, there is a fusion of the horizons of subjectivities into a unity, a harmonious oneness, a wholeness—a bunch of "I's" becoming a groupy "we." There is something nice and fuzzily warm about it.

Two short comments I wish to offer:

1. At a larger contextual level, the "self and other" can become "selves and others." And the selves and others may, in turn, become "we who are inside," and "others who are outside." In its structure, it is no different from the "self and other" we explored in Voice #1. An example at a national level might be appropriate. Those of you who have been to Japan know how the Japanese are prone to a groupy we-ness that tends to label nonJapanese gai-jins—outside people.

2. The second comment is with respect to what happens to the "and" in this brand of "self *and* other." In "self and other" becoming "we," the "and" virtually disappears, and in the wake of its disappearance, there lurks danger that we may become indifferent to the differences between self and other that ought not to be erased.

VOICE #3. Ethicality in "Self and Other" (Emmanuel Levinas)

Let us move to the third understanding of "self and other," the one that leans on Emmanuel Levinas,[8] who is deeply concerned with the authentic relationship between a human self and a human other. His is a concern for the ethicality in the relationship between "self and other." He interprets this ethicality by giving primacy to "the self's responsibility to others." "Responsibility before rights" was his firm belief, and he even spoke of one's responsibility to others whom one hasn't yet met.

For Levinas, the "and" in the "self and other" becomes an intertwining movement of "responsibilities" and "rights." And for him, the otherness of others is the ethical binding that allows us to be human.

With Levinas we see cracks in the individualistic "self and other" of modernity. The self is no longer centered; the center no longer holds. Individual identity begins to dissolve and the "and" in "self and other" becomes loaded with ethicality.

VOICE #4. "Self and Other" in a Divided Subject (Julia Kristeva)

So far, in voices 1, 2, and even 3, "self and other" are in different degrees individualized; there is the individualized self and the individualized other, each undivided, although self and other are related in differing ways. I now turn to the voice of Julia Kristeva, who questions the "undivided individual" and proposes what she calls a *divided subject,* no longer an "individual." Kristeva, raised at the margins of Bulgarian Communistic culture and regime, upon becoming a student in Paris of the 1960s became a part of the postmodern scholarship of Derrida, Lyotard, Deleuze, Foucault, Guattari, and so on, all of whom, like Charles Taylor, questioned the modernist bent for centering things and people. Kristeva resisted the notion of the centered and *undivided subject* and proposed a radically different notion of the *divided subject.* By this she meant that one's *subjectivity* is constituted by *both* self and other. She would say that each one of us is *both* self and other; each subject is inhabited by *both* self and other. In each one of us there is always a part that is a stranger to the self—other than self. To those who are under the spell of the undivided individual, Kristeva's divided subject will be a shocker as she denies the possibility of an "individual."

And so it is she wrote *Strangers to Ourselves.*[9] For Kristeva, our world is filled with strangers—whether we call them foreigner, aliens, or simply

---

[8] Levinas, Emmanuel. (1981). *Otherwise Than Being or Beyond Essence.* The Hague: Martinus Nijhoff.
[9] Kristeva, Julia. (1991). *Strangers to Ourselves.* New York: Columbia University Press.

"others." She tells us that we shall never be able to live at peace with the strangers around us if we are unable to tolerate the otherness in ourselves. The otherness in ourselves, the strangers in ourselves—such is Kristeva's understanding of "self and other." Each one of us is a divided subject, constituted by both self and other.

What Kristeva says about the divided subject resonates with Hélène Cixous, a noted French feminist scholar who says: "In the beginning is difference." For the modernist who believes in stable foundations we stand on, Cixous will be upsetting. She would say with us, we are always in the midst of differences, the betweens and Ands.

Kristeva also resonates with a Chinese word, a Chinese calligraph: a person 人 . We in the West love to translate 人 as "individual," "person," "self," pointing to the inevitable coloring of translations according to the translator's culture. In the past, I used the Chinese calligraphic 人 to begin to put into turbulence the notion of the "undivided individual." I used to say the two strokes of 人 indicate a self leaning on another. With Kristeva and Cixous, I am emboldened to say: 人 reflects a divided subject, constituted by both self and other.

Even in this cursory excursion into the landscape where voices of "self and other" sing polyphonically, we can begin to see how one particular meaning among many of "self and other" is culturally inscribed in the "child" of the "child-centered curriculum." So when *Year 2000* subscribes to one meaning of self among many, making it *the* meaning where shall we as teachers of *Year 2000* stand?

A LINGERING NOTE

At the outset, I told you how Janet pressed me into delivering a title for this talk, and how in the midst of the media-saturated situation came forth "The Child-Centered Curriculum: Where Is the Social in Pedocentricism?" By *social* I meant the social context, that is, the self/other context, the dialogical context, within which any person, including the child, dwells. And the call to indwell in the title more deeply led me to the question: "What is the condition that makes it possible to say 'child-centered curriculum?'"

The question moved us in and out of three linguistic landscapes: the language world of curriculum centers, the language world of "individualism," and the language world of "self and other." Surely, there are others.

I reread the text of my talk and while I was reading, another question came forth: "Where is the site that made the text of the talk possible?"

For us it is the site of "between" where, according to Charles Taylor, the hold of modernity weakens, showing its signs of malaise. It is a site at the edges of modernity, a site where the privileging of "centers" could be questioned; a site where the notion of child-as-individual could be questioned; a site where the privileged meaning of "identity as substance" could be questioned; a site where multiple meanings of "self and other" could make their appearance.

Chapter 16

Humiliating the Cartesian Ego[1] (1993)

One of Tom Wilson's 1971 cartoons shows Ziggy studying a computer printout card. The card reads "I think; therefore, I am." I have shown this cartoon to school educators, administrators, nursing educators, and others. On each occasion, almost inevitably, in that textured space between the viewers and the text of the cartoon, there erupt muffled chuckles, an enigmatic laughter of sorts, a gesture touched by ambiguity. I am both drawn into the chuckles and puzzled by them. And I wonder: Could these chuckles be a sign of a touch of humour in a high-tech world? High-touch? Low touch?

Positioned in the midst of my puzzlement, I wonder what is at work that produces these chuckles?

Could it be that when we look at the Ziggy cartoon, we chuckle at the vintage mainframe computer of the 1960s and 1970s? I recall the time I struggled to learn the *Fortran* language for giant-sized computers, housed in a room about a quarter the size of a school gym. Today, most of us have a home computer, and some of us, I'm sure, pack a laptop computer. Are our chuckles touched with the look of proud owners of hypermodern technology as we gaze on a Model T technology of 20 long years ago?

Or could it be that we chuckle at seeing Ziggy puzzled by the computer, which, in its own effort to understand, prints out the Cartesian logo, "I think; therefore, I am"? Could Ziggy be asking, "Who should be thinking, me or the computer?"

Or could it be that we experience humour in the predicament of humans who, humbled by the very machines we created, are giving way most humbly to the machine's intelligence, artificial though it may be?

Or could it be . . .?

It seems then that our chuckles, as in laughter following a joke, are a product of a collision of things that refuse to be bound together neatly. They clang about, not fitting right. So understood, could it be that the structure of our chuckles is the structure of a bind, a site of tension between this and that, a site of difference that speaks of two or more things at the same time? Could it be that what is at work is a situational paradox of sorts? Could it be that awareness

---

[1] Dr. Aoki originally presented this paper at the conference on Values and Technology: High Touch in a Hi-Tech World sponsored by the Religious and Moral Education Council, Edmonton. April 22, 1993. It is reprinted from: Aoki, Ted T. (1993). Humiliating the Cartesian ego. *SALT: Journal of the Religious and Moral Education Council* (The Alberta Teachers' Association), *15*(2), 5–11.

of binds is a call to remind us that we, as humans, live in a divided way, in a realm of both this and that?

I think it is this kind of bind, although not necessarily humorous, that Mike Dean spoke of, when, back in November, he scribbled a thought about self and technology: "I was thinking of the tremendous enjoyment I get from my high-tech movie systems. At the same time, I'm a little worried about the same technology stifling the imagination of youth." I would like to ask Mike: "What is it like to be caught up in the tension of a bind of this kind? What is it like to be *both* enjoying *and* worrying? Why doesn't this bind produce a laugh? Maybe it's no laughing matter. Which does it produce?"

Like Mike, our colleague Sister Elaine Cole wrote of her experiences of relationship with technology that affirm the realm of both this and that. Listen to her words, and, as you listen, place yourself in between this and that and see what meaning can be produced there:

As I contemplate my relationship to technology, I affirm that it is both a blessing and a burden.

- It is a blessing when I can duplicate material for my classes and save my time retyping passages.
- It is a burden when I have to develop a filing system to retrieve all this information. It is also a burden when one uses sheets of paper for an activity, and students only have to fill in a few blanks with a few words.
- It is a blessing when you can learn what is going on all over the world as it happens. However, it is a burden when you feel helpless and begin to distance yourself from painful realities such as famine and war.
- It is a blessing when you can call people easily by telephone, but it is a burden to have to talk to a tape recorder at the other end of the line.
- It is a blessing to be able to cook meals quickly in microwave ovens, but it is a burden when families do not have time to share a meal together. The family members all know how to heat up leftovers.
- It is a blessing to have a variety of leisure activities, but more and more of these activities cut off people from communicating. For example, how much talking can you do when you are cross-country skiing? How much effort is made to have a conversation when loud music is playing?
- Technology is a blessing when I can travel a couple of thousand miles in a few hours but is a burden when the time saved is wasted or, worse still, when the time saved is used being impatient. The great burden of technology

is the way I tie into it and depend on it. For example, clocks regulate my day.

- It is a blessing when you can store three years of work on a computer disk, but it is a burden, even a humiliation, to find it is erased accidentally and no back-up copy was made.

From the outset, Sister Cole affirmed that, in her relationship with technology, she experienced both blessings and burdens, and she offered us concretely lived experiences in the language of "both this *and* that." We can ask of Sister Cole, "What was it like to dwell in the *and?*"

IN THE REALM OF THE CARTESIAN EITHER/OR

I return to the cartoon where we found Ziggy trying to make sense of the text of the computer printout: "I think; therefore, I am." That triggers a personal anecdote. When I first started teaching many years ago, I was an enthusiastic teacher trying to make it in the vocation of teaching. The war was still on, and the Hutterites, who lived about 96 km east of Calgary, were the only people who would hire me, a Japanese Canadian, as their teacher. Talk about vintage; the school was a genuine one-room schoolhouse and there I taught Grades 1A and 1B and more—Grades 2, 3, 4, 5, 6, 7, and 8. And I recall this brand new teacher being pretty well wiped out by the end of the day.

But I recall best my reading lessons with my Grade 1 students using a basal primer, *We Think and Do.* As a teacher of reading, I applauded the children when they read without too much fumbling—"They're beginning to read." I said, and I was disappointed when they fumbled with words—"unable to read," I said. Naively I taught, for naively I failed to realize that an instrumental understanding of reading is based on a narrow instrumental understanding of language—language understood merely as a tool of communication, that is, techniques and skills to facilitate communication—such that, in curriculum talk, teaching language means how to read, how to spell, how to write, how to think instrumentally.

Moreover, as a teacher of reading, I was a blind reader, unable to read thoughts and ideas already inscribed in the text of *We Think and* Do. I couldn't read between the lines where it said unsaid that *We Think and Do* is a mundane version of "I think; therefore, I am." I was, in effect, an illiterate reader. What a teacher of reading! Humiliating!

Some decades later, now that I don't teach Grade 1, I am a little wiser, maybe a little more humble. Now I can say that *We Think and Do,* as a version of "I think; therefore, I am," is historically grounded in the Age of Enlightenment, illuminating the shape and texture of the Western epoch we have come to know as Modernism. And, of course, we know how Western Modernism flourished as the disciplines of science and technology, which today hold a privileged position.

But what are some features of modern society inscribed in the logo "I think; therefore, I am?" Most fundamental, I feel, is the notion of dualism, in whose fabric we have come to inhabit by habit. Many of us have been schooled that way. Many of us have been schooled to teach that way, as you saw me as a teacher of reading. A prominent dualism is the subject–object binary, in which each segment is understood to be a separate entity, complete in itself. Furthermore, the subject "I" is seen as a preexistent ego capable of thinking about the objective world out there, outside the self. This "I" is saturated with the ego's will to control and master the world through thought and action. Such an ego-centered universe is reminiscent of da Vinci's "Canon of Man's Proportions," symbolic of the modernist's valorizing of anthropocentricism.

The binary of subject–object reminds us of other commonplace binaries:

(subject)	(object)
I	other
leader	follower
good guys	bad guys
right	wrong
yes	no
secular	spiritual
positive	negative
on	off

All these binaries are frameable in an either/or opposition, often structured as a hierarchy with privilege bestowed to the first named. In Western culture, this either/or framework has become dominant, so prevalent that we have tended to adopt it as a reality, forgetting that it has been constituted historically and culturally.

What is worrisome about this framework that valorizes the either/or binary is the way it seduces many of us into the language of either "boosters of technology" or "knockers of technology." Trapped within the either/or realm, we can become either promoters or opposers of the value of technology. We can become technophiles or technophobes. And by becoming so polarized, we might unconsciously slip into an oppositional zero-sum game. What is dangerous is that we could begin to believe that this is the only game worth playing. Most important, by participating in such a game as boosters or knockers, we might fail to realize that in the very participation we are supporting the either/or framework.

In all this, let us be mindful of the way in which the ego "I" is complicit in the either/or dualism that prevails. The Cartesian world of either/or is an ego-centered world, Indeed, it is timely that we question the privilege we have bestowed on the either/or framework and the individualized ego so deeply in the grain of the modernist landscape. In this questioning, we might lean on our colleagues like Mike Dean and Sister Cole who can speak of an alternative to the landscape of either/or like the landscape of "both this and that, and more . .

." that does not exclude the either/or but regards it as one among many ways of being in the world.

IN THE LANDSCAPE OF
"BOTH THIS AND THAT, AND MORE"

Let us return to Mike Dean, who said in his anecdote that he experienced tremendous enjoyment from his high-tech system and, simultaneously, worried that the same technology might stifle imagination. He experienced enjoyment and worry at the same time, and he spoke of both this and that. He did not say either this or that.

Let us also return to Sister Cole who said that her experience with technology was simultaneously a blessing and a burden. She experienced both blessings and burdens at the same time—and she spoke of both this and that. She did not say either this or that.

From such a juxtaposition, we begin to sense that the either/or world is a more clear-cut world, a more definable world, where we can bring closure by arguing for either one side or the other. It is an appositional world, a confrontational world. In certain situations in our lived world, no doubt the either/or framework will function well for us, particularly in a technical, instrumental situation where positive is positive and negative is clearly negative.

But in other situations, particularly in nontechnical human situations, we find ourselves thrown into a realm of open possibilities with much uncertainty and ambiguity, indeed, a very human realm. We are all familiar with this realm in our classes at school, where students insist on being different, where students come to us with multiple abilities and multiple interests. We are familiar with such a situation, and yet we teachers are reasonably composed, even amidst difficulties. Here we struggle and do our best, we say.

This is the landscape of "both this and that, and more"—a realm in which there is no finite end. We say, "Let's call it O.K. for knowing that possibilities are there ad infinitum, never-ending, evermore."

What does all this say to a curriculum person like me? What does the landscape of "both this and that, and more" say to the landscape of curriculum? Remember how in North America the word *curriculum* entered into the language of education as a management category set up by school administrators. We are told that the first curriculum staff person was named "curriculum director" in the Denver school system. So originating, from the outset, curriculum was cast in a management framework of "ends–means," a striated instrumentalism inscribed in the curriculum landscape even today. Curriculum designing has been textured often within the language of input and output within a production system. The consequent reduction of human designers to instruments was not at all surprising, as it mirrored the technical and technological ethos that prevails in the Western world, wherein even the notion of "education" has become instrumentalized.

With these words, I have already intoned a curriculum landscape inscribed by striated linearity, a landscape dominated by a single master curriculum that stands in splendor as a tree stands in its own landscape. All else, like branches, becomes derivative. In such a landscape, curriculum words like *implementation, instruction* or *assessment* flow derivatively from the curriculum. I call such a landscape a C and I landscape (a curriculum and instruction/implementation landscape). This is the established landscape for many curriculum designers.

FIG. 16.1 C and I landscape.

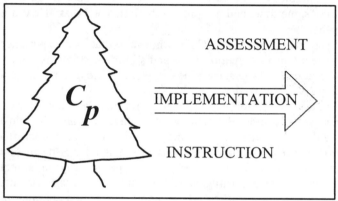

But let us pause and weigh with care how limited this landscape might be. Allow me to take a short detour. We all know that if we were to ask students the question "What is your Social Studies 9 curriculum like this year?" We would get responses such as the following (from British Columbia):

> We're into multiculturalism, and because so many of the kids in our class are from Pacific Rim countries, we hear lots about what it's like to be ethnic. We learn a lot from each other. Some of the ethnic students have a tough time mixings. I like Socials 9 except when we have to stuff into our heads a lot of facts about China, Japan, Thailand and so on to get ready for the big test at the end.
>
> We find Socials 9 mostly exciting. We discuss things like the meaning of what it is to experience prejudice. At one time I thought all prejudices were bad, until I learned that every understanding has some kind of prejudgment, some kind of prejudice. The challenge is to learn to see which prejudgments are acceptable, which ones are not.

These students' sayings reflect lived experiences, what to them are their *lived curricula*. So understood, we can see that if there are 25 students in the class, there are apt to be 25 lived curricula. Quite a multiplicity! Each lived curriculum deserves the label "curriculum" as much as the "curriculum-as-plan" deserves the label "curriculum."

Acknowledging both the lived curricula of students and the designed curriculum places us in a different landscape, one populated by a multiplicity of curricula. For want of a name, I call it the C and C landscape (the *c*-as-plan and *c*-as-lived landscape). This is but a version of "both this and that, and more."

FIG. 16.2   C and C landscape.

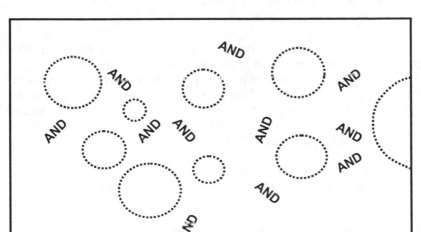

Let us bear in mind that the curriculum-as-plan is one of the multiplicity of curricula.

The acknowledgment of the landscape of multiplicity is, in my view, a paradigm shift, a big move beyond the singular curriculum of the arboreal curriculum landscape.

But now that we are in a landscape of multiplicity, I think we are ready for more things to happen. Here, I wish to lean on Deleuze for a turn in thought— Deleuze who, like the Greek Heraclitus, believes that life is ever in flux. In keeping with his thought that everything is in motion, he said: "Multiplicity is not a noun." Deleuze puts into turbulence our traditional dictionary meaning of multiplicity, asking us simultaneously to place ourselves at a site different from the usual. Where is such a place of multiplicity? Deleuze (Deleuze & Parnet, 1988, viii) states: "In a multiplicity what counts are not the elements, but what there is between, the between, a site of relations which are not separable from each other. Every multiplicity *grows in the middle.*"

Deleuze urges us to displace ourselves from our fondness of noun-oriented, thing-oriented entities that give us a thing-oriented view of curricular multiplicity, to decenter ourselves from such an established modernist view and to place ourselves in the midst, between and among the curricular entities.

Where are we? We are now at a place where the *and*s are not mere conjunctions, as usually understood, but understood differently. And I wonder if *and* might be a place where we can think differently. Can it be a place where human's ego can become decentered, can become dissolved a bit? At this point, I lean on Michel Foucault (1973), who thinks quite differently from Descartes:

> It is no longer possible to think in our day other than in the void left by man's disappearance. For this void does not create a deficiency; it does not constitute a lacuna that must be filled. It is nothing more and nothing less than the unfolding of a space in which it is once more possible to think.

How reminiscent of Heidegger, who said: "The most thought-provoking thing about our thought-provoking times is that we are not yet thinking."

Positioned in an "and," how shall we begin to think anew? One way might be to remember Deleuze, who said that in multiplicity what counts are not the elements but the space between, a place of difference, a place of bind, a place of tension. In noting the *and* as a place of difference, we might listen more fully to what Deleuze (Deleuze & Parnet, 1988) has to say about difference:

> We tend to think in terms of more or less, that is to see difference in degree where there are differences in kind. (p. 21)

> Each time that we think in terms of more or less, we have already disregarded difference in kind between the two orders, or between beings, between existants. (p. 20)

> Considering everything in terms of more or less, seeing nothing but difference in degree . . . where, more profoundly, there are differences in kind is perhaps the most general error of thought, the error common to science and metaphysics. (p. 20)

Deleuze, in calling on us to think differently, alerts us to how differently "difference" might be understood and, further, how to be seduced to understanding "difference" as difference in degree may be to become indifferent to difference in kind.

To offer my sense of lines of thought that move within differences in kind, allow me to sketch two lines of movement I have found growing in the middle between the curriculum-as-plan and the lived curriculum.

One line of movement is itself the intensity that lies in the difference between two kinds of discourse: the discourse of the curriculum-as-plan and the discourse of the lived curricula. We all know of the rather disembodied, prosaic language of the typical curriculum-as-plan that speaks of goals and objectives, teacher and student activities, and teaching resources. The discourse of the lived curricula, on the other hand, speaks a somewhat different language—more concretely situated, embodied and incarnated, often narratively told.

Given these discourses, what new kind of discourse can designers grow in the middle that is neither the discourse of the curriculum-as-plan nor the discourse of the lived curriculum? For one thing, this language cannot be indifferent to the possibilities of lived curricula, which vary depending on the situated lives of teachers and students. It will have to be a language of humility, as the curriculum has to await the invitation of the teacher and students in the classroom. An interesting discursive challenge awaits curriculum designers situated within the C and C landscape, a landscape of multiplicity.

This leads to a second line of movement: indeed, what the C and C landscape itself may be asking of curriculum designers. As has been mentioned, curriculum developers are often placed such that they are in a sense "condemned" to design for faceless teachers and students. On the other hand, teachers in their classroom situation are in a more intimate face-to-face setting with students. Curriculum developers in a landscape of multiplicity are asked to heed their relationship with others, primarily the teachers and the students somewhere out there.

In the rather disembodied language world of the C and I landscape, the *others*—teachers and students—are only implied in words like *implementation, instruction,* and *assessment.* These *others* become secondary to the curriculum-as-plan being designed. Further, these others become faceless and thus are reducible to some kind of sameness. This becomes discernible when assessment time comes, when all students are subjected to districtwide, provincewide, or even nationwide tests.

You can see how the *and* in the curricular landscape of multiple curricula, the space similar to the one that Mike Dean and Sister Cole opened up for us in their language of "both this and that, and more," is a tensioned place that could vibrate in differences. It need not be a closed place but a place open to many possibilities. It is a place where new lines of thought can spring forth, running in many directions simultaneously. As such, it is a fertile place.

I am hoping that some of you are saying, "Hey, what Aoki has been saying sounds like my class when it's alive!" Such is the way I am reading the space of *and* that sprang from "both this and that, and more."

HUMILIATING "HUMILIATION"

Many of you may be asking, and rightly so, why I have not dealt with the word *humiliation.* It is true I have not been explicit, but this is, in part, because I have been sliding about in my talk with the word *humiliation* in my back pocket, looking for a site that might allow the word itself to erupt somewhere with new meaning.

From the outset, I have wanted to reunderstand the word *humiliation,* guided by the notion that a word as signifier shifts in meaning from discourse to discourse. I have been wanting to move into a space that is not anthropocentric, not caught in a discourse where humans are central, frozen into the subject–object dualism wherein humans, the subject, hold sway with their will to control and master others. For, in such a discourse, it is too easy for the "I," the arrogant "I" to act on another, to humiliate the other. I have wanted to escape from that bind of space. So I have been looking for a site where the usual meaning of humiliation connected with human-centeredness dissolves somewhat, so there is room for the emergence of new lines of meaning.

But I have just noticed that over the journey so far, I have had a hole in my back pocket. Pieces of humiliation have been slipping out, growing new sprouts of meaning at different sites, so it seems. One such piece slipped out, I think, when we saw Ziggy and chuckled a bit. That piece seems to like places where people join in laughter, finding humour in things that collide, changing in differences. Another piece slipped out when Mike Dean spoke of finding himself in a very human bind of both enjoyment and worry. And I know several pieces slipped out when Sister Cole spoke of human sorts of dilemma, caught between blessings and burdens. More pieces of humiliation slipped out when I was telling you of my humbling experiences teaching Grade 1, when I came to realize years later that I mistaught the innocent Grade 1 students that language is merely a tool of communication. I now shudder at my humiliating complicity with Cartesian dualism and the Cartesian ego. Still more pieces slipped out, landing on the fertile soil of *and*. And lingering in this space of lived tensionality of difference, I am able to hear the rhythmic measure of the earth, our place of dwelling, where its earthy humus provides nurturance to new meanings of humiliation that are springing forth.

And here, positioned at the site of one of the many *and*s where the human-centered meaning of humiliation moves in tension with a different meaning of humiliation—one where the human is no mere ego, no mere subjective "I" that thinks it thinks: Here, *humiliating* shifts its meaning, admittedly ambiguously, to one that is concerned with lived space where people dwell communally, where dwelling is a dwelling with others on earth under the sky, where we find *humus* that nurtures *humans*, where *humans* caught up in binds sometimes chuckle, where we can hear laughter at the thought of humans thinking they can master the world.

What kind of a place is this? A place where there is room for words like *humour, human, humus, humility* to live together. In such a place, to be humiliated is to be reminded that we are communally ecologic, that the rhythmic measures of living on Earth come forth polyphonically in *humour* and *human* and *humus* and *humility*.

I have taken this time to come to a place named *and*, a place of lived tension between this and that. And here, I hope, *humiliation* is no longer a word that merely sounds negative; in its repositioned sense, *humiliation* can indeed be a sign of our humanness.

REFERENCES

Deleuze, G., & Parnet, C. (1988). *Dialogues*, Trans. H. Tomlinson & B. Habberjam. New York: Columbia University Press.

Foucault, M. (1973). *The order of things: An archaeology of the human sciences* New York: Random House.

Chapter 17

In the Midst of Doubled Imaginaries: The Pacific Community as Diversity and as Difference[1] (1995)

REMEMBERING A SAYING

"The Pacific Rim," "the Asia Pacific," "the Pacific community"—these and other newly coined signifiers slide about with shifting images as global attention turns at the end of this century to this oceanic space we call the Pacific. Such a turn of interest leads me to a saying that resonates within me:

大平洋の 時代は來たり

(The regime of the Pacific will come.)

This saying was cited often early in this century by my parents both teachers from Tokyo, at the Japanese language school I attended dutifully in Cumberland on Vancouver Island, a namesake of Cumberland, we were told, in northern England. In this small but thriving mining community settled migrant coalminers and their families in diverse mining towns—an Italian town, a Chinese town, and two Japanese towns—all situated in clearings carved out for them in the periphery of the main English town, lorded by the huge estate of the Dunsmuirs.

Schooling? Daily during the morning and early afternoon I attended what we called 白人學校 (a "school for whites" would be a translation), and after that, in late afternoon, I attended 日本學校 Japanese Language School). Thus, students like me were schooled in two schools, a doubled schooling that positioned us in the midst of twofold Pacific languages and histories. No wonder I was, since very early, a mixed-up hybrid kid.

At the public school, teachers had to deal with a language problem. I still remember how, to encourage us into the discursive world of English, the school set up a language code for recess breaks: "Anyone speaking Japanese during recess shall be strapped!" With such a code of conduct, we learned to speak English out loud and to speak Japanese silently, erupting into Japanese at the

---

[1] This paper was originally an invited address to "Imagining a Pacific Community: Representation and Education" Conference, April 23-26, 1995, at the University of British Columbia, Vancouver, Canada. It is reprinted here from: Aoki, Ted T. (1995). In the midst of double imaginaries: The Pacific community as diversity and as difference. *Contents: Pacific Asian Education, 7,* (1 & 2), 1–7.

end of the public school day as we hiked off to Japanese school jabbering in Japanese all the way.

At this school, I remember reading the story of a young but dedicated Japanese dreamer and activist from, 山 口 県 (Yamaguchi)-Ken at the western end of Honshu, later venerated as Yoshida Shoin. I remember how in the story, he as a young man resisted vociferously Japan's ideology of "island isolationism" pronounced by the Tokugawa Shogunate, was caught attempting to leave Japan for the West, and was promptly executed, samurai fashion. (Let me add in keeping with the ethnic addiction to heritage that I married a Yoshida who in the Netherlands of her heritage claims Yoshida Shoin as ancestor. A hybrid that she, too, is, she loves and practices Chinese and Japanese calligraphy and tai-chi but she resists Japanese patriarchy, particularly the principle of primogeniture.)

At this school, I also remember enjoying the essays in Japanese of Lafcadio Hearn, an eccentric migrant from England to the New England States to Japan, who in adopting Japan came to be known better by his adopted name, Koizumi Yakumo (eight floating clouds over a fountain). The ambivalence in his writing, which I found fascinating, I now find more fascinating, now that my space time positioning is at the end of this millennium colored by what some call postmodern space and postcolonial time.

At the other school, the public school, I remember being schooled into the excitingly gung-ho narratives of Western discoveries and exploits: the discovery of continents new to Europeans, named the Americas after Amerigo Vespucci, an Italian cartographer; of the discoveries of Christopher Columbus, an Italian in the hire of Spain (interested in big game, not in little fish), who in meeting the Indians thought he discovered Marco Polo's riches of the East; of the daunting exploits of Ferdinand Magellan, who in a post-Atlantic navigation, cut through the turbulence of the rough waters between Tierra del Fuego and Cape Horn and opened up to the peaceful expanse of waters, which he promptly named "Pacificus Oceanus," filled with the promise of penetration through the waters to the Far East ("Far" from where? from the center of the geopolitical regime that measured and named others as those in the Near East, the Far East).

And today on this side of the Pacific, we find the coast dotted with traces of Iberian naming: Ecuador, Costa Rica, San Diego, Los Angeles, Juan de Fuca, Quadra Island (not too far from Cumberland), Bella Bella, Bella Coola— appellations inscribed in the narratives of the authority of "God and country," heralding the Renaissance of the First World's hegemonic rise of the geopolitical economy of Western Modernity.

But here, where we now are, the British and the English language prevailed and prevails, their prestige acknowledged by the academic bastions that bear the names not of Spanish but British Columbus/Columbia, of Queen Victoria, and of Simon Fraser, the explorer.

So today, as I hear the echo of the saying

太平洋の時代は来たり

"The Regime of the Pacific will come," I see how the imaginary of this saying was inscribed in the geopolitics of the curriculum at work, legitimating the binary of the Occident and the Orient, the primacy of the first named, and the universalizing of the English language, that is, the Canadian version of Oxonian English, brilliantly written about in postcolonial fashion in a book entitled *Empire of Words: The Reign of the OED*, by John Willinsky, cohost of the conference.[2]

Here, today, in British Columbia, new language codes are at work, for within the public schools' curricular scene exist legitimated spaces for East Asian languages such as Japanese, Mandarin, Cantonese, and Korean. At U.B.C., in the recently inaugurated Asia Pacific Education Graduate Program directed by Stephen Carey, another cohost of this conference, studies in education oriented to the Pacific are under way. Among them is an ongoing study by Bruce Russell, a teacher of Japanese at Templeton Secondary School in Vancouver, whose pedagogical interest has led him to a thesis titled "Kanji no Satori" ("Wisdom Embedded in the Compositioning of Chinese and Japanese Characters") relying, in part, on Roland Barthes's imaginary of Japan as signifier in his well-known book, *Empire of Signs*.[3] And there is an ongoing study by Kimiko Hirose of Steveston Secondary School in Richmond, BC, who writes of her tensioned experiences as a Japanese Canadian teacher both in Japan and in Canada, and, as well, of her experiences as a teacher of English in Kyoto and a teacher of Japanese in Richmond.

Indeed, we are in a position to transform the saying

大平洋の時代は来たり

from the future tense, "The Regime of the Pacific Will Come," into the present tense, "The Regime of the Pacific Has Come"—a transformational feat that is accomplished without changing a word in the Japanese version (which might be saying something about "temporality" in the Japanese imaginary).

DISRUPTING THE LINEARITY OF A HISTORICAL NARRATIVE: FROM THE MEDITERRANEAN TO THE ATLANTIC TO THE PACIFIC

So far I have not mentioned that our saying is often enframed within the imaginary of a linear historical movement of centers of civilization: from the Mediterranean to the Atlantic, and then to the Pacific. Likely, this thesis was

---

[2] Willinsky, John. (1994). *Empire of words: The reign of the OED*. Princeton, NJ: Princeton University Press.

[3] Barthes, Roland. (1982). *The empire of signs*. Toronto: McGraw-Hill Ryerson.

appropriated by the Japanese in their yearning for modernization, which, some Japanese scholars say, paralleled the beginning of the Meiji era.

Let me juxtapose to the foregoing what I recently heard at a lecture at the Asian Center on campus in which Dr. Rafik Aliev, a Russian linguist, anthropologist and Japanologist, told us that the linear Mediterranean–Atlantic–Pacific thesis is attributable to a European scholar, Karl Marx. There are two versions. What we might note is that both versions are inscribed within the linear imaginary of the extension of the same, merely a shifting of location.

Last year I heard Dr. Richard Cavell, a postcolonial scholar at U.B.C.'s Department of Comparative Literature, speak to Ritsumeikan students on this campus of the different imaginaries that constitute the Atlantic and the Pacific. For the Atlantic, he deployed the metaphor of the garrison state with its expansionary policy and diplomacy as discussed by Northrop Frye, and for the Pacific, he deployed Marshall McLuhan's metaphors of the global village and the media as message. For Cavell, the regime in the Pacific is no mere linear extension of the Mediterranean–Atlantic–Pacific thesis: his imaginaries disrupt this linearity. It is with such disruptive admonition that I now approach the term "Pacific Community."

The Conventional Imaginary: The Pacific Community as Diversity

When I first saw the title of the conference, "Imagining a Pacific Community," I was drawn to the word "Pacific." I now recognize in the title the little article "a"—a Pacific community—a sign of indeterminacy and indefiniteness, situating us in a space of ambiguity and ambivalence. So positioned, I see inscribed in the word "community" the words "common" and "unity," which I sense are prevailing signifiers in articulating the conventional imaginary of "community."

We in North America, wherein our national and cultural makeup is construed as "multicultural Canada" or "multicultural USA," have become beholden to an image of community constituted within the metaphorical language of diversity. Within such imaginary rests a notion of community as a totality such that in its heterogeneity exists some kind of homogeneity, a unity that is community/unity. "Unity in diversity" has become a geopolitical slogan we often hear. Hence, when we speak of the Pacific Community, we find ourselves predisposed to slip into the metaphor of diversity.

So disposed, we texture the Pacific community as a community of diverse cultural and national entities, to borrow Homi Bhabha's apt phrase, "a land of musée imaginaire"[4] (an imaginary museum), an anthropological museum of national cultures often exoticized, categorized, and labeled. So inclined, we recall this imaginary at work when we saw portrayed in media 2 years ago the

---

[4] See "The third space: Interview with Homi Bhabha." In Rutherford, Jonathan (Ed.). (1990). *Identity: Community, cultures, difference*, p. 208. London: Lawrence & Wishart.

gathering of national leaders of the Pacific community in Seattle, Washington, and last year again in Jakarta, Indonesia, leaders of Pacific nations attired in the sameness of silk shirts native to the host country, projecting for us an image of a community united in diversity.

In the field of education, the endorsement of cultural diversity has become the "bedrock of multi-cultural, multinational education"[5] that flourishes in our school curricula as exotic studies of Japan, China, Korea, Taiwan, Hong Kong, and so on, and as heritage-day programs on multicultural days often celebrated in schools. And at the university level this curriculum of diversity appears as an arrangement in Asian Studies Programs—diversified into a disciplined array of Japan Studies, China Studies, Korea Studies, S.E. Asian Studies and others—entrenched entities in Asian Studies centers.

But if we heed postcolonial scholars such as Stuart Hall and Homi Bhabha, both of whom speak from the liminal margins of Eurocentric modernity, we need to question this very imaginary that construes the Pacific Community as diversity. Listen to Bhabha who says, "It is a common place of plural democratic societies to say that they can encourage and accommodate cultural diversity."[6] Such encouragement and accommodation are seen as signs of the "cultured" or the "civilized" attitude that can appreciate cultures by locating them in a universal time frame that acknowledges their various historical and social contexts. But such an imaginary that gives birth to the metaphor of community as diversity produces, in its seeming liberal openness and tolerance of other, a silent norm that both contains and constrains differences on the underside of diversity.

In discussing this trope of community as diversity, Bhabha reminds us of Hanna Arendt, who articulated a liberalist form of social living in these words: "People are with others,"[7] a social relationship articulated in the preposition "with." But such an imaginary of society as a community of diverse entities compels Hanna Arendt, in spite of her liberal openness, to be silent about a crucial feature. Says Bhabha, "Arendt's form of social mimesis does not deal with social marginality as a product of the liberal state."[8] He insists that the entertainment of an image of community as diversity, as a liberalist image, is inevitably coupled by a constraint, that is, "a norm is constituted—a norm given by the host society or dominant culture which says that these or other cultures are fine, but we must be able to locate them within our own grid"[9]—a grid reified in the liberal vision of community as diversity, but one that tends to be indifferent to community as difference. That is to say, the universalist pluralism espoused by liberalism paradoxically permits diversity but masks differences.

---

[5] Rutherford (p. 208).
[6] Rutherford (p. 208).
[7] Bhabha, Homi. (1994). *Location of culture*, p. 190, London: Routledge.
[8] Bhabha (p. 190).
[9] Rutherford (p. 208).

An Imaginary With a Difference: The Pacific Community as Difference

What is needed, then, is a disruption, a displacement that relocates us away from the space of demographic plurality inscribed in diversity to a borderline space that permits "negotiations of cultural translation."[10] Such repositioning is a movement away from the imaginary of community as diversity to the imaginary of community as difference, to an enunciatory space of language in movement, a space of signifying activity, a space of interlanguage translation. It is an enunciatory space of cultural and language differences—in my case, the space that is neither Japan nor Canada, neither Japanese nor English, but that interspace where the otherness of others cannot be buried as is done within the imaginary of community as diversity.

The enunciatory spaces of difference in the Pacific Community are signifying spaces marked by different kinds of cultural histories, different lineages, different languages, all involved somehow in articulating in multiple ways, positively and negatively, progressively and regressively, often conflictually, sometimes even incommensurably. Such spaces are liminal places, inhabited often by the colonized, the minorities, the migrants in a diasporic community whose productive voices are now beginning to come forth.

To provide a lived view of this enunciative space of community as difference, allow me to tell you a narrative of a conversation I experienced.

Having been schooled within the "civitas" of Western civilization, Western modernity, and Western liberalism, I've been engaged in questioning some imaginaries I've been schooled. In this deschooling, which is also a reschooling, I have been reading works such as:

> *The Unsettling of America* by Wendell Berry:[11]
> *White Mythologies: Writing History and the West* by Robert Young:[12]
> *Religion and Nothingness* by Keiji Nishitani:[13]
> *The Location of Culture* by Homi Bhabha:[14]
> *The Malaise of Modernity* by Charles Taylor.[15]

In the last book, I have been drawn to Taylor's concern for the malaise in the texture of our lives. He claims that at the heart of this malaise is the Western

---

[10] Rutherford (p. 209).

[11] Berry, Wendell. (1986). *The Unsettling of America*. San Francisco: Sierra Club Books.

[12] Young, Robert. (1990). *White mythologies*. London: Routledge.

[13] Nishitani, Keiji. (1982). *Religion and nothingness*. Berkeley: University of California Press.

[14] Bhabha, Homi. (1994). *Location of culture*. London: Routledge.

[15] Taylor, Charles. (1991). *The Malaise of modernity*. Concord, ON: Anansi Press.

imaginary that has created the notion of the "individual." Taylor insists that we have become too comfortable with the liberal ideology of "individualism."

I was dwelling in this mood when Jan Walls of Simon Fraser University, a long-time friend, a Japanologist and Sinologist I deeply respect, invited me to a dim-sum lunch. Our conversation took place in a polyphonic space of English and a smattering of Japanese, punctuated by Chinese whenever Jan ordered dim-sum dishes.

It was in the midst of a double happiness of tasty food and conversation that I mentioned to Jan about my reading of Charles Taylor's concern with the Western ideology of "individualism." That comment sparked a conversation about how when the Frenchman, de Tocqueville, was asked following his visit to the United States, "Who are Americans?" He responded: "Americans are individuals." Jan then told me that when Japan opened up to the language of the West, Japanese were both entranced with and puzzled by the strange word "individual," but amid the familiar and the strange came into being a new word, 個人 (ko-jin), a solidified self, a unified person, an entity unto itself.

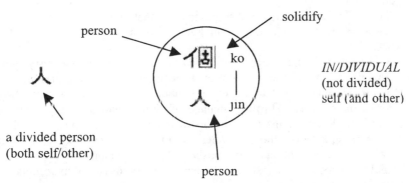

It was while we were in this intertextual conversation that Jan told me of how his father named him Jan after the Greek God Janus, a double-visioned figure that sees two images at once. I remember responding, recalling William Blake, "twofolded always." We chatted a bit about how different this is from the imaginary of the monovisioned, whose desire for clarity and the singular characterize their epistemology.

The story does not end here. For later, at a graduate seminar of the Asia Pacific Education Graduate Program, when I retold the story of my conversation with Jan Walls, alert as he always is, Albert Zhou, a doctoral student from mainland China who has taught in Tokyo, told us that the Chinese borrowed the word 個人 (ko-jin) from the Japanese (a reversal in language movement), becoming very much a part of the Chinese lexicon. Languages in intercultural movement, I thought, a to-and-fro of languages in enunciatory spaces of translation.

So, bolstered, I return to re-visit the enunciatory space of 個人 (ko-jin). For the translators, culturally accustomed 人 (hito), its two strokes often interpreted as a twofold in one (it takes at least two to make a person, or one cannot stand alone), the very notion of an "individual self" must have been strange to them. In this context, to read 個人 (ko-jin) simply as a synthetic compositioning of 人 (hito) and "individual" is, I believe, to be indifferent to the inevitable ambivalence of translation. One segment 固 of 個人 (ko-jin) does say a solidified unity, an undivided individual, but the juxtapositioning of 人 (hito) in 個人 (ko-jin) causes the supposed solidity of the entity to quake a bit. For, now, we can see that 個人 says that it is both divided and undivided, an admission perhaps that in translation there is ever some slippage, something left untranslated, and thus ever incomplete. So interpreted, 個人 (ko-jin) as an articulation in that enunciatory space between Japanese and English, is seemingly Japanese but not all Japanese. It is a hybrid; it is both Japanese and English yet it is neither Japanese nor English. It is a space of paradoxical ambivalence with its built-in contradiction. Yet, it is a generative space of difference, an enunciatory space of becoming, a space where newness emerges.

What is this all about? I remind myself that our focal interest is in recognizing different articulations of the Pacific Community as diversity and as difference.

What I now see in the foregoing is how articulating in the enunciatory space of the imaginary of difference requires a positioning at a margin. In our situation we are challenged to be explicit about the imaginaries that allow articulations of the *other*. In the language of "individualism," the "other" is beyond the self, distanced and objectifiable as in a display, no matter how close the other is brought before the self, whereas in the language of 人 (hito), the other is already present, albeit ambiguously, within the person.

Thus I have become interested in the language of those who, in articulating the Pacific community as difference, are positioned at the margins, sensitive to multiple articulations of "others" and "othering." In the Pacific are emerging those who seem so positioned. Allow me to cite just three.

There is Trinh Min-ha, an Asian American (Vietnamese, I believe) now at the University of California at Berkeley, whom I heard speak recently on this campus. In her provocative book, *Woman Native Other*,[16] she locates herself at the juncture of a number of different fields and disciplines—in true interdisciplinary fashion that shatters disciplinary borders—pushing and fracturing boundary lines. So positioned, she challenges Western regimes of knowledge. Further, bringing to her writings many meanings of the marginalized others, she argues that the multiple hyphenated peoples in Asia are not simply placed in a binary of cultural heritages. Trinh portrays the predicament of having to live a difference that has no name and too many names

---

[16] Trinh Min-ha. (1992). *Woman, Native, Other*. Bloomington, IN: Indiana University Press.

already, and she argues for nothing less than a revision of knowledge that is based on the imaginary of community as diversity. Hers is a resonant voice from the margins of what we've been calling the imaginary of community as difference.

And then there is Rey Chow, another postcolonial feminist, educated in both the British colony of Hong Kong and the United States. As professor of comparative literature at the University of California in Irvine, she has written *Writing Diaspora: Tactics of Interventions in Contemporary Cultural Studies.*[17] From her postmodern space and postcolonial time, sensitive to 1997, she questions the legacies of European imperialism and colonialism, particularly of popularized notions about "others." She questions essentialist notions of culture and history: conservative notions of territorial and linguistic propriety, and the notion of "otherness" ensuing from them. Her writings, springing from the enunciatory spaces in the midst of differences, articulate the cultural temporality of contingency and indeterminacy contained within discourses of so-called civil society.

And now I mention Masao Miyoshi, who teaches comparative literature and Japanese literature at the University of California in San Diego. In a book dedicated to Oe Kenzaburo even before he was named the Nobel Literature Prize winner, and titled *Off/Center: Power and Culture, Relations Between Japan and the United States,*[18] he adopts a post-colonial marginal perspective that he labels off/center—one that allows the assymetrical historical relations between Japan and the United States from Commodore Perry to Douglas MacArthur—to investigate the blindness that has characterized relations between these two cultures.

This blindness is the kind of blindness considered earlier in this paper when we saw how the imaginary of the Pacific Community as diversity, conceals and constrains the imaginary of difference.

Trinh Min-ha, Rey Chow, and Masao Miyoshi have helped me much in repositioning myself within the Pacific Community. In so doing, they have helped me to transform the sting of the strap I got for speaking Japanese at school during recess decades ago into a generative rhythm such that the sting is no more. Instead, in my own becoming, I feel I am beginning to speak a vitally new language.

A MEDITATION

I have been interpreting the holding of this conference as a sign not only of educators' acknowledgment that we are already entangled in the midst of the regime of the Pacific, but also of their involvement as curriculum workers and

[17] Chow, Rey. (1993). *Writing diaspora: Tactics of intervention in contemporary studies.* Bloomington: Indiana University Press.

[18] Miyoshi, Masao. (1991). *Off/center: Power and culture, relations between Japan and the United States.* Cambridge, MA: Harvard University Press.

teachers in articulating the shape of curricula and pedagogy that is in tune with the emerging imaginaries of space/time in the Pacific.

For some years now the Ministry of Education in British Columbia has been promoting what we have come to call the Pacific Initiatives. Under such supportive promotion, we have seen the to-and-fro movement of teachers and students spanning the Pacific; we have seen curricular activities inspired by the initiatives; we have seen teacher education institutions participating through programming and reprogramming.

Amid all these enervating activities, the conference has challenged us through its title: "Imagining a Pacific Community, Representation and Education," to pause a while, prompting us to become aware of the adopted imaginaries within which we are enacting our curricular and pedagogical actions.

As I have indicated, the title of the conference certainly challenged me, coaxing me to resituate myself and to reflect upon my own narrative imaginary within which I've been inventing my stories of personal experiences of my schooling days, and, as well, upon my own life experiences as a Canadian with the label of an Asian minority.

But for me, most significantly, the conference title has challenged me to consider possible imaginaries within which the very notion of the Pacific Community is constituted. It was at this juncture that I began to sense that the conventional imaginary of the Pacific Community as diversity constituted within the space/time of modernity may be inadequate, begging displacement and reconstitution.

Fortunately, I have come upon the writings of people like Charles Taylor, Homi Bhabha, Trinh Min-ha, Rey Chow, and Masao Miyoshi who are engaged in rewriting features of the entrenched imaginaries of modernity, simultaneously urging us to become sensitive to the limitations of the imaginary of the Pacific Community as diversity. So it was that I repositioned myself in a new enunciatory space, the imaginary of the Pacific Community as difference.

I now seek further help. Hence, I look forward to coming sessions of this conference over the next few days and plan to join you as you engage in articulating   your   imaginaries   of   the   Pacific   Community.

Chapter 18

Imaginaries of "East and West": Slippery Curricular Signifiers in Education[1] (1996)

IN THE MIDST OF MODERNIST IMAGINARIES

Earlier in this century, my parents, then living on the Pacific Coast of North America, insisted that the era of the Pacific will come. Influenced in part by their urgings, I became a commerce student focusing on international trade at the University of British Columbia. For me, international trade meant plying the Pacific east and west. For the professor and the course, international trade meant plying the Atlantic. I mention this as a trace of dreams that surfaced in other guises.

Then the War came and my dream was shattered, beckoning a physical displacement that landed me in the prairies of Alberta in the field of education. In the latter years I was "professing" education as a member and, later, chair of a curriculum department at the University of Alberta. While so situated, suppressed traces of the dreams about the Pacific surged forth. Let me offer two short narratives.

A BINARY IMAGE OF EAST AND WEST

I recall the time I served as a university representative on a ministerial curriculum committee engaged in revising a humanities program. Recognizing that the time had come to enlarge our students' vision of the world, the committee was toying with new words in the lexicon such as "internationalization" and "globalization." At the committee meeting the time came for entitling the new course. Came the first suggestion through the mouth of the chair: "Western and non-Western Civilizations."

The silence that followed suggested approval. I teasingly broke in and offered "Eastern and non-Eastern Civilizations." There was a shuffling of words and bodies indicating concern for the disappearance of the word "West." Next day, the committee compromised and settled for: "Western and Eastern Civilizations."

---

[1] Aoki, Ted. T. (1996). Imaginaries of "East and West:" Slippery curricular signifiers in education. In the proceedings of the *International Adult and Continuing Education Conference* (pp. 1–10). Sponsored by the Office of Research Affairs, Chung-Ang University Korea Research Foundation.

This retitling seems to suggest an equitable recognition of both West and East. The title indeed suggests a balancing. But when we note in the texture of the course the words "Near East" and "Far East," the adjectival "near" and "far" tell us that in this geopolitical imaginary, "near" and "far" are measurements from some central point in the West.

No doubt, then, under the semblance of equivalence in the title "Western and Eastern Civilizations," the stuff of this humanities course was somehow complicit in Eurocentricism, the kind of imaginary that in recent years, Edward Said (1978) styled *Orientalism*—an ideological imaginary that insists on seeing the "Orient" as the other side of the West.

Naive as my image may be, the structuring of the title of the humanities course "Western and Eastern Civilizations" can be seen as a Hegelian *syn*thesis, with "Western and non-Western Civilizations" as the *thesis*, "Eastern and non-Eastern Civilizations" as the *anti*thesis. I now see what we on the committee had done was to employ the working of an oppositional binary, which in seeming transformation was very much complicit in sustaining naively a dualistic image with which we had begun.

One more comment: in our interest in "East and West," we have completely ignored the key word "civilization" in the title, assuming, I presume, that the word "civilization" is a universal. Today, we know of the turbulence being experienced by this signifier, so associated it is with the Western imaginary of liberal democracy.

ASIAN SCHOLARS MEET WESTERN SCHOLARS

Fortunately, on the staff of the University of Alberta was a Korean media scholar, Dr. C. Y. Oh. When he told us that he was visiting Korea, we requested him to be open to possibilities of meaningful contacts with educational life in Korea. He brought forth two notions:

1. With increasing interest in English as a second language (ESL) he began to arrange summer visitations of ESL teachers to improve their speaking and writing.

2. With increasing interest in Korean educators' Western scholarship, he sought out possible graduate students. The keen interest of these Korean scholars leaving Korea to come to us compelled us to ask seriously, "What is the meaning of education in an East–West context?"

Certainly, we said, they ought to come into contact with Western scholarship. But the very thought of them coming to us from Korea to study Western scholarship and return the same was, it seemed, reducing education to a commodity view of education.

When they arrived we asked them why they had come to the West. We tried to remind them that their space of life lies between Korean/Asian scholarship and Western scholarship and that merely to carry home a commodity called Western scholarship seemed wanting. We asked, insistently, that in their dissertations each include at least a chapter on the experiences of Korean scholars living life at a Western University. For us it was an opportunity to question ourselves seriously: What is it to invite Eastern scholars in our midst?

Thus began our long-standing contact with Korean scholars, with the University of Alberta becoming a beneficiary in the warm scholarly and cultural interchange that is still ongoing.

"EAST AND WEST"
WITHIN THE IMAGINARY OF CULTURAL IDENTITY

I return to the key signifier of the title of the conference—"East and West." Somehow within my imaginary, I am pulled by the capitalized terms, "East" and "West." Why am I so attracted? I respond, "I must be habituating an imaginary attuned to the substantive." By this I mean that within this imaginary, each of "East" and "West" is articulated assuming presence of its own identity—geographically, culturally, and linguistically.

Stuart Hall provides us the following. Within this imaginary, according to Hall (1990, p. 223), cultural identity is defined in terms of "one shared culture, a sort of collective . . . which people with a shared history and ancestry held in common." Further, "our cultural identities reflect the common historical references and shared cultural codes which provides, as one people, with stable, unchanging and continuous frames of reference and meaning. . . ." For Hall, this oneness is "the truth, the essence . . . of [people's] experience. It is the identity, which we must discover, excavate to bring to light and express through representation."

The labels "East" and "West" suggest two distinct cultural wholes, "Eastern culture" and "Western culture," each identifiable, standing distinctly and separately from each other.

The earlier curriculum narrative of "Western and Eastern Civilizations" was premised on this imaginary within which these two separate civilizations were claimed to be fashioned.

So understood, the term "East and West" is rendered as a binary of two separate preexisting entities, which can be bridged or brought together to conjoin in an "and." This imaginary has been the dominant Western modernist imaginary deeply ingrained in the works of historians, anthropologists and the like.

Even more, at the University of British Columbia, this imaginary is dominant in the culture of Western education. For example, with interest, in the Asia Pacific, UBC has established "the Center for Asian Studies" consisting of the subcategories of Korean Studies, Chinese Studies, Japanese Studies, South-

East Asian Studies and Indo-Asian Studies—each a solitude formulated into a separate identity. I cite this illustration to indicate the legitimacy of this imaginary in university educational programs in the West.

THE IMAGE OF "CROSSING" BETWEEN EAST AND WEST

Another term in the lexicon of the "East and West" has been the word "crosscultural," emphasizing movement in getting across from one culture to another. A few years ago, in Vancouver, an international conference in the Humanities was held under the label "Pac Rim." This label pointed to the conference's interest in movement at the rim of the Pacific Ocean. For the conferees, it seems, the rim portion of the Pacific was considered significant.

By invitation, I wrote a short article titled "Bridges that Rim the Pacific." Concerned that educators, like tourists or businesspeople, may be overly emphasizing "crossing" from one nation to another, from one culture to another, i.e., in bridging across from land to land, I chose to play with the signifier "bridge/bridging" to query the prevailing imaginary that allows such language.

I pondered the usual meaning of the word "bridge" in our daily locution. Bridges abound—small bridges, long bridges, ships and planes that bridge the Pacific moving goods and people. Today, we revel in the remarkable speed, lifelines we call them, and give thanks to all these bridges (if we remember to thank them) for helping us to move from one place to another, the speedier the better, the less time wasted the better.

But if I go to an Oriental garden, I am likely to come upon a bridge, aesthetically designed, with decorative railings, pleasing to the eyes. Such a bridge is very unlike the many bridges that cross the Han River in Seoul. But on this bridge, we are in no hurry to cross over; in fact, such bridges lure us to linger. This, in my view, is a Heideggerean bridge, a site or clearing in which earth, sky, mortals, and divine, in their longing to be together, belong together. I wrote: "Bridges in the Pacific are not mere paths for human transit, nor are thy mere routes for commerce and trade. They are dwelling places for people. The Pacific Rim invites . . . educators to transcend instrumentalism to understand what it means to dwell together humanly" (Aoki, 1988).

In the language of this episode, I can see myself trying to move away from the identity-centered "East and West" and into the space between East *and* West. And in so doing, I leaned on Heidegger's well-known critique of instrumentalism and technology, trying to undo the instrumental sense of "bridge." But have I succeeded in moving away from the identity sense of bridge?

A SHORT INTERLUDE ON SIGN THEORY

At this point let us lean on sign theory that may assist us in understanding our imaginaries. Ferdinand de Saussure showed us that the meaning of a sign is an artifact based on the relationship between signifier and signified. Jacques Lacan reworked Saussure to enable him to split signs into double meanings.

$$S \quad \text{(signifier)}$$

$$\overline{}$$

$$s \quad \text{(signified)}$$

Within the first imaginary, the meaning of a sign assumes a vertical relationship between signifier and signified, wherein the bar between signifier (S) and signified (s) is transparent. The signifier has direct access to the signified. For example, my identity can be portrayed by showing forth the deep me. In the past, ethnographers claimed the possibility of accurate portrayals of existing cultures through contact with their essences. The signifiers "East" and "West" that I have dealt with so far have been understood within this vertical imaginary.

Even when I attempted to shift to the bridging space between East and West, my portrayal, based on Heidegger's ontological essentialism—a bridge as a site of being—was framed vertically.

But Lacan's second imaginary assumes opaqueness of the bar between signifier and signified; the signifier is barred from access to the signified. Within this imaginary, meaning arises in the midst of signifiers, horizontally arranged. In the midst of signifiers "East" and "West"?

RETURNING TO "EAST AND WEST"

I return to the terms "East and West," to try to dissolve my identity-oriented imaginary to one that allows me into the space between "East and West," to the site of "and" in a nonessentialist way.

In order to loosen my attachment to East or West as "thing," I call upon a Chinese character, 無 (wu). It reads "nothing" or "no-thing." But I note that in "no-thing" there is already inscribed the word "thing," as if to say "nothing" cannot be without "thing," and "thing" cannot be without "no-thing." For me, such a reading is already a move away from the modernist binary discourse of "this or that," or the imaginary grounded in an essence called "thing." And now I am drawn into the fold of a discursive imaginary that can entertain "both this and that," "neither this nor that"—a space of paradox, ambiguity and ambivalence.

So textured, I return to the "and" between "East *and* West," reunderstanding "and" as "both 'and' and 'not-and,'" that allows a space for both conjunction and disjunction.

So reframed, I revisit Heidegger's bridges, bridges of the Pacific Rim, and rethink of them as being both bridges and non-bridges. I revisit the Korean graduate students who studied with us, and rethink of their spaces as third spaces between Western scholarship and Eastern scholarship.

Here, "identity" is no mere depiction of the vertical but more so "identification," a becoming in the space of difference. Of this imaginary on identity/identification, Stuart Hall (1990, p. 223) states:

> It belongs to the future as much as to the past. It is not something which already exists, transcending place, time, history and culture. Cultural identities come from somewhere, have histories. But like everything, which is historical, they undergo consistent transformation. Far from being eternally fixed to some essentialized past, they are subject to the continuous play of histories, culture and power. Far from being grounded in a mere recovery of the past, which is waiting to be found . . . identities are the names we give to the different ways we are positioned by, and position ourselves within . . ..

So understood, the tensioned space of both "and/not-and" is a space of conjoining and disrupting, indeed, a generative space of possibilities, a space wherein in tensioned ambiguity newness emerges.

WHERE NEWNESS EMERGES

Allow me to bring forth a small example of how languages and cultures interplay in the third space of "and/not and." In a conversation with a Canadian Sinologist, our talk turned to the generative space of ambivalence between the Chinese language and the English language.

The word "individual" (an undivided person, a whole person) is alien to Orientals. Hence, in that space between the English language and the Chinese language, a term was created:

(divided person) 人   個
                              人   individual (not-divided)

In composing the term, fragments were juxtaposed. The fragment 古 means, "The past is a reality that can be accessed and boxed." The fragmer 亻 and 人 mean "person," with the two lines saying that it takes at least two to make a person. In other words, a person is divided. So here is a version of "individual" transformed in the space between languages with traces of both individual identity and doubled identity—indeed, a hybrid. What kind of newness is this?

Of such a construct, Ernesto Laclau (1995, p. 16) has this to say:

> Hybridization does not necessarily mean decline through a loss of identity; it can also mean empowering existing identities through the opening of new possibilities. Only a conservative identity, closed on itself, could experience hybridization as a loss.

Indeed, this imaginary allows envisaging of third spaces between "East *and* West," between and among diverse segments of the East, or between and among diverse segments of the West, as spaces of generative possibilities, spaces where newness can flow.

The title of the conference suggests to me that Korean scholars in education are alert to the postmodern deconstruction of Western modernity. And in the doubled movement which goes on in deconstruction—that is, the questioning of modernist imaginaries and their displacements—interesting work has been ongoing.

But in this doubled movement, there seem to be scholars on the double to cross from the modernist to the postmodern. In this hurry, there may have been a neglect to consider the space between doubled moves. This is the Third Space (using Homi Bhabha's [1990] term) of 間 that Asians seem to know about in their traditions of wisdom.

I mark the third space as an ambivalent space of both this and that, of both East and West, wherein the traditions of Western modernist epistemology can meet the Eastern traditions of wisdom. Could it be that such a space is the ambivalent space of modernism and non-modernism? The ambivalent space of "East and West?"

REFERENCES

Aoki, T. T. (1988). *Bridges that rim the Pacific.* Washington, DC: National Council for the Social Studies (NCSS), Social Education.

Bhabha, H. (1990). The third space. In J. Rutherford (Ed.), *Identity: Community, culture, difference.* London: Lawrence & Wishart.

Hall, Stuart. (1990). Cultural identity and diaspora. In J. Rutherford (Ed.), *Identity: Community, culture, difference.* London: Lawrence & Wishart.

Laclau, Ernesto. (1995). Subject of politics, politics of the subject. *Differences: A Journal of Feminist Culture Studies, 7.*

Said, E. (1978). *Orientalism.*   London: Routledge and Kegan Paul.

Chapter 19

Language, Culture, and Curriculum . . . [1] (2000)

We look at the title of our presentation, giving it readings. In our first reading, likely by habit, we see three master signifiers—"language," "culture," and "curriculum"—each a legitimated discipline in academe, the last named, "curriculum," a young newcomer in the family of disciplines. In our second reading, we are drawn into spaces: first, the space between "language" and "culture" where a graphic mark we call "comma" urges us to pause a moment, then the space between "culture" and "curriculum" where we locate the word "and" claiming a conjoining, and then, the space marked ". . ." suggesting "more to come" and "incompleteness."

And now, as we move into our third reading, we listen to Leonard Cohen's refrain in his poem, "The Anthem." He sings,

> There's a crack, a crack in everything;
> That's how the light comes in.[2]

Heeding Cohen, we re-read our title, which now reads:

language . . .culture. . . curriculum . . .

making us wonder what it may be like to be enlightened, living in the spaces of between, marked by the cracks in the words.

We move into the midst of these readings and attempt to dwell in five living metonymic moments.

METONYMIC MOMENT #1: MIDST CURRICULUM-AS-PLAN/CURRICULUM-AS-LIVE(D)

Claiming to be curriculum oriented, we take the word "curriculum" and heeding Leonard Cohen, we graphically mark it

---

[1] Ted Aoki and Ken Jacknicke presented this paper at the Canadian Association of Curriculum Studies President's Symposium, CSSE Conference, May 27, 2000, Edmonton, Alberta.
[2] From Leonard Cohen's poem "The Anthem."

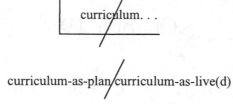

curriculum-as-plan/curriculum-as-live(d)

So attuned, we note that the "crack" offers us two understandings of curriculum: curriculum-as-plan and curriculum-as-live(d).

Such a folded view of curriculum reminds us of stories of pedagogy by thoughtful teachers who tell us of lived experiences struggling amid the plannable and the unplannable, the predictable and the unpredictable. Pedagogy is the fold between the two?

Curriculum-as-plan is the conventionalized notion of curriculum, understood as mandated school subjects like mathematics, social studies, science, and so on. In British Columbia, teachers know curriculum-as-plan as IRPs (Integrated Resource Packages), prescripted for implementation. So framed, teaching becomes linearized as instruction, and assessment becomes measuring of learnings with standards set in the prescription.

Curriculum-as-live(d) is the curriculum experienced by students and teachers as they live through school life. Much of this curriculum is unplanned and unplannable, as thoughtful teachers tell us, remarking that pedagogy is located in the vibrant space in the fold between curriculum-as-plan and live(d) curricula, at times a site of both difficulty and ambiguity and also a site of generative possibilities and hope.

METONYMIC MOMENT #2:
MIDST PRESENCE /ABSENCE

When Dennis Samara and Brent Davis of York University, then editors of *JCT* (*The Journal of Curriculum Theorizing*) requested an appropriate calligraphic work for the cover of a special issue, we submitted 有無 (yû-mu)— presence/absence—symbolizing the postmodernist flavor of the articles.

To help the editors, we submitted the following purporting to contextualize the Chinese characters.[3]

---

[3] The calligraphic work is from the cover of *JCT* [*The Journal of Curriculum Theorizing, 11*(4), 1996]. The extract on presence/absence is from the back cover of the same issue.

Calligraphed on the cover of this issue is 有 無. (Yû-mu)–Yû 有 presence / mu 無 absence.

Yû-mu as both "presence" and "absence" marks the space of ambivalence in the midst of which humans dwell. As such, Yû-mu is non-essentialist, denying the privileging of either "presence" or "absence," so deeply inscribed in the binarism of Western epistemology. As the groundless ground in traditions of wisdom, the ambiguity textured in yû-mu is understood as a site pregnant with possibilities.

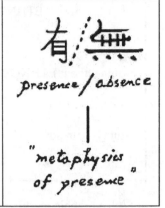

Such an interpretation was inspired by David Smith, University of Alberta, who wrote an article he titled "Brighter Than a Thousand Suns: Facing Pedagogy in the Nuclear Shadow," originally presented at the WCCI (World Council for Curriculum and Instruction) Conference in Hiroshima, Japan (Smith, 1994). In it, he dwelt on a metonymic theme insisting that in the presence is absence, questioning the modernist imagery that, by privileging presence, erased absence by placing it in the shadow.

This critical stance is echoed by Maxine Greene (1994), who has been calling upon us to be mindful of our essentialist bias in her article "Postmodernism and the Crisis of Representation in Curriculum." Challenging as it may be, she is calling upon us to tarry in the space between modernist and nonmodernist discourses

METONYMIC MOMENT #3:
OPENING UP TO THE THIRD SPACE MIDST
REPRESENTATIONAL/
NONREPRESENTATIONAL DISCOURSES

In the realm of curriculum inquiry, interest in narrative writing has led us to keen interest in ethnographic writing. Again we heed Leonard Cohen by "cracking" the signifier, "ethnography."

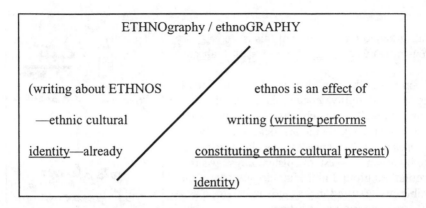

Such a graphic marking allows a doubled reading graphically textured: ETHNOgraphy and ethnoGRAPHY.

ETHNOgraphy, with emphasis on Ethnos (ethnic cultural identity), can be read as writing <u>about</u> "ethnos," an object of study already present awaiting uncovering and discovering. In such a discourse, language is understood as a tool to represent the already present but hidden from view that precedes language; language is secondary to thought.

In contrast, ethnoGRAPHY suggests that "ethnos" (i.e., ethnic identity) is an effect of writing. Here writing actively performs in the formulation of "ethnos." Within this discourse, language is no mere communication tool; the very "languaging" participates in creating effects. Within this discourse, identity is not disclosed but constituted in a signifying practice labeled "identification." Such an interpretation is nonrepresentational, questioning the hegemony of "presence" in the contiguous figure of "presence/absence."

Here we are reminded of Dorinne Kondo, whose ethnographic study she did at Harvard University is titled *Crafting Selves: Power, Gender and Discourses* (University of Chicago Press, 1990). More poignant is the book edited by Clifford and Marcus titled: *Writing Culture: The Poetics and Politics of Ethnography* (University of California Press, 1986). In these books the performativity of language is emphasized such that linguistic activities as writing inactively performs, crafting "selves" in the case of Dorinne Kondo, and constituting "culture" in the book by Clifford and Marcus.

Embedded in the texture of these remarks, we turn for a moment to developments in sign theory that speaks to verticality and horizontality in significations.

First we turn to a noted linguist, Saussure, who claimed that a signifier (S)— a word—is in direct relation with the signified (s) —the reality or truth, and that the signified is accessible because the bar between the signifier and the signified is transparent. But, Saussure added, such an imagery of relationships is arbitrary.

```
S          (signifier, word)

....       transparent bar

(s)        signified (concept, reality)
```

Roman Jacobson, another renowned linguist, urged that language can be understood in terms of two axes—a vertical axis (metaphoric) and a horizontal axis (metonymic). So reading, we can see that Saussure by relating the signifier directly to the presence of the signified reality, favored verticality.

We now consider Jacques Lacan, a noted but controversial psychoanalyst who reinterpreted the semiotic positions of Saussure and Jacobson. For Lacan, signifiers are in a horizontal contiguity of signifiers in a signifying chain. For him, the bar between signifier (S) and signified (s) is opaque. The signified is erased, hence, absent. Meanings, always partial and incomplete, are constituted in the spaces of difference between signifiers in a signifying chain.

```
S...  S...  S...  S...
_____
                    ↖
                        opaque bar

(s) - signified is erased and
thus absent
```

Such is Lacan's nonrepresentational imagery of signification in which so-called "reality" is constituted arbitrarily in the intertextual spaces midst signifiers. Such a reality we might call virtual reality constituted midst spaces of horizontality.

This interpretation leads us to the metonymic space of verticality and horizontality, that is, the space between representational discourse and nonrepresentational discourse, into what Homi Bhabha, a postcolonial scholar, calls a "third space of ambivalent construction."

METONYMIC MOMENT #4: MIDST WESTERN
KNOWLEDGE/ABORIGINAL KNOWLEDGE

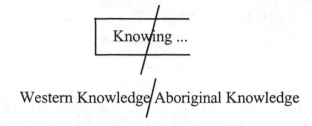

Western Knowledge/Aboriginal Knowledge

As we crack the word knowing, we are left with different readings: "What is it to know?" or "Differing ways of knowing."

When Europeans landed on the shores of North America in the late 15TH century, it marked a meeting of two divergent worldviews, Aboriginal and Western. The ideology of a culture directs the gathering and creating of information and knowledge, and determines the method and purpose of knowing. Western ideology dominated for five centuries as the only valid source to "knowing." There were indications that Aboriginal peoples were attaining knowledge of a very different nature and purpose from Western peoples. These differences manifested themselves in both language and culture.

Recently, a wider acceptance of differing worldviews is becoming evident. Aboriginal educators have moved towards transforming education and recapturing their culture and traditions (Battiste & Barman, 1995).

A major difference between the Aboriginal and Western worldviews is the emphasis of Western ideology on physical presence or objective reality, what some authors call "outer space." Contrast this to Aboriginal ideology, which is much more metaphysical and places a premium on the spirit, self, and being, or "inner space" (Ermine, 1995). A result is that there is likely to be more emphasis on the isolated individual in Western culture, whereas Aboriginal cultures support inclusiveness and connectedness through the life force in all living things.

At the University of Saskatchewan, Dr. Glen Aikenhead, a Western science educator, has been working with Aboriginal communities for a number of years, attempting to understand Aboriginal ways of knowing while developing cross-cultural science programs. In an article in which he contrasts Aboriginal and Western notions, Aikenhead (1997) notes that [science] knowledge is developed by Aboriginal and Western cultures for differing social goals, such as the survival of a people versus the gaining of knowledge for power over nature and other people; differing intellectual goals of coexisting with the mystery of nature versus cause-and-effect explanation; holistic First Nations perspective versus reductionist Western science (the "highest" form of knowledge) with its aggressive mechanistic and analytic explanations.

As we Westerners come to more fully understand Aboriginal knowing, we note the differing emphases on language. Aboriginal languages suggest inwardness, where the real power lies (Ermine, 1995). For example, "mystery" in the Cree language (Muntou) connotes a higher power and a connection to the greatest mystery of all, life.

Aikenhead's latest work is in collaboratively developing cross-cultural science and technology units with six aboriginal teachers from northern Saskatchewan. This attempt to "move in the cracks" Aikenhead calls "crossing cultural borders."

As we better understand and appreciate worldviews, we can better understand what it means to move into the cracks and see curriculum as a living entity.

METONYMIC MOMENT #5:
TRANSLATION/TRANSFORMATION

A favorite story I often tell is one told by Dr. Jan Walls, a prominent Sinologist at Simon Fraser University.

I had been reading *The Malaise of Modernity*, by the well-known McGill philosopher, Charles Taylor. A key malaise of Western modernists would be in their addiction to the signifier "individualism," and the related ideology, whose logos is centered on the "in-divisible self." Says Taylor:

> The first source of worry is individualism. Of course, individualism also names what many people consider the finest achievement of modern civilization. We live in a world where people have a right to choose for themselves their own pattern of life, to decide in conscience what conditions to espouse, to determine the shape of their lives in a whole host of ways that their ancestors couldn't control. And these rights are generally defended by our legal systems. (p. 2)

When I mentioned Charles Taylor's comment during a conversation with Jan Walls, he told me of a time over a century ago when Commodore Perry opened up the closed gates of feudal Japan. It is said that Japanese linguists became fascinated but puzzled with the word "individualism" as apparently no such word existed in the Japanese lexicon.

For the Japanese, a person was a 人 (HITO), the graphic strokes signifying that it takes at least two to make a person—a person is a twofold of self and other. The English word "individual," in contrast, is an entity unto itself, a self "in-divisible," a totalized self.

The Japanese linguists, so it is said, moved into the inter-textual space between "individual" and 人 (hito) and their translateral activity of translation, coined the word 個人 (KO-JIN), the 固 in the first character signifying a bounded boxable whole, an entity called the "self"; attached to the left is 亻—a

—radical—combined with 🈀 to form 🈁 and below, the character
人 (HITO). Together the newly constituted word reads 個人 (KO-JIN), a
word supposed to say "individual" but haunted by traces of non-individual.
個人 (KO-JIN), then, looks Japanese but it is only partly Japanese. It carries
traces of English. It is of a hybrid form constructed in an inter-linguistic and
inter-cultural space of difference.

The forming of 個人 (KO-JIN) suggests that in translation a complete
absolute translation is an impossibility, that translation as transformation is not
completely old nor completely new. Translation as transformation is an
ambivalent construction, as Homi Bhabha stated—a signification that is ever
incomplete and ongoing.

A LINGERING MOMENT

We began boldly enunciating the title "Language, Culture, and Curriculum . . . "
In journeying in/through metonymic moments, our boldness trembled and
quaked a bit, transforming both ourselves and our understandings of the words.
In our meanderings we experienced metonymic moments that were moments of
transformation, wherein form and formlessness insistently interplayed. We
revisit the title "Language, Culture, and Curriculum," which has been
transformed to a less noun-oriented signification to living moments of life. We
leave you with a new title: "The Interplay of Languages and Cultures Midst
Curricular Spaces: Five Metonymic Moments."

REFERENCES

Aikenhead, G. (1997). Towards a First Nations cross-cultural science and
    technology curriculum. *Science Education, 81*, 217–238.
Battiste, M., & Barman, J. (Eds.). (1995). *First Nations education in Canada:
    The circle unfolds*. Vancouver: University of British Columbia Press.
Clifford, J., & Marcus, G. E. (Eds.). (1986). *Writing culture: The poetics and
    politics of ethnography*. Berkeley: University of California Press.
Ermine, W. (1995). Aboriginal epistemology. In M. Battiste, & J. Barman,
    (Eds.), *First Nations education in Canada: The circle unfolds* (pp. 101-
    112).Vancouver: University of British Columbia Press.
Evans, D. (1996). *An introductory dictionary of Lacanian psychoanalysis*.
    London: Routledge.
Greene, M. (1994). Postmodernism and the crisis of representation. *English
    Education, 26*(4).
Kondo, D. (1990). *Crafting selves: Power, gender and discourses*. Chicago:
    University of Chicago Press.
Makaryk, I. (1993). *Encyclopedia of contemporary literary theory*. Toronto:
    University of Toronto Press.
Smith, D. G. (1994). Brighter than a thousand suns: Facing pedagogy in the

nuclear shadow. In *Pedagon: Meditations on pedagogy and culture* (pp. 166–188). Bragg Creek, AB: MAKYO Press.

Part III

Sounds of Pedagogy
in Curriculum Spaces

Chapter 20

Reflections of a Japanese Canadian Teacher Experiencing Ethnicity[1] (1979)

A few years ago at the curriculum conference in Richmond, British Columbia, devoted to Multiculturalism, Ethnicity, and Curriculum, I asked an assembled group of about 200, "How many of you are ethnics?" About 50 hands went up. I assumed, perhaps wrongly, that the remaining 150 considered themselves non-ethnic. I thought it likely the latter group felt that ethnics are those people over there, *about* whom we write, *about* whom we talk, *about* whom we film, *about* whom we package into curriculum, *about* whom we conference.

So much of what we see and read about ethnicity are object studies *about* ethnic people, and by being factual, they tend to conceal the experiences of life-as-lived earthly. Hence, my interest here is to disclose even to some extent that which we tend to conceal, by attempting to bring into fuller view reflection upon what, for me, experiencing ethnicity has been like. I regard experiencing ethnicity as experiencing subjectively one's lived situation from one's own ethnic perspective. From my personal standpoint, and this is the only standpoint I experientially know, experiencing ethnicity has been and is experiencing being a Japanese Canadian in the time-space coordinates of my own historical situation into which I was born, and within which I have lived and am now living.

EXPERIENCING ETHNICITY AS A JAPANESE CANADIAN IN JAPAN

What has the subjective experience of my own ethnicity as a paramount experience been like? When, as a youth, I first walked the sidewalks of crowded Tokyo, I experienced a strange feeling that stemmed from being thrust into a sea of black heads, a feeling of belonging and not belonging. For the Japanese throng, their "geographical *here* among black heads" must have been taken for granted whereas for me "my *here* among black heads" (at least at that moment)

---

[1] Adapted from T. T. Aoki, "Experiencing Ethnicity in British Columbia," an address presented at the Biennial Conference of the Canadian Ethnic Studies Association, Vancouver, October 12, 1979, and "On Being and Becoming a Teacher in Alberta," a paper presented at the Conference on *the Japanese Canadian Experience in North America,* The University of Lethbridge, Alberta, commemorating a century of Japanese Canadian experience in Canada, in the fall of 1979.

was vivid to me. Why was I so conscious about being among black heads when the native Japanese were not? Why wasn't I one of them with them? Perhaps it was because for me to be one with the dominant mainstream group has never been my way of life, ever since I was born. Perhaps the personal histories of these Japanese people and my history were quite different. They, I'm sure, shared their common histories such that *their past, their present, and their future* together made sense, whereas for me, even if I could have shared with them in part *my present* and a bit of *my future, my personal past* was totally irrelevant to their daily existence. In other words, from their perspective, my history counted little or not at all. What was the meaning of this to me? I felt myself to be somewhat of an ahistorical being in this situation, virtually a personal shorn of a part of his own history. Put another way, the space-time coordinates of their lived experiences, that is, *their here* and *their past*, didn't ring too well with *my own here* and *my past*. Maybe that's what being a Japanese Canadian in Japan means—at least that's what it meant for me in Tokyo.

And yet . . .

And yet when I traveled north from Tokyo, I felt at times a vibrant resonance with certain things and people of Japan. For instance, when I meandered along the pebbled trails of Nikko, I couldn't help but recall a Chamber of Commerce type slogan that I learned in a Japanese language school my father operated in Cumberland, Vancouver Island. The commercial went: "Don't say you're fulfilled until you've seen Nikko." In spite of the commercial (and I hate commercials), Nikko appealed to me. I experienced a oneness with Nikko's temples and gardens, which by enfolding earth and sky, man and the divine, seemed to transcend the merely physical and to come close to what is humanly true.

But what appealed to me more so was Matsushima, some miles north of Nikko, where the blue sea and the dotted islands sing a song of unspeakable but bounteous beauty and joy. A haiku that I learned—again in Cumberland— surged through me.

> Matsushima ya,
> A Matsushima ya,
> Matsushima ya.

I felt that the poet was saying to me: So prosaic are we that much of what we deeply experience, we know not how to say.

But what appealed to me more than Nikko and more than Matsushima, and therefore is more vivid in my memory, was my visit to Hirosaki Castle at the northern end of Honshu, whence my mother came. We were approaching the castle from the open plaza, at the end of which, etched against the white walls of the castle, stood a sculptured figure. I recognized it as "my grandfather in his usual armour," for grampa, who had been a samurai attached to Lord Tsugaru, stood in as model for the lord. To help the sculptor, he was photographed. This photograph had been a part of our family album since Cumberland days, and thus "grampa in armour" was the way I knew him. I was told, later, that when I saw the "dozo" (statue), I shouted "ojisan" (grandfather) and ran to him across the plaza to be with him. In some mysterious way, I felt, through that piece of ground, a presencing in oneness of both him and me, of both his past and my past, of both Cumberland and Hirosaki. That I richly and deeply remember. All of these, Nikko, Matsushima, and Hirosaki, struck a resonant chord within me.

And yet . . .

And yet, back in Tokyo, I recall watching, puzzled, parades of elementary school children, boys and girls, toting on their shoulders wooden guns, led by lady teachers also toting wooden guns, marching along the streets of Tokyo to the rhythm of "oichi-ni, oichi-ni" (one-two, one-two). This was shortly after the Manchurian episode. A few weeks later at Ujina in the Inland Sea, we visited the Japanese naval yard, with "Matsu," the flagship, bedecked, ready for some maneuver. . . . This was the time when the Japanese populace was devouring the book *Nichi-Dei Mushi Tatakawaba (Should Japan and America War)*.

As a preteen Japanese Canadian youngster, I couldn't make sense of school and marching; they didn't seem to go together. Nor could I make sense of a naval fleet in the beautiful Inland Sea. . . .

A British Columbia-born Japanese Canadian in Japan? In Japan I felt that as a Japanese Canadian, I was both Japanese and non-Japanese. I felt I was both insider and outsider, "in" yet not fully in, "out" yet not fully out.

EXPERIENCING SCHOOLING AS A JAPANESE CANADIAN IN BRITISH COLUMBIA

As a Japanese Canadian born in British Columbia, schooled in public schools on Vancouver Island and in Vancouver and at the University of British Columbia (U.B.C.), but for some time not having lived in British Columbia, partly because of unusual circumstances in Canadian history called the "evacuation," I have had opportunities to experience occasional homecomings. My coming home had often been a reexperiencing of my lived experiences in British Columbia.

As a Japanese Canadian in British Columbia, I have experienced the dialectic of the individual being and the social being that I simultaneously am. For me, it has been to become sensitive to the tension between the being of my humanness of lack thereof, and the social condition within which I interethnically dwelled. And as a Japanese Canadian, I occasionally felt my humanness crushed or disturbed.

I don't remember too well what I learned in Grade 1, but what I do remember is etched vividly in my memory. In my school at Cumberland, British Columbia, there were two Grade 1 classes. I was, for some reason, in the "regular class" consisting mostly of occidentals; the other class was strictly for Orientals, Japanese and Chinese Canadians. I recall that all of us passed at the end of the first year; the kids in my class passed to Grade 2 and the kids in the other class "passed" to Grade 1-A. That school experience of leaving my ethnic colleagues behind in Grade One was my first "learning" experience of social division by ethnicity—an example of a hidden curriculum at work.

I jump a little better than a dozen years to tell of similar experiences I experienced. They occurred on the campus of the University of British Columbia. My ethnic colleagues and I experienced a sense of not belonging when we learned that the faculties of law, applied science, and medicine on the campus, and the School of Education, then downtown, disallowed the entrance of Japanese Canadian students. The power of the gatekeepers of the professions of law, engineering, medicine, and education held sway. We were, in a sense, permitted to pursue fully "liberal" studies as long as we knew where the "illiberal" fence was. Hence, for us, U.B.C.'s motto "Tuum Est" ("It is up to you") held only within a zone of freedom ethnically defined by some mysterious someone. For me, "Tuum Est" has that kind of distorted meaning.

But where does a Japanese Canadian like me belong? At this time Pearl Harbor was yet to be. For 2 years as a cadet in the Canadian Officers Training Corps, I marched toting a relic Lee Enfield (as lifeless as the wooden guns the Japanese school children carried), with a "professor" lieutenant up front barking the rhythm of "left, right; left, right." This was the real thing. What more can I offer my homeland than myself? So I reasoned. We were tested on *the common to arms* exam, *the special to arms* exam, and were well on our way to a couple of pips on our epaulettes. Early in the fall of 1941, our Commanding Officer, Colonel Shrum, summoned me. In the basement of the present University Administration Building I appeared before him. He fired me a terse question with his typical bark: "Aoki, what would you do should there be a war between Japan and Canada?" I responded in what I thought was a voice assured: "I am a Canadian, Sir." That was a damn good honest answer, I thought. But I guess my old physics professor didn't think so. For about two weeks later I received a piece of paper—an honourable discharge from His Majesty's service—this before Pearl Harbor! (Not being a historian, I ripped up that curriculum document!)

Rough? Yes! Rough! Rough on a fellow seriously trying to find meaning in his life, a reason for being. Yet I call U.B.C. my foster mother, my alma mater, for even with the few hurts it might have given me, it has helped me in my human transformation. (Mind you, I'm not subscribing to the "blessing in disguise" hypothesis.) It has compelled me to probe more deeply into what it means to be a Japanese Canadian in Canada. And the more I probed, the more I felt I was beginning to touch the essence of what it means to be human—the essence of what it means to become more human. I guess I was on a search for the inner meaning of my "isness"—what Viktor Frankl was later to call aptly *Man's Search for Meaning.*

This kind of opportunity for probing does not come easily to a person flowing within the mainstream. It comes more readily to one who lives at the margin—to one who lives in a tension situation. It is, I believe, a condition that makes possible deeper understanding of human acts that can transform both self and world, not in an instrumental way, but in a human way.

ON BEING AND BECOMING A TEACHER IN ALBERTA

I speak now from the perspective of a Japanese Canadian Nisei and an evacuee. Hence, I speak from the perspective of a Nisei who experienced the evacuation, and who as an "evacuee" holds a special experiential relationship with those who relocated me, the "evacuators."

A Biographical Sketch

I lived for 13 years in Lethbridge, Alberta, for 22 years in southern Alberta, for 37 years in Alberta. Hence, when I speak of my lived experiences in Alberta, I speak not from the standpoint of a "visitor" looking on, but from the standpoint of an "insider" who lived his life with fellow Albertans for a third of a century.

Allow me to recall a slice of my lived experiences that of being and becoming a teacher in Alberta, dating back to 1945, the closing year of World War II, including my experiences as a teacher trainee at the Calgary Normal School, as a teacher for 1 year at a Hutterite School east of Calgary, as a teacher for 2 years at Foremost south of Lethbridge, as a teacher for 3 years at Taber, for 13 years as a teacher and vice-principal at Lethbridge Collegiate Institute in Lethbridge, prior to my becoming a teacher educator at the University of Alberta.

A Typical "Becoming a Teacher"

What does it mean to become a teacher? I learned, from becoming one, that to become a teacher one undergoes a ritual that allows one entry into a culturally shaped and culturally legitimated world in which are prescriptions of years of training, certification, automatic membership in a teachers' association, apprenticeship, scrutiny and evaluation by legitimated seniors, and so on. Once allowed into this culturally shaped world one is governed by rules of conduct and socially accepted behaviour, which are presumed to be "becoming" of people called teachers, and by codified ethical prescriptions of personal and interpersonal action. It is a domain of conduct governed socially by a codified School Act, provincially legislated, which sets out the bounds within which typical teachers are expected to act out their typical roles. Those who learn the roles well are typified by being labeled "teachers."

However, looking at typicalities ignores the untypical, the unique flavour of the experiences of becoming a teacher in my time and in my own historical situation. My experiences are centered within my own experiential horizon and undergirded by my own biography of past experiences and my own aspirations and hopes.

A Dialogue With Chief Maurice Wolfe

In the fall of 1971, I chanced to meet Maurice Wolfe, Chief of the Ermineskin Band, the largest of the four bands of the Hobbema Indian Reserves south of Edmonton. A friend of mine, Dr. Ralph Sabey, and I were at that time jointly seeking an opportunity to work with the people of Hobbema on a Native Indian Curriculum Project, firmly believing that a new curriculum development conception based on Native Indian involvement was sorely needed to develop meaningful school programs by Indians for Indian children attending Indian schools. Only by so doing could we begin to include in the curriculum the insider's perspective on what it means to be schooled.

On the appointed day, I met Chief Wolfe, and we talked freely of many things, mainly about matters other than mounting a curriculum project—so I thought, naively, at that time. Although many of the details of our conversation have faded from my memory, I still remember vividly three items about which we chatted:

1. We talked of judo—in passing, we learned that our sons were in judo training at that time. Our discussion about judo led us to the notion of the dialectic between "defense" and "offense," between "the active" and "the passive," between "the gentle" and "the strong," between "the positive" and "the negative." We felt good about this dialectic talk, a momentary enjoyment of a nonpositivistic world.

2. Chief Wolfe led me to a discussion of a book on his shelf, Dr. Nitobe's, *Bushido*. We dwelt to some extent on the meaning of being and becoming a warrior in the truest sense. We felt and experienced deep thoughts about being a human being and about human becoming, and for a moment I thought he would be expounding to me the meaning of Zen. I wish he had, for I had often listened to my father telling of his experiences of being a disciple of Daizetsu Suzuki, a Zen master.

3. Then, he talked to me of what he knew about the experiences of the Japanese Canadian evacuees—the expropriation of their properties on the Coast and their forced evacuation. He drew a parallel between the Japanese Canadian experience and his own forbearers' experience—the expropriation of their lands and their appropriation of reserve lands—and of his own people, then working as seasonal labourers on the sugar-beet farms in southern Alberta. Then he asked me of my

experience and my fellow Japanese Canadians' experience as sugar-beet workers in southern Alberta, but particularly, he asked me how the Japanese Canadians transcended "the state of being economic objects" (that is how he viewed sugar-beet workers), and how they transformed themselves "to become beings with increased control of their own destinies." I thought he was in search of a way—possibly resembling the way of a warrior—to help his people transform themselves.

Shortly thereafter as I reflected upon our conversation, I could not help but envisage Chief Wolfe viewing humanity in a dialectical relationship between one's subjective being and one's objective world in contrast to a popular view of people as strictly economic beings, that is, an objectified and "thingified" view of humankind, shorn of much of one's humanness and human dignity. I reinterpreted Chief Wolfe's earlier question to me in Freirian terms as follows: "How did the Japanese Canadian evacuees liberate themselves from the objectified condition, having been partially stripped of their history, of their familiar surroundings, of their circle of friendships and acquaintances? How did they move to a position where they, the Japanese Canadians, could conduct themselves with promise, with dignity, as subjects of their thoughts and actions?" Chief Wolfe wanted to know of the Japanese Canadian experience in this regard. I told Chief Wolfe of my personal experience in the only way I knew.

Job Offers in the Spring of 1945

The invocation in Canada of the Emergency War Measures Act in 1941 undoubtedly brought about an abrupt change in the life of most Japanese Canadians. But it was yet another Emergency Measure, a little known one, that provided the setting for what turned out to be, for me, my personal transformation from a sugar beet worker to a teacher.

The Emergency Measure I am referring to is the Alberta Government's School Emergency Measure. During the War, the province faced a critical shortage in the teaching force and there was an urgent need to devise a way to throw warm bodies (labeled teachers) into many teacher-less classrooms. The Normal School entrance requirement was lowered to allow entry of Grade 11 graduates, who with a 3-month crash program (including 9 days of practicum in teaching) were enabled as graduates to receive a temporary license which, followed by two summer schools at the University of Alberta, opened the way for a "bona fide" teaching certificate.

During the winter 1944, a group of Japanese Canadians—Niseis most of us—were at Burmis in the Crows Nest Pass area felling timber as a winter "pastime." It was there I saw a newspaper advertisement calling upon Grade 11 students to become teachers. I wrote to Mr. Monroe, the principal of the

Calgary Normal School, indicating my qualifications (a bachelor of commerce degree from U.B.C.), to which he responded, "fully qualified." So I dropped my bucking saw and double-bit axe and off I went to Calgary. Here, I faced an unanticipated problem—a becoming a teacher problem for a Japanese Canadian, that of "where to live?" Calgary's bylaws forbade residence of any Japanese Canadian within the confines of Calgary city proper.

A kind Japanese couple working at Hay's Dairy just outside the city limits allowed me to stay with them. So, for a brief while, as a daily ritual I commuted to Calgary on the 7:00 a.m. milk wagon and I "Greyhound bussed" home at night.

In the meantime I applied to the City Council for temporary permission to reside within Calgary. A report of the City Council deliberations hit the *Calgary Albertan* and the *Calgary Herald* on February 7, 1945, an event that catapulted me into a "cause célèbre" at the Normal School. I felt good that the council took time to discuss my application; I did not feel good about some of the comments that flew about in the City Council Chambers.

> One alderman referred to Japanese Canadians as "well-educated cultural devils" and shouted "If I had my way I'd take them all out to the middle of the Pacific Ocean and pull the cork." Another alderman stated: "They are treacherous. They are our enemies. And I don't like them—yellow bellies! And if there are no black marks against them, they will make good spies."

A six-to-five vote of the council referred my case to the city commissioners and suggested that "if in conference with Royal Canadian Mounted Police and city police, there be no objection to the individual's character, he is to be permitted to attend Calgary Normal School for a period of two and a half months."

From this experience I gained one important piece of knowledge, which I promptly offered freely to my Japanese Canadian friends. I told them—find a city or town where Japanese Canadians are forbidden to live and apply for permission to reside there. One predictable outcome will be receipt of official information about their own character—gratis, at that!

By April of that year, I had a temporary ticket as a teacher. I learned quickly that when the government spoke of a shortage of teachers, they had in mind "typical" teachers. There was no shortage of Japanese Canadian teachers. In fact, there was one too many.

I know, however, that the Normal School principal tried hard to locate a job for me. He did find one for me, eventually, at a Hutterite colony 60 miles east of Calgary—a one-room school, Grades 1 to 8.

Interestingly enough—and remember this is in the Spring of 1945—out of the blue I received two other job offers:

1. A job as radio broadcaster at B.B.C., London, to do propaganda broadcasting in Japanese to Japan for the British Army.
2. A job in Vancouver as an officer-instructor of the Japanese language, giving instruction to the Canadian Intelligence Service. (Previously I had done a 2-year stint of Canadian Officers Training Corps duties at U.B.C. but had received from C.O. Colonel Shrum an honourable discharge, essentially, I believe, for being of Japanese extraction.)

What job did I choose? I actually had no problem in deciding. I found that no real alternative faced me. I accepted the job at the Hutterite school—as caretaker, teacher, principal, all wrapped up in one package—and launched a pedagogic career—a move that by the way, I have never regretted taking.

However, I found that teaching on a Hutterite colony was a stranger's existence in that the residents permitted me to enter only that sector of their world associated with the "English" school (the other school being the German school). Further, it was a life with little contact with fellow teachers or the mainstream of the community's social world, although, for me, the latter was not an unaccustomed kind of experience—for living apart from the mainstream had been the lot of most Japanese Canadians.

Shifting to Foremost

In the spring of 1946, I scouted for another job. I had come to know the superintendent of schools in Foremost. I asked him for a job. I got an answer. Even a portion of that letter will give you the flavour of my lived world at that time. The letter is dated April 13, 1946.

Dear Mr. Aoki:

> I have your letter of April 8th enquiring about vacancies in the Foremost Division for the next school year. My personal opinion is that men should be judged on their individual merits irrespective of race or creed. However, the problem of community reaction must be taken into account in teacher appointments. I will take up the matter of your appointment at the next Board meeting and I will advise you immediately as to their stand. Probably the only position available in any event will be in a rural school.

> Yours sincerely,

I received an appointment in the town school.

Teachers' Convention, Lethbridge, 1947

The Marquis Hotel in downtown Lethbridge holds a special meaning for me. It revolves around a special episode 36 years ago, in the fall of 1947.

I was teaching in Foremost—just a year and a half out of Normal School—and had come to the city of Lethbridge for the annual teachers' convention. A group of my cronies from Normal School settled in a circle around a little round table in the Marquis Hotel to seek strength, courage and sustenance to continue the tough life as green teachers. The roundtable conference had an aborted life. The beer hop spotted me as a Japanese and served notice that "It is the policy of the management of the Marquis not to serve Japs."

I don't remember anything of the happenings at the teachers' convention—but I do have a strong indelible memory of that ten-second episode at the Marquis.

Summer Session 1947, University of Alberta

During the winter of 1946 I was already considering going to the 1947 summer session Studies at the University of Alberta. Earlier that year Deputy Minister Fred McNally had informed me: "I have telephoned the city authorities who assure me that there are no longer any restrictions on students of Japanese ancestry so far as residence in Edmonton is concerned." In spite of this, I received word from the Registrar of the University of Alberta that registration was impossible unless the city granted me permission to reside within the city. I dispatched a letter to which I received a reply from Mayor Harry Ainlay of Edmonton:

> Replying to your letter of the 27th instant, the City of Edmonton has granted your application for permission to reside in Edmonton temporarily, for the purpose of attending the 1947 Summer Session of the University of Alberta.

To all my children, Douglas, Michele, and Edward, Harry Ainlay means a large composite high school in Edmonton (dedicated to one-time mayor Ainlay)—and it has for them mixed memories there of life as Sansei students. For me, however, the name Harry Ainlay means "he who granted me the privilege of temporary residence" in Edmonton to attend summer school in 1947.

I feel sure that Niseis of my vintage will be able to recall episodes somewhat akin to the ones that I have cited. They add "charm" to the generalized reports and studies about Japanese Canadian experiences that are making their way into public view. These experiences I narrate and the experiences of my fellow Japanese Canadians attest to the psychic walls and constraints that kept us caged in or caged out depending on one's perspective—unwanted strangers in our own homeland.

These experiences we experienced; silently but bone deep we experienced them.

Departure/Entry—Lethbridge

For 13 years I taught in Lethbridge. They were good years. But I left it in 1964 when I was a budding assistant principal of the Lethbridge Collegiate Institute—in charge of locker keys, student attendance, student assemblies and not really enjoying being assistant principal.

During those 13 years, mostly happy years, the world of Lethbridge became very familiar and comfortable for me. I even dug into Lethbridge's past—for as a master's study I had done a history of Lethbridge School District #5I. I was even becoming familiar with many of my predecessors in Lethbridge. I was becoming one of many; I did the many things that many did; I had come to own many things that many owned; I had come to value the many things that many valued. I was becoming very comfortable in the city, yet discomforted by the very comfort that seemed to surround me. So I struck out anew—I became a stranger again, in a new surrounding—in a university setting as a junior professor at the University of Alberta. This time I became a stranger of my own volition.

Thinking about my departure from Lethbridge reminds me of the time I came to Lethbridge as a stranger 13 years earlier. The year was 1951. Although I was a stranger as a teacher, I was no stranger as a "consumer" in the business end of town—Fifth Street, Third Avenue, and so on. But as a teacher, I was a total stranger in Lethbridge's world of teachers and teaching.

I applied for a teaching job—I was in Taber then—in answer to a want ad that appeared in the *Lethbridge Herald* calling for a junior high school social studies and physical education teacher. I was appointed to the staff of Hamilton Junior High School there.

They tell me I was the first teacher of oriental origin to be hired in Lethbridge—this I knew. What I did not know was the fact that I was hired as a test case—to see how the people of Lethbridge, parents and children, would react to the presence in their midst of a Japanese Canadian teacher. This I learned several years later from Superintendent L. H. Bussard. This was confirmed for me by Professor Nora Sinclair, one-time teacher in Lethbridge, later assistant to the dean, Faculty of Education, U.B.C.

But remember 1951 was 2 years after 1949. What about 1949? A Japanese Canadian high school student said at a Japanese Canadian Citizens Association's Annual Oratorical Contest in the early '1950s held at the Capitol Theatre in Lethbridge:

> March 31, 1949. To most Canadians this is a significant
> historical date, for on this day, Newfoundland became the tenth

province of Canada. However, to twenty-two thousand
Canadians of Japanese ancestry, this day meant something
more for the hard, long struggle for enfranchisement was
finally won. On that day, the Japanese Canadians became
Canadians in the truest political sense.[2]

This rings somewhat of the romantic but beautiful idealism of a young high
school student in 1949. The real struggle for enfranchisement in the minds of all
people was undoubtedly still going on in Lethbridge in 1951 if the fact of my
test case is true. But my presence in Lethbridge as a test case in itself reflects a
new mood, a questioning of the walls erected, a reexamination of the Japanese
Canadians in southern Alberta society.

We in our turn tested out the attitude of the bigger world. Here is an
illustrative case, which occurred in 1952.

This same high school girl who spoke of the meaning of 1949 and her
fellow Nisei students brought to my attention a high school social studies text in
use at that time, Dr. L. A. Bagnall's *Contemporary Problems* published by the
Western Canada Institute Ltd, Calgary. Their complaint was the reference of
Japanese as "Jap" and "Japs." (Interestingly, the 1939 edition is clean; it is the
1946 edition that is contaminated.)

As a result, I submitted a brief to the Lethbridge Local of the Alberta
Teachers' Association in the matter of the use of the terms "Jap" and "Japs" in a
recommended reference book in social studies in Alberta. The resolution read in
part:

> Be it resolved that the Alberta Teachers' Association strongly
> urge the Department of Education and offices concerned to
> take steps to withdraw from the list of recommended reference
> books in Social Studies the book entitled *Contemporary
> Problems* (Revised Edition) by Bagnall and Norton, until such
> time that terms "Jap" and "Japs" are revised to read
> "Japanese."
>
> And Further Be It Resolved that the Alberta Teachers'
> Association notify of their action and attitude to the authors
> and publisher of the aforementioned book.

If the fire and heat of the activists of the 1960s were lacking, the spirit and
the soul were there. The book ceased to be used as a social studies reference
book.

---

[2] Mary Aoki, a high school student at the Lethbridge Collegiate Institute,
Lethbridge, Alberta.

Being a Professor at UBC

For 3 years, from 1975 to 1978, I served the University of British Columbia as a professor of curriculum studies. To seek momentary refuge from routinized activities and from life in the "huts," I often wended my way to Nitobe's Garden.

Walk with me now.

We stroll along the walk toward the Asian Studies Building. As we approach the garden gate, we walk in the shade of a row of tall poplar trees— trees arranged in a straight line in measured repetition, and spaced in measured evenness of distance between them. This row of poplars guards the even, ordered grid of the parking lot. I find this scene a paradigm of orderliness reflecting interest in efficiency and effectiveness—values embedded in our very technological world.

Soon I reach the garden and I slip in, wherein I find no two things alike, yet together possessing a unity of their own. To me this garden talks the language of a dialectic world, a paradigm of reciprocity of differences, a dialectic world of positives and negatives, of things and no-things— a world that invites the viewer to become one with it.

These two scenes, the poplar scene and the garden scene, are juxtaposed scenes. How should we approach them, these two scenes? Schleiermacher, an eminent theologian, once said that multifold are the ways in which man can approach his universe. There are many ways we might approach our two scenes. Let's consider just two.

First, these scenes can be approached as jarring opposites. "Incongruent" is a common term used for those who approach them this way. No doubt about it, this is one way of approaching the two scenes.

There is another way to approach them—as a conjunction of two cultural paradigms, separate folkways that find unity in their reciprocal influences. Viewing the two scenes as a face-to-face situation allows possibilities of a dialectical unity.

To explore this approach a bit more, let me go back to Dr. Nitobe, and to his book *Bushido: The Soul of Japan,* wherein he reflects upon two flowers: the sakura and the rose. I look at a passage that my son Douglas brought to my attention. In it Nitobe speaks as a Japanese, showing the bias of his own ethnicity. Nevertheless, of interest to us is how he allows the two flowers to symbolize for him two lifestyles—two ways of seeing, two ways of knowing, that is, as two metaphors.

Reflecting upon the sakura, Dr. Nitobe wrote:

> The sakura has for ages been the favourite of our people and
> the emblem of our character . . .. The Yamato spirit is not a
> tame, tender plant, but a wild growth; it is indigenous to the
> soil; its accidental qualities it may share with the flowers of

other lands, but in its essence it remains the original, spontaneous outgrowth of our clime.

The refinement and grace of its beauty appeal to our aesthetic sense as no other flower can. We cannot share the admiration of the Europeans for their roses, which lack the simplicity of our flower. Then too, the thorns that are hidden beneath the sweetness of the rose, the tenacity with which she clings to life as though loth or afraid to die rather than drop untimely, preferring to linger on her stem; her showy colours and heavy odours—all these are traits so unlike our flower, which carries no dagger or poison under its beauty, which is ever ready to depart life at the call of nature, whose colours are never gorgeous, and whose light fragrance never palls. Beauty of colour and of form is limited in its showing; it is a fixed quality of existence, whereas fragrance is volatile, ethereal as the breathing of life. . . .

In Nitobe's view of the sakura, seen as a being "ready to part with life at the call of nature," is reflected—without a touch of morbidity—the dialectic between life and death. Such a view illuminates the notion that without life there is no meaning in death, and that without death there is no meaning to life. It is that thought-style that embraces the notion: "Positive is negative" and "negative is positive." This thought-style rooted in a dialectic mode is somewhat alien to the dominant thought mode in Western cultural tradition.

In his view of the rose as a being "clinging to life, loth or afraid to die" is reflected a worldview in which there is an attempt to shunt death into the periphery of our vision or even beyond, as if that were possible. Within such a worldview, one tries to understand and to define "life" by looking at "life" itself. Within this scheme of things life is defined by life; death is defined by death. Such a view is rooted in a mode of thought and action in which the "positive is positive" and the "negative is negative." Further, often, the negative is seen to be instrumental to the positive. It is the thought-style that underlies positivism—a thought mode. That has given birth to science and technology, as we know them, a thought-style that permeates mainstream Western culture.

In Nitobe's view the sakura and the rose are root metaphors within which we could dwell and which in our daily lives guide and help us to interpret our world and to act. We live by metaphors. But most of the time we take our root metaphors for granted without realizing the assumptions we unconsciously hold. If we want to come to know the assumptions we make about humanity and world, we need to learn to stop our ongoing world, and to reflect upon how we make sense of our world by uncovering and thus discovering the root metaphor(s) to which we unconsciously subscribe. The method of stopping the world is akin to that pedagogical approach that Don Juan used in order to help Castaneda uncover the world of reality into which he himself was thrust upon birth, and within which he has dwelt and learned as a way of life. Such an uncovering may well be a way for a person to find out for himself who he is, why he sees the world in the way he does, why he acts within and upon his world in the way he does.

It seems to me that for a Japanese Canadian like myself, I have alternative possibilities in making sense of my world using, for example, Nitobe's sakura metaphor and/or the rose metaphor.

As one possibility, I could make sense by adopting the nondialectic *either–or* attitude and could try to become totalized into either one metaphor or the other, thus coming to view my world either in the sakura way or in the rose way. This totalization is reductionist in that other possible metaphors and perspectives are reduced out. In totalizing, one converts *a* way of life into *the* way of life. This sense-making approach is equivalent to opting for a monovision existence. I won't go for it. I feel it will cripple me.

As another possibility, I could make sense of my world by regarding my world as a homogenized reality, wherein I can try to persuade the sakura and the rose to merge into a single being—a hybrid. It may be zoologically possible, but as a construct of human beingness, it smacks too much of the "melting pot" concept. Further, I am not too sure whether a conception like "hybridization," which is appropriate in making sense in the natural and the physical world, is appropriate in the human, social, and cultural world. The baggage of assumptions carried over, when a metaphor is borrowed from another world, may be inappropriate as well as being risky.

Another possibility—and this is the last I like to consider: I could try to give meaning to my lifestyle keeping the rose and the sakura in view simultaneously. Instead of the power of monovision, the power of double vision may be what I should seek. The significance to me of making sense of ethnicity as a Japanese Canadian in this way may well lie in the ever-present dynamic between the sakura way and the rose way. It may well be that I should learn to make sense of life, not only within the clarity and certainty of a monovision that either metaphor may provide me, but, more importantly, I should learn to see life within the fullness of a double or even a multiple vision. Such an approach may reveal more fully within my lived human condition self-imposed or socially-imposed distortions that call for action—action that in the very acting will empower me to become a maker of my own history, a historical being engaged in his own personal and human becoming. Maybe being a Japanese Canadian is just that — maybe experiencing ethnicity as a Japanese Canadian is just that.

A LINGERING NOTE

I have a daughter; rather, I had a daughter. Three years ago, Michele Novuko, like a cherry blossom that had its brief moment, parted with life, untimely, at the call of nature. Of her 19 years, she spent 3 years in Vancouver, one of them on the campus of the University of British Columbia. How she felt experiencing being a Sansei in B.C., we really didn't have a chance to converse too much about. But when in 1978 we moved back to Alberta, she came with us, but urged us to retain our house in Vancouver as a symbol of "home." We did.

We have taken her home and have buried her on the coast. Beside her is a plot. It is mine. I intend to come home to B.C., and when I come home, I will want to view the sakura and the rose, so beautiful and bountiful are they in British Columbia. But in seeing them, I will be seeing myself — for I know that what I see and how I see is because of who I am. I am what I see. I am how I see. And when I see them, I will likely reflect upon what it means for me to experience ethnicity in British Columbia as a human being endeavouring to become more human.

For me, being and becoming a teacher and teacher educator has been an experience made richer by the fact of my ethnicity. I regard it as my personal world of my lived experiences, a world in which I participated with others in its very construction.

In my being and becoming the tensions that were there created a dynamic world within which I acted which has, after all is said and done, turned out to be my life as I have experienced it. I reflect upon it as a unique life in many ways, at times distorted, but nevertheless a life which on occasions by my very acting within them, I used to give meaning to my being, doing my damnedest in my own personal becoming.

Chapter 21

Revisiting the Notions of Leadership and Identity[1] (1987)

Who are we, we Japanese Canadians of the first, second, third, and fourth generations, who from far and near have here assembled? What calls us to this communal venturing wherein we gather to hear and to offer voices regarding our mutual concerns? What are the personal and communal stories that have been told, are being told, and will yet be told? Who are we that tell these stories, and what indeed do these stories tell? And, I add, what are the questions to which these stories are answers?

As for me, what authorizes me, silver-haired and vintage Nisei that I am, to stand before you and ask you to hear my voice rather than other voices more elegant, eloquent, and thoughtful than mine? I present myself not so much to tell stories, but rather to participate in a questioning of the questions we typically ask when we, in and through our very living, tell our stories—stories that inevitably tell who we are and, as well, our understanding of how our world is. In a sense, I assume somewhat of a distanced but hopefully reflective stance—a stance that may allow us to question anew questions we have become so fond of. Some of you wedded to a particular tradition will question whether my sort of questioning is needed or desirable; others more attuned to our own personal and cultural historicity, as historical beings, may be more solicitous to my form and way of questioning.

Over the generations the question, "Who are we, we who call ourselves Japanese Canadians?" appears not to have changed. Seemingly it recurs and is considered to be the central question by each generation. But I feel that although the question may sound and appear the same, the question is inevitably understood differently by each generation, for the context within which the question is interpreted changes.

I have been asked to participate in the questioning of two of the themes of the workshop on "generations" this afternoon—the notions of "identity" and "leadership."

In this questioning, you will have to forgive me for situating my task as I understand it in my own lived situation—that of a Japanese Canadian who devoted more than four decades to the fields of public education and teacher education. Inevitably, my bias will show. What follows, then, are two sets of questionings—questionings that hopefully will help us move beyond the typical understandings of "leadership" and "identity."

---

[1] An invited address presented at the National Conference of the National Association of Japanese Canadians held in Vancouver, British Columbia, May 16 and 17, 1987.

QUESTIONING LEADERSHIP

"What is it to lead?"

I pose this question knowing full well that for there to be leaders, there must be followers. For me, "leader" and "follower," like "mother" and "child" or "teacher" and "student," need to exist only together. They make sense only when in each set the two are held together.

It seems a bit odd to me that in the case of leadership, it is often detached from the twofold of leadership and followership. We know attempts have been made to make sense of leadership separated from followership particularly in discourses in organizational theory, in management theory and the like.

We can see something of this sort in the British Columbia political situation of educators, where in Bill 20, the place of a school principal as leader has become an issue.

A principal of a school at one time was understood as the *principal teacher*, a leading teacher. In this sense, the principal was a specially recognized teacher, but first and foremost, a teacher. How, from that, the word "principal" became detached and turned into a noun in its own right is a bit of a mystery.

But we can see how that separation was a prelude to the linking of "principal" to "administration," a term *au courant* in the world of business. In educational administration, the principal-become-administrator is endowed heavily with organization theory, or leadership theory, each a part of management theory. In education, educational leadership became couched heavily in the becoming, language of business and industry, and so education became a business, an educational enterprise to be managed.

We can see why, then, that in Bill 20 the principal has been named "administrative manager" and dissociated from membership in the teachers' group, the B.C. Teachers Federation. I find it a bit hilarious that in the bill, provision is being worked out so that when a principal (remember, "principal teacher" at one time) fails as administrator, the school board must make room for his or her demotion to "teacher."

Just as amusing in British Columbia is how deputy ministers in the Provincial Government seem to be understood. We used to think that the position of deputy minister was the top leadership role for a professional in a field—of education, of finance, of forestry, of mining, and so on.

But that kind of thinking, at least in British Columbia has passed. Deputy ministers, like principals, are mere administrative managers—and the substance of the field managed has become of minimal importance. Otherwise, how could there have been the musical chair, the shifting about of practically all the deputy ministers in the B.C. government? It can only happen in Fantasyland!

In my world of education, the notion of "educational leader" is a redundancy, repeating the same thing twice, for "to educate" itself means, in the original sense, to lead out (*ex-ducere*). To lead is to lead others out, from where they now are to possibilities not yet.

But a question remains: How does a good leader know which path or way he or she and others should tread? It is at this juncture that we need to restore the two-fold of "to lead" and "to follow." A leader must be a true follower—in leading, he must follow. But follow what? If he is a leader, he must lead by following that which is true to that which is good in the situation within which he dwells.

We might understand the meaning of leadership a little better if we listened with care to a mother's true leading of a child, a leading that follows the voice of the hand-in-hand of mother and child as they cross a busy street. Here, the leading is attuned to and follows the care that dwells between mother and child. And it is in the following of this logos of care that allows mother to lead from where the child now is to where the child is not yet. For the mother, her hand will ever be there, and even in those times hand does not touch hand, there is a touching that flows from mother's care for the child. And the mother knows that when the child, no longer a child, takes leave, mother's watchful touch in absence will ever be there.

And so when we inquire what leadership is, we are led to ask, "What authorizes a person to be leader?" We seek in a leader not so much that sort of authority that is present invested authority by appointment or position, or authority vested in paper credentials, but more so that form of authority that flows from insightfulness and wisdom that knows the good and the worthy in a situation that must be followed. In knowing what to follow, a person merits being leader. Hence, when we ask, "What authorizes a person to be leader?" we must not be swayed by the management sort of authority—for that is not being true to what authority truly is—but be guided more by the deep sense of authority that speaks to leadership linked to authentic followership. It is in this way that we can question the typical way of understanding leadership and indeed move to answer authentically the question, "What authorizes a person to be leader?"

QUESTIONING IDENTITY

Now as I submit myself to the questioning of the notion of "identity," allow me to work myself through three concrete episodes.

Episode 1: Canadian Japanese? Japanese Canadians?

Late 1986 I was asked by the University of Toronto to serve as an external examiner for a doctoral dissertation. The title of the study by a young Hebrew scholar from Israel was "Ethnic and National Identity among Jewish students in Ontario." What struck me from the outset of my reading was the way in which the Canada-born Jewish students, the subjects of his study, were referred to by the author of the dissertation. Through some 300 pages, these students were referred to as "Canadian Jews."

The question that first came to mind was, "What does it mean for these Canadians to be identified as Canadian Jews?" "How do they indeed understand themselves under this name?"

So as external examiner, usually given the privilege of opening a conversation (called "examination") with the candidate, I began as follows:

> Mr. Shamai, I have been calling myself a Japanese Canadian, and people like me have become accustomed to being called Japanese Canadians, not Canadian Japanese. This mode of naming seems different from the identifying label "Canadian Jews," the mode of speaking you use to portray the identity of the youngsters you discuss in the dissertation. I ask you, "In the Canadian context, does it make a difference whether Canadian is a noun or an adjective? As some might say, 'Is it merely a semantic matter?'"

That was the first question put. Personally, I was speaking from a way of understanding that allows us to speak of "the world in a word" much in the fashion that Paulo Freire, the great Latin American educator, understands. I have a sense that the question seemingly simple is a complex and subtle one.

From the foregoing allow me to draw the following question: "What is it about us that allows us to call ourselves or to be called Japanese Canadians?"

Episode 2: Reunderstanding the Question "Who Are Japanese Canadians?"

Recently, I was asked for help in a small study at the University of British Columbia. There exists a program called the Ts'kel Educational Administration program for Native Indian graduate students aspiring to be educational administrators. The question they asked me to explore was a question of curriculum relevance: "Is the program the Native Indian graduate students are experiencing relevant?"

Of course, we immediately ask, "relevant to what?" I, too, asked, and put a question in this way, "Is the program relevant to who they are as Native Indians?" Within it is a basic question, "Who are Native Indians?"

I pressed further and asked, "How shall I understand the question, 'Who are Native Indians?'" And out of such questioning emerged two questions: "Who are *Native Indians*?" and, "Who *are* Native Indians?"—indeed two different questions, for they are embedded in two different worlds. The first question, "Who are *Native Indians*?," urges me to be attuned to the "whatness" of the question, beckoning an indwelling in a world of whatness, of things and objects, of names and nouns. As a Japanese linguistic scholar recently said, the world of whatness is a world of the language of having, a have-language world, typical of Western cultures.

The second question, "Who *are* Native Indians?" (with "are" underlined, associated with the verb "to be"), urges me to be attuned to a different world, a world of being and becoming, a world of human beings. In this world the nouns tend to conceal themselves. This is, as the same Japanese scholar said, a world of the language of being, a being world. In this world the question searches for understanding of the meaning of what it means to be alive, the meaning of life in the lived human situation. New questions appear: "What does it mean to be a Native Indian in Canada? What is it like to live in a situation where across the road non-Indians dwell?"

Where, indeed, is the dwelling place of Native Indians inmost places in Canada? On the Native Indian side of the road? On the non-Indian side of the road? Or right in between on the road?

Now, I turn this question to our own situation: Indeed, "Who are Japanese Canadians?"

Ask the question, "Who are *Japanese Canadians*?" Given this question, likely we will respond offering features and characteristics.

Ask the question, "Who *are* Japanese Canadians?" Given this question, likely we will respond by saying something like "Being a Japanese Canadian is like this, and like that"—drawing upon existential themes of our lives.

Episode 3: Beyond Identity

Many of you saw in a recent *Time Magazine* (March 30, 1987) an article entitled, "What makes Seiji run?" with a subcaption, "At the peak of his career, Ozawa remains a man of two worlds."

The article begins:

> On a terrace overlooking a lake near Salzburg, Seiji Ozawa and Yo-yo Ma are deep in conversation. "Remember that discussion about whether an Oriental can do Western music?" asks the Japanese conductor in heavily accented English. Ma does "Music can be learned really, by anybody who cares to know it well enough and deeply enough," says the cellist who is of Chinese parentage but American as a baseball cap.
>
> "In Asia," Ma notes, "conforming is more important than being an individual." That becomes hard when you have talent. You have to speak up, you have to say, "I have an opinion." Ozawa, 51, looks at his young colleague uneasily. "Can you do that?" he wonders.

The article moves on to describe Ozawa:

> "The first East Asian to succeed in a quintessentially Western Art form remains solidly Japanese outlook and temperament. It is a clash of cultures—and its effect on music making—that makes him a provocative figure."

Ozawa recounts some experiences. When early in his career he went to Europe, he commented, "I realized that what I was doing was strange only when I got to Europe." This when he realized that the Germans were suspicious enough when an Italian performed Beethoven, let alone a Japanese.

Later, after studying with van Karajan in Berlin and after serving as assistant to Leonard Bernstein of the New York Philharmonic, Ozawa returned to conduct the N. H. K. Symphony in Tokyo. Ozawa is said to have experienced standing alone on a podium in front of an ensemble of empty chairs. It reminded him of the Japanese saying, "The nail that sticks out is hammered down."

The article goes on to say that Ozawa is "torn between his two lives, although he speaks confidently of his future with the Boston Symphony Orchestra." Ozawa claims he is content. The writer of the article asks, "Is he really content?," and wonders as he notes Ozawa's "divided life, symbolizing at many levels the duality that every Japanese musician in the West faces."

To his own question, "Why I became a Western Music musician," Ozawa muses, "I think that makes my life much more interesting and much more exciting . . .. Maybe, there is a way to make a marriage between this Oriental blood and Western music."

In what way do Ozawa's experiences speak to us? Where, indeed, is his dwelling place, his home? The author of the article says that Ozawa lives two lives in two worlds.

Personally, I feel that the author may be correct to a point, but not true to the essence of Ozawa's being. I feel that Ozawa's meaningful dwelling place is that place that makes his life more "interesting" and more "exciting" as a place worthy of a person of Japanese origin living a life of Western music.

Indeed, where is his place of worthy living? It is, as he did say, "between two lives," "between the East and the West," between his Oriental blood and Western music.

I see his dwelling as a dwelling in tensionality in the realm of between, in the tensionality of differences. It is the difference that really matters and for Ozawa, as for us, it is not so much the elimination of the differences, but, more so, the attunement of the quality of the tensionality of differences that makes a difference.

Recently, my son (of the third generation, 44 years my junior) advised me to read *Identity and Difference* by Heidegger. In it Heidegger points to how the traditional notion of "identity" tends to truncate the situational context of our lives, leaving the possible danger of reducing our life reality to an abstracted totality of its own, pretending to wholeness. He cautions us that such reduction seduces us to forgetfulness of the possibilities for a fuller life, of our living in differences. He advises us not to limit ourselves, not to submit ourselves to mere identity, but to enlarge and to deepen our place of dwelling so that both identity and difference can dwell complementarily. There, he says, would be a human place of openness wherein humans may struggle in their dwelling aright. And it is the quality of this struggle that really matters.

If the foregoing makes sense, a question comes into being: "Is not the reality of our being Japanese Canadians better understood if we were to move beyond the sense of identity to dwell within a twofold of identity and difference?"

The guiding interest of my talk was to question the notions of "leadership" and "identity" in an effort to understand better who we are as Japanese Canadians.

With respect to "leadership," I pose the question, "What authorizes a person to be a true leader?" With respect to the notion of "identity" the following questions are now before us:

1. What is it about us that allows ourselves to be called Japanese Canadians?
2. Who are *Japanese Canadians*? Who *are* Japanese Canadians?
3. Will not our understanding of who we are as Japanese Canadians be enlarged and deepened if such an understanding reflects the twofold of *identity* and *difference*?

Chapter 22

Inspiriting the Curriculum[1] (1987)

My teaching career began more than 40 years ago at a Hutterite school near Calgary. It was in 1945, when the war in the Pacific was still raging, that I found myself in a one-room school, the sole teacher of 40 in Grades 1 to 8.

What I remember most about that year were the reading lessons I thought I taught to the children in Grade 1. Using a primer, *We Work and Play*, I thought I did a fair job of following the reading curriculum. What I did not realize then was that I was teaching an ethic—an ethic that separated work from play, that sublimated work and deemphasized play, and sanctified the rather simple-minded attitude of either work or play, but never, never, work and play together. I taught naively, not understanding the hidden curriculum I was teaching.

Today, I am pleased to say, "play" is being recognized in certain quarters as a legitimate human experience, and curriculum builders, aware of the taken-for-granted bias against play, are beginning to provide alternative understandings of the relationship between work and play.

In that same reading class, many years ago, I used another primer entitled *We Think and Do.* From it, too, I taught naively—pleased whenever the children were able to mouth the words, "We think; we do," and unhappy whenever they stumbled over words, unable "to read," I thought.

How naively I taught, thinking that reading was mere "doing," that reading was a skill that could be acquired or not acquired. Obediently following the curriculum guide, I helped students "attack" words and sentences as if reading were a war game. So, as in warfare, I and other teachers indulged in "strategies" and "tactics," guided by targeted ends (many of them behavioural), the achievement of which meant victory and the failure to achieve, defeat.

How was I, as a novice teacher, to know that understanding "reading as skills" stemmed from an understanding of "language" as a mere tool of communication? How was I to know that this instrumental view of language led inevitably to an instrumental view of reading, reducing it to mere skills and techniques, transforming reading to a halflife of what it might be?

---

[1] This article is adapted from a speech given at an ATA curriculum seminar on March 4, 1989. It was printed in two places: Aoki, Ted T. (1990). Inspiriting the curriculum. *The ATA Magazine*, January/February, pp. 37–42 and in Aoki, Ted T. (1991). Inspiriting the curriculum. In Ted T. Aoki (Ed.). *Inspiriting Curriculum and Pedagogy: Talks to Teachers* (pp. 17–22). Curriculum Praxis, Department of Secondary Education, Faculty of Education, University of Alberta, Edmonton, Alberta.

More significantly, how was I to know that in teaching reading as a mere skill, I was being caught up unconsciously in a technological ethos that by overemphasizing "doing," tended toward a machine view of children as well as a machine view of the teacher? Within this ethos, was I not understanding people, teachers, and children not as *beings* who are *human* but rather as *thing beings?* Is this not "education" reduced to a half-life of what it could be?

And, most significantly, how was I to know that I was really teaching a hidden curriculum when I taught from *We Think and Do* that (1) "thinking and doing" are highly prized acts of first importance to our culture and (2) "thinking and doing" is a way of life in which one says, "First you think; then, you do," a way of life in which "thinking" is primary and "doing" is derivative, a way of life that edifies *one* understanding of "thinking," to the neglect of other possibilities.

Philosophers among us will see in this view echoes of Descartes's *Cogito, ergo sum* ("I think, therefore, I am"); historians among us will see in it a tradition rooted in the Age of Reason; artists will see in it the famous sculpture by Rodin, "The Thinker"; the academics will see in this view the model of a university whose "thinkers" are held in high esteem.

FROM THEORY TO PRACTICE QUESTIONED

What I was teaching was a way of life that sees thinking as theorizing and doing as practicing. Hence, *We Think and Do* can be seen as merely a mundane version of what could be entitled *We Theorize and Practice.*

For educators, it is a way of life that regards teacher preparation in education curriculum and instruction courses as theorizing and the practicing of theories as *practicum.* At the university level, it is a way of life that sees theorizers within basic faculties (such as the Faculty of Science and the Faculty of Arts) and practitioners in the applied faculties, which we have typically labeled professional schools (such as medicine, law, commerce, nursing and education). At the school level, it is a way of life that sees schools as being divided into academic programs and vocational programs. At the advanced education level, it is a way of life that splits universities and technological institutes—universities, where thinking is emphasized, and the technological institutes where practice (doing) is emphasized.

If we grant that "thinking and doing" are important human acts, is it always the case that we should think first and then act? Must we be caught up totally in the linearized form of "from theory into practice"? I think not. Without rejecting this approach totally, we should be freed to explore other possibilities for understanding theorizing and practicing, as well as the relationship between "theory and practice."

The time is ripe to question the traditional way of understanding *We Think and Do*, and move forward to embrace a more edifying and inspired sense of theorizing.

We live today a mid voices of concern about many forms of alienation. Among these voices of despair rings that of Urie Bronfenbrenner, a noted American humanistic scholar, who, in a 1986 article entitled "Alienation and The Four Worlds of Childhood," pointed to a number of societal problems in the United States that bring despair. These include the highest rate of teenage pregnancy of any industrialized nation, the highest divorce rate in the world, the highest incidence of alcohol and drug abuse among adolescents of any country in the world, fewer support systems for individuals in all age groups, including adolescents, than in any other industrialized nation, and the highest number of infants and preschool children who live in families with incomes below the poverty line.

These problems are not unique to the United States. We on this side of the border are compelled to concur, and in concurring, we too despair and agonize.

Bronfenbrenner notes that problems such as these go hand in hand with the unravelling of the social fabric that has been taking place since World War II, or even earlier. So he pleads that if we are to take seriously the education of our youth, we must not be blind to circumstances in which we ask our young to live—within the family, within the community, within the peer group, within the school, within the classroom.

Examining the disintegration of the social fabric, Bronfenbrenner identifies a twofold sense of alienation: (1) a disconnectedness that brings about the diminishing of the soul of the family, the community, the peer group, and the school, and (2) a disconnectedness that diminishes the soul of each person, or what Christopher Lasch, in his 1979 book *The Culture of Narcissism: American Life in an Age of Diminishing Expectations,* calls a minimalization of the self. Lasch describes this result as a self in whom whatever soul is left is secondary to the body, a self that is no longer a being that is human, but a diminished being on the way to becoming a thing.

Bronfenbrenner worries about the transformation of North American schools into what he calls "academies of alienation."

If what Bronfenbrenner and Lasch are saying is taken seriously, education that alienates must be considered "miseducation," and education must be transformed by moving toward a reclaiming of the fullness of body and soul.

TOWARD AN INSPIRITED CURRICULUM

The B.C. music curriculum is an example of one that is potentially inspirited with the soul of which I speak.

Some remarks by Brian Orser after he was crowned the men's world figureskating champion in 1988 provide a sense of what it means for a curriculum to be inspirited—a quality of body and soul intertwining in their fullness. When asked by interviewer Barbara Frum how calm he was during his 4 ½minute freeskating performance, Brian answered, "No, I was not calm; calmness was not what I wanted. I was in tension—in a good tension that surged throughout my whole body." Then he spoke of the practice sessions that had been geared to allow him to experience different forms of tension, while always understanding that skating well means not the presence of calmness or tranquility but the appropriate tension that allows his body and soul to resonate well with the surface of the ice, with the music, with the spectators.

When, later in the interview, Barbara Frum commented on how in his performance his skating seemed to reflect well the shift in mood of the music, Brian responded, "When I skate well, as I feel I did in my number, I become the music. I do not skate to music as if it were outside of me. I become the music. My skating is the music."

Orser's comments lead us to feel that to be alive is to be appropriately tensioned and that to be tensionless, like a limp violin string, is to be dead. Curriculum developers need to be sensitive to ways in which the curriculum can influence the ways people can be attuned to the world.

When Orser said that when he skates well, he does not skate *to* music, he was saying he does not find music distanced from him; he *becomes* the music. In the B.C. music curriculum, this twofold attunement is provided in two strands. One is a study *about* music, wherein music is held at some distance as an object and studied abstractly; the other calls for *experiencing* or living music.

In this curriculum, that which is distanced is apparently recognized, but it is allowed to have the potential to sink into the lived world of music.

LAYERED WORLDS OF CURRICULUM AND PEDAGOGY: HELPFUL FOR DEVELOPERS

The ideas of Bronfenbrenner and Orser foreshadow a layered world of curriculum and pedagogy, an understanding of which may be helpful to curriculum developers concerned with the question of attunement.

The ideas of Schleiermacher, a great theologian and hermeneutic scholar who once said, "Multifold are the ways a person relates to the universe," can point out possible worlds of curriculum and pedagogy to which curriculum developers can be attuned. Schleiermacher tells us of how a theoretician (such as an architect), a practitioner (such as a carpenter), and a practicing worshiper might relate to a cathedral.

A theoretician, like an architect of edifices, experiences the cathedral conceptually and theoretically. Within his intellectual scheme of things, he classifies the cathedral as a special type of church building and, likely by the shape of it, can indicate when it was built, its architectural style, and the materials that entered into its construction. If the architect theoretician is a good scholar, he will have a store of factual and theoretical knowledge about it. He will have a good intellectual command of the cathedral as an object of study. He will be evaluated as a good scholar of architecture if he knows much. For him, the cathedral is as an object to be subordinated to his intellect, mainly in the form of analysis.

A practicing carpenter walking into the same cathedral likely will look for whatever needs making and fixing. He will be bent on making the cathedral serviceable for practical purposes. If the roof leaks, he will fix it. If a window is broken, he will fix it too. If an altar is needed, he will make it, following a blueprint. He is a technician, and he experiences the cathedral practically. He would be judged as a good carpenter if he has good technical skills and is efficient in making and fixing things.

When a true worshiper enters the cathedral, the person likely experiences the cathedral existentially and poetically in a fundamental sense. The person experiences the world as a whole with the self included, as the person seeks the meaning of what it is to live and to be human. For this person, the cathedral is likely an embodied spiritual dwelling place wherein the fourfold of mortal self, divinity, earth and heaven gather together and shine through as one. The meaning of lived experiences undoubtedly is the person's utmost concern. The person would be judged to be a good worshiper if his or her quality of being is revealed as deeply human.

If we substitute *school* for *cathedral*, we begin to have three understandings of *school*. View 1 is a school given primarily to "rational thinking," a school where the curriculum emphasizes intellectual skills. The curriculum likely will be a thinking curriculum. It is a school that understands a teacher or student as split into mind and body. Teaching is seen essentially as mind building, accomplished by filling containers with factual and theoretical knowledge; being a student is being like a blotter, absorbing knowledge, the more the better and the faster, the better, as the assessment people get closer. An appropriate metaphor, as mentioned earlier, is Rodin's sculpture, "The Thinker," symbolic of the Age of Enlightenment.

View 2 is a school given primarily to "doing," a school that emphasizes practical skills, like the three R's, a school that nurtures skills for productive purposes. This school is utilitarian oriented; usefulness in the postschool workplace is the guide to curriculum building. The school is a preparation place for the marketplace, and students are moulded into marketable products. Predominant is the interest of the market. Adult life is the model, and the adolescent is understood as an "immature adult" yet unskilled.

At the secondary school level, these market-oriented schools are often called vocational schools; at the higher education level, they are called institutes of technology or professional schools at universities (schools of engineering, medicine, business, law, education, and the like).

View 3 is a school given primarily to being and becoming, a school that emphasizes and nurtures the becoming of human beings. Such a school will not neglect "doing" but asserts the togetherness of "doing" and "being" enfolded in "becoming." Here, it is understood that to do something, one has to be somebody. The teacher or student is seen as being simultaneously an individual and a social being. But as it is a school given to becoming, it emphasizes a reflective reviewing of self and world, as well as the taken-for-granted assumptions that make possible our seeing and acting.

Moreover, teaching is understood not only as a mode of doing but also as a mode of being-with-others. Teaching is a relating *with* students in concrete situations guided by the pedagogical good. Teaching is a tactful leading out—leading out into a world of possibilities, while at the same time being mindful of the students' finiteness as mortal beings. Although the View 1 school and the View 2 school are grounded in a fragmented view of persons (body *and* mind), the View 3 school sees its origin in an understanding of teachers and students as embodied beings of wholeness. View 3 restores the unity of body and mind, body and soul.

CAN A CURRICULUM TRULY INVITE?

For it to come alive in the classroom, the curriculum itself has to contain, said or unsaid, an invitation to teachers and students to enter into it. Not only that, there needs to be a reciprocal invitation. The curriculum-as-plan must wait at the classroom door for an invitation from teachers and students. And when the curriculum, teachers, and students click, we are likely to find a live tension that will allow the teacher and the students to say, "We live curriculum," in much the same way that Brian Orser was able to say, "I become the music."

To curriculum developers, the question is a challenging one. "How can a curriculum be so built that it will touch something deep that stirs teachers and students to animated living?" "How can a curriculum-as-plan be so built that it has the potential for a curriculum-as-lived that is charged with life?" "How can a curriculum be built so invitingly that teachers and students extend a welcoming hand?"

UNDERSTANDING CURRICULUM IMPLEMENTATION

In typical curriculum talk, "curriculum implementation" comes after "curriculum development." Typically, when a curriculum is built, curriculum developers poise themselves to ask, "Now, how shall we implement this curriculum?"

This typical question illustrates the way in which curriculum activities are caught up in an industrial metaphor that sequences linearly curriculum policymaking, curriculum development, curriculum implementation, and curriculum evaluation, all in that order. It is a process–product model that may be appropriate in a commodity-production oriented world, where implementation is understood as a reproductive task. The teacher as implementer becomes a mere reproducer, a person reduced to a technical practitioner, much in the way that a carpenter might be viewed in Schleiermacher's cathedral.

Such an understanding of implementation allows the possibility of curriculum imperialism that calls for a sameness throughout the province. What we must guard against is that a curricular demand for sameness may diminish and extinguish the salience of the lived situation of people in classrooms and communities. We need to nurture the interpretive powers of teachers and students, without which, teaching and learning may not have the chance to become inspirited. We need empowered curriculum developers.

As they are engaged in working out the curriculum, or even before, developers are urged to be sensitive to how they understand curriculum implementation, for that understanding inevitably influences curriculum development.

In understanding implementation, what becomes central for curriculum developers is to understand who teachers are and what teaching is.

STRIVING FOR THE SECRET PLACES OF THE SOUL

A report of a recent UNESCO research project on "curriculum balance" concluded, "There is a need to reorient educational systems towards a closer connection between abstract knowledge and everyday activities."[2]

I interpret this concern as a questioning that flows from an awareness of the distancing between abstractions at the conceptual and theoretical level within a curriculum and the world of everyday life of teachers and students. Implicit in the call for a closer connection between the two is an invitation to curriculum developers to attempt to seek ways of understanding the relationship between the abstract and the concrete.

The typical understanding of the relationship between the abstract and the concrete is reflected in a key word, *application.* In North America, there is increasingly a call for a renewal and redirection of science education. For example, the B.C. biology program includes the following statement: "The 1984 Science Council of Canada report on Science Education . . . Called for curriculum that . . . Emphasizes the science–technology–society connection."[3]

And the B.C. social studies curriculum states:

> The curriculum attempts to present knowledge and concepts
> . . . in a context to which students can relate their expanding
> life experiences . . . by the application of knowledge. Concepts
> and skills . . . culminate in the ability to transfer knowledge to
> a real-life situation.[4]

The implicit linear notion of "from theory to practice" prevails in much of the B.C. curriculum documents; it is reminiscent of the primer, *We Think and Do,* I used almost 50 years ago. This general notion, Aristotilean in origin, gives primacy to theory and secondariness to practice.

---

[2] "Study on Distribution and Balance of the Content of General Education." UNESCO Division of Educational Sciences Contents and Methods of Education, May 1986.

[3] *Biology Curriculum Guide Grade 11 and 12,* pp. 11 and 12.

[4] *Elementary Social Studies Guide,* pp. 5 and 10.

Curriculum developers need to be aware that curriculum balance between the abstract and the concrete understood as *application* is by tradition so dominant that it may suppress an equally significant approach.

In contrast to this, it should be noted that there are in the B.C. curriculum documents occasional references to a notion of relationship between the abstract and the concrete that breaks with the notion of application. These occur in subtle ways in the B.C. curriculum documents.

For instance, the new B.C. curriculum for science and technology states, almost cautiously, that "technology may actually precede science."[5] To one accustomed to the phrase "science preceding technology," hearing the words "technology preceding science" invites a double take, making one wonder if it isn't a slip of the tongue.

Recall the B.C. elementary music curriculum, which speaks of two strands: (1) the "learning about music strand" in which children study "about music and the role of music in society past and present" and (2) the "living music strand" wherein children are "actually involved with music through activities involving singing, listening, playing, etc."

Although the curriculum calls for coexistence of the two strands, one senses which layer is the ground because the curriculum guide, leaning on Plato, states, "Education in music is most sovereign, because more than anything else, rhythm and harmony find their way into the secret places of the *soul*."[6] That in curriculum talk there is such interest in reclaiming the soul is excitingly satisfying.

All of these ideas about curriculum development are embedded in notions of what education is. For each curriculum stance, for each pedagogical sense, there seems to be in the shadow some notion of an educated person.

The B.C. Ministry of Education offers to curriculum developers and to teachers, in its publication, *Let's Talk About Schools*, the following image of an educated person—a composite of the opinions of the people of British Columbia:

> The educated person is one who is a thinking individual, capable of making independent decisions based on analysis and reason. The individual is curious, capable of, and interested in learning, capable of acquiring and imparting information, and able to draw from a broad knowledge base. The individual appreciates and is able to contribute to creative expression. The individual is self-motivated, has a sense of self-worth, pursues excellence, strives to be physically healthy and is able to achieve satisfaction through achievement. The individual has sound interpersonal skills, morals and values, and respects others who may be different, understands the

---

[5] Ibid.

[6] *Secondary Music Curriculum/Resource Guide (1–12),* 1980.

rights and responsibilities of an individual within the family, community, nation and the world and is aware of Canada's cultural heritage. The individual is flexible and has skills necessary to function in and contribute to the world of work.

Thomas Berger, the noted public-spirited former judge and royal commissioner, when asked what he thought of this image of an educated person said, "I think the minister's definition of the educated person is so comprehensive as to be virtually meaningless."

To me, an educated person, first and foremost, understands that one's ways of knowing, thinking, and doing flow from who one is. Such a person knows that an authentic person is no mere individual, an island unto oneself, but is a being-in-relation-with-others, and hence is, at core, an ethical being. Such a person knows that being an educated person is more than possessing knowledge or acquiring intellectual or practical skills, and that basically, it is being concerned with dwelling aright in thoughtful living with others.

An educated person thus not only guards against disembodied forms of knowing, thinking, and doing that reduce self and others to being things, but also strives, guided by the authority of the good in pedagogical situations, for embodied thoughtfulness that makes possible a living as a human being.

Moreover, a truly educated person speaks and acts from a deep sense of humility, conscious of the limits set by human finitude and mortality, acknowledging the grace by which educator and educated are allowed to dwell in the present that embraces past experiences but is open to possibilities yet to be. Thus, to be educated is to be ever open to the call of what it is to be deeply human, and heeding the call to walk with others in life's ventures.

Chapter 23

Sonare and Videre:
A Story, Three Echoes and
a Lingering Note[1] (1990)

BOBBY SHEW JAZZES UP A CURRICULUM SEMINAR:
A STORY

It was during a winter session in 1981 at the University of Alberta. In a chance conversation on campus, I learned that Bobby Shew, the jazz trumpeter from California, was being invited as a visiting scholar to the music department across campus.

As chair of the Department of Secondary Education, a department given to curriculum and pedagogy, I was delighted to hear of Bobby Shew's coming. I jumped on the phone to the chair of the Music Department to see if we could borrow Bobby Shew for a couple of hours for our grad and staff curriculum seminar. On the phone I could feel a questioning tone: "A curriculum seminar? Bobby Shew at a curriculum seminar?" His voice sounded bewildered: "A curriculum department in the Faculty of Education interested in a jazz trumpeter?" So before the questioning tone became a question, I cut in: "There are two questions we would like Bobby Shew to speak to, sing to, or play to. The first question is, 'When does an instrument cease to be an instrument?' and the second question is, 'What is it to improvise? What is improvisation?'"

Having lived through my college days here in Vancouver taking in the big jazz bands—Duke Ellington, Lionel Hampton, Benny Goodman, Count Basie, Tommy Dorsey, Gene Krupa (these are the ones I remember)—Bobby Shew meant for me a reconnection with that world.

When Bobby Shew arrived on campus, I was invited to chat with him. I walked over to the Music Department. I don't know what Bobby Shew thought when a bespectacled Japanese Canadian, a nonmusic educator to boot, walked in. Beckoned by his cordiality, I repeated the two questions of our interest.

---

[1] This talk was presented as a keynote address at Ensemble '91, Annual Conference of the British Columbia Music Educators' Association held on February 7–9, 1991, at Hotel Vancouver in Vancouver, BC. Reprinted here from: Aoki, Ted T. (1991). Sonare and Videre: A Story, Three Echoes and a Lingering Note. In Ted T. Aoki (Ed.). *Inspiriting Curriculum and Pedagogy: Talks to Teachers* (pp. 29-34). Curriculum Praxis, Department of Secondary Education, University of Alberta, Edmonton.

Intensely he listened and responded: "Even we musicians don't talk too much about these things. They're philosophical questions you ask. Sounds like fun."

I told him how in the field of curriculum we have come under the sway of discourse that is replete with performative words such as goals and objectives, processes and products, achievement and assessment—words reflective of instrumentalism in modernity—and that some of us were exploring ways of breaking out of such instrumentalism. Perhaps, if we can come to know how an instrument can cease to be an instrument, maybe that might provide us clues for a way out.

And why "improvisation"? I told him that in education, and in curriculum particularly, under the hold of technological rationality, we have become so production oriented that the ends–means paradigm, *a* way to do, has become *the* way to do, indifferent to differences in the lived world of teachers and students. Could improvisation be a way to create spaces to allow differences to show through?

Bobby Shew listened to me intently. With a big smile, he said, "I'll be there."

The day for Bobby Shew's curriculum seminar came. Students and staff crowded the seminar room. Then Bobby Shew strode in with his trumpet, blew a few licks to announce that he and his trumpet were here.

Then he began to tell us how he introduces a new student to the world of trumpet playing. He told us how he would allow the student to hold the gleaming trumpet, not in front, but at his back, and to withhold him from bringing the trumpet to his lips. The first few lessons would be all lip and scat-singing work. And only when Bobby Shew felt that the trumpet in joining lips would become a part of the body—become an embodied trumpet—would he allow trumpet and lips to meet. He insistently said, "The trumpet, music, and body must become as one in a living wholeness."

We were impressed by Bobby Shew's pedagogy that seemed to say that musicianship is more than a matter of skills and techniques, that music to be lived calls for transformation of instrument and music into that which is lived bodily.

On improvisation, he resorted to his trumpet and, although handicapped by the absence of fellow musicians, he gave us a few renditions of improvisations, no two alike. He spoke of how in improvising he and his fellow musicians respond not only to each other, but also to whatever calls upon them in that situational moment, and that, for him, no two situational moments, like life lived, are exactly alike. He said thoughtfully, "Exact repetition, thank God, is an impossibility. It's a remarkable feature that ought not be suppressed!"

It was an inspirited curriculum seminar that we truly lived and enjoyed, a seminar whose resonant echoes, even now, 10 years later, sound and resound.

ECHO 1: THROUGH DISEMBODIED
INSTRUMENTALISM TO EMBODIED MEANING

When we asked Bobby Shew, "When does an instrument cease to be an instrument?," he offered us a thoughtful response: "When music to be lived calls for transformation of instrument and music into that which is bodily lived." In these remarks, he gives us in the field of curriculum a reason to reflect upon the ambience within which we have been toiling as curriculum workers. What Bobby Shew has done for us is to open up a sonorous clearing so that we might recognize instrumental words in curriculum and seek curriculum words that can sound and resound in an inspirited way.

All of us know that in education we have come to be in the seductive hold of a technological ethos, an ethos that uncannily turns everything virtually into "how to do's," into techniques and skills. We know that many curriculum courses we have taken in teacher education have become "methods" courses. Bobby Shew would say, I'm sure, that such a technical ethos is a cultural version of instrumentalism—a way of life that is not fully bodily lived.

As educators, we all know that the very word "curriculum" was coined as an administrative category, sponsored by management interests. No wonder, then, at the prominence of instrumental language in curriculum talk, populated by expressions like "curriculum development," "curriculum implementation," "curriculum integration," "curriculum piloting," and the like. The danger in speaking this language is that we become the language we speak. And in so becoming, we might become forgetful of how instrumental language disengages us from our bodies, making of us disembodied, dehumanized beings, indifferent to the nihilistic drying out of inspiritedness.

We are reminded of Milan Kundera, the Czechoslovakian novelist who wrote *The Unbearable Lightness of Being*,[2] a portrayal of dispirited lives lived daily by Czechoslovakians in a regime that, in its exercise of instrumental totalitarianism, became indifferent to the beingness of humans. The result, nihilistic existence—disembodied existence, hollow existence.

So when we are called upon as teachers to "implement" a curriculum, we ought to recognize implementation as an instrumental word, and then we ought to ask not "How do I implement?" but "What is it to implement?" Here we should recall Bobby Shew, whose notion of improvisation reverberates within us and animates us. Instead of "curriculum implementation," how about "curriculum improvisation"? Such a change provokes in us a vitalizing possibility that causes our whole body to beat a new and different rhythm.

What "curriculum improvisation" does for me is twofold. First, it reminds me more clearly that curriculum implementation asks teachers to be mainly

---

[2] Milan Kundera wrote *The Unbearable Lightness of Being* (New York: Harper & Row, 1984) based on the Nietzschean theme of the eternal return and the Heideggerian theme of the forgetfulness of Being.

installers, primarily interested in fidelity to the curriculum to be installed. The danger lies in the possibility of indifference to the lives of teachers and students in the situation. Second, "curriculum improvisation" rings differently. In curriculum improvisation teachers are asked to shift from being installers to being improvisers, sensitive to the ongoing life and experiences of themselves and students in the situation. The quality of the curriculum-as-lived becomes a leading concern. "Curriculum improvisation" so understood helps us move beyond the hold of instrumentalism of curriculum implementation.

If what I have been saying is worthy of Bobby Shew's teaching to us, then more than ever we need the help of music educators such as you to help us in the creation of a new curriculum language—a language that resounds bodily.

ECHO 2: POLYPHONIC CURRICULUM:
RESPONDING TO THE CALL
FOR CURRICULUM INTERGRATION IN "YEAR 2000"

A curriculum talk in British Columbia that doesn't mention "Year 2000"[3] risks being labeled "irrelevant." I have been noticing, from a comfortable distance, a flurry of activities that "Year 2000" has precipitated. One such activity involves "curriculum integration."

We all know how "Year 2000" speaks to multiple curriculum strands and substrands that teachers are asked to integrate. I have a teacher friend in Richmond who at this moment is writing a narrative of his experiences integrating Grade 8 social studies and English. I attended recently a tri-university session where the professors assembled were setting up courses for teachers concerning concepts and theories about integration and their application to practice. I didn't see Bobby Shew there. As a visitor, I kept my mouth shut except to ask one question, "Is integration always good?" I was asking the question of the *integrity* of the very notion of "integration" in curriculum talk.

"Integration." How do we usually feel when we hear the word? It feels warm; it feels inherently good somehow, and we get the sense that integrating things leads to a harmonious, tranquil world. We are given this sense of "integration" by no less an authority than Plato, whose words appear in a BC Music Curriculum: "Education in music is most sovereign because more than anything else . . . rhythm and harmony find their way into the secret places of the soul."

Harmony, as Plato, an early metaphysicist, understood it, is a fitting together, a con-c(h)ord, an integration of sounds—a sonic univocity. In our Western tradition, we are given to this quietest sense of "harmony" as a natural goodness, thought to be in accord with all that which is valued and true. It may

---

[3] *Year 2000: A Curriculum and Assessment Framework for the Future* is a publication of the British Columbia Ministry of Education, issued as a discussion paper.

well be. But could it be that such an understanding of "integration," of conjoining, of belonging together, is a reflection of our caughtness in our own creation—good as it may be—a metaphysical notion of oneness, a harmonic oneness, an integrated totality? I wish to let Daisetz Suzuki, a Zen scholar, put into turbulence this quietest sense of "harmony." He said of Nature:

> It is not a sense . . . of tranquility that Zen sees . . . in Nature.
> Nature is always in motion, never at a standstill. . . . To seek
> tranquility is to kill nature, to stop its pulsations, and to
> embrace the dead corpse that is left behind. Advocates of
> tranquility are worshippers of abstraction and death.[4]

Two summers ago, I heard Edwin Dumas, a music teacher from Maple Ridge, speak of contrapuntality in certain of Bach's fugues. Speaking to curriculum-oriented people who, like me, are nonmusicians but fascinated with the notion and sounds of the contrapuntal, he had us listen to the contra-ness of five lines of a fugue. Edwin pointed to a sonic realm in which five lines coexist in polyphonic tensionality, whose openness within its own space contrasted sharply with the closedness of synthetic, integrated harmony.

Edwin will be happy to know that because of him, just before Christmas, my wife and I attended a remarkable concert, the Tallis Scholars' Christmas Concert, at St. Andrews-Wesley Church just up Burrard Street. It featured Palestrina, who, as you know better than me, is the grand master of the polyphonic style. Of the Tallis singers, Michael Scott of the *Vancouver Sun* glowed:

> It is a mark of the technical prowess of the Tallis Scholars that
> they do not resort to tricks of volume or vocal drama to
> animate such meaningful material [of the program]. Instead,
> they immersed their individual characters in its braided
> polyphony, winding a complex skein that glows white-hot
> from within.[5]

I am in ecstatic awe. But I return to our multiple curriculum strands and to the question of curriculum composition. Shall we integrate the strands into a sonic unity? Shall we allow the strands to sing polyphonically and pray that, on occasion, they glow white-hot from within?

I return to Bobby Shew and tune in to one of his jam sessions. And lingering in the sonorous shadow, I wonder if he would approve me speaking of his jamming as polyphonic improvisation? I wonder.

---

[4] This saying by Daisetzu Suzuki, a noted Zen scholar, is quoted by Roloff Beny, *Japan in Colour* (London: Thames and Hudson, 1967) p. 8.
[5] From the *Vancouver Sun,* December 10, 1990, p. B7.

An Interlude: Conversation Pieces

Before we listen to Echo 3, whose theme is *sonare and videre,* let's linger a while and listen to a few conversation pieces, short sayings about listening, the ear, and the world of sound. Most of them are gems from books I've been reading: *The Third Ear: On Listening to the World* by J. E. Bererndt[6]; *The Ear of the Other* by Jacques Derrida[7]; and *The Listening Self* by David Levin.[8]

> We understand only half of the world if we . . . comprehend it only by seeing. (Berendt, *The Third Ear*)
> We are given two ears and one mouth so we can listen more than we talk. (Native Indian proverb)
> The eye takes a person into the world. The ear brings the world into a human being. (Lorenz Oken, cited by Berendt)
> Vision is a spectator; hearing is a participation. (Dewey, cited by Levin)
> The beginning is not "the word." The beginning is hearing. (Daly, cited by Berendt)
> Everything comes down to the ear you are able to hear me with. (Derrida, *The Ear of the Other*)
> The ear is the most spiritually determined of the senses. (Kierkegaard, cited by Levin)
> The echo is the essence of the thing. (David Levin)
> The echo has much to teach us. If we listen for echoes, and listen to them, our listening can grow in wisdom. The echo is a precious gift to hearing. (David Levin)
> Listen not to me; listen to the Logos. (Heraclitus, cited by Levin)
> We do not hear because we have ears. . . . We have ears because we are hearkening and . . . need to listen to the Song of the Earth. . . . The need to hear the Song of the Earth requires that our hearing be a sensuous one which involves . . . the ears. (Heidegger, cited by Levin)

---

[6]Joachim-Ernst Berendt, *The Third Ear: On listening to the World* (Longmead, Shaftesbury, Dorset: Element Books, 1988). I was introduced to this book by Dr. Betty Hanley of the Music Education Department, University of Victoria.
[7]Jacques Derrida, *The Ear of the Other: Otobiography, Transference, Translation* (Lincoln: University of Nebraska Press, 1985).
[8]David Levin, *The Listening Self: Personal Growth, Social Change and the Closure of Metaphysics* (New York: Routledge, 1989).

ECHO 3: SONARE AND VIDERE

I pause to reflect. Lingering in the reflection, I confess that over the years of schooling and teaching I have become beholden to the metaphor of the I/eye—the I that sees. I have come to accept without questioning the primacy of the disembodied, objective world with its nexus of subject and object in which the prime integrating mode is the subject observing the object. I have come to accept the metaphor of the eye at times resplendent with the glamour of the scientific, the instrumentalist and the technological, embraced almost lovingly by curriculum workers. For myself, I too had become enamoured of the metaphor of *videre* (to see), thinking and speaking of what eyes can see. And I had come to revel in words such as "images," "speculation," "insights," "visions," "supervisions," and "light that illuminates our seeings."

I am convinced now that in becoming enchanted with the eye, there lurks the danger of too hurriedly foreclosing the horizon where we live as teachers and students. I am reminded of Ludwig Wittgenstein,[9] who late in his life as scholar taught school so that he might be nearer to understanding how students come to understand language. He spoke of how in the West the world of language has come to over emphasize and overly rely upon visuality, thereby diminishing the place of other ways of being in the world.

The time is ripe for us to call upon *sonare* to dwell juxtaposed with *videre*. It seems urgent that we come to be more fully sonorous beings than we are. It is imperative that the world of curriculum question the primacy of *videre* and begin to make room for *sonare*.

I return to the Tallis Scholars' concert and to Michael Scott, the music critic of the *Vancouver Sun*, who, we remember, glowingly reported:

- "They immerse their individual characters in its braided polyphony, winding a complex skein that glows white-hot from within." But he said more. He said, "Paradoxically, the power of the music comes not from the voices . . . but from the pure geometries of the music itself."
- "The power of the music comes . . . from the pure geometries of the music itself."
- "The geometries of the music."
- Geometry.

The word "geometry" refuses to let me go. For many of us, the word "geometry" invokes a visual/calculative realm of mathematics. But when Michael Scott speaks of the "geometry of music," he transcends such

---

[9] For an interpretation of the self-transformation of Ludwig Wittgenstein's own thoughts on language, see Allen Thiher, *Words in Reflection: Modern Language Theory and Postmodern Fiction* (Chicago: University of Chicago Press, 1984).

visual/calculative realm.   Surely, he is beckoning us to understand "geometry" within the fold of a sonorous world.

So, if we carefully hearken, we may begin to hear the tonality of the word "geometry" as the Greeks understood it. Let's listen. Geometry is geo-metron. "Geo" is "eco"; it is earth, this earth on which we dwell, this earth whose humus nourishes us. For the Greeks, this sacred earth was graced by Gaia, the goddess of Earth—the Earth Mother.

The "metron" of "geometry" is "measure."   But this measure is of the sonorous world, unmeasurable in terms of the disembodied measure of the visible, calculable world. Rather, the measure is sonorous; it is the sound of the beat and rhythm of the earth; it is the sound of Gaia's pulsation—the inspirited, embodied beat of life; it is Gaia's gift of life.

So when Michael Scott said, "the power of the music comes . . . from the pure geometries of the music itself," was he not beckoning us to draw ourselves nearer to the place where we can begin to hear the earth's elusive but true measure?

We recall Bobby Shew, who in describing improvisation told us how improvising musicians listen not only to the sound of the improvisations of others, but also to the call of the music itself. In so saying, was not Bobby Shew also saying that in the call of the music dwells geo-metron, the earth's true sonorous measure?

I feel awed and I am stilled.

But having opened ourselves to the Occidental tonality of "geometron," allow me to in-tone an Oriental counterpoint for whatever sound it may reveal.

I begin with the Chinese character for "poetry," a character that refuses linearity but promotes its own polyphony. In the presence of this word, I ask: "What does it mean to dwell poetically?"

At the top right is   土   (earth).

Below it is   寸   (measure).

They together read "geo-metron."   Earlier we gave it a Greek reading as Gaia's pulsation. In the Orient, (tera) earth/measure means "temple," a sacred place where one may be allowed to hear the true measure of earth beings, mortals in the nearness of divinity.

On the left side of the character is   言   (to speak/to sound)

Within   言   is the "mouth" that sounds forth or sings, over layered with three echoes and a lingering note.

Earth, measure, temple, mouth, echoes, to speak/to say—these are the polyphonic strands of poetry.

What does it mean to dwell poetically?

Allow me an Occidental reading of an Oriental word. To dwell poetically is to be in the dwelling place of mortals where one may hear the inspirited beat of earth's measure. So inspired, in the sounding forth, may echoes of geo-metron sound and resound.

Sound waves (echoes)

geo

temple

mouth

metron

POETRY

Now, I am beginning to understand Heidegger who told us: "We do not hear because we have ears. . . . We have ears because we are hearkening, and by way of this heedfulness, we are allowed to listen to the Song of the Earth."

I began with a story, "Bobby Shew Jazzes Up a Curriculum Seminar." Then we lingered in three echoes. We first listened to Echo 1: *Through disembodied instrumentalism to embodied meaning.* Here, we lent our ear the instrumentalist of "curriculum implementation," and played with the inspiriting possibilities of "curriculum improvisation." Then we listened to Echo 2: *Polyphonic curriculum: Responding to the call for curriculum integration in Year 2000.* Here, without rejecting curriculum integration, we sought space for a way of composing curriculum that allows for polyphony—a polyphonic curriculum. Then we lingered a while in Echo 3: *Sonare and videre.* Here we sought legitimation for *sonare* to coexist with *videre.* But in opening up to *sonare*, we sensed an opening up to a deeper realm beyond the reach of the eye, a realm where we might begin to hear the beat of the earth's rhythm.

A LINGERING NOTE

Allow me now to close with a lingering note, which hopefully, like the ring of a temple bell, echoes and re-echoes as it fades into silence.

It is a short prose poem by Mary Wilke about a first-grade experience in music—"All I Wanted Was To Sing."

All I Wanted Was To Sing[10]

When I was in first grade
I loved to sing.
When it was my turn I'd stand up
and sing clearly and happily,
thoroughly enjoying myself.
My teacher declared me singing champion.
Why did something as innocent and joyful
as the music of small children
have to be turned into a contest?
The voices should have been
sources of joy, not pride or shame.
But my first grade teacher thought
that my talent should be brandished
in front of my peers . . .
My joy became of mixture
of pride and shame,
and as time went on
shame overshadowed pride . . .
My teacher was the one who wanted
a champion;
all I wanted was to sing.

(Mary Wilke in *Seen Through Our Eyes*)

---

[10] Mary Wilke's "All I Wanted Was to Sing" is from Mark Link (Ed.), *In the Stillness is the Dancing* (Niles, IL: Argus Communications, 1972), p. 53.

Chapter 24

Taiko Drums and Sushi, Perogies and Sauerkraut: Mirroring a Half-Life in Multicultural Curriculum[1]

ENGATHERED IN MULTIFLAVOURED NOURISHMENT

Over these two days we have been nourished by many flavoured foods for our thoughts and our bodies. We feel nurtured and revitalized. The Chinese know how to say all this in one sweeping character. We who frequent Chinese restaurants have seen displayed on a prominent wall,

orienting us to an Oriental meaning of what it is to be nourished. Many of us know that this character reads "double happiness, two-folded happiness or enfolded joy."

A Japanese Canadian like myself who speaks no Chinese, but who can read some Chinese characters because the Japanese, renowned borrowers that they are, borrowed the Chinese language holus bolus, might try to offer a reading in English of this Chinese character. Here is an attempt.

well being

plants

mouth

mouth

"Double happiness is a dwelling in the midst of life where people engathered partake in the nourishing gifts of the earth."

---

[1] This talk was given at the ATA's Multicultural Education Council's Annual Conference at Barnett House in Edmonton, November 1990. Reprinted here from: Aoki, Ted T. (1991). Taiko drums and sushi, perogies and sauerkraut: Mirroring a half-life in multicultural curriculum. In Ted T. Aoki (Ed.), *Inspiriting Curriculum and Pedagogy: Talks to Teachers* (pp. 35–39). Curriculum Praxis, Department of Secondary Education, University of Alberta, Edmonton, Alberta.

I cling to this gustatory metaphor that wets our mouths to say that our conference has offered many-flavoured gifts resplendent in their heritaged multiplicity.

I must have been attuned to this mouth-watering metaphor of multiculturalism when I was asked by Mary Anna Harbeck, your conference director, to say a few words. With the kind of title I gave Mary Anna, some of you must be saying, "For Aoki, multiculturalism must mean multi-foods. His understanding of multiculturalism is in his stomach!" I respond, "You are right on—particularly if you add to sushi, sauerkraut and perogies, a flask of sake, a keg of German beer, and a bottle of Ukrainian rye whiskey. Double, double happiness."

囍　囍

Seriously (and here, I pause for an aside, wondering why it is that when we become serious, we have to move away from our stomachs), more seriously (I pause for another aside, remembering Milan Kundera, a Czechoslovakian novelist known for *The Unbearable Lightness of Being*, who, commenting on how man becomes overly serious, recalls a Jewish proverb: "Man thinks; God laughs"), I ask, "What is it about this word 'multiculturalism' that is powerful enough to gather us together for serious thoughts at a conference such as this?"

I am reminded of an address given by Vaclav Havel, a name that has come into the global vocabulary only within the last year. Shortly before he became president of Czechoslovakia, this literary playwright become politician gave an acceptance talk on the occasion of a literary award presented to him by the German Booksellers' Association (October 15,1989).

Havel, titling his talk, "Words on Words" (1989), focused on one word whose meanings for Czechoslovakians made many twists and turns. This word is "socialism." Guided by his understanding that every word has multiple possible meanings ever changing in the flux of historical time, he spoke of how "socialism" as a word once rang through with a call for revolutionary and emancipatory change; of how the word later became a totalitarian, ideological, political slogan under whose meaning Vaclav Havel himself experienced life in jail; of how recently in Czechoslovakia "socialism" had become a laughable word. He exclaimed, "What a weird fate can befall certain words" (1989, p. 6).

Reflecting upon what happened to the word "socialism" in his country, Havel thoughtfully said of "words":

> No word . . . comprises only the meaning assigned to it by an etymological dictionary. The meaning of every word also reflects the person who utters it, the situation within which it is uttered, and the reason for its utterance. The selfsame word can at one moment radiate great hopes; at another, it can emit lethal rays. The selfsame word can be true at one moment and

> false the next, at one moment illuminating, at another
> deceptive. On one occasion it can open up glorious horizons,
> on another, it can lay down the tracks to an entire archipelago
> of concentration camps. The selfsame word can at one time be
> the cornerstone of peace, while at another, machine-gun fire
> resounds in its every syllable. (1990, p. 6)

Havel's words on words provoke us to thought. Can we stomach all this talk—happy talk and serious talk—when we partake our word of interest, "multiculturalism?"

Just a month ago when the new TV series titled "Diversity" was launched in British Columbia, a program supported by Multiculturalism and Citizenship Canada, the *Vancouver Sun* carried a news article that caught my eye. The caption read, "TV Program offers Diversity minus the dirty culture words." The article began:

> For the staff of "Diversity," the dirty words are the M-word
> and the E-word. They don't want words like "multicultural" or
> "ethnic" used to describe their new information series. Such
> words conjure up scenes of festive clothing, special holidays,
> Easter egg painting contests, clog dancing festivals and other
> happy imagery of Canada's vertical mosaic. So we won't use
> these words here. (*Vancouver Sun*, October 6, 1990, B-1)

These words caused me to pause and wonder. Are the bread-and-butter words for Multiculturalism and Citizenship Canada, words like "multiculturalism" and "ethnicity," in a bit of turbulence? I think they are. Havel's remarks on "words" echo and reecho.

MULTICULTURALISM AS MULTIPLE IDENTITIES

Many of us remember curriculum efforts of the early 1970s involving Canadian multiculturalism. Out of OISE in Toronto emerged a book reflecting the curriculum thrust of the day. Titled *What Culture? What Heritage?* (Hodgetts, 1968), it lamented the softness of the whatness of Canadian cultural and historical studies in school curricula. Reflecting the heyday of the curriculum slogan, "the structure of the disciplines," supported by gurus such as Jerome Bruner, J. J. Schwab, Zaccharias, and so on, the Canadian authors of *What Culture? What Heritage?* were calling for disciplined studies of multiculturalism parallel to what was happening in the New Math, Chem Studies, BSCS (Biological Sciences Curriculum Study), and so on.

In the West a few of us were claiming we were open to the emerging political consciousness reflected in the writings of people like Ivan Illich (*Deschooling Schools*), Paulo Freire (*The Pedagogy of the Oppressed*), Jurgen Habermas (*Knowledge and Human Interests*), Mike Apple (*Curriculum and*

Ideology), and Bill Pinar (*Reconceptualizing Curriculum*). Hence, when we had the opportunity to explore the multicultural and ethnic content in Canadian social studies programs, we chose to interpret the texts of the curriculum documents for underlying ideological interests and assumptions. So while the OISE book was titled *What Culture? What Heritage?* we titled ours *Whose Culture? Whose Heritage?* (Werner, Connors, Aoki, & Dahlie, 1977). You can see how we were concerned about whose voices were being heard or neglected and how these voices were being portrayed.

But in the study we were also keenly interested in how multiculturalism was understood by curriculum developers across Canada. We labeled the dominant perspective we found "the museum approach"—an approach within which was reflected the manyness of cultural and ethnic identities in Canada. Like a museum display, the interesting cultural curios were arrayed as objects of study.

It is this flavour of multiculturalism that led me to the title of this talk: "Taiko Drums and Sushi, Perogies and Sauerkraut." These words reflect, you will agree, the understanding of multiculturalism in terms of heritage-day celebrations, ethnic festival days often held in schools, of curriculum texts devoted to a chapter each for Japanese Canadians, Ukrainian Canadians, German Canadians, and so on, the cultural identities arranged as many-colored people, languages, habits, and customs, about whom and about which students are asked to study.

We recall that for the TV *Diversity* program producers, the museum approach was not for them. In a newsletter, *Together*, published by Multiculturalism and Citizenship, we find described their favoured curriculum orientation for the program:

> *Diversity* will bring the positive aspects of multiculturalism to
> the screen. . . . Instead of dwelling on ethnic food and exotic
> costumes, this program will present multicultural news items,
> in depth reviews of current affairs and studio interviews.
> (*Together*, Multiculturalism and Citizenship Canada, Fall
> 1990, p. 19)

On reading this, I asked myself, "Do I add to the dirty M-word and E-word, T, S, P and S words?" ("Taiko Drums," "Sushi," "Perogies," and "Sauerkraut").

No matter how we feel about "multicultural curricula à la museum," we need to grant that it has helped us in moving beyond the hold of the monocultural/monolingual and bicultural/bilingual. By opening up into the world of multiplicity and heterogeneity, we have sensed beginnings of cracks in the vertical edifice of homogeneity.

But although multicultural curriculum that emphasizes manyness and diversity opens up the closedness of the monocultural/bicultural worlds, we need to be mindful of the way it tends to reduce life to a half-life. The museum approach assumes the structure of the viewer–viewed, of subject–object separation. As such, it is reductive—reducing others to objects, allowing a study about. And we know that the preposition "about" calls for objects.

We hurry to listen to Heidegger, who said, "Objective meanings hide lived meanings. The latter become silent and man becomes heedless of this silence."

No doubt, the museum approach promotes objective meanings requiring us to be mindful of how attractedness to objective meanings may seduce us such that we become forgetful of lived meanings. In this way can occur the oblivion of Being.

There is a related concern, for this oblivion of Being applies not only to the people objectified but also to the subject that objectifies. Usually unconsciously, the subject diminishes itself to a half-life. An oppressor becomes oppressed by the half-lives he or she produces.

A concern for a related but different sort of reductionism arises when people closet themselves into solitudes of ethnic identities. We are familiar with the narcissistic "I" of the "me" generation, which flows from a regard for the identity of self as an ego-centered individual. In like way, does not understanding multiculturalism as solitudes of identities promote ethno-narcissism by regarding others strictly as "them," outside?

In the context of these thoughts I look at myself. I have been told that I am a Japanese Canadian with a Japanese Canadian identity. For many years I have been in search for this identity—searching into my heritage, searching for the ground on which I stand. At one time, I objected to the hyphenization of Japanese-Canadians. On another occasion, seeking ethnic purity, I dropped my name "Ted" and returned to my given ethnic name "Tetsuo," until people started to ask me, "Where's Ted?" As you can see, I've been having difficulty and I have come to believe that it may well be that the elusive Japanese Canadian identity I am searching for may not be where people, including me, think it is.

BEYOND MERE MANYNESS TO CROSS-CULTURALISM

A key theme word of this conference is "cross-culturalism." I am drawn to it for the way it promises to open up to others.

Although the following anecdote moves beyond the bounds of Canada, its theme is appropriately cross-cultural. In a thoughtful anecdote, Carol Taylor, an elementary teacher from Kelowna, BC, revisiting Korea last summer, this time under British Columbia's Pacific Rim Initiative, writes of a short episode. She writes:

> "Americans, go home!"
>
> It is an old man who shouts at us as we stroll through Pagoda Park in central Seoul.
>
> "But I'm Canadian!" I retort, pulling into closer range my small maple leaf pin. I would not have been able to make that claim 28 years ago when I was working in South Korea as an American citizen. We were a decade away from signing an armistice ending the fighting of the three-year Korean War.

> Division between North and South Korea was as much of an
> issue then as unification is today. (*Teacher*, BCTF, October
> 1990, p. 16)

Carol's portrayal of how, in Seoul, she called upon her maple leaf lapel pin to help reorient an Oriental in his view of Carol and her colleagues reminded me of my first visit to Korea (1982), when the first question asked of me was, "Are you Japanese or are you Canadian?" Carol, true to her theme that a distinction is not so much a place as a "new way of looking at things," urges us to be mindful of how others help us to open ourselves to who we are as Canadians. Others help us in our own self-understanding. In this, I feel, is the power and thrust of cross-culturalism.

MULTICULTURALISM AS DWELLING
IN THE MIDST OF INTERCULTURALISM

In the previous section, multiculturalism as cross-culturalism took us to the crossings over the between. But now I slide away from the crossing, and sink into the lived space of between—in the midst of many cultures, into the *inter* of interculturalism. Indwelling here is a dwelling in the midst of differences, often trying and difficult. It is a place alive with tension. In dwelling here, the quest is not so much to rid ourselves of tension, for to be tensionless is to be dead like a limp violin string, but more so to seek appropriately attuned tension, such that the sound of the tensioned string resounds well.

To get a more concrete sense of tension in the midst of differences, allow me to lead you to such a place in two episodes.

Episode 1: Canadian Jews? Jewish Canadians? Canadian Japanese? Japanese Canadians?

Two years ago I was asked by the University of Toronto to serve as an external examiner for an interesting study in multicultural education. The title of the study by a young Hebrew scholar from Israel was "Ethnic and National Identity Among Jewish Students in Ontario." What struck me from the outset of my reading was the way in which the Canada-born Jewish students were referred to by the author of the dissertation. Through some 300 pages, these students were referred to as "Canadian Jews."

The question that first came to mind was, "What does it mean for these Canada-born to be identified as Canadian Jews?" "How do they indeed understand themselves by these words?"

So as external examiner, usually given the privilege of opening a conversation (called "examination") with the candidate, I began:

> Mr. Shamai, I have been calling myself a Japanese Canadian,
> and people like me have become accustomed to being called

Japanese Canadians, not Canadian Japanese. This mode of
naming seems different from the identifying label "Canadian
Jews," and the words you use to portray the identity of the
youngsters you discuss in the dissertation. I ask you, "In the
Canadian context, does it make a difference whether Canadian
is a noun or an adjective? Or, as some might say, is it merely a
semantic matter?"

Does the episode draw you into what we have been calling the tensionality
in the midst of differences in the "inter?"

Episode 2: "Canadian," "Nation," "Land"— More Turbulent Words: In the Midst of Polysemic Differences

Two summers ago in my graduate seminar in curriculum studies at the
University of Victoria was present an able Native Indian scholar-educator, a
superintendent of Band Schools. He taught us much—like the meaning of what
it is for a chief to stand tall as a leader, and the way in which he, as a Native
Indian, sees Western individualism as a narcissistic "I."   In one of our
discussions, and we had many of them, our conversation turned to the question
of who we are. I told him that I saw myself as a Japanese Canadian, still in
search for the lived meaning of who I am.   And within a turn in the
conversation, someone asked him, "Are you a Canadian?" He was thoughtfully
silent. Somehow we brushed over the silence and moved on to something else.
But that silence has never left me. It keeps echoing and reechoing within
me.
I return to the silence where now I find more questions. What do we mean
by *"nation"* when we say *"the Canadian nation?"* I remind myself that the
notion of nation-state is a Western cultural artifact, constituted and instituted.
We know some nations prospered as nations, but in places in Africa, the
imposition of the nation-state has created havoc in a Euro-African cultural clash.
And here in Canada, I ponder the word "nation" in "the founding *nations*," "the
first *nations*," "the Canadian *nation*." I am pulled into the tensionality of
differences of meaning. I ask more. How is the word "land" understood within
the different word/worlds of nation? I suspect differences. And I ask: What is
land when it becomes "property" possessed? What is *land* when the question is
asked, "Does man deserve this earth?"
Beneath me, I feel the earth tremble as the words "Canadian," "nation,"
"land" breed uncertainty and ambiguity.

Moving into the Midst of Differences Through Stories

Let these two episodes suffice to portray what might be meant by "inter" in
interculturalism, a living in the midst of differences. I hurry to return to the
conference's guiding question, "What can I do for this child?" And in returning,

I need to move to a concretely lived place with an actual teacher and child. Allow me to share with you a short story of a pedagogic moment in the lived experiences of real people.

EXPERIENCING DIFFERENCES IN THE MIDST OF TWO LANGUAGE WORLDS: A CHILD'S STORY OF A PEDAGOGICAL EXPERIENCE

This first story is told by Lucy Colby, an ESL instructor at Malaspina College, Nanaimo, BC. She recalls her early experiences as a Ukrainian Canadian child, pauses, and lingers reflectively in the story. (It is not a story of perogies.)

The story is titled, "Experiencing Language: Who Am I Who Speaks Two Languages?" Let me read a segment of Lucy's story.

My Story: I Squirmed as My Teacher Paused to Talk to My Parents

> As a child, I lived in a home where Russian was spoken by my father and Ukrainian by my mother, in a Ukrainian community within the larger English-speaking community in Niagara Falls, Ontario. We spoke both of these languages at home or a quasi interlanguage, which married English with these two languages: *Za parkyvay kary b garajay.* On the street where I lived were many Ukrainian families and it was not uncommon to hear parents calling their children home to dinner in their mother tongue. We were very much involved in the Ukrainian community. I called and still do call myself a Ukrainian Canadian.
>
> My birth certificate reads: Ludmilla Nikifortchuk. My driver's license reads: Lucy Colby. I speak what I call "kitchen Russian" reasonably well. I speak English. English is the language in which I am most fluent. It is the language I live in the most. Maurice Merleau-Ponty (1961) wrote, "I may speak many languages, but there remains one in which I live" (p. 103). But still. . ..
>
> It was the year that I discovered that my parents spoke broken English. I had not been aware of it before this year.
>
> I was grocery shopping with my parents at the corner Loblaw's. I was in grade 3 or 4. I had been having a lot of fun. The weekly shopping was always fun as my father and I played silly games and looked for the "new" item to be purchased that week, like strawberry-flavoured Nestlé Quik straws, while my mother did the serious shopping. She always greeted our discovery with mock horror. In the midst of this, I saw my teacher, Miss Buck, whom I adored. I was overtaken

by acute embarrassment. I tried to steer my parents into another direction. It didn't work and my teacher stopped to chat with us as I squirmed.

My parents didn't say anything to me at the time but were perfectly aware of what I was feeling. A few days later, my father talked to me about pride in being oneself and how one cannot hide her origins even if it is convenient. He talked about the difficulties he had had learning new languages: German in Germany, French in Belgium and English in Canada. He also talked about his ability to speak two languages fluently even though the other three were always expected to be a problem.

Dwelling In My Story

I pause to dwell in this story. This was my first sense of language defining who I am. In the grocery store, I was trying to keep my two language worlds separate. I was comfortable in each one. The colliding of my worlds caused tension for me. My father was leading me to recognize that I lived between two language worlds and that I had an authentic dwelling place there. He was allowing for my unfolding.

Looking and relooking at this memory, I am able to remember that this story did not end here. I celebrated two Christmases as a child. One was English Christmas on December 25th; the other, following the Gregorian calendar, was Ukrainian Christmas on January 7th.

When I brought in the annual note from my parents to be excused from class on January 7th, Miss Buck greeted it with much enthusiasm and interest. At least a month had passed since we had met her in Loblaw's. There was also another Ukrainian girl in my class. Miss Buck helped us lead a discussion with our classmates about the celebrating of Ukrainian Christmas and the traditions. She later asked us to wear our Ukrainian costumes to class and perform Ukrainian dances. I can remember feeling special and proud as my classmates admired my costume with its long colourful ribbons from the crown.

Miss Buck picked up the pedagogical good of the grocery store encounter. She also was aware of the tension in me when I was trying to keep my language worlds separate. She allowed for my further edification. Both Miss Buck and my father walked back along the path to meet me and my living tension. They gave me the support and guidance I needed to live in my world between the two language worlds (T. Aoki & M. Shamsher, 1991).

The foregoing story is an exploration of what it is to be pedagogic in the midst of intercultural lived experiences. In it, we are visited by a deep sense of teaching, not so much as a mode of doing, but more so as a mode of being, human to the core, inspirited by the thoughtful care the teacher has for the child. We are moved away from the voices of the storyteller to the voices of the logos of teaching.

A LINGERING NOTE

I linger now in the midst of the story and the question of the conference, wondering how they belong together. I now sense that the guiding question of the conference, "What can I do for this child?"—not any child, but *this* child — can come forth meaningfully only from a lived, situated place where teachers and children dwell. It is the place where Miss Smith lives with Tamotsu, Mary, Anatasia, Henrik, and others; it is the place where Miss Buck of our story lived with Lucy.

So situated, the question comes forth not so much from someone's head but from life lived thoughtfully, questioningly, and pedagogically with children.

I relive in the question, "What can I do for this child?," more mindful that *doing* that diminishes teachers and students into half-lives is surely not pedagogic. And I have become sensitive to the notion that a concern for *doing* needs to be accompanied by a concern for *not doing*, for holding back, for withdrawing, for letting go, for letting be. And as I become more thoughtful this way, I begin to see more deeply how Miss Buck held herself as she was beholden to the life of the situation in which she found herself. I am indebted to Miss Buck for her insightful teachings.

I know it—in my stomach, I know it—that I'll be face to face again with the question, "What can I do for this child?" But when I do face the question in the future, I will not feel alone, for that question will insistingly remind me of all you people who dwelt in this question at this conference—at times with laughter, at other times with deep seriousness. I wish you doubly double happiness.

But through it all a question lurks beneath and beckons to us: How shall we understand "multiculturalism?" As manyness of cultures? As cross-culturalism? Or. . .? It seems that the quest for inspiriting multicultural curriculum and pedagogy calls for our openness to the historicity and multiplicity of meanings of the word "multiculturalism."

REFERENCES

Aoki, T., & Shamsher, M. (Eds.). (1991). *Voices of Teaching*, Vol. 2,
    Vancouver, BC: British Columbia Teachers Federation.
Havel, V. (1990, January 18). Words on words, *New York Book Review*, pp. 5–8.
Hodgetts, A. B. (1968). *What Culture? What Heritage?* Toronto: Ontario
    Institute for Studies in Education.
Teacher (1990, October). Pacific Rim Initiative p. 16. Vancouver, B.C: British
    Columbia Teachers Federation.
Together (1990, Fall). Newsletter, p. 19. Ottawa, Canada: Multiculturalism and
    Citizenship Canada.
Vancouver Sun (1990, October). TV program offers diversity minus the dirty
    words. P.BIO. Vancouver, British Columbia, Canada.

Werner, W., Connors, B. Aoki, T., Dahlie, J., *Whose Culture? Whose Heritage? Ethnicity within Canadian Social Studies Curricula* (Centre for the Study of Curriculum and Instruction, University of British Columbia, 1977).

Chapter 25

The Sound of Pedagogy in the Silence of the Morning Calm[1]

Listening to Pedagogic Being—Anjin's Story

Many times have I savoured the story I am about to share with you. Every reading has nourished me in a different way, helping me to understand and re-understand more deeply the insistently enduring question for us who profess to be educators—the questioning of what it means to be truly pedagogic.

Before this moment at home, on the other edge of the Pacific Rim, I read this story in the calm of the early dawn to engender within me, if it will, a sense of what it may be like to listen in the morning calm to the call of our calling, teaching. But that, I know, was pretending to be in Korea. Hence, I have been anticipating this very moment to savour the reading of this story that may allow for me a listening to the sound of pedagogy emerging from the earthy silence of the land of the morning calm. For the story I am about to read blossomed forth here, in Seoul, written of Mokwol nim, your eminent poet and teacher, by his student, now a noted poet herself, Anjin Yoo of Seoul National University. And doubly fortunate that I am, Anjin's younger sister, Hae-Ryung (together with Kwon-Jahng Jin, a scholar from the Korean Educational Development Institute), happened to be present in my last graduate seminar at the University of Alberta in Canada, and there, I asked her to bridge the Pacific by translating her sister's story into English. This reading, thus, is in a way a homecoming.

I have listened and relistened to the sound of pedagogy that resounds in each reading of this touching story. It is titled, "Dear Mokwol nim: My Esteemed Teacher," an inspiring human story, a story of teaching told by a student whose deep esteem for her teacher shimmers. Here, then, this Korean story offered in the context of the international gathering that is the texture of this conference.

---

[1] This invited paper was presented at the International Conference on Korean Studies sponsored by the Academy for Korean Studies, Seoul, Korea, June 1990. It appears in the Academy's publication in 1991. Reprinted here from: Ted T. Aoki. (1991). The Sound of pedagogy in the silence of the morning calm. In Ted T. Aoki (Ed.). *Inspiriting Curriculum and Pedagogy: Talks to Teachers* (pp. 43-48). Curriculum Praxis, Department of Secondary Education, University of Alberta, Edmonton, Alberta.

DEAR MOKWOL NIM,[3] MY ESTEEMED TEACHER—BY ANJIN YOO

Today, I again visited thee in Yong-In.[4] But I still feel unsatisfied, unfulfilled. Perhaps it is thus that I am writing this letter. Thou might remember that I have not written to thee for a long time. More than ten years ago, I wrote thee the first letter, sending my poems, hoping to receive thy recommendations. This then may be the second one. From now on, when my mundane life occupies me much, I wish to write to thee instead of making a trip to Yong-In.

When all of us had to leave thee alone on the cold, windy mountain, I could not resist weeping a flood of tears. But, today, on my second visit to thee in Yong-In, I was rather glad to realize that the place where thou art dwelling is not Wonhyoro[5] but Yong-In. I told myself, "Of course, for thee, Yong-In may be much better than Wonhyoro. There, thou can walk in a pine grove, sing a poem with the songs of reeds. . . ." But while talking so to myself, I am again falling into deep sorrow.

At first, It[6] was so rueful as if I had experienced the sky fall in on me, as if I had become an abandoned orphan. But now, I rethink of It again, and have come to know that we are not abandoned or left behind. Not at all. Rather, thou have gone in order to exist forever in our hearts and thou have left us because of thy deep concern for our future. Thou already knew that we as mature poets must stand alone in the near future, with the attitude of a teacher, living life in our poems. Hence, I believe, like a faith toward God, that thou, even after a thousand years, will live as a man one or two over sixty, with hair of beautiful silver, writing poems in the envy of the white

---

[3] "Nim" is a suffix commonly attached to one's name to call a person with respect and politeness.

[4] The name of the area where Mokwol's grave is located.

[5] The name of the area where Mokwol had lived till his death.

[6] "It" refers to Mokwol's death. In the original, Korean version of this essay, the author seems to refer to Mokwol's death in an implicit and indirect way throughout the essay rather than using straightforward and direct terms such as "death." This kind of indirect expression of one's death is also seen in the Korean custom of consoling the bereaved family. By murmuring in a small voice comforting words to the family instead of articulating clearly, guests try to avoid recalling the death and thus hurting the family.

clouds seen in the limpid eyes of an innocent roe,[7] enjoying an April day with the blowing wind of pine tree flowers.[8]

Mokwol nim, my dear teacher, in this way would we like to console ourselves over the sorrow of March 24th, and in this way I would like to relieve myself from the bottomless despair watching thine encoffining. Upon my entering thine place in Wonhyoro, with a desperate wish for the miracle of thy resurrection, it was not thee any more but only the picture[9] that greeted me, "You have come, Yoo kun!"[10] Grieving and resenting God taking thee away from us, I have tried to remove this heartfelt emptiness. Even while walking in a street, I often had a sudden feeling of defeat, a hollow emptiness as in my childhood when I realized all of a sudden my empty hand after a strong bully had taken a delicious cookie from my hand. But, now, I dwell in a belief that thou has just moved to a new place, the nearest as well as the most beautiful, the eternal home of poems and songs. There, we can visit and see thee whenever we desire, and there thou, like the moon passing by the clouds, can go to the Yong-In market fair[11] or walk to the neighbouring village through a wheat field,[12] wearing a flapping white coat and rubber shoes of size nineteen and a half.[13]

There, in the sunshine on a sloped filed of a mountain thou will greet me, "You have come, Yoo kun!" And there, thou will discuss poetry with me and show me recent writings of thine, or tell me that thou have read my new poems in a certain journal. Sometimes, thou will pause from work in a field and walk to church in thy bare feet. Then, I may wish to follow

---

[7] "Clouds seen in the limpid eyes of an [innocent] roe" is a phrase in one of Mokwol's poems.

[8] "An April day with the blowing winds of pine tree flowers" is a phrase in Mokwol's poem, "Embolism's April." This phrase "an April day" refers to Embolism's April, the fourth month of the lunar calendar, and is usually May or June by the solar calendar.

[9] This picture or portrait of a dead person is one that Koreans, according to their custom, place on a specially prepared table for at least 49 days after the death in the memory of the dead person.

[10] "Kun" is a word usually attached to a male youngster's name to call a person in a manner of expressing respect and care. By calling the author "Yoo kun" even though the author is female, Mokwol expresses his care toward the author.

[11] "Yong-In market fair" is a phrase in Mokwol's poem.

[12] "Like the moon passing by the clouds... walk [to the neighbouring village] through a wheat field" is a phrase in Mokwol's poem, "A Wayfarer."

[13] "Rubber shoes of size nineteen and a half" is a phrase in a Mokwol poem.

thee and kneel down behind the pious poet in prayer. Thy
prayer will be so interwoven with the songs of pine trees and
the wind of reeds that it may not be easily understood. But I
would not mind it at all since I know that thy prayer will be
short.

On a serene autumn day, sitting together on a deck in the
backyard and offering buckwheat jelly[14] to me, thou may ask
us about our stories in Seoul. And perhaps thou will start
talking again about our first meeting more than ten years ago.

Then, please let me tell thee about those white and
dazzling heaps of wild roses on the left side of the hill at
Hanyang University[15] on my first visit to thee with my poetry
exercise books. And even if thou start talking again of my
foolishness at the small restaurant behind the Hwashin
Department Store, I will not be ashamed any more. But about
your opening that story[16] to the people at the celebration party
of my first poetry book publication, I feel now at last able to
complain to thee. I would also like to listen to the reason why
thou thought, "She can be a poet," as thou looked at me
struggling with that unseasoned soup.

After glancing again and again at Milady's[17] face reluctant
against my long talk with thee, I may have to stand up, despite
the desire of being together with thee longer, and walk a path
to the bus stop to return to Seoul. I will look back, over and
over again, at the small violet-tinted hills and rocks sitting at
the back of thine house. I will see through the bus window,
thou still standing there to see me off near the stepping-stones
in the brook. Hence, Mokwol nim, my dear teacher, I have
made up my mind not to grieve any more, not to stay in sorrow
any more. Although I may not be able to see thee very often, I
will still think of thee as I sit under the white magnolia
blossom on a spring day reading thine writings thou gave me; I
will think of thee while looking at the poem on the wall written
and framed by thine hands especially for me. I will sing a song
of parting joining a wild goose's cry on an autumn evening or
amid the falling snow, now on a wintry day. When some of us

---

[14] One of the traditional Korean folk foods.
[15] One of the universities in Seoul. Mokwol had taught at this university until his
death.
[16] "In the restaurant since I was too shy before thee to pick up the salt container,
I had to finish the beef soup without any seasoning." (This part is originally
included in this essay, but for the sake of convenience of translation, the
translator removed it from the essay.)
[17] This refers to Mokwol's wife.

gather at the "Shimsahngsa" some Saturday afternoon or on the Lord's day, we will visit and see thee in Yong-In, the eternal dwelling place of the poet. The next time I write to thee, I will talk about our recent stories in Seoul. My dear, dear teacher, Mokwol nim, may thou have a peaceful rest. May thou have a peaceful rest.

(Translated by Hae-Ryung Yeu and Kwon-Jahng Jin, in Edmonton, Alberta, Canada, May 1987)

THEME 1: LINGERING IN THE STORY'S PEDAGOGICAL THEME

The story you just heard is for us a treasured story that over the past few years, graduate students in curriculum and pedagogy at the University of Victoria, the University of Alberta, and at Louisiana State University have come to know fondly as "Anjin's Story."

Picture me, if you will in a seminar of master's and doctoral students, calling upon them to read the story. They read in silence. Then ensues a hushed silence, a different silence. But talk-oriented as we professors are in our pedagogic situations, I break the silence and beckon them to a discussion. Silence continues to prevail. I sense their hesitation to break the sanctity of the silence, preferring instead to allow the story to linger where it seems truly to belong—in the silent mystery that is teaching.

Pedagogical Taking Leave

As I return to dwell in Anjin's story, I am gathered into a saying about the esteemed teacher, Mokwol nim. Anjin said of him "thou have left us because of thy deep concern for our future."

I linger in this saying, which speaks to a teacher's leaving in the midst of his deep concern for the student. I am led to ask, "What is it for a teacher to leave in the midst of a deep concern for students?"

Such a leaving seems vastly different from a leaving that emanates from a situation wherein a teacher lacks concern for students, a leaving that is a leaving behind, a turning away from students, a walking away with the turning of one's back.

Let us recall that within the Western tradition, "pedagogy," in its Greek origin, meant leading the young or leading the less mature (understood latterly in this paper) (from *agogue* "to lead," and *pedae* "the young or immature"). Within the understandings of pedagogy as leading, how shall we understand "leaving" or "taking leave"?

Often, a pedagogical tactic in teaching is to say to a student, "I leave it to you," suggesting a letting go of decision making to the student. Such an understanding reflects teaching understood as delegating or allocating power assumed to reside in the teacher. Hence, "I leave it to you" suggests, as we often hear in educational leadership talk, power sharing, given to the understanding of teaching as political activity. Without doubt this is a dimension of the activity we call teaching.

But in relation to the foregoing, we pause to consider another question, "What authorizes a teacher to teach?" What commonly appears is the generally accepted notion of the authority of the teacher resting in an official certificate received from an educational bureaucracy, or a notion of authority vested in a position assigned by a still higher authority. But in Anjin's story, we do not sense at all Mokwol nim's authority in the senses I have mentioned. Rather, it seems that this pedagogical authority flows from somewhere else altogether— from the wisdom of having lived well, from the being that deeply understands what it is to live truly, a poet who not only wrote and sang poetry but who also lived piously and dwelt poetically on this earth, on this land of the morning calm. Authority so understood is not concerned with delegating or sharing power, as if it were a commodity, but, rather, it leads us to understand authority in terms of the wisdom that comes from having lived well as a very human being.

For Mokwol nim, our esteemed teacher, it is not for him to be concerned about sharing power; rather, it is for him to know, as a sage knows, that as pedagogue, at times, he must take leave, that he must withdraw, such that in the very event of withdrawal, there may inhere a pedagogic creativity, a coming into being of a clearing that is vibrant with pedagogic possibilities. Hence, pedagogic withdrawal may, within a seeming negating of self, confer in the silence of the pedagogue's absence an opening wherein the student can truly learn what it is to stand, what it is to be in one's becoming. Such I understand when I read again in Anjin's story of Mokwol nim's taking leave: "Thou have left us because of the deep concern for our future. Thou knew that we as mature poets must stand alone."

Allow me to lean on a Latin American I admire, Octavio Paz, who, in his essay "The Poetic Revelation" (1973) gave us a hint of the way poets must stand on their own. He wrote:

> By a path, in its own way . . . the poet comes to the brink of language. And that brink is called silence. . . . A silence that is like a lake, a smooth and compact surface. Down below, submerged, the words are waiting. And now one must descend, go to the bottom, be silent, wait. Sterility precedes inspiration, as emptiness precedes plenitude. The poetic word crops out after periods of drought. But whatever its express content may be, whatever its concrete meaning, the poetic word affirms the life of this life. (p. 13)

To be standing humanly, according to Octavio Paz, is to be not only at the brink of silence, but also to be in the depth of silence, awaiting the arrival of the poetic word that affirms the life of this life. If this be so, what is the pedagogic knowing that opens a student to a path which in her own way, not the pedagogue's way, enables affirmingly a living of this life?

I understand Mokwol nim, whose own pedagogic knowing was itself a living of a pedagogic life, being open not only to the pedagogic world that itself poetic, but also to the student's poetic living of her life. The tone I hear of Mokwol nim's pedagogy emerges from the silence at the brink of his lived language, the silence of withdrawal that knows that it is the student's own path that allows a coming into her own as a poet.

I am inspired by Mokwol nim's pedagogy — a pedagogy that knows deeply what it is to shepherd the mystery that is life.

THEME 2: (PEDAGOGICAL) BELONGING TOGETHER: AN EXCURSUS INTO HEIDEGGER'S *KEHRE*

Anjin's story allowed us an initial unfolding of a pedagogical theme: pedagogical taking leave. Allow me now an excursus into Heidegger's twofolded venture: (1) unfolding the themes of "belonging *together*" and "*belonging* together"; and (2) Heidegger's *Kehre*, an attempt to think the unthought.

I appeal to Heidegger's celebrated book, *What Is Called Thinking* (1968), for two sayings, so that we may pause, one about thinking and the other about teaching:

> Most thought provoking in our thought-provoking time is that
> we are still not thinking. (p. 6)
> Teaching is even more difficult than learning . . .. Teaching is
> more difficult than learning because what teaching calls for is
> this: to let learn . . .. If the relation between the teacher and the
> learners is genuine . . . there is never a place in it for the
> authority of the know-it-all or the authoritative sway of the
> official . . .. It . . . is an exalted matter . . . to become a
> teacher—which is something else entirely than becoming a
> famous professor . . .. We must keep our eyes fixed firmly on
> the true relation between teacher and taught. (pp. 15-16)

"We must keep our eyes fixed firmly on the true relation between teacher and taught." So said Heidegger in his celebrated lecture: "What Calls for Thinking." For Heidegger, "Keeping our eyes fixed firmly" surely did not mean observing keenly with our naked eyes. What he meant was this: that we need to think in a way we have never thought before. Thinking what? Thinking the isness of the true relationships between "belonging" and "together" in "belonging together."

Belonging *Together*

The habitual way many of us understand "belonging together" is "belonging *together*," enframed in the primacy of togetherness. Belonging is thus secondary; belonging is a fitting of elements into an order—an order that is of man's making, a fitting that is of man's making. So understood, "belonging *together*" is a belonging in the totality of sameness, reflecting representational thinking characterized by representation of a thing in terms of its categories, held together in a nexus—within connections wherein categories are intertwined in a unity of togetherness. So understood, "belonging *together*" falls within a metaphysical frame that orders the many into a unity mediated by synthesis, a unity of a systematic totality with its onto-theological ground, as Heidegger would say.

Within this framework what are related assumes priority over the notion of relation. This is the usual way in which we understand relationships. For example, first, there are the teacher and the taught as two separate entities that come together in a relationship we call pedagogy. This way of thinking, caught within a metaphysical framework of totality and foundation, fails to see or hear a happening nearby, and in the failing occurs the oblivion of Being.

Taking our own historical situation, Heidegger (1969) shows us how in this atomic age, we imagine the world of technology as a conjoined totality of physical "energy, the calculating plans of man and automation" (p. 34). Within such a framework, thinking of any human situation (like our pedagogical situation) falls short of the mark for we become overtaken by the thought that the world is of man's own making. And the quest for understanding grinds to a halt with the incessant debate on whether man is the master of his plan or its servant.

What is lost in this thinking that falls short of the mark? What is lost is our hearing; we become deaf to the call of Being, so caught up are we with the matter of the essence of technology. And this loss of hearing is, according to Heidegger, inevitable as long as we are caught in the univocity of metaphysical totality.

How, then, are we to be released from the hold of this metaphysical totality that reduced "belonging together" to the eminence of togetherness in belonging *together*? By thinking differently.

Belonging Together

> "To think metaphysically is to stop thinking halfway" (Heidegger, 1969, p. 40). "Where are we? In what constellation of man and being are we?" (p. 40). "We do not

dwell sufficiently as yet where we in reality already are" (p. 33).

Heidegger calls upon us to step out of thinking that, by habit, steps out half way.   Simultaneously, he calls upon us to move away from the constellation wherein the subject thinks its object.   And further, he calls upon us to dwell more sufficiently where we already are, where we are thoughtlessly blind or deaf to the near where we already are.

Heidegger acknowledges that this realm of where we are, although more original, is more difficult to be in its fold.   Yet it is the realm wherein the relation of belonging together may be granted to us as *belonging* together.

In his quest to be in this realm, Heidegger does not resort to reasoned moves; instead, he delivers himself to the experience of *Kehre,* what Albert Hopstadter (1979) calls "a reversal with a surprising turn" (p. 17).

For Heidegger, *Kehre* is a leap that allows a break away from metaphysical thought in understanding "belonging together"; it is a leap that acknowledges the face of the challenge of "letting things appear" within the horizon of the calculable; it is a leap that, paradoxically, is a moving away that is a coming nearer into the neighbourhood where resides the call of Being; it is a leap from the metaphysical ground into an opening—an abyss that is neither empty nothingness nor murky confusion.   It is an event of appropriation.   It is a leap wherein occurs a transformation of "belonging *together* as enframing" into "*belonging* together as an event of appropriation."

In this event, belonging's homage to "together" is loosened, making possible recovery of belonging in its fuller sense.   In this recovery, belonging, which was understood as productive action becomes not so much making or producing; instead, it becomes appropriating—a listening to the call of the active nature   of   "letting-belong-together."   In   this   "letting-belong-together," "belonging" takes precedence over "together," thereby allowing the revealing in a more originary way what belonging is.   Understood in this way, the event of appropriation is that realm "vibrating within itself, through which man and Being reach for each other in their nature, achieve their active nature by losing qualities with which metaphysics had endowed them" (p. 37).

Joan Stambaugh, a translator of a number of Heidegger's works, helps us in understanding "belonging" by way of *ereignis*, a common word in the German language meaning simply "event."   She shows us how in Heidegger's language, *ereignis* opens itself up to two parallel understandings:

1.   It is abstract in its being distant from everyday life, yet being so close to us we cannot see or hear it;

2.   It is concrete in its etymology, which shows that "*ereignis*" is rooted in "*eigen*" (to own), offering us the notion of coming into one's own, that is, coming to where one truly belongs.

Indeed, the event of appropriation is a letting-belong-together, a letting be into one's own. It is, as Albert Hopstadter likes to emphasize, enownment. Belonging as enownment is a reaching out to each other, an extending of a gift one to each other, such that in the reaching one can, if appropriately attuned, catch sight or hear the claim of Being. Viewed in this way the event of appropriation appropriates man and Being in their essential togetherness, which rests not in togetherness but in belonging.

THEME 3: DESCRYING THE DAWN IN THE EVENING LAND OF THE OCCIDENTAL

> Is not pedagogy in the twilight of modernism—repressive modernism which both the West and the recent East are now experiencing? (Hae-Ryung Yeu—in personal letter)

> The irony of Japan's success in the technological sphere is that it has led to the attrition of local traditions and spiritual imitation. (Beittel, 1989)

The excursion into the realm of "(pedagogical) belonging together" offered us an opening that may enable us, particularly of the West, to savour the questioning of the centricism of metaphysical thought in the garb of modernism. We in the West are now beginning to feel the turbulence of the ground of two thousand years of Western tradition beginning with Plato and Aristotle. Is this the twilight of the primacy of modernism of which Hae-Ryung Yeu speaks?

In the context of this question, we might heed the voice of David Krell, a Heideggerean scholar, who in the book *Nietzsche by Martin Heidegger, Vol. 1* (1978) portrayed Heidegger situated at "the outermost point in the history of the Occident or Evening-land . . . descrying the land of dawn" (see Heidegger, 1979, p. 250). By the land of dawn is meant a source, wherever it may earthly be, that allows thinking of the yet unthought in Western thought. We know that in his quest, Heidegger sought such a source in pre-Socratic thought such as that of Parmenides or Heraclitus. But we also know that Heidegger, through his conversations with Asian scholars who sought his thoughts, had himself been stirred to thought by the nonmetaphysical attunement of certain Asian thought.

For instance, we might listen to Paul Shih-Yi Hsiao (1987), the Taiwanese scholar, who with Heidegger began in 1946 to translate the *Tao Te Ching*. Attuned as he was to Oriental ways of thought, Hsiao was urged to say that what Heidegger "brought to language has frequently been said similarly in the thinking of the Far East" (p. 94). But also of interest to us is how Hsiao felt that although the eight chapters of the *Tao Te Ching* that he and Heidegger jointly translated are only a small portion, yet "they exerted a significant influence on Heidegger" (p. 98).

Graham Parkes (1987), who has had a deep interest in bridging Heidegger and Asian thought, wrote of Heidegger's frequent references to Taoism:

> In the late fifties . . . he makes . . . reference to Taoism in print. In the lecture, "The Principle of Identity," he mentions the Chinese Tao in the same breath as the Pre-Socratic Greek logos. Two years later, in "Underway to Language" (1959) . . . he offers a brief discussion of the idea of Tao in the poetic thinking of Lao Tzu. (p. 106)

One wonders about the interplay between Tao and Heidegger's Being. It is understandable, then, why Hwal Yol Jung, a Korean scholar of Heidegger, sees possibilities of interweaving texts of the East and the West. He saw Heidegger:

> revisioning and subverting the long-cherished meta-physical tradition of the West—the logocentricism that coincides often with ethnocentricism or Occidentalism of one kind or another . . . that tradition of inherited thought (in the West) which is at the brink of unleashing awesome, destructive forces ranging from thermonuclear power to cybernetics—that almighty tradition of calculative power which may summarily be called "politology." An alternative to illusionary and fateful "politology" is the "piety of thinking" . . . which may serve as the yarn to weave the woof of Heidegger's own thought and the ways of Eastern thought—Confucianism, Taoism, Ch'an or Zen Buddhism, and others. (Jung, 1987, pp. 283–289)

What Jung, Parkes, and Hsiao are promoting is the cultivating of dialogue that may help us open ourselves to the pretextual realm that welcomes the belonging together of the language of the East and the language of the West. Within this event of appropriation, we who are interested in understanding pedagogy may be let into the texture of the dialogue, there to be allowed to partake in thinking of pedagogy in ways yet unthought, possibly allowing us to become more pious in our thinking.

A dreamer's dream? Allow me now to return to Anjin, whose words inspirited us to venture forth to dwell in three thematic petals of thought. Before I withdraw, I turn again to Anjin to collect her words.

In the preface of *What Makes Us Eternal*, where "Anjin's story" has its treasured place, Anjin Yoo gently advised her readers:

> I am a poet, but here I offer my stories . . . .. I am by vocation an academic . . . .. But what I present here about life can never be resolved with logic . . . .. Would that I could enter your thoughtful depths amid pleasant laughter, tingling pain, and pungent taste of life.

As I ponder about thinking of the unthought within the thoughtful depths Anjin Yoo speaks of, I recall a moment in her story when she, following her master to church, knelt "down behind the pious poet in prayer . . . so interwoven with the songs of pine trees and the wind of reeds." I am drawn into what we are now beginning to call "pious thinking," that which Heidegger disclosed as "piety of thinking."

I am reminded of Hwal Yol Jung (1987), who thoughtfully said that pious thinking like poetic thinking "is attuned to the topology of Being," and as such is "the acme of thinking. It does not surmount the earth in order to exploit and conquer it. Rather, it brings man onto the earth and makes him belong to the earth: it brings him dwelling on earth" (pp. 234–235).

For Anjin, as for us, the taste of life and for life is made possible not so much through logicality whose language of thought, as Krell (1979) aptly said, flows from a belonging to the earth that is "cut loose from the sun, deprived of her horizon, and a dwelling that lovers in holy dread before the raging discordance of art and truth" (p. 250). Rather, the taste of life and for life comes to its own as a gift through the grace of the piety of thinking that is truly of the earth—the earth that knows the sun of the dawn, the calm of the morn, the silence of its mystery. In its poeticity and its linguisticality, Anjin's story allowed us to follow the open hand that gently gestured toward the topos of pedagogical Being, that pedagogical relationship that reverentially knows its attunement to Being.

As I now see it, the gentle lesson that is Anjin's story is that to those who are sufficiently attuned to where we already are is granted piety of thinking that allows a revealing of the truer measure of pedagogy, freed of the calculated measure of logic. For is it not true that face to face with the primal mystery of Being, we are brought to an awareness that language which has served us well to describe the phenomena of the world begins to falter; at best, it merely points and then passes into silence.

I am left with a petal of thought that the appropriate topos for such piety of thinking is the silence of the morning calm. Anjin Yoo, a pedagogue that she is, has led me by her hand to the brink of this silence. And at this moment in the shimmering presence of her absence, I stand—midst the silence—alone but not alone.

REFERENCES

Beittel, K. (1989). Mind and Context in the Art of Drawing. New York: Thompson International.

Heidegger, M. (1968). *What is called thinking?* (J. Glenn, Trans.). New York: Harper and Row.

Heidegger, M. (1969). Principle of identity. In *Identity and difference* (J. Stambaugh, Trans). New York: Harper and Row.

Heidegger, M. (1979). *Nietzsche, Vols.* I–IV (D. Farrell Krell, Trans.). New York: Harper and Row.

Hopstadter, A. (1979). Enownment. In W. V. Spanos (Ed.), *Martin Heidegger and the question of literature*. Bloomington: Indiana University Press.

Hsiao, P. S. (1987). Heidegger and our translation of the *Tao Te Ching*. In G. Parkes (Ed.), *Heidegger and Asian thought*, Honolulu: University of Hawaii Press.

Jung, H. Y. (1987). Heidegger's way with Sinitic thinking. In G. Parkes (Ed.), *Heidegger and Asian thought*. Honolulu, HI. University of Hawaii Press.

Krell, D. F. (Trans.). (1979). Analysis. In M. Heidegger, *Nietzsche Vol. I: The will to power as Art*. New York: Harper and Row.

Parkes, G. (1987). Afterwords—Language. In G. Parkes (Ed.), *Heidegger and AsianThought*. Honolulu: University of Hawaii Press.

Paz, O. (1973). The poetic revelations. In *The bow and the lyrei*. Austin: University of Texas Press.

Chapter 26

Narrative and Narration
in Curricular Spaces[1] (1996)

A SUBLIME IMAGE:
A FLAG WITH A HOLE IN THE CENTER

Ljubljana. I first heard of Ljubljana just 2 years ago when an artist friend, Elysia Dywan, then a fine arts graduate student at the University of Alberta, told me that her work of art was accepted at an international art exhibit. Where? Ljubljana. Where? Slovenia.

I was both happy and shocked. What is it, I asked, that makes it possible to hear of an art exhibit in Slovenia, while next door in other dismembered segments of old Yugoslavia, we were hearing stories of ethnic cleansing, of separatist nationalism, and of battles for "democracy," whatever that meant.

A few weeks ago, I received a surprise postcard from Ljubljana with a warm one-line message: "Ted all the best from Slovenia. From Terry and Jan." Terry Carson and Jan jagodzinski, both of the University of Alberta, traipsing around in Eastern Europe.

The card with the sparse memo was accompanied by a letter, long as the card was short. In it was mention of Jan's interest in entering a tightly knit circle in Ljubljana—Zizek's Circle—a circle almost impossible to penetrate, so the letter said.

Coincidentally, when the card and letter from Ljubljana arrived, I was in the midst of a slow reading in the early pages of a book titled, *Tarrying with the Negative*—the author, Slajov Zizek.[2] His book opens with an uncanny image, what he calls "the most sublime image," reflecting the political upheaval in Eastern Europe in our time. He is reliving the unique image of the moment of the violent overthrow of Ceausescu in Romania. And the image? In Zizek's words:

> The image of the rebels waving the national flag with the red star, the communist symbol, cut out, so that instead of the symbol standing for the organizing principle of national life, there was *nothing but a hole in its centre*. (Zizek, 1995, p. 1, emphasis added)

---

[1] An invited address presented at the conference titled "Curriculum as Narrative/Narrative as Curriculum: Lingering in the Spaces." Held at Green College, University of British Columbia, May 2 and 3, 1996.

[2] Zizek, Slavoj. (1995). *Tarrying with the Negative.* Durham, NC: Duke University Press.

A flag with nothing in the center. Zizek continues:

> It is difficult to imagine a more salient index of the "open"
> character of a historical situation in its becoming . . .of that
> intermediate phase when the former Master Signifier, although
> it has already lost the hegemonic power, has not yet been
> replaced by the new one. (p. 1)

Zizek alerts us to the sublime enthusiasm of that sublime moment when
"the masses who poured into the streets of Bucharest 'experienced' the situation
as 'open,' participated in the unique intermediate state of passage from one
discourse to another, when for a brief, passing moment, the hole in the big other,
the symbolic order, became visible" (p. 1). The enthusiasm that carried them
was the enthusiasm over this hole, not yet hegemonized by any positive
ideological project.

Indeed, a sublime moment tarrying with "nothing" at the center, tarrying
with the negative. Ljubjlana.

DISJUNCTURE BETWEEN MODERNIST
AND POSTMODERNIST DISCOURSES

I have been calling the Asia Pacific Education Graduate Program straddling the
CSCI and LANE (the Centre for the Study of Curriculum and Instruction and
the Department of Language Education) my home on this campus over the last
couple of years. On the program brochure are three master signifiers,
"language," "culture," and "curriculum," and we have been open to that space
where we can reconstitute meanings of these signifiers. With such interest
aglow, we have been positioning ourselves in an interdisciplinary space, mindful
of Roland Barthes's admonition:

> Interdisciplinary work, so much discussed these days, is not
> about confronting already constituted disciplines (none of
> which, in fact, is willing to let itself go). To do something
> interdisciplinary, it's not enough to choose a subject or a theme
> and gather around it two or three sciences. Interdisciplinary
> consists in creating a new object that belongs to no-one.
> (Barthes, 1986, p. 26)[3]

We in the program have been asking, where is this interdisciplinary space,
where is creation of newness possible?

Early this year LANE held a departmental colloquium, a session given to a
discussion under the title "Standard Academic Research and Postmodern

---

[3] Barthes, Roland. (1986). *The Rustle of Language*. New York: Hill and Wang.

Discourse." I heard people say, "exciting times," "about time," "what's up? or down?," "have we no norms?"

The story goes that two doctoral students in LANE took bold turns in their dissertations. At the oral, both did well, I'm told, but in the department, their bold turns raised the question of the stability of the master signifier in graduate studies, the word "research." One of these was Laurie Jardine,[4] whose dissertation was titled, "Reading Gavin Bolton: A Biography of Education."

The other was Erika Hasebe-Ludt,[5] whose dissertation title read, "In All the Universe: Placing the Texts of Culture and Community in Only One School." On Erika's Examination Committee I sat as "university examiner," whatever that meant, and David Smith of the University of Lethbridge served as the absent external examiner, although his words were very much present at the oral.

I was invited to participate in the departmental colloquium together with a scholar from the English Department who was appointed by the Dean of Graduate Studies to chair one of the orals and to report to the dean. Carl Leggo of LANE responded to the two talks. He performed by dancing a neat response.

I talked. Studiously, looking at the title of the session, "Standard Academic Discourse and Postmodern Research," I wondered where best I could tarry. First, I tarried with the Asian negative 無 (wu in Chinese; mu in Japanese).

無 reads "nothing," that is, "no-thing." Noting that in "nothing," "thing" is already inscribed, I reread: 無here can be no-thing without thing," and "There can be no thing without nothing."

So retextured, I returned to the title of the colloquium: "Standard Academic Discourse and Post-modern Research." I avoided the "things" in the title, and positioned myself in the "and," which I quickly retextured into both "*and*" and "*not-and*," into both conjunction and disjunction, into both continuity and discontinuity.

Drawn into this space, I leaned on a few writers. I mentioned Jean François Lyotard, who by publishing the book *The Post-modern Condition*[6] popularized, so it has been said, the signifier "postmodern." I found it interesting that the later Lyotard re-worked the word "postmodern," first by erasing the pre-fix "post" and replacing it with "re," his way of undoing the linearity inscribed in "post." Then he erased "modernity," displeased with the substantive in modernist epistemology, replacing it with the performative version of "writing."

---

[4] Jardine, Laurie. (1995). *Reading Gavin Bolton: A Biography of Education.* Unpublished doctoral dissertation, Department of Language and Literacy Education, University of British Columbia.

[5] Hasebe-Ludt, Erika. (1995*). In All The Universe: Placing the Texts of Culture and Community in Only One School.* Unpublished doctoral dissertation. Department of Language and Literacy Education, University of British Columbia.

[6] Lyotard, Jean François. (1984). *The Post-modern Condition.* The University of Minnesota Press.

So with Lyotard "postmodern" became "rewriting modernity" (Lyotard, 1991).[7] Neat!

We visited, next, Deborah Britzman of York University, who, in a recent article, "The Question of Belief: Writing Post Structural Ethnography," played with the word "ethnography" usually linked with cultural narrative writing.[8] She claimed that in the Modernist tradition of ethnographic research, *ethno*graphy is understood as writing (graphing) *about* "ethnos" (writing *about* identifiable and representable cultures), whereas in ethno*graphy* in the postmodern sense interest is in the performativity of writing in the midst of signifiers.

Then, we noted Homi Bhabha, who, in his article "Interrogating Identity," marked out the space between writing about the identity of the "deep me" and identification of a subject, that is, constituting of a subject as the "written me." For Bhabha,[9] the crucial space is that ambivalent space—the third space—between the "deep me" and the "written me," between the discursive space of "identity" and the discursive space of "identification."

At the colloquium, I noted that out in the open are signs of both conjunction and disruption occurring in the "and" between the norms of academic research and the non-normality of post-modern research—signs of transformative possibilities. And in this transformative agenda, it seems, graduate students appear actively involved—quite a shift from the days when concerning research in the Centre for the Study of Curriculum and Instruction, I was told by an ex-graduate student of U.B.C., "We were told we could do phenomenological narrative research as long as we don't use the word 'phenomenology.'"

NARRATING WITH DIFFICULTY IN THE MIDST OF ORIGINAL DIFFICULTY

In the summer of 1993, John Willinsky of CSCI invited me to teach a graduate level course in curriculum. For the course, I chose two texts to help texture the flow of the course.

The first was *The Call of Teaching*, [10] published by the B.C. Teachers Federation, which is a collection of curricular narratives—experimental writings by teachers. The other text was one edited by Pinar and Reynolds titled,

---

[7] Lyotard, Jean François. (1991). *The Inhuman*. Stanford, CA: Stanford University Press.

[8] Britzman, Deborah. 1995. "The Question of Belief: Writing post structural ethnography." *International Journal of Qualitative Studies in Education,* 8 (3). London: Taylor and Francis.

[9] Bhabha, Homi. (1994). Interrogating identity: Frantz Fanon and the postcolonial prerogative. In *The Location of Culture*. London: Routledge.

[10] Aoki T. T., and Shamsher, M. (1993). *The Call of Teaching*. Vancouver: B. C. Teachers' Federation.

Understanding Curriculum as Phenomenological and Deconstructive Text "divided" into two parts.[11] Loaded with Canadian authors, there are articles by Margaret Hunsberger of the University of Calgary, Terry Carson of the University of Alberta, David Jardine of the University of Calgary, Jan jagodzinski of the University of Alberta, and Jacques Daignault of the University of Quebec.

Right in the middle of the book, at the very end of Part I, is an article by David Jardine titled "Reflections on Education, Hermeneutics and Ambiguity: Hermeneutics as a Restoring of Life to Its Original Difficulty."[12] My class discussed whether the article belonged to Part I or Part II, or whether it might be better located in the "and" between Part I and Part II. Neither strictly phenomenological nor postmodern, most students felt it was "growing" in the ambivalent space of "and/not and," between Part I and Part II.

From the outset, in the article, David Jardine set out polar questions: (1) "How are we (as educators) to educe new life in a way that conserves what already is?" and (2) "How are we to educe the new?" Asking us to set these questions aside for a moment, Jardine urged us, "Underlying both of these . . . is a more fundamental question, How are we to respond to new life in our midst in such a way that life together can go on, in a way that does not foreclose on the future?" (Jardine, p. 118).

With this question, Jardine alerted us to the groundless ground of ambiguity that marks the human condition, a site of vibrant original difficulty, at times agonizingly difficult. He was showing us, it seemed to us, how life's difficulties relate to this ambiguity, how life in its ongoing becoming constitutes and is constituted in the site between life and life, and at times, between life and not-life where the negative tarries.

For Jardine, the word "original" in "original difficulty" does not mean a sort of nostalgic longing for some unspecified past, nor a longing for one's own past echoingly heard in some phenomenological narratives. Yet, for him, longing is nevertheless a longing a desire for the fundamental "question of how life together can go on in such a way that even in difficulties, new life is possible."

Among the students in this class were George Fedoruk and Margo Rosenberg, both of whom were to experience life's extreme difficulties. In the course, I had students read my narrative effort, "Being and Becoming a Teacher

---

[11] Pinar, W. & Reynolds, W. (1992). *Understanding Curriculum as Phenomenological and Deconstructed Text.* New York: Teachers College Press.

[12] Jardine, David. (1992). Reflections on education, hermeneutics, and ambiguity: Hermeneutics as a restoring of life to its original difficulty. In W. F. Pinar & W. M. Reynolds. (Eds.), *Understanding Curriculum as Phenomenological and Deconstructed Text.* New York: Teachers College Press (Columbia University).

in Alberta: A Personal Curriculum," an early effort of mine in narrating live(d) experiences.[13] Near the end of a pedagogical journey, I wrote:

> We have a daughter; rather, we had a daughter. Michele Novuko, like a cherry blossom that had its brief moment, parted with life untimely at the call of nature. Of her 19 years she spent three years in Vancouver, one of them on the campus of the University of British Columbia. . . .
> We have taken her home and have buried her on the coast . . ., and when I come home, I will want to view the sakura. . ., so beautiful and bountiful are they in British Columbia. (Aoki, pp. 334-335)

Since the course in 1993, George Fedoruk has been experiencing grief, losing a son in a car accident near Squamish, B.C. He visits me occasionally, and we share stories, midst tears at times. Margo Rosenberg came to me on the last days of the course to ask of me permission to leave so she could fly to Chicago to be with her very ill mother. She feared the worst. Later, she came to me to tell me of the loss of her mother. Now, wanting to write narratively the meaning of suffering in grief, so that she, as teacher, might be able to help others should they desire help, she asked me for a reading or two to assist in her writing. I was lost, unable to help.

Later I met Margo at Rosa Mastri's thesis oral and I told her I would like to send her an article that David Smith sent me very recently. It is titled "Person as Narration: The Dissolution of 'Self' and 'Other' in Ch'an Buddhism."[14] I sent a copy to both Margo and George.

In the article is a poignant story about narration and narrative. It is simply titled, "Kisagotami's Story":

> Once, there was a young woman named Kisagotami . . . who had apparently lost her mind because of the death of her child. Carrying the tiny corpse, she wandered from house to house in her village, begging her neighbours to give her a medicine capable of reviving the baby. Finally, someone referred her to the Buddha, who was staying at Jevalana.
> She approached the Buddha and . . . begged his assistance. He agreed to help, and told her that in order to heal the child, he needed four or five mustard seeds from a house where no

---

[13] Aoki, T. T. (1983). Being and becoming a teacher in Alberta: A personal curriculum. *Journal for Curriculum Studies*. New York: Teachers College Press (Columbia University).

[14] P .D. Hershock. "Person as Narration: The Dissolution of Self and 'Other' in Ch'an Buddhism." *Philosophy East and West*, Vol. 44, No. 4., Oct. 1994, University of Hawaii Press.

son, father, mother, daughter had died. Thanking the Buddha, Kisagotami set out, going from door to door in search of a house where death had never entered. Finally, she reached the very outskirts of town without having found a family that had not been visited by death. She returned to the Buddha and in his quiet presence, her mind cleared. She understood the meaning of his words and from that day on was one of his devoted followers. (Hershock, pp. 688–689)

Moved by the short but elusive narrative, I lingered in the words: "She understood the meaning of his words . . . ." I wondered, could it be that what she understands includes what the narrative is not?

I read on in Hershock's article, as his text holds me. At the outset, he says, we may be tempted to an understanding that suffering loss and grieving is universal—that suffering as grieving is an experience common to us all, one that is inevitable, given our nature as sentient human beings.   But such a universalistic understanding, Hershock reminds us, clings to the traditional Western modernist belief in "the objectivity of identity, and in the reality of essence or universals." In the place of such an understanding, Hershock offers a doubled interpretation within the Ch'an tradition of Asian wisdom.

First, he rejoins Kisagotami in the midst of her visits through the town where she comes to realize that there is no home where impermanence and suffering do not reach. This is not to say that impermanence and suffering are the same, but rather that there is no place where one can go to avoid the vexations of the negative. Yet, at a more profound level, Hershock states that the ubiquity of impermanence assures us that no matter how hopelessly stricken we feel in a situation, there is promise of hope that can arise in the seeming bondage between life and nonlife.   According to Hershock, that is one understanding that Kisagotami likely reached.

For another, Kisagotami came to realize that suffering always occurs in the context of a consciously articulated story. Hershock reminds us that the Buddha does not tell her that everyone experiences grief. Rather, he asks her to go from house to house inquiring people whether death occurred there. And when she knocks on a door and asks if death has occurred in the home, rather than being answered with a brusque "yes" or "no," she is more apt to linger as the pain of her suffering calls for the pain of the suffering her neighbour is experiencing. Likely, she is invited into the home where a conversation ensues, including narratives of sufferings of people with "names, birthdates, distinctive traits and dreams" (p. 690). And in these conversations, narratives begin to intertwine. Hershock says, "In this sense, suffering is . . . neither objective nor subjective but profoundly and immediately personal and shared." Kisagotami is granted the possibility of opening herself to their stories, entering back into them in full reciprocity by reincluding them once again as active participant in her own. As such, and this is crucial, Kisagotami's personhood becomes a *centerless space of dramatic interplay.*

If that be so, although my suffering is always uniquely embedded in a story in which I am the seeming narrator, it is never mine alone but always ours. The locus of suffering is not the objective so-called "natural" world of individual people and things, but, rather, the *fathomless intimacy of narration. Person is narration, a centerless space of dramatic interplay.* Narrator? Narrative? Narrative and narration?

IN THE METONYMIC SPACE OF "NARRATIVE AND NARRATION"

I now find myself located in the space of what for me is a metonymic site of "narrative and narration," a site midst doubled signifiers. How was this space so constituted?

It was born, if at all born, in that curriculum class of 1993 when it found itself located in that space of ambiguity and original difficulty David Jardine spoke of. It was within this space that George Fedoruk and Margo Rosenberg began to tell their experiences of loss and grief, later nourished by the tale of suffering Kisagotami experienced and came to understand.

And, now, dwelling in the midst of "narrative and narration," with images of a person as a centerless space, and person as the fathomless intimacy of narration, I return to Zizek of Ljubljana, beckoned by his sublime image of the centerless flag—the flag with the master signifier cut out.

In Romania, Zizek noted the brevity of the sublime moment of the centerless master signifier, for quickly the Romanian people were clamouring to fill the void with new hegemonic signifiers. This is what he saw happening in Romania. Thoughtfully, Zizek tells us that when we experience loss, often our desire is to fill the space of loss such that the "empty" space, the space of the negative, becomes invisible. We tend to replace the lost master signifier with another master signifier, itself claiming its own hegemonic power.

Concerned, very concerned, Zizek challenges us with these strong words:

> The *duty* of the critical intellectuals—if in today's post-modern
> universe, this syntagm has any meaning left, is *to occupy all
> the time*, even when the new order stabilizes itself and . . .
> renders invisible the hole as such, the place of this hole; i.e., to
> maintain a distance toward every reigning master-signifier.
> (Zizek, p. 4)

How might we, who dwell midst the doubling of "narrative and narration," read and interpret Zizek's poignant remarks? If, indeed, we are, each of us, centerless narration, yet, in our moment of all too human desire we rush to fill the void of narration with narratives, what then?

It is here I hear Zizek urging us that we, as humans, are duty bound, ethically bound, to undergo the difficulty—to try to occupy all the time the centerless space of narration. This indeed might be a way "that life together can go on, in a way that does not foreclose on the future" (Jardine, p. 116).

Short as this paper is, I experienced, in the writing of narratives, of life/not life, many pauses, spaces where I was drawn to linger a while. Where were these moments? Most of them were occasions when I tarried with negatives embedded in the doubling of "things and no-things," of "and and not-and," of "enjoining and disjoining," of the ambiguity of "this and that" instead of "this or that," of the difficult space of "life and not-life," of "center and the centerless," of "the visible and the invisible," but, most lingeringly, in the metonymic space between "narrative and narration."

Chapter 27

Spinning Inspirited Images in the Midst of Planned and Live(d) Curricula[1] (1996)

GEO-METRON IN DOUBLED IMAGINARIES

Within me, the sounds of Davis Thiaw's drumbeats[2] sound and resound. And in this special space we call Timm's Centre on the University of Alberta campus, the earthy rhythmic beats continue to pulsate in thunderous rolls and in fingertip whispers, dancing to and fro, insistently, echoing vibrantly within me and beyond me. Held in awe by the drumbeats that linger, I find myself indwelling this moment, earthily, spiritually, and poetically.

So inspired and so inspirited by the Senegalese drumbeat, I am beckoned by another rhythm, this from far-off Asia. Join me in a play with images and sounds of just one word—詩 —an ideograph that comes to us as a Chinese character.

In Japanese, it reads "shi," literally translated as "poetry" or "that which evokes earthy rhythm."

INDWELLING IDEOGRAPHICALLY

- 詩 (shi) as an ideogram is, linguists tell us, both whole and fragmented. Fragments of thoughts are juxtaposed into a compositioning that yields meanings cumulatively.

- 土 (tsuchi) means earth, the earth on which we stand and walk. It is "eco" of "ecology," a discourse concerning life on earth. It is "geo" of "geography," earth writing or earthy writing. To the Greeks, it is the dwelling place of Gaia, the goddess of earth. It is the *humus* of the earth, which nurtures us as *humans*, a place where *humans* are

---

[1] Reprinted from: Aoki, Ted. (1996). Spinning inspired images in the midst of planned and live(d) curricula. *FINE: Journal of the Fine Arts Council of The Alberta Teachers' Association*, fall, pp. 7–14.

[2] This article was originally presented as the keynote address at the Fine Arts Council Conference in April 1996. The address was preceded by a drum performance by Davis Thiaw, originally from Senegal, Africa. Ted Aoki was introduced to the stage by Thiaw's drumbeats.

beckoned to dwell in *humility*, yet with a sense of *humour* where joyous pleasure and laughter can commingle with serious living.

- Under 土 (tsuchi) is 寸 (sún), which means measure; in Greek, "metron." it appears as metered measure in music, as pacing in acting, as measured brush strokes in painting, as rhythmic movement in dancing. It is the tectonic pulsation inscribed in the humus and rock formations of the earth's crust—not still, always astir, sometimes beating thunderously, at other times beating whisperingly.

- In 寺 (tera), earth and metron conjoining give us "geometron," earth's measure, earth's rhythm. It marks the place where earth's true measure sounds forth. So composed, it reads, in Chinese, "temple," an inspirited place, a sacred place. In ancient Greece, it was the setting where the goddess Gaia daily dwelt touching all.

- 口 (kuchi). On the other side, we find: 口 (kuchi — mouth—an opening through which sounds come forth. It symbolizes the voicing of stories and songs within which inspirited dreams are spun.

- 亠 and the lines above 口 (kuchi) are sound waves and echoes, with the mark above signifying the lingering of echoes.

- 言 So on the left side, ir 言 (yúú), the mouth and the sound waves and echoes conjoin to say "saying," "telling," or "singing" of live(d)[3] experiences, already saying that such a space is a dialogical space, where selves and others indwell.

- 詩 And when earth (   ), rhy 寸), temple (寺), mouth (口), sound waves (亠) and echoes come together,(言), the whole jointly reads "poetry" or "that

---

[3] "Live(d)" in "lived experiences" marks the double meanings of experience. The first of these is "*lived* experience," referring to past experiences that are assumed to be historically recollectable. The second is "*live* experience," referring to ongoing experiences of the moment.

which is poetic" or "indwelling inspirited within earth's rhythm."

INDWELLING CALLIGRAPHICALLY

Now may I ask you to dissolve the foregoing image of *ideo*graphic writing, that is, writing thoughts and ideas, and displace it with another imaginary—writing that might be called calli*graphic* (writing artistically). Within this imaginary, envisage 詩 (shi) as a work of calligraphic practice, done by a one-time student here at the University of Alberta, her degree in sculpture.

June, my wife, has long been fond of Chinese and Japanese calligraphy (which she prefers to call "brush sculpting"), and for over a decade, she has been an understudy to Chinese and Japanese calligraphy masters. Every morning from six to seven, she has been at the desk "writing." What has long puzzled me is how she stays at her desk writing and rewriting, repeating the same word or words 10, 20, and even more times. In this seemingly tensioned repetition, she appears not so much concerned with what is being written but, rather, seems enraptured in a world of sculpturing in space with her brush and ink as partners. Writing as sculpturing in space? Calligraphy?

IN THE MIDST OF DOUBLED IMAGINARIES

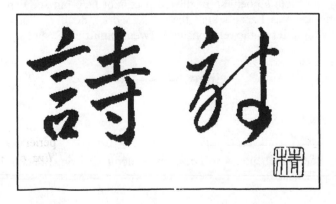

Now as I pause to reflect, I find myself lingering in the fold of doubled imaginaries—the *ideo*graphic 詩 (shi) and the calli*graphic* 詩 (shi). I find myself in a vibrant tension of in-between, the seemingly same word refusing to fuse—a pleasant confusion! Similar, yet different at the same time!

Such a doubled imaginary reminds me of poetic work I used last summer to begin a graduate course in curriculum studies at the University of Victoria:

To
write
is to
write
is to
write
is to
write
is
to write is to write is
to write is to write.

— Gertrude Stein

And now, as I speak, I can almost hear each of you, transforming Gertrude Stein into your idioms of preference:

- To act is to act is to act . . .
- To dance is to dance is to dance . . .
- To paint is to paint is to paint . . .
- To sing is to sing is to sing . . .
- . . .

What multiple meanings Stein anticipated, I hesitate to venture even a guess. But I do note the way in which she textured ideographically and calligraphically the space that was the empty page. In noting the verticality and horizontality in Stein's poem so displayed, I cannot help but see Ferdinand de Saussure and Jacques Lacan's sign theory[4] at work—doubly. For Lacan, the meaning of a sign lies in the relationship between signifier (S) and signified (s):

$$\text{Sign} = \frac{S}{s}$$

---

[4] Note, for example, chapter 4 in *Lacan* by Malcolm Bowie (London: Fontana, 1991, pp. 88–121).

One meaning arises from the vertical relationship between S and s wherein the bar between them is assumed to be transparent. The meaning of what it is "to write" is seen to be located vertically in the deep, challenging us to make present the essence that lurks below. But if the bar is opaque, the meaning of the signifier "to write" is understood to be generated in the space between it and another signifier adjacent to it horizontally, that is, metonymically. Within this understanding, meaning arises; for instance, between and among the words (signifiers) in a sentence. Meaning vertically generated: meanings horizontally generated? Gertrude Stein takes us into an ambiguous space. More later.

DISTURBING "CURRICULUM" AS MASTER SIGNIFIER

The consideration of the word *poetry*   (詩 —shi) led us to at least two meanings of the word, suggesting that any word as signifier can have multiple meanings, each meaning framed within its own imaginary. We say the ideographic and the calligraphic at work in different imaginaries, each with its own language.

In this context, allow me to recall an astute article "Words on Words" by Vaclav Havel (1990), one-time president of Czechoslovakia, now, since the split, president of the Czech Republic. Havel wrote of how the word *socialism*, once virtually sacred in Eastern Europe, became tainted by the collapse of the Soviet Union and then eventually became a dirty word to be uttered with disdain. Havel, a one-time literary dramatist, said that any word as signifier changes its meaning over time and, further, that at any single moment several meanings of a word can coexist; he emphasized that how a meaning of a word becomes *the* meaning is a political, legitimating act.

So reminded, let us move into the realm of "curriculum." So positioned, we ask, "Why is it that we seem to be caught up in a singular meaning of the word *curriculum*?"

I find that the word *curriculum* typically conjures forth a conventional landscape of school curricula dotted with school subjects, such as mathematics, social studies, the sciences, and literary studies, usually legitimated as the core, and others, such as home economics, the shops, drama, music, painting, and dancing, marginalized as noncore. Within this imaginary of curriculum, an array of curricula exists, typically categorized by some authority into "compulsory" courses and "options."

Such a landscape so familiar to us suggests a diversity of offerings. But the seeming curricular diversity is an illusion because "they" are manifestations of a singular meaning of curriculum: curriculum-as-plan. In this conventional landscape, when we say curriculum ("the mathematics curriculum"), we typically envision a singular curriculum for each grade, a master curriculum planned under an authority, authorizing sameness and homogeneity throughout the province. Likening the single curriculum to a single tree dominating the landscape, I call such a landscape "arboreal" (Fig. 27.1). Within this landscape, the lone tree casts its benign shadow over the landscape such that "teaching" becomes "implementation" and "instruction" becomes in-structuring students in the image of the given.

FIG. 27.1   Arboreal curricular landscape.

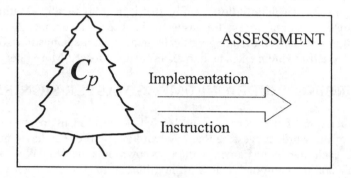

What we see here is the conventional linear language of "curriculum and instruction," of "curriculum implementation," of "curriculum assessment." This is the world in which the measures that count are preset; therefore, ordained to repeat the same—to dance the same, to paint the same, to sing the same, to act the same—a world in which proper names of students tend to be reduced to "learners," psychologically enframed, where learning is reduced to "acquiring" and where "evaluating" is reduced to measuring the acquired against some preset standardized norm. This metron, this measure and rhythm, is one that, in an overconcern for sameness, fails to heed the feel of the earth that touches the dancing feet differently for each student.

We are aware of the foregoing linear instrumentation, a landscape that will persist as an arboreal landscape as long as the word curriculum is defined solely as plan. This landscape needs a bit of earth quaking such that other meanings of "curriculum" can surface.

THE LIVE(D) CURRICULUM: A NEW SIGNIFIER

Let us, then, shift our attention from the image of the arboreal landscape of planned curriculum to the image of live(d) curriculum. By live(d) curriculum, I mean the situated image of the live(d) curricular experiences of teachers and students.

Let me take a short aside to touch on the split character of *live(d)* in "live(d) curriculum," of "curriculum as live(d) experiences." The word *experience* is a hybrid, including the notions of "past experiences" (*lived* experiences) and "ongoing experiences" (*live* or *living* experiences).   But what matters significantly lies beyond mere "past" and "ongoing."

Here, I lean on Jonathan Culler (1982, p. 82), who wrote: "Experience is divided and deferred—always behind us as something to be recovered, yet still before us as something to be produced." What is he saying? First, past experiences, assumed to lie in the depth of the past, await recovery through careful archaeology. We sense here an image of verticality we noted in Gertrude Stein's poem. For the other, Culler is saying that meanings of experiences ongoing horizontally are being produced in the spaces between signifiers. Again, we recall Gertrude Stein's horizontal writing of "to write is to write is to write."

Without getting involved in the complexity of signifying practice, let us speak of "live(d) curriculum" as a situated image, not of an abstract classroom but of a concretely situated live classroom.

In such a situated image, a person called teacher has a proper name, for example, Miss O, and students are no longer abstractions but have names and personalities (feisty Sarah, can't-sit-still Johnny, daydreamer David, quiet-and-thoughtful Martha, friendly Mary, and so on), all 25 of them—experiencing classroom life similarly and differently. In such a classroom, Miss O tries to be mindful not only of the planned curriculum but also of the 26 live(d) curricula including her own. It is a very complex, quaky curricular milieu within which Miss O dwells. Practicing teachers can relate to Miss O readily, themselves having experienced what Miss O is experiencing.

FIG 27.2 Rhizomean curricular landscape

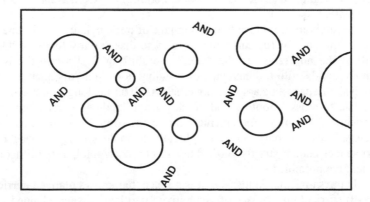

Such a curricular landscape is replete with a multiplicity of curricula. I call this landscape "rhizomean" (Fig, 27.2), not only to signify the multiplicity of curricula but also to recognize that textured web of connecting lines that, like rhizomean plants, shoot from here to there, and everywhere working through, nourished by the humus. In creating such an image, we ought to heed Gilles Deleuze (Deleuze & Parnet, 1987), who reminds us that "multiplicity is not a noun." He says, further, "In a multiplicity what counts are not the elements, but what there is between, the between, as site of relations which are not separable from each other. Every multiplicity *grows in the middle.*"

Such a rhizomean landscape comes into being by recognizing and legitimating live(d) curricula that in the imaginary of the arboreal landscape have been rendered invisible. If living on earth as humans, experiencing being and becoming, matters in education, it behooves us to transform the language of school life such that multiple meanings of the word *curriculum* can prevail.

IN THE MIDST OF AND BETWEEN
PLANNED AND LIVE(D) CURRICULA

In gazing on the newly framed landscape, what stands out linguistically is the expression, "planned curriculum and live(d) curriculum." Almost by habit, I focus on the elements (two things): *planned curriculum* and *live(d) curriculum.* Why so? I have been habituated to dwell in a noun-oriented world, a world populated by "people" and "things": this thing, that thing, these things, those things—possibly a sign of our Western epistemological imaginary that centers on naming things, commodity-oriented as we have become. In such a discursive world, even people are apt to become things.

To shake myself loose of the habit, let me attend to an East Asian word: ("wu" in Chinese, "mu" in Japanese). Anglicized, the word says "nothing" or "no-thing." What I find in the word *nothing* is that "thing" is already inscribed, almost to say paradoxically that "nothing" cannot be without "thing" and, as well, a "thing cannot be without nothing." Confusing? Ambiguous? Ambivalent?

So retextured, I return to the language of our curricular landscape: "planned curriculum and live(d) curriculum." I try to dissolve my focus on "things" and shift to the nonthing—to the "and." So shifting, I slip into the language of "and/not and," into the language of "conjunction" and "disjunction," a difficult ambivalent space but a space nonetheless. It is no longer a space where it is possible to cross smoothly and quickly from "planned curriculum" to "live(d) curriculum" through "implementation or instruction:" it is now a space textually accented with a mark: /, a graphically tectonic space, a space marked by differences neither strictly vertical nor strictly horizontal, a space that may allow generative possibilities.

In our curricular landscape, it is a space that knows planned curriculum and live(d) curriculum, a space of generative interplay between planned curriculum and live(d) curriculum. It is a site wherein the interplay is the creative production of newness, where newness can come into being. It is an inspirited site of being and becoming.

It may be ancient history to you, but I recall when Brian Orser, following his victorious skating at the World Figure Skating Championships in Cincinnati, was interviewed by the late Barbara Frum. When asked "How are you listening to the music when you are skating?" he promptly replied, "When I'm skating, I don't listen to the music; I become the music." Brian Orser's inspirited skating.

I recall another occasion some years ago when Bobby Shew, a jazz trumpeter from California, visited the Music Department in the Department of Fine Arts here at the University of Alberta. I was chair of the curriculum department then, and I tried to woo him to a curriculum symposium. When he expressed curiosity about why a curriculum person was interested in him, I posed two questions: "When does an instrument, like a trumpet, cease to be an instrument?" (If it were today, I would also ask him what is happening in that space of "and" between instrument *and* noninstrument.) Second, "To a jazz trumpeter, what is 'improvisation'?" (If it were today, I would also ask him what is happening in improvisation, in that space of "and" between the music score and lived music.) Thanks to Bobby Shew's talk, his trumpeting and lively conversations with him, our curriculum symposium was inspirited and memorable indeed. I continue to linger in its echo.

Next, let us linger a moment with a work of art (Fig. 27.3). Titled "Quadrant of Arms: Drawing, Mixed Media,"[5] what you see here is a page from an art catalogue of an exhibit held in 1993 at Over-Seas House on St. James Street, London, sponsored by the Royal Over-Seas League. The work was done by Elysia Dywan, then a master's student in fine arts at the University of Alberta. Accompanying the work, Dywan (1993) writes, "I see my work as commenting on the ambiguous nature of the human condition." Her focus is on life's ambiguous condition. Mindful of the space between viewer and the texture of the painting, she writes of the four quadrants: "These disparate visual elements are not intended to denote a specific reading into the nature of the human condition, but instead, it is my hope that the resulting ambiguity [creates] a dynamism in the formation of meaning." These words indicate her interest in the creation of newness in that generative space of ambiguity in the space between the texture of the painting and the texture of the viewer.

With the help of people such as Brian Orser, Bobby Shew, and Elysia Dywan, I have come to better understand the generative although ambiguous, ambivalent space between this and that, between planned curriculum and live(d) curriculum.

- I now see inspirited hybrid brush writing that occurs in that space of ambivalence between ideographic writing *and* calligraphic writing.
- I see inspirited dancing that happens in that space between dancing about an event *and* dancing as performative.
- I see inspirited singing as that creative singing in the space between singing a song *and* live(d) singing.

---

[5] Elysia Dywan's "Quadrant of Arms" is originally in colour, here reduced unfortunately to black and white. It is reproduced with the artist's permission from the 1993 Annual Open Exhibition catalogue.

- I see inspirited acting as enaction in that space between acting by script *and* live(d) acting.
- I see inspirited painting as that generative creation in that space between painting an object *and* painting as living experience.

Such spaces are edgy spaces, located at margins and boundaries, spaces of doubling, where "this or that" becomes "this and that," ambiguously, ambivalently—difficult places but nonetheless spaces of generative possibilities.

Poststructuralists and postcolonialists, such as Homi Bhabha (1990), call such spaces "the third space," spaces where newness can enter the world. Bhabha speaks of spaces of possibilities in ambivalent spaces between life and *non*-life, between the known and the *un*known, between universals and particulars (nonuniversals), even between possibilities and impossibilities where inspirited newness is ongoingly constituted and reconstituted.

This is the space where all humans as artists creatively indwell. And this is the space that I wish to call on artists and art educators to kindle afire the all-too-often deadening weight of scholasticism and academicism that too much blanket the interspaces in monochrome.

FIG. 27.3 *Quadrant of Arms* by Elysia Dywan 1983. Drawing mixed media.

A PLEA TO ART EDUCATORS

Recognizing the shortcomings of a curriculum imaginary characterized by the hegemony of curriculum-as-plan, many educators over the years have toiled to improve what they have seen as limitation and partialities. Some have expended effort to sharpen and to detail complexities of the planned curriculum. Others have moved sideways, exploring different and fuller dimensions of the word *instruction* in the expression "curriculum and instruction." Still others have left the word *instruction,* preferring the word *teaching* in its gerundial formulation. A few have participated in restoring the word *pedagogy,* for so long in the lexicon of European educators but shunned for some reason in North America. Still others have taken to the word *education,* resisting commodification as in the language of "getting an education" or "acquiring an education," opening it to deeper and richer meanings. No doubt much good and promising work has gone on and is ongoing.

But so oriented and so directed, many have neglected the word *curriculum,* and by their neglect, they may have been complicit in solidifying the hold of the meaning of curriculum-as-plan. It is with this benign complicity that I am here concerned.

As I have suggested, the word *curriculum* is yearning for new meanings. It feels choked, out of breath, caught in a landscape wherein "curriculum" as master signifier is restricted to planned curriculum with all its supposed, splendid instrumentalism. I call on fine arts educators in particular, with their strong sense of poetics, to offer inspiration and leadership in the promising work of creating a new landscape wherein "live(d) curricula" can become a legitimated signifier. We seek your guiding hand in reshaping and reconstituting the landscape such that in generative third spaces earth's rhythms can be heard, at times in thunderous rolls and at other times in fingertip whispers, not only in fine arts classes but also throughout the school wherever teachers and students gather in the name of inspirited education.

REFERENCES

Bhabha, H. (1990). The Third Space. In J. Rutherford (Ed.) *Identity:*
   Community, Culture, Difference. London: Lawrence & Wishart.
Culler, J. (1982). *On Deconstruction: Theory and Criticism After Structuralism.*
   Ithaca, NY: Cornell University Press.
Deleuze, G., & Parnet, C. (1987). *Dialogues.* (Trans. H. Tomlinson & B.
   Habberjam) New York: Columbia University Press.
Dywan, E. 1993. [Commentary in catalogue.] *1993 Annual Open Exhibition.*
   London: Royal Over-Seas League.
Havel, V. (1989). Words on words." *New York Review of Books,* 1990.

Chapter 28

Locating Living Pedagogy in Teacher "Research": Five Metonymic Moments[1] (2003)

For a teacher researcher, an insistent question is, "Where is living pedagogy located?" Such a question invites a Lacanian anecdote.

Jacques Lacan, a noted but controversial scholar and psychoanalyst, regarded the situation of the analyst and analysand as a pedagogical situation, a site of teaching/learning. But for him such a site is not merely a topographical site of the doctor's office or clinic, not merely a social site of doctor and patient, but more so a discursive site—a site of the to and fro flow of language is discourse. For Lacan, the discourse of the master doctor and the patient is inadequate; instead, he opts for the to- and-fro discourse of teaching/learning. For him, listening to "what" is being said requires listening to "where" the "what" is being said. Then, the "what" can be interpreted in terms of the "where." To help understand the where, allow me to journey through five metonymic moments.

MOMENT #1: LIVING PEDAGOGY MIDST CURRICULUM-AS-PLAN/ CURRICULUM-AS-LIVE(D)

As one interested in curriculum and pedagogy listening to Lacan's anecdote, I recall Leonard Cohen, a Canadian, who in his poem, "The Anthem," repeated the following refrain:

> Ring the bells that still can ring,
> Forget your perfect offering.
> There is a crack, a crack in everything,
> That's how the light gets in.

Enlightenment? Where? In the middle, in the midst of meditation?

---

[1]This paper was first presented at the Teacher Research Conference, Baton Rouge, LA, April 2000. This article is reprinted with permission from Aoki, Ted. T. (2003). Locating Living Pedagogy in Teacher "Research": Five Metonymic Moments. In Erika Hasebe-Ludt & Wanda Hurren (Eds.), *Curriculum Intertext; Place/Language/Pedagogy*, (pp. 1–10). New York: Peter Lang.

Heeding Leonard Cohen, I allow the signifier "curriculum" to appear and then allow a graphic mark to crack the word.

Curri⁄ulum

curriculum-as-plan/curriculum-as-live(d)
IRPs (integrated resource packages)
plannable/unplannable
predictable/unpredictable
(sayable) . . . (unsayable)
prescriptive/nonprescriptive

In/through this graphic marking, "curriculum" unfolds into "curriculum-as-plan," which we typically know as the mandated school subject, and into curricula-as-live(d)—experiences of teachers and students—a multiplicity of curricula, as many as there are teachers and students.

Here, I recall stories of thoughtful teachers who speak of their pedagogic struggles in the midst of the plannable and the unplannable, between the predictable and the unpredictable, between the prescriptible and the nonprescriptible. They're pedagogical where?—between the curriculum-as-plan and the live(d) curriculum. Sites of living pedagogy?

MOMENT #2: INDWELLING MIDST PRESENCE/ABSENCE

Five years ago, Dennis Sumara and Brent Davis, then co-editors of JCT[2] asked me to ask June, my wife, for a calligraphic work on the cover of a special issue. After perusing the articles, which referred to scholars such as Foucault, Lyotard, Derrida, Lacan, bell hooks, and so on, we decided on (yû-mu)—presence/absence. Thinking I would be helping the editors, I scribbled a memo:

> Calligraphed on the cover of this issue is (yû-mu)—yû (有)
> presence/ mu (無) absence. Yû-mu as both "presence" and
> "absence" marks the space of ambivalence in the midst of
> which humans dwell. As such, Yû-mu is non-essentialist,
> denying the privileging of either "presence" or "absence," so
> deeply inscribed in the binarism of Western epistemology. As
> the groundless ground in traditions of wisdom, the ambiguity
> textured in yû-mu is understood as a site pregnant with
> possibilities. (The calligraphic brushwork is that of June
> Aoki).

---

[2] Reference is made to *JCT* (*Journal of Curriculum Theorizing*), 11 (4), 1995.

Surprisingly, this appeared on the back cover.

What I have implied but left unsaid is the way discipline-oriented discourses of curriculum plans are grounded in the metaphysics of presence—privileging presence over absence. So valenced, the discourse assumes the presence of reality or truth hidden in the depth below, calling researchers to search and research, with successful engagement resulting in findings that provide insights into the essence of reality. To research, then, is to represent the presence of the essence of reality. This is the language of the discourse of representation, which in Western modernity has held hegemonic sway.

It is the hegemony of this discourse that Maxine Greene of Columbia University questions in her powerful article, "Postmodernism and the Crisis of Representation."[3] She calls upon us to move to the edgy edges of representational discourse, and there, open ourselves to discourses beyond.

Then Elvi Whittaker, an anthropologist at the University of British Columbia, questions the "thingifying" of the presence of culture in her noted article "Culture: Reification Under Siege."[4]

Both Greene and Whittaker are writing at the edges of modernist representational discourse, questioning the hegemony of the metaphysics of presence.

MOMENT #3: REPRESENTATIONAL DISCOURSE/NON-REPRESENTATIONAL DISCOURSE: GEOGRAPHY, DISCIPLINE, AND DISCOURSE

I now turn to Dr. Derek Gregory, a professor of geography at the University of British Columbia, Vancouver, Canada. On his move from Cambridge University in England, he brought with him a manuscript ready for the press. It was titled *The Geographical Imagination*. The story goes that during his first year of teaching at UBC, he became disenchanted with the manuscript and discarded it. Over the next few years, he rewrote the book, now retitled *Geographical Imaginations*.[5] In the transformation, he noted the multiplicity of imaginations, and, most acutely, the absence of "the," the definite article in which is inscribed the claims of finitude, the presence of the finite. In the new title, the definite article is dissolved, and in its place are indefinite articles "a . . .a . . .a . . ." — assuming indefiniteness and infinitude.

In the introduction of his book, Derek Gregory says, "I am now more interested in the discourse of geography than in the discipline of geography." Here, I recall Dr. Trevor Barnes and James Duncan, colleagues of Derek

---

[3] Greene, Maxine. (1994). Postmodernism and the Crisis of Representation. *English Education*, XXVI (4).

[4] Whittaker, Elvi. (1996). Culture: Reification under Siege. *Studies in Symbolic Interaction*, XIII, 107–117.

[5] Gregory. Derek. (1994) *Geographical Imaginations*. Oxford, UK: Blackwell.

Gregory, who published a book titled *Writing Worlds: Discourse, Text, Metaphor and the Representation of Landscape*.[6] Such a focus on discourse and language urges me to recall Lacan in his pedagogical discursive space. Allow me a brief excursion into sign theory.

A BRIEF EXCURSION INTO SIGN THEORY

Let's begin with Saussure, structural linguist, who provided us with an image of a sign as a relationship between a signifier (S) and a signified (s), between a word and a concept of reality. For Saussure, the signifier (S) has access to the signified(s) because the bar between is transparent.

$$
\text{Sign} = \quad \frac{(S)}{(s)} \quad \begin{array}{l} \text{signifier} \\ \text{(transparent bar)} \\ \text{signified} \end{array}
$$

But Saussure added that such an understanding of relationship is arbitrary.

Next, let's acknowledge Roman Jacobson, a Russian American linguist, who claims that language has two axes—the vertical (metaphoric) and the horizontal (metonymic).

Lacan with his psychoanalytic interest in language, recognizing the arbitrariness of Saussure's representational verticality, provided us with a horizontal image, in which signifiers (words) are horizontally arranged in a signifying chain:

$$
\text{S...S...S... (signifying chain)}
$$

$$
===== \quad \text{opaque bar}
$$

$$
(s) \quad \quad (s) \text{ is erased/absent}
$$

For Lacan, the bar between signifier and signified is opaque, erasing the signified(s). Thus, for him, signification is enacted in the spaces of differences between signifiers. Meanings are constituted in the inter-textual play midst signifiers. Here, language participates and performs to constitute effects. It is a discursive world of floating discourse, nonrepresentational with risks of anarchism and relativism. It is suggestive of the floating world of hypertext with its virtual realities.

Here, we must not forget our key question. Where is living pedagogy located?

---

[6] Barnes, T. & Duncan, V. (Eds.). (1994). *Writing Worlds: Discourses. Text Metaphor in the Representations of Landscapes*. London: Routledge.

MIDST THE VERTICAL AND THE HORIZONTAL

I suggest that the site between representational and non-representational discourses is the site of living pedagogy. This is the site that post colonial literary scholar, Homi Bhabha[7] calls the Third Space of ambivalent construction: the site that Trinh Minh-ha, a postcolonial feminist, calls, "a hybrid place."[8] It is a site that David Jardine, University of Calgary, calls a site of original difficulty, of ambiguity, ambivalence and uncertainty, but simultaneously, a site of generative possibilities and hope—a site challenging us to live well. It is a site that David Smith,[9] University of Alberta, writes about in his book *Pedagon*,[10] pedagogy in the site of agon(y). It is the site Derrida speaks of in his recent book, *Aporias*.[11] It is a site that Aristides Gazetas portrays in his recent book, *Imagining Selves: The politics of Representation, Film Narrative and Adult Education*.[12] It is the site that Marylin Low and Pat Palulis describe in their article "Teaching as a Messy Text: Metonymic Moments in Pedagogic Practice."[13] For Bill Doll, it is the site of chaos in which dwell transformative possibilities. As for me, it is a site of metonymy—metaphoric writing, metonymic writing.

MOMENT #4: SELF/OTHER

A few years ago, I was immersed in reading *The Malaise of Modernity* by Charles Taylor of McGill University.[14] He boldly claimed that within Western Modernity, the greatest malaise is "individualism."

---

[7] See Rutherford, J. (1990). "The third space," an interview with Homi Bhabha. In J. Rutherford (Ed.), (pp 207–221). London: Lawrence and Wishart.

[8] See Mayne, Judith (1990) "From a hybrid place," an interview with Trinh Minh-ha. In *Feminism*, September–October.

[9] Jardine, David. (1992). Reflections in education, hermeneutics and understanding. In W. Pinar & W. Reynolds. (Eds.), (pp. 116–127). *Understanding Curriculum as Phenomenological Deconstructive Texts.* New York: Teachers College Press.

[10] Smith, David G. (1999). *Pedagon.* New York: Peter Lang.

[11] Derrida, Jacques. (1993). *Aporias.* Stanford, CA: Stanford University Press.

[12] Gazetas, Aristides. (2000). *Imagining Selves: The Politics of Representation, Film Narrative, and Adult Education.* New York: Peter Lang.

[13] Low, Marylin and Palulis, Patricia. Teaching as a messy text: Metonymic moments in pedagogic practice. *JCT* (Journal of Curriculum Theorizing), in press.

[14] Taylor, Charles. (1991). *The Malaise of Modernity.* Concord, On: House of Anansi Press.

I was pondering about his remarks when Dr. Jan Walls, a Sinologist at Simon Fraser University in Canada, invited me to a dim-sum luncheon. I told Jan what Charles Taylor said of "individualism." He told me a story.

When over a century ago, Commodore Perry of the United States "opened up" Japan, the Japanese linguists were puzzled by the notion of a person as an individual—an individual entity, a self unto itself with its own identity. For the

Japanese, a person is graphically textured as 人 (hito), the two strokes saying that it takes at least two to make a person, self and other together. The Japanese linguists were puzzled with the notion of the undivided individual.

Moving into the space of interlanguage and intercultural difference, our Third Space, they allowed intertextual play and coined a new word—個 人 (ko-jin), supposedly meaning "individual." Graphically, the 固 in the first character says a past then can be isolated and boxable, reflecting the isolated self of the individual. But, on the left, they placed イ (a radical of 人) and they added 人 (hito) to 個 combining to constitute 個人 (ko-jin).

To us, 個人 (ko-jin) looks Japanese but it is not strictly Japanese. There are traces of both English and Japanese, indeed, a hybrid constituted in the third space. Such an interpretation suggests that absolute translation is an impossibility, that translation is ever incomplete and partial, and further that ongoing translation is ever-ongoing transformation, generating newness in life's movement

MOMENT #5: A DOUBLE READING OF A ZEN PARABLE

In an article titled "Haiku: Metaphor Without Metaphor," German philosopher G. Wohlfart[15] interprets Basho's haiku with the help of a well-known Zen parable:

> For those who know nothing about Zen, mountains are but
> mountains, trees are but trees, and people are but people.
> When one has studied Zen for a short time, one becomes aware
> of the invalidity and of the transitoriness of all forms, and
> mountains are no longer mountains, trees are no longer trees,
> and people are no longer people. For while the ignorant
> believe in the reality of material things, those who are even
> partly enlightened can see that they are mere apparitions, that
> they have no lasting reality, and that they disappear like

---

[15] Wolfart, G. (1997). "Haiku: Metaphor Without Metaphor." A talk presented at Simon Fraser University, Burnaby, B.C.

> fleeting clouds. Whereas—as the parable concludes [he] (sic) who has gained full understanding of Zen knows that mountains are once again mountains, trees are once again trees, and people are once again people. (from A. Watts, *Von Geist des Zen*, Basel, 1986, pp. 69f)

A few years ago, I was invited to teach a course at McGill University titled "Curriculum Foundations." I replied acceptance, providing I could change the title to "Curriculum Foundations Without Foundations."

In the course, we included Wohlfart's article, "Haiku—Metaphor Without Metaphor." We dealt with a distinct society without distinctiveness, purity of language without purity, sovereignty without sovereignty.

In the midst all this, I visited the famous art gallery at the foot of the mountain down University Street. My son and his wife, both University of Alberta fine arts graduates, guided me quickly through chambers of paintings to a special exhibit—an installation of two paintings by Gerhart Richter, a postmodern German painter. And there, I faced two paintings on adjacent walls.

My son asked me, "Where are you positioned when you are looking at the paintings?" I responded intelligently, or so I thought. I gazed absorbingly at this painting on the left, then shifted to gazing at the other trying to make sense of the paintings. Then, Edward suggested, "place yourself in the space between."

So located, I tried a doubling: listening to the Zen parable and viewing the paintings simultaneously.

FIG. 28.1 *Wuesenthal* 1985 by Gerhard Richter.

FIG. 28. 2 *Meditation* 1986 by Gerhard Richter.

Located in the between with my eyes leaning to the left I hear, "For those who know nothing about Zen, mountains are but mountains, trees are but trees, and people are but people." Then, following my eyes leaning to the right, I heard, "For one who has studied Zen for a short while, mountains are no longer mountains, trees are no longer trees, and people are no longer people." So enlightened, one eye to the left and the other eye to the right, I listened: For those who understand Zen, "mountains are again mountains, trees are again trees, people are again people."

Indeed, my son taught me a lesson on "where"—the site of living pedagogy.

Part IV

Appendix: Short Essays

Principals as Managers:
An Incomplete View[1] (1991)

*Some highlights from a discussion held with the
Coldsteam Community (Vernon) parents on April 15,
1987, on the occasion of a seminar with them on
ways to understand evaluation.*

- To understand *principals as managers* is to understand principals
  within the metaphor of business/industry. The world of education is
  likened to the management and control to accompany the goals of
  effectiveness and efficiency. Education does entail, in part,
  management, and in that sense, education is like a business. Correct.
  But such a partial understanding is not true to what education is. We
  need to be mindful when metaphors are borrowed; dangers—lurk when
  one thing is likened to another.

- The word *principal* was at one time understood as *principal teacher*—
  first or leading teacher. *Principal* was at one time an adjective. How
  did it become a noun? What happened when the adjective *principal*
  was separated from *teacher?*

- The separation made it easy for principals to be labeled administrators,
  usually understood within the business framework as managers. Such
  an understanding, which might be satisfactory for business, is
  inappropriate for educational ventures. Business deals with materials
  and people as resources—as *beings that are things* (note,
  dehumanization). Education deals with people—with *beings that are
  human,* making education a venture different from business.
- When we hear "principals are administrators," there is evident
  forgetfulness of the original meaning of what it is "to administer." The
  original meaning of *administer* was ["ad" to; "minister" serve] to serve.
  To serve others, "to be servants," "to minister to the well-being of
  others" was the original meaning of administration. Somewhere along
  the line, there occurred a reduction through truncation. We need a

[1] These are sketched notes sent to Mrs. Elsie McMurphie, then president of the
B.C. Teachers Federation, on the occasion of discussions of Bill 19 that allowed
the creation of an administrators' association separate from the BCTF. Reprinted
from: Aoki, Ted T. (1991). Principals as managers. In Ted T. Aoki (Ed.),
Inspiriting Curriculum and Pedagogy: Talks to Teachers (pp. 11–12).
Edmonton, Alberta: Department of Secondary Education, University of Alberta.

recovery of the original meaning if we are to speak of *educational administration.*

- What authorizes a person to be administrator? In the truest sense, "authority" does not flow from assignment of position by powered people, nor from receipt of certified pieces of paper. Authority flows from being true to whatever phenomenon claims the person.

- Administrators often talk of leadership. What authorizes a person to be an *educational leader?* What is it the lead? To lead is to follow the authority of the true. A leader in education must lead as he or she follows the essence, the true, of what education is.

- At the heart of education is pedagogy. Fortunately, both *pedagogy* and *education* speak to the meaning of leading. *Pedagogy* means ["agogue" lead; "pedae" young children] *leading the young. Education* means ["ex" out of; "ducere" lead] *a leading out.* Leading in education means, essentially, the leading of people from where they are now to new possibilities. To lead in such a way requires that *the leader follow the essentially true of what education is.* (Leading and following is a dialectic.) The principal as leading teacher must be one who leads others to new possibilities by following the essentially true of what education is.

- *Principal as manager* is correct insofar as education is a business, but not true insofar as education is not a business. *Principal as manager*, by itself, misunderstands education. As such, it is dangerous.

Bridges That Rim the Pacific[1] (1991)

When I was a child, a map of the world hung in the living quarters of our home. My father, an Issei educator in Canada, reminded us persistently that, in the generations of Niseis and Sanseis, the globe would be our world.

I recall how our Mercator map, centered on the Atlantic, split the Pacific Ocean, and relegated the Orient and the Occidental Americas to the map's extremities.

Today, we witness the dawn of the era of the Pacific, calling upon us who dwell on the Pacific Rim to reorient ourselves. We have before us now a newly textured map on which the Pacific claims dominance, compelling us to become attuned to the view that the Orient is to the west and the Occidental Americas to the east. The dawning of this new era invites us to inquire what it means to dwell humanly on the Pacific Rim.

"It is my wish to serve as a bridge over the Pacific Ocean." These words of Dr. Inazo Nitobe are inscribed on a cairn in Beacon Hill Park in Victoria, Canada, overlooking the expanse of the Pacific. Nitobe was a noted Japanese visionary who devoted a large part of his life to the international efforts of the League of Nations. He dreamed of the coming Age of the Pacific.

As we approach the end of the 20th century, I am prompted to ask what Dr. Nitobe meant when he said he wished to serve as a bridge. In what ways can a person be like a bridge? What does it mean to be a bridge? What indeed is a bridge?

In our everyday activities, we walk over bridges, drive over bridges, and build bridges. If we pause to ask what a bridge is, some will wonder what there is to ask. The answer seems too obvious. A bridge is a bridge! Why ask about what we already know?

We are accustomed to think that bridges link lands. Bridges allow us to cross from bank to bank, from one land to another, and even cross the wide Pacific.

I recall sailing by ship for eleven days and nights, bridging the distance from Vancouver to Yokohama.

Today, we fly the arc from Vancouver to Narita Airport in a mere nine hours. By phone, we bridge the Pacific instantaneously. We glory in the technological prowess that enables us to bridge the arc of the Pacific Rim from

---

[1] This invited article was first published in HCSS's *Social Education*, March 1988, in conjunction with the Pacific Rim and the Social Studies Conference sponsored by the National Council for the Social Studies and the BC Social Studies Teachers Association. The International Conference was held in Vancouver, BC. Reprinted from: Aoki, Ted T. (1991). Bridges that Rim the Pacific. In Ted T. Aoki (Ed.), *Inspiriting Curriculum and Pedagogy: Talks to Teachers* (pp. 41–42). Curriculum Praxis, Department of Secondary Education, University of Alberta, Edmonton, Alberta.

Australasia to Tierra del Fuego. Ships plough the ocean and planes fly the Pacific skies, moving people and goods and making the Pacific a vibrant mosaic of human activity. Impressed by our own achievements, we undauntedly pursue new heights that seem endless.

The foregoing is, at best, a partial answer to the question, "What is a bridge?" Merely to describe and characterize physical bridges and their metaphorical extensions in transportation and communications, however, even when one includes in the account the wonders of science and technology that make them possible *and* their implications for commerce, trade, and culture, falls short of capturing the *essential* properties of the physical structure of bridges, transportation, and communications. It falls still farther short of grasping the human meaning of the bridges for humankind. That is what Nitobe had in mind when he spoke of serving as a bridge.

JAPANESE GARDEN

Near one end of the Nitobe Japanese Garden on the campus of the University of British Columbia is a small, unassuming bridge—several well-trodden, weather-bleached planks, slightly angled, bridging a shallow pond. There are no guardrails.

As strollers approach the bridge, they forego strolling to pause a while. As they pause, the bridge gathers into a unity the hundred iris plants in the shallow water reaching for the sunbeams that pass through the foliage of the pines sheltering the bridge, the landscapes beyond that acknowledge their bond with the bridge and the sky above, and the strollers themselves receive inspiration as they sense the link between their mortal finitude and the divine infinitude.

Such a moment is authentic dwelling, as Heidegger would say, made possible by the way mortals *are*, on this earth beneath the sky, beings who belong together in neighbourhood. When Inazo Nitobe spoke of his wish to serve as a bridge, his meaning was surely more than a physical structure than connects two masses of land. He spoke of what a bridge means humanly.

TRUE BRIDGE

In interpreting the Pacific Rim, social studies educators may be tempted to understand it in terms merely of the lands, the people who dwell in those lands, and the ways in which people have technically overcome distances between them. They will do well to remember that any true bridge is more than a merely physical bridge. It is a clearing—a site—into which earth, sky, mortals, and divinities are admitted. Indeed, it is a dwelling place for humans who, in their longing to be together, belong together.

Bridges on the Pacific Rim are not mere paths for human transit; nor are they mere routes for commerce and trade. They are dwelling places for people.

The Pacific Rim invites social studies educators to transcend instrumentalism to understand what it means to dwell together humanly.

Interview (2003)

Ted Aoki/ Doug Aoki[1]

The interview is conventionally a numbers game, or, more exactly, a conjuring trick: it is constituted by *two* people (the interviewer and the interviewee) but defined by only *one* subject (the interviewee). It also conventionally orients social space. The interviewer asks questions and the subject answers, establishing a direction *from* the former *to* the latter. It is no coincidence that this discursive orientation is recapitulated rhetorically: the interviewer *directs* the interview and thereby the interviewee. The interview enacts a politics of radically asymmetrical and unequal partners. The irony is that the asymmetry of the interview is conceptually weighted in precisely the opposite direction, for an interview is generally framed in terms of the interviewee. This is why s/he is the only subject. In academic journals, if not the pop cultural worlds of Barbara Walters or Larry King, the interviewer is often rhetorically effaced, becoming so much the representative of an organization or institution that her/his very name is overwritten by the title or initials of the journal involved. But appearances can be deceiving; power is subtle in its discursive moves and disguises. Judith Butler is pertinent here. In *The Psychic Life of Power*, she brings Foucault, Althusser and Lacan together to argue that the subject only comes to exist through her/his discursive subjection. This is the very definition of Butler's conception of performativity: the conjuring of the subject through the summons by authority, the *interpellation* that Althusser famously figures by the hail of a police officer. The interview, with its only subject generated by the direction of someone who has ceased to be a subject, is a classic exemplification. Years ago, Barbara Frum became uncharacteristically flustered while interviewing Margaret Atwood when the latter started asking her own questions. The evident disruption of the interview, the unexpectedness of Atwood's inversion, proved that she had turned herself into a *bad subject*.

This text—the one you are reading—is supposed to be an interview of Ted Aoki by Doug Aoki. But you will find no helpful, identifying initials labelling any paragraph; you will be given no explicit distinctions between the "interviewee" and the "interviewer." Does this interview then fail to be one? Or can an interview productively escape the discursive structures and markers that define it? More generally, what necessity drives the attribution of words to names? Will you "win" something valuable if you determine that one idea is Ted's and another is Doug's? Is the demand for attribution motivated by something more profound than the standards of scholarship? Or does scholarship

[1] Reprinted from: Aoki, Ted T. / Aoki, D. (December 2003). Interview. *Educational Insights*, 8(2). [Available: http://ccfi.educ.ubc.ca/publication /insights/v08n02/celebrate/interview.html]

anxiously call for attribution to sustain its own respectability, and thereby lose the chance to be something more than respectable? Do we so desperately *want* names? Do we so desperately *desire* them? And what do we think we have learned when we have learned them? What do we think we have been taught? When Ted's first grandson, Alex, was born, Doug asked Ted to give him a Japanese name. Ted's suggestion was *Tetsuyoshi*, which translates as, "Obligated to philosophy." The usual response by those who learn that translation is to feel sorry for Alex. What passionate expectations do we have in general for names and other words?

> But there's this angel in her eyes that tells such desperate lies,
> And all you want to do is believe her . . .
> Oh, she's the One.
>
> Bruce Springsteen

Today's successor to Frum's interview segment on CBC's *The Journal* is *One on One with Peter Mansbridge*. The title begs the question, what is "the One"? Among other things, "the One" is an abbreviation of "the one and only," an emphatic advertisement of the subject's assumption of singularity. The One isn't just anyone; s/he is the one worthy of (or made worthy by) being interviewed by Peter Mansbridge. More fundamentally, the One is the subject staking claim to its own existence, at least in the constitutively discursive form of its identity. Butler again provides the key, one habitually missed by academic readers: she opposes *performance* to *performativity*. For her, the former presumes the subject, while the latter puts into question the very concept of the subject. This is why those who assert she explicates a theory of performance are so very wrong. Instead, she theorizes performativity as the radical undermining of the subject-as-performer, echoing previous declarations by Barthes and Foucault of the death of that definitive academic performer, the author. This is also why every Mansbridge interview should be recognized as performance: not because it is a theatrical "act" and therefore not serious journalism, but rather because it is far *too* serious. The journalistic interview must be sufficiently serious that its viewers/listeners/readers attend to the substance of its discourse, and thereby never become aware of how the form of that discourse both produces its subjects and displaces them. The failure of the academics who misread Butler works through a parallel logic. That failure is no mere accident or slip; its necessity is as profound as its error. Professors and students who enthuse over her "theory of performance" are invariably *too* enthusiastic. Their fervour testifies to how they must misread, mis-teach and mis-learn Butler so their own positions as both subjects and subjects-supposed-to-know are reinforced, rather fatally destabilized. Each of them wants to be the One to Know; each of them *needs* to be the One.

Before John Carpenter found fame as the director of the definitive Hollywood blockbuster slasher film, Halloween, he made a short science-fiction comedy, Dark Star, the adventures of an eponymous starship. The Dark Star is

armed with very smart bombs—so smart that they can converse with the crew.
When the technology of the future inevitably malfunctions and one of the bombs
decides it is going to blow up while still onboard ship, the commander, unable to
disarm the weapon, asks his senior advisor what else he can do:

> ADVISOR: *Teach it phenomenology.*
> COMMANDER: *Sir?*
> ADVISOR: *Phenomenology.*
>   . . .
>
> COMMANDER: *Hello, bomb, are you with me?*
> BOMB: *Of course.*
> COMMANDER: *Are you willing to entertain a few concepts?*
> BOMB: *I am always receptive to suggestions*
> COMMANDER: *Fine. Think about this one, then: how do you*
>   *know you exist?*

Phenomenology has been historically stuck in its frame of intentionality as
the subject conscious of the object, suggesting the possibility of lived experience
as absolute knowledge qua consciousness. The painstaking attention to what is
conscious is an equally painstaking turning away from the unconscious. This is
where psychoanalysis meets deconstruction, for the phenomenological
metaphysics of presence is the matriculation of making the subject present.
Phenomenology is an attempt to break from the objectivity of the subject by
attention to intentionality as lived experience. The interview is thus
thoroughly—if often crudely—phenomenological: it presents the subject to an
audience by provoking the autobiographical narration of lived experience.

The problem is that narration is yet another performance and that
autobiography is yet another presumption of the presence of the narrating
performer. To put this another way, the problem with the narration of the subject
is not the inevitability of its failure, but rather the possibility of its success. The
performative caution is not that the narration cannot make the subject present,
but rather that narration is *the only way to do so.* That is, the subject is never
present in and of itself. In Lacanian terms, before the subject is positioned in the
symbolic order—before it is written into social existence—the subject is only
present as lack. It is only produced (as present) through discursive gestures
whose archetype is the narration of the self. This is the pertinent lesson of the
Derridean, "there is nothing outside the text": the subject only comes to be
through its inscription; the subject would fade away without its inscription. This
is also why Lacan symbolizes both the subject and the signifier with an "S." At
the same time, Lacan distinguishes between them by slashing the "S" of the
subject, making it divided and placing it under erasure. That lexical difference
asserts that the subject only appears as fully itself— as an unslashed "S"—in its
discursive representation.

The relationship between the lack of a subject and its narration as present is
more closely coupled than mere incoherence, however, for it is the very lack of

the subject which drives its narrative production. That is, it is *because* the subject is not "there" that its story gets told. For Butler, social identity only persists because it continuously fails. The incessance of failure necessitates the iteration of its recuperation. Hence the characteristically repetitive nature of social life: we need to "perform" the same social gestures again and again, often on a daily basis, to be able to sustain the images of ourselves as female or male, gay or straight, teacher or student. For example, sex may appear to be biologically determined, and it is generally taught as such, but even its factuality demands discursive support. Alex—our pitied grandson and son—is a six year-old boy with very long hair. Another boy in his swimming class, when queried by a parent, responded, "I don't know if Alex is a boy or a girl, but he's got one of these," and pointed between his own legs. Even what Lacan has most problematically privileged as the phallic signifier loses its categorical power without the support of the social story establishing its signified and significance.

> *I think where I am not, therefore I am not where I think.*
> Jacques Lacan

There is a further crucial complication. A discursive representation like an interview only makes the subject *appear* to be fully itself. In Lacanese, the fullness of social identity is a quintessentially imaginary moment, in which the unifying image of the subject is coincident with its utterly unreal status. In Lacanian psychoanalysis, there is a deep divide between the logics of the image and the word. A celebrated news photograph is compelling because it makes viewers "feel as if they were *there*"—which is exactly what theory means by *presence*: the utterly convincing sense of being (in its most fundamental sense) where one is not. The image is the defining instance of re-presentation. The paradigmatic operation of the image is to make the subject *appear* in words, casually conflating what Lacan is determined to keep distinct as the imaginary and symbolic orders. Making the subject visible means making it enter the discursive scene. Hence the *view* in *interview*. Does this mean that the *inter*view stages an interchange *between* views? But appearances, as usual, are deceiving. The two views are mediated and framed by a third, a meta-view, if you will: the humanist view of what it means to be human. The foundational image is the portrait.

The logic of the word is exactly the opposite, as Derrida forced us to recognize nearly forty years ago. Deconstruction is not and has never been an esoteric, academic, literary-theoretical technique. Instead, it is a precise description of how language in its everyday usage (*parole*) constantly undermines its presumption to communication. For deconstruction, no text or word, in or out of the academy, is immune to *différance*: difference and deferral. The psychoanalytic version is that a chain of signifiers always slips away. In either account, language never stands still: it defies every attempt to nail it down. In particular, it defies every attempt to pin it to a subject, to make meaning one's own—with two crucial consequences: (1) the attribution of words to names, as in a regular interview, must inevitably fail, and (2) we endlessly desire attribution *because* it is ultimately impossible, and therefore always lacking. The interview is always caught in the basic tension between the conflicting logics of the image and the word, teetering on the brink of the chasm between the imaginary and symbolic orders, between desire and the impossibility of its fulfillment.

> *The humanist's greatest delusion is that "I am here" and "you*
> *are there."*
>
>   Zen saying

> *I am he as you are he as you are me and we are all together*
> *See how they run like pigs from a gun, see how they fly. . . .*
> *I am the eggman they are the eggmen*
> *I am the walrus*
> *Goo goo g'joob*
>
>   Lennon & McCartney

The very concept of identity is the exemplary assertion of such an impossibly definitive meaning of and by the self: "I am *x*" or "She's the one." Identity is exactly the presumption that a person can be pinned to a unique and fundamental story. Directly ignoring the insights of a sweeping range of contemporary cultural theories—deconstruction, Lacanian psycho-analysis, French feminist theory and queer theory, to name a few—the seemingly self-evident faith in the existence of identity is actually an extraordinarily sweeping semiotic presumption. Not only does it reconstitute the sign by uniting the signifier (the name) and signified (the concept of a specific person), it fastens that sign to the referent (that person in her/his "real-word" existence). Identity, therefore, constitutes a radically "vertical" space of the subject, as if one's body, mind and soul were not only perfectly aligned, but also located in a very specific place on the map of the social world. Hence the notion of the "grounded self," whose "down-to-earth" appeal masks the ferocious desperation by which identity clings to its defining place. The championing of the liberatory power of metaphor depends on the same disingenuousness because the verticality of identity also structures that trope. The apparent abandon of metaphor belies the severity of its demand: each of its poetic terms must replace another *in the same place*, so that every instance of metaphor, no matter how creative or original, implacably returns to the same place to reinforce it. The subjective site—the longitude and latitude of the symbolic order, the place from which One speaks, the supposedly postmodern "subject location"—remains the same, regardless of the changes that take place there. Again, it's sleight of hand: celebrating the virtuosity of performance keeps us from questioning the status of the performer. It is no accident, therefore, that metaphor is the paradigmatic figure of speech, for its paradigmatic place is that of the subject figured in terms of its identity.

Metonymy, on the other hand, is perpendicular to the humanist figuration of metaphor. Metonymy generates a "horizontal" or lateral space of discourse, one that does not fix a "subject location," but rather enacts the subjective consequences of *différance*. The curious and revealing thing about metonymy is how people invariably find it much harder to understand than its partner, metaphor. Metonymy, like deconstruction, gets misconstrued as some exotic intellectual abstraction, when it is actually immanent to every utterance ever made. Insofar as one word is spoken after another, "laterally" in time, insofar as one word follows another horizontally on a page, the relation between each of those words is metonymic. Metonymy is the most ordinary thing in the world, the basic spatial relation of discourse, whether spoken or written, "high" academic or everyday. That metonymy nonetheless appears so baffling is powerful testimony to our unconscious perceptiveness, for despite its ordinariness and ubiquity, metonymy's implications are radical, general and deeply disturbing to our subjective ground. If discourse is characterized by difference and deferral rather than signification, then the subject, insofar as it is subject to language, is always different and deferred from itself. If the chain of signifiers eludes the multiple-choice/dictionary logic of the correctness of meaning, then the subject always slides away from its own identity. Metaphor grounds the subject; metonymy lets it take flight.

As always, the way we speak teaches us about ourselves. The well-intentioned who valorize that common academic figure of speech, grounding or anchoring—as in "grounded research," "anchored in the disciplinary literature," "a well-grounded argument"—demonstrate the deep perils of being blind to the lateral connections of our own discourse. Anchoring and grounding are, of course, familiar nautical metaphors. Yet academics rigorously ignore how an anchored vessel stays in the same place and how one that runs aground mires itself through negligence or bad navigation. Neither can go anywhere until they hoist anchor or un-ground themselves. Even the most conventionalized of academics admit as much when they laud cutting edge research as "ground-breaking."

The conventional interview broadens into a metonymic space despite itself. The identity of its subject is taken for granted as coincident with the place of the interviewee, but the very success of an interview turns on its ability to generate a new vision of the subject *in the space of its own discourse*. This subject thus "appears" in this new light and new place, not in her or his studio chair, but rather in the "lateral" space in-between interviewee and interviewer. The inter-space of the interview is not the empty separation of bodies; it is the paradigmatic discursive space in its performative fecundity and complication. From this point of view, the intriguing spatial aspect of the interview is the distance between the interviewee and her/his appearance, and how that distance is negotiated as an engagement with (and evasion of) the subject. The discretion of the interview lies not only in the courtesy of the interviewer—the distance between Peter Mansbridge and Howard Stern—but importantly in the discreteness attributed to the identities of interviewer and interviewee. To reinvoke and redeploy Butler, this is the discretion of performance.

We can put it this way: the mission of the interview structured by the logic of metaphor is to teach us what the subject (putatively) *is*. This is the communication of knowledge established (or taken for granted) as truth. The mission of the interview working through the logic of metonymy is to teach us the fraught operation and promise of subjectivity itself. This is much more exhilarating and dangerous than methodologically sound research (the *–ology* of any methodology defines it as logocentric). This is neither biography nor autobiography; this is not, in fact, the narration of any life. This is living itself.

Postscript/Rescript

A

It was in 1964 that I, a junior vice-principal and secondary school social studies teacher, received an invitation to become a teacher educator in the Faculty of Education, University of Alberta, Edmonton, Alberta. The faculty was established in 1945 as a professional school on campus, the first such faculty of education in Canada.

Housed in the Department of Secondary Education, I noted that all the courses carried the prefix "Ed.C.I." (Educational Curriculum and Instruction.) I assumed "curriculum" to mean prescripted mandated school program by the provincial (state) Ministry of Education, and "instruction" to mean teaching interpreted as transmitting to students the substantive knowledge, skills, and attitude prescribed as a normative standard for all students in the province. With such an instrumental view, teaching was cast into a transmissive mode.

In our department, it was primarily the graduate students, who began to question the ideology of instrumentalism within which the language of teaching was embedded. Boldly moving beyond the courses offered within the Faculty of Education, a few of them ventured out to seek modalities of thought and practice that moved beyond instrumentalism. It was they, the graduate students, who brought to the staff's attention Continental European ideologies, particularly the neo-Marxist critical social theory with interest in reflection and emancipation, and further, they brought to us the language of hermeneutics and phenomenology so new to many of us.

Among these students was Max van Manen, who in his undergraduate teacher education program at the University of Utrecht, Utrecht, the Netherlands, sought opportunities to explore new understandings of teaching as lived experiences, calling for attention to "intentionality" understood in terms of "subjectivity conscious of objects," thus breaking with the positivists over emphasis of objectivity. Our language began to shift to include both curriculum-as-plan and curriculum-as-live(d.)

Today I recall the day when Max van Manen in the midst of the writing of his dissertation phoned me, the chair of his supervisory committee, asserting that he could not continue unless he was allowed to use the first-person subject in his study. He was questioning the canon of objectivity in dissertation writing, insisting on the place of subjective interpretative narratives of personal lived experience. It seemed he was calling for legitimation of phenomenological writing in dissertations. I agreed to support the venture, which by introducing phenomenology marked an opening up to what has come to be known as qualitative inquiry.

It was at this time that we learned of the efforts of William F. Pinar, then of the University of Rochester, Rochester, New York, who began to question the overreification of curriculum. He was drawing our attention to "currere," which emphasized movement in the flux of pedagogical life. He boldly began a new journal, titling it *Journal of Curriculum Theorizing,* emphasizing the transformative movements in constituting theories of curriculum. And when he launched the annual conferences in Bergamo, Ohio, we joined his efforts, Bergamo becoming synonymous with the reconceptualization of curriculum thought and practice. So when his book *Curriculum Theorizing: Phenomenological and Deconstructive Texts* was published, we felt a kinship predominantly in the textured context of phenomenological discourse.

B

In 1986 William Reynolds, then editor of *JCT* (*Journal of Curriculum Theorizing*), asked me to locate a calligrapher to design the cover of a special issue. I sought out Woo May, a noted artist and calligrapher in Edmonton, Canada, who was a recent migrant from Mainland China. I requested her to graphically write the word 道 (the way) (*Tao* in Chinese, *Do* in Japanese). She asked me quietly, "Just one word?" She hesitated a moment but agreed.

At this time, for me, Tao signified the way. The graphic character in Chinese reads a person in movement, in a way a form of "currere." I saw it as a central concept in Buddhism, manifested as Taoism in China and as Zen Buddhism in Japan, and as a concept I had assumed it to be a master signifier, harbouring the essence of human reality. Here I feel that I am echoing Saussure's notion of structuralist signification in which signifier (word) is transparently linked with the signified truth or reality.

Today as I recall the occasion, two untold stories emerged.

Story #1: "Just One Word?"

Woo May's quiet words silently but insistently have haunted me over these years, particularly as I became increasingly sensitive to the linguistic semiotics of curriculum and pedagogy.

I had been accustomed to questions like, "What is curriculum?" "What is teaching?," without awareness of discursive preconditions that allowed me to utter these words. I had not realized that I already dwelt in a meta-discourse artifactually constructed—a discursive world we have come to name Western Modernism.

Turning again to 道 (Tao), I reread the sketch of Woo May on the reverse side of the cover page of the journal. As a migrant artist, she immediately noted she now had access to Western water-colour paint as well as her own mineral-colour paint. And in her interest (inter/ease), she allowed the interplay of the Western and Oriental colour media. I now view her artwork hanging in our living room as a vivid hybridity of two colour schemes, a hybrid of the East and the West. I see in her painting what it means to be a Chinese Canadian artist.

I add a further reading of Woo May's calligraphic work. Interested in enlivened script, she set aside her calligraphy brushes and turned to tissue paper, dipping it in black ink, allowing it to meet rice paper in an enlivened way. She was vitally concerned with the movements as ink met paper. She wished to allow the black of the ink and the white of the paper to liven each other, conjoining and disjoining. As a calligrapher she was not only interested in artist scripting on paper. She was also interested in the interplay of ink and paper, of black and white, of stability and instability, an inscription that is an interscription.

Story #2: Experiencing Refiguration of the Word "Way"

A few years ago at Century College, a private Taiwanese college in Vancouver, British Columbia, I taught a course titled "Shifting Figurations of Identity and Difference Midst Discourses of Curriculum and Pedagogy."

Early in the course, I told students Woo May's story. At the following session, a Taiwanese student presented me a copy of *Tao Te Ching* by the famous Taoist sage, Lao Tze, in both Chinese and in English. I immediately recalled reading about Heidegger, who, many years ago, began translating with his Chinese student the eighty-one verses. They managed to translate the first eight verses. It must have involved much dialogue midst slow reading and slow rewriting.

That evening I opened *Tao Te Ching* and began to read. The first line read

- The way that can be described is not the Eternal Way.

I read and reread: The way described/not the way.

I was drawn away from the image of one word and drawn into a texture of contiguity away from seeking the essence of the words, "Tao," to a sensitivity of metonymic context: word/no word.

The very reading repositioned me such that I was located in the ambivalent site of difference between the word way and no word, indeed a liminal space of aporia.

A few words of thought on "just one word."

C

In 1995, I was contacted by Dennis Sumara and Brent Davis, then coeditors of *Journal of Curriculum Theorizing*, inviting my wife June to do a calligraphic artwork on the cover of a special issue. Wanting to reflect on intercultural space between the Orient and the West or between Western modernist and far Eastern non-modernistic figurations, we returned again to the first verse of Lao Tze's *Tao Te Ching*. Lines 3 and 4 read as follows:

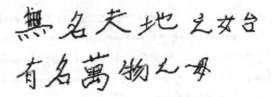

Absence of name is the condition of Heaven and Earth;
Presence of name is the Mother of Ten Thousand Things.

Taking the first character in each line June calligraphically brushed (Yû-mu)

I forwarded June's graphic work to the editors, together with a handwritten note.

有無

Calligraphed on The cover of this issue is 有無 (yū-mu) — Yū (有) presence/mu (無) absence. Yū-mu as both "presence" and "absence" marks The space of ambivalence in the midst of which humans dwell. As such, Yū-mu is non-essentialist, denying The privileging of either "presence" or "absence", so deeply inscribed in the binerism of Western epistemology. As The groundless ground in traditions of wisdom, The ambiguity textured in yu-mu is understood as a site pregnant with possibilities (The calligraphic brushwork is that of June Aoki)

The note reappeared on the back cover of the issue.

Consideration of this work led us to recall Maxine Greene's article, "Postmodernism and the Crisis of Representation."[2] By representation she was referring to the modernism discourse grounded in the metaphysics of presence, which presumes the preexistence of reality, often hidden in the deep but inviting search and re-search, so success leading to findings. I felt that by crisis she was critical of the hegemony of representative discourse erasing the non-representational. In effect, she was calling for a retexturing this acknowledged the metonymic figuration such as "yû-mu", presence/absence.

But she was mindful of dualism that clings to the ground of metaphysics. She was urging us to consider spatial sites of difference, entangled in ambiguity and aporia, difficult but with generative possibilities. So oriented, we began to consider metonymic contiguity, as a cursive figuration often invoking the "is not."

In recent years, doctoral students on whose dissertation committee I served as a member have provoked me to domains of signification—the ways in and through language, graphics, film, sounds, and so on. They have alerted me to

---

[2] Greene, Maxine. (1988). *Post Modernism and the Crisis of Representation.* (pp. 206-218). New York: Teachers' College Press.

signs and figurations—subjectively and culturally constituted—always partial and incomplete, always in movement.

I list here the titles of the last six dissertations I was involved with, feeling that even the language of the titles begins to invoke the signifying figurations within which the graduate students and their dissertations were positioned.

1. "Imagining Selves: The Politics of Representations, Film Narratives and Adult Education" (1997) by Aristides Gazetas, Department of Educational Studies, Faculty of Education, University of British Columbia.

    Interested in semiotic realms including film images and linguistic discourses, Aristides Gazetas felt that figurations of language and culture were significant in theories of signification. With particular interest in textual and graphic images of human relations, he explored the postmodernists efforts in reunderstanding "self and other," displacing the identity centered image of self and other.

    He undertook to examine five metonyonic images of self and other, attending to the interpretations of Jacque Lacan, Michel Foucault, Jacques Derrida, Baudrillard, and Jean-François Lyotard.

    His dissertation lead me to a moment of thought in which I could see in the postmodern articulations, a reflection of Taoist (Zen) metonymy of presence/absence. In his dissertation he boldly insisted that discussion formulations are necessary illusions, linguistically and culturally constituted.

2. "Difficulties of Intergrative Evaluation Practices: Instances of Language and Content as/in Contested Space(s)" (1999) by Marylin Grace Low, Department of Language Education, University of British Columbia.

    In the midst of her study, Marylin Low sensed discomfort located in the liminal space of linguistic studies centered on content, thereby suppressing context. Thus, she questioned the hegemony of the configurations of conventional linguistics as understood in educational discourses. She insistently called for inclusion of the contextual, thereby allowing consideration of the metonymic configuration in discourses.

    She claimed that hegemonic understanding of evaluation in language education was restrictive, incomplete, and inadequate—quite a challenge when universal testing of reading, for example, is the political norm in many Western countries. For her the cultural texture inevitably embodied in language systems is a dimension that needs to be considered seriously in any evaluation.

3.   "Tarrying in Metonymic Sites of Pedagogy: The Space of Language and the Language of Space" (2001) by Patricia Palulis, Centre for the Study of Curriculum and Instruction, University of British Columbia.

Patricia Palulis attempted to break through the confines of structuralist linguistics by including the poststructuralist discourse of signification, a semiotic domain wherein language is no mere tool of communication.   In her rereading and rewriting she allowed language to constitute meanings and subjectivity, thereby recognizing the limitation of the conventional understanding of language in language programs.   Her work beckoned many of us to question the notion that a dissertation is essentially an assertive representation.   Her doubled sense of performativity in the space of language and the language of space is refreshingly new to many of us.

4.   "Music for Living or Music as Art?   Disrupting the Dominant Discourse that Marginalizes Music in Education" (2002) by Sheila Sim, Faculty of Education, University of Victoria, British Columbia.

As a committee member I was invited into the curricular domain of music education in public schools. As one new to the domain of semiotics, I relished the opportunity to enter in to the figurations of sound images. Sheila Sim de-constructed the dualism of masculinity and femininity.   Articulating the language of established music in music education programs, she pointed out the patriarchal hegemony in legitimation of "music" in music education   program.   Leaning   on   writings   of postcolonialists like Homi Bhabha, she called upon music educators to consider this site Homi Bhabha labeled the Third Space to displace dualistic discourse.   To be introduced in a figurative domain of sound and listening was a rich experience for me.

5.   "Re/constituting   Educational   Administration: Hermeneutic Dispositions(s) of the Interpretative Gesture and Situations-at-Hand in Daily School Life" (2001) by Craig Worthing, Simon Fraser University, British Columbia.

As a principal of an elementary school, Craig Worthing, discomforted by the conventional interpretation of the term "educational administration" upholding John Caputo and others, opened us to hermeneutic discourses, giving shifting meanings of "educational administration."

There he discussed three discourses of hermeneutics of closure, of disclosure and Ebranler. By so naming he reconstituted meanings of both the term "educational administration" and the subjectivity of school "principals."

6.   "Abiding in Liminal Space(s): Inscribing Mindful Living/Dying with(in) End-of-Life-Care" (2002) by Anne Bruce, School of Nursing, Faculty of Graduate Studies, University of British Columbia.

Focusing on palliative care in nursing, Anne Bruce contextualized her study to include Taoist meditation midst metonymy of life and death, each separately identifiable.   Her doctoral program included Zen meditation and Zen hospice care at an institute in San Francisco, which led her to a transformed articulation of nursing theory and practice.

In her articulation of nursing in a metonymic context, I felt that we who dwell in the field of teaching and learning have much to consider as a way to reconstitute the discourse within which we define teachers, teaching, and teaching/learning.

D

In the first year of the new millennium, year 2000, William Pinar initiated a recursive movement in *currere* in Baton Rouge, the home of Louisiana State University. He convened a conference, "Internationalizing Curriculum Studies." A surge of international interest led to the announcement of the formation of the International Association for the Advancement of Curriculum Studies. A simultaneous pronouncement indicated that the first triennial conference would be held in Shanghai in the year 2003.

Shanghai is situated on the Pacific Rim, on the borderline, in the space of "inter"—often midst vibrant ambivalent metonymic figurations. This Third Space provokes semiotic signs wherein linguistic and cultural signs in interludic play could generate newness and hope. *Currere* in recurring movement?

CURRICULUM VITAE FOR TED TETSUO AOKI, Ph.D.

Professor Emeritus, University of Alberta

ACADEMIC DEGREES

Doctor of Philosophy, University of Oregon (Curriculum and Instruction), 1969
Master of Education, University of Alberta (Educational Foundation), 1963
Bachelor of Education, University of Alberta (Social Studies Major), 1949
Bachelor of Commerce, University of British Columbia, 1941

HONORARY DEGREES

Honorary Doctor of Laws, University of Western Ontario, 1999
Honorary Doctor of Laws, University of Alberta, 1992
Honorary Doctor of Laws, University of British Columbia, 1991
Honorary Doctor of Laws, University of Lethbridge, 1988

TEACHING AND ADMINISTRATIVE EXPERIENCES

Professor Emeritus, University of Alberta, 1985–
Honorary Professor, U.B.C. 1994–
Adjunct Professor, University of Victoria, 1987–1996
Re-appointment as Chairman, Department of Secondary Education, University of Alberta, 1983–1985
Professor and Chairman, Department of Secondary Education, University of Alberta, 1978–1983
Professor and Coordinator, Centre for the Study of Curriculum and Instruction, Faculty of Education, University of British Columbia, 1975–1978
Professor, Department of Secondary Education, Faculty of Education, University of Alberta, 1972–1975
Associate Professor, Department of Secondary Education, Faculty of Education, University of Alberta, 1967–1972
Assistant Professor, Department of Secondary Education, Faculty of Education, University of Alberta, 1964–1967
Assistant Principal, Lethbridge Collegiate Institute, Lethbridge, Alberta, 1962–1964
Teacher, Public Schools in Alberta, 1945-1964 (Rockyford, Foremost, Taber, and Lethbridge) at Elementary, Junior High School and Senior High School levels.
"Evacuated" to Alberta immediately following Pearl Harbor, 1942

SELECTED PUBLICATIONS AND PRESENTATIONS

Aoki, T. T. (2000). Locating living pedagogy in teacher "research." Five metonymic moments. Invited paper presented at the Teacher Research Conference, Baton Rouge, LA, April.

Aoki, T. T. & Jacknicke, K. (2000). *Language, culture and curriculum.* Paper presented at the Canadian Association of Curriculum Studies President's Symposium, CSSE Conference, May 27, Edmonton, Alberta.

Aoki, T. T. (1999). Toward understanding "Computer Applications." in W. F. Pinar (Ed.), *Contemporary curriculum discourses: Twenty years of JCT* (pp. 168–176). New York: Peter Lang, 1999.

Aoki, T. T. (1996). *Narrative and Narration in Curricular Space.* Invited Address presented at the conference: "Curriculum as Narrative/Narrative as Curriculum: Lingering in the Spaces," Green College, University of British Columbia, Vancouver, BC, May 2 and 3.

Aoki, T. T. (1996, fall). Spinning inspirited images in the midst of planned and live(d) curricula." *FINE: Journal of the Fine Arts Council of the Alberta Teachers' Association*, pp. 7–14.

Aoki, T. T. (1996). Imaginaries of "East and West": Slippery curricular signifiers in education. In *Proceedings of the International Adult and Continuing Education Conference* (pp. 1–10). Sponsored by the Office of Research Affairs, Chung-Ang University Korea Research Foundation.

Aoki, T. T. (1995). In The midst of language education and global education. In M. Chapman & James Anderson (Eds.), *Thinking globally about language education.* Centre for the Study of Curriculum and Instruction, University of British Columbia.

Aoki, T. T. (1995). In the midst of double imaginaries: The Pacific community as diversity and as difference. *Contents: Pacific Asian Education* 7(1&2), 1–7.

Aoki, T. T. (1993). Legitimating lived curriculum: Re-mapping the curricular landscape. *The Journal of Curriculum and Supervision*, 8 (3).

Aoki, T. T. (1993). (Ed.) *Teachers narrating narratives teaching: Pacific Rim experiences.* Victoria: Department of International and National Education, Ministry of Education and Ministry Responsible for Multiculturalism, British Columbia.

Aoki, T. T., & Shamsher, M. (Eds.). (1993). *The call of teaching.* Vancouver: British Columbia Teachers Federation.

Aoki, T. T. (1993). The child-centered curriculum: Where is the social in pedocentrism? In T. Aoki & M. Shamsher (Eds.), *The Call of Teaching.* Vancouver. BC: British Columbia Teachers' Federation.

Aoki, T. T. (1993). In the midst of slippery theme-words: Living as designers of multicultural curriculum." In Ted T. Aoki & M. Shamsher (Eds.), *The call of teaching,* Vancouver, British Columbia Teachers' Federation.

Aoki, T. T. (1993). Humiliating the Cartesian ego. *SALT: Journal of the Religious and Moral Education Council* (The Alberta Teachers'

Association), 15(2), 5–11.

Aoki, T. T. (1991). *"Inspiriting curriculum and pedagogy: Talks to teachers.* Edmonton: Faculty of Education, University of Alberta. Published by the Department of Secondary Education as a part of the celebration of the fiftieth anniversary of the Faculty of Education, University of Alberta.

Aoki, T. T. (1991). Five curriculum memos and a note for the next half-century. In Max van Manen (Ed.), *Phenomenology & pedagogy.* Edmonton: Publication Services of the Faculty of Education, University of Alberta.

Aoki, T. T. (Ed.). (1991). *Voices of Teaching, Vol. II.* Vancouver, BC Teachers' Federation.

Aoki, Ted T. (Ed.). (1990). *Voices of Teaching, Vol. I.* Vancouver, BC Teachers' Federation.

Aoki, T. T. (1991). Layered understandings of orientations in social studies program evaluation. In J. Shaver (Ed.), *Handbook of research in social studies teaching and learning.* Washington, DC. National Council for the Social Studies.

Aoki, T. T. (1992). Layered understandings of teaching: The uncannily correct and the elusively true. In W. F. Pinar & W. M. Reynolds (Eds.), *Understanding curriculum as phenomenological and deconstructed text.* New York: Teachers' College Press.

Aoki, T. T. (1990). The sound of pedagogy in the silence of the morning calm. The Academy of Korean Studies, Papers of the Sixth International Conference on Korean Studies: Its Cross-Cultural Perspective. Seoul, Korea.

Aoki, T. T. (1992). *In the midst of slippery theme-words: Living as designers of Japanese Canadian curriculum.* Invited paper presented at Designing Japanese Canadian Curriculum Conference, May 21, 22, and 23, North York, Ont.

Aoki, T. T. (1991). Signs of vitality in curriculum scholarship. In T. T. Aoki (Ed.), *Inspiriting curriculum and pedagogy: Talks to teachers* (pp. 23–28). Edmonton: Curriculum Praxis, Department of Secondary Education, Faculty of Education, University of Alberta.

Aoki, T. T. (1991). Teaching as in-dwelling between two curriculum worlds. In T. T. Aoki (Ed.), *Inspiriting curriculum and pedagogy: Talks to teachers* (pp. 7–10). Edmonton: Department of Secondary Education, University of Alberta.

Aoki, T. T. (1991). Ted Aoki in conversations. In L. Berman (Ed.), *Towards curriculum for being: Voice of educators.* New York: SUNY Press.

Aoki, T. T. (1991). Sonare and videre: A story, three echoes and a lingering note. In T. T. Aoki (Ed.). *Inspiriting curriculum and pedagogy: Talks to teachers* (pp. 29–34). Edmonton, Alta: Curriculum Praxis, Department of Secondary Education, University of Alberta.

Aoki, T. T. (1991). Taiko drums and sushi, perogies and sauerkraut: Mirroring a half-life in multicultural curriculum. In Ted T. Aoki (Ed.), *Inspiriting curriculum and pedagogy: Talks to teachers* (pp. 35–39). Edmonton, Alta.:

Curriculum Praxis, Department of Secondary Education, University of Alberta.

Aoki, T. T. (1991). The sound of pedagogy in the silence of the morning calm." In Ted T. Aoki (Ed.). *Inspiriting curriculum and pedagogy: Talks to teachers* (pp. 43–48). Edmonton: Curriculum Praxis, Department of Secondary Education, University of Alberta.

Aoki, T. T. (1990, January/February). Inspiriting the curriculum. *ATA Magazine*, pp. 37–42.

Aoki, T. T. (1990). Sonare and videre: Questioning the primacy of the eye in curriculum talk. In W. Schubert & G. Willis (Eds.), *The arts as a basis for curriculum*. New York: SUNY Press.

Aoki, T. T. (1989). Themes of teaching curriculum. In J. T. Sears & J. D. Marshall (Eds.), *Teaching and thinking about curriculum: Critical inquiries*. New York: Teachers College Press.

Aoki, T. T. (1989). Thoughts from a threshold. In F. H. Hultgren & D. L. Coomer (Eds.), *Alternative modes of inquiry in home economics research*. American Home Economics Association Yearbook.

Aoki, T. T. (1988). Towards a dialectic between the conceptual world and the lived world: Transcending instrumentalism in curriculum orientation. In W. F. Pinar (Ed.), *Contemporary curriculum discourses*. Scottsdale, AZ: Gorsuch Scarisbrick Publishers.

Aoki, T. T. (1988, March). Bridges that Rim the Pacific. *Social Education*.

Aoki, T. T. (1987). The dialectic of mother language and second language: A curriculum exploration. *Canadian Literature, A Quarterly of Criticism and Review*.

Aoki, T. T. (1987). Revisiting the notions of leadership and identity. Invited Address presented at the National Conference of the National Association of Japanese Canadians held in Vancouver, May 16 and 17.

Aoki, T. T. (1987). Toward Understanding "Computer Application." *Journal of Curriculum Theorizing, 7*(2).

Aoki, Ted. T. (1987). Reflections of a Nisei educator. *Greater Vancouver Japanese Canadian Citizens' Association Bulletin, XXIX, 3, 4 & 5*.

Aoki, T. T. (1986). Teaching as in-dwelling between two curriculum worlds. *B.C. Teacher, 65*(3).

Aoki, T. T. (1986). Interests, knowledge and evaluation: Alternative approaches to curriculum evaluation. *Journal of Curriculum Theorizing, 6*(4), 27–44.

Aoki, T. T. (1987). In Receiving, a giving: A response to the panelists' gifts. *The Journal for Curriculum Theorizing*, special issue, "Curriculum Praxis as Teaching, Research and Administration: The Work of Professor T. Aoki," a Symposium held at Bergamo, Ohio, 1985.

Aoki, T. T. et al (Eds.). (1986). *Understanding curriculum as lived: Curriculum Canada VII*. Centre for the Study of Curriculum and Instruction. University of British Columbia. (Proceedings of The Canadian Association for Curriculum Studies Sponsored Symposium held in 1985.)

Aoki, T. T. (1986). A Response to a symposium on the conversation and company of educated women. In L. Peterat (Ed.), *In the conversation and company of educated women: A colloquy on home economics education.* Urbana, IL: University of Illinois at Urbana-Champaign.

Aoki, T. T., Carson, T. & Favaro, B. & Berman, L. M. (1983). *Understanding situational meanings of curriculum in-service acts: Implementing, consulting, inservicing. Curriculum Praxis Monograph Series, Monograph 9* (pp. 3–17). Edmonton: Department of Secondary Education, Faculty of Education, University of Alberta.

Aoki, T. T. (1984). Towards a reconceptualization of curriculum implementation. In D. Hopkins & M. Wideen (Eds.), *Alternative perspective on school improvement.* London: The Falmer Press.

Aoki, T. T., et al. (1984). Whose culture? Whose heritage? Ethnicity within Canadian social studies curriculum. In J. R. Mallea & J. C. Young, (Eds.), *Cultural diversity and Canadian education: Issues and innovations.* Ottawa, Ont.: Carleton University Press.

Aoki, T. T. (1984). Competence as instructional action and practical action. In E. C. Short (Ed.), *Competence: Inquiries into its meaning mid acquisition in educational settings.* New York: University Press of America.

Aoki, T. T. (Ed.). (1981). *Re-thinking education: Modes of enquiry in the human sciences.* Edmonton: Department of Secondary Education, University of Alberta.

Aoki, T. T. (1981, March). Toward understanding curriculum talk through reciprocity of perspectives. Paper presented at a symposium; Toward understanding trans-national curriculum talk: An exploration in cross-paradigmatic communication. Annual conference of the Association for Supervision and Curriculum Development, St. Louis, Missouri.

Aoki, T. T. (1978). Toward Curriculum Inquiry in a New Key. In J. Victoria & E. Sacca (Eds.), *Phenomenological description: Potential for research in art education.* Montreal, Que.: Concordia University.

Aoki, T. T., et. al. (1978). Six reports on BC social studies assessment published by the BC Ministry of Education.

Aoki, Ted T. (1977). On being and becoming a teacher in Alberta: A Japanese Canadian experience. *RIKKA, 4.*

AWARDS AND RECOGNITIONS

Honorary life membership awarded by the Social Studies Council of the Alberta Teachers' Association, 2001, with the following citation: "For meritorious and significant contributions to Social Studies Education in Alberta and for exemplary service as a leader in the ATA Social Studies Council."

Mentoring award presented by the International Institute for Qualitative Methodology, University of Alberta with the following citation: "In recognition of your life long pedagogical contributions in building a community of scholarship in qualitative inquiry."

An honorary award presented by the Curriculum Theory Project of Louisiana State University, April 29, 2000, with the following citation: "For his lifetime of achievement in the Internationalization of Curriculum Studies."

Inducted as laureate member, Kappa Delta Pi, an international honor society in education, at its biennial convocation held in Orlando, Florida, 1993.

Inducted into the Professors of Curriculum Circle (125 membership) at its annual meeting in Boston during the Annual Conference of the Association for Supervision and Curriculum Development, March 1988.

The distinguished service award, presented by the American Educational Research Association, Division B, presented at the Annual AERA Conference in Washington, DC, April 20, 1987.

The *Journal of Curriculum Theorizing* award, presented at the Annual Conference on Curriculum Theory and Curriculum Practice, Ohio State, Bergamo, October 18, 1985, with the following citation: "*The Journal of Curriculum* Theorizing honors Professor Ted T. Aoki for distinguished contribution to curriculum studies in the United States and Canada by establishing the Annual Aoki Award."

CEA Whitworth Award for Research in Education presented by the Canadian Education Association. Awarded at the Annual Canadian Education Association Conference, Quebec City, September 17, 1985.

PDK of the Year Award, presented by the University of Alberta chapter of Phi Delta Kappa, Edmonton, AB, May 21, 1985.

The Distinguished Service Award, presented by the Canadian Association for Curriculum Studies presented at the Annual Canadian Society for Studies in Education Conference, Montreal, Canada, May 28, 1985, with the following citation: "For outstanding contributions to the intellectual, practical, and human aspects of our field."

Certificate of appreciation presented by Dr. Young Sik Kim, President of the Korean Educational Development Institute, December 3, 1984, later Minister of Education, South Korea, with the following citation: "Presented to our respected international colleague and Chairman, Department of Secondary Education, University of Alberta, with gratitude and appreciation for the dedication, commitment and friendship in the promotion of international exchange between Canada and the Republic of Korea, and in particular, for the warm hospitality and generosity to our colleagues and students from KEDI."

AUTHOR INDEX

A

B

C

E

SUBJECT INDEX

A

Anthropocentrism, 49, 300
Aporia, 452
Application, 32, 110, 154, 155,
156, 232, 363, 364
Art education, 92
Assessment (see also curriculum
assessment), 168, 177, 182, 184,
224, 259, 271, 272, 274, 299, 367
Attunement, 165, 360, 398
Auditory (the), xvi, xvii, 64, 65, 80,
82, 375
Autobiography (autobiographical),
36, 57, 232, 447

B

Belonging (together), 67, 68, 84,
371, 395, 396, 397, 398
Bridge (bridging), 1, 6, 28, 52, 53,
75, 79, 81, 83, 84, 219, 228, 316,
317, 318, 437, 438
Business metaphor, 113, 431, 435

C

Calligraphy (calligraphic), 71, 72,
73, 265, 289, 304, 415, 421, 426,
450, 451, 453
Call of calling, 213
Call of teaching, 406
Citizenship, 65
Commonplaces, 232, 233
Competence (competency), 5, 6, 7,
8, 77, 113, 125, 126, 127, 129, 130,
132, 133, 224
Computer, 11, 236
    application, 11, 12, 151, 153,
    154, 156, 157
    education, 151
    literacy, 152

technology, 12, 152, 153, 154,
156, 157
Conferencing, 103
Control, 102, 141, 170
Conversation, 21, 28, 29, 30, 53, 80,
81, 82, 83, 180, 214, 214, 220, 221,
222, 227, 228, 239
Critical Theory, xvi, 3, 7, 8, 29, 30
Cross-culturalism, 65, 219, 381,
382
Currere, 257, 449, 457
Curriculum, 47, 54, 62, 69, 72, 73,
90, 111, 114, 121, 128, 142, 145,
159, 204, 219, 222, 227, 229, 230,
231, 232, 233, 244, 249, 251, 264,
271, 273, 295, 321, 322, 333, 357,
360, 361, 362, 363, 370, 417, 420,
423, 426, 449, 450, 451
    Action, 232
    anecdote, 199
    architects, 16, 164
    as-ideology, 257
    -as-lived, xxi, 15, 23, 24, 27,
    32, 39, 74, 76, 78, 159, 160,
    161, 162, 163, 201, 202, 205,
    211, 231, 232, 273, 321, 322,
    418, 423, 425, 426, 449
    -as-plan, xxi, 5, 9, 14, 15, 23,
    24, 27, 32, 39, 43, 73, 74, 76,
    78, 144, 159, 160, 161, 162,
    163, 201, 202, 204, 205, 206,
    208, 209, 211, 231, 257, 274,
    276, 297, 298, 299, 321, 322,
    417, 423, 425, 426, 449
    assessment, 20, 39, 44, 257,
    418
    balance, 363, 364
    building, 361
    centers, 45, 281, 282
    child-centered, 94, 279, 280,
    282, 283, 285, 289